Blueprints for High Availability
Second Edition

Blueprints for High Availability
Second Edition

Evan Marcus
Hal Stern

WILEY

Wiley Publishing, Inc.

Executive Publisher: Robert Ipsen
Executive Editor: Carol Long
Development Editor: Scott Amerman
Editorial Manager: Kathryn A. Malm
Production Editor: Vincent Kunkemueller
Text Design & Composition: Wiley Composition Services

Library of Congress Cataloging-in-Publication Data is available from the publisher.

ISBN: 0-471-43026-9

For Carol, Hannah, Madeline, and Jonathan
—Evan Marcus

For Toby, Elana, and Benjamin
—Hal Stern

Contents

Preface
For the Second Edition

The strong positive response to the first edition of *Blueprints for High Availability* was extremely gratifying. It was very encouraging to see that our message about high availability could find a receptive audience. We received a lot of great feedback about our writing style that mentioned how we were able to explain technical issues without getting too technical in our writing.

Although the comments that reached us were almost entirely positive, this book is our child, and we know where the flaws in the first edition were. In this second edition, we have filled some areas out that we felt were a little flat the first time around, and we have paid more attention to the arrangement of the chapters this time.

Without question, our "Tales from the Field" received the most praise from our readers. We heard from people who said that they sat down and just skimmed through the book looking for the Tales. That, too, is very gratifying. We had a lot of fun collecting them, and telling the stories in such a positive way. We have added a bunch of new ones in this edition. Skim away!

Our mutual thanks go out to the editorial team at John Wiley & Sons. Once again, the push to complete the book came from Carol Long, who would not let us get away with slipped deadlines, or anything else that we tried to pull. We had no choice but to deliver a book that we hope is as well received as the first edition. She would accept nothing less. Scott Amerman was a new addition to the team this time out. His kind words of encouragement balanced with his strong insistence that we hit our delivery dates were a potent combination.

From Evan Marcus

It's been nearly four years since Hal and I completed our work on the first edition of *Blueprints for High Availability*, and in that time, a great many things have changed. The biggest personal change for me is that my family has had a new addition. At this writing, my son Jonathan is almost three years old. A more general change over the last 4 years is that computers have become much less expensive and much more pervasive. They have also become much easier to use. Jonathan often sits down in front of one of our computers, turns it on, logs in, puts in a CD-ROM, and begins to play games, all by himself. He can also click his way around Web sites like www.pbskids.org. I find it quite remarkable that a three-year-old who cannot quite dress himself is so comfortable in front of a computer.

The biggest societal change that has taken place in the last 4 years (and, in fact, in much longer than the last 4 years) occurred on September 11, 2001, with the terrorist attacks on New York and Washington, DC. I am a lifelong resident of the New York City suburbs, in northern New Jersey, where the loss of our friends, neighbors, and safety is keenly felt by everyone. But for the purposes of this book, I will confine the discussion to how computer technology and high availability were affected.

In the first edition, we devoted a single chapter to the subject of disaster recovery, and in it we barely addressed many of the most important issues. In this, the second edition, we have totally rewritten the chapter on disaster recovery (Chapter 20, "A Disaster Recovery Plan"), based in part on many of the lessons that we learned and heard about in the wake of September 11. We have also added a chapter (Chapter 21, "A Resilient Enterprise") that tells the most remarkable story of the New York Board of Trade, and how they were able to recover their operations on September 11 and were ready to resume trading less than 12 hours after the attacks. When you read the New York Board of Trade's story, you may notice that we did not discuss the technology that they used to make their recovery. That was a conscious decision that we made because we felt that it was not the technology that mattered most, but rather the efforts of the people that allowed the organization to not just survive, but to thrive.

Chapter 21 has actually appeared in almost exactly the same form in another book. In between editions of *Blueprints*, I was co-editor and contributor to an internal VERITAS book called *The Resilient Enterprise*, and I originally wrote this chapter for that book. I extend my gratitude to Richard Barker, Paul Massiglia, and each of the other authors of that book, who gave me their permission to reuse the chapter here.

But some people never truly learn the lessons. Immediately after September 11, a lot of noise was made about how corporations needed to make themselves more resilient, should another attack occur. There was a great deal of discussion about how these firms would do a better job of distributing their data to multiple locations, and making sure that there were no single points of failure. Because of the economy, which suffered greatly as a result of the attacks, no money was budgeted for protective measures right away, and as time wore on, other priorities came along and the money that should have gone to replicating data and sending backups off-site was spent other ways. Many of the organizations that needed to protect themselves have done little or nothing in the time since September 11, and that is a shame. If there is another attack, it will be a great deal more than a shame.

Of course, technology has changed in the last 4 years. We felt we needed to add a chapter about some new and popular technology related to the field of availability. Chapter 8 is an overview of SANs, NAS, and storage virtualization. We also added Chapter 22, which is a look at some emerging technologies.

Despite all of the changes in society, technology, and families, the basic principles of high availability that we discussed in the first edition have not changed. The mission statement that drove the first book still holds: "You cannot achieve high availability by simply installing clustering software and walking away." The technologies that systems need to achieve high availability are not automatically included by system and operating system vendors. It's still difficult, complex, and costly.

We have tried to take a more practical view of the costs and benefits of high availability in this edition, making our Availability Index model much more detailed and prominent. The technology chapters have been arranged in an order that maps to their positions on the Index; earlier chapters discuss more basic and less expensive examples of availability technology like backups and disk mirroring, while later chapters discuss more complex and expensive technologies that can deliver the highest levels of availability, such as replication and disaster recovery.

As much as things have changed since the first edition, one note that we included in that Preface deserves repeating here: Some readers may begrudge the lack of simple, universal answers in this book. There are two reasons for this. One is that the issues that arise at each site, and for each computer system, are different. It is unreasonable to expect that what works for a 10,000-employee global financial institution will also work for a 10-person law office. We offer the choices and allow the reader to determine which one will work best in his or her environment. The other reason is that after 15 years of working on, with, and occasionally for computers, I have learned that the most correct answer to most computing problems is a rather unfortunate, "It depends."

Writing a book such as this one is a huge task, and it is impossible to do it alone. I have been very fortunate to have had the help and support of a huge cast of terrific people. Once again, my eternal love and gratitude go to my wonderful wife Carol, who puts up with all of my ridiculous interests and hobbies (like writing books), our beautiful daughters Hannah and Madeline, and our delightful son Jonathan. Without them and their love and support, this book would simply not have been possible. Thanks, too, for your love and support to my parents, Roberta and David Marcus, and my in-laws, Gladys and Herb Laden, who *still* haven't given me that recipe.

Thanks go out to many friends and colleagues at VERITAS who helped me out in various ways, both big and small, including Jason Bloomstein, Steven Cohen, John Colgrove, Roger Cummings, Roger Davis, Oleg Kiselev, Graham Moore, Roger Reich, Jim "El Jefe" Senicka, and Marty Ward. Thanks, too, to all of my friends and colleagues in the VERITAS offices in both New York City and Woodbridge, New Jersey, who have been incredibly supportive of my various projects over the last few years, with special thanks to Joseph Hand, Vito Vultaggio, Victor DeBellis, Rich Faille, my roomie Lowell Shulman, and our rookie of the year, Phil Carty.

I must also thank the people whom I have worked for at VERITAS as I wrote my portion of the book: Richard Barker, Mark Bregman, Fred van den Bosch, Hans van Rietschote, and Paul Borrill for their help, support, and especially for all of those Fridays. My colleagues in the Cross Products Operations Groups at VERITAS have been a huge help, as well as good friends, especially Dr. Guy Bunker, Chris Chandler, Paul Massiglia, and Paula Skoe.

More thank-yous go out to so many others who I have worked and written with over the last few years, including Greg Schulz, Greg Schuweiler, Mindy Anderson, Evan Marks, and Chuck Yerkes.

Special thanks go, once again, to Pat Gambaro and Steve Bass at the New York Board of Trade, for their incredible generosity and assistance as I put their story together, and for letting me go back to them again and again for revisions and additional information. They have been absolutely wonderful to me, and the pride that they have in their accomplishments is most justified. Plus, they know some great restaurants in Queens.

Mark Fitzpatrick has been a wonderful friend and supporter for many years. It was Mark who helped bring me into VERITAS back in 1996, after reading an article I wrote on high availability, and who served as my primary technical reviewer and personal batting coach for this second edition. Thank you so much, Marky-Mark.

Last, but certainly not least, I must recognize my coauthor. Hal has been a colleague and a good friend ever since our paths happened to cross at Sun too many years ago. I said it in the first edition, and it's truer now than ever: This book would still just be an idea without Hal; he helped me turn just-another-one-of-my-blue-sky-ideas-that'll-never-happen into a real book, and for that he has my eternal respect and gratitude.

From Hal Stern

If Internet time is really measured in something akin to dog-years, then the 4 years since the first edition of this book represent half a technical lifetime. We've seen the rise and fall of the .com companies, and the emergence of networking as part of our social fabric, whether it's our kids sending instant messages to each other or sipping a high-end coffee while reading your email via a wireless network. We no longer mete out punishments based on the telephone; in our house, we ground the kids electronically, by turning off their DHCP service. Our kids simply expect this stuff to work; it's up to those of us in the field to make sure we meet everyone's expectations for the reliability of the new social glue.

As networking has permeated every nook and cranny of information technology, the complexity of making networked systems reliable has increased as well. In the second edition of the book, we try to disassemble some of that complexity, attacking the problem in logical layers. While many of the much-heralded .com companies didn't make it past their first hurrahs, several now stand as examples of true real-time, "always on" enterprises: ebay.com, amazon.com, travel sites such as orbitz.com, and the real-time sportscasting sites such as mlb.com, the online home of Major League Baseball. What I've learned in the past 4 years is that there's always a human being on the other end of the network connection. That person lives in real time, in the real world, and has little patience for hourglass cursors, convoluted error messages, or inconsistent behavior. The challenges of making a system highly available go beyond the basics of preventing downtime; we need to think about preventing variation in the user's experience.

Some new thank-yous are in order. Through the past 4 years, my wonderful wife Toby, my daughter Elana and son Benjamin have supported me while tolerating bad moods and general crankiness that come with the author's territory. Between editions, I moved into Sun's software alliance with AOL-Netscape, and worked with an exceptional group of people who were charged with making the upper levels of the software stack more reliable. Daryl Huff, "Big Hal" Jespersen, Sreeram Duvvuru, and Matt Stevens all put in many hours explaining state replication schemes and web server reliability. Rick Lytel, Kenny Gross, Larry Votta, and David Trindade in Sun's CTO office added to my knowledge of the math and science underpinning reliability engineering. David is one of those amazing, few people who can make applied mathematics interesting in the real world. Larry and Kenny are pioneering new ways to think about software reliability; Larry is mixing old-school telecommunications thinking with web services and proving, again, that strong basic design principles stand up over time.

While on the software side of the house, I had the pleasure of working with both Major League Baseball and the National Hockey League on their web properties. Joe Choti, CTO of MLB Advanced Media, has an understanding of scaling issues that comes from hearing the (electronic) voices of millions of baseball fans. Peter DelGiacco, Group VP of IT at the NHL, also lives in a hard real-time world, and his observations on media, content, and correctness have been much appreciated. On a sad note, George Spehar, mentor and inspiration for many of my contributions to the first edition, lost his fight with cancer and is sorely missed.

Finally, Evan Marcus has stuck with me, electronically and personally, for the better part of a decade. Cranking out the second edition of this book has only been possible through Evan's herculean effort to organize, re-organize, and revise, and his tireless passion for this material. Scott Russell, Canadian TV personality, has said that if you "tell me a fact, I forget it; tell me the truth and I learn something; tell me a story and I remember." Thank you, Evan, for taking the technical truths and weaving them into a compelling technical story.

Preface from the First Edition

Technical books run the gamut from code listings sprinkled with smart commentary to dry, theoretical tomes on the wonders of some obscure protocol. When we decided to write this book, we were challenged to somehow convey nearly 15 years of combined experience. What we've produced has little code in it; it's not a programmer's manual or a low-level how-to book. Availability, and the higher concepts of resiliency and predictability, demand that you approach them with discipline and process. This book represents our combined best efforts at prescriptions for developing the disciplines, defining and refining the processes, and deploying systems with confidence. At the end of the day, if a system you've designed to be highly available suffers an outage, it's your reputation and your engineering skills that are implicated. Our goal is to supplement your skills with real-world, practical advice. When you see "Tales from the Field" in the text, you're reading our (only slightly lionized) recounts of experiences that stand out as examples of truly bad or truly good design.

We have sought to provide balance in our treatment of this material. Engineering always involves trade-offs between cost and functionality, between time to market and features, and between optimization for speed and designing for safety. We treat availability as an end-to-end network computing problem—one in which availability is just as important as performance. As you read through this book, whether sequentially by chapter or randomly based on particular interests and issues, bear in mind that you choose the trade-offs. Cost, complexity, and level of availability are all knobs that you can turn; our job is to offer you guidance in deciding just how far each should be turned for any particular application and environment.

We would like to thank the entire editorial team at John Wiley & Sons. Carol Long believed in our idea enough to turn it into a proposal, and then she coached, cajoled, and even tempted us with nice lunches to elevate our efforts into what you're reading now. Special thanks also to Christina Berry and Micheline Frederick for their editorial and production work and suggestions that improved the overall readability and flow of the book. You have been a first-rate team, and we owe you a debt of gratitude for standing by us for the past 18 months.

From Evan Marcus

This book is the product of more than 2 years of preparation and writing, more than 7 years of working with highly available systems (and systems that people thought were highly available), and more than 15 years of general experience with computer systems. Having worked in technical roles for consulting companies specializing in high availability and for software vendors with HA products, I found myself answering the same kinds of questions over and over. The questions inevitably are about getting the highest possible degree of availability from critical systems. The systems and the applications that run on them may change, but the questions about availability really don't. I kept looking for a book on this subject, but never could find one.

In 1992, I became intimately involved with Fusion Systems' cleverly named High Availability for Sun product, believed to be the very first high-availability or failover software product that ever ran on Sun Microsystems workstations. It allowed a predesignated standby computer to quickly and automatically step in and take over the work being performed by another computer that had failed. Having done several years of general system administrative consulting, I found the concept of high availability to be a fascinating one. Here was a product, a tool actually, that took what good system administrators did and elevated it to the next level. Good SAs worked hard to make sure that their systems stayed up and delivered the services they were deployed to deliver, and they took pride in their accomplishments. But despite their best efforts, systems still crashed, and data was still lost. This product allowed for a level of availability that had previously been unattainable.

High Availability for Sun was a tool. Like any tool, it could be used well or poorly, depending on the knowledge and experience of the person wielding the tool. We implemented several failover pairs that worked very well. We also implemented some that worked very poorly. The successful implementations were on systems run by experienced and thoughtful SAs who understood the goals of this software, and who realized that it was only a tool and not a panacea. The poorly implemented ones were as a result of customers not mirroring their disks, or plugging both systems into the same power strip, or running poor-quality applications, who expected High Availability for Sun to solve all of their system problems automatically.

The people who successfully implemented High Availability for Sun understood that this tool could not run their systems for them. They understood that a tremendous amount of administrative discipline was still required to ensure that their systems ran the way they wanted them to. They understood that High Availability for Sun was just one piece of the puzzle.

Today, even though the product once called High Availability for Sun has changed names, companies, and code bases at least three times, there are still people who realistically understand what failover management software (FMS) can and cannot do for them, and others who think it is the be-all and end-all for all of their system issues. There are also many less-experienced system administrators in the world today, who may not be familiar with all the issues related to rolling out critical systems. And there are managers and budget approvers who think that achieving highly available systems is free and requires little or no additional work. Nothing so valuable is ever that simple.

The ability to make systems highly available, even without failover software, is a skill that touches on every aspect of system administration. Understanding how to implement HA systems well will make you a better overall system administrator, and make you worth more to your employer, even if you never actually have the chance to roll out a single failover configuration.

In this book we hope to point out the things that we have learned in implementing hundreds of critical systems in highly available configurations. Realistically, it is unlikely that we have hit on every single point that readers will run into while implementing critical systems. We do believe, however, that our general advice will be applicable to many specific situations.

Some readers may begrudge the lack of simple, universal answers in this book. There are two reasons for this. One is that the issues that arise at each site, and for each computer system, are different. It is unreasonable to expect that what works for a 10,000-employee global financial institution will also work for a 10-person law office. We offer the choices and allow the reader to determine which one will work best in his or her environment. The other reason is that after 15 years of working on, with, and occasionally for computers, I have learned that the most correct answer to most computing problems is a rather unfortunate, "It depends."

We have made the assumption that our readers possess varying technical abilities. With rare exceptions, the material in the book is not extremely technical. I am not a bits-and-bytes kind of guy (although Hal is), and so I have tried to write the book for other people who are more like me. The sections on writing code are a little more bits-and-bytes-oriented, but they are the exception rather than the rule.

* * *

When I describe this project to friends and colleagues, their first question is usually whether it's a Unix book or an NT book. The honest answer is both. Clearly, both Hal and I have a lot of Unix (especially Solaris) experience. But the tips in the book are not generally OS-specific. They are very general, and many of them also apply to disciplines outside of computing. The idea of having a backup unit that takes over for a failed unit is commonplace in aviation, skydiving (that pesky backup parachute), and other areas where a failure can be fatal, nearly fatal, or merely dangerous. After all, you wouldn't begin a long trip in your car without a spare tire in the trunk, would you? Busy intersections almost never have just one traffic light; what happens when the bulbs start to fail? Although many of our examples are Sun- and Solaris-specific, we have included examples in NT and other Unix operating systems wherever possible.

Throughout the book, we offer specific examples of vendors whose products are appropriate to the discussion. We are not endorsing the vendors—we're just providing their names as examples.

* * *

First and foremost, my gratitude goes to my family. Without the love, support, and understanding (or at least tolerance!) of my wife Carol and my daughters Hannah and Madeline, there's no way I could have written this book. A special note of thanks, too, to our family and friends, who pretended that they understood when I missed important events to stay home and write. See, it really was a book!

Additional thanks to Michael Kanaval (we miss you, Mike) for his inspiration and some excellent examples; to Joseph J. Hand, who helped with some of the NT material; to Michael Zona and John Costa for some of the backup stuff; to Mark Fitzpatrick and Bob Zarrow for some of my early and ongoing education in failover and general HA stuff; and to Mindy Anderson and Eric Burgener for clustering and SANs. Thanks, too—for general support, enthusiasm, and tolerance—to my parents Roberta and David Marcus, my in-laws Gladys and Herb Laden (now can I have that recipe?), and Ed Applebaum, Ann Sheridan, and Dinese Christopher, and everyone else at VERITAS and elsewhere who made suggestions and showed general enthusiasm and interest in this project. Special thanks to Mark Fannon and Evan Marks for excellent technical review and general help.

Thanks go out to the countless customers, users, and technical colleagues I've worked with over the years, with special thanks to the people at Morgan Stanley Dean Witter, Bear Stearns, Deutsche Bank, J. P. Morgan, Sun Microsystems, VERITAS Software, Open Vision, and Fusion Systems.

And a really big thanks to Hal Stern for being my personal door opener. In mid-1997 I finally made the decision to write this book. Having never written a book before, I knew that I needed help. I emailed Hal, looking for initial guidance from someone who had written a successful book. He wrote back and asked if perhaps we could collaborate. I thought long and hard for about 2 nanoseconds and then replied with an enthusiastic "Yes!" It was Hal's idea that we begin the writing process by creating a slide presentation. Our original set of 250 slides quickly grew to over 400, which we still present at technical conferences each year. By presenting the slides, we were able to determine what content was missing, where questions came up, and how the content flowed. It was a relatively (very relatively) easy job to then turn those slides into the book you see before you. Hal also originally contacted Carol Long at Wiley, got us on the agenda at our first technical conferences. This book would still just be an idea in my head without Hal.

From Hal Stern

My introduction to reliable systems began nearly 10 years ago, when I worked with the Foxboro Company to port their real-time, industrial control system from proprietary hardware to the Sun platform. You never really consider the impact of a hung device driver or failed disk drive until the device driver is holding a valve open on a huge paint mixing drum, or the disk drive is located along the Alaskan oil pipeline under several feet of snow. As the Internet has exploded in popularity, reliability and "uptime engineering" are becoming staples of our diet, because web surfers have caused us to treat most problems as real-time systems. As system administrators we have to decide just how much money to pour into reliability engineering, striving for four-nines (99.99 percent) or five-nines (99.999 percent) uptime while management remarks on how cheap hardware has become. There are no right answers; everything is a delicate balance of management, operations, money, politics, trust, and time. It's up to you to choose the number of nines you can live with. I hope that we help you make an informed choice.

This book would not have been possible without the love and support of my family. To my wife Toby and my children Elana and Benjamin, a huge thank-you, a big hug, and yes, Daddy will come out of his study now. I also want to thank the following current and former Sun Microsystems employees for educating me on various facets of availability and for their ideas and encouragement: Carol Wilhelmy, Jon Simms, Chris Drake, Larry McVoy, Brent Callaghan, Ed Graham, Jim Mauro, Enis Konuk, Peter Marcotte, Gayle Belli, Scott Oaks, and Wendy Talmont. Pete Lega survived several marathon sessions on complexity, recovery, and automation, and his inputs are valued. Chris Kordish and Bob Sokol, both of Sun Microsystems, reviewed the manuscript and offered their comments and guidance. Larry Bernstein, retired vice president of network operations at AT&T, challenged me to learn more about "carrier grade" engineering; it was an honor to have had discussions with a true Telephone Pioneer. Avi Nash and Randy Rohrbach at the Foxboro Company gave me a firsthand education in fault tolerance. Various individuals at Strike Technologies, Bear Stearns, Fidelity Investments, Deutsche Bank, Morgan Stanley Dean Witter, and State Street Bank proved that the ideas contained in this book really work. I thank you sincerely for sharing engineering opportunities with me, even if confidentiality agreements prevent me from listing you by name. A special thank-you to George Spehar, a true gentleman in every sense, for offering his sage management and economic decision-making advice. Ed Braginsky, vice president of advanced technology at BEA Systems, has been a good friend for eight years and a superb engineer for longer than that. His explanations of queuing systems, transaction processing, and asynchronous design, along with the thoughts of BEA cofounder Alfred Chuang, have been invaluable to me. Of course, thanks to Mom and Pop for teaching me the importance of being reliable.

Finally, a huge thank-you to Evan Marcus. We became acquainted while working on a customer project that required sniffing out performance problems during the wee hours of the morning. I'd never met Evan before, yet he was driving me around New Jersey and providing a steady patter at all hours. I should have recognized then that he had the stamina for a book and the power of persuasion to have me join him in the endeavor. Evan, thanks for your patience, understanding, and unique ability to prompt me out of writer's block, winter doldrums, and extreme exhaustion. It's been a pleasure traveling, working, and teaching with you.

About the Authors

Evan Marcus is a Principal Engineer and the Data Availability Maven at VERI-TAS Software. His involvement in high-availability system design began in 1992 when he codesigned a key piece of the first commercial Sun-based software for clustering. After a stint as a system administrator for the equities trading floor at a major Wall Street financial institution, Evan spent over 4 years as a sales engineer at VERITAS Software, servicing all sorts of customers, including Wall Street financial firms. Since then he has worked in corporate engineering for VERITAS, consulting and writing on many different issues including high availability, clustering, and disaster recovery. He has written articles for many magazines and web sites, including, most recently, TechTarget.com, and is a very well-regarded speaker who contributes to many industry events. Since completing the first edition of *Blueprints*, he was an editor and contributing author for *The Resilient Enterprise*, a 2002 VERITAS Publishing book on disaster recovery that was the first VERITAS published book that involved a collaboration of industry authors. Evan holds a B.S. in Computer Science from Lehigh University and an M.B.A. from Rutgers University.

Hal Stern is a Vice President and Distinguished Engineer at Sun Microsystems. He is the Chief Technology Officer for Sun Services, working on design patterns for highly reliable systems and networked applications deployed on those systems. In more than 10 years with Sun, Hal has been the Chief Technology Officer for the Sun ONE (iPlanet) infrastructure products division and the Chief Technologist of Sun's Northeast U.S. Sales Area. Hal has done architecture, performance, and reliability work for major financial institutions and electronic clearing networks, two major professional sports leagues, and several of the largest telecommunications equipment and service companies.

Hal served as contributing editor for *SunWorld Magazine* for 5 years, and was on the editorial staff and advisory board of IDG's *JavaWorld* magazine. Before joining Sun, Hal developed molecular modeling software for a Boston area startup company and was on the research staff at Princeton University. He holds a B.S. in Engineering degree from Princeton University. When not at the keyboard, Hal coaches Little League, plays ice hockey, cheers for the New Jersey Devils, and tries desperately to golf his weight.

Introduction

A journey of a thousand miles begins with a single step.
—Confucius

Despite predictions in the 1970s (and extending into the 1980s) that computers would make everyone's lives easier and give us all more leisure time, just the opposite seems to be taking place. Computers move faster, thanks largely to faster and faster CPUs, yet as fast as computers are, the business world seems to move even faster. Computers are expected to be operational and available 7 days a week, 24 hours a day. Downtime, even for maintenance, is no longer an option.

With the unprecedented growth and acceptance of the Internet, average people expect to be able to buy clothing or office supplies on the Web at 4:00 A.M., while in their underwear. And if they can't buy from your web site, they will buy from your competitor's. Uniform resource locators (URLs) are part of the culture; they are written on the sides of city buses, and even some two-year-olds know www.nickjr.com and www.disney.com.

Adding to the complexity is the globalization of the Internet and the Web. Even if there are quiet times for web servers in the United States, those times are filled by users in Europe and the rest of the world. National borders and time zones essentially disappear on the Web.

The amounts of data that businesses are being called on to save and manage are growing at astounding rates. The consulting organizations that monitor such things estimate that online data will continue to grow at 70 to 75 percent per year for the next few years. That data must be accessible quickly at all hours of the day or night, if not for your company's European operation, then for its U.S. personnel. As the amount of data grows, the price of storage devices continues to drop dramatically, making it feasible for companies to store all their data.

But what happens when the systems crash? What happens when disks stop turning? What about when your network stops delivering data? Does the business stop? Must your customers visit your competitor's web site to order their Barbie dolls? Should you just send your employees home? For how long? Can you recover? When? And how come this stuff never seems to happen to your competitors? (Don't worry—it does.)

The media frenzy surrounding the Y2K nonevent did do some good. The fear of all computers everywhere failing made the average Joe appreciate (even if just a little bit) the direct effect that computers have on his daily life. Although that lesson may have fallen from the society's day-to-day consciousness, at least the impact was there for a short time. As a result, the people who allocate money for the management of computer systems have a little bit more of an appreciation of what can happen when good computers do go bad.

Why an Availability Book?

The Y2K problem is certainly not the only issue that has caused problems or at least concerns with computer availability; it just happens to be the best-known example. Some of the others over the last few years include:

- Worldwide terrorism, including the September 11, 2001, attacks on New York and Washington, DC
- Satellite outages that brought down pagers and other communication devices
- Attacks by various computer viruses
- Natural disasters such as floods, tornadoes, and earthquakes
- The introduction of the euro
- The emergence of the Internet as a viable social force, comparable to TV or radio as a mass-market influence

Obviously, the actual impact of each of these issues has varied from negligible to serious. But again, each calls attention to the importance and value of computers, and the impact of failures. Downtime on the Internet is like dead air on a television station; it's embarrassing and a mistake that you work hard to prevent.

Our Approach to the Problem

In this book, we will look at the elements of your computer systems that can fail, whether because of a major event such as the ones just listed, or because of rather mundane problems like the failure of a network router or corruption of a critical file. We look at basic system configuration issues, including, but not limited to, physical placement of equipment, logical arrangements of disks, backing up of critical data, and migration of important services from one system to another.

We will take an end-to-end perspective, because systems are an end-to-end proposition. Either everything works or nothing works. Rarely is there any middle ground. Your users sit in front of their computer screen, trying to complete a task. Either the task runs or it doesn't. Sometimes it runs, but too slowly. When an application runs too slowly, that may still be an availability issue, since the user cannot get his job done in a timely manner.

We also take a business-oriented approach, never losing sight of the fact that every bit of protection—whether mirrored disks, backup systems, or extra manpower for system design—costs real money. We have tried to balance costs and benefits, or at least help you to balance costs and benefits. After all, no two sites or systems are the same. What may be important to you may not matter a bit to the guy down the hall. One of the hardest jobs facing designers of highly available systems is scoping out the costs of a particular level of protection, which are frequently higher than the people running the business would like. In an era where computer hardware prices shrink logarithmically, it's hard to explain to management that you can't get fault-tolerant system operation at desktop PC prices. Our goal is to help define the metrics, the rules, and the guidelines for making and justifying these cost/benefit trade-offs. Availability is commonly measured in "nines"—99.99 percent uptime is "four nines." Our goal is to help you increase the number of nines you can achieve within your engineering constraints, and the number you can afford within your budget and cost constraints. At the same time, we'll question the industry's dependence on nines as the only gauge of availability.

We'll frequently refer to cost/benefit or cost/complexity trade-offs. Such decisions abound in technology-driven companies: Buy or build? Faster time to market or more features? Quick and dirty or morally correct but slower? Our job is to provide some guidelines for making these decisions. We'll try to avoid taking editorial stances, because there are very few absolutes in engineering design.

What's Not Here

Many things are missing from this book, some of which may be missed, but all of which were omitted for specific reasons:

- We mention products, but we do not judge them. Product references are not endorsements; we mention them so that you have the opportunity to evaluate the best-known players in a particular market. Products change rapidly, vendors change rapidly, and we prefer not to make judgment calls about products. After all, we both work for vendors of these products. We prefer to outline the questions to ask, to make you a better evaluator of your own issues.

- There aren't prescriptions or recipes that you can copy and try out in your machine room. Partly this is because there are no one-size-fits-all solutions, and partly it's because describing only the solution evades a discussion of the skills needed to build it.

- There's not much code, as in programming snippets. When you're customizing a failover solution, you're going to be writing some code and fine-tuning scripts to match your environment. Our goal is to convey discipline, process, and methodology to establish the requirements for this code-slinging. You'll find this book a level more abstract than a programmer's guide.

- You won't find absolute and complete answers to all of your questions. Some topics can only be addressed in your machine room, with your business, your budget, and your management. If we help you make choices you can live with, we feel that we've done our job.

- We do not offer guarantees for specific levels of uptime. We do not say, "Do this and you'll achieve 99.99 percent uptime." There are no guarantees; there are trends. If you do the right things, and protect your systems against the right types of outages, you will increase your system's uptime. If you protect the wrong things, you will spend money and get nothing in return.

Our Mission

This book actually comes with a mission statement. It's not a rambling paragraph about curing all the world's ills; it's a short, snappy reflection on what we're prompting you to do. When we wrote the book, this statement was never far from our thinking, and, in fact, it was in many ways the driving force behind the entire project. We believe that every bit of information in the book is related to this statement:

> *High availability cannot be achieved by merely installing failover software and walking away.*

In fact, the best way to ensure that you stick to our mission statement is to follow this piece of advice: Build your systems so that they never have to failover. Yes, of course they will failover, but if you make failover the very last resort, you will truly maximize your availability.

Of course, some sanity must be added to the last statement. You can't just throw money at your systems to make them work better. At some point, the additional money will not provide commensurate benefits. The key is to:

- Price out your downtime

and then use that figure to:

- Determine how much you can afford to spend to protect against service outages

Remember that reliability engineering costs money; it's far more than what you'll spend on hardware or system software. It's an operating-system-independent cost, and one that hasn't come down as a function of cheaper memory or larger disks. When you spend this money, you are not throwing good money after bad. You are investing money in the critical systems that run your operations so that they can run those operations more of the time.

Those messages are probably the most important statements in this entire book. Together they build a message that balances system needs with the harsh realities of budget limitations.

The Availability Index

Another way of making the point about balancing downtime with cost is to look at availability as a curve. The more you spend, the higher you move up the curve. Be sure to note, however, that the incremental costs to move from one level to the next increase as you move up the curve.

As you go through the technology chapters, which make up the heart of the book, you'll find that each chapter begins with a picture of the Availability Index. A detailed explanation can be found in Chapter 3, "The Value of Availability," but fundamentally, it shows the relationship between availability and cost. The line is curved because the relationship is not linear; the higher the level of availability you require, the more it costs to move to the next level. Costs accelerate as you move up the Index. Another way to look at it is that the curve reflects the law of diminishing returns. After you protect against the cheaper and easier-to-fix problems, the cost (and complexity) of the next level of protection increases, flattening out the curve. You may also notice that the curve never quite makes it to 100 percent; that's because we believe that 100 percent availability cannot be attained over the medium and long term. More on that later.

Summary

Computer systems are very complex. The solutions that make them work best are complex too. They require planning, work, testing, and a general ongoing effort by knowledgeable people at every level of implementation. Applications must be tolerant of failures and inappropriate inputs. Hardware must be able to automatically recover from failures. And since systems change, if you want this functionality to always be present, you must regularly test your recovery procedures. Do they still work? Do they still work as quickly as they should? If they do not work as expected, the time to find out is not when something has gone wrong and the pressure is on.

Our goals are to help you design your systems for maximum availability and predictable downtime and recovery times. We will look at these systems from end to end, and from network, system, and application perspectives.

Organization of the Book

We take a very layered approach to systems, and that layered approach follows in the organization of this book. We look at each type of component separately, starting with disks and moving up through systems into software and finally disaster recovery.

In many of the chapters, you will find sidebars that we call "Tales from the Field." They are generally true-to-life experiences that we have lived through ourselves or have seen real users of computer systems go through. Some of them are funny; all of them help make a point clearer. We hope that you learn from the mistakes and examples that we have seen and sometimes suffered through.

Chapter 2, "What to Measure," takes a look at the numbers and statistics that go into measuring availability, as well as what can go wrong with the various components of your system. This chapter also looks at measurement trends, such as six sigma and "nines," that are becoming more common metrics for system quality.

Chapter 3 introduces the Availability Index in some detail and looks at the business case for availability.

Chapter 4, "The Politics of Availability," is a primer on how to introduce the concept of availability into your organization and how to deal with some of the politics and other potential organizational roadblocks.

Chapter 5, "20 Key High Availability Design Principles," is a cornerstone for the whole book and contains our 20 key design principles for attaining resilience and high availability. We refer back to these principles throughout the book.

Chapter 6, "Backups and Restores," focuses on the last line of defense between you and irrevocably lost data. How do you take backups, why do you take them, and how do you handle the tapes and the hardware?

Chapter 7, "Highly Available Data Management," looks at data storage. We discuss disks and disk arrays, and the ways to logically arrange them to maximize your protection against hardware failures, including the use of RAID (redundant array of independent disks) hardware and software.

Chapter 8, "SANs, NAS, and Virtualization," introduces some newer technology: Storage Area Networks (SANs), Network-Attached Storage (NAS), and virtualization.

Chapter 9, "Networking," reviews networking concepts and discusses the various elements of making your networks survive failures at the physical or logical layers, including router redundancy and load balancing

Chapter 10, "Data Centers and the Local Environment," looks at the environment around your computers, including your data center, power issues, cabling, maintenance plans, cooling, system naming conventions, and physical space.

Chapter 11, "People and Processes," looks at some people and process issues related to system resiliency, such as system administrators, maintenance plans, patches, documentation, vendor management, and security.

Chapter 12, "Clients and Consumers," examines clients as consumers of high-availability services and as resources to be managed.

Chapter 13, "Application Design," focuses on application reliability. What are the issues involved in making your applications recover properly after a server has failed and recovered? What should you do to make your applications more resilient to external system faults and internal (logical) problems?

Chapter 14, "Data and Web Services," details high-availability models for web and network services such as web, application, and directory servers, along with some thoughts on making XML-based web services more reliable.

Chapter 15, "Local Clustering and Failover," introduces the concept of clustering, the technology that is often viewed as the core of high availability.

In Chapter 16, "Failover Management and Issues," we look at failovers and the software that manages them. We look at the implications of building your own failover software, and at some of the inherent complexities that accompany the use of this software.

Chapter 17, "Failover Configurations," examines the myriad of different failover configurations—the good, the bad, and the ugly.

Chapter 18, "Data Replication," reviews techniques for replicating critical data to remote systems across a network.

Chapter 19, "Virtual Machines and Resource Management," covers resource management and machine partitioning, tools used in ensuring service levels to users who may define a slow or unpredictable system as one that's not meeting its availability requirements.

Chapter 20, "The Disaster Recovery Plan," examines disaster recovery issues, ranging from legal and personnel issues to practical issues like whose application gets restored first at the DR site.

Chapter 21, "A Resilient Enterprise," is a case study of the New York Board of Trade, who lost their building and systems in the attacks on September 11, 2001, and were ready to get back to business by 8 P.M. that night.

Chapter 22, "A Brief Look Ahead," is our look at technology trends that will shape high-availability design.

And Chapter 23, "Parting Shots," is a quick wrap-up and some parting shots.

Key Points

We end each chapter with a few bullet points that we believe sum up the key messages. For Chapter 1, it's really quite easy:

- High availability cannot be achieved by merely installing failover software and walking away.
- The availability problem domain spans the entire data path from client to network to server.

CHAPTER

2

What to Measure

What would you think about, if it were you, sitting there in an oversized suit, strapped to an intricate and complex network of components, wires, circuits and engines, all procured by the government, from the lowest bidder?
—John Glenn, on his thoughts before his first spaceflight

We have become obsessed with data. If we can measure it, in theory, we can control it and improve it. Data collected and analyzed becomes the basis for resource allocations and prioritization decisions, ranging from whether or not to buy an additional 10 terabytes (TB) of disk space for marketing, to which server pairs should be turned into clusters for improved availability. Our goal for this chapter is to present some common measurements of availability, and to provide a framework for interpreting those measurements. In Chapter 3, "The Value of Availability," we'll ascribe pricing and business benefit to this data.

In this chapter we discuss the following topics:

- How we measure availability

- The failure modes, or typical things that can and do go wrong

- Situations in which measurements may not be valid

Throughout this book we use *resiliency* in terms of overall system availability. We see resiliency as a general term similar to high availability, but without all the baggage that HA carries along with it. High availability once referred to a fairly specific range of system configurations, often involving two computers that monitor and protect each other. During the last few years, however, it has lost much of its original meaning; vendors and users have co-opted the term to mean whatever they want it to mean.

To us, resiliency and high availability mean that all of a system's failure modes are known and well defined, including networks and applications. They mean that the recovery times for all known failures have an upper bound; we know how long a particular failure will have the system down. Although there may be certain failures that we cannot cope with very well, we know what they are and how to recover from them, and we have backup plans to use if our recoveries don't work. A resilient system is one that can take a hit to a critical component and recover and come back for more in a known, bounded, and generally acceptable period of time.

Measuring Availability

When you discuss availability requirements with a user or project leader, he will invariably tell you that 100 percent availability is required: "Our project is so important that we can't have any downtime at all." But the tune usually changes when the project leader finds out how much 100 percent availability would cost. Then the discussion becomes a matter of money, and more of a negotiation process.

As you can see in Table 2.1, for many applications, 99 percent uptime is adequate. If the systems average an hour and a half of downtime per week, that may be satisfactory. Of course, a lot of that depends on when the hour and a half occurs. If it falls between 3:00 A.M. and 4:30 A.M. on Sunday, that is going to be a lot more tolerable on many systems than if it occurs between 10:00 A.M. and 11:30 A.M. on Thursday, or every weekday at 2:00 P.M. for 15 or 20 minutes.

Table 2.1 Measuring Availability

PERCENTAGE UPTIME	PERCENTAGE DOWNTIME	DOWNTIME PER YEAR	DOWNTIME PER WEEK
98%	2%	7.3 days	3 hours, 22 minutes
99%	1%	3.65 days	1 hour, 41 minutes
99.8%	0.2%	17 hours, 30 minutes	20 minutes, 10 seconds
99.9%	0.1%	8 hours, 45 minutes	10 minutes, 5 seconds
99.99%	0.01%	52.5 minutes	1 minute
99.999%	0.001%	5.25 minutes	6 seconds
99.9999% ("six 9s")	0.0001%	31.5 seconds	0.6 seconds

One point of negotiation is the hours during which 100 percent uptime may be required. If it is only needed for a few hours a day, that goal is quite achievable. For example, when brokerage houses trade between the hours of 9:30 A.M. and 4:00 P.M., then during those hours, plus perhaps 3 or 4 hours on either side, 100 percent uptime is required. A newspaper might require 100 percent uptime during production hours, but not the rest of the day. If, however, 100 percent uptime is required $7 \times 24 \times 365$, the costs become so prohibitive that only the most profitable applications and large enterprises can consider it, and even if they do, 100 percent availability is almost impossible to achieve over the long term.

As you move progressively to higher levels of availability, costs increase very rapidly. Consider a server (*abbott*) that with no special protective measures taken, except for disk mirrors and backups, delivers 99 percent availability. If you couple that server with another identically configured server (*costello*) that is configured to take over from *abbott* when it fails, and that server also offers 99 percent availability, then theoretically, you can achieve a combined availability of 99.99 percent. Mathematically, you multiply the downtime on *abbott* (1 percent) by the uptime on *costello* (99 percent); *costello* will only be in use during *abbott*'s 1 percent of downtime. The result is 0.99 percent. Add the original 99 to 0.99, and you get 99.99 percent, the theoretical uptime for the combined pair.

Of course, in reality 99.99 percent will not occur simply by combining two servers. The increase in availability is not purely linear. It takes time for the switchover (usually called a *failover*) to occur, and during that period, the combined server is down. In addition, there are external failures that will affect access to both servers, such as network connectivity or power outages. These failures will undoubtedly decrease the overall availability figures below 99.99 percent.

However, we only use the "nines" for modeling purposes. In reality, we believe that the nines have become an easy crutch for system and operating system vendors, allowing them to set unrealistic expectations for uptime.

The Myth of the Nines

We've seen a number of advertisements proclaiming "five nines" or more of availability. This is a nice generalization to make for marketing materials, because we can measure the mean time between failures (MTBF) of a hardware system and project its downtime over the course of a year. System availability is based on software configurations, load, user expectations, and the time to repair a failure. Before you aim for a target number of nines, or judge systems based on their relative proclaimed availability, make sure you can match the advertised number against your requirements. The following are considerations to take into account when evaluating the desired availability:

Nines are an average.   Maximum outages, in terms of the maximum time to repair, are more important than the average uptime.

Nines only measure that which can be modeled.   Load and software are hard to model in an average case; you will need to measure your actual availability and repair intervals for real systems, running real software loads.

Nines usually reflect a single system view of the world.   Quick: Think of a system that's not networked but important. Reliability has to be based on networks of computers, and the top-to-bottom stack of components that make up the network. The most reliable, fault-tolerant system in the world is useless if it sits behind a misconfigured router.

Computer system vendors talk about "nines of availability," and although nines are an interesting way to express availability, they miss some essential points.

All downtime is not created equal. If an outage drives away customers or users, then it is much more costly than an outage that merely inconveniences those users. But an outage that causes inconvenience is more costly to an enterprise than an outage that is not detected by users.

Consider the cost of downtime at a retail e-commerce web site such as amazon.com or ebay.com. If, during the course of a year, a single 30-minute outage is suffered, the system has an apparently respectable uptime of 99.994 percent. If, however, the outage occurs on a Friday evening in early December, it costs a lot more in lost business than the same outage would if it occurred on a Sunday at 4:00 A.M. local time in July. Availability statistics do not make a distinction between the two.

Similarly, if an equities trading firm experiences a 30-minute outage 5 minutes before the Federal Reserve announces a surprise change in interest rates, it would cost the firm considerably more than the same outage would on a Tuesday evening at 8 P.M., when no rate change, and indeed, little activity of any kind, was in the offing.

Consider the frustration level of a customer or user who wants to use a critical system. If the 30-minute outage comes all at once, then a user might leave and return later or the next night, and upon returning, stay if everything is OK. However, if the 30 minutes of downtime is spread over three consecutive evenings at the same time, users who try to gain access each of those three nights and find systems that are down will be very frustrated. Some of them will go elsewhere, never to return. (Remember the rule of thumb that says it costs 10 times more to find a new customer than it does to retain an old one.)

Many system vendors offer uptime guarantees, where they claim to guarantee specific uptime percentages. If customers do not achieve those levels, then the vendor is contractually bound to pay their customers money or provide some other form of giveback. There are so many factors that are out of the control of system vendors, and are therefore disallowed in the contracts, that those contracts seldom have any teeth, and even more seldom pay off. Compare, for instance, the potential reliability of a server located in a northern California data center where, in early 2001, rolling power blackouts were a way of life, with a server in, say, Minnesota, where the traditionally high amounts of winter snow are expected and do not traditionally impact electric utility service. Despite those geographical differences, system vendors offer the same uptime contractual guarantees in both places. A system vendor cannot reasonably be expected to guarantee the performance of a local electric power utility, wide area network provider, or the data center cooling equipment. Usually, those external factors are specifically excluded from any guarantees.

The other problem with the nines is that availability is a chain, and any failed link in the chain will cause the whole chain to fail. Consider the diagram in Figure 2.1, which shows a simple representation of a user sitting at a client station and connected to a network over which he is working.

If the seven components in the figure (client station, network, file server and its storage, and the application server, its application, and its storage) have 99.99 percent availability each, that does not translate to an end user seeing 99.99 percent availability.

To keep the math simple, let's assume that all seven components have exactly the same level of expected availability, 99.99 percent. In reality, of course, different components have different levels of expected availability, and more complex components such as networks will often have lower levels. The other assumption is that multiple failures do not occur at the same time (although they can, of course, in real life); that would needlessly complicate the math.

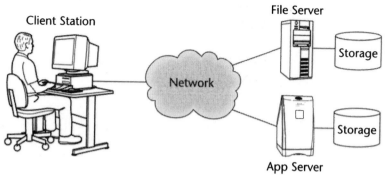

Figure 2.1   A user of a simple network.

Availability of 99.99 percent over each of seven components yields a simple formula of 0.9999 to the seventh power, which works out to 99.93 percent. That may not sound like a huge difference, but the difference is actually quite significant:

- Availability of 99.99 percent spread over a year is about 52 minutes downtime.

- Availability of 99.93 percent spread over a year is over 6 hours of downtime.

Another way to look at the math is to consider that for all practical purposes, the seven components will never be down at the same time. Since each component will be responsible for 52 minutes of downtime per year (based on 99.99 percent availability), 7 times 52 is 364 minutes, or just over 6 hours per year, or 99.93 percent.

The actual path from user to servers is going to be much more complicated than the one in Figure 2.1. For example, the network cloud is made up of routers, hubs, and switches, any of which could fail and thereby lower network availability. If the storage is mirrored, then its availability will likely be higher, but the value will surely vary. The formulas also exclude many other components that could cause additional downtime if they were to fail, such as electric power or the building itself.

Consider another example. Six of the seven components in the chain deliver 99.99 percent availability, but the seventh only achieves 99 percent uptime. The overall availability percentage for that chain of components will be just 98.94 percent. Great returns on investment can be achieved by improving the availability of that weakest link.

So, while some single components may be able to deliver upwards of 99.99 percent availability, it is much more difficult for an entire system, from user to server, to deliver the same level. The more components there are in the chain and the more complex the chain, the lower the overall availability will be.

Any bad component in the chain can lower overall availability, but there is no way for one good component to raise it above the level of the weakest link.

Defining Downtime

Definitions for downtime vary from gentle to tough, and from simple to complex. Easy definitions are often given in terms of failed components, such as the server itself, disks, the network, the operating system, or key applications. Stricter definitions may include slow server or network performance, the inability to restore backups, or simple data inaccessibility.

We prefer a very strict definition for downtime: If a user cannot get her job done on time, the system is down. A computer system is provided to its users for one purpose: to allow them to complete their work in an efficient and timely way. When circumstances prevent a user from doing this work, regardless of the reason, the system is down.

Causes of Downtime

In Figure 2.2 and Figure 2.3, we examine two different views of the most common causes of downtime, from surveys conducted by two different organizations. In Figure 2.2, which comes from the computer industry analysts Gartner/Dataquest, the greatest cause of downtime is system software failures, but just by a little bit (27 to 23 percent) over hardware failures. In Figure 2.3, provided by CNT, hardware failures cause 44 percent of downtime, more than triple their estimate for software downtime (and still more than double if you include viruses among their software causes).

The conclusion that we draw from these two very different sets of results is that if you ask different groups of people, you'll get widely varying results.

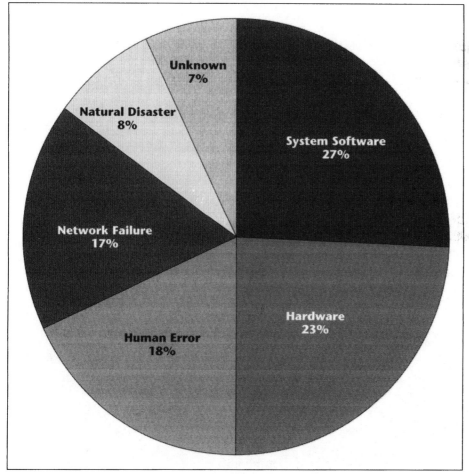

Figure 2.2 The most common causes of unplanned downtime (one view).

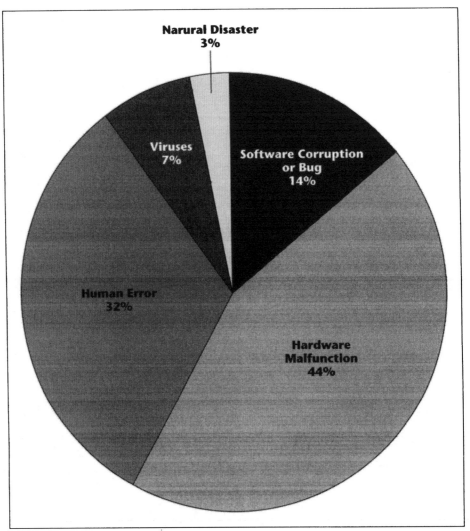

Figure 2.3 The most common causes of unplanned downtime (alternate view).

Both surveys agree that human error is a major cause of downtime, although they disagree on the degree of downtime that it causes. People cause downtime for two closely related reasons. The first reason is that they sometimes make dumb or careless mistakes. The second reason is that they do not always completely understand the way a system operates. The best way to combat people-caused downtime is through education combined with simple system design. By sending your people to school to keep them up-to-date on current technologies, and by keeping good solid documentation on hand and up-to-date, you can reduce the amount of downtime they cause.

The wide variance in the downtime caused by hardware according to the two surveys is most interesting. We believe that hardware is causing less downtime than it used to, as hardware components are getting more and more reliable over time, and because the most delicate components (disks and power supplies) tend to have the greatest amount of redundancy applied to them. When a disk or power supply fails on a critical system, its workload is often switched over to an identical component with little or no evident down-time being caused.

The most obvious common causes for system outages are probably software failures. Software bugs are perhaps the most difficult source of failures to get out of the system. As hardware becomes more reliable, and methods are employed to reduce planned outages, their percentages will decrease, while the percentage of outages attributed to software issues will increase. As software becomes more complex, software-related outages may become more frequent on their own. Of course, as software development and debugging techniques become more sophisticated, software-related outages should become less prevalent. It will be very interesting to see whether software-related downtime increases or decreases over time.

What Is Availability?

At its simplest level, availability, whether high, low, or in between, is a measure of the time that a server is functioning normally. We offer a simple equation to calculate availability:

$$A = \frac{MTBF}{MTBF + MTTR}$$

Where A is the degree of *availability* expressed as a percentage, MTBF is the *mean time between failures*, and MTTR is the *maximum time to repair or resolve* a particular problem.

Some simple observations:

- As MTTR approaches zero, A increases toward 100 percent.
- As MTBF gets larger, MTTR has less impact on A.

For example, if a particular system has an MTBF of 100,000 hours and an MTTR of 1 hour, it has a rather impressive availability level of 100,000/100,001, or 99.999 percent. If you cut the MTTR to 6 minutes, or ⅒ of an hour, availability increases by an extra 9, to 99.9999 percent. But to achieve this level of availability with even 6 minutes of downtime, you need a component with an actual duration between failures of 100,000 hours, which is better than 11 years.

Let's restate that last statistic. *To achieve 99.9999 percent availability, you are permitted just 6 minutes downtime in 11.4 years.* That's 6 minutes in 11.4 years over your entire system, not just the one component we happen to be examining. Given today's technology, this is, for all practical purposes, unachievable and a completely unrealistic goal. Downtimes of less than 10 minutes per year (about 99.998 percent) are probably achievable, but it would be very difficult to get much better than that. In addition to well-designed systems, a significant degree of luck will surely be required. And you just can't plan for luck.

Luck comes in many flavors. Good luck is when your best developer happens to be working late on the night that his application brings down your critical servers, and he fixes the problem quickly. Good luck is when the water pipe in the ceiling breaks and leaks water over one side of your disk mirrors but doesn't affect the other side. Bad luck (or malice) gets you when someone on the data center tour leans on the power switch to a production server. Bad luck forces a car from the road and into the pole in front of your building where the power from both of your power companies comes together. Bad luck is that backhoe outside your window digging up the fiber cable running between your buildings, as you helplessly watch through your office window.

M Is for Mean

The key term in MTBF is mean time. A mean time between failures number is just that, a mean. An average. If a disk drive has an MTBF of 200,000 hours (almost 23 years), that does not mean that every disk rolling off the assembly line is guaranteed to work for exactly 23 years, and then drop dead. When the government announces life expectancy figures, it certainly doesn't mean that every person in America will die when he reaches the age of 76.9 years. For every person who doesn't make it to his 50th birthday, there is going to be someone whose picture makes it onto *The Today Show* for surpassing her 100th birthday.

Means are trends. If you look at all the disks that roll off the assembly line during a given period of time, the average life expectancy of a disk, before it fails, is about 23 years. That means, however, that some disks may fail the first day and others may last 40 years (obsolescence aside). It also means that if you have a large server, with, say, 500 disks in it, on average you will lose a disk every 200,000/500 or 400 hours. Four hundred hours is only about 16½ days. So, you will be replacing a disk, on average, every 2½ weeks.

A statistical mean is not enough to tell you very much about the particular members of a population. The mean of 8, 9, 10, 11, and 12 is 10. But the mean of 1, 1, 1, 1, and 46 is also 10. So is the mean of 12,345, -12,345, 47,000,000, -47,000,000, and 50.

The other key number is standard deviation, or sigma (σ). Without going into a long, dull explanation of standard deviation calculations (go back and look at your college statistics textbook!), σ tells you how far the members of a population stray from the mean. For each of the three previous examples (and treating each like a complete population, for you statistics nerds), σ is as follows: 1.414214, 19.6, and 29,725,411. For the sake of completeness we offer one more example: the mean of 9.99, 10.01, 9.999, 10.002, and 9.999 is still 10, and the standard deviation is 0.006419. As these comparisons illustrate, the closer the members of the population are to the mean, the lower σ becomes. Or in other words, the lower σ is, the more indicative of final results the mean is. (You can unclench your teeth now; we have finished talking about statistics.)

When looking at hardware components, therefore, you'll want MTBF figures that are associated with low standard deviations. But good luck in obtaining MTBF numbers; most hardware vendors don't like sharing such data. If you can get these numbers, however, they will tell you a lot about the quality of the vendor's hardware.

Let's apply this logic to the server with 500 disks example. What we said about replacing disks every 2½ weeks isn't really true, because half the disks will last longer than 23 years. But, if it were true, you would still not be replacing a disk on schedule every 2½ weeks. The distribution of disk failures would look more like a bell curve, with the amount of failure increasing as the MTBF date approached. The height of the bell curve increases as σ decreases, and vice versa.

The same guidelines that apply to MTBFs also apply to MTTRs. If it takes your administrator an average of 15 minutes to recover from a particular problem, that does not necessarily mean it will take him 15 minutes every time. Complications can set in during the repair process. Personnel change, and recovery times can increase while the new people learn old procedures. (Conversely, as an administrator becomes more adept at fixing a particular problem, repair times can decline.) System reboot times can increase over time, too, as the system gains additional components that need to be checked or reinstalled at boot time.

Many aspects of MTTRs can be out of your control. If you need a critical component to repair a server, and that component is on back order at the vendor, it could take days or possibly weeks to acquire it. Unless you have alternative sources or stock your own spare parts, there isn't anything you can do but wait, with your system down. In many shops, system administration is a separate job from network administration, and it is performed by a totally separate organization. If the system problem turns out to be network related, you may have to wait on the network folks to find and fix the problem so that you can get your system running again. Or vice versa.

What's Acceptable?

Balancing the cost of improved availability and shorter MTTR against your business needs is the subject of Chapter 3. The following are some vignettes to think about before we discuss the range of failures that your systems may experience:

- In general, you don't hear about local phone service outages. The phone companies have mastered the art of installing upgrades to their infrastructure without causing any perceptible interruptions to phone service. Acceptable outages in a telephone network are in the subsecond range; anything longer gets counted as a User Impacted Minute (UIM) that typically gets reported to the FCC.

- On a trading floor, outages in the subminute range can be tolerated (usually not well, though) before impact is felt. Regulatory issues concerning on-time trade reporting kick in within two minutes. The market moves every few seconds, possibly making a profitable trade less interesting only a few seconds later.

- If a decision support system is driving a mass mailing that has a deadline 48 hours away, and it takes 4 hours to finish a single query, your uptime requirements are stronger than if the mailing deadline is in the next month.

- If your users believe that the system will be down for an hour while you fix a problem, and you can fix it in 20 minutes, you are a hero. But if the users believe it should take 10 minutes, the same 20-minute fix makes you a goat. Setting expectations drives another downstream system, namely, what the users will do next. If they're convinced they'll be live again in an hour, you have to deliver in that hour. In *Star Trek III: The Search for Spock*, Captain Kirk asked Engineer Scott if he always multiplied his repair estimates by a factor of 4. Scotty's response was, "Of course. How do you think I keep my reputation as a miracle worker?"

You need to know what can break, how those failures appear to the user and to the administrators, before you analyze what you'll do in each case.

Failure Modes

In this section, we take a quick look at the things that can go wrong with computer systems and that can cause downtime. Some of them, especially the hardware ones, may seem incredibly obvious, but others will not.

Hardware

Hardware points of failure are the most obvious ones—the failures that people will think of first when asked to provide such a list. And yet, as we saw in Figure 2.2 and Figure 2.3, they only make up less than half (possibly just a little more than a quarter, depending on whose numbers you like better) of all system outages. However, when you have a hardware outage, you may be down for a long time if you don't have redundancy built in. Waiting for parts and service people makes you a captive to the hardware failure.

The components that will cause the most failures are moving parts, especially those associated with high speeds, low tolerances, and complexity. Having all of those characteristics, disks are prime candidates for failures. Disks also have controller boards and cabling that can break or fail. Many hardware disk arrays have additional failure-prone components such as memory for caching, or hardware for mirroring or striping.

Tape drives and libraries, especially digital linear tape (DLT) libraries, have many moving parts, motors that stop and start, and extremely low tolerances. They also have controller boards and many of the same internal components that disk drives have, including memory for caching.

Fans are the other components with moving parts. The failure of a fan may not cause immediate system failure the way a disk drive failure will, but when a machine's cooling fails, the effects can be most unpredictable. When CPUs and memory chips overheat, systems can malfunction in subtle ways. Many systems do not have any sort of monitoring for their cooling, so cooling failures can definitely catch many system administrators by surprise.

It turns out that fans and power supplies have the worst MTBFs of all system components. Power supplies can fail hard and fast, resulting in simple downtime, or they can fail gradually. The gradual failure of a power supply can be a very nasty problem, causing subtle, sporadic failures in the CPU, memory, or backplane. Power supply failures are caused by many factors, including varying line voltage and the stress of being turned on and off.

To cover for these shortcomings, modern systems have extra fans, extra power supplies, and superior hardware diagnostics that provide for problem detection and identification as quickly as possible. Many systems can also "call home." When a component fails, the system can automatically call the service center and request maintenance. In some cases, repair people arrive on-site to the complete surprise of the local staff.

Of course, failures can also occur in system memory and in the CPU. Increasing numbers of modern systems are able to configure a failed component out of the system without a reboot. This may or may not help intermittent failures in memory or the CPU, but it will definitely help availability when a true failure occurs.

There are other hardware components that can fail, although they do so very infrequently. These include the backplane, the various system boards, the cabinet, the mounting rack, and the system packaging.

Environmental and Physical Failures

Failures can be external to the system as well as internal. There are many components in the environment that can cause system downtime, yet these are rarely considered as potential points of failure. Most of these are data center–related, but many of them can impact your servers regardless of their placement. And in many cases, having a standby server will not suffice in these situations, as the entire environment may be affected.

The most obvious environmental problem is a power failure. Power failures (and brownouts) can come from your electric utility, or they occur much more locally. A car can run into the light pole in front of your building. The failure of a circuit breaker or fuse, or even a power strip, can shut your systems down. The night cleaning crew might unplug some vital system in order to plug in a vacuum cleaner, or their plugging in the vacuum cleaner may overload a critical circuit.

The environmental cooling system can fail, causing massive overheating in all of the systems in the room. Similarly, the dehumidifying system can fail (although that failure is not going to be as damaging to the systems in the room as a cooling failure).

Most data centers contain rats' nests of cables, under the floor and out the back of the racks and cabinets. Cables can break, and they can be pulled out. And, of course, a sudden change in the laws of physics could result in copper no longer conducting electricity. (If that happens, you probably have bigger problems.)

Most data centers have fire protection systems. Halon is still being removed from data centers (apparently they get one more Halon incident, and that's it; Halon systems cannot be refilled), but the setting off of one of these fire protection systems can still be a very disruptive event. One set of problems ensues when the fire is real, and the protection systems work properly and put the fire out. The water or other extinguishing agent can leave a great deal of residue and can leave the servers in the room unfit for operation. Halon works by displacing the oxygen in the room, which effectively chokes off the fire. Of course, displaced oxygen could be an issue for any human beings unfortunate enough to be in the room at the time. Inergen Systems (www.inergen.com) makes newer, more environmentally sound, and friendlier to oxygen-breathing life systems, that can be dropped directly into Halon systems (there are competing systems as well). The fire itself can cause significant damage to the environment. One certainly hopes that when a fire protection system is put into action, the fire is real. But sometimes it isn't, and the fire protection system goes off when no emergency exists. This can leave the data center with real damage caused solely by a mistake.

The other end of the spectrum is when a fire event is missed by the protection system. The good news is that there will be no water or other fire protection system residue. The bad news is that your once-beautiful data center may now be an empty, smoldering shell. Or worse.

Another potential environmental problem is the structural failure of a supporting component, such as a computer rack or cabinet. Racks can collapse or topple when not properly constructed. If shelves are not properly fastened, they can come loose and crash down on the shelves beneath them. Looming above the cabinets in most data centers are dusty ceilings, usually with cables running through them. Ceilings can come tumbling down, raining dust and other debris onto your systems, which get sucked into the systems by cooling fans.

Many data centers have some construction underway while active systems are operating nearby. Construction workers in work boots bring heavy-duty equipment in with them and may not have any respect for the production systems that are in their way. Cables get kicked or cut, and cabinets get pushed slightly (or not so slightly) and can topple. While construction workers are constructing, they are also stirring up dust and possibly cutting power to various parts of the room. If they lay plastic tarps over your equipment to protect it from dust, the equipment may not receive proper ventilation and may overheat.

And then there are the true disasters: earthquakes, tornadoes, floods, bombs and other acts of war and terrorism, or even locusts.

It is important to note that some high-end fault-tolerant systems may be impacted by environmental and power issues just as badly as regular availability systems.

Network Failures

Networks are naturally susceptible to failures because they contain many components and are affected by the configuration of every component. Where, exactly, *is* your network? In the switch? The drop cables? Bounded by all of the network interface cards in your systems? Any of those physical components can break, resulting in network outages or, more maddeningly, intermittent network failures.

Networks are also affected by configuration problems. Incorrect routing information, duplicate hostnames or IP addresses, and machines that misinterpret broadcast addresses can lead to misdirected packets. You'll also have to deal with redundancy in network connections, as you may have several routers connecting networks at multiple points. When that redundancy is broken, or its configuration is misrepresented, the network appears to be down.

When a network that you trust and love is connected to an untrusted or unmanaged network, you run the risk of being subject to a denial-of-service attack or a network penetration attempt from one of those networks. These types of attacks happen within well-run networks as well. Security mogul Bill Cheswick asks the attendees at his talks if they leave their wallets out in the open in their offices. Nary a hand goes up. Then he asks how many leave unprotected network access points like twisted-pair wall jacks in open offices, and you see the tentative hands raised. Access to the network is valuable and has to be protected while still allowing user activity to proceed without onerous overhead.

Finally, networks use a variety of core services or basic information services that we lump into the network fabric. Naming systems like NIS or DNS, security and authentication servers, or host configuration servers for hosts requiring DHCP to boot and join a network will bring down a network if they are not functioning or are giving out wrong answers. As we'll see in Chapter 9, "Networking," building resilient networks is a complex task and requires many cost/benefit choices.

File and Print Server Failures

When file and print servers fail, clients will hang or experience timeouts. A timeout can mean that a print job or a file request fails. The timeout can also lead to wrong answers or data corruption. For example, using Network File Systems (NFS) soft mounts, a write operation that times out will not be repeated. This can lead to holes in data files that will only be detected when the file is read. NFS soft mounts, and other misbehavior by NFS clients, is discussed more in Chapter 13, "Application Design."

The failure of a print server can result in lost, hung, or damaged print jobs that require resubmitting. All the while, the user who has requested the job is not being served; based on our definition of downtime, the print server is down to the user.

Database System Failures

Like any complex application, database systems contain many moving parts. These moving parts are not found in fans or disk drives, however: They are the interrelated subapplications that make up any large enterprise application. The heart of a database system is the server process, or database engine, the main and primary database component that does the reading and writing to the disk, manages the placement of data, and responds to queries with (we hope) the correct answers. If this process stops working, all users accessing the database stop working. The database engine may be assisted by reader-writer or block manager processes that handle disk I/O operations for the engine, allowing it to execute database requests while other processes coordinate I/O and manage the disk block cache.

Between the users and the database server sits the listener process. The listener takes the incoming queries from the users and turns them into a form that the database server can process. Then, when the server returns its answer, the listener sends the answer back to the user who requested it.

The users, at their client workstations, run their end-user application, which is almost always one level removed from the actual SQL (structured query language) engine. The end-user application translates the user's request into SQL, which is then sent across the network to the listener. Well-written end-user applications also shield the user from the dreary complexities of the nearly perfect grammar that SQL requires, and from ordinary problems with the database, such as server crashes and other widespread downtime.

Obviously, the failure of any of these processes in the chain will cause the database to be unavailable to its users. Possible failures can include the following:

Application crashes.   The application stops running completely, leaving an error message (we hope) that will enable the administrators to determine the nature of the problem.

Application hangs.   A more insidious problem with databases or other systems that have significant interaction with the operating system is when a component process, such as a listener, reader-writer process manager, or the database kernel, hangs waiting for a system resource to free or gets trapped in a deadlock with another process. Some very long-running database operations (such as a scan and update of every record) may appear to make the system hang when they are really just consuming all available cycles.

Resource shortfalls.   The most common resource shortfall to strike most database environments is inadequate disk space. If the space allocated to the database fills up, the database engine may crash, hang, or simply fail to accept new entries. None of these is particularly useful in a production environment. If the database itself doesn't fill, the logs can overflow. There are logs that are written into the database disk space itself, and others that may be written into regular filesystem space. When data cannot be written to either type of log, the database will not perform as desired; it could hang, crash, stop processing incoming requests, or act in other antisocial ways.

Database index corruption.   A database server may manage terabytes of data. To find this data quickly on their disks, database servers (and filesystems, for that matter) use a confusing array of pointers and links. Should these pointers become corrupted, the wrong data can be retrieved, or worse, the attempt to retrieve data from an illegal space can result in the application or the system crashing completely. Data corruption problems are fairly unusual because most good RDBMSs have consistency checkers, which scan the database for corruption on startup.

Buggy software.   Almost by definition, software has bugs. (There is an old saw in computing that says all programs have at least one bug in them and can be shortened by at least one line. By extension, that means that all programs can be cut down to one line in length, and that line will have a bug in it.) Software is written by humans, and most of us, from time to time, make mistaks. Bugs can impact the system in various ways, from a simple misspelling in a log entry to a fatal bug that crashes the server and/or system. When trying to solve a problem, always consider the possibility that it was caused by a bug. Don't just assume that all problems were caused by bugs, but at the same time, don't strike bug from the list of possible causes for almost any problem. And these bugs can occur at any point in the subapplication chain, server processes, listener processes, client SQL engines, user applications, or even with the user's keyed input.

Web and Application Server Failures

The bugs that can strike a database can also affect a web server. Of course, many web servers are part of client/server applications that query back-end database servers to service client requests. So, anything affecting the database server will have an adverse effect on the web server as well. However, there are many other places within the web server environment where things might go awry.

There are many new places for bugs to crop up, including in the Common Gateway Interface (CGI), Perl, Java, JavaScript, or Active Server Page (ASP) code that manages the web page. If some set of circumstances causes a CGI program to get stuck in a loop, the web page it manages will never display, most likely causing the user to try another site.

New technology turns up all over the world of web servers. Much of this technology has been tested in a relatively short time by lots of users, and so it is often quite reliable. However, *web server* refers to a collection of applications: the httpd or web server that handles requests for items on a web page (hits) and returns the HTML or image files; the CGI scripts that get executed to generate web pages or take action on forms or other postings from web clients; and whatever back-end database or file servers are used to manage the content and state information on the web site. A failure in any of these components appears to be a web site failure.

Sitting in front of the web server, load-balancing hardware and software may be used to distribute requests over multiple, identical web servers, and on the client side a proxy cache server sits between a client and server and caches commonly accessed pages so that requests don't have to go outside of the client's network. Again, these systems can fail, making it appear that the web server has gone away.

Much like database servers, disks, filesystems, and logs can fill; memory or CPU can be exhausted; and other system resources can run out, causing hangs, crashes, unresponsiveness, and other nasty behavior. How do your CGI programs react if they cannot write to a required file? Or if they don't get a necessary response from some upstream application? Make sure they continue to operate.

Usually a web server is a front end for an application server, that nexus of business logic, data manipulation routines, and interfaces to existing back-end systems that does the "heavy lifting" of a web site. In the Java world, application servers are the frameworks that run the J2EE environment. The overall reliability of the application server is a function of all of the components that are layered on top of it. If you're using J2EE, for example, but call a non-Java native method written in C or C++, that code poses a risk to the application server. Step on memory with some poorly written native code and it's possible to corrupt the memory footprint of the application server.

Since web and application servers represent the top of the software stack, they're affected by the reliability and correct operation of all of the network pieces underneath them. Peter Deutsch, networking, security, and risk evaluation expert, points out that you can't control the security, reliability, or latency of a network. Furthermore, there's rarely a single point of control or single point of accountability for a network of systems. We'll look at how each piece of the networked system fits into the puzzle of making the overall system more reliable, based on the Availability Index that we'll introduce in Chapter 3.

Denial-of-Service Attacks

Not all problems involve the failure of a component. Making a resource unavailable to requestors is just as harmful to system availability as having that resource crash or fail. For example, a web server that is being bombarded by an exceptionally high request rate, absorbing all of the network connection capacity of the servers, appears to have failed to any web users attempting to access it. It hasn't failed in the downtime sense, but it has been made unavailable through a denial-of-service (DoS) attack. DoS approaches have been well known in security circles for several years, and in February 2000, the first wide-scale distributed DoS (DDoS) attack known as trin or trin00 affected several popular web sites. DoS attacks consume all available bandwidth for a given resource, ranging from network bandwidth and network connections to web server request handling and database requests.

ON LINE BECAUSE OF ONLINE

At the end of January 2003, my parents called me from Newark Airport, proud that their routine of arriving more than two hours early for their flight paid off handsomely. They had waited in line close to an hour for check-in because the counter agents were reduced to writing paper tickets and checking passengers in manually. A DoS attack that affected web and database servers had impacted one of the airline's ticketing systems, slowing service to a crawl. The Web brought immediate access to a wide variety of back-end systems directly to the consumer, and it also exposed those systems to all of the vagaries of the Internet.

—Hal

The following are some characteristic DoS attacks:

Network bandwidth flooding.   A torrent of packets, valid or garbage, consumes all of your incoming network bandwidth. This type of attack typically causes routers or switches to begin dropping legitimate traffic.

Network connection flooding.   An attempt by an attacker to send a series of ill-formed connection requests, filling up the incoming connection queue on web servers, database servers, or other back-end machines. The half-completed connection requests remain enqueued until they timeout, and of course more requests arrive during that interval, keeping the server's network stack overloaded.

CGI or web interface abuse.   A script or utility accessed by your web server is called repeatedly, or called with arguments that cause it to consume CPU, memory, or network resources. In many cases, these attacks may be signs of a security intrusion, with an attacker looking for a mail relay or other unsecured entry point. The SQLslammer attack in early 2003 fit this model loosely, with incoming requests attempting to access back-end database servers through well-known interfaces on public-facing web sites.

DoS attacks are likely to become more common. Vendors frequently offer patches or workarounds for the more common DoS approaches; for example, one way to combat the network connection flooding attack is to put in-progress connections in a separate queue and then prune the badly behaved connections out of the queue at shorter intervals, freeing up connection slots for real work.

Confidence in Your Measurements

Measuring the availability of a system, or making investment decisions aimed at improving that availability, depends on having confidence in the data you collect. The relative value of your measurements is colored by three factors: Is the metric the right one, is the metric valid over time, and can you use the metric to drive a process of improvement?

Renewability

Let's say your system fails because the operating system panics. It reboots, restarts applications such as web servers and databases, and continues on as before the failure. What's the probability of another failure due to an operating system panic? In all likelihood, it's exactly the same as it was before the reboot. There are many cases, however, in which repairing a system changes the

MTBF characteristics of the system, increasing the probability of another failure in the near-term future.

When you replace a punctured tire on your car with the "doughnut" spare tire, the MTBF for tire problems isn't the same as when you were running on four original tires; the doughnut has speed and distance restrictions on it that make it less reliable than a new tire. You've repaired your car so that it's functional again, but you haven't restored the car to its original MTBF specifications.

The concept of repairing a system such that its MTBF remains the same is called *renewability*.[1] Systems that aren't renewable degrade over time. Software, in general, may not be renewable because of issues like memory leaks or memory corruption that increase the probability of failure over time. Fixing one failure may not restore the system to its original state; if you've ever done a regular reboot or preventative maintenance reboot, you've aimed to make a system renewable the brute force way.

In all of the examples and scenarios we describe, we are aiming to make systems renewable. Repairing a failed component, whether hardware or software, shouldn't affect the expected time before the next failure. When evaluating an availability technique, the key question to ask is "Will this repair restore the system to its original state so that all of my assumptions about failure modes, failure rates, and repair processes are the same as they were before I made the repair?" Answer "yes" and you can have confidence that your MTBF numbers will stand up after a series of failures and associated repairs. We'll discuss the trade-offs involved in these evaluations more deeply in Chapter 3.

Sigmas and Nines

Six-sigma methodology is another popular trend that drives us to be data-focused and process-intense. The heart of six-sigma methodology is to measure something, find out where defects are being introduced, and then remove the source of the defects so that the resulting process shows less than six defects per million opportunities for a defect (six sigmas or standard deviations away from the mean). Though this methodology is most commonly used for manufacturing processes and hard goods, it has applicability to reliability of networked systems as well. Instead of thinking about six sigma as a search-and-destroy process for defects, think about it as a way of reducing variation.

---

[1] Renewability, and the statistics that support it, are covered in exquisite detail by Paul Tobias and David Trindade in *Applied Reliability*, published by Kluwer Academic Publishers (1995). The math is intense but complete. If you want to explore any of the concepts of MTBF, and the more proper ideas of failure rates and incidents over time, immerse yourself in their work.

- What are the values that users find most critical in your systems? Response time? Consistent behavior? Correct behavior? These are the critical-to-quality (CTQ) variables that you can measure.

- Define failures, or defects, based on these CTQs. If a transaction is expected to complete in 10 seconds, and it runs for 30 seconds but eventually completes correctly, is that a failure? Is it a defect?

- Can you relate these user CTQs to components in the system? Where are the defects introduced? What are the sources of variation, and how can you control those system components by changing their availability characteristics?

Six-sigma methodology can take your thinking about availability from the binary uptime-versus-downtime model to one in which you look at the user experience. It requires that you measure variables that are related to things you can control, reducing variability by removing the cause of defects in the process. If you've defined a long-running transaction as a defect, then capacity planning and resource allocation become part of your remediation. If that variability in response time is caused by system behavior during a failover, then you may have to design for a more complex recovery model. Deciding where to start the process—what gives you the most benefit for the effort—is at the heart of our Availability Index that debuts in Chapter 3. Think of it as a Pareto of availability techniques for the six-sigma-minded.

Key Points

- Components fail. Face that fact, plan for it, and be sure that you know the different failure modes of all of your components, from disks to systems to applications.

- MTBF only applies if your system is renewable. If a failure changes the probability of future problems, your availability planning isn't based on valid data.

- Failure modes change and get more complex over time. Each new network-based attack or discovered security flaw becomes another possible failure that you need to consider when predicting the availability of your entire system.

The Value of Availability

Price is what you pay, value is what you get.
—Warren Buffett

Fundamentally, high availability is a business decision. Computers cost money to operate. They cost additional money should they fail to operate when they are expected to. But the fundamental reason enterprises invest in computers (or anything else, for that matter) is to make them money. Computers enable an organization to perform tasks it could not perform without the computer. Computers can do things that people cannot; they do things faster and more cheaply and more accurately than people can. (Not everything, but many things.) When a computer is not performing the function for which it was purchased, it is not making its owners money; it is, instead, costing them money. Since downtime can, unchecked, go on forever, there is ostensibly no limit to the costs that a down computer might generate.

What Is High Availability?

There was a period of time when your authors debated taking the phrase "high availability" out of the title of this book. The argument for doing so was that the term had become so muddied by vendor marketing organizations it had lost all meaning. The argument against removing it was that there was no other term that so well summed up what we were trying accomplish with the book. In the end, we decided that if we took "high availability" out of the title, nobody would ever be able to find the book, and if we let it stay, we would have the opportunity to define it ourselves. So we left it in. Think of it as a marketing decision.

If you ask around, you'll find that there really is no hard definition for high availability or a firm threshold that determines whether or not a particular system has achieved it. Vendors have molded the term to fit their needs. Just about every system and OS vendor with a marketing department claims to deliver high availability in one form or another. The truth is that despite claims of $7 \times 24 \times$ whatever, or some number of nines, those claims mean remarkably little in practical day-to-day system availability.

The Storage Network Industry Association (SNIA) has an excellent online technical dictionary (`www.snia.org/dictionary`), in which they define high availability as follows:

> *The ability of a system to perform its function continuously (without interruption) for a significantly longer period of time than the reliabilities of its individual components would suggest. High availability is most often achieved through failure tolerance. High availability is not an easily quantifiable term. Both the bounds of a system that is called highly available and the degree to which its availability is extraordinary must be clearly understood on a case-by-case basis.*[1]

It is a rare definition that admits its own vagueness.

So, in the hunt for the true definition of high availability, we must take a different approach. Breaking the term into its components, we have

High, adj.   Greater than normal in degree or amount

Availability, n.   The quality of being at hand when needed[2]

Availability is pretty clearly defined, but it's *high* that is the problem. Is a 20-story building high? In Manhattan, Kansas, it would be, but in Manhattan, New York, a 20-story building is lost in the crowd. It's very much a relative term. How high is up? How up is high? How available does something have to be for it to be highly available? Greater than normal? What is normal, and who defines it? Again, not much help in these definitions. Developing a practical definition for high availability will require still another approach.

Consider why someone implements a computer system. Someone spends money to purchase (or lease) a computer system. The goal, as it is with any business expenditure, is to get some sort of return, or value back, on that spending. Money that is spent with the intent of getting value back is an investment. The goal, then, is to achieve an appropriate return on the investment made to implement the computer system. The return on that investment need not be

---

[1] `www.snia.org/education/dictionary/h`

[2] `www.dictionary.com/cgi-bin/dict.pl` (citing WordNet ® 1.6, © 1997 Princeton University)

directly monetary. In an academic environment, for example, the return may be educational. A computer science department at a university or high school buys computers with the noble goal of teaching their students how to use those computers. Of course, in the long run, a computer science department that develops a good reputation gets a financial return in increased attendance in classes and tuition.

IT'S ACADEMIC

During one of my high-availability tutorials, I was explaining the basics of the financial aspects of availability to my audience. A gentleman in the front row raised his hand and complained that the enterprise he was concerned about was a university, and so he didn't have to be concerned about finances.

I did my best to respectfully disagree with his position, explaining that the money to purchase the computers and the software and all the other system components still had to come from somewhere. I explained that choices have to be made, and if his department bought a computer, that may translate to one less teaching assistant or professor they can hire. He was adamant that this material did not apply to him, and during the first break, he left and did not return.

What he failed to realize, I fear, is that money spent now is money he can't spend later. There are always going to be trade-offs, no matter how much or how little money an organization has. Money and budgets are always finite.

—Evan

The educational computers at a university would not be considered critical by most commercial enterprises, but if those computers are down for so much of the time during a semester that students are unable to complete their assignments, then the computers are not able to generate an appropriate return on the financial investment placed in them. If these outages occur often enough, and last long enough, the department may develop a reputation for having lousy computers, or lousy computer administration, which, in either case, reflects very poorly on the department and could, over time, affect enrollment. The same is true for any computers at any enterprise; computers that are down are not doing the job for which they were implemented.

Consider, then, that a system is highly available when it is available enough of the time to generate the return for which it was implemented in the first place. To be fair, it requires a clear vision of the future to know whether a system is adequately protected against all possible events, and that is plainly impossible. So, we consider high availability to be a design goal rather than an actual design. When a system is designed, it should be clear to its designers what requirements it has for availability. If the system is truly designed to those requirements, then the system is highly available. Our definition of high availability, therefore, is as follows:

> **High availability, n.**   A level of system availability implied by a design that is expected to meet or exceed the business requirements for which the system is implemented.

High availability, then, is a trade-off between the cost of downtime and the cost of the protective measures that are available to avoid or reduce downtime.

The Costs of Downtime

The only way to convince the people who control the purse strings that there is value in protecting uptime is to approach the problem from a dollars-and-cents perspective. In this section, we provide some ammunition that should help make the case to even the most stubborn manager.

Direct Costs of Downtime

The most obvious cost of downtime is probably not the most expensive one: lost user productivity. The actual cost of that downtime is dependent upon what work your users perform on the affected systems.

If your users are developers, then perhaps the cost seems to be nothing more than the time and carrying cost for the idled developers. Of course, for a large development organization, those costs can be quite significant. A developer may be paid $800 to $1,500 a day, though that figure may vary significantly, depending upon innumerable factors. It is quite reasonable to assume that idling a group of 50 developers for a week could cost $400,000 or more.

But even the $400,000 is nothing more than the direct cost of the developers' idle time. Not taken into account is the overtime required to make up for the lost time to ensure that delivery deadlines do not slip. If your developers are consultants, or other hourly employees, then at time-and-a-half, the overtime costs could exceed an additional $600,000. These figures do not take into account factors such as fatigue from working all that overtime or the impact on morale.

On the other hand, rather than pay the overtime, you might elect to slip your project deadlines a week to make up for the outage. (Does that ever actually happen?) The costs of slipping deadlines are not as obvious or as easily stated as employee carrying costs, but they are just as real.

For production users, costs will obviously vary depending on the line of work performed on the affected servers. For equities traders in large trading firms on Wall Street, the number often quoted for downtime during the trading day is $2 million per trader per 20-minute outage. One assumption in that $2 million number is that all trades made on the trading floor are profitable. Consider that the outage could have prevented a trader from making a money-losing deal, thus saving the firm money. Wall Street firms are oddly loath to discuss this possibility.

Of course, the traders' salaries and carrying costs are lost, and while many traders do make a lot of money for both themselves and their firms, very few of them can consistently bring in $2 million dollars every 20 minutes. A trading firm's loss is not as easily quantifiable as the loss to the development organization, because the trading firm's losses are also composed of opportunity losses.[3]

Other industries' direct costs of downtime, as reported by various services, are listed in Table 3.1. Over time, of course, these values will change; the actual values are less important than the orders of magnitude of the values, and how much the costs can vary by industry. You don't need to precisely quantify a loss to know that a significant loss has occurred.

Table 3.1 The Direct Costs of Downtime

INDUSTRY	AVERAGE DOWNTIME COST PER HOUR
Brokerage services	$6.48 million
Energy	$2.8 million
Credit card	$2.58 million
Telecomm	$2 million
Financial	$1.5 million
Manufacturing	$1.6 million
Financial institutions	$1.4 million
Retail	$1.1 million
Pharmaceutical	$1.0 million
Chemicals	$704,000
Health care	$636,000
Media	$340,000
Airline reservations	$90,000

Sources: Network Computing, the Meta Group, and Contingency Planning Research.

[3] Opportunity losses are the loss of a chance to do something, regardless of its outcome. The something could be trading shares of stock, verifying a credit card transaction, or something more mundane like selling a product on the Internet. Without close monitoring, it is almost impossible to know what the opportunity losses are when a system goes down.

Indirect Costs of Downtime

As expensive and unpleasant as the direct costs of downtime are, the indirect costs can be significantly higher and have much greater long-term impact on the enterprise.

Imagine that you wish to order an $80 sweater from one of those catalog clothing stores via telephone (or the Internet). When you call, the operator politely tells you that their systems are down, so could you please call back in a couple of hours? But you want your sweater now.[4] So you call a different catalog company and order your sweater there instead. The direct loss to Company 1 is clear; it is the price of the sweater that you didn't buy from them. But there are other, more indirect costs. You took your business to its competitor; this helps the competitor, so not only did Company 1 lose $80, but Company 2 made an extra $80. Assuming that Company 2 serviced your order satisfactorily, which company will you call next time you want a sweater? Most likely, Company 2. More losses to Company 1. And when your friends ask you where you got that nice new sweater, and you tell them Company 2, the losses to Company 1 increase. They increase further if you tell the whole story to your friends, convincing them to take their business to Company 2. Multiply that by the number of customers who may call during the system outage, and you can see that the impact is significant, though perhaps impossible to quantify precisely.

The following are some examples of indirect costs:

Customer satisfaction.   As in the preceding example, if a customer visits a web site intending to purchase something, or to take part in the activities that the web site delivers, and he cannot, he will surely be frustrated. Depending on his past experience, he may decide to go away and do other things, returning to the site later. If he is a first-time visitor to the site, he may never return. If he has experienced downtime on other occasions, he may or may not ever return. If he is a happy customer, he will likely return later. But there are few better ways to turn happy customers into unhappy ones than repeating bad experiences. Remember the rule of thumb: It costs 10 times as much to bring in a new customer as it does to retain an old one.

Bad publicity and press.   Although the news media's feeding frenzy has diminished from 1999 and 2000, when large companies' web sites experience significant downtime, it still makes the news, though generally not the front page. Keeping your systems running for years at a time is not newsworthy (perhaps it should be), but one outage can make it onto the evening news and injure a company's reputation. When you see availability stories on the evening news, beware: The networks tend to

---

[4] For the proper effect, this sentence must be whined, in the style of a spoiled child.

skip over the technical details in favor of sensationalism and attempts to scare their viewers. As far as we know, no TV networks employ specialized availability consultants. (Your authors can recommend a couple, though, if any networks are interested.)

Stock price.   A common follow-on to the bad publicity and press from downtime is that Wall Street may perceive a corporate weakness and sell the company's stock. This can have a wide-reaching effect throughout the company, personally affecting everyone all the way up to the CEO.

Legal liability.   Stockholders routinely bring lawsuits against companies whose stock has taken precipitous drops. Many of these are dismissed as frivolous, but others are not. The likelihood of corporate officers being demonstrably liable will increase when there is the perception that those officers of the company did not take appropriate measures to maintain computer system reliability. Corporations can be held liable if their officers do not deliver on their obligations of fiduciary responsibility. An extended and expensive outage can certainly throw into question whether or not the officers have done so. There are also many laws that have been on the books for years that require corporations to take adequate steps to protect their critical resources; failure to do so could create a morass of legal issues.

Employee morale.   Some bad press, a stock drop, and a few liability cases can easily create serious morale problems around a company, as employees start to wonder what will go wrong next. Some talented employees may leave, and others may not work as hard if they believe things are going bad at their company.

External reputation.   If word gets out that key people are unhappy and are leaving the enterprise, that can further hurt its reputation, putting the enterprise into a vicious cycle where bad news makes the reputation worse, and the bad reputation causes things to get worse inside the company.

The Value of Availability

Downtime costs money. It can cost big. It can cost entire companies.

Unfortunately, it can also cost big money to protect systems against downtime. There is no free lunch. Later in this book, we discuss in detail the technologies that can improve system availability and allow your critical systems to achieve high availability. In this section, we are going to justify the use of these technologies from a business and financial perspective.

This is a fairly math-heavy section. If math is not your strong suit, you can safely skip it. But please take away our conclusions: There are many technologies that make great sense to implement to increase availability, even in less critical environments. As your needs for availability increase, you will need to implement more expensive and more complex protective technologies. Not every system needs those technologies; it depends where the systems fall on the Availability Continuum, as presented in the next section.

As we discussed in Chapter 2, "What to Measure," the following is the formula for availability:

$$A = \frac{MTBF}{MTBF + MTTR}$$

There are two ways, based on that formula, to improve availability. Either extend MTBF (keep the systems' components from failing) or extend MTTR (shorten the recovery time when they do fail). The easier one for system administrators to affect is, of course, MTTR. Components are going to fail when they fail; it is difficult to significantly influence how often they fail.

If you approach the problem with the basic premise that some outages and downtime are inevitable, you can seriously reduce your downtime by taking steps to minimize the duration of your outages. By mirroring disks, for example, you can reduce the downtime caused by a failed disk from hours to zero. By setting up clustering and failover, you can reduce downtime from a systemwide hardware failure from (potentially) days to just a few minutes.

If you have only one outage in a particular week, and you can reduce its duration from 4 hours to just 10 minutes, you have increased availability for that system during that week from 97.6 percent to better than 99.9 percent. As we've said, implementing protective measures costs money, but consider the example in the previous paragraph. If the cost of downtime for the system in question is $100 per minute (a reasonable and often low number), reducing the outage's duration from 240 minutes (4 hours) to 10 minutes saves the company $23,000. If you could expect this outage to occur once a month, then implementing this one protective measure can save the company $276,000 per year. Would it be worth spending $25,000 to achieve these savings? Would it be worth spending $200,000? Would it be worth spending $500,000? What if the life span of the system (and therefore the investment) were 5 years? What if the cost of downtime for the system were $500 per minute? What if we could only reduce the outage from 4 hours to 2 hours?

If we apply some arithmetic to these questions, we can come up with some fairly concrete answers. For this analysis, we will look to reduce the risk of downtime. In the analysis, the goal is to evaluate the potential savings after we apply a particular protective measure, when we compare the current situation to the situation we are thinking about implementing. So, Savings (S) equals Risk Before (R_B) minus Risk After (R_A). Mathematically, that's $S = R_B - R_A$.

And then, once we've determined Savings, we can look at the cost of implementation (C_M), and compare it to the savings, and calculate the Return on Investment (ROI) in percent:

$$\text{ROI} = S / C_M$$

The calculation of risk is a little more complicated. To determine risk, it is necessary to consider every event on which the measures being considered might have an effect. Each event is made up of three factors: likelihood, duration, and impact, which are defined as follows:

Likelihood.   The number of times the particular outage event being considered is expected to occur over the remaining life of the system. This number could be large: An event that occurs weekly over a 5-year life span would have a likelihood of about 260. A rare event that might never occur, such as a total site disaster, could have a likelihood factor of 0.01 or less. In determining likelihood values, you are making predictions. Obviously, predicting specific incidents of downtime (or any future event) is risky. Physicist Niels Bohr once said, "Predictions are hard. Especially about the future." To determine likelihoods, examine history, speak with other people who operate similar systems, and use your own experience.

Duration.   The length of time users will be unable to work as a result of the outage. It includes the time the affected systems or related networks and dependent systems are down, plus the time that might be necessary to make users aware that the systems are available again. (It is unlikely during an extended outage that users will sit at their desks, fingers poised over their keyboards, eagerly awaiting the system's return.) When calculating downtime for the total loss of a filesystem, for example, you must include the time necessary to locate and then restore the complete set of backups, which could take days. When calculating durations, stay conservative and estimate on the high side, because unforeseen complications are almost always associated with large-scale outages. We consider duration in units of minutes; the units you choose are not important, as long as you are consistent with their use throughout the analysis.

Impact.   The percentage of the user community that the outage will affect. Most outages will affect all users, but the loss of a single filesystem might affect only 20 percent of your users. A scheduled reboot in the middle of the night might affect only half the users. If a single user deletes a key file that must be restored from tape, the impact may be as low as 1 percent or 2 percent, depending on the size of the user community. It's also not hard to imagine that some impacts could exceed 100 percent if they occur at times of unusually high system load.

Each event under consideration has two states: the before state and the after state. And each of those states is made up of likelihood (L), duration (D), and impact (I). Mathematically, the effect (E) of a particular event is as follows: $E = L \times D \times I$. To be mathematically proper, we must break these effects into before and after cases and do so for each event being considered. So, the before case formula would be the following:

$$E_{Bx} = L_{Bx} \times D_{Bx} \times I_{Bx}$$

and the "after" case formula would be:

$$E_{Ax} = L_{Ax} \times D_{Ax} \times I_{Ax}$$

The other critical factor for both the before and after cases is cost of downtime (C_D). C_D (expressed in dollars per minute) tells us how much downtime costs and, by extension, how much you can afford to spend on your systems to protect them against such downtime. Many businesses do not know how much it costs when their systems are down. Some of the industry consulting companies (Meta, Gartner, IDC, and so on) publish downtime costs, but those are generally businesswide values rather than for a single system.

An interesting mathematical aside is that the units associated with E are minutes. Likelihood and impact are scalars (free-standing numbers without associated units). Duration is, of course, expressed in minutes. So the effect of a particular outage is expressed in time. When you include cost of downtime in these calculations, multiply minutes by dollars per minute, and you wind up with a value expressed in dollars.

To build the risk formula for the before case, you must add up all the effects and multiply that result by the cost of downtime. So the formula for risk in the before case looks like this:

$$R_B = C_D \times (E_{B1} + E_{B2} + E_{B3} + \ldots + E_{Bx})$$

The formula for the after case is slightly more complicated because you must also consider the cost of implementation (C_M). The cost of implementation must include the cost of all hardware and software purchased for the implementation, as well as any professional services, support, training, additional personnel, downtime required for the implementation, and any other costs to the business. The after formula looks like the following:

$$R_A = C_M + (C_D \times (E_{A1} + E_{A2} + E_{A3} + \ldots + E_{Ax}))$$

Now that we have the formulas, let's plug in some numbers.

COST OF DOWNTIME IS NOT A CONSTANT

Further complicating matters is the fact that the cost of downtime is not a constant. We will assume it to be constant for the purposes of our calculations (it makes them much, much simpler), but in reality, the cost of downtime increases as the duration of an outage increases.

Consider again the effects of downtime on an e-commerce site. If the site suffers a brief outage (a few seconds), the cost will be minimal, perhaps even negligible. An outage of a minute or less probably will not affect business too badly: All but the most disloyal users will simply hit their browser's reload button and try again. A 30-minute outage will cause some customers to take their business to a competitor's site; others will be patient and keep trying. An outage of several hours will likely cause all but the most loyal customers to take their business elsewhere and will cause some of them to never return. An outage that lasts days could result in the total failure of the business. Once a customer is lost and that customer has a more pleasant experience on a competitor's web site, the customer will bookmark the other site and likely not return to yours.

Depending on the nature of your business, an outage at 1:00 A.M. may cost less than an outage at 1:00 P.M. (Then again, it could cost more.) An outage in mid-December may cost a lot more than an outage in mid-August. Repeated, intermittent failures of 15 minutes apiece that total two hours will likely cost you more than a single two-hour outage because multiple outages can cause more user frustration than one-time outages.

For the purposes of the calculations in this chapter, we will keep things simple and assume that cost of downtime is a constant. As a rule of thumb, consider the costs of downtime for an outage of roughly an hour. (If you have calculated more precise values, then by all means use them.) What's more, the added complexity of trying to develop a formula for a variable cost of downtime will not help make our points in this chapter any better.

Please note that in these examples, we make a lot of assumptions that may not fit your reality. Please plug your own numbers into the formulas to develop models that fit your implementation.

Two implicit assumptions in our examples are that hardware failures will be repaired quickly and that they can be repaired in clustered configurations without stopping services. By making repairs in a timely manner, you can ensure that if a second component fails, your system will be able to survive. By replacing or repairing failed components quickly, you will significantly reduce the likelihood that a second failure will occur and cause more extended downtime. The quicker you can make the repair, the higher the level of service you will be able to provide. If it becomes necessary to shut down systems or services to replace hardware—a disk on a shared SCSI bus, for example—then our estimates of downtime in cluster configurations will be low. If you have a two-node cluster sharing SCSI disks, and a disk needs to be replaced, it will be necessary in most cases to shut down both systems while making the repair. When fiber connections are employed, disks and systems can usually be removed without affecting other systems on the same cabling.

Example 1: Clustering Two Nodes

A large restaurant supply company has a file server that has a logical volume manager (LVM) and enhanced filesystem product running on it. They are considering adding a second, identical server and clustering the two servers together using a standard commercial clustering software product. The expected life span of the system is 5 years, and the cost of downtime is $75 per minute or $4,500 per hour.

To implement this cluster, several actions and purchases are required. The company must do the following:

- Purchase a second server.

- Install the logical volume manager (LVM) software and filesystem on the new server.

- Install the clustering software on both nodes.

- Implement a pair of heartbeat networks between the nodes.

- Configure the option in the clustering software to enable automatic switchover to a standby network card. This option will protect them from the failure of a NIC by moving the IP addresses associated with that NIC to dedicated standby NIC in the same node, without requiring a system-to-system failover. The hardware requirements for these additional networks is four NICs, two per node.

For more detailed information about clustering and failover, please see Chapter 15, "Local Clustering and Failover."

Estimated costs of implementation:

- Second server: $42,000

- Two licenses and media for clustering software: $12,100

- Extra NICs and cables: $4,500

- 5 years of vendor support for the clustering software: ($3,132 per year): $15,660

- Clustering software training for two students: $6,000

- Clustering software implementation services: $12,000

- LVM and filesystem software for the second node: $6,000

- 5 years of LVM and filesystem software support for the second node ($1,380 per year): $6,900

The total cost of implementation is $105,160.

Note that these costs are for the first cluster. Additional clusters will cost less because implementation costs will drop. Once their system administrators have been trained, there will not be any need to send them to training every time they implement a cluster. Plus, after a few installs, it will probably not be necessary to employ implementation services for every cluster. Per-server costs also decline as cluster sizes increase.

Because we are considering implementing clustering software, we must examine all the outages that it will affect. Table 3.2 lists the outages we will consider, along with their durations and likelihoods before the clustering software is implemented.

Given all the statistics in Table 3.2, we get:

$$R_B = \$75 \times 9{,}360 = \$702{,}000$$

The 99.644 percent availability in the last box in Table 3.2 is the level of availability that your system would attain if it had all of these outages and no others over the five-year life span of the systems. It is the best possible level of availability, given these outages. Additional outages would cause that level to drop even further.

In Table 3.3, we examine the same values after the clustering software has been installed. We make the conservative assumption that we will recover from any outage in 5 minutes with a reliable failover. In reality, failover times will vary depending on your application. Some failovers will be longer than 5 minutes, whereas others will be shorter. The duration of the failover will depend mostly on the time it takes to restart the application on a different host. File service, shown in this example, is particularly adept at failing over quickly. We assume that likelihood and impact values have not changed and that only the duration of the outage is affected by the presence of clustering software.

Table 3.2   Effects of Outages before Clustering Software Is Installed

OUTAGE TYPE	BEFORE DURATION (D)	BEFORE LIKELIHOOD (L)	BEFORE IMPACT (I)	BEFORE EFFECT (D × L × I)
Crash and reboot	60 minutes*	10†	100%	$E_{B1} = 600$ (during the day)
Crash and reboot (off-hours)	120 minutes‡	10†	75%§	$E_{B2} = 900$
Scheduled reboot	30 minutes	60‖	50%§	$E_{B3} = 900$
Motherboard or other major hardware failure	24 hours (1,440 minutes)#	2	100%	$E_{B4} = 2,880$
Network card failure	4 hours (240 minutes)**	2	100%	$E_{B5} = 480$
Application failure	60 minutes	20††	100%	$E_{B6} = 1,200$
Scheduled maintenance	4 hours (240 minutes)#	20	50%	$E_{B7} = 2,400$
Failover testing	0§§	0	0	$E_{B8} = 0$
Total effect of outages:				9,360 minutes (99.644 percent availability over 5 years)

* Assumes manual reboot, allowing time for the administrator to reach the system, reboot it, and deal with other hazards along the way.
† Twice a year for 5 years.
‡ The 60 minutes beyond the "during the day" case is to allow time for the administrator to get from home to the office, where the system is.
§ Since the incident occurs off-hours, we assume that the impact is less than it would be during the workday.
‖ Once a month for 5 years: a prudent rebooting schedule.
We assume that this will require opening a service call with your hardware support provider, waiting for an engineer to arrive, and an additional delay while waiting for parts to be shipped. Your mileage may vary.
** We assume that the replacement of a NIC card can be done by a good system administrator, without having to wait for an engineer or parts to be shipped. If the case is not so, then the duration will be longer than 4 hours.
†† We are assuming that this occurs once per quarter over 5 years. This will vary on the basis of many factors, including the nature, complexity, and reliability of your application.
# The duration of the scheduled maintenance depends on many factors. 4 hours is a reasonable estimate.
§§ Because no failover mechanism is in place, no failover testing is required in the before case.

Table 3.3 Effects of Outages after Clustering Software Is Installed

OUTAGE TYPE	AFTER DURATION (D)	AFTER LIKELIHOOD (L)*	AFTER IMPACT (I)*	AFTER EFFECT (D × L × I)
Crash and reboot	5 minutes†	10	100%	$E_{A1} = 50$ (during the day)
Crash and reboot (off-hours)	5 minutes†	10	75%	$E_{A2} = 37.5$
Scheduled reboot	5 minutes	60	50%	$E_{A3} = 150$
Motherboard or other major hardware failure	5 minutes	2	100%	$E_{A4} = 10$
Network card failure	2 minutes, then 5 minutes‡	2	100% then 50%	$E_{A5} = 9$
Application failure	3 minutes§	20	100%	$E_{A6} = 60$
Scheduled maintenance	5 minutes	20	50%	$E_{A7} = 50$
Failover testing	5 minutes‖	20	50%	$E_{A8} = 50$
Total effect of outages:				416.5 minutes (99.984 percent availability over 5 years)

* Likelihood and impact will be the same after clustering software is installed. Only the duration will be affected.
† Because failover is automatic, no administrator need be present.
‡ Good failover software should be able to respond to the failure of a NIC without a failover, and therefore the duration should be shorter than it would be for a full failover. The two durations are because the first is the automatic switchover to a working NIC. The second duration is a failover to replace the failed card, which can be done off-hours.
§ Applications can usually be restarted in place, without a failover, on a system with clustering software.
‖ Since no failover mechanism is in place, no failover testing is required in the before case.

Given the statistics in Table 3.3, we get the following:

$$R_A = \$105,160 + (\$75 \times 416.5)$$
$$R_A = \$105,160 + \$31,237.50 = \$136,397.50$$

When we calculate our savings and subtract R_A from R_B, we get:

$$S = \$702,000 - \$136,397.50 = \$565,602.50$$

Implementing clustering software as described in the preceding text saved the restaurant supply company $565,602.50, or 80.6 percent. And that $565,602.50 savings (or return) on our $105,160 investment yields a return of 537.8 percent. The time to payback (P) for this five-year investment is 339 days[5] (about 11 months). Most corporate financial analysts would find such a return extremely appealing.

Example 2: Unknown Cost of Downtime

A big assumption in the first example is that the cost of downtime is a known quantity. Most organizations have no idea what their downtime really costs, particularly on a per-system basis; they just know that they don't like it. That's OK. By starting with all of the other values, with a little (gasp!) algebra, it's not too tough to solve for cost of downtime. (This is the last serious math in the whole book. We swear! But if you take a few minutes and roll up your sleeves, you'll find that the math here isn't too bad, and it's most worthwhile.)

Let's go back and use the data from Example 1, but leave the cost of downtime as an unknown:

$$R_B = C_D \times 9,360$$
$$R_A = 105,160 + (C_D \times 416.5)$$
$$S = R_B - R_A = C_D \times (9,360 - 416.5) - 105,160$$
$$S = (C_D \times 8,943.5) - 105,160$$

If we set savings to zero ($S = 0$) and solve for C_D, we get:

$$C_D = 105,160 / 8,943.5 = \$11.76 \text{ per minute (or \$705.50 per hour)}$$

The $705.50-per-hour figure is a very low one for cost of downtime in most organizations.

Of course, most businesses would not be satisfied with a savings of zero dollars over a five-year project. In Table 3.4, we offer some cost of downtime, savings, return on investment, and days to payback values. If required savings was $100,000, then:

$$C_D = 205,160 / 8,943.5 = \$22.94 \text{ per minute, or \$1,376.37 per hour}$$

[5] Calculated as $P = \text{Days}/\text{ROI}$.

If the required savings was $1 million, then:

$$C_D = 1,105,160 \ / \ 8,943.5 = \$123.57 \text{ per minute or } \$7,414.28 \text{ per hour}$$

Table 3.4 Cost of Downtime and Return on Investments

REQUIRED SAVINGS	COST OF DOWNTIME PER MINUTE (C_D)	RETURN ON INVESTMENT	DAYS TO PAYBACK ON A FIVE-YEAR INVESTMENT
$0	$11.76	N/A	N/A
$100,000	$22.94	95.1%	1,919 days (Just over five years)
$250,000	$39.71	237.7%	768 days (A little over two years)
$500,000	$67.66	475.8%	384 days
$1,000,000	$123.57	950.9%	192 days
$2,000,000	$235.38	1,901.9%	96 days
$5,000,000	$570.82	4,754.7%	38 days

Determine your required savings and solve for the required cost of down-time to see if it's reasonable for your environment. However, if you are seriously considering implementing measures to increase your availability, it's a good bet that your cost of downtime exceeds $11.76 per minute ($705 per hour) by quite a bit.

The Availability Continuum

Taken to its logical limit, the definition of high availability cited in the preceding text implies that every system can potentially have a different threshold of availability before it achieves high availability. This is absolutely correct. Computer systems vary widely in their tolerance of downtime. Some systems cannot handle even the briefest interruption in service without catastrophic results, whereas others can handle brief interruptions, but not extended ones, and others can even handle extended outages while still delivering on their required returns on investment. Consider the following examples:

- Computers whose failures cause a loss of human life, such as hospital life support systems or avionics systems, generally have the highest requirements for availability.

- Slightly less critical computers can be found running e-commerce web sites such as amazon.com and ebay.com, or managing and performing equities trading at brokerage institutions around the world.

- Systems that operate an assembly line or other important production activities, whose failure might idle hundreds of workers, while other parts of the business can continue.

- Computers in a university's computer science department may be able to stand a week's downtime, while professors postpone assignment deadlines and teach other material, without a huge impact.

- The computer that manages the billing function at a small company could be down through a whole billing cycle if backup procedures to permit manual processing are in place.

- A computer that has been retired from active service and sits idle in a closet has zero availability.

In fact, there is a whole range of possible availability levels that range from an absolute requirement of 100 percent down to a low level, where it just doesn't matter if the computer is running or not, as in the last bullet. We call this range the Availability Continuum, and it is depicted graphically in Figure 3.1.

Every computer (in fact, every system of any kind, but let's not overextend) in the world has availability requirements that place it somewhere on the Continuum. The hard part is figuring out where your system's availability requirements place it on the Continuum, and then matching those requirements to a set of protective technologies. Although it is best to determine the appropriate level availability that is required for each system and not change it, the reality is that over time just about all systems tend to drift higher on the Continuum. In Figure 3.1, we chose a few different types of systems and indicated where on the Continuum they might fall.

It is best to determine an appropriate point on the Continuum for a critical system and leave it there, because it is simpler and more straightforward to design availability into a system when it is first deployed rather than add incremental improvements over time. The incremental improvements that follow reevaluations of availability needs invariably cause additional downtime, and in many cases the enhancements are not as reliable as they might have been if they had been installed at the system's initial deployment.

Systems drift higher on the Continuum over time because cost of implementation is an important aspect of determining exactly how well protected a system needs to be. Less enlightened budget holders tend to give less money for needed protective measures than they should. When a failure occurs that falls outside the set of failures that the system has been designed to survive, the system will go down, probably for an extended period. When it becomes apparent to the budget holder that this outage is costing his business a lot of money, he will likely approve additional spending to protect against future failures. When he does that, he is nudging the system up the Continuum.

The higher a system needs to be on the Continuum, the more it costs to get it there. The higher cost is necessary because in order to achieve higher levels of availability, you need to protect against more varieties of more complicated and less frequently occurring outages.

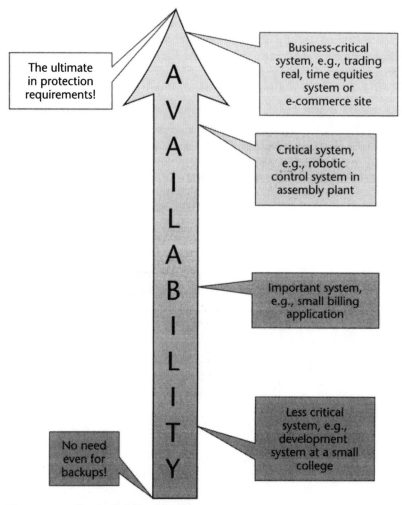

Figure 3.1 The Availability Continuum.

At about this point in the process, the people who approve budgets get upset because they see that the cost of their critical system is about to rise considerably. They are right. But they should not feel cheated. The system they are buying is going to make money for the enterprise, either through direct income opportunity (for example, e-commerce) or through improvements in efficiency, and so it is natural that there be expenses associated with the system. (Please refer to Chapter 5, "20 Key High-Availability Design Principles," *#20: Don't Be Cheap*, and *#19: Assume Nothing* for further discussion of the need to spend money to achieve high availability.)

Putting additional money into an enterprise's critical systems to increase their availability is often viewed by some as throwing good money after bad. That is not the case. The systems were purchased to perform a particular function. If they are unable to perform that function to an appropriate degree, then the money spent on the systems may be wasted. Instead, consider the additional spending as an investment in the critical systems that run your business.

With that in mind, we offer Figure 3.2, which is an attempt to graph investments in availability increases against different levels of availability. Close examination of Figure 3.2 reveals that costs increase until the cost curve nearly flattens out along the top, which represents the highest levels of availability. This is because the highest levels of availability approach but never quite reach 100 percent, which we believe is impossible to achieve over a long period of time.

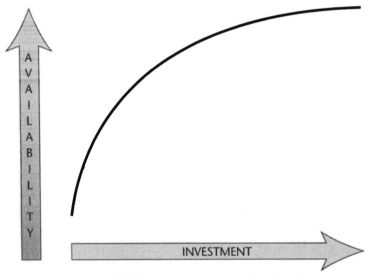

Figure 3.2   The Availability Continuum graphed against investment.

The Availability Index

The graph in Figure 3.1 is an attempt to demonstrate the relationship between investment (spending) and availability. It is conceptual in nature and does not attempt to graph particular levels of availability (nines) against specific dollar amounts. There are many reasons why no specific data points are on the graph. Many of them were discussed in Chapter 2, in the section *The Myth of the Nines*. But another important reason is that the actual level of availability you will see is dependent on too many factors to allow for any sort of accurate predictions.

Nevertheless, the trend is certain. Reaching higher levels of availability will cost more money, and the amount of money it takes to get from one level to the next is more than it took to get from the last level to where you are now.

In Figure 3.3, we have overlaid the graph with a layered list of 10 technologies, ranging from Good System Administration Practices at the bottom, all the way up to Disaster Recovery at the top, creating the Availability Index.

There are two important messages in the Index. First is the relationship between cost and availability. Second, when properly applied, the technologies that enable increased availability do form a stack. It is best to apply them in order, from bottom to top.

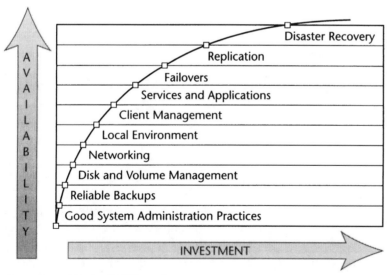

Figure 3.3   The Availability Index.

BEWARE THE ITCHY HA TRIGGER FINGER

I received a call from an end user, who was complaining about his production application. "It goes down once or twice just about every day, and it usually brings my server with it," he said. "Do you think we could use clustering software to enable failover and get the application back in service faster when it crashes?" I explained that while this might work, it's not the right approach. Failovers still generally cause interruptions to users, and so will not be tolerated. The right approach is to repair the problems with the application so that it keeps running more than a few hours. Once the system is more stable, then we can look at clustering and other technologies that will help improve availability even more.

—Evan

Note the relative positions among different technologies. In particular, clustering, the technology that is most commonly associated with increasing availability, is at Level 8. Attempting to start your efforts to increase availability with clustering and without the underlying levels in place is like starting to build a skyscraper on the eighth floor. It simply will not stand.

The Availability Index is the single most important graphic in this book. Beginning with Chapter 5, we have arranged the remaining chapters in the order in which the technologies appear on the Index, and we will use the Index as an introductory graphic to those chapters to indicate where on the layer of technologies the following chapter falls. Successive chapters will be higher on the Index than previous ones. Some levels require more than one chapter. Use the Index and the associated chapters ordering to help determine how highly available your systems need to be.

The Lifecycle of an Outage

Figure 3.4 shows a simple timeline. The bolt of lightning at time T_1 is used to indicate that Something Bad has happened, usually a component failure, that can cause some system downtime. Since we are maintaining our end-to-end approach to availability, it does not matter which component fails for the general case; it could be a network card, a disk, a whole system, a network, an application, or any other critical component whose failure will cause an interruption in service.

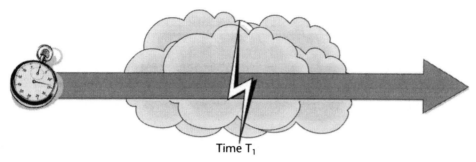

Time T_1

Figure 3.4 The outage lifecycle timeline.

Downtime

When the lightning bolt strikes at T_1, that is the beginning of the outage. The duration and effect of the outage will be determined by the nature of the outage and by the protective technologies that have been put into place to attempt to keep the systems running. As a result of the component failure, an outage begins that lasts until T_2, as shown in Figure 3.5.

One of the main objectives of designing a highly available system, and probably the most obvious, is to reduce the duration of this downtime. The acceptable amount of downtime is formally called the Recovery Time Objective, or RTO. The recovery time is a function of both the type of outage that occurs as well as the technologies that are in place to protect against it.

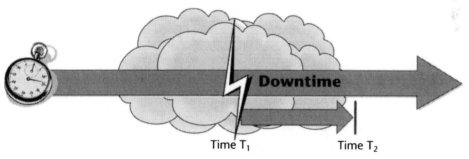

Downtime

Time T_1 Time T_2

Figure 3.5 The outage lifecycle: The downtime interval.

Different protective technologies will result in different amounts of down-time, as shown in Figure 3.6. In that example, we have chosen a serious outage: a lost data center. In this case, there are at least three different technologies[6] that can be employed to return the critical applications that ran in the failed data center to service. (There are surely other technologies that might be included, and other levels of granularity that could be applied, but this model makes the point adequately.) If a data center is lost, and operations must be migrated to a new data center, the following three technologies can be employed:

Tape restore.   Assuming it is possible to recover backup tapes after the calamity that rendered the data center unusable, the slowest path to recovery is to load each tape into a tape drive and restore it, one at a time. Depending on the size of the data center, the number of tapes, and the number of drives available for restores, a recovery by restoring backup tapes could take days, or in many cases even weeks. For more information on backups and restores, please refer to Chapter 6, "Back-ups and Restores."

Replication with manual migration.   Using one of the replication tech-niques described in Chapter 18, "Data Replication," the critical data and applications can be sent to your secondary data center so that it is not necessary to restore data from backup tapes. Since the data is already there, the greatest effort will need to be put into starting the applications at the secondary data center. Depending on manpower, the number of systems, and the number of applications, this recovery could take any-where from a few hours to a week or more.

Extended cluster.   There are several variations on shared clusters, as described in Chapter 17, "Failover Configurations." Implemented properly, clustering and replication between the primary and secondary data centers can ensure that critical applications are back online in min-utes or even seconds in some extreme cases with a minimum of manual intervention.

There is actually a fourth technology that might be used in this situation: nothing. If no effort at all is made to prepare for a disaster, then it is quite likely that after a significant failure such as the one in this example, data will be lost forever, and the downtime will effectively last forever.

---

[6] The details about these technologies can be found in later chapters in the book. The details should not be required in order to understand how they can affect recovery times.

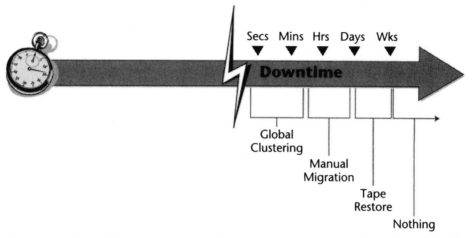

Figure 3.6 Four different technologies that can reduce downtime after a data center failure.

This example only considers one type of outage. There are, of course, any number of failures that can cause system downtime, and each of them has its own set of protective measures. For many failures, proper protection will mean zero downtime—for example, the failure of a disk in a system where disks are protected with RAID technology, such as disk mirroring. For a detailed discussion of RAID technology, please refer to Chapter 7, "Highly Available Data Management."

Lost Data

Figure 3.7 shows that outages don't only reach forward in time; they can also reach backwards and affect data that users have already entered and believed was committed. Sometimes the data may have been acted upon by other processes. For example, an e-commerce site could bill a customer's credit card and then lose the data that would have permitted them to ship product to the customer. That's bad for everybody.

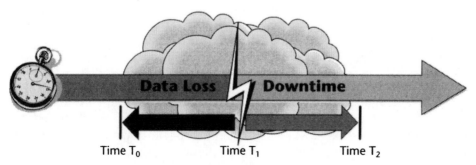

Figure 3.7 The outage lifecycle timeline: The lost data interval.

The lost data duration reaches backwards in time from Time T_1 to Time T_0, the time of the last relevant data protection event. Depending on the nature of the outage, that event could be the most recent tape backup, data replication, or mirrored disk write.

As with downtime, though, there are technologies that can protect critical systems against lost data; the type of frequency of the data protection events will ultimately determine how much data will be lost in an outage. Some of these technologies, once again using a lost data center as an example, are shown in Figure 3.8. In this case, many of the same technologies that can reduce downtime also reduce lost data. That will not be the case for all types of outages. The technical term for lost data is Recovery Point Objective, or RPO.

The technology choices that can affect the amount of lost data after the loss of a data center are as follows:

Synchronous replication.   Under synchronous replication, data arrives at the secondary host as soon as it is written to the primary data center. The downside to synchronous replication is in performance; since data must be sent across the network to the remote site, and then confirmation must come back, for each write, performance can be seriously impacted. More information on replication can be found in Chapter 18.

Asynchronous replication.   With asynchronous replication, you get back the performance that you lose with synchronous replication, but in return, a small number of transactions may be delayed in being sent to the secondary site. That could mean a small amount of lost data (usually less than a minute's worth), but in return for the performance boost, many enterprises consider the lost data a worthwhile trade-off.

Periodic or batch replication.   The data is sent from time to time under periodic replication. This means that the network load is reduced, but the data at the secondary data center could be hours, or even days out of date.

Tape backup.   Because backups are not taken continuously, it is almost impossible for them to be up-to-date. Backups are normally taken once a day or so, so a restore from such a backup tape will, on average, be half a day out of date. If backup tapes are not shipped off-site every day, as is often the case, then the data loss could be considerably more than half a day.

Nothing.   If the only copy of a data set is lost, then there is nothing to recover from, and work must restart from the time that the system and its applications went into service.

Different systems running different applications across an enterprise will have different requirements for downtime and lost data, and those requirements, balanced with the cost of implementing the desired solutions, will lead the decision as to what technology will be implemented.

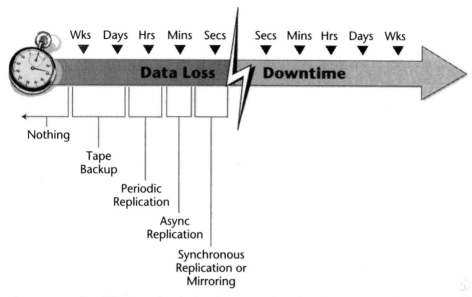

Figure 3.8   Five different technologies that can reduce lost data after a data center failure.

Degraded Mode

Although downtime and lost data are the most serious and dangerous parts of the lifecycle of an outage, they are not the whole story. The third part of the lifecycle is degraded mode. During the degraded mode, the enterprise would be unable to withstand another outage similar to the first. The backup system or resource has already been used, and so there is nothing more in reserve.

A data center that has already migrated to its secondary site, for example, could not stand the loss of the secondary site. When a new secondary site has been designated, the data center is no longer operating in degraded mode.

Once again, depending on the nature of the failure, and the precautions put in place, the duration of degraded mode can range from zero to forever. In a high-end disk array, if one disk drive fails, the array can automatically swap a dedicated spare in its place. If the array has multiple spares, then there will not be any degraded mode at all. In the preceding example, if an enterprise decides not to replace its primary data center after a disaster, then it would remain in degraded mode forever.

Scheduled Downtime

The final piece of the lifecycle of an outage is scheduled downtime. Like degraded mode, scheduled downtime is not part of every outage. Scheduled downtime is required in some cases to end degraded mode and return operations to a normal state, but once again, not in all cases. In a high-end disk array, for example, a failed disk can be replaced through a hot swap, without removing or shutting down the array.

However, downtime is downtime. Scheduled downtime is a little less intrusive to your users, especially local ones, because its onset can be controlled, and because users can be notified so that they expect the outage. Scheduled downtimes can, of course, be scheduled for times of the day when usage is reduced so that the impact to the users is minimized. But, as we said, downtime is downtime, and downtime will generally cause unhappiness and stress among users and likely have an effect on the bottom line.

This particular example of scheduled downtime is not the same as preventative maintenance, which is an entirely different class of scheduled downtime. Preventative maintenance generally occurs before an outage and is performed to prevent an unscheduled outage from occurring at all.

Figure 3.9 shows the completed outage lifecycle timeline, and all of the effects that a single component failure can have on a system.

To maximize the long-term health and availability of critical computer systems, it is important to look at potential outages with an eye toward reducing the impact of the outages all across the lifecycle. It is not enough to just consider the potential downtime that an outage might cause. Consider the lost data, the system's vulnerability to an additional failure, and the time and effort that may be required to return all of its components and systems to full working order.

In Table 3.5, we compare the outcomes of two occurrences of the same outage. In this example, we look at what can happen after a disaster in each phase of the outage lifecycle. The specific disaster we have chosen is the loss of a data center. With superior protective measures in place, the amount of downtime is minimized, whereas with inferior protective measures in place, the amount of downtime can be quite dramatic. Each of the technologies mentioned in the example is discussed in more detail in later chapters of this book.

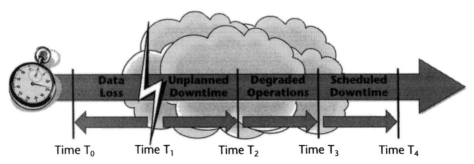

Figure 3.9 The completed outage lifecycle timeline.

Table 3.5 Comparing Two Sets of Technologies and Their Effects on Downtime after the Same Outage

LIFECYCLE PHASE	WITH SUPERIOR PROTECTION	WITH INFERIOR PROTECTION
Lost data	Synchronous data replication results in data being up-to-date and available at the disaster recovery site. There should be no lost data whatsoever.	Weekly full backups that are sent off-site must be retrieved and restored at the remote site. The restore process can take days or weeks. Data written after the most recent weekly backup is lost.
Downtime	Through remote clustering, applications are automatically brought up at the disaster recovery site.	System administrators must manually bring up each application at the disaster recovery site. This process could take days.
Degraded mode	The operations are in degraded mode while the primary site is down. But work can continue normally using systems at the disaster recovery site. If another disaster should occur, the results would be catastrophic.	The operations are in degraded mode while the primary site is down. But work can continue normally using systems at the disaster recovery site. If another disaster should occur, the results would be catastrophic.
Scheduled downtime	When the primary site has been restored to service, a brief amount of downtime, similar to the amount of downtime when the outage occurred, will be incurred as data and applications are migrated back.	When the primary site has been restored to service, a downtime, similar to the amount of downtime when the outage occurred, will be incurred as data and applications are migrated back.

In truth, of course, the outage lifecycle model is a very simple one. Outages and failures do not occur in a vacuum. While the effects of a second outage that is related to the first are accounted for in the lifecycle's Degraded Mode, one outage can bring about another in less predictable ways. One failure can cause another failure because of the additional load that the first failure puts on some other component—for example, a clustered database server that handles all of the load on a single node may run out of log space or suffer from network connection loading problems. The formal analysis for evaluating multiple failure modes, and how a system moves from one state to another based on the probability of an individual failure, is known as a *chain analysis*. Chain in this context refers to the sequence of events that take the system from one state to another. If we assume that the first failure of any component in the system is sufficient to cause user-visible disruption and we concentrate on repairing those failures, then we can take a simplified view of the world and treat the overall system health, over time, as a series of single lifecycle events described previously. As mentioned in Chapter 2, making sure your system is renewable—that it has the same MTBF characteristics after a failure has been repaired—will allow you to simplify your view of the outage lifecycle to that of a series of individual events.

NO MATTER WHERE YOU GO, THERE YOU ARE

It helps to know what failure is most likely, or what you should plan for in sequence. When I was about 10 years old, I was infatuated with Estes model rockets, spending at least one Sunday a month launching—and frequently losing—them into nearby fields. Estes sold a low-end movie camera that could be mounted on the rocket, giving you a shaky bird's-eye view of the flight. The proprietor of our local hobby shop told me that shelling out the $100 for the camera was a no-lose proposition, because if you ever lost the rocket, you could simply "develop the film, watch the movie to see where the rocket landed, and then go pick it up—it's impossible to lose the camera." It took me longer than it should have to decide that my $100 was better spent on something else.

—Hal

Key Points

- Fundamentally, high availability is a business decision.

- High availability is a level of system availability implied by a design that is expected to meet or exceed the business requirements for which the system is implemented.

- The decision to implement high availability is purely a business decision that is based on the value to an enterprise that a computer system has, and the cost of ensuring that the computer is available when needed to deliver that value.

CHAPTER

4

The Politics of Availability

One of the penalties for refusing to participate in politics is that you end up being governed by your inferiors.

—Plato

When discussions about implementing high availability get past the technical, they almost invariably turn to the political. Administrators tell us, "Yes, we all know it's important to implement this stuff, but I can't convince my management to take it seriously." Although most technical decisions come down to money, and we discussed the direct financial benefits of implementing availability in Chapter 3, "The Value of Availability," in this chapter, we take a look at some of the other ways you can get the people who control the purse strings to take the whole concept of availability more seriously.

The process begins as you start to collect information to help you build the case that will persuade them to see the value of your ideas.

Beginning the Persuasion Process

To persuade others of the value of your ideas, it is necessary to delve into the dark, shadowy world of organizational politics. Fundamentally, this means that you achieve your goals by helping (or if you aren't particularly scrupulous, appearing to help) others around you achieve their goals, so that they then help you achieve yours.

Start Inside

Probably the best way to convince others of the value of your ideas is to first convince them that your ideas will help them achieve their own goals. To do that, you must understand what their goals are. The development manager's goals are going to be different than the goals of the marketing manager, which will in turn be different from the goals of Human Resources. The good news is that to impress most managers, you need only demonstrate a high rate of financial return on the required investment to get their attention, but that is not always the case.

You must also understand the organization's overall goals. If the organization is a public company, there is a wealth of information available about the organization and its business. The annual report is an excellent place to determine what is important to a company, and what projects are perceived to be the most important to the company's future (they are usually the ones with the nice color pictures of smiling people near their descriptions). Other ways to find information about a company include reading through press releases, looking for published interviews with executives, and surfing the Web for financial statements that companies are legally obligated to generate. In the United States, these include the 10-K and 10-Q forms, which are available on the Web. It is always good if you can demonstrate how your ideas can add value to popular internal projects.

After you understand and have confirmed the manager's and the organization's goals and objectives, you must work out how your ideas will make them more successful. How will increasing the availability of their computer systems allow them to perform their jobs better?

Remember that if you are asking for money, you are competing with everyone else in your organization who has an idea that costs money. Money is an extremely limited resource in most organizations, especially when the economy is suffering. You may run into people in your organization who do not want your proposal to succeed because if it does, it will reflect badly on them. Beware of such people.

Learn to speak the language of business. In formal writing and presenting, messages are generally delivered calmly or with mild enthusiasm. Slang and street language are unwelcome. Remember that most organizations are businesses. (There are exceptions, of course, in academia, government agencies, and nonprofits, where goals may be different, but saving money is a high priority in just about any organization.) To impress businesspeople, messages must be delivered in terms that they understand without technical buzzwords, lingo, or acronyms, and they must solve problems of the people receiving the message. The gospel of high availability is an important one, but if you deliver it to the Human Resources manager, it is unlikely he or she will be interested, and it's even less likely that the manager would be able to help you.

If your message will help someone above you in the organization to be more successful and to look good to their management, they will be happy to help you. If your message makes them look bad, they will be unwilling to help you.

Then Go Outside

Once you have an understanding of your organization's goals, it's time to go outside the organization and get an education about high availability. If you have enough money to afford outside training, attend conferences. USENIX (www.usenix.org) and its technical subgroup SAGE (The System Administrators' Guild) hold conferences throughout the year to help raise and address issues that commonly affect system administrators. If your interests are in the area of disaster recovery, *Disaster Recovery Journal* (www.drj.com) publishes an excellent magazine and holds two conferences a year, attended by experts on all aspects of disaster recovery.

If you lack the budget to attend conferences, then read books (you are off to an excellent start!) and magazines on high availability. Visit web sites like www.techtarget.com, which has about 20 different web sites dedicated to many different aspects of system administration. Their whatis.com companion site is a tremendous resource for understanding complex technical terminology and concepts.

Learn about real problems that plague real companies. Disasters are the most colorful and newsworthy problems, and they are certainly very important, but there are countless other events that can cause outages. Is your enterprise prepared for them? How well prepared is your organization to handle a nasty worm or virus attack? What if your Internet provider were to go out of business tomorrow? Are you prepared for a hardware failure in your business's most critical computer servers?

Legal Liability

There are many laws on the books in the United States (and in other countries as well, although we only discuss American laws here) that legally obligate public companies and certain other organizations to do all they can to protect their enterprises, their critical systems, and their data. These include the following:

- The Health Insurance Portability and Accountability Act, or HIPAA, which was passed by the U.S. Congress in 1996, affects just about everyone who delivers any sort of health-related services in the United States. The impact on data and information technology from HIPAA is huge. It affects patients' privacy rights and the way data relating to patients, procedures, and insurance records is stored, managed, and protected, with specific attention paid to patients' privacy and data retention. Failure to comply with some of the more serious HIPAA guidelines can result in fines of up to US$250,000 and up to 10 years in jail; others will only result in fines of up to US$25,000.

- The Foreign Corrupt Practices Act of 1977, a federal law in the United States, requires all public companies to have formal DR plans. If your public company does not have an emergency contingency plan or a security program, they can be found in violation of this law. Further, they must be able to demonstrate that these plans were implemented and tested on a regular basis.

- The Securities and Exchange Act of 1934 is full of requirements as to data and record retention. To oversimplify the requirements, the act says that all records of publicly held companies and the firms who audit them must be retained for at least 7 years.

- Internal Revenue Service ruling number 71-20 requires that corporate tax records must be retained for as long as they are relevant. The IRS does not want to hear about system crashes or bad backups; they just want to make sure that you have all of the data that you are supposed to have.

The good news is that criminal prosecutions under these acts are pretty much unheard of. There are many other corporate malfeasances that have gotten the attention in the last few years.

However, there's bad news too. We live in an extremely litigious society (at least in the United States), where law firms routinely file class action suits against public companies just about any time the company's stock price goes down. It is not hard to imagine a scenario where a public company suffers a major financial loss due to a lack of preparation for systems problems, which results in further losses when the lawyers begin to file suits. In the end, the result of the civil litigation could cause a greater financial loss than any system problem or data loss.

There are even cases where corporate officers could be held personally liable for significant business losses due to outages. If nothing else gets their attention, this will.

Cost of Downtime

We discuss the cost of downtime in other places around the book, but no discussion of the business impact of downtime and availability is complete without mentioning it once again. The Meta Group, an industry consulting firm, estimates the cost to a business of total system downtime at just over *$1 million an hour*.

A University of Minnesota study says that a 48-hour outage would put 20 percent of the Fortune 500 out of business. And a study from Contingency Planning Research Inc. says that the average time to recover a business's systems after a disaster is four days.

The University of Minnesota study also said that of companies that suffer a major outage from a disaster and do not have a working recovery plan, just 43 percent of them will ever resume operations. Of that 43 percent, just 29 percent of those will still be in business two years later. Relax, we've done the math for you: *87 percent of companies that have a disaster and do not have an adequate plan will be out of business within 2 years.*

So, how long will it take your enterprise to recover? Do you have a plan?

Start Building the Case

Once you have learned what you need to know, the next step is to begin to put together a calm and rational case that explains in nontechnical terms what the vulnerabilities, risks, and costs are. The case must include a discussion of the risks of inaction.

Find Allies

Ask around your organization. Look for friends and colleagues who share your concerns. Maybe you'll find someone who has tried to convince management of something in the past. At the very least, though, it is best if you can find people in other organizations who agree with you and who can help build the case.

If you are a Windows system administrator, speak to the Unix system administrators and see if they agree with you. Contact database administrators, as well as network and storage administrators. If the problem that you have identified is a real one, it surely affects some of these other people. Maybe you can also identify some end users who share your concerns and invite them to join the fight. If your organization is large enough to have multiple facilities, contact peers in other facilities and see if you can find allies there.

If you can demonstrate to management that your concerns are shared in different parts of the organization, your case will be much stronger. On the other hand, if you can't find allies in a medium- to large-sized organization, that may be an indication that your efforts will not succeed and that you should probably reconsider your efforts.

One problem that can arise when you bring in additional people is that different people have different perceptions of a problem, as well as different priorities. To be successful, you must take input from every member of the team and make sure that their concerns are addressed in the final presentation. It may become necessary to compromise and change the level of priority that certain issues receive. But if you aren't willing to compromise, you run the risk of having some of your allies drop from the effort or, worse, form a competitive group. If that happens, both movements will likely fail.

Which Resources Are Vulnerable?

Now you have some idea of what's important to the business, and what some of the costs and risks associated with downtime are. The next step is to develop a list of potential vulnerabilities. Consider anything that could interrupt critical services, from the minor to the very large. The following are some of the typical vulnerabilities (your list will surely be much larger) that an enterprise's computer systems might have:

- A failed disk
- A blown CPU
- Corruption in a database
- Unreadable backups
- Network component failures
- A fire in the data center
- An extended power outage
- Flooding
- A chemical truck spill on a nearby highway
- A tornado
- A blizzard
- A bioterrorist attack

It is likely that protection is already in place for many of the vulnerabilities on your list. You should still include those, as they will help make your case for implementing protection against other vulnerabilities.

Once you have the list, and it should be as long as possible, rate each vulnerability on two characteristics: likelihood and impact. Use a simple scale for each characteristic, such as a rating from 1 to 3; there's no reason to go out and research the expected dollar loss to the enterprise for each type of outage at this early stage. We offer a very basic example in Table 4.1.

Table 4.1 Worksheet Describing Vulnerabilities, Likelihoods, and Impacts at a Fictitious Organization

VULNERABILITY	LIKELIHOOD (1–3)	IMPACT (1–3)	LEVEL OF CONCERN (LIKELIHOOD × IMPACT)	COMMENTS
Failed disk	3	1	3	Critical systems already have mirrored disks.
Blown CPU	2	2	6	Systems are not clustered; a failed CPU will result in major downtime for one server.
Database corruption	2	3	6	Corruption in a critical database could shut down the web site for hours.
Unreadable backups	1	2	2	Only an issue if we lose data from our disks. Then it could be quite serious.
Network component failure	2	2	4	We have a very complex network, with many single points of failure.
Data center fire	1	3	3	Could cause the loss of our entire computing infrastructure.
Extended power outage	2	2	4	Won't damage data, but could keep us down for a long time.
Flooding	2	3	6	This area has a history of flooding. With the data center in a low floor, results could be catastrophic.
Chemical spill	1	3	3	An interstate highway goes within 200 yards of the front door. Always a small risk.
Tornado	1	2	2	Would have to hit the building to be a major problem.
Earthquake	2	3	6	Can, of course, be a major disaster.
Bioterrorism	1	3	3	Unlikely, but if it happened, could be serious.

Be conservative in your ratings; everything can't be a 3, or you will lose credibility. Build the list and the ratings so that it would be very difficult to poke holes in your reasoning or logic. By being conservative and calm, you take away some of the ammunition of your potential critics, and you will make a much more persuasive case.

When trying to develop your list of vulnerabilities, it is wise to employ brainstorming techniques and include several people in the process. There are many methods to assist with creative thinking beyond brainstorming that will help you generate a more complete list.

Develop a Set of Recommendations

Once your list of vulnerabilities and ratings is complete, it's time to develop a list of recommendations. If you have made a solid and sober case, and you can follow that with some equally well-thought-out recommendations, you will maximize the likelihood that you'll get the resources you are looking for.

Choose no more than three or four of the most serious vulnerability scenarios—the ones with the highest likelihoods and impacts. Develop complete plans to address each of them, with alternatives at different cost levels. Choose one that you like best, and recommend it the most strongly, but make sure that all of the alternatives are palatable.

The recommendations should include a pure business discussion of costs versus risks, along with those old business school chestnuts *return on investment* and *time to payback*. (We discussed these in some detail in Chapter 3.) What are the objectives? Why are we discussing this? What is the potential benefit to the business? Be as specific as possible. Discuss the impact on current ongoing operations of implementing your solution; will there be downtime? How much? What will it all cost?

When estimating costs, be sure that your numbers are realistic. If someone challenges you on acquisition or implementation costs, be sure that you can defend your numbers. Cite sources for your information.

Discuss the hidden benefits of your proposal. For example, will having better recovery plans result in a reduction in the enterprise's business interruption insurance premiums? (You may not be able to accurately determine this, but it's something to include as a potential hidden benefit. For example, a completed and tested disaster recovery plan can reduce these very expensive premiums by 20 percent or more.) If the plan includes purchasing additional computer equipment or real estate for a disaster recovery site, what additional benefits can these resources provide the organization? Will you be able to off-load backups from primary systems? Will you be able to house additional personnel? Is there a chance the property value will rise? Remember that financial arguments are most likely to get attention from upper management.

Some of the key questions to ask include how long could our business/enterprise/organization survive without:

- Our web site?
- Our customer service representatives?
- Our LAN, SAN, MAN, or WAN?
- Our accounts payable and receivable departments?
- The payroll department?
- Telephones?
- Electricity?
- A place for employees to come to work?

Be sure you also consider the short- and long-term business impacts of extended outages to the organization's reputation. Will there be front-page articles on our experiences? How will those articles affect future business?

And then there are the intangibles, like loss of market share and investor confidence. Your outage could put you in violation of all sorts of industry regulations, including some of the ones we discussed before. Your outage could even tarnish the reputation of your entire industry. It could also alienate customers, either present or future.

Your Audience

Before you can assemble your message and its associated deliverables into their final form, you must first deal with two critical aspects of your audience. First, you must obtain an audience, and then you must know who they are so that you can target your message to them.

Obtaining an Audience

There is not much point in doing all of the work to put together a strong and persuasive message if you don't have anyone to deliver the message to. You'll need to go through your own manager, and then possibly through other levels of management, in an attempt find the right people to deliver the message to.

Be sure that you don't go around levels of management. There aren't many more certain ways to anger managers above you than by going around them. If you learn that you have inadvertently gone around someone during the process, be sure that you tell him or her what happened at your first opportunity.

In the process of speaking to different managers, you'll be asked for a brief summary of your main message. Have a clear 50-word verbal overview that you can deliver from memory without stammering anytime someone asks you to. You will appear to be well organized and to have thought through your ideas well, and this is likely to impress the people you are speaking to. If you receive feedback on your overview, take it seriously and consider incorporating the comments into your work, especially if it comes from important and influential people.

Know Your Audience

The single most important thing to know when you are delivering a message of any kind is whom you are delivering the message to. It is imperative that you know your audience, so that you can learn what their concerns are. If you can know their concerns, what kinds of proposals they have responded well to in the past, and (perhaps most important of all) what they don't want to hear, you can tailor your message to meet those requirements.

If the members of your audience are interested in technology, you can make your message a little more technical in nature. If they are not especially technical, then it is very important to remove all jargon, acronyms, and geek talk from the message. Forcing technical terminology and concepts on a nontechnical audience is a surefire way to frustrate and alienate them.

If you are unable to get a good read on your audience before you meet with them, concentrate on the financial aspects of your proposal. Never forget that the universal language of management is money. In many organizations, management receives bonus compensation based, at least in part, on how much money they save.

Delivering the Message

When it comes time to deliver the message, the preferred method is to do so in two parts. Prepare a slide presentation and a paper.

The Slide Presentation

Prepare a presentation that will run no longer than 20 minutes, unless you are told otherwise. And if you can keep it shorter, then by all means do so. Remember that the people you are presenting to are very busy, and you do not want to waste their time. If you respect their time, they will be more likely to respect you. You can also show respect in the way you dress; it may be wise to put on a suit and tie for the occasion. In addition, many organizations use a standard template for slide presentations; if yours does, you should use it.

Before you start the presentation, explain why you are there and what you hope to accomplish by taking up some of their valuable time. It is important to be respectful and polite, especially if you have never presented anything to these people before. Remember to speak slowly and to clearly enunciate all of your words.

Choose two or three especially critical problem areas, and concentrate on those for about 10 to 12 minutes. Don't worry about the other issues in an initial presentation. If your ideas are well received, you'll have time to discuss other issues later. If they are not well received, why waste everyone's time? For each of the areas you've chosen to concentrate on, discuss the vulnerabilities and risks to the enterprise from each and then your ideas to fix them. Finish with some very rough financial estimates that include both costs and return on investment. Remember that if you are just asking for money, without any promise of return, you will not get any. Well-run companies will spend money when there is a good chance they will make that money back and more in a reasonable amount of time.

At the end of the presentation, wrap up with a brief (one slide) review of what you just said. The cliché about delivering presentations still holds: "Tell 'em what you're going to tell 'em, tell 'em, and then tell 'em what you just told 'em." Make sure you emphasize the financial returns that your proposal will generate.

If you are not an experienced presenter, it is best to practice your presentation several times in front of a video camera or, even better, in front of friends who will be honest with you about the strengths and weaknesses of the presentation and your delivery style. If you are very uncomfortable presenting, perhaps one of your allies has more presentation experience and would be willing to do it instead.

In presentations such as these, it is best to stay away from jokes and animated slides. They distract from your main message, and the wrong kind of joke could offend someone you are trying to impress. Avoid negative statements. Don't insult people, products, processes, or companies. Be positive. Remember that you are there to help make the company money, which can make everyone in the room more successful.

If you believe in what you say and can show some enthusiasm and confidence, you'll have an excellent chance of success.

The Report

At the meeting where you deliver the presentation, you should also deliver a written report. The report should contain all of the gory details about your proposal and should not be limited to just the two or three points you make in the presentation. Hand copies out to all of the attendees. Bring a few extra copies just in case you need them.

When you write anything longer than a quick email, it is best to begin the process with an outline. An outline helps you keep your thoughts organized and ensures that you hit all the points you want to. When the outline is complete, you should plan on showing it to a couple of chosen allies. After you have received comments on the outline, it's time to begin writing the actual report.

The basic organization of the report should be similar to the presentation's. Open with a brief overview, called an executive summary, of what the report contains (no more than a page), with an emphasis on the conclusions that you will draw. Assume that many of the people who read your report will only read the executive summary, so make it as punchy and compelling as possible.

Follow the opening with a clear statement of the problems, risks, and vulnerabilities. Behind that should come the proposed solutions, including costs and returns. If there are a great number of problems and solutions to discuss, it may be best to open the paper with a detailed discussion of a few of the most important ones, along with their proposed solutions, and then have another section later in the report that discusses lesser issues. Working papers such as the scoring chart of vulnerabilities should be included as appendices.

Be sure not to use too many horror stories. If you overload the paper with scary scenarios, you will most likely turn your audience away, and they will not take your message as seriously as they would with just a couple of good stories. IT professionals still harbor some Y2K-induced distrust of gloom-and-doom driven planning.

If the report is longer than about seven pages, it should also include a table of contents. If your organization has a preferred style for reports, that style should be strictly adhered to. The front cover of the report should always include the date and current version number. Put the company logo on the cover and the appropriate confidentiality messages on the bottom of each page.

If you are concerned about your ability to write (and this is not at all an unusual problem among technical people), it may be worthwhile for you to identify someone in your organization who can write well and whom you trust and ask for that person's help in preparing the report.

Make sure that you have a place in the report where you can list the names of every single person who helped you, whether they gave you a huge idea that really helped develop the message or just helped you spell a word. People love to see their name in print, and it's a very nice way to publicly show your gratitude to people who genuinely helped you. Keep a list as you go along; don't trust your memory. Then make sure the people you thanked see the final report.

After the Message Is Delivered

If you did a great job of getting your message across, everyone in the room heard you, understood you, and was totally won over by your outstanding presentation and written report. You've been given all the money you need to implement the project, you got a big raise and promotion, and that really attractive person in the cubicle down the hall from yours is calling you for a date. (Okay, that probably didn't happen.)

If you've merely done a good job of getting your message across, then you have persuaded at least some of the people who heard and read your message that at least some of your message was valid. The next step is to work with the people you convinced and get their assistance in implementing the plan and in persuading the others to see the value of your proposal.

Most likely, your work is just getting started. Once you have convinced everyone of the importance of implementing high availability, you will probably be put in charge of the effort. Now the real fun begins. Good luck!

Key Points

- Managers, even senior managers, are people just like you, with their own interests and agenda. If you can appeal to their interests, you can usually gain their support for your projects.

- Don't be afraid to contact other people in your organization to build a consensus.

- A clear, calm, and concise message that is not full of jargon and buzzwords will likely produce the best results.

- Know your audience and do your best to tailor the message for that audience.

CHAPTER

5

20 Key High Availability Design Principles

From the home office in Wahoo, Nebraska...
—David Letterman

In Chapter 3, "The Value of Availability," we introduced the idea of the Availability Index. As shown in Figure 5.1, the first level of the Index is called "Good System Administration Practices." Since these practices are the first level of the Index, they are the least expensive to implement. Being on the first level doesn't make them the easiest, it just means that they lay the foundation for all of the other technologies that we will discuss in future chapters. We believe that there is no good reason to skip over these most basic system administrative practices. Some of the practices that we'll discuss in this chapter are easy to implement, while others can be difficult and tedious. The difficult ones are no less important than the easy ones.

Most, though not all, of these topics will only be discussed here. Later sections of the book discuss technologies and principles of availability that rank higher on the Index, and therefore are more expensive and complex.

For no particular reason, we present this list in reverse order, from #20 down to #1.

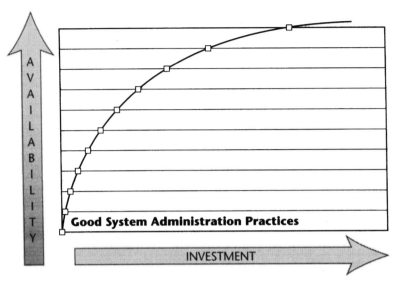

Figure 5.1   Level 1 of the Availability Index.

#20: Don't Be Cheap

Mugger: *Your money or your life!*
Jack Benny: *I'm thinking, I'm thinking...*
—The Jack Benny (radio) Show

One of the basic rules of life in the 21st century is that quality costs money. Whether you are buying ice cream ("Do I want the Ben & Jerry's at $4.00 per pint, or the store brand with the little ice crystals in it for 79 cents a gallon?"), cars (Rolls-Royce or Saturn), or barbecue grills, the higher the quality, the more it costs.

As we explained in Chapter 3, the decision to implement availability is a business decision. It comes down to dollars and cents. If you look at the business decision to implement availability purely as "how much will it cost me," then you are missing half of the equation, and no solution will appear adequate. Instead, the decision must also consider how much the solution will save the business and balance the savings against its cost.

When considering the return on investment of a particular availability solution, look at how it will increase uptime and increase the value of your systems because they are up more. Consider the increase in productivity among the users of the critical system and how, because the system is up, they won't have to work overtime or be idled during the workweek. There is no question that implementing a protective measure will cost money; the key is to balance that against the ROI. In Chapter 3, we discussed a model to estimate ROI. That model is not perfect because it requires making predictions, but educated guesses will get you figures that are close to reality. Over time, you can revisit the figures and improve them for the future.

It probably doesn't make sense to spend a million dollars to protect a development system in most shops, although there are surely enterprises where that level of protection is necessary.

The extra hardware and software required to implement a redundant data center, clustering, and mirrors will surely cost quite a bit of extra money. Hiring the skilled personnel who will make the right decisions on system implementation and management will cost extra money. But the hardware, software, and people, properly deployed, will save the company money in reduced downtime. The trick is to find the appropriate balance between cost and value.

#19: Assume Nothing

When you assume, you make an ass out of you and me.
—The Odd Couple (TV)

Despite marketing claims to the contrary, high availability does not come with computer systems. Achieving production-caliber levels of end-to-end system availability requires effort directed at testing, integration, and application-level assessments. None of these things are done for you by the vendor directly out of the box. Very few products can simply be dropped into an environment and be expected to add quality of availability. In fact, without up-front engineering efforts and costs, the opposite is true: Poorly implemented new products can reduce overall system availability.

Don't expect product features that work in one situation to continue to operate in other, more complex environments. When you add reliability, you add constraints, and you'll have to test and verify the new bounds of operation.

Don't assume that application developers are aware of or sensitive to your planned production environment or the operational rules that you'll impose there. Part of the job of availability design is doing the shuttle diplomacy between application developers, operations staff, and network management crews.

Beyond that, vendors do not just throw in clustering or replication software; it has to be purchased at additional cost above the systems that require protection. (To be fair, at least one OS vendor does include clustering software for free with their high-end OS. You can be certain that the price is just hidden in the price of the OS.) Without extra work and software, data will not get backed up, systems won't scale as needs increase, and virus and worm protection will not be implemented.

Achieving production-quality availability invariably requires careful planning, extra effort, and additional spending.

#18: Remove Single Points of Failure (SPOFs)

You are the weakest link. Good-bye.
—Anne Robinson

A *single point of failure* (SPOF) is a single component (hardware, firmware, software, or otherwise) whose failure will cause some degree of downtime. Although it's a cliché, it's an apt one: Think of the SPOF as the weakest link in your chain of availability. When that one link breaks, regardless of the quality of the rest of the chain, the chain is broken. There are obvious potential SPOFs, such as servers, disks, network devices, and cables; most commonly these are protected against failure via redundancy.

There are other, equally dangerous, second-order SPOFs that also need attention. Walk through your entire execution chain, from disk to system to application to network and client, and identify everything that could fail: applications, backups, backup tapes, electricity, the physical machine room, the building, interbuilding ways used for network cable runs, wide area networks, and Internet service providers (ISPs). Reliance on external services, such as Dynamic Host Configuration Protocol (DHCP) or Domain Name Service (DNS), can also be a SPOF. After you have identified your SPOFs, make a concerted effort to eliminate as many of them as possible, by making them redundant or by getting them out of the chain, if possible.

It is, in fact, not possible to remove every single SPOF. Ultimately, the planet Earth is a SPOF, but if the Earth suffered a catastrophic failure, you probably wouldn't be thinking about your systems anymore. And no amount of preparation could protect you against that particular failure.

On a more realistic level, if you run parallel wide area networks to connect a primary site with a secondary or disaster recovery site, the networks are very likely to run through the same building, conduit, or even shared cable somewhere upstream. Wide area bandwidth is generally leased from a small number of companies. WAN service providers are usually quite reluctant to admit this fact, but that is the way things are.

A NET BY ANY OTHER NAME

While we were teaching our availability course, a system administrator related his experience with redundant Internet connections. Insisting on no single points of failure in its entire networking chain, his company had routers from different manufacturers connected to different ISPs so that they'd be safe from router bugs or ISP headaches. Nevertheless, his primary connection to the outside world had failed. It turned out, unfortunately, that the secondary ISP chosen happened to resell access from the same upstream provider as the failed primary ISP. Both Internet connections were down because the SPOF was located at the Internet access wholesaler.

—Hal

There are many other SPOFs to consider, and many of the ones discussed briefly in the preceding text have many other facets we have not yet addressed. We will address many of these through the course of the book.

#17: Enforce Security

*I opened that virus just like you told us
not to.*
—A recent TV commercial

Entire books and multiday seminars have been written on maintaining a high level of system security. It is not our intent to replace any of them. However, making your systems secure is still a fundamental element of achieving overall system availability.

We will discuss security in more detail in Chapter 11, "People and Processes," but here we introduce some of the basic things that should be done on all systems to tighten up their security:

Keep unnecessary users off of critical systems. If a user logs onto a system where he does not need to be, he cannot be doing any good. If he does not need to be there, then he should not be able to get there.

Use sudo or similar tools to restrict privileged activities. The Unix tool sudo can be used to limit privileged access on Unix systems, so that DBAs and other users who need privileged access can have it even while their actions are restricted to a fixed set of commands, and their actions are logged. That functionality can be achieved on Windows through several mechanisms, including the Windows Scripting Host (WSH). Some Windows administrative commands have a Run As option on the right-click menu that allows changing users.

Use firewalls.   A fundamental way to keep unwelcome visitors out of your network and off of your critical systems is through the use of firewalls. Firewalls are not the be-all and end-all of security, as there are almost always ways to sneak through them, but they are an effective starting point.

Enforce good password selection.   Lots of freeware and shareware utilities enforce good password selection. Some of them attempt to decrypt passwords through brute-force methods, using common words and variations on those words. Others do their work when the passwords are created to ensure that a sufficient variety in characters is used, thus making the password difficult for a guesser to figure out. Another common tool is password aging, where users are forced to change their passwords every 30 or 90 days, and they cannot reuse any password from the last set of 5 or 10. Beware, though, when combining password aging with other requirements; you may unintentionally force users to write down their passwords.

Change default system passwords.   Old Digital Equipment Corporation (DEC) Virtual Memory System (VMS) systems had a default password set for the administrator (privileged) account. Since the world was not networked, this was not a big security hole, but with the Internet, it becomes frighteningly easy to access systems on other networks, especially when firewalls are not adequately deployed. Some versions of Microsoft SQL have a default password for the administrator account; it is critical that this password be changed to keep hackers out of your systems.

Train your users about basic system security rules.   Not long ago, there was a TV commercial where a user proudly says to her system administrator, "I opened that virus just like you told us not to." Users need to be instructed in the rules of basic security. They should not open email attachments from unknown sources, and they should be very careful opening attachments from known sources. They need to be wary of using certain file extensions. They should never give out or write down their passwords.

Delete logins and files of ex-employees after they leave.   Beware of a disgruntled employee who departs her employment on bad terms. If she is clever and really angry, she may leave behind a time bomb (a program that destroys files or other data at a later date) or some sort of back door permitting her to access your systems at a later date. Don't just delete files from the ex-employee's home directory or primary server; search the network for other files that she may have owned.

Use virus checkers, and keep them up-to-date. Like firewalls, a virus checker is a good first step in protecting your system, but if you don't keep the virus definitions up-to-date, a newly released virus can still incapacitate your systems. There was a time when the conventional wisdom was that you needed to update your virus definitions monthly. Today, conventional wisdom says that you should update your virus definitions no less than weekly, and more often when you hear of a new virus being released. Unix and its variants (including Linux) are much more virus-resistant than Windows systems are; generally, Unix administrators do not need to be nearly as concerned with viruses as Windows administrators do.

Check the Web for alerts. Sometimes you can keep up on security issues and new viruses by reading the news, but in general, you need to keep an eye on web sites like www.cert.org where you can get reliable, unbiased, and timely security information.

#16: Consolidate Your Servers

The fool says, "Don't put all your eggs in one basket," by which he means that you should spread your resources and energy around. The wise man says, "Go ahead, put all your eggs in one basket. Then watch that basket!"
—Mark Twain

The trend over the last few years in many computing circles has been to consolidate servers that run similar services. Instead of having many small single-purpose machines or lots of machines running a single instance of a database, companies are rolling them together and putting all the relevant applications onto one or more larger servers with a capacity greater than all of the replaced servers. This setup can significantly reduce the complexity of your computing environment. It leads to fewer machines that require backups; fewer machines that require reboots; and overall, fewer things that can fail. As a result, the labor and cost associated with administering systems is reduced. It is cheaper and easier to manage fewer larger systems that are configured similarly, using today's technologies, than it is to manage many smaller systems, especially ones that run disparate operating systems.

Consolidation is, however, a powerful force for improving the simplicity and manageability of an environment. It comes with the cost of having to invest even more engineering effort in making the larger, consolidated server more reliable and robust. The moral of the story is "Go ahead and put all your eggs in one basket; just make sure the basket is built out of titanium-reinforced concrete."

A new trend is emerging, though, that may render this particular principle moot in a few years. Vendors are linking together hundreds or even thousands of very small systems called blades, and developing pseudo-backplanes and shared networks to connect them together, enabling these blade computers to act as a massive cluster. The biggest obstacle so far is administration; few mainstream tools allow easy administration of hundreds of systems, even ones that share applications and operating systems. Those technologies will likely appear in the next few years. We'll discuss blade technology further in Chapter 22, "A Brief Look Ahead."

#15: Watch Your Speed

Either this man is dead, or my watch has stopped.
—Groucho Marx

When people speak of the end-to-end nature of availability, they usually think of all of the components between the user and the logically most distant server. While those components are, of course, all links in the chain of availability, they are still not the whole story. After all, either a piece of equipment is functioning, or it is not.

If we maintain our user perspective on availability, another element needs to be considered: performance. Since our user cares about getting his job done on time, the performance of the system that he is attempting to use must also be considered. If the system is running but is so overloaded that its performance suffers or that it grinds to a halt, then the user who attempts to work will become frustrated, possibly more frustrated than he would if the system were down.

So, in addition to monitoring system components to make sure they continue to function, system performance must be monitored from a user's perspective. Many system tools can be used to emulate the user experience, as well as to put artificial loads on systems so that high-water marks for acceptable levels of resource consumption can be determined.

We believe, however, that benchmarks are not nearly as useful or practical as vendors would have you believe. In general, benchmarks can be tweaked and modified to get almost any desired results. At least one disk array vendor has a sales agreement that specifically prohibits its customers from running or publishing any benchmarks related to the vendor's equipment, and the vendor has enforced this prohibition in court on more than one occasion. Benchmarks rarely measure what people actually do on their systems. They seldom mimic multiuser systems, where users are working in a manner in which users actually work. And, unfortunately, benchmarks become less and less valid the more that the testing environment differs from reality, and it doesn't take a lot of differences to make the benchmark totally worthless.

To a user who is trying to use a computer system, very little difference can be detected between a down system and a very slow one, and as the system slows down more and more, no difference is discernible at all.

Back in the heyday of the Internet, an Internet consulting company, Zona Research, estimated that $4 billion a year was lost due to users attempting to buy things on slow web sites, then giving up and canceling their purchases. Although that number has surely come down in the time since the Internet boom, even a single cancelled transaction should be enough to give a company reason to stop and think.

#14: Enforce Change Control

Plus ça change, plus c'est la même chose.
(The more things change, the more they are
the same.)
—Alphonse Karr (1849)

When you call system support or your help desk to complain about something being wrong with your computer, the first question the helpful person on the other end of the phone asks is always the same: "What was the last thing you changed?" The most common answer to this question is, of course, "Nothing." But most of the time, something has changed, and it's usually something fairly serious.

Mature production environments should have change committees that include representatives from every relevant organization, including the users, networking, system administration for each operating system, database administration, management, and every internally developed application. Other groups may be required as well, depending on the environment. When someone requests a change, it is brought before the committee for approval and implementation scheduling. With a solid change control system in place, everybody's needs can be taken into account, including schedules and deadlines. Conflicting or contradictory changes can be identified early in the process. The change control process should be such that any rejection of a change is justified and explained so that the requester has a chance to resubmit it at a later date. But no change, regardless of how small, can be made unless it has been approved in writing by all members of the committee.

Any change request should include, as a minimum, the following items:

- Executive summary of the change
- Detailed description of exactly what will be changed
- The source of the code to be changed (if the changes are in software)
- Why the change is required
- What the risks are, if the change goes badly
- A back-out plan, in case the changes go badly
- The time that will be required to implement the plan
- Requested schedule for the implementation

Some enterprises impose additional restrictions on changes to production, including requiring that changes be made in a test environment first and allowed to run there for a week or more before they can be introduced to production.

Another aspect to change control is keeping track of changes to files, particularly system files. Fortunately, there are utilities that can help out in this regard. One excellent utility for monitoring changes to system files is Tripwire (`www.tripwire.org`), which is available on many different operating systems. Tripwire is a tool that checks to see what has changed on your system. It monitors key attributes of files that should not change, including binary signature and size, and reports those changes when it detects them.

#13: Document Everything

The only thing worse than no documentation
is bad documentation.
—Unknown

The importance of good, solid documentation simply cannot be overstated. Documentation provides audit trails to work that has been completed. It provides guides for future system administrators so that they can take over systems that existed before they arrived. It can provide the system administrator and his management with accomplishment records. (These can be very handy at personnel review time.) Good documentation can also help with problem solving.

System documentation includes run books, procedures, development documentation, operation manuals, application error guides, and anything else that a new developer or SA might need in order to get systems to work. It should be well written, with no assumptions about applications or processes, and should be aimed at multiple audiences over time.

1. The first audience is the author himself. Documentation aimed at the software author makes it much easier for the author to go back and debug problems in his own code that may occur years later. When you look back at your own two- or three-year-old work (system or network design or programs, for example), it can be almost impossible to remember why you did something a particular way, and not another way, despite having excellent reasons at the time. Write comments in your code. Write manuals, even if they are just a couple of pages long.

2. The second audience is sometime in the future. The people who maintain the systems and the applications today aren't going to be around forever. And you can't assume that any experienced personnel will be around to mentor newcomers. You must prepare for a massive exodus of your experienced people. A popular sign on many system administrators' desks reads: "Remember, 100 years from now, all new people!"

3. The third audience is management. Keeping good notes and documenting your work helps demonstrate to management that you have been diligent and shows what measures have been taken to keep the systems running and productive. If a system does not meet the requirements set forth in the documentation, it should be easy to figure out why and to determine what must be done to make the system compliant. Even if your management does not understand the value of the services you provide to the organization, they will usually understand the value when it is presented as a thick stack of documentation.

Make sure that documentation is stored on paper too. If the system is down when you need the manuals, you're not going to be able to get to them. Keep them in binders so that they can be easily changed and updated. After the documentation is written, don't forget to review it and update it on a regular basis. Bad documentation is worse than none at all. In a crisis, especially if the most knowledgeable people are not around, documentation is likely to be followed verbatim. If it's wrong, things can go from bad to worse.

A common question about preparing documentation is at what technical level it should be written. One school of thought says that documentation should be written so that anyone in the organization, from a janitor to the CEO, can follow it and, if required, bring the systems up after a disaster. After all, the system administrative staff may not be available at the time, and someone has to do it. While that is a noble goal, it is an impractical one. The state of the critical systems changes all the time. The more detail that is included in that documentation, the quicker it becomes out-of-date. In order to write documentation so that an untrained smart person could bring systems up or do other critical work on them in time of crisis, it would have to be so detailed as to be unmanageable.

If the task at hand is to edit a file to change one variable to another, for an appropriately trained system administrator, the documentation would only need to say, "Change ABC to XYZ in /directory/file.txt." For an untrained smart person, the documentation would need to say:

1. Change directory to /directory by typing "cd /directory".

2. Open the vi text editor by typing "vi file.txt".

3. Move the cursor down to line 300 by typing "300G".

and so on (in whatever operating environment is appropriate). Every time the line number in the file changed, the documentation would have to be changed. Many error conditions would need to be handled for the inexperienced person as well; for example, if the terminal type or line count is set wrong, the vi editor may have trouble dealing with it. In that event, what should the inexperienced person do?

The right answer, therefore, is to write documentation so that an experienced system administrator could use it. Don't expect the administrator to have a great deal of experience in your shop, just general experience. In a Windows environment, target a Microsoft Certified Engineer (MSCE). In Unix environments, target experienced system administrators. If something happens to the current system administrative staff, you can reasonably assume that they will be replaced by experienced people.

Documentation is a lot like a fine piece of literature. Everybody wants to say that they have read *Moby Dick*, but nobody wants to actually sit down and read *Moby Dick*.

THE BOOK OF EVAN

When I worked for a Wall Street trading firm several years ago, the tradition was for departing system administrators to create, say, The Book of Evan, in which the soon-to-be-dearly-departed describes in detail all of his projects, past and present. In this way, whoever takes over the projects has a starting point and a way to know quickly what's going on. Once a system administrator gave notice, he'd spend the last two weeks of his employment writing his book. This is an excellent way to ensure a clean passing of the torch from one generation to the next.

—Evan

#12: Employ Service Level Agreements

... And so we've agreed together that we
can't never agree.
—Will Carleton

Before disaster strikes, many organizations put written agreements in place with their user community to define the levels of service that will be provided. Some agreements include penalties for failing to meet, and rewards for greatly exceeding, agreed-to service levels.

Service-level agreements might deal with the following areas:

Availability levels.   What percentage of the time are the systems actually up? Or, how many outages are acceptable during a given service period? And how long can each outage be?

Hours of service.   During what hours are the systems actually critical? On what days of the week? What about major holidays? What about lesser holidays? What about weekend holidays?

Locations.   Are there multiple locations? Can all locations expect the same levels of service? What about locations that do not have on-site staff?

Priorities.   What if more than one system is down at the same time? Which group of users gets priority?

Escalation policy.   What if agreements cannot be met? Who gets called? After how much time has elapsed? What are the ramifications?

Limitations.   Some components of service delivery will be outside local control. Do those count against availability guarantees anyway?

These agreements are usually the result of considerable negotiations between (and often significant pain to) both customer and service provider.

When designing SLAs, beware of ones that commit you to deliver nines of availability. You are betting the success of your job (if not the job itself) on whether or not the system will go down. Nines are a sensible approach only if you know exactly how many times the system will go down over a given period of time. Unfortunately, though, managers, especially non-technical managers, really like to use the nines as an approach to SLAs because they are simple, straightforward, and easily measurable. They are also easy to explain to other non-technical people. If your performance is being judged on your ability to fulfill SLAs, avoid nines-based SLAs.

A much more sensible way to design an SLA is to discuss specific types of failures and outages, and how long the system will be down as a result of them. When estimating downtimes, be conservative; everything takes longer than you think it will.

#11: Plan Ahead

*If it weren't for the last minute, nothing
would get done.*
—Unknown

Planning is a vital component to any significant project. When you are dealing with critical systems that have dozens or hundreds of users, their requirements must be taken into account any time a system is changed. Crisis situations, such as disasters, require significant planning so that everyone who is responsible for the recovery knows exactly where to go and what to do.

In addition, no matter how good your automated protection tools are, there will occasionally be events that are outside of their ability to cope. Multiple simultaneous failures will stretch most software and organizations to their limits. By having plans in place that are the result of calm and rational thinking well in advance of the calamity, a smooth recovery can be facilitated. Without a good plan, you'll find yourself prioritizing and coordinating in real time and leaving yourself open to myriad variations on the theme of "fix it now!"

Any kind of documented recovery plans should be approved by management and key personnel and may be part of a service level agreement. Keep these plans offline, in binders, and in multiple locations so that the acting, senior person on-site can execute them when required. Make sure they are kept current. If they contain confidential or personal information, be very careful with the distribution of the plans, and limit access only to those who need it.

Planning also includes coordination. If you are planning to bring down some critical systems for scheduled maintenance, be sure you coordinate that downtime with the users of the systems. They may have deadlines of their own, and your scheduled downtime could interfere with that downtime. In most shops, a wise approach is to give the same level of scrutiny to scheduled downtime as to changes; a committee should bless scheduled downtime periods.

GET I.T. RIGHT!

In a sales organization where I once worked, the IT department announced via email that it would be taking the internal email system down for the entire upcoming weekend. As the upcoming weekend was the last weekend of the calendar quarter, and because the sales organization worked on a quarterly calendar, a very angry email was quickly and publicly issued from the Senior VP of Sales. The IT department quickly found a reason to reschedule the downtime.

—Evan

#10: Test Everything

An untested plan is just a piece of paper.
—Unknown

Not only do crisis plans need to be tested, so do all new applications, system software, hardware modifications, and pretty much any change at all. Ideally, testing should take place in a production-like environment, with as similar an environment to the operational one as possible, and with as much of the same hardware, networks, and applications as possible. Even better, the same users should perform the tests. The tests need to be performed with the same production network configuration and loads, and with the same user inputs and application sets. User simulation and performance modeling tools may help to generate the first few tests in a quality assurance environment, but you're going to want to test out an application in an environment that looks and feels live before really turning the system on.

Be sure that you test at the unit level (what if this disk fails?); at the subassembly or subsystem level (what if we unplug this disk array or pull out this network connection?); at the complete system or application layer; and then on a full end-to-end basis.

Testing should always be based on a clear and well-thought-out test plan, with specific goals, and acceptance and failure criteria. All test plans should be documented so that they can be referenced in later tests and so that tests can be researched without having to be duplicated. Significant testing efforts should be followed by postmortem meetings, where the test results, and the test procedures themselves, can be discussed. When considering the results of tests, always remember what was being tested. A common mistake that is made in testing is the assumption that if the test didn't go well, it was the people who messed up. People are people; if the test goes badly, then it is the test that has failed and that must be changed.

Tests need to be repeated on a regular basis. Environments change, and the only way to be sure that everything works and works together is to test it. Otherwise problems will occur in production that will inevitably lead to downtime. Adopting a regular testing policy is akin in popularity to regular rereadings of *Moby Dick*. But no matter how unpopular or distasteful documentation and testing are, they are still preferable to downtime. You'll catch many problems in the earlier tests that may be buried or harder to find in the more complex, later tests, or that don't turn up until production rollout.

One way to increase the value of testing is to automate it. Automated testing can provide a level of thoroughness that is difficult to achieve through manual testing. Testers can get bored or tired, and they may not test every permutation of testing parameters, especially after several go-rounds of testing. Many tools are commercially available to help automate testing; these tools will not have boredom issues.

#9: Separate Your Environments

The flapping of a single butterfly's wing today produces a tiny change in the state of the atmosphere. Over a period of time, what the atmosphere actually does diverges from what it would have done. So, in a month's time, a tornado that would have devastated the Indonesian coast doesn't happen. Or maybe one that wasn't going to happen does.

—Ian Stewart, *Does God Play Dice?*

Keep your production and development environments separate and independent of each other—not just the servers, but the networks and the users. Development users should never be permitted routine access to production systems, except during the first few days of a new rollout (and even then, only under carefully controlled and monitored conditions) and when a critical problem occurs that requires their attention. Without separate environments, change control cannot be enforced in your production environment. Ideally, a well-designed environment should contain as many as six different environments:

Production.   In production, changes are made only with significant controls. Everything in production needs to work all the time. If something doesn't work, there must be a way to roll back to a version that did work. Changes must be made smoothly, and with a minimum of interruption to the production workflow. Any changes should go through a change control committee, as described previously.

Production mirror.   The production mirror is more properly called a production time warp. It should be an accurate reflection of the production environment as it was two or three weeks ago. Any updates to production, whether approved or otherwise, should be applied to the mirror after an agreed-upon period of time has passed. This environment permits production to roll back to a working production environment in the event that defective software is installed in production. As noble an idea as this is, it is very seldom used in practice.

Quality assurance (QA).   This is a true test environment for applications that are believed to be production-ready. Quality assurance is the last stop for code before it goes live. Changes made to this environment should be as well controlled as changes made to production or to the production mirror.

Development.   Clearly this environment is for works in progress. Change need not be monitored very closely or approved with the same degree of procedure as production, but at the same time, the environment must be maintained properly and cleanly for developers to work. In development, code can be installed and run that may not work 100 percent. It may be genuinely buggy. That's okay here, as long as the software is running only in development and its bugginess does not affect the other environments in any way.

Laboratory.   Often called a sandbox, the laboratory is a true playground. This is where SAs get to play with new hardware, new technologies, new third-party applications, and whatever else comes along. An interesting side benefit of a good lab environment is that it works as a change of pace for your system administrators. With all the automation and procedures that are in place on many production systems, it's healthy to allow a bored or burned-out SA to have a place to go where the rules aren't so strict. The lab may contain new cutting-edge equipment or be used to set up and solve duplicated thorny production problems in a nonproduction environment. Labs can be a wonderful opportunity for your SAs to develop some real hands-on experience and to exercise their coding or hardware skills.

Disaster recovery/business contingency site.   This site is located some distance, possibly thousands of miles, away from the main production site. In the event that some major catastrophe takes out the production site, a reasonably quick switchover can be made and production can resume from the disaster recovery site. We will discuss disaster recover issues in much more detail in Chapter 20, "The Disaster Recovery Plan."

Not every company will need, or can afford, all six environments. If no code is developed in-house, then you may not need a development environment, for example. You still should test out externally developed applications before implementing them, but that integration function may be combined with a QA environment in a single staging area.

The production mirror is a luxury that many sites cannot afford, so if it is used at all, it is most often combined with the DR site, and not maintained two or three weeks in the past as discussed previously. Combining these two environments does introduce some risk, of course, and limits the ability of the DR site to recover from a bad change that has been made to production.

#8: Learn from History

What's past is prologue.
—William Shakespeare, *The Tempest*

In order to see what changes to make on your system to make it more resilient, you need to look at the recent history of your system. Why does your system go down? What are the most common causes? Don't just rely on anecdotal information ("Well, it sure does seem to go down a lot on Thursdays"). Keep real records. Check them often. Look for patterns. (Maybe the system really does go down a lot on Thursdays. Now you need to figure out why!) Maintain availability statistics over time.

Account for every incident that causes downtime. Understand the root cause of the failure and the steps needed to fix it. If you've invested in failure isolation, you should have an easier time finding root causes. Look closely at the MTTR, and see if something can be done to improve it. Did it take two days for key parts to arrive? Was there a single person whose expertise was critical to the repair process—and was he unavailable?

Use the evaluations to identify your most common problems, and attack them first. Don't waste your time protecting the CPU if the most common cause of downtime is an application bug. The old 80/20 rule of thumb works here. Roughly 80 percent of your downtime is likely to be caused by 20 percent of the problems. Fix that 20 percent and you should see a tremendous improvement in availability. Then you should be able to reapply the 80/20 rule on the next 80 percent of downtime.

The other quote that we considered for this principle is the one from the mutual fund commercials: "Past performance is no guarantee of future success." However, that is not quite the message that we wanted to get across. On the other hand, that quote does help prove the adage that for every saying, there is an equal and opposite saying. Consider the combination of "look before you leap" and "he who hesitates is lost" or "out of sight, out of mind" and "absence makes the heart grow fonder."

#7: Design for Growth

A gas will expand to fill all available space.
—The definition of a gas

Computer utilization will expand to fill all available space.
—The definition of a gas, applied to IT (Evan Marcus)

Experience tells us that system use always expands to fill system capacity. Whether it's CPU, memory, I/O, or disk space, it will all get consumed. This means that the 2TB of disk you just bought for that server will be all used up in a few months. That's just the way of the world.

If you go into the design of a computer system with this experience in mind, you will build systems with room for easy growth and expansion. If you need 8 CPUs in your server, buy a 16-CPU server, and only put 8 CPUs in it. If you buy and fill an 8-CPU server, when it's time to add more CPUs, you may have to purchase a whole new server, or at least additional system boards (if there is room for them) to obtain the additional capacity. Some system vendors will even put the extra 8 CPUs in your server and leave them disabled until you need them. When you need them, the vendor will activate them and charge you for them then. (Beware of this practice: You may be buying hardware that will be outmoded by the time you actually need it.)

If you buy a large disk array completely full of disks, when it is time to expand your disk capacity, even by a single disk, you will need to buy another array. If you find that you don't have enough I/O slots in the server, you're in trouble.

The industry buzzword for this is scalability. Make sure that your system will scale as your requirements for those systems scale. The incremental cost of rolling in a new systems or storage frame is considerable. The downtime implications for adding new frames or adding boards to the backplane will also be significant. By spending the extra money up front for the additional capacity, you can save yourself both downtime and cost when you need to grow the systems.

#6: Choose Mature Software

A new broom sweeps clean, but an old
broom knows where the dirt is.
—Unknown

Let's say that you have a choice between two relational database management systems (RDBMSs); for our purposes, we'll say the choices are the current release of Oracle and Joe's Database v1.0, from Joe's Database and Storm Door Company of Ypsilanti, Michigan. (We are not endorsing Oracle; the same rules would apply to any mature software product. As far as we know, Joe has not yet released a database.) Joe's product has a couple of features that make it a little easier to use, and it comes in a lot cheaper than Oracle does. You like Oracle, but Joe's sales rep got you courtside seats for the NCAA finals last year.

No offense to Joe or his sales rep, but in the end, you will almost certainly be better served by going with the product from a large company like Oracle (or Sybase, IBM, or Microsoft). The large-company products have benefits that you simply cannot get from a small-company product like Joe's. Established RDBMSs have 24×7 telephone support, fly-to-site support, informative web sites, user groups, user conferences, magazines, and other mature services. A small company like Joe's is unlikely to have any of those things. Established support structures make it easier to get help from many different sources. You can find users with whom you can discuss various implementation options, performance optimization, problems you may have encountered, and all sorts of other interesting issues, real and imagined. You can also more easily find reference sites that are willing to show you what they have accomplished with their product.

Mature software has been tested by its customers (and internal testers) for a long time, and problems that newer software, written by less experienced developers, may run into have probably been taken care of. In some cases, more mature software will have availability features written right into it. Oracle's RAC features are one example of such a feature.

However, like so many other good rules, this one does not apply universally. Just because a product has achieved wide acceptance, that does not ensure that it is high quality. All wide acceptance ensures is that a lot of people use it. Wide acceptance is an excellent first qualifier when examining your choices in a given marketplace, but it should never be the only factor that gets consideration.

When designing for availability, sometimes you'll have to sacrifice the latest-and-greatest technology for something established because you know you'll have to fix it when it breaks, and because cutting-edge products are not generally as reliable as the tried-and-true.

There's an intermediate ground, however, in the area of publicly available software. Software that has large user bases and many developers working on fixes and improvements is likely to be easily obtained, fixed, and managed, because you'll find a reference model for its use in your application. Windows utilities, Unix tools, cross-platform languages like Perl, browsers, and even web authoring tools can be obtained by looking and evaluating carefully. This is one of the advantages that the Open Source movement provides: many eyes and hands looking at the code.

You should always have reservations about dot-zero, or first major revisions of software. Not that you shouldn't put these releases into your test bed or laboratory environments and evaluate the new features and their integration with your world. But hesitate to put them in production until you've done the shakedown. When dealing with Internet software and startup companies, sometimes you need the latest killer application. The enabling technology may be brand-new to the market, forcing you to deal with version 1.0 products. In that case, refer back to Key Design Principle #10 repeatedly.

Of course, it's not always easy to tell when software is brand-new. Vendors have figured out that their customers are often reluctant to use version 1.0 and so give their software all kinds of other version numbers. Some vendors hide massive rewrites of old products by giving them the next release number in sequence. Other vendors don't use release numbers at all, preferring instead to identify versions by the year or by some other name, number, or abbreviation. And still others synchronize the releases of many of their products and give all products released together the same version numbers, regardless of their relative maturity. With a little research, though, you should be able to determine how mature different releases of software are.

#5: Choose Mature, Reliable Hardware

It is sad to grow old, but nice to ripen.
—Brigitte Bardot

Statistical information about mean time between failures (MTBFs) for particular hardware units can be difficult to obtain, and the data is often considered proprietary by its vendor. What's more, the accuracy of MTBF numbers have often been called into question; how can a vendor reliably claim that a disk drive that was developed six months previously has an MTBF of 200,000 hours (which is more than 23 years)?

Nevertheless, when purchasing new hardware, make an effort to secure and compare MTBF data. The data will help you get an idea of how often the various pieces of hardware will fail. Obviously, using more reliable hardware components will result in more reliable systems.

Building for easy repair is more a matter of selecting hardware that is easy to fix and easy to access. It is much easier to swap out a client computer if its disks are located outside the box, rather than inside. If they are outside, you need only swap out the computer and plug everything back in to get the client's user back in business. If the disks are inside the client computer, the old computer must be opened and the disks removed. Then the new client computer is opened, and its disks are removed and replaced by the older disks. All the while, the user is unable to work at his desk.

BURIED TREASURE

In 1978, my dad bought me my very first car, a used 1974 Camaro. For the most part, it ran just fine. One day, though, it began leaking oil. We brought it in for service and were told that the cause was a faulty engine gasket, a 79-cent part. The only problem was that to get to the gasket, they would have to pull the engine out of the car and take the whole thing apart. The end result was that I lost the car for a week, and it cost me (okay, my dad) about $800. By providing either an easier access point or a higher-quality gasket (it was a cheap part that failed quite often, we were told), the manufacturer could have saved us time and money, and the MTTR would have been much shorter. The same lesson applies to computer system design.

—Evan

Another way to reduce MTTRs is to manage your spare parts properly. Know what spares you are likely to need, and determine how long it will take your vendor to supply them. Also consider what will happen if the vendor has certain key parts on back order.

In the days that followed September 11, 2001, all air traffic in the United States was shut down. People who were waiting for shipments had to wait several days longer. Can your business handle that eventuality? Does it make sense for you to inventory certain key spare parts? Balance the extra cost of the parts and the space and inventory overhead with the convenience and the potential reduction in MTTR.

#4: Reuse Configurations

Plagiarize, plagiarize; never let another's work escape your eyes. But always call it research.
—Tom Lehrer

If you have success with a particular system configuration, reuse it everywhere! Replicate it throughout your enterprise. Pick a handful of configurations for different situations, and just use those. It will be necessary to revisit the specific technology choices over time, as technology evolves, but by limiting the number of different models, fewer elements will need to be revisited, and overall, fewer configurations will need to be running in your enterprise.

The following are some of the advantages of using replicated configurations:

Ease of support.   Fewer configurations mean fewer permutations of hardware and software, fewer things to learn, and fewer things that can go wrong.

Pretested configurations.   If the same exact configuration works in 20 other places, how much additional testing is required before rolling it out the 21st time? And if some elements actually have changed, only those changed elements need significant testing.

High degree of confidence for new rollouts.   If you know that a particular configuration has worked in other rollouts, it makes it much easier to justify using it for future rollouts.

Bulk purchasing.   It is often easier (and cheaper) to purchase large quantities of a single component than to purchase smaller quantities of many different components. This situation is especially true when multiple vendors are involved.

Fewer spare parts.   Fewer different components mean fewer spare parts to stock (if you choose to stock them at all). This lowers the overall cost of the spare parts, decreases the storage space required to stock them, and simplifies the inventorying process.

Less to learn.   Perhaps the biggest benefit of replicating configurations is in how much less there is for incoming system administrators to learn. Giving your SAs less to learn means that they can come up to speed on the way your company does things much faster, and as a result, they can be productive much sooner.

The advantages of replicating configurations can be achieved in other ways as well. Many shops use a centralized OS server; if a new system needs to join the network, or if something happens to an old one, the OS can be reinstalled on it quickly and easily, and in a way that is just like all of its neighbors on the network. This feature, often called Jump Start, Kick Start, or Remote Installation Services, is available from most operating system vendors.

Embedding more and more software, such as volume managers, databases, popular GUIs, and browsers into the Jump Start means that the post–Jump Start work is greatly reduced, and systems can rejoin the network that much more quickly.

#3: Exploit External Resources

A paperclip can be a wondrous thing. More times than I can remember, one of these has gotten me out of a tight spot.

—MacGyver

Most likely, whatever problem you are trying to solve, or whatever product you are trying to implement, someone has done it before you. The vendor probably has a consulting or professional services organization that, for a fee, will visit your site and implement your critical solutions for you, or at least offer advice on how to architect and implement your plans.

Arrange for on-site consultation from vendor resources or independent contractors, and be sure a transfer-of-information or technical exchange is part of the planned work. If vendors offer training classes on a product, make sure the right people attend them so that you learn the pitfalls and issues before you start implementation.

Read books (we know an excellent one on high availability) and magazines, both on paper and online. Scan the Web; the TechTarget collection of web sites (www.techtarget.com) is an excellent set of resources for the system and database administrator on every major platform. Attend conferences; for example, the USENIX and LISA conferences (www.usenix.org) offer consistently excellent training and support services for Unix, Linux, and Windows administrators, on a variety of general and very specific topics.

If you are a significant user of a particular vendor's products, see whether they have user conferences; they represent an outstanding opportunity to meet other people who use similar products and who may have run into similar problems. Auburn University in Auburn, Alabama, maintains a collection of mailing lists, many of which are relevant to system administrators. For more information, visit http://mailman.eng.auburn.edu/mailman/listinfo. Countless other examples of mailing lists and valuable web sites can be found all over the Internet.

User documentation is often a good starting point for information, although some product documentation can be less useful than others. Many vendors have local user groups in major cities or where there are concentrations of their users. Salespeople are usually happy to point interested users to these groups.

An often overlooked and yet very valuable resource for all sorts of technical information is something we think of as the grandparent of the World Wide Web, Usenet. Often simply called newsgroups, Usenet is an immense collection of bulletin boards on thousands of different topics. A recent check showed that there are over 35,000 different newsgroups on practically every topic imaginable, serious or recreational, from medical issues to current events, from macramé to professional wrestling. A huge percentage of Usenet is devoted to technical topics of all sorts (although there does not appear to be a newsgroup dedicated to high availability). Any of the major web browsers can be used to access Usenet. At `http://groups.google.com/groups`, you can search the Usenet archives dating back to its very beginnings in the 1970s. If you have never visited Usenet, you should do so at your first opportunity. It is a tremendous storehouse of knowledge. Unfortunately, like the rest of the Internet, it has been badly contaminated in recent years by junk postings and spam. But if you can filter out the junk, there is a lot of value in Usenet.

Another way to gain knowledge in your organization is to hire experienced people. If someone else has sent them to training, and they have learned most of what they need to before they joined your organization, then you can save money on training. It will likely cost you more money to hire well-trained and experienced people, but it is almost always worth the expense.

Vendor salespeople represent another useful resource. Although their product-specific information may be somewhat slanted, they can often obtain experts in their specific field of interest who can come and give non–sales-specific talks. Salespeople can also provide reference sites, where you can verify that their solutions work as they advertise them and you can learn about the vendor and the product at a level that the sales team can be reluctant to provide.

#2: One Problem, One Solution

I do one thing at a time, I do it extremely
well, and then I move on.
—Dr. Charles Emerson Winchester III *(M*A*S*H)*

Someone once said that a good tool is one that has applications that even its inventor did not foresee. Although that's true, most tools are designed for a single purpose. Although a butter knife can turn a screw, you wouldn't use one as a screwdriver and expect the same results. The same holds true for software; you should not try to shoehorn software into performing a function it was not designed to do.

Don't try to make a solution fit if the designers did not intend it to be used in the way you propose. Complex problems have many aspects (subproblems) to them and may require more than one solution. Examine one subproblem at a time, and solve it. If your solution happens to help solve another subproblem, that's serendipity. But don't expect it to happen every time. In fact, one solution may create other unforeseen problems, such as incompatibility with other products.

BE CAREFUL WHAT YOU ASK FOR

A prospective customer of mine wanted to replicate a database from a site in New Jersey to a remote site in Kansas. My company offered a perfectly satisfactory solution to implement this replication. However, he also wanted the replication software to hold the replicated data for four hours before applying the updates to the remote site. This way if a database administrator accidentally corrupted the database by, say, deleting a table, he wanted to have his worldwide user base switch its access point to the delayed copy in Kansas.

At the time, our software could not do this. Even though my company offered three other products through which he could achieve his goals, he insisted that we provide the solution through the replication software. He did not want to hear about the issues associated with reinitializing the New Jersey copy of the database after switching to Kansas, nor in considering our detailed alternate proposals.

In the end, after my consulting organization did a lot of custom work to our replication software, the customer did not select our product. He felt that the solution was cobbled together. It was. In the end, his chosen solution could not do the job adequately either. If he had been willing to consider a different approach, his problems could have easily and quickly been solved.

—Evan

If you have faith in your vendor and its sales force, then when the salesperson recommends against your using his product in a certain way, it is best to listen to his advice. Consider the salesperson's motivation (assuming that he is a good and honest salesperson). He ultimately wants happy customers. Happy customers buy more, and when they buy more, he makes more money. If he tells you something that discourages you from buying a product, he is turning down short-term gain for a long-term gain. That is the mark of a good salesperson; he is attempting to build a trusting relationship with his customer. When a salesperson or a sales engineer does this, consider the advice carefully; it is probably valid.

#1: K.I.S.S. (Keep It Simple . . .)

*Things should be made as simple as
possible, but no simpler.*
—Albert Einstein

We live in an immensely complex world. We have technologies and tools about which our parents and certainly our grandparents never dreamed. And our children will likely see similar technological advances in their lifetimes.

TV OR NOT TV? I DON'T UNDERSTAND THE QUESTION

A couple of years ago, my family bought a complete home theater system, with a satellite dish, a big-screen digital TV, surround sound, and a DVD player. Back when we had cable TV, if you wanted to watch TV, you turned on the TV, and maybe the set-top cable box, and you were ready to go. Not anymore. Now, if you want to watch TV, you have to turn on the TV, make sure it is set to the right input source (satellite, DVD, antenna, or VCR, which are helpfully labeled ANT A, ANT B, and Video 1 through 3), turn on the satellite converter box, turn on the stereo, and make sure it is set to the proper input (TV, DVD, AM, FM, CD, tape, and so on). Then you have to choose a channel from the nearly 150 different choices that we can get, numbered between 2 and 999.

There are seven remote controls sitting on my coffee table (including ones for the TV, satellite box, stereo, VCR, and DVD player). Some of these remote controls have more than 50 buttons on them. There are also two specially purchased multifunction remote controls that we bought to try and rein in the whole mess. They did not work as well as we'd hoped.

My wife and I came home from a night out and found her parents (who were baby-sitting) watching TV with no sound (they couldn't figure out how to get the sound to come on; they had been watching it that way for over two hours). As a result, I decided to write a manual for operating the whole system, which I call, "So You Wanna Watch TV?" It contains digital photos of each remote control, the TV, the satellite box, and the cabinet that contains the stereo components, with circles and arrows, and detailed instructions.

My in-laws can once again watch TV in my house.

—Evan

In order for technology to become generally accepted into society, it has to be simple. If a complex technology is made sufficiently simple to use, it will be adopted. When automobiles first came out, you needed to be a mechanic to keep them operating. Nowadays, you do not need to know anything about the workings of a car to drive one. As a result, in much of the world, cars are totally pervasive. They remain complex, and have gotten much more complex over the years. But they are easy to use. The same cannot be said of computers.

However, beyond adoption, simplicity allows technology to work. The fewer parts that something has, everything else being equal, the more likely it is to work. By removing unnecessary components, you reduce the number of components that can fail.

Computer systems today are immensely complex, and they are likely to become more complex over time. When you sit down to work on your networked computer, you are using your computer and all of its software components, including the operating system, the applications, and all of the other administrative applications like antivirus software, the computer's hardware components (CPU, memory, network card, and so on), your storage (whether direct-attached, networked-attached, or SAN-attached), your local LAN and all of its components (routers, hubs, switches, and so on), whatever servers your applications require, and all of their software and hardware components, and so on.

All this complexity means that in any computer network, there are a large number of individually complex components that can fail, often causing larger failures.

Unless special precautions have been taken (and we will spend a significant percentage of the remainder of this book discussing what we mean by "special precautions"), if any one of those components fails, work on the systems will be interrupted. What's more, even if protective measures have been put into place, the failure of one component may hasten the failure of another component that has become overworked due to the first failure.

Simplicity means many things. To help introduce simplicity into computer systems, do the following relatively easy tasks:

- Eliminate extraneous hardware on critical systems. Get the scanners off the production systems—unless your production work involves scanning, of course. If your servers don't need graphical screens and mice, then remove them; they add nothing and are just two more things that can break.

- Slim down servers so that they run only critical applications. Stop playing Doom on production systems, even if the game does run faster there. Don't run screen savers on production systems; modern monitors don't get burn-in (which is what screen savers were originally employed to defend against). Today's screen savers are nothing but CPU suckers.

- Disconnect servers from networks where they don't need to be. There's no reason for development or QA networks to be connected to production servers. A network storm or other problem on those networks can have an adverse effect on production.

- Select hostnames that are easy to remember and easy to communicate on the telephone. Admittedly, hostnames like *ha4pv56a* may communicate a lot of information about a host, but they are hard to remember, especially for new people. Imagine a situation where the boss says, "Quick, run up to the data center and reboot the ha4pv56a file server! It's hung, and everybody is locked up!" You run to the elevator, then ride it up to and wait for the second set of elevators in order to get to the data center. When you finally get there, you are confronted by four servers: *ha4pb56a*, *ha4pd56a*, *ha4pt56a*, and *ha4pv56a*. If you reboot the wrong one, you'll affect 100 otherwise-unaffected users, who'll be pretty angry.

  If instead of those hard-to-remember names you choose pronounceable and memorable names from a theme, you'll get it right every time. Rule of thumb: If you have to read out more than three characters in the name of a system, it's probably a bad name.

- Automate routine tasks. Human error is one of the leading causes of system downtime. Computers are really good at doing mundane and boring tasks. By automating them once, you significantly reduce the chance of error when the task must be repeated.

- Remove ambiguity from the environment. If it's not clear whom you should call when something breaks, or who has authority to take a network down, the wrong thing will happen.

The bottom line is that you want to minimize the points of control and contention, and the introduction of variables. The fewer things that are there, the fewer things that can break.

Since human error is a leading cause of downtime, one important way to improve availability is to reduce the number of mistakes that humans (administrators) make on critical systems. The best way to do so is to give them less opportunity to make mistakes (even honest ones). By making systems simpler, you do just that. Simpler systems require less administrative attention, so there is less reason for administrators to interact with them, so there is less chance for them to make a mistake that brings the system down.

Key Points

- You can do many things to increase your system's availability that are neither expensive nor complicated.

- Never assume that the people who manage the system today will be the people who manage it tomorrow. Leave documentation for them, and make things as simple as possible so that the next generation of administrators is able to take over with a minimum of difficulty.

- Past performance is an indicator of future success, at least when analyzing downtime patterns on critical computer systems.

CHAPTER

6

Backups and Restores

Never underestimate the bandwidth of a station wagon
full of tapes hurtling down the highway.
—Andrew Tannenbaum

In this chapter, we look at backups, perhaps the greatest nuisance task in system administration, and yet one of the most important. Backups represent the last line of defense against lost data; if you have no backups, you could lose significant chunks of your data. The real value of backups, of course, is in the restore. The first time you are forced to turn to backups to restore a piece of critical data, and you succeed, all the time and effort you have put into backups will be justified.

With backups, we reach Level 2 of the Availability Index, as shown in Figure 6.1.

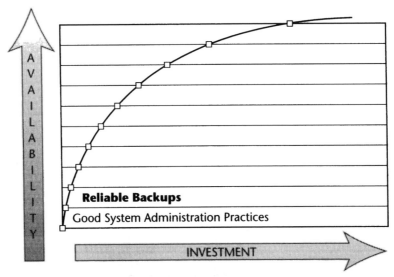

Figure 6.1   Level 2 of the Availability Index.

The Basic Rules for Backups

In many ways, backups are the heart of any design of critical systems. Handled properly, they represent the last line of defense against just about any catastrophe. Even if your building or your entire city is wiped out, your business can be restored on other computers from properly generated and protected backup tapes. But there are several "if" conditions that must be satisfied for everything to work out properly and data to be recoverable.

There are a number of basic backup guidelines. By keeping them in mind as you design your backup environment, you will make the best advantage of your backups, and they will serve you best when you need them:

Mirroring does not replace backups.   This hard fact runs counter to a very old and unfortunate myth. Mirroring protects against the failure of storage hardware, but it does nothing at all to protect you from a deleted or corrupted file. If a file is deleted on one side of a mirror, it is gone from both sides and therefore must be retrieved through some external means. The most common (but by no means the only) external means of recovery is restoring a backup tape.

The most common use of restores isn't after a catastrophe.   Yes, of course catastrophes do happen, but it is much more likely that a user will accidentally delete or damage a single file, or even a directory, than it is for the contents of both sides of a mirror, or two disks in a RAID stripe, to fail at the same time, or for a sitewide disaster to occur. So, design your backups to optimize restore times for a single file.

Regularly test your ability to restore. Backups are very important, of course, but if you cannot restore them, you have wasted a lot of time and effort creating useless tapes. You shouldn't need to test every backup tape that you create, but certainly every tape drive should be tested regularly to ensure that the backups it makes are readable, and a random sampling of tapes should be tested to ensure that they can be read and restored properly.

Keep those tape heads clean. Dirty tape heads may cause backups to appear to complete successfully when, in fact, only garbage has been written to the tape. Clean the tape heads as often as the manufacturer recommends, if not slightly more often. If your backup utility reports tape read and/or write errors, clean the heads immediately. If errors continue, see if they are present on other tapes, and if they are, then contact the vendor.

Beware of dirty tapes. No, not adult videos, but rather the tapes themselves. Sometimes a single bad spot—a crease, a fold, or a smudge of dirt—on a tape can prevent the entire tape from being read. Store the tapes in their cases in relatively clean rooms, and test a sample from time to time.

Pay attention to MTBF numbers for tapes. If the manufacturer suggests that a tape's useful life is 1,000 backups, then use it 1,000 times, and get rid of it. The time to find out that a tape has gone bad is NOT during a restore. Good backup management software will keep track of tape access counts for you and tell you when it's time to dispose of a tape.

Tapes decompose over time. Do not assume that the tape you made five or six years ago is still readable today. Tapes break down; they get exposed to weak magnetic fields that affect their quality, and some simply age badly. It is very difficult for manufacturers who are introducing new tape formats to accurately determine the shelf life of such a tape. If they were to perform definitive tests, introduction of such tapes could be delayed for several years. Test your tapes on a regular basis, and copy them to new media from time to time. To help extend the shelf life of your tapes, pay attention to the tape's storage requirements; avoid extremes in temperature and humidity.

Make two copies of critical tapes. Tapes are much less expensive to purchase and maintain than is re-creating the data that is on the tapes. To better ensure the longevity and safety of your tapes and data, it is wise to store one copy of your tapes off-site.

Make sure you can still read old media.   It's nice having a record album collection, but if you don't have a turntable with a good needle, the records are pretty useless. The same is true of old magnetic tapes; if you can't read your old nine-track tapes, there's no point in keeping them. When new technology comes along, copy the old tapes that you need onto new media.

DRUM ROLL, PLEASE

A museum in California was producing an exhibit showing the development of a particular chunk of land over a period of several decades. The exhibit curators asked NASA and three-letter government agency contacts for satellite photos of the area, and were thrilled when told they could have the actual data in its original form. What arrived, much to the museum's chagrin, was a set of data drums: decades-old rotating storage without a device to mount or read it. The bits of data representing bits of land might have been a stellar addition, but without the ability to make sense of it, the data was effectively lost. Beware of the longevity of the media format, as well as the media's magnetic properties.

—Hal

Do Backups Really Offer High Availability?

The kinds of debates and arguments that an author of a book can get sucked into are quite interesting. Sometimes they are of the hairsplitting variety. One of the more recent debates is whether or not backups qualify as high availability at all. As with the definition of high availability itself, different groups and organizations have their own answers to this question.

Until recently at VERITAS Software, for example, the software engineering organization was split into two groups: the Availability Products Group (APG) and the Data Protection Group (DPG). All VERITAS backup products were grouped into DPG, suggesting that backups are not perceived as high availability.

In fact, we believe quite strongly that backups are high availability. As discussed in Chapter 3, "The Value of Availability," the ability to successfully restore data that has been lost or damaged can shorten recovery time from forever to merely hours or days. Since properly implemented backup and restore software can shorten downtime, it is most definitely high-availability software.

What Should Get Backed Up?

Every file on every system should get backed up, from the obviously critical to the seemingly trivial. If a file could ever be needed at a later date, for any reason, then it should be backed up. If it would take any time at all for a user to re-create the data in a file, then the file should be backed up. If losing a file would be a nuisance to a user, the file should be backed up.

Obviously, servers must be backed up. The data on servers can be shared by dozens, hundreds, or even thousands of users, any number of which could be inconvenienced by the loss of that data. Unfortunately, in many shops, the backup effort ends with the server. Servers should just be the beginning of backup efforts.

It's hard to imagine a laptop or other client system that should not be backed up. Some studies claim that 60 percent of all critical data is on laptops. Laptops get stolen. They break. They get dropped. Because they move around so much, their disks are much more prone to damage than systems that are stationary. Yet remarkably few enterprises take the time and effort to back up their laptops. Some excellent software packages are on the market for backing up and restoring laptops. Some can restore a laptop's entire contents to a CD-ROM for easy shipment to a road warrior in just a few hours.

In addition, some systems contain hidden files that need to be backed up, and they may require special efforts. On Windows nodes, be sure that the Registry is being backed up properly. Make sure that configuration files stored on network devices are backed up. Make sure that the configurations for your logical volume manager are backed up, and can be easily restored. Otherwise, some significant manual effort will be required to bring systems back online.

Just about all commercially available backup software uses a catalog or an index to allow for quick restores of single files, or groups of files. If the catalog is lost or damaged, restores will either be delayed immensely while the catalog is rebuilt or they will be completely impossible to restore. Catalogs can generally be rebuilt, but doing so requires reading the contents of every relevant backup tape along the way. That process can easily take several days of round-the-clock tape changing. By backing up the catalog, and storing that backup tape off-site, the restore process can be greatly sped up. Some shops prefer to replicate the backup catalog to their DR site (see Chapter 18, "Data Replication") to further enhance their ability to recover their systems.

Back Up the Backups

It isn't enough just to take the backups, though. In order to restore lost data quickly, the backup tapes must be stored near the tape drives. Otherwise, downtime can be extended by the time it takes to retrieve the tapes. In that event, a traffic jam on a local highway could be the cause of a system being down longer than it should have been. Because the backups should be stored near the tape drives, what happens if there is a buildingwide disaster and the contents of the building are lost?

If the building, or just the closet that stores the tapes, is damaged or lost, the only way to recover critical systems and data is by having a copy of the backup tapes stored off-site. To get backups off-site, you must back up the backups. That means making copies of backup tapes and sending them off-site. Many enterprises take daily backups but only send tapes off-site once a week, or once a month. That's fine if the enterprise could handle losing a month's worth of data. If the data center is lost, and the only copy of the critical data is a month old, then users will have to spend their time reentering old data, assuming that they have records of this data that survived the loss of their building. Otherwise, that data may never be recovered.

Getting Backups Off-Site

There are two primary methods to get copies of backed up data off-site for safe storage. Both involve copying tapes.

The first is to copy the tapes on a local tape drive, generally during the production day, when the tape drives are unused. It's best to keep at least one or two drives free at all times, in case an emergency restore is required, though. Once the tapes are copied, they are then hand-carried or shipped off-site to a storage facility or to the DR site.

The second method is to copy the tapes across a WAN to a remote system with its own tape drives. This method does not require the use of a shipping agent to deliver the tapes off-site; however, it consumes a great deal of network bandwidth, which can be extraordinarily expensive on WANs.

Both methods can be fairly expensive, since a service that carries tapes off-site and retrieves them as needed is likely to charge a lot of money, and since sufficient WAN bandwidth to copy nightly backup tapes is likely to be considerable.

Other methods for getting critical data off-site will be discussed in Chapter 18.

DATA THAT SWIMS WITH THE FISHES

There is at least one financial services firm located in the New York metro area that has rather cleverly solved the problem of getting their backup tapes off-site while still keeping them easily accessible for routine restores. They have production sites in Lower Manhattan and in nearby New Jersey, and have extended a SAN across the Hudson River between them. Lower Manhattan's backups are performed in New Jersey, and the tapes are stored there. New Jersey's backups are performed in Manhattan, and those tapes are stored there. They feel that with this model, they do not need to copy tapes for further off-site storage.

One potential source of concern is that you can see each building from the other. They are reluctant to discuss what their plans are if something should happen to both sites simultaneously.

—Evan

Backup Software

Many of the key design principles that we discussed in Chapter 5 come into play in the following discussion of backup software.

Commercial or Homegrown?

Many factors lead users to consider implementing homegrown backup software rather than using commercial software. Probably the most common factor is cost: There is a mistaken belief that creating one's own backup software will result in a savings in cost, especially on Unix systems. (Windows systems are bundled with fairly intelligent backup solutions, so homegrown solutions in that space are usually a nonissue.) Homegrown backup solutions are almost always wrappers around standard OS backup tools like dump or tar and as such exhibit the shortcomings of those tools. For instance, many versions of the Unix tar utility cannot handle long filenames, or backups that span more than one tape, especially if they don't start at the beginning of a tape.

GROWING MY OWN

A few years ago, I was called on to write a backup utility for a development group to whom I was consulting as a system administrator. (In the end it turned out to be a roughly 500-line Perl program.) Maintaining the program, not to mention the backups themselves, wound up taking an inordinate amount of my time because the requirements for the backups were constantly changing. (The requirements document read: "Dear Evan, Please write a backup program for the developers. Love and Kisses, The Boss") What's more, I never got around to adding the rather complex code that would have enabled my program to handle backups that spanned more than one tape. Fortunately for me (though perhaps not for my customer), I left that consulting assignment shortly before the backups outgrew a single tape.

My program also made no allowances for backing up open files. This came back to bite us all very badly, as the development group used a development environment product that required precise consistency across hundreds of tiny files throughout the filesystem. When the filesystem needed to be completely restored from tape, the backups did not contain a consistent view of the filesystem, and so the development environment could not be restored. The developers were down for a week.

And there were other problems. Some nights the backup would complete in three or four hours, while other nights it would continue from 8:00 P.M. until 10:00 or 11:00 the next morning. When that happened, we had no choice but to abort the backups, as they put such a load on the server that performance became unacceptable. On those nights, backups simply failed. We never did find out why. Admittedly, I did not have that much experience with backups at the time I did this work, but most likely, the system administrator being asked to develop a homegrown backup system at your site hasn't very much more. High-quality commercial backup software will have ways to address these issues.

—Evan

Poor and inconsistent performance are just two issues that mature commercial backup solutions have run up against and solved over the years. A homegrown solution is unlikely to have solved very many at all, leaving its users to settle for a second-rate product. In the sections that follow, you will see more cases where a homegrown backup solution will not suffice.

Examples of Commercial Backup Software

The backup and restore arena is filled with commercial products. Some of the leaders, and some of the operating systems they will back up, are:

- *VERITAS NetBackup.* Solaris, Windows, HP/UX, AIX, Linux, SGI, Novell NetWare, NDMP, OS/2, Compaq Tru64

- *Tivoli Storage Manager (formerly IBM ADSM).* AIX, Solaris, Windows, HP/UX, AS/400, OS/2, MVS, VM

- *Legato Networker.* Solaris, Windows, HP/UX, AIX, SGI, Novell NetWare, OS/2

- *Computer Associates ARCserve.* Windows, Novell NetWare, some Unix

There are many other entrants in the field, including VERITAS Backup Exec, SyncSort, EMC's EDM, and others.

Commercial Backup Software Features

What follows is a list of some features that are valuable when you are evaluating a backup product. This is by no means a complete list, and different users will surely assign different values to some of these features. Your mileage may vary:

100 percent hardware utilization.   We spend quite a bit of time in this chapter discussing the best way to lay out your hardware to achieve the backup performance that you need. All that is for naught if your backup software cannot drive your hardware at its maximum speeds. Tape drives are designed to spin as much as possible, and will last longer and deliver better performance when they do. Most likely, you have a lot of backup hardware. Tape drives, tape libraries, dedicated backup networks, and tapes themselves are only a few of the expensive assets required to take and maintain backups. Surely the people who sign your purchase orders would prefer that you make full use of the hardware you have before you invest additional money on hardware that you may not actually need. Good backup software will drive your hardware at its maximum capacity and will scale well as new hardware is added.

Hot backups.   You should be able to back up filesystems and databases, as described previously, without having to take them offline and without an obvious performance impact to your applications.

Open tape format. In an emergency, you should be able to read and restore tapes without needing specialized software or license keys. The delay in obtaining software and keys will increase your MTTR in a crisis.

Speed. Benchmark backup and restore performance in your environment. Even if backup performance isn't critical today, you can safely assume that it will be tomorrow.

Centralized management. It should be easy to administer your entire backup environment from a single console, if that is the configuration you select. If you prefer a few administrative consoles, that option should be available to you.

Reliability. There should be no single point of failure in your backup environment. If a tape server or a controlling server fails, its functions should be picked up by another server on the network.

Quick disaster recovery. Some backup products require the rebuilding of their tape databases or catalogs before a post-disaster recovery can begin. If rebuilding indices requires prereading every tape in the library, it could add days to your recovery times. Make sure you understand the entire process for initiating a recovery from a major outage on new systems.

Hardware support and flexibility. When you are implementing a new wide-scale backup project, it is unlikely that you will have the luxury of purchasing all new tape hardware. Any backup solution you choose to implement should support as much of your existing backup hardware as possible.

Multiple platform support. You should not need to buy one backup solution for your Windows boxes, another for your Solaris boxes, and a third for your Novell servers. One backup product should suffice across all your major platforms.

Mature products with reference sites. Just as we said in Key Principle #6 in Chapter 5, always select your products with an eye toward mature products, with a proven record of successful implementations, and reference sites.

Media management.   Although media management seems like an obvious feature, many vendors do not include such capabilities with their software. Media management includes features like tape labeling, bar code management, a database of tape locations, management of off-site media as well as on-site, robotic controls, and sharing.

A REAL DISASTER

In 1993, when the World Trade Center in New York was attacked by terrorists the first time, many system administrators who worked in the building found themselves with nothing more than a bag of backup tapes from which to rebuild their business. Some backup vendors took several days before they were able to provide their customers with license keys that would enable them to begin the restore process. There was nothing those SAs could do except to wait for the keys to be delivered.

—Evan

Backup Performance

In order to get the best-possible performance out of your backup software, you need to get the best-possible performance out of all of your backup hardware. As you consider the issues presented in this section, we offer a simple rule of thumb: "Backups are only as fast as the slowest link in the chain." To that end, Table 6.1 takes a look at the speed at which backup (or any kind of) data can traverse your networks to your media or tape servers.

Table 6.1 Realistic Network Throughputs

NETWORK MEDIUM	LINE SPEED MEGABITS/ SEC	THEORETICAL MEGABITS/ SEC	THEORETICAL MEGABYTES/ SEC	THEORETICAL MEGABYTES/ HOUR	REALISTIC UTILIZATION	REALISTIC MEGABYTES/ SEC	REALISTIC GIGABYTES/ HOUR
10Base-T Ethernet	10	10	1.25	4,500	60%	0.75	2.7
100Base-T Ethernet	100	100	12.5	45,000	60%	7.5	27
Gigabit Ethernet	1,250	1,000	125	450,000	60%	75	270
Fibre Channel 1x	1,062.5	800	100	360,000	75%	75	270
Fibre Channel 2x	2,125	1,600	200	720,000	75%	150	540

We also need to examine the speed with which data can make it from a system (whether it has come across a network or from local disks) to a locally attached tape drive. There are two components to this: the speed with which the tape drive can write (see Table 6.2) and the speed at which data can be sent to the tape drive, across a directly attached bus connection (see Table 6.3).

Table 6.2   Capacity and Performance of Selected Tape Drives

TAPE DRIVE	TAPE CAPACITY IN GIGABYTES (COMPRESSED)	WRITE PERFORMANCE PER SECOND (COMPRESSED) IN MEGABYTES/ SECOND	WRITE PERFORMANCE PER HOUR (COMPRESSED) IN GIGABYTES
DLT 4000	20 (40)	1.5 (3.0)	5.4 (10.8)
DLT 7000	35 (70)	5 (10)	18 (36)
DLT 8000	40 (80)	6 (12)	21.6 (43.2)
Super DLT	160 (320)	16 (32)	57.6 (115.2)
8-mm tape	14	1	3.6
StorageTek 9840	20 (80)	8 (20)	28.8 (72)
AIT	50 (100)	6 (12)	21.6 (43.2)
LTO Ultrium 1	100 (200)	20 (40)	72 (144)
LTO Ultrium 2	200 (400)	40 (80)	144 (288)

Table 6.3   Performance of Selected Local Data Buses

CONNECTION TYPE	SPEED
Narrow SCSI	10MB/second (36GB/hr)
Wide SCSI	20MB/second (72GB/hr)
Ultra SCSI	40MB/second (144GB/hr)
Ultra2 SCSI	80MB/second (288GB/hr)
Ultra160 SCSI	160MB/second (576GB/hr)
Ultra320 SCSI	320MB/second (1.15TB/hr)
Fibre Channel	100MB/second (360GB/hr)
Infiniband	2.5GB/second (9TB/hr)

Properly tuned and configured backups are really just an exercise in moving data. The process is very much analogous to moving water through pipes. You have to move a certain amount of water, but you are limited by the capacity of the pipes. If you want to move more water faster, you need fatter pipes or more pipes, or you need to make better use of the pipes you already have (get the hair out of the drain!). You can put a 100MB/second LTO Ultrium 2 drive on a system, but if the backup data is sent across a 10 Base-T network, then the drive will only be able to write data at about 750KB/second (or less than 1 percent of the drive's capacity), because that's how fast the data arrives on the network.

Improving Backup Performance: Find the Bottleneck

Let's say that you have to back up 60GB of data located on five systems, as shown in Figure 6.2. There is 40GB on one system, and 5GB each on the remaining four. The systems are networked to a dedicated backup server, with no data of its own via an old-fashioned 10Mbit/second (10Base-T) Ethernet link. The backup server has a single DLT 7000 tape drive on it, which can write compressed data at 10MB/second. (Some data cannot be compressed as well as others, and so the 10MB/second is an estimate. Some sites report bursts of up to 12 or 13MB/second, while others see no more than 7 or 8.) The game, then, is to find the bottleneck.

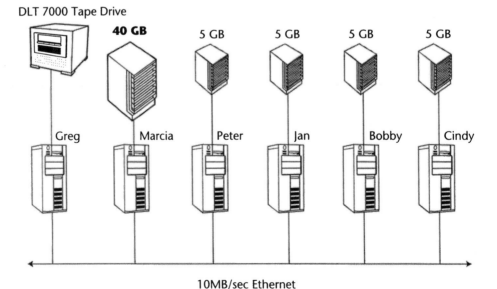

Figure 6.2   Basic networked backup configuration.

Regardless of how fast your tape drive can write, it will only be fed data at 750KB/second, and that assumes that your data is the only data flowing on the network cable; in real life, your throughput will probably be less. 60GB at 750KB/second will take roughly 80,000 seconds, which is over 22 hours. And that assumes maximum efficiency from every other element in the backup chain. In this example, the bottleneck is very much the network.

If we magically change the network to 100Base-T (see Figure 6.3), then backup times are cut by an order of magnitude to about 8,000 seconds, or about 2 hours and 10 minutes. But since 100Base-T can only send data at about 7.5MB/second and the tape drive can handle data at about 10MB/second, the network is still your bottleneck.

What if we move our tape drive from the dedicated backup server (*greg*) and attach it directly to the 40GB server through a nice Ultra Wide SCSI interface that can pass data at 40MB/second? We have eliminated *greg* from the picture; *marcia* is now our media server. (See Figure 6.4.)

Now the 40GB from *marcia* will go directly to the tape without hitting the network, and will do so at tape drive speed. 40GB at 10MB/second will take 4,000 seconds, or about 1 hour and 5 minutes. The remaining 20GB from the clients must still flow over the 100Base-T network at 7.5MB/second, and so will take an additional 45 minutes, for a total of about 1 hour and 50 minutes.

The other advantage to putting the tape drive directly on the server is that the 40GB of backup data no longer goes across your LAN, freeing network bandwidth for other applications.

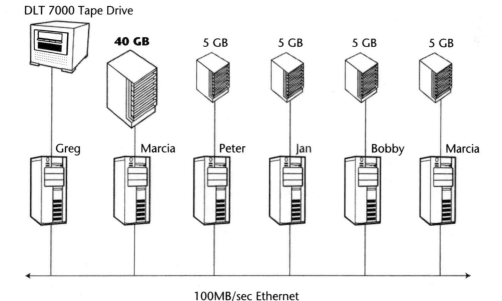

Figure 6.3 Backup with 100MB/second network.

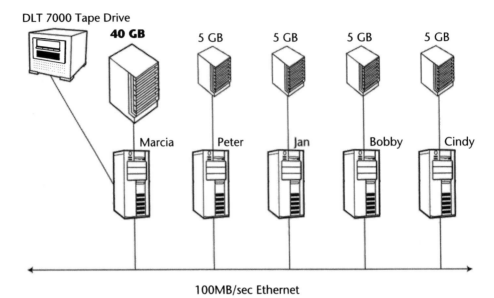

DLT 7000 Tape Drive

40 GB   5 GB   5 GB   5 GB   5 GB

Marcia   Peter   Jan   Bobby   Cindy

100MB/sec Ethernet

Figure 6.4 Backup with the tape drive on the main server.

To increase our network performance so that it approaches the performance of our tape drives, we can introduce a switched network (see Figure 6.5). In a switched network, a private 100Mbit/second tunnel is opened between two of the network cards on the network. If we put four network cards in our main server and connect them all to a 100Base-T switched network hub, then each client can send data to the server at 7.5MB/second at the same time, for a theoretical total of 30MB/second reaching the server at the same time. 20GB at 30MB/second takes about 11 minutes. However, since our tape drive can only write at 10MB/second, our bottleneck has moved from the network to the tape drive. Assuming that we can throttle back our network usage, or limit the amount of data being sent over our networks to maximize the utilization of our single tape drive, we can write our 20GB of client data in 2,000 seconds, or about 33 minutes.

We can cut still more time off of the backup by adding a second tape drive (Figure 6.6). Since the Ultra SCSI bus can handle 40MB/second (and Wide SCSI can write at 20MB/second), and our one tape drive only uses 10MB/second, we can add a second tape drive to the SCSI bus and effectively double our write performance. Used properly, our local backups are down to just 34 minutes. With our switched network still in place, the clients will back up their 20GB at 20MB/second, or 1,000 seconds, which is a little less than 17 minutes. Adding the second tape drive cuts the total backup time to just 51 minutes. The bottleneck for our clients is still the tape drives, not the network.

DLT 7000 Tape Drive

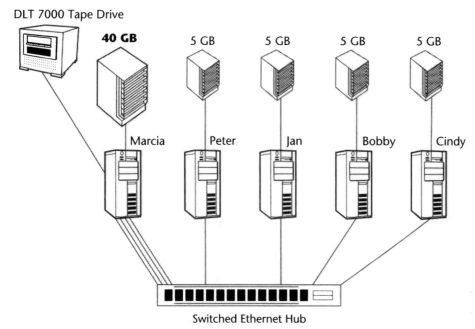

Figure 6.5   Backups over a switched Ethernet.

DLT 7000 Tape Drive

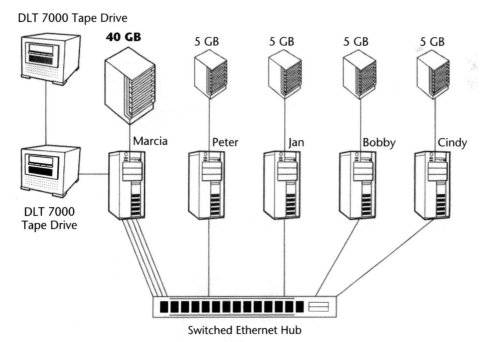

Figure 6.6   Backup over switched Ethernet with a second tape drive.

Adding a third tape drive to the server, which would require a second Wide SCSI adapter card but not another Ultra SCSI card (due to Ultra's additional capacity), reduces the time for the local backups to just 22 minutes. Our clients will send their data at the same 30MB/second that the tape drives can write, so backing up that additional 20GB will take another 11 minutes, giving us a total of 33 minutes for the entire backup.

In these examples, we have shown that you could back up the exact same 60GB of data spread across five machines in times ranging from 22 hours down to a little over half an hour. It's all in the hardware. More tape drives, more SCSI buses, and faster and more efficient networks will yield faster and faster backup times. To achieve faster times, of course, more money must be spent on hardware. It's a model very similar to the availability model, where cost increases with availability.

Again, all of these idealized numbers are based on a fundamental assumption that all the other elements in the backup chain (networks, memory, CPU, disks, and tape drives) are used as efficiently as possible and that your backup software uses the hardware that it's been given as efficiently as possible. Your mileage will surely vary.

The other assumption we are making is that you are backing up all of your data every time. For most environments, that is unrealistic. Backup times can be cut drastically further by reducing the amount of data that is backed up each time. (See *Backup Styles*, later in this chapter.) The trick is to reduce the amount of backed-up data without compromising system reliability or lengthening beyond an acceptable level the amount of time it takes to recover lost data.

Solving for Performance

Most often, you will be given a set of systems with a particular amount of data on it, and a backup window, during which you must complete a full backup. Let's say you maintain a network, as in Figure 6.7, with one server, *elephant*, that has 300GB on it; a second, *moose*, with 100GB; two more, *cow* and *pig*, with 60GB each, and 10 clients with 2GB each on them. And you've been given a window of just 6 hours to complete your backups.

Due to the wide acceptance of DLT 7000 tape drives, we are going to stick with them for our examples, and with 20MB/second SCSI buses. We also assume that our network consists of switched 100Base-T. The exercise would be similar if different hardware were employed. We also assume that you get the full level of compression that the manufacturers claim. Your mileage will vary, based on the kind of data you are storing, your hardware, your backup software, and nearly everything else in the configuration.

The first thing we must do is to figure out how much data we're backing up:

$$300GB + 100GB + (2 \times 60GB) + (10 \times 2GB) = 540GB$$

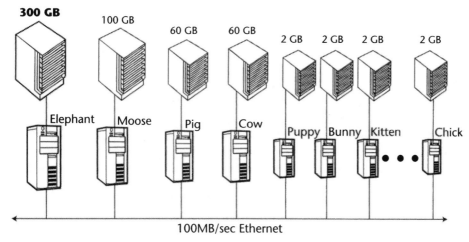

300 GB

100 GB

60 GB   60 GB

2 GB   2 GB   2 GB   2 GB

Elephant   Moose   Pig   Cow   Puppy Bunny Kitten   Chick

100MB/sec Ethernet

Figure 6.7 The backup problem.

In order to back up 540GB in 6 hours, we must achieve a backup rate of 90GB/hour.

Our solution includes a deployment of local tape drives, as well as backups across the network. We make no assumptions about network traffic outside of backups. Many users approach this style of solution through the use of dedicated backup networks, although many users do not have this luxury. If your backups will go across the same networks as your regular networked data, be sure to take that into account.

Another important timing issue to take into account is tape changing. We are also not going to count tape changing times in our calculations. The most efficient way to change tapes is to use an automatic tape changer, usually a library or a stacker.

To limit network traffic, and to speed up backups as much as possible, we will put tape drives onto *elephant*. In order to back up 300GB of data in no more than 6 hours, we must install two local tape drives. At 10MB/second, one tape drive would take 500 minutes, or 8 hours and 20 minutes. Two drives would cut that in half, to 4 hours and 10 minutes, which meets our backup window requirement. Remember that *elephant's* 300GB of data requires five tapes (four for the first 280GB, plus a fifth for the leftovers). We must be sure that whatever method we use to change tapes does not cause us to run past our backup window.

On *moose*, a single tape drive can back up the 100GB in a little less than 3 hours onto two tapes, easily meeting our backup window.

Solutions for *cow* and *pig* are not as clear-cut. If we choose to put a local tape drive on each of them, they can each complete their backups in 1 hour and 40 minutes. If we put a tape drive only on *cow*, and back up *pig's* data across the network, then *cow's* backup would still take 1 hour 40 minutes, but *pig* would take 2 hours and 20 minutes. Both backups would complete in an even 4 hours, and require two tapes.

There are other options for *cow* and *pig*. *Moose* still has 3 hours of unused backup window, and so we could network *pig's* backup there, still leaving about 40 minutes within the backup window. Assuming that we want to make the best use of our hardware, that would be the most efficient solution. *Cow* would still need a local tape drive, though.

We still have our ten 2GB clients that need to be backed up. The 20GB of client data could be completed in 35 minutes. The clients could all be backed up to the tape drives on *elephant*, where we still have almost 2 hours of backup window still available.

So, the configuration requires four tape drives—two on *elephant*, one on *moose*, and one on *cow*. Of course, the tape drive on *cow* is very underused. There are a number of options:

- You might choose to leave it underused, keeping it free for growth, or for restores that may be required during the backup window.

- You might choose to back up *cow's* data across the network to *moose*, and overrun your backup window by a small amount. The difference is the cost of that tape drive and SCSI bus.

- Or, you might choose to put the extra tape drive onto *elephant*, adding flexibility to *elephant's* configuration, and leave it underused over there instead.

Our preference is the last choice. Put the extra drive onto *elephant*, back up *cow* to *elephant* over the network, and give yourself a little extra capacity for growth. Remember, putting the third tape drive on elephant will require an additional SCSI card.

The completed configuration is shown in Figure 6.8. A summary of the configuration is in Table 6.4.

Table 6.4   Summary of Backup Solution

HOST	AMOUNT OF DATA	SENT TO WHICH HOST AND DRIVE?	DURATION OF BACKUP
Elephant	300GB	2 local DLT 7000s	4 hr, 10 min
Moose	100GB	1 local DLT 7000	2 hr, 45 min
Cow	60GB	3rd DLT 7000 on elephant	2 hr, 20 min
Pig	60GB	DLT 7000 on moose	2 hr, 20 min
Ten 2GB clients	20GB	DLT 7000s on elephant	50 min

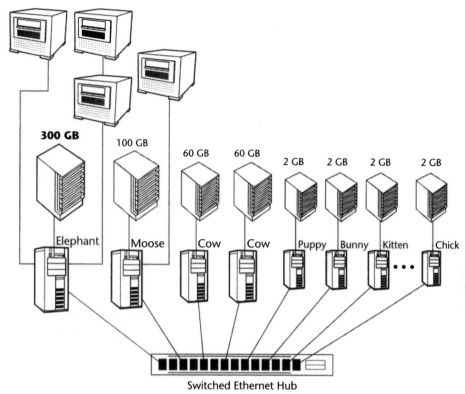

Figure 6.8 A solution to the backup problem.

We were able to complete this design by using just four DLT 7000 drives, and we have capacity to spare. As we discussed, it could have been done with three DLT 7000s, but that would have left no room for growth and would have been an extremely tight fit. Since three drives would have a combined throughput of about 108MB/hour, all three drives would have to be operating for almost the entire backup window to complete the backups in the allotted time. Adding the fourth allows for additional growth and for tape changing, and makes it much easier to fit the backups in the window, especially if a tape drive failure or other problem interrupts the normal process.

Backup Styles

In this section, we look at a bunch of different ways to back up data beyond full backups, including differential and cumulative incrementals, hot backups, hierarchical storage management, archives, synthetic full backups, host-free backups, third-mirror breakoff, backups directly to disk, snapshots, multiplexed backups, and fast and flash backups.

Incremental Backups

When we discussed completing backups within a narrow time window, we did not discuss the use of incremental backups. A full backup, as discussed in the last section, is a backup where every bit of data on the disks is copied to tape. Though extremely reliable, full backups can be slow, since they back up all the data, regardless of whether it has changed since the last full backup. An incremental backup only copies the files or data that have changed since the last backup was taken.

There are, in fact, two kinds of incremental backups. The first is a *cumulative* incremental, where all data that has changed since the last full backup is backed up. The other is a *differential* incremental, where all data that has changed since the last differential is backed up. Since differentials back up less data than cumulatives, they run faster.

In Table 6.5, we compare three differing backup styles. For the purposes of our example, we made a few assumptions:

- The total amount of data is 60GB.

- Of the 60GB, 5GB changes each day.

- Each day the amount of data to be backed up by the cumulative incremental grows by a smaller and smaller amount (for example, some of the same data that changed on Tuesday also changed on Wednesday).

- For simplicity's sake, we are not going to change the quantity of data being backed up.

- We can back up the data at 20GB an hour.

The conclusion one can draw from Table 6.5 is that differential backups are faster.

There are other varieties of the incremental backup. One of those is found in the standard Unix utility called dump or ufsdump. Dump permits up to 10 levels of backups to be taken; a level 5 backup backs up everything since the last lower-level (say, level 3) backup was taken. In shops where dump is employed, a common strategy calls for a level 0 (the whole disk) backup to be taken once every few months, level 1s once a month, level 3s every week, and level 5s every night.

The need for so much flexibility in backup strategies is apparent when we examine the requirements that are introduced when we need to restore the data. (For simplicity in this example, we assume that each backup fits on a single tape and is the only backup on that tape. In reality, neither of these assumptions will likely hold.)

Table 6.5 Durations of Different Backup Styles

	SUNDAY	MONDAY	TUESDAY	WEDNESDAY	THURSDAY
Weekly fulls and daily differential incrementals	Full backup (60GB; 3 hours)	Changes since Sunday's full (5GB; 15 minutes)	Changes since Monday's incremental (5GB; 15 minutes)	Changes since Tuesday's incremental (5GB; 15 minutes)	Changes since Wednesday's incremental (5GB; 15 minutes)
Weekly fulls and daily cumulative incrementals	Full backup (60GB; 3 hours)	Changes since Sunday's full (5GB; 15 minutes)	Changes since Sunday's full (9GB; 27 minutes)	Changes since Sunday's full (12GB; 36 minutes)	Changes since Sunday's full (14GB; 42 minutes)
Daily fulls	Full backup (60GB; 3 hours)	Full backup (60GB; 3 hours)	Full backup (60GB; 3 hours)	Full backup (60GB; 3 hours)	Full backup (60GB; 3 hours)

Again, for the examples in Table 6.6 to work, we need to make some assumptions:

- Restores run at 15GB/hour. (Filesystem restores almost always run slower than backups, because the filesystem must place the data on the disk and create a map to retrieve it again later.)

- It takes up to 2 minutes to unmount, remount, and position a new tape to begin restoring from it.

- The failure of our filesystem occurred on Friday, after Thursday's backups were completed.

In a shop where full backups are taken every day, only one tape will need to be restored after a catastrophe. Restoring only one tape makes the process much simpler and much less labor-intensive.

When fulls and cumulative incrementals are the rule, two tapes need to be restored—the full and the most recent cumulative. This model is roughly twice as complex and labor-intensive as the full backup method.

In the multilevel backup just described, three tapes are required to perform a complete restore—the level 1, the level 3, and the latest level 5.

To restore differential incremental backups, after the full backup tape is restored, all of the differential tapes must be mounted and restored, one by one.

TOO MANY TAPES

One user I know did a full backup on the 1st of the month, and differential incrementals every day after that. As Murphy's Law would have it, their disk crashed on the 30th of the month. To do the restore, they needed the 1 full and 29 incremental tapes. Since each incremental was on its own tape, in addition to taking time to actually read and restore the data, each tape had to be mounted individually (fortunately, all the tapes were stored in a single tape library). It took roughly 3 minutes to unmount one tape, and mount and position the next. Multiply that by 30 tapes, and the restore already takes 90 minutes before a single byte has been restored. The users could have saved a lot of time by putting more than one differential on each tape. That admittedly can make the tape a single point of failure, so beware. But if MTTR is critical, time can be saved by minimizing the number of tapes that require mounting in a restore.

—Evan

Table 6.6   Durations of Restores

TYPE OF BACKUP	NUMBER OF TAPES TO READ FROM	OVERHEAD TO MOUNT AND UNMOUNT ALL THE TAPES	AMOUNT OF DATA TO RESTORE	TIME TO RESTORE THE DATA	TOTAL TIME REQUIRED
Weekly fulls and daily differential incrementals	5 (Sunday full, and incrementals from Monday through Thursday)	15 minutes	80GB	5 hours, 20 minutes	5:35
Weekly fulls and Thursday cumulative incrementals	2 (Sunday full and incremental)	6 minutes	74GB	5 hours	5:06 daily
Daily fulls	1 (Thursday's full)	3 minutes	60GB	4 hours	4:03

When selecting the method that is best for you, you must strike a balance between the duration of your backups, which are probably nightly events, and the duration and effort required to perform a complete restore. Complete restores may only be required once or twice a year. But the duration of the restore is your MTTR. As we have said so many times before, you want to keep your MTTRs as low as possible, as some portion of your system is out of service until the effort is completed.

Incremental Backups of Databases

In general, incremental backups are limited to filesystems, although some backup vendors do have technology that will permit the incremental backing up of databases. Specifically, to do an incremental backup of a filesystem, the blocks that have changed must be backed up. Once they are backed up, pointers and indices must be maintained so that the blocks can be put back into the database upon restore.

Some solutions require a complete scan of the database for changed blocks. At least one solution (VERITAS NetBackup with the VERITAS File System, only available on Unix) keeps track of the blocks that have changed and does not need to do a full database scan in order to perform an incremental backup.

As with all incremental backups, in order to perform a full restore, the tapes from the full and all of the incrementals (or only the most recent cumulative incremental tape) are required.

Shrinking Backup Windows

A backup window is the amount of time that systems can be affected by a backup. That used to mean the time that the systems were unavailable while backups were taken. Nowadays, systems can remain operational while backups go on, but they will likely suffer a performance impact unless special precautions are taken.

The bottom line on backup windows is that they are getting smaller and smaller, approaching zero. In many shops, they already are zero; backups cannot cause any service interruption at all. Fortunately, even tiny backup windows are no excuse to give backups short shrift.

In this section, we look at some of the techniques for shortening the duration of the interruptions caused by taking backups. Some of these techniques reduce the amount of data being backed up; others require additional specialized hardware or software to get their job done. Some techniques are specific to one vendor or another, and others work only on databases, or only on filesystems.

Hot Backups

The ultimate in backup windows is one that causes no interruption whatsoever. This can be achieved on databases, and can very nearly be achieved on filesystems.

The biggest problem in achieving hot backups is one of data consistency. Since it takes time for a backup to run and complete, files or data can change within the data store (filesystem or disks) being backed up. In order for a hot backup to be successful, there must be a mechanism inserted between the data store and the application that may be writing there.

Most good commercial backup utilities support online, or hot, backups of filesystems and databases. (Homegrown solutions generally do not.) To achieve reliable hot backups, the backup utility must interface, often at a very low level, with a utility specifically designed for the application or filesystem being backed up. For example, the Oracle database makes two different utilities available (depending on the version of Oracle you are running). The backup utility that writes data to tape (or other backup medium) must know how to speak with OEBU (Oracle Enterprise Backup Utility) or RMAN (Recovery Manager) and turn the data that those utilities provide into data that can be written to (and later read from) tape. MS-SQL, DB/2, Sybase, and Informix all have similar utilities to allow hot backups. In addition, some commercial backup products have their own agents that work with the published database APIs to enable hot backups without the need for utilities like RMAN or OEBU.

Normally, during a hot database backup, the database is put into a state where database writes are locked out of the actual database and only written to a log. When the backup completes, the contents of the log are run as a batch job and are added to the database. There are some performance implications with this method, because of the batched nature of the additions. There is also usually some performance overhead associated with logging the changes.

Hot database backups are very vendor-specific and are an almost constantly changing technology. They are generally quite reliable and so should definitely be considered when you are evaluating ways to shrink backup window requirements.

As for filesystem backups, there is a consistent problem across both Unix and Windows filesystems. Filesystem backups are usually taken in two passes—a first pass that determines and backs up the file and directory layout, and a second pass that backs up the files and their contents. If a file changes between the two passes, inconsistent results can occur, but the most likely result is that the file will not be backed up properly. Another problem will occur if an application requires that two or more files are consistent. If they change during the backup, different versions may be backed up as the backup utility walks through the filesystem, resulting in inconsistent versions on the backup tape.

Filesystem backups vary by operating system. On Windows, there is an issue with backing up open files. If an application has a file open, the file is locked. A locked file cannot be accessed by any other applications. Obviously, in order to back up a file, a backup utility must access the file. If the utility cannot access (or lock) a particular file, it will timeout in its attempt to back up the file, and move on. When this occurs, the locked file will not get backed up at all.

There are at least two utilities for assisting in the backing up of open Windows files: St. Bernard's Open File Manager and Columbia Data Systems' Open Transaction Monitor. Some Windows backup manufacturers integrate one of these products right into their software, while others deliver their own. These utilities operate in kernel mode, filtering I/O for calls to open or locked files. They keep a copy of the open file in cache memory and present that copy to the backup software. In this way, this software guarantees that a consistent copy of the file gets backed up. The open file management software may also be able to cache the entire filesystem in memory (or on another disk) and present a consistent and unchanging copy of the filesystem to the backup utility.

On Unix, open files are not as much of an issue. A file that is written to disk can be backed up by reading it off the disk. If a file is open and being written to, then the disk copy of the file may not reflect its most recent contents, but your backup will get the most recent copy that is on the disk. Several products that do hot filesystem backups make multiple passes over the filesystem's inodes to be sure that file sizes and modification times have not changed during the course of the backup; if they have, the files that were being written to are dumped to tape again.

Of course, running backups while production is going on can have a discernible impact on overall system and network performance, so even if backups can be done online, we still want to keep them as brief as possible, which leads back to the earlier discussion of incremental versus full backups. There are other ways to shorten the duration of your backups, which are discussed next.

Have Less Data, Save More Time (and Space)

There are at least two ways to reduce the amount of data that gets backed up in a filesystem. Both involve removing older and less used data from the filesystem, and storing it someplace else.

Hierarchical Storage Management

A very interesting exercise for the system administrator in your spare time (ha ha) is to use OS utilities to generate an aging report for all of the user files in the various home directories under his or her watch. Search for files that have not been accessed in each of 2 weeks, 1 month, 3 months, 6 months, and 1year. Go back further if your systems have been around that long.

Consider this: Those files that haven't been touched in 6 months or more still take up valuable time, space, and bandwidth during your backups and once again during restores. Apart from simply deleting them, what can you do to recapture the resources that these files consume?

Welcome to the world of *Hierarchical Storage Management* (HSM). Hierarchical Storage Management is a grossly underused utility that provides a sort of automated archival system. An HSM process examines the most recent access date of the files in a filesystem and, based on rules set up and maintained by the system administrator, automatically migrates the files to a less expensive, more permanent, and slower medium. This medium may be specially dedicated tapes, writable CDs, magneto-optical disks, or some other not-quite-online storage medium. Left behind in the filesystem is a stub file, which is a special file that tells the HSM process to find the real file. Stub files are usually about a couple of kilobytes in size.

Once a file is migrated, a user need only access the old file in the usual manner, and the system will either locate and mount the appropriate tape or place an operator request for a particular tape to be mounted. Once accessed, the file is returned to the local disk, and the clock on it starts again. While a file is migrated, it is no longer backed up; only its stub is. Obviously, the trade-off is that the first time a user needs to access a file, it may take several minutes, or longer, to retrieve the file from the offline medium. But once the file has been retrieved from the remote storage, it will be stored locally, and future accesses will take place at the normal rate.

TUNING IN CHANNEL Z

There's a less-than-ideal way to test out the prospective benefits and user reactions to a Hierarchical Storage Management system. Find large files that are more than six months old, and compress them in-place on the disk. You may reduce their size by anywhere from a factor of two to five times, and you haven't removed any data—only introduced a new access step for users who really need to get at the uncompressed original file. We tried this once without warning the user base, and results were good; few people noticed that their large, unloved files now had a ".Z" extension (due to the Unix `compress` utility's work), and the few engineers who found the files ran `uncompress` as needed. Of course, we had one employee who was complaining about all of "those stupid .Z files cluttering up [his] system," so of course he deleted all of them. Compression doesn't replace backups, but it sure can make the files being backed up smaller and easier to handle.

—Hal

There is a significant additional benefit to implementing HSM: Since files are not being stored on active disks, the disks will be used more efficiently. If 20 percent of the space on a filesystem can be migrated with HSM, then it's as if the disks have grown by 20 percent, with no need to buy new disks.

If properly implemented, apart from the delay in retrieving a file, HSM should be totally transparent to your users. A directory listing does not indicate that anything is unusual. The files appear to be present. Only when a user actually tries to access a file can any difference be detected.

If, like so many other systems, your user directories are littered with large files that have been untouched for months, and you need to shrink your backup windows and loads, HSM may be worth a look.

Archives

Archives are similar to, though somewhat less sophisticated than, HSM. To archive a file, the file is written to tape (or some other offline medium) and deleted from the filesystem completely. Some external mechanism must be employed to maintain the location of archived files. Otherwise, there is a very real risk that the file could get lost.

In some environments, users are allowed and even encouraged to maintain their own archive tapes. In others, the administrators maintain archives.

Synthetic Fulls

Incremental backups, as we discussed, are a very efficient way to back up file systems, since they require copying far less data to tape then fulls. Data that have not changed since the last full need not be backed up.

Unfortunately, cumulative incremental backups can grow in size over time, until their size approaches that of a full. The number of tapes required to restore a set of differential incremental backups can also grow over time until the sheer number becomes overwhelming. The remedy to these problems is the same: Take full backups from time to time.

What if you never had to take full backups of your production servers again? You can with *synthetic full backups*. In a synthetic full backup model, you keep a full copy of your filesystem on another node. You take a full backup of your system (*curly*) once, and restore it on a separate system (*shemp*). Then, you take nightly differential incremental backups of *curly* and restore them onto *shemp*. Then, you take a full backup of the filesystem from *shemp*. If something happens to *curly*, you can replace him with *shemp*. *Shemp*'s data should be identical to what was on *curly*, and since all the data is on a single tape, the time it takes to complete the restore will be greatly reduced, as compared to restoring a full and a bunch of incrementals.

For additional protection, you may choose to keep *shemp* at a different site from *curly*, although that's not necessary if you send *shemp*'s backup tapes off-site. (No need to keep an on-site copy, since *shemp* itself fills that role quite admirably.)

This model is certainly not for everyone, since it requires a great deal of extra hardware (system, disks, and tape drives), but it is a very effective way to reduce backup windows and restore times, a very elusive combination.

Use More Hardware

Vendors are developing new techniques and technologies, and exploiting old ones, to speed up backups through the use of additional hardware or clever software tricks. These techniques are of varying usefulness, depending on your environment. Some will surely work, while others could actually slow you down.

Host-Free Backups

The marketing hype for host-free backups (sometimes called backdoor or direct backups) says that they allow the backing up of data directly from disk to tape, without requiring an intervening CPU. The reality of host-free backups is that there must be a CPU someplace. There is no technology today that we have found that allows data to simply copy itself to tape. There must be a CPU to initiate and perform the copying work.

Some hardware arrays have embedded CPUs that perform the work. Other solutions use dedicated data movers from companies like Chaparral, ADIC, or Crossroads, which contain CPUs that take care of the data copying. Other solutions use the host's CPU to copy the data. While there may be advantages to using off-host CPUs to copy the data, it is not an absolute given, as many people assume, that the use of host-based CPU is bad. Some CPU must be used in order to move the data. The external CPU that is included in a disk array or data mover may be quite expensive, and it may be completely unnecessary if there are enough idle CPU cycles in the host CPU. And most systems have some extra CPU cycles to spare.

What's more, no matter which CPU does the work, the storage will still be called upon to perform I/Os, and there will likely be some overhead incurred from that work. If the copying (backing up) is done from disks that have been split off of the original copies, I/O overhead may still be evident in the SCSI or Fibre Channel connections and/or host bus adapters (HBAs), or over the networks between the clients, hosts, and tape drives.

Today's technology simply does not support true host-free backups. In the future, enough intelligence will be placed inside the disk arrays to allow them to push their data directly out to a tape drive, but even then, there is still a CPU involved. The advantage that any host-free backup offers is that the backup can be performed without impacting the CPU or memory performance of the host holding the data. However, that CPU may be the cheapest in your system. In many cases it will cost less to get some additional CPU for your host than it would to get additional CPU for your disk array or data mover. It is not automatically evil if a small amount of extra CPU host is consumed.

If the backups are also performed over a dedicated backup network or a storage area network (SAN; for more on SANs, see Chapter 8, "SAN, NAS, and Virtualization"), then little impact should be felt on production resources. EMC Symmetrix arrays have embedded PCs, and they offer off-host backups when combined with certain commercial backup utilities. More and more backup software vendors are adding this capability to their software.

Third-Mirror Breakoff

Some hardware and software vendors have implemented a backup model that involves keeping three active disk mirrors of a filesystem or database. When it's time for a backup, the third mirror gets split off from the first two. New transactions continue to be written to the first two mirrors, while the backup is started using the data on the third mirror. At the end of the backup, the third mirror must be resynchronized with the other two copies, so that it's ready for the next backup.

The good news about third-mirror breakoffs is that the backup can be taken without taking the database or filesystem out of service for more than a few seconds (and that is only to ensure that the third-mirror copy is clean and consistent).

The downside is the additional disk space required. Instead of the 100 percent disk space overhead that is required for regular mirrors, third-mirror breakoff requires a 200 percent disk space overhead. To mirror 100GB of disk space, you need 200GB of total storage space. To perform third-mirror breakoff, you need 300GB of disk. In addition, the act of resynchronization is very I/O-intensive, and it can be CPU-intensive too, depending on the implementation, there may be a very noticeable CPU performance impact caused by the resynchronization process.

The other variation of third-mirror breakoff is to create the third mirror before the backup begins, instead of after it is completed. The I/O and CPU overhead is greater in this case, since all of the work must be done up front, rather than gradually over time. The potential is there to save disk overhead, as one set of disks could be reused as the third mirror for more than one filesystem.

EMC Symmetrix arrays use a utility called TimeFinder that allows this resynchronization to be performed off-host, eliminating the impact to your server's CPU and allowing much faster performance than when the resynchronization is performed on a server. There will still be some I/O impact on the disks being copied.

Third-mirror breakoff is a method that is especially appetizing to companies who make their livings selling expensive disk drives. It allows them to sell a lot more disk to perform functions that do not necessarily need extra disk space.

DOING IT CAFETERIA-STYLE

File restore requests are fairly common in a university environment. Too many late nights mixed with too few trips to Starbucks and you're looking at heavy-handed data corruption due to sleepy students. At Princeton, we did incremental dumps to disk to provide an online cafeteria-style restore system. It wasn't faster than dumping to tape, but it reduced restore times because you didn't have to look for the tape with the right files on it. Few things are more frustrating than slogging through four tapes to find a file, only to have a sleep-deprived, deadline-fearing undergraduate tell you it's the right file from the wrong date and he needs it 3 hours ago. Put the backup indices online, in such a way that each user can only read his or her own index files, and let the users self-select what they want backed up from the data available online. This will reduce your effective MTTR, but only if you do this in conjunction with a solid tape-based backup system. Disk-based backups are not a substitute for tapes (it's hard to get those disks off-site), and they're not ideal for large volumes of data, but they provide a nice middle ground between *snapshot* or point-in-time solutions and full, tape-based backups.

—Hal

From time to time, a disk vendor will release a new fast disk that is faster than current tape technology, for a while. But tape vendors soon leapfrog those advances. Note, too, that high-speed disks are going to cost a lot more money per megabyte than tapes, and a significant cost savings can be realized by taking advantage of the low cost of writing data to tapes instead of disks.

Sophisticated Software Features

Some commercial backup software offers features that can significantly reduce the overhead and the duration of backups too.

Copy-on-Write Snapshots

A filesystem is nothing more than a collection of data blocks on a disk, with pointers to them so that data can be located and retrieved after it is written to disk. To create a clean copy of a filesystem, so that it can be backed up, the filesystem is copied in its entirety to a new location. That method is acceptable, but it consumes a great many system resources, including I/O and disk space.

A newer method of copying a filesystem, called a *copy-on-write snapshot*, has been developed that addresses the issues associated with doing a complete filesystem copy. Since a filesystem is, as we said previously, a collection of data blocks that are organized through the use of pointers, by manipulating the pointers and creating some new ones, you can effectively copy a filesystem without requiring the additional disk space and I/O overhead.

As shown in Figure 6.9, in a snapshot-style backup, pointers are created that point back to the data's original location. When a snapshot is enabled, and a transaction is about to overwrite a data block that must be preserved, four things happen:

- The original block is read.
- That original block is written to a new location, in a specially reserved snapshot region of the disk.
- The snapshot pointer is changed to point at the new location of the old block.
- The new data overwrites the original data in the filesystem.

Figure 6.10 depicts what happens after three writes have been made to a snapshotted file system.

The snapshotted version of the filesystem preserves the state of the filesystem as it looked when the snapshot was taken, no matter how many more writes are made to the filesystem. The space requirement for the snapshot region depends almost entirely on how many blocks have been changed in the original filesystem. In Figure 6.9, no additional data has been stored, just a collection of pointers. In Figure 6.10, three additional data blocks have been stored.

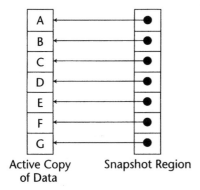

Figure 6.9   A copy-on-write snapshot before any writes have been made.

The new set of pointers always points to a consistent copy of the data as it looked when snapshot was turned on. Of course, these steps are only necessary the first time a block is overwritten after snapshot is enabled; after that, we don't need to save the intermediate versions of the filesystem, as shown in Figure 6.11, where A1 has been overwritten by A2. As expected, and as would happen if no copy-on-write were in progress, A1 has been lost.

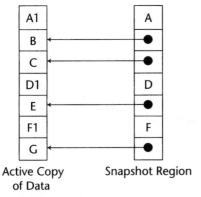

Figure 6.10   The copy-on-write snapshot from Figure 6.9 after three writes have been made to the filesystem.

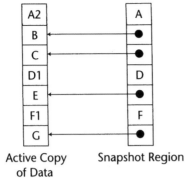

Figure 6.11 The copy-on-write snapshot from Figure 6.10 after block A has been overwritten a second time.

The end result is that we can take a clean backup of a filesystem even though it is continuing to receive new data. When the backup is completed, no resynchronization process is required. And the disk space overhead for a copy-on-write backup is greatly reduced. Instead of adding an additional 100 percent, only 10 to 15 percent is usually required, although that figure will vary depending on how much data actually changes during the backup. If the snapshot is left active long enough, it could require as much disk space as the original. If it looks like that might happen to you, then snapshots are probably not the right way to back up your data.

Multiplexed Backups

Some commercial backup software is smart enough to take streams of data from more than one source, whether network connections or local disks, and stream the incoming data onto tape. This is especially useful in an environment where the tape drives can write much faster than any one client can send data to the tape server.

By keeping the tape drive spinning, data transfer rates will be much faster; each time the tape drive stops spinning, it must take time to reposition the tape against the head. This repositioning puts extra stress and strain on the tape and its transport mechanism and will shorten the lives of the drives and the tapes.

Multiplexing can be slow to restore because the utility that reads the tape must read many more times the amount of data off the tape to get the same amount of useful information. Use of multiplexing may also counteract your backup software's ability to write in an open and generally readable format.

Fast and Flash Backup

The fast and flash methods of backups read the contents of a filesystem and write it directly to tape, as it sits on the disk, including portions of the disk that have no actual data on them. In a more traditional filesystem, backup files are backed up one at a time, which means that there is significant filesystem overhead associated with the retrieval of the file. Parts of files can be scattered all over the filesystem, and it is up to the filesystem to locate and retrieve the files. Fast and flash backup can read at raw speed, transferring data as fast as possible, without regard for file boundaries or locations. It also retrieves and stores the pointer (inode) map to the files, and stores that on the same tape.

To retrieve a file from a fast backup tape, the restore software must rebuild the map, and then rebuild the file from its potentially scattered parts on the tape. By putting the rebuild load on the restore end instead of the backup end of the process, backups are sped up dramatically.

Of course, in environments where filesystems are primarily empty, flash backup may not be the right answer, because all that empty space must be backed up too. These methods work best on filesystems where there are lots of small files, because small files introduce the most overhead during a backup.

Fast backup is available on Auspex hardware; flash backup is available for Solaris and other Unix platforms from VERITAS NetBackup.

Handling Backup Tapes and Data

Backup tapes are among the most valuable resources your company has. If they can rebuild your business after a major outage, they also can enable a competitor to steal your business when no outage has occurred. They must be treated at all times like the crown jewels of your company, because that is just what they are.

The goal in handling backup tapes and data is achieving the proper balance between protecting them from inappropriate access and providing easy access for rapid recovery when the tapes are truly needed:

Restrict physical access to tapes.   Access to a physical backup tape is about the same as root access to the disk on which the original filesystem or database resided. Give an unprotected tape to someone, and she can read it back anywhere else. Only personnel who have business seeing and touching tapes should have that access.

Magnetically erase tapes before they are reused.   Many shops recycle tapes after they have expired. Since tapes can cost more than $100 each, that makes sense. But if you just toss an expired tape into a box, then whoever picks it up has access to all the data on the tape. If there is a recycled tape box, tapes must be erased before they are put into the box. In especially secure environments, recycling should be carefully evaluated; destruction of the tapes may be the wiser approach.

Encrypt backup data.   If backup data can be picked up off the network, networked backups are also as dangerous as granting someone access to your raw disks. If you go to the trouble of securing user-level access to data, and database-level access by user, be sure that you secure access to backup data in transit over the network. It's the same data, perhaps with a trickier access mechanism, but you're still basically spewing the contents of a raw disk out in public unless you take the steps to encrypt it. Encryption may be as simple as doing network backups through an ssh tunnel or creating a disk-based backup image that is encrypted and then sent to a remote tape drive. Some backup utilities will encrypt the data before it flows over the network, if the option is enabled. Be aware that encryption will almost certainly have a negative impact on the performance of the backup process. Make sure that you keep track of your encryption keys; otherwise you'll be unable to read the tapes, and they may as well be blank.

RADIO DAYS

Back in college, I worked in radio. Besides being on the air, I spent a lot of time working in the production studio, putting taped promotional and public service messages onto small tape cartridges, called "carts," that looked a lot like old-fashioned 8-track tapes. Like most college radio stations, good old WLVR (Stereo 91.3 FM) operated on a shoestring budget, and carts were expensive, so we constantly reused them. Before you could record something new onto an old cart, you had to erase the previous contents. Otherwise, the new material would overlay the old. We had a small electromagnetic cart eraser on the floor, with a foot-pedal switch. You would hold your wristwatch behind your back, step on the foot-pedal, and rub the cart across the magnet, erasing the cart. To this day, I cannot understand why data centers do not use a similar method to erase old backup tapes.

—Evan

> ## THERE'S GOLD IN THEM THAR TAPES
>
> When I worked at a Wall Street brokerage firm, there was a box of scratch tapes in the data center. If someone needed a tape, they could just take one and use it; there was no security or checkout process involved. One day, I decided to read one of those tapes and see what was on it. It was full of equities trading floor production data from just 2 weeks before. A competitive firm would have been very interested in the contents of that tape.
>
> —Evan

Do not allow user-initiated restores without authorization.   If you choose to allow users to run their own data restores, make sure they are restricted to data that they normally have access to. Make sure the right levels of passwords are required to restore data.

Protect tapes that leave your site.   After a tape is shipped off-site for long-term storage, what happens to it? Can you be certain that nobody ever has unauthorized access to these tapes? Would you bet your job, or your company, on it? If you have the bandwidth, consider duplicating your tapes across the network (encrypted!), rather than physically transporting them.

Don't store originals off-site.   You should only need to access off-site tapes in the event of a true emergency. Keep original tapes on-site. If they are stored remotely, then the MTTR is increased by the time it takes to find the tape off-site and then transport it back home.

Balance safety and rapid access.   The ultimate in safe storage for your tapes might be in a locked, hidden, waterproof, airtight, underground vault halfway around the world. However, since it might take 2 or 3 months to transport the tape back to you if you need it, that is probably unacceptable. The ultimate in rapid access for off-site tapes might be to store them next door. But a neighborhood-wide catastrophe might wipe the backup tapes out, too. Your solution should achieve a practical balance between these two extremes.

Label every tape.   Unlabeled tapes may as well be blank. There's no easy way to determine what's on them, and they will get reused by some other operator.

BLANKED OUT

In my house, we have a rule by the VCR. If a tape is unlabeled, it's fair game for reuse. Nobody should be expected to take the time to put the tape in the VCR and watch it to determine if there's anything of value on it before they record over it. If it matters, label it.

—Evan

Use bar codes.   If you have a large library or silo, take full advantage of its ability to read bar codes, and use those codes to identify tapes. Bar codes are a simple, reliable, and uniform way to identify all your backup tapes.

General Backup Security

Backups are very valuable to an ongoing operation, but they can also represent a significant potential security hole. Everything you do to organize your backups, and make them easy to search through, and easy to restore from, also works against you. Those well-indexed backups are also easy for an enemy to rummage through, enabling him to examine and steal the very same data.

Can an intruder add an unauthorized client to your backup network? If he does, can he then spoof the identity of a valid client? Once he has spoofed a valid client, if the proper security is not enabled within your backup software, this intruder can restore from critical backups, or even erase backup tapes. Some backup software offers users the ability to initiate their own backups and restores. User-initiated restores can open a real security hole if intruders can gain access to your backup network. After all, good backup software makes the restores as easy as possible, finding the right tape, and either inserting it or requesting that an operator insert the tape, with little or no direct user involvement. If restores require security clearance and passwords, it becomes much more difficult for unauthorized restores of backed up data.

Most backup data travels across a network, whether a dedicated backup network, or just the regular internal LAN. If the data is not encrypted on the client side, this data can be read right off the network. If it can be read, it can be reassembled and viewed by inappropriate persons.

Restores

There is a real trade-off between backup and restore speed. A lot of the things you can do to speed up backups will slow your restores. Here we offer a few ways to speed up restores—but beware, some of them will increase your backup durations.

Do fewer incremental backups.   Of course, fewer incrementals mean more fulls. More fulls mean that backups take longer. This can be a tricky balancing act. The best approach is probably to do cumulative incrementals once a week or so and daily cumulative incrementals. Then you need only restore three tapes after a total failure. If you alternate between two or three cumulative incremental backup tapes, then the cost of losing one of those tapes will also be reduced. If you put all your incrementals on the same tape, then if that tape is lost or unreadable, you will lose all work performed since the weekly full.

Make the tapes accessible.   Recovery time grows while the operator looks for the right tape to mount. Don't let that happen. Keep the tapes near the drives, and keep the library neat and well organized.

Speed up disk writes.   Build your systems with disk hardware that maximizes write speed. Some disk arrays use cache memory to capture large chunks of data before writing it to disk. If the writes are filesystem based, use a filesystem that optimizes performance.

Use the fastest path from tape to disk.   Dedicated high-speed switched networks will move the data fastest across a LAN. Direct connections via 40MB/second Ultra Wide SCSI beats 100Base-T (at 100Mbit/second) better than four to one. 100MB/second (or faster) Fibre Channel beats them both. The downside here is expense. More hardware costs money.

Try not to have to do restores at all!   The best way to speed up restores is not to have to do them at all. Since most restores are of a single file, rather than a complete restore of a catastrophic filesystem loss, by storing a snapshot or a checkpoint of a filesystem it may be possible to go back in time and restore a deleted file from an online copy rather than from a backup tape. The VERITAS File System is one product that supports this sort of filesystem snapshots. Note that this scenario does not eliminate the need to take backups at all; they are still needed as a last resort against a catastrophic loss of a filesystem.

LESSONS LEARNED FROM SEPTEMBER 11, 2001

In speaking with organizations that were forced to recover their IT infrastructure in the wake of the terrorist attacks on September 11, 2001, I heard one lesson that was learned more than any other. Data centers found that they did not have enough tape drives for their restores. Restores, by their nature, take longer than backups, and shops that had enough tape drives for backups found that they needed more drives to do their restores. Other organizations had fewer tape drives in their DR sites than they had at their original sites, which made the restores take even longer.

Disk Space Requirements for Restores

Imagine the following scenario:

- On Sunday, we take a full backup of our accounting department filesystem, containing 8GB of data, out of a possible 10GB of space.

- On Monday, we learn that Joe, formerly in database design, is transferring to accounting, and he is bringing 4GB of critical files with him. Before Joe's 4GB can be added to our filesystem, which has just 2GB of free space, at least 2GB must be deleted. Word is given, and our friends in accounting delete 3GB of files containing pictures, music, and games downloaded from the Internet. An incremental backup of our newly reduced 5GB filesystem is taken.

- On Tuesday, Joe arrives, and his 4GB is added to our file system, bringing the total to 9GB. Another incremental backup is taken Tuesday night.

- On Wednesday, a disk crash occurs, so we must perform a full restore of the filesystem. (For the sake of this example, this filesystem is not mirrored.)

At the time of the crash, the filesystem contained 9GB. However, most backup software will try to restore all 12GB that existed during the course of the week. Because a 10GB filesystem is not large enough to hold 12GB, your restore will fail. If you know this is going to happen, you can sit at the keyboard and re-delete those large music, picture, and game files as soon as they are restored, but that wastes your time and increases restore times. You also

run the risk of missing one or two that got restored in error, and still overflowing the filesystem. An overflowing file system will cause your restore to fail,
and it will have to be restarted. (On some Windows operating systems, an
overflow may cause your system to crash entirely.) Chances are, if you are
doing a full restore, you have other things on your mind besides sitting and
deleting files that were restored in error.

The solution is to make sure that your backup software is smart enough to
not only keep track of which files have changed from backup to backup, but
also to keep track of which files have been deleted. Good backup software will
simply skip over those unwanted music files.

Summary

Backups are tedious, dull, and a real pain in the neck, but they are your last
line of defense against total loss of data in many types of disasters. Whether
you suffer the crash of an unmirrored disk, the deletion of critical files, or the
total loss of your data center, your backup tapes are the last thing between you
and the irretrievable loss of this data. Sometimes, backups are necessary simply to reload a machine that has suffered hopeless data corruption and can't be
brought back online with failovers because there's nothing left to failover. Last
line of defense doesn't mean last priority; good, clean, regular backups must
be a high priority.

The tapes containing the data must be treated as very real and very valuable
company assets, and they must be given an appropriate amount of protection.
The processes that perform the backups must be trusted and tested on a regular basis to make sure that they really work. If they don't, the time to find out
is not when you need to restore from a tape that turns out to be invalid.

The software that does the backups must be fast enough to complete the
backup cycle inside whatever window you have. It must manage the tapes
properly so that they can be easily located. This is a job that should not be
trusted to homegrown code. There are several examples of commercial backup
software; compare them against each other for the speed and other features
that you need; that comparison is a better use of your time than writing
backup code with no support, no references, and inadequate testing.

If your backups work, but your restores don't, then you are wasting your
time taking backups. Restores need to be quick, easy, and reliable. Make sure
that whatever tool you use for backups creates tapes that can be reliably
restored.

Key Points

- Design backup systems to fit within your time window and tape space restrictions, while also optimizing the time to restore a single file from those backup tapes.
- Disks are not a substitute medium for tapes.
- Examine all of the facets of commercial backup software to be sure it handles your data service requirements, tape formats, and operating systems.
- Handle backup tapes, even old ones, like the valuable resources they are.
- Take the time to do the math and figure out the performance impact that backups will have on your network.
- Every so often, perform spot tests to make sure that the backups you think are being taken are really being taken.

CHAPTER 7

Highly Available Data Management

Since the invention of the microprocessor, the cost of moving a byte of information around has fallen on the order of 10-million-fold. Never before in the human history has any product or service gotten 10 million times cheaper, much less in the course of a couple decades. That's as if a 747 plane, once at $150 million apiece, could now be bought for about the price of a large pizza.

—Michael Rothschild

Disks, and the data stored on them, are the most critical part of just about any computer system. Our discussion of disks and data move us to the third level of the Availability Index, as shown in Figure 7.1.

In this chapter, we discuss many of the options you have for storing data on these disks, and ways of protecting the data against inevitable failures of disks, cables, interface cards, and so forth. We spend a lot of time defining terms in this chapter; the definitions act as a framework for the availability and design lessons that follow. They also introduce and reintroduce some technologies with which you may not be as familiar as you'd like.

To that end, in this chapter we discuss:

- Disk hardware
- RAID levels
- Data redundancy
- Disk space
- Filesystems

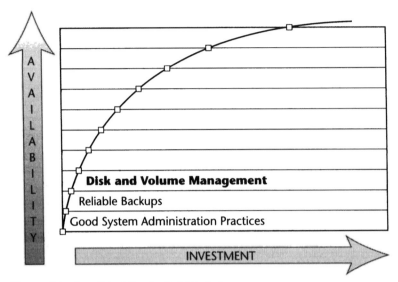

Figure 7.1 Level 3 of the Availability Index.

Four Fundamental Truths

Four fundamental truths relate disk storage to overall system availability:

1. Disks are the most likely component to fail.
2. Disks contain data.
3. The data must be protected.
4. Data accessibility must be ensured.

These are discussed in the sections that follow.

Likelihood of Failure of Disks

Most systems are connected to many more physical disks than they are to any other component. If your system has 100 disks in it, each with an MTBF of 200,000 hours (almost 23 years), that doesn't mean that you'll be error-free for two decades and then, on one really bad day, all 100 disks will fail at once. Each disk has the same probability of errors, but as the number of disks increases, the probability that no disk will have an error goes down exponentially. The actual MTBF for a system with that many disks can be calcuated by combining the probability distributions and determining the new mean and standard deviation for the system with 100 interrelated components in it. This approach is beyond the scope of this and, thankfully, most other books.

Instead we propose a very rough, and very conservative, rule of thumb: Divide the MTBF for a specific component by the number of those components in the system, and you have something of a worst-case time to your first failures. With a 200,000-hour MTBF, you should expect a 50 percent chance of failure per disk in the first 200,000 hours, but over 90 percent of those failures fall within one standard deviation of the mean. With 100 disks, our simple math works out to 200,000/100, or about 83 days for a 50/50 chance of at least one disk failing.

With MTBFs in the 30,000 hour range,[1] power supplies tend to have the worst MTBF figures for any component in the system. But since you only have a few of them, the overall frequency of failures will be lower than for disks. Your system may only have six power supplies, giving you a good shot at a failure in just over 200 days, using the same voodoo math approximation we used for disks.

Data on Disks

The incredibly obvious observation that disks contain data transfers the value of the data, which in most companies is their one of their two most valuable assets (the other being their people), to the disks, the media on which the data is stored. Disks themselves have very little intrinsic value (and that value is dropping all the time, as disks get cheaper and cheaper); their primary value comes from the data that is stored on them.

Protecting Data

If you lose the hardware components of your system, they can be replaced pretty easily. If you lose your data, however, it could take years to recover, if it can be recovered at all. If a company's key data is truly lost, the company may never recover from that loss. Probably the single most important action you can perform to protect your systems, and therefore your data, and therefore your job, is taking regular backups. That means backups that are successful, that are tested, and that are done with the regularity of breathing. We discussed backups and restores in detail in Chapter 6.

Ensuring Data Accessibility

If the data is critical, and it has been backed up to tape, then your next-most-important job is to ensure that the data can actually be reached by the user community. Data that cannot be read is not doing anyone any good. This calls for data redundancy via RAID, data path redundancy via multiple pathways and the appropriate management software, and storage management software that notifies you when a component has failed or is failing.

[1] 30,000 hours translates to about 3½ years.

Six Independent Layers of Data Storage and Management

There are six independent layers of data storage and management, as shown in Figure 7.2. The terms introduced in the description of these layers are discussed and properly defined in the next section.

Physical disks. These are the actual disks where data is read and written.

Storage area networking. A new addition to this layered model, SANs take either the physical disks or the LUNs (if present) and make them available via a network (often called a *fabric*) to the host systems on the SAN. Over the next few years, RAID capabilities will be added directly to the SAN, allowing centralized management of RAID levels, rather than requiring management in either a disk array or the host. We'll discuss SANs further in Chapter 8, "SAN, NAS, and Virtualization."

Hardware RAID. Hardware RAID services take the physical disks and organize them into logical units (LUNs), as explained in the preceding text. Management of Hardware RAID is generally performed from within a disk array, and has its own management tool. Management and configuration of LUNs fall outside the control of the host's operating system.

Software RAID/volume management. Software RAID and volume management, which are usually so closely connected as to be inseparable, allow the host that uses the storage to take the disks, in whatever form it sees them, and build RAID configurations on them. The disks may be seen as simple disks or LUNs. The host system does not generally differentiate between the two, so Software RAID and volume management products cannot differentiate either.

Filesystem or raw device. A host system builds its filesystem on top of the volume created by a volume manager, on a LUN, or on a simple disk, depending on which of the preceding layers have actually been employed. Not all applications require filesystems; some applications, notably image processing and data collection, use raw disks for pure speed, treating the volume (or LUN or disk) like a tape drive that has no real formatting and is a continuous stream of bytes from beginning to end.

Application or database. The application writes its data to whatever type of device it has been configured to write to. The device could be a filesystem or a raw device. The raw device, in turn, could be a LUN, volume, or physical disk.

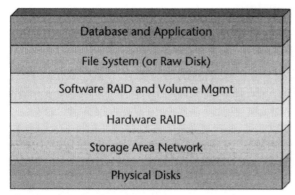

Figure 7.2 The data management layers.

We have illustrated this layered model to demonstrate the independence between each of the layers. The choice to use, for example, a SAN should not in any way impact the choice of one application over another. Hardware RAID does not necessarily eliminate the need for Software RAID, and vice versa.

Disk Hardware and Connectivity Terminology

In this section we introduce some disk hardware terminology.

SCSI

Small Computer Systems Interfaces, or SCSIs, come in many varieties: Narrow SCSI, Wide SCSI, and UltraSCSI, each of which refers to the amount of data that can be sent across the bus (data cable or transport) in parallel. Narrow is 8 bits, Wide is 16 bits, and Ultra is 32 bits; the wider the bus, the faster the data can get across it. Theoretical maximum speed for Narrow is 10MB/second, for Wide is 20MB/second, and for Ultra Wide is 40MB/second; in reality, top speeds will usually run 10 to 15 percent slower because of the overhead of the SCSI data transport protocol. In addition, there are differential and single-ended SCSI varieties, and Ultra, Fast, Fast/Narrow, and Fast/Wide SCSI varieties. There are speed enhancements being made all the time, with transfer rates usually doubling with each enhancement. We have attempted to create an exhaustive list of SCSI varieties, but we may have missed one or two:

SCSI-1. This is the original SCSI technology, developed in the early 1980s. It only supports 3 to 5MB/second transfer rates, and only allows one disk and one system on a bus. You'd be hard-pressed to find SCSI-1 hardware on production systems today.

SCSI-2. Work started on this update in 1986. It is faster and more reliable than SCSI-1, comes in several varieties, typically has an 8-bit-wide data path, and uses a 50-pin connector. The theoretical maximum throughput of SCSI-2 is 10MB/second.

Single-ended SCSI-2. This is the "regular" version of SCSI (so identified to separate it from Differential SCSI). Because of line noise, transfer speeds rarely exceed 5MB/second.

Differential SCSI-2. Differential SCSI uses a much more complex method of transmitting signals, which results in longer supported cabling distances (up to 25 meters), easier termination, and faster transmission speeds (up to 10MB/second) because differential SCSI puts less noise on its data cables. Not all SCSI devices are compatible with differential SCSI.

Fast/Narrow SCSI-2 (also called, simply, Fast SCSI-2). Cable lengths are limited to 6 meters. A 10MB/second throughput is possible.

Fast/Wide SCSI-2. Fast/Wide SCSI-2 doubles the 8-bit width to 16 bits, doubling throughput to 20MB/second at the same time. Fast/Wide can come in either differential or single-ended varieties. Because 16-bit Fast/Wide uses a 68-pin connector (instead of the 57 pin that its predecessors used), it is easy to recognize.

SCSI-3. At 8 bits wide, SCSI-3 (also called UltraSCSI) can transmit data at 20MB/second. Once again, SCSI-3 is available in differential or single-ended varieties.

Wide UltraSCSI. This takes the 8-bit SCSI-3 bus and doubles its width to 16 bits, giving it 40MB/second throughput.

Ultra-2 SCSI. Ultra-2 offers 40MB/second at 8-bit widths, and 40MB/second at 16-bit widths. It no longer comes in a single-ended variety.

Wide Ultra-2 SCSI. The wider data bus allows more data, increasing throughput to 80MB/second.

Ultra-3 or Ultra160. This once again doubles throughput, potentially to 160MB/second. From this point forward, all SCSI is of the wide (16-bit) variety.

Ultra320. This doubles the throughput again to 320MB/second.

Ultra640. This doubles it yet again, to 640MB/second.

For more detailed information on these varieties of SCSI, as well as any future innovations, and other technical information, visit www.scsita.org.

A SCSI bus is an electrical circuit that requires a terminator on both ends. A system generally acts as the terminator on one end. If there is only one system on the bus, then a terminator device is required on the other end. Because a SCSI bus is a circuit, it should never be broken (unplugged) while in use. If it is, data loss can, and almost certainly will, occur.

Two kinds of devices can sit on a SCSI bus: initiators and targets. Generally, initiators are computers; they place commands onto the bus that targets respond to by reading or writing data. Targets are usually disks and tape drives, although other devices are possible. Every device on the bus must have a unique address. The range of valid addresses on a narrow bus is from zero to 7. On a wide bus, the address can go to 15.

SCSI resets occur when an initiator ID is changed, when a system connected to the bus reboots, or when an operation in progress is interrupted. SCSI resets can, in some cases, result in the loss of data in transit. To ensure the integrity of data, it is generally best not to mess with an active SCSI bus.

Traditionally, host adapters on servers have a default address of 7. When more than one initiator (a multi-initiated SCSI) is placed on a single SCSI bus (as in Figure 7.3), one of the initiators must change its address. This is usually a manual operation.

From one terminator to the other, a differential SCSI bus cannot exceed 25 meters or 82 feet in length, including the short runs of cable within enclosures. The newest types of SCSI (Ultra160 and above) only support 12-meter (about 40 feet) cable runs. Single-ended SCSI buses cannot exceed 6 meters, or about 20 feet in length. At the higher data rates of Fast/Narrow SCSI, long single-ended SCSI bus chains can introduce reliability problems due to noise. Electrical and noise requirements constraining the length of a SCSI bus put a serious limit on the maximum distance between a server and its storage.

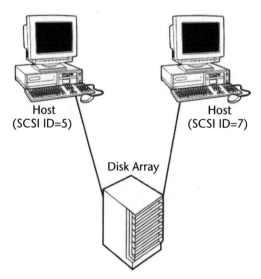

Host
(SCSI ID=5)

Host
(SCSI ID=7)

Disk Array

Figure 7.3   Multi-initiated SCSI.

In addition to defining an electrical standard, SCSI also defines a command set for moving data across the bus that has been adopted by other connection media, including Fibre Channel.

Fibre Channel

Fibre Channel (FC) is a newer technology for connecting servers to disks. At this writing, Fibre Channel supports speeds up to 2GB/second. The 2GB/second data transfer rate is expected to increase to, and probably exceed, 10GB/second over time. Since FC uses a 24-bit addressing scheme, approximately 16 million devices can be connected to a single FC network or fabric.

FC supports much greater distances for disk connectivity than does SCSI. The formal FC specification says that devices can be up to 10 kilometers apart, but vendors are exceeding the specification, and spreads of 80 kilometers and more are being achieved when long-wave optics are used to enhance the optical signal sent on the fiber. This distance limitation (as well as the maximum throughput) will likely be a moving target for some time. Moreover, differential SCSI's 82 feet is the limit for the *total length* of a SCSI bus; while in an FC environment, the 10 kilometer limit is the maximum separation between an end device (server, disk array, etc.) and its network connection point.

FC also supports its own versions of all of the networking hardware normally associated with LANs, such as switches, bridges, hubs, and routers. The devices in a LAN are not interchangeable with those in a SAN, but SAN devices are basically functional equivalents of LAN devices. As mentioned earlier in the chapter, this arrangement of devices on a SAN is commonly called a fabric. FC cables are thin and light because they transmit a single beam of light, and so do not need the 50 to 67 separate wires running in them that SCSI cables require. Unlike SCSI, FC offers complete electrical independence of its devices, allowing them to be unplugged or plugged in without affecting the other devices on the bus.

In spite of all the physical differences between SCSI and FC (see Table 7.1), FC uses SCSI's mature and well-known interdevice communication protocol, making it easier for vendors to migrate their products to the new standards.

We will discuss Fibre Channel in more detail in Chapter 8.

Table 7.1   SCSI versus Fibre Channel

TECHNOLOGY	DATA TRANSFER RATE	NUMBER OF DEVICES	MAXIMUM DISTANCE
Ultra640 SCSI	640MB/sec	16	82 feet end-to-end
Fibre Channel	2GB/sec	No limit	80 kilometers between devices and beyond with new technologies

Multipathing

Multipathing is the connection of a single host to a single disk array with more than one data path. This technology requires multiple interface cards in the host, and a disk array that has sufficient inputs to support all the connections.

Data transfer rates can be increased nearly linearly (that is, two 80MB/second connections yield an effective transfer rate of almost 160MB/second) if both connections are active all the time. If one of the connections fails, the other should be able to take over the full data transfer load without interruption, limited only by its own remaining throughput.

Connections may fail due to a cable breaking or being removed, or because an interface card or controller in either the disk array or in the host has failed. All of these failures will be transparent in a properly configured multipathed environment.

Commercial examples of multipathing include VERITAS's DMP feature in their Volume Manager product, and EMC's PowerPath.

A simple example of multipathing can be found in Figure 7.4.

Multihosting

Multihosting is the connection of one set of disks to two or more servers at the same time. Both servers can see and access the disks, but generally will not at the same time. Multihosting is most commonly used in a clustered environment, enabling the takeover server to get data that is as up-to-date as possible. For more on clustering, please see Chapter 17, "Local Clustering and Failover."

In a SCSI environment, multihosting, accomplished through multi-initiated SCSI, is an exception that is generally found only in clustered environments. It is the norm in the FC world.

Disk Array

A disk array is a single enclosure or cabinet, containing slots for many disks. The array may use SCSI or Fibre Channel internally to address its disks, and may use SCSI or Fibre Channel to connect to its host(s). The same array may have SCSI disks internally, while connecting to its host(s) via Fibre Channel.

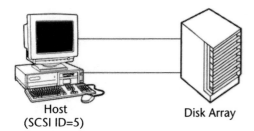

Host
(SCSI ID=5)   Disk Array

Figure 7.4   Multipathing.

Most disk arrays have some intrinsic intelligence that permits disks to be mirrored or striped together (see *RAID Technology*, coming up in this chapter), and usually have disk cache that is used to speed up write access to the array's disks.

Arrays may have additional features that increase their availability. Common hardware features may include multiple, redundant power supplies and hot-swappability. Additional software features may include replication or the ability to break off a mirrored copy of data, for additional processing.

Hot Swapping

A disk array that allows a failed disk to be removed and a new disk added without requiring the array to be shut down supports hot swapping. Arrays that support hot swapping disks are a fundamental requirement for most highly available applications. Hot swapping is also referred to as hot plugging.

Logical Units (LUNs) and Volumes

We get a little bit ahead of ourselves by defining logical unit (LUN) here, but we need it for our discussion of SANs. A LUN is a logical grouping of physical disks into a RAID construct. When the grouping is done inside an intelligent disk array, and passed to connected hosts as a unit, that unit is called a LUN (see *Hardware RAID*, later in the chapter). When that grouping is done outside of a disk array, and in the attached host instead, the group is called a *volume* (see *Software RAID*, later in the chapter).

JBOD (Just a Bunch of Disks)

JBOD (pronounced "JAY-bod") refers to a collection of disks without any sort of hardware intelligence or real organization. Often, JBODs are literally a stack of small disk cabinets that each contain a disk or two. On a critical system, these disks will require some sort of logical volume management and Software RAID capability.

Hot Spares

A *hot spare* is a disk that sits in reserve, waiting for a critical disk to fail. The hot-sparing software agent migrates the data that was on the failed disk to the hot spare. Hot spares require some sort of RAID so that the contents of the failed disk can be re-created on the replacement. Hot sparing can be performed by either the disk array or by logical volume management software.

Write Cache

Many disk arrays contain some specialized memory that acts as a staging area for disk writes. Since memory is much faster than disk, writes to this cache can complete many times faster than writes to disk. Write cache can increase the cost of a disk array, and unless the disk array has a reliable battery backup, it can cause data loss if the data written to the cache never makes it to disk. Data that's written to the write cache is flushed to disk on a regular basis, usually every few seconds.

Storage Area Network (SAN)

A storage area network is a new model for interconnecting storage and computing systems into a shared pool that many different hosts can access. Although many SANs are based on Fibre Channel, FC is not a requirement. SANs can be based on a number of different underlying technologies, including IP-based networks. We will discuss SANs in more detail in Chapter 8.

The storage devices on the SAN are usually limited to disks and tape drives, although other devices, such as CD and DVD drives, are expected to be available in the near future. Through the use of protocol bridges, legacy SCSI-based storage devices can join a SAN as well.

In Figure 7.5, we offer a diagram of a simple SAN.

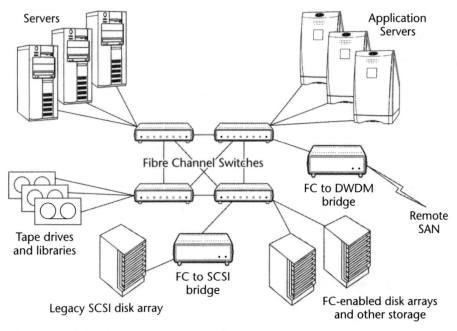

Figure 7.5 A simple storage area network.

In a SAN, newly purchased storage can be put into a storage pool and allocated as needed between the hosts on the SAN. As a result, storage purchasing becomes much more efficient. When you request a disk purchase, and management complains that "you just bought 2TB of storage," you don't have to say, "Yes, but we put that 2TB on that server over there; now I need disks for this server over here." All the storage can be shared and easily allocated among all of the servers on the SAN. (This argument assumes that some of the 2TB remains unused so that there is actually something to allocate between the hosts.)

The following are other SAN advantages:

Centralized management and allocation.   The storage pool and its allocation can be centrally managed from one host in the SAN. This means that a single collection of disks can be allocated in chunks, generally allocated as whole disks or LUNs, are required, and can easily be reallocated among hosts as needs change.

Intrinsic resilience and high availability.   Disks can be centrally RAIDed and allocated to SAN hosts premirrored. This will help ease the storage management burden on each individual host. Storage will usually have dual connections to the SAN, so that the loss of a single controller or connector will not cause a failure. Disk pools can be spread out over multiple locations, so that the loss of a single location will not affect the availability of the data that is on that storage.

Disks need not be colocated.   Since the permitted distances for FC are so much greater than those for SCSI, disks can be mirrored (see *RAID Technology* later in this chapter) between multiple locations on the same SAN, or centrally located. The SAN model gives administrators much more flexibility in how they physically layout their storage, allowing them to balance availability with convenience.

Smart and more efficient failover.   More complex failover configurations, such as N-to-1, N-to-N, cascading, and service level failovers are much more practical in a SAN environment. We will discuss clustering configurations in much more detail in Chapter 17, "Failover Configurations."

Efficient resource deployment.   The resources on a SAN are visible to all the members of the SAN, so a tape silo or other expensive backup device can be shared between all the members of the SAN. This makes the purchase of large, expensive backup devices much more practical and justifiable.

LAN-free backups.   With a tape drive on the SAN and some high-quality backup software that supports this capability, you can back up your server directly to tape by putting the data on the SAN rather than on the LAN, thus reducing the impact of backups on your user community.

As SANs mature, more features will develop, and implementation costs will drop. For example, there are products that allow parallel applications to read and write from more than one server at the same time. The result is increased performance and reliability. Oracle's enhanced version of their database, called Oracle 9i RAC, is a parallelized application, and VERITAS's SANpoint Foundation Suite allows the simultaneous reading and writing of disks by the members of a SAN. There are not, however, many applications that can take advantage of this capability.

RAID Technology

The RAID standard describes several ways to combine and manage a set of independent disks so that the resultant combination provides a level of disk redundancy. Five levels of RAID are defined, plus an additional loosely defined level that does not provide any redundancy. RAID functionality can be provided from within a disk array or on a disk controller (Hardware RAID) or from the host system (Software RAID). In general, Software RAID requires cycles from the host system's CPU; Hardware RAID is performed on a separate dedicated CPU. More on the differences between the two is discussed in the sections that follow.

RAID Levels

The RAID Advisory Board has defined six official levels of RAID. Five of them (RAID-1 through RAID-5) provide various levels of increased disk redundancy. One more (RAID-0) does not provide any redundancy.

Several other levels of RAID fall into one of two classes: combined levels and marketing-created levels. Combined levels, such as RAID 0+1 or RAID 5+0, indicate, as you might guess, a combined approach. Other levels, such as RAID-6 or RAID-S, are not recognized by the RAID Advisory Council, and generally come from one company's marketing department or another. We discuss these topics in more detail in the paragraphs that follow.

As explained in the data management layers at the start of this chapter, RAID functionality is totally independent of the data stored on the disks. The data could be stored in a filesystem or in raw format (non–filesystem-based); it could be user data, application data, source code, or any other sort of data. RAID simply manages where and how many times the data is written, and what, if any, calculations are performed on the data to protect it.

RAID-0: Striping

RAID-0 is another name for disk striping. In a striping model, each chunk of data to be written to disk is broken up into smaller segments, with each segment written to a separate disk. Because each disk can complete the smaller writes at the same time, write performance is improved over writes to a single disk. Performance can be enhanced further by striping the writes between separate controllers too.

The size of each segment is called the *stripe width*. In general, the optimal size of a stripe width is the average size of a disk write, divided by the number of disks in the stripe. However, if the disk array has its own cache, the rules may change.

The first and most important thing to know about RAID-0 is that, unlike all the other levels of RAID, RAID-0 does not increase your system or data availability. In fact, when used by itself, RAID-0 decreases availability. In order for a stripe set to function, all of its member disks must be available. If any disk in a stripe fails, the entire stripe fails and cannot be read or written. Consider a 2GB filesystem, and disks with a 200,000-hour MTBF. If the filesystem lives on a single 2GB disk, the MTBF in is simply 200,000 hours. If the filesystem is striped across four disks, with 500MB of data on each disk, the MTBF is reduced significantly due to the increased probability that at least one of the disks will fail.

Because RAID-0 adds no redundancy, it does not require any additional disk space.

Please note that when we use the term RAID throughout the book as a generalized way of adding disk redundancy, we are specifically excluding RAID-0 from that discussion, since RAID-0 reduces overall system availability and all other levels increase it.

RAID-1: Mirroring

RAID-1, or mirroring, is a model where a copy of every byte on a disk is kept on a second disk. The copy is (normally) 100 percent in sync. In this model, if one disk fails, the other disk continues to operate without interruption.

A common misconception of RAID-1 is that a master/slave relationship exists between the disks, and if one disk fails, the other takes over. This is not the case: Both copies in a mirror act as peers. A better way to think about this relationship is to imagine a logical disk that sits on top of the mirrored copies and sends all read and write requests to both disks at the same time. If a disk fails, the logical layer is not affected; it continues reading and writing to the surviving disk. Reads are usually requested of both underlying copies, and the logical layer returns the data that comes from the first physical disk to reply, resulting in a slight improvement in performance under RAID-1.

In fact, mirrors are not limited to two copies. Many shops will keep three or four mirrors of their data, and split one off from time to time for backups, or to provide production-like data to their development, quality assurance, or disaster recovery environments.

Another, slightly less common misconception about mirroring is that if your disks are mirrored, you don't need to take backups. This is not true. Mirrors will protect your users from hardware failure, but they will not protect you from the careless or malicious deletion or corruption of critical data. All mirrored copies will be affected by the deletion. Point-in-time copies or checkpoints, however, will protect your users from such a deletion; we discuss those later in this chapter.

Besides the minor performance improvement, the main advantage of RAID-1 is data protection when the inevitable failure of a disk occurs. If a disk fails in a RAID-1 configuration, users and applications will continue to receive their data, with no interruption in service.

RAID-1 has disadvantages as well. The primary disadvantage is in the added expense. Each mirror requires 100 percent disk overhead. It takes an additional 10GB to mirror 10GB. There are no economies of scale possible with RAID-1. The other disadvantages are performance related. Resyncing a failed or new RAID-1 disk usually requires a block-for-block complete copy of the contents of the original disk. This takes time, and it also requires a tremendous amount of I/O, which can slow down the service times for regular requests that have nothing to do with the resync. Some RAID vendors have developed hardware or software solutions that can speed up the resyncing (or "resilvering") of mirrors.

Write performance will generally also suffer a little with RAID-1 because all disks must be written to, and the write request will not complete until the slowest disk has finished writing. Slowest in this regard doesn't only refer to the transfer rate of the disk but rather to the rotational and seek latencies incurred in setting up the write head to move the data. The minor slowing in performance should be more than offset by the increase in read performance, which, though very small, does occur more often than the write performance penalty (because reads are generally much more common than writes). When the disks are in a disk array with a large write cache, performance will probably not be affected in this way, and write performance generally will be much better than it would have been without the cache (your mileage may vary).

Combining RAID-0 and RAID-1

Unlike in the world of mathematics, addition of RAID levels is not commutative. RAID 0+1 is significantly different from RAID 1+0. RAID 1+0 (sometimes inappropriately called RAID-10) is a superior method of combining these technologies, but it is often harder for vendors to implement, or at least to implement well, and as a result, many vendors have allowed the confusion between 0+1 and 1+0 to stand uncorrected. Fortunately, your authors are here to remedy this situation.

MAYBE IT IS COMMUTATIVE . . .

As I said in an earlier *Tales from the Field,* when you write a book like this one, people assume you are an expert on every issue related to the topic, and so you get pulled into all sorts of technical debates and arguments. Some are interesting, some are hairsplitting. One of the more interesting (and yet hairsplitting) debates was over which name, 0+1 or 1+0, actually referred to mirrored stripes, and which referred to striped mirrors, and for that matter, whether mirrored stripes meant that the mirroring took place first or the striping did.

The nomenclature that we use in this section was based on some research, as well as on what we see in marketing literature from companies who have products that actually deliver RAID 1+0 and 0+1.

My worthy opponent in the debate was a colleague, friend, and prolific author, Paul Massiglia, who served on the original RAID Advisory Board, and who had helped name the levels of RAID, including 1+0 and 0+1, back in 1989. The Board had, unfortunately, named them the other way around, and Paul and I were being asked to reach a consensus on the names for VERITAS's marketing department.

We agreed that the names striped mirrors and mirrored stripes were very confusing, largely because it's hard to remember which is which (and the numbers don't help either). When the board assigned the names, they decided that 0 (striped) + 1 (mirrors) was a sensible naming convention. Unfortunately, the convention evolved differently in the marketplace.

In the end, the argument came down to style rather than any technical issue. We decided to use the style that you see in this book, after a discussion that ran on and off for several months and that was briefly revived (for about the 10th time in the last few years!) as I put this Tale together.

—Evan

The difference in layouts between the two models depends on which of the two methods is employed first. As shown in Figure 7.6, in RAID 0+1 (or mirrored stripes), the stripes on one side of the mirror are built first and then they are mirrored to the other side. Figure 7.7 shows RAID 1+0 (or striped mirrors); the mirrors are built separately first, and then are striped together as if they were separate disks.

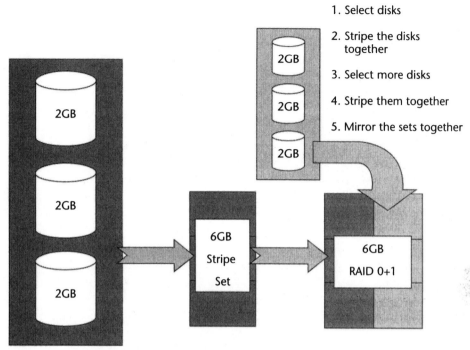

1. Select disks

2. Stripe the disks together

3. Select more disks

4. Stripe them together

5. Mirror the sets together

Figure 7.6   Building RAID 0+1: Mirrored stripes.

The differences between 0+1 and 1+0 are not particularly apparent in the description of how they are built. But when you look at how they handle failures and how they recover from those failures, the differences, as well as the advantages of one over the other, become much more striking.

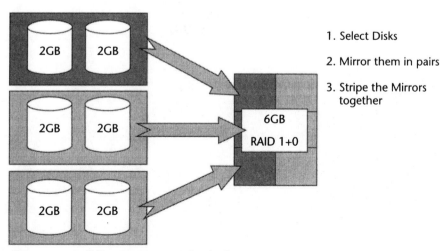

1. Select Disks

2. Mirror them in pairs

3. Stripe the Mirrors together

Figure 7.7   Building RAID 1+0: Striped mirrors.

As shown in the RAID 0+1 example (see Figure 7.8), the loss of any member of a stripe causes the loss of the entire stripe. If disk A, B, or C fails, all of stripe 1 is lost. If disks D, E, or F fail before the first failed disk can be recovered and the data refreshed, the entire data set is lost.

In the RAID 1+0 example in Figure 7.9, if A or B fails, there is no data loss. If C or D fails, there is no data loss. If E or F fails, there is no data loss. However, if A and B fail at the same time (or C and D, or E and F), then and only then the entire RAID device is lost.

One might note that either RAID composition could sustain the loss of one half of its disk members and still survive. However, the odds for surviving are very much in favor of 1+0. If disk A fails in either figure, both compositions will survive. In the RAID 1+0 example, of the five disks that remain after disk A fails, the failure of only one of them (B) could cause a catastrophic outage. In the RAID 0+1 example, if A fails, then a catastrophic failure will result if D, E, or F fail. So, in our examples, the chance that a second disk failure will cause a catastrophe in RAID 1+0 is only 20 percent (1 in 5), while in 0+1 the chance is 60 percent (3 in 5). And since B and C are not actually in use once A fails, the chances for catastrophe are even greater.

The other issue when comparing the two combined RAID levels is recovery time. Once disk A has failed in RAID 0+1 (Figure 7.8), and the entire stripe is lost, all three disks in the stripe (A, B, and C) must be synced with D, E, and F in order to bring stripe 1 back on line. To recover from the loss of disk A in the RAID 1+0 example (Figure 7.9), only disk A needs to be resynced.

The reliability advantage of 1+0 over 0+1 is clear. The only real downside to 1+0 is that each of the stripe components needs to be the same size. That can be inconvenient when designing the layout. RAID 0+1 does not have that requirement, and only requires that all sides of the mirror be the same size.

Stripe 1   Stripe 2

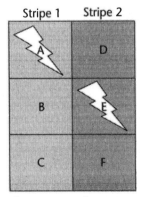

1. Disk A fails

2. All of stripe 1 is lost;
   data remains available via stripe 2

3. Disk E fails

4. Stripe 2 is lost; data is no longer available

Figure 7.8 When RAID 0+1 disks fail.

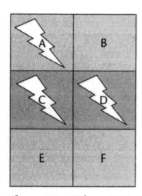

1. Disk A fails

2. No other disks are taken offline; data still available

3. Disk C fails

4. No other disks are taken offline; data sill available

5. Disk D fails

6. **Then** data is lost.

Figure 7.9   When RAID 1+0 disks fail.

RAID-2: Hamming Encoding

We include this RAID level purely for completeness. RAID-2 uses the same Hamming encoding method for checking the correctness of disk data as is used by Error Correcting Code (ECC) memory. We have been unable to find even one commercial implementation that uses RAID-2. Next.

RAID-3, -4, and -5: Parity RAID

RAID levels 3, 4, and 5 are all different styles of parity RAID. They do not require maintaining a complete copy of the original data on a second set of disks, and the associated 100 percent overhead. Instead, each RAID volume requires extra space equivalent to one extra disk. This additional disk's blocks contain calculated parity values, which are generated by taking XORs (eXclusive Ors, a logical Boolean operation) of the contents of the corresponding data blocks on all the other disks in the RAID volume. If any one disk (including the parity disk) in the RAID set is lost, its contents can be calculated based on the contents of all the other disks in the set. If two disks are lost at the same time, or a second disk is lost while the first disk is being rebuilt, all the data on the RAID stripe is lost and must be restored from a backup. The overhead in a parity RAID model is generally only about 20 to 25 percent, depending on the number of disks in the stripe.

Parity RAID requires that each member disk in the RAID volume be the same size.

Parity RAID introduces significant performance penalties under most conditions. When a write is generated, not only must the write complete, but the updated parity must be recalculated. To recalculate parity, data has to be read from otherwise unaffected disks in the set so that the correct parity value can be written to the parity disk region. This means that in a five-disk RAID-5 stripe, a single write that fits on one disk causes four reads, five XORs, and two writes. RAID writing, therefore, especially when the writes are small, is generally pretty slow. RAID read performance is basically the same as if no RAID was present, because no parity calculations are required.

When a disk fails, its replacement must be rebuilt from the data on the surviving disks, all of which must be read and then processed. Because a rebuild requires reading every block on every disk in the RAID-5 stripe and performing the parity calculations, rebuilds can be extremely time- and CPU-consuming. If Hardware RAID is employed, a lot of CPU cycles will still be required, they will just be on a different CPU, with different performance and cost characteristics from the CPU on the host.

The performance of a RAID set is also dependent on the number of disks in the set. Once you exceed six or seven disks in a RAID set, performance will really fall off, because the number of additional reads and calculations that must be performed becomes excessive.

The differences between RAID-3, RAID-4, and RAID-5 are primarily in exactly how they implement the parity between the disks.

RAID-3: Virtual Disk Blocks

In RAID-3, virtual disk blocks are created and striped across all the disks in the RAID-3 volume. Every disk operation touches all the disks, regardless of the size of the write. The RAID stripe can only process one disk I/O at a time.

RAID-3 performance depends on the nature of the writes. If the I/Os are small and random (all over the volume), performance will be poor. If the I/Os are large and sequential, performance will be fast; streaming I/Os work best.

Commercial implementations of RAID-3 are generally in hardware rather than software. Storage Technologies (Storage Tek), Medea, and Baydel are three disk array vendors that implement RAID-3 in hardware. For the most part, the vendors use large disk caches to ease any issues with performance.

RAID-4: Dedicated Parity Disk

In RAID-4, one entire disk is devoted to RAID volume parity, as shown in Figure 7.10. Whenever a write is performed to any data disk in the RAID set, the parity disk is also written to, so that its parity data can be updated. On a write-intensive system, that can make the parity disk a performance bottleneck.

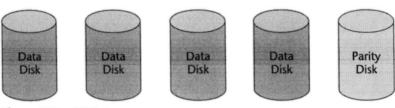

Figure 7.10   RAID-4.

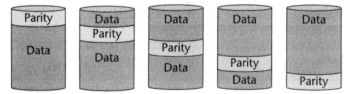

Figure 7.11 RAID-5.

Much like RAID-3, small writes are especially poorly performing on RAID-4. Larger writes aren't quite as bad, but since parity must be recalculated whenever any write occurs, performance will suffer.

Commercial examples of RAID-4 are also generally limited to Hardware RAID vendors, and can be found in Network Appliance's NAS-based storage devices (we'll discuss NAS in Chapter 8). As with RAID-3, most hardware vendors ease any performance issues by placing a battery-backed-up memory-based disk cache logically in front of the disks.

RAID-5: Striped Parity Region

RAID-5 works almost identically to RAID-4, except that the bottleneck imposed by the presence of a single parity disk is eliminated. As shown in Figure 7.11, the parity space is striped across all the disks in the RAID set. Because RAID-5 is a little better suited to general applications than RAID-3 or RAID-4, you will see software implementations of RAID-5. VERITAS Volume Manager and Sun Solaris Disk Suite have software implementations of RAID-5. However, software implementations of RAID-5 will generally still be slow for any sort of write-intensive application.

The rule of thumb is that for applications with more than 15 to 20 percent writes, RAID-5 performance will probably not be acceptable without some sort of disk cache in place.

Since recovery from a disk failure requires a complete read of all the surviving disks in the stripe set, plus XORing them together, recovery from the loss of a RAID-5 disk can be very time-consuming. During that time, system performance will suffer noticeably, and if another disk fails (more likely than average because the disks are so busy), all of the data in the stripe will be lost, and it will be necessary to restore it from backups.

Other RAID Variants

There are several other variants of RAID offered by a number of different vendors. What follows is not an exhaustive list, but rather just a survey of some of the better-known RAID variants.

RAID-6. RAID-6 takes the striped parity region from RAID-5 and duplicates it. Each disk in a RAID-6 stripe has two parity regions, each calculated separately. The advantage of RAID-6 is that even if two disks fail, the RAID stripe would still have a complete set of data and could recover the failed disks. The biggest disadvantage is in performance. The performance impact of RAID-5 is roughly doubled, as each set of parities is calculated separately. Where RAID-5 requires one extra disk for parity, RAID-6 requires two, increasing the cost of the implementation.

RAID-7. RAID-7 is a trademarked term, owned by Storage Computer Corporation. They appear to have the only commercial implementation, which involves proprietary disk array hardware with an internal CPU, and a combination of striping and a RAID-5–like model.

RAID-S. EMC Symmetrix disk arrays offer an alternate, proprietary method for parity RAID that they call RAID-S. While detailed documentation on RAID-S is proprietary, it appears to be similar to RAID-5, with some performance enhancements as well as the enhancements that come from having a high-speed disk cache on the disk array.

RAID-10. RAID 10 is just a renaming of RAID 1+0, which was discussed previously.

RAID 5+0. By building a series of RAID-5 groups and then striping them in RAID-0 fashion, you can improve RAID-5 performance, without reducing data protection.

RAID 5+3. It would be more accurate to call this RAID 0+3, but it has come to be called RAID 5+3, and it is defined by striping (in RAID-0 style) RAID-3's virtual disk blocks.

RAID. A commercial insecticide best known for killing bugs dead. We know of many software developers who could benefit from its use.

Hardware RAID

The difference between Hardware and Software RAID is where the disk management is performed. Hardware RAID functions are performed, as the name implies, within the disk hardware. The disk array has dedicated internal CPU, I/O, and memory, to perform these functions without impacting the host computer. Management of Hardware RAID is performed through an interface program that runs on the host computer; but any management work that is to be performed is done within the disk array.

If you take another look back at Figure 7.2, you'll see that Hardware RAID performs its functions independently from the operating system and independently of any software-based disk management. The output of a Hardware RAID function is a LUN, which looks exactly like a disk to the host system, regardless of whether its underlying configuration is a 9-disk RAID-0 stripe, a 14-way RAID-1 mirrored set, a 6-way RAID-5 stripe with cache in front, or something else entirely.

In general, users need not be concerned with the RAID level that is used on a Hardware RAID array. The assumption that data is being properly managed should be adequate for most situations. Of course, your mileage may vary.

Some of the advantages of Hardware RAID are:

Performance.   The performance of parity RAID is more acceptable in a Hardware RAID configuration than in a Software RAID configuration. The CPU overhead is offloaded from the host system to the dedicated outboard CPU.

Operating system neutrality.   No special software is usually required on a host to connect to a Hardware RAID system, so arrays can be connected to just about any kind of system that knows how to speak to disks. If you can connect a disk array to your Amiga or your Xbox, it should work with all of its native features intact.

Disk cache.   Many disk array vendors put cache memory in their arrays. This cache will greatly improve write performance and can improve read performance when the data that is being searched for remains in the write cache. Other enhancements, such as read-ahead, where the array prereads data from the disk it expects will be requested soon, will also generally improve read performance. Putting disk cache in front of a slower parity RAID model usually counteracts the performance disadvantages they impose.

Advanced features.   Some Hardware RAID manufacturers offer features like wide area data replication, or the ability to share expensive disk hardware between multiple hosts.

There are also disadvantages to Hardware RAID. Depending on the vendor you choose, some or all of these may be present. They are all conditions to ask your vendor about.

The following are some of the disadvantages of Hardware RAID:

Expensive CPU cycles.   One of the most often-touted advantages of intelligent disk arrays is that they have their own CPUs and therefore can offload storage and RAID management tasks from their associated hosts. However, the CPU cycles must come from somewhere, and it is likely that disk array CPUs and their cycles are more expensive than CPU cycles in a host. Beware of hidden costs.

Limited to one disk array.   Since Hardware RAID cannot manage disks that are in different arrays, the disk array itself can introduce a single point of failure.

Difficult to resize or reconfigure LUNs. If a LUN is full, the only solution is to dump its contents to tape (or to another LUN), destroy and rebuild the original one larger, and restore the data to it. The associated downtime can be considerable, especially for a large LUN. Disk array vendors are aware of this rather significant problem and are working to overcome it.

No management interface standard. Every Hardware RAID vendor has its own management interface. Learning to use one is no guarantee that you will be able to use another.

May limit the number or size of LUNs. Some disk arrays have implicit hardware limitations, such as to the number of LUNs that they support, that will force system administrators to make design and configuration decisions that are less useful than they would have liked.

May lock you into a single vendor. Adding a new Hardware RAID vendor to your configuration will introduce a new management interface, with an associated learning curve. By adding more of the same kind of hardware to your environment, management will be simpler, but you may lock yourself out of another vendor's new hardware or management features, or into your chosen vendor's pricing scheme.

Potential single points of failure. Not every disk array will have all of these points of failure, but when deciding which disk array vendor to purchase from, you should be aware of the following potential single points of failure:

Internal cache memory. In many disk arrays, the memory cache can fail, effectively causing a total loss of the entire array. Data that has been written to the cache, but not yet flushed to disk can be lost if the cache fails.

Power supply. A power supply is the likeliest component to fail over time. A good array will have more than one power supply, with standby components that are powerful enough to seamlessly assume the full load if one supply fails.

Cooling. The failure of a fan can be very subtle. Overheating equipment does not usually fail in obvious (or even in predictable) ways. Ensure that if a fan fails, its companions can take over for it, and that you will be notified of the failure.

Power cord. Cord security is important: If a clumsy system administrator, a member of the cleaning crew, or a visitor on a data center tour trips on your disk array power cord and pulls it out, your array goes down, without warning.

Fuses.   These are not generally a problem, but if an internal fuse blows, resolution can be quite confounding. A blown fuse could cause large portions of the array to shut down.

Internal disk controllers.   These provide internal connectivity and some of the intelligence that makes the array function. If they fail, what are the consequences? Are there backups if one board fails?

Cache memory battery power.   There are reports of some disk arrays that fail without warning because the battery on the cache dies, even when ample electric power is being supplied to the array.

Backplane.   Virtually every piece of computing equipment has an internal central pathway over which its data moves. Generally these pathways do not fail, but, like all complex system components, they can. What are the implications if yours does?

Easy-to-lean-on power switch.   Where is the power switch located? Is it protected by a door or a lock? Can it be accidentally kicked, leaned on, or backed into? What happens if someone hits the switch; is there any sort of user-level confirmation? These switches are especially vulnerable to data center tours.

The enclosure itself.   Cabinets of all varieties can topple over. They can be moved, forcing cables to be pulled out or broken. There are even reports of fires breaking out inside a disk array cabinet. Something external can fall onto or into the cabinet. Look for strong, well-constructed cabinets that will stand up to disasters. And fasten them down.

Disk Arrays

Hardware RAID, when it is present, is usually only one feature that a disk array might offer. As has been discussed, many disk arrays offer cache memory for performance improvements, often mitigating the performance impact of underlying hardware parity RAID protection.

Disk arrays may offer the following additional features:

Wide area data replication.   Data is copied across a WAN to a remote site, where it can be read (usually not written to) by another application or maintained offline for use in a disaster. Commercial examples: EMC's SRDF, and Hitachi's TrueCopy. (We'll discuss replication in much more detail in Chapter 18, "Data Replication.")

Intelligent disk buses.   If two hosts are connected to the same disk array, it is critical that only one host access a particular disk at a time; otherwise, data corruption can result. Intelligent disk buses can lock out one host when the other is actively working on a disk or a bus. As parallel applications reach market, though, it is important that this protection can be overridden.

Parallel buses. A single host can be connected to the same set of disks via more than one connection. In some cases, this means increased throughput, since all of the buses can be active at the same time. On other arrays, only one bus is active, and the other remains passive until the active one fails.

Connections to many hosts at the same time. Often combined with intelligent disk buses, some disk arrays allow connections from several servers at the same time, enabling disks to be allocated to several hosts. This can result in major savings when compared to purchasing a disk array for each host. This capability essentially makes your array into a small SAN.

Operating system support. Connecting a hardware disk array to a new operating system will not generally require porting any software. If the hardware can be connected and the host system made to see the disks, then the disk array and all of its advanced features should work. If you can connect a Hitachi disk array to your Palm PDA, you can probably make it work.

Hot-pluggable disks. If a disk fails, it can be removed and replaced without affecting the function of the other disks in the array.

Hot spares. If a disk fails, its data can be automatically moved to another disk in the array without affecting the function of the other disks in the array, allowing the failed disk to be hot swapped for a new one.

Read-ahead buffers. Performance gains can be achieved when a smart disk array reads more than the data requested. Statistics demonstrate that a high percentage of reads are sequential, so by reading the next block of data and storing it in memory, when that next block is requested, it can be returned at memory speed, not at disk speed. (Memory speed can be hundreds or thousands of times faster than disk speed.)

Internal data copies. Though doing so will introduce significant additional hardware costs, some disk arrays support making internal copies of active data or splitting off of mirrors of a critical LUN. The copy can then be used for backups, feeding data to development or QA, for disaster recovery, or for handing off to another server.

Storage administration. Some disk array vendors bundle complete and total array management services with their arrays. These may manage the array for you from afar and simply show up on-site when a problem requiring hands-on access occurs.

Phone-home capabilities.   Your disk array may be smart enough to pick up the phone and call its manufacturer's support center when it detects that it has a problem.

Many of these features have additional costs associated with them, and not all are available from all vendors.

Software RAID

Software RAID moves the disk management functions off of the disk array, allowing more flexibility in the choice of disk hardware. However, since the functions are performed on the host computer, additional load is added to that system. If parity RAID is involved, then significant CPU overhead will result. Regardless of the method employed, though, there will be some additional I/O, CPU, and memory load on the server.

Disk management is often packaged with logical volume management for additional features. Just as the output of Hardware RAID operations is a LUN, as mentioned, the output of Software RAID operations is a *volume*. A volume is the object on which filesystems are written, or on which databases write their data. As we discussed earlier in the section entitled *Six Independent Layers of Data Storage and Management*, the filesystem and database don't care how a volume is organized.

The following are advantages of Software RAID:

Flexibility.   You can mix and match vendor disk hardware. You can combine LUNs when one fills up. Your purchases are not locked to a single disk vendor who can charge what he wants for his disks; instead, you can shop around for the least expensive disks that meet your requirements.

Removal of hardware limitations.   You can mirror and stripe disks from different arrays into logical volumes, and resize and rearrange LUNs without restriction.

Costs scale better.   When buying additional disks, you are not limited to potentially expensive Hardware RAID–capable hardware. Any disks, even JBODs, will do. Therefore, as a system's storage capacity grows, the additional storage hardware you need to purchase is much less expensive; it need not include the Hardware RAID intelligence.

The biggest downside to Software RAID is reduced performance, but this does not occur in all cases. If you must do parity RAID, then it is probably best to do so with Hardware RAID. Writing in software-based RAID-5 is generally too slow for most high-volume, insert- or update-intensive production environments. When Software RAID-1 is used, the performance is generally fine for most applications.

The other downside worth mentioning is that in order to bring Software RAID to a new operating system, its code must be ported. This can delay the availability of such products on emerging operating systems or prevent their availability altogether.

Logical Volume Management

Software RAID is often just one feature of logical volume management (LVM) software. LVM offers many other features besides Software RAID. While each LVM product is different, here are some of the more useful features:

Online reconfiguration.   This feature includes the ability to add and remove mirrors, to expand and, in some cases, shrink a volume or filesystem, and rearrange the disk layout of data, and to do so without interrupting user service.

Removal of OS-imposed limitations.   For example, in Sun's Solaris operating system, a disk cannot be divided into more than seven "slices." A good LVM would remove that restriction, allowing whatever slicing is desired.

Hooks into system management tools.   When the LVM detects failures or performance issues in monitored devices, the information should be automatically shared with system monitoring tools. The LVM might even offer suggestions on how to better layout data for improved performance.

Hot sparing.   If one disk fails, a dedicated spare disk can be automatically moved into its place, transparent to the users.

Some commercial examples of LVMs are VERITAS Software's Volume Manager, which runs on Solaris, HP-UX, AIX, Windows, and Linux, and Sun's Solstice Disk Suite.

Disk Space and Filesystems

When designing a system, subscribe to the physics definition of a gas as applied to disks: Disk usage will always expand to consume all available resources. Extra disk capacity, especially disks kept offline, are vital to stave off disaster. A full filesystem presents the same problems with nonavailability of data storage as a down system. If a user needs to save a file and cannot, then the system may as well be down. In fact, the inability to save critical work after it has been performed may be worse than the system being down. It is certainly more frustrating to the average user, due to the wasted time.

So, when you purchase system resources, look toward optimal disk performance, not storage capacity. Once you have determined the optimal number of platters to maximize performance, buy another 25 to 40 percent of disk capacity for growth and availability. A clever system administrator will keep a certain percentage of unused disk space offline so that in the event of an unexpected critical disk space shortage, he will still be assured of an adequate reserve.

When you arrange the physical layout of your disks, consider the following factors:

Hot-pluggable disks.   If you have to bring your system down whenever a disk fails or new disks are added to the system, your overall system availability will be seriously impacted. Hot-pluggable disks will allow your system to continue running while maintenance is being performed.

Physical capacity.   How much data can you store on each disk? How many disks can you fit on each controller? How many disks can you fit in each disk cabinet? If you use RAID, you will lose a significant portion of that disk capacity, and you must purchase additional disks to make up for the shortfall.

Performance.   Just because you can put six disks on that controller, does that mean you should? What will the impact be to system performance? If the disks are busy, will that exceed the capacity of the disk bus?

Cabinet space.   If there are no empty slots for new disks in your disk cabinet, then as soon as you need to buy more disks, you will have to buy a new cabinet. The incremental costs will stun your purchasing agent. By providing extra space for expansion, the large incremental cost can be better planned for sometime down the road.

Data center floor space.   The new cabinet will also require a chunk of floor space in your data center; be sure that you have it available and that it is physically located within the distance limitations for the technology you are using. If not, there may be no way to make it work. (Remember SCSI's 82 foot cable length limitation.)

Cable runs and conduits.   Make sure that your cable conduits have the necessary space for the additional cables that will be required, and that parallel cables do not run along the same paths.

Power requirements.   More hardware means more power. Be sure that your data center (or other physical location) has sufficient power for all of the incoming hardware.

Backplane slots.   Make sure that if you add more disks, you will have slots for the cards to connect the disks to the host.

Cooling capacity.   While it is unlikely that one more disk will be the straw that breaks your cooling system's back, it is definitely best to make sure that the air-conditioning can handle the extra load.

Planning for costs.   Be sure to build all the costs, both short- and long-term, into your growth plan. Be sure to include support and any training costs in your estimates.

Large Disks or Small Disks?

Disk vendors revel in being able to squeeze more and more bits onto their disks. At this writing, 250GB disks are relatively commonplace and available for about 1 U.S. dollar per gigabyte. By the time you read this, disk sizes may double, and pricing could halve. The marketplace has been led to perceive the constant increases in disk density as a good thing.

We question this wisdom.

In order to fit more data into a smaller space, disk manufacturers must use smaller and smaller components. Those components are likely to be more fragile, and designed with lower physical tolerances, than earlier generations, and therefore more subject to failure.

Since disks are larger, most organizations tend to buy fewer of them. After all, if you can fit three separate databases on one pair of large mirrored disks, why buy two disk pairs? There are at least three good reasons to continue to run applications on separate disks regardless of the size of the disks:

1. Early generations of larger disks tend to spin more slowly than later generations, resulting in slower performance, even under the very same load conditions. At this writing the common speed for 250GB disks is 5,400 rpm. Smaller disks spin faster (7,200 or even 10,000 rpm) and therefore are able to serve up requested data faster.

2. Putting all of the applications on a single disk will increase the load on that disk. An increased load will slow the average response time to any single request, even if the disks were to spin at the same speed. Since higher-density disks spin at slower speeds, performance will be doubly impacted.

3. Since each disk is likely to be working harder, fetching two or three different applications worth of data, rather than just one, the hardware is more likely to fail.

We find ourselves wishing that vendors continued to make older, faster, and less-dense disks available. There would likely be a market for disks as small as

2 to 10GB for smaller applications. Unfortunately, it probably makes little economic sense for manufacturers to keep a factory tooled to build older, smaller disks.

What Happens When a LUN Fills Up?

If you fill up a Hardware RAID LUN, your fate will be decided by how you've planned for such an eventuality. If you have a good LVM and hot-pluggable disks, things won't be so bad. If you don't, then plan on spending the weekend on the job.

If you don't have a good LVM and hot-pluggable disks, then you will probably have to follow these steps:

1. Get your users off the system.

2. Halt the system.

3. Add your new disks to the disk array.

4. Reboot.

5. Take a full, clean backup. (You might choose to verify the backup, but that can be incredibly time-consuming.) Good backup software will allow you to take your backups online, of course, and so you could take your backups as the first step. See Chapter 6, "Backups and Restores."

6. Wipe out the old LUN.

7. Build a new LUN with the appropriate amount of disk space including the newly added disks.

8. (If appropriate) build a new filesystem on the new LUN.

9. Restore the contents of your backup.

10. Check that everything works okay. Note that if you're using this LUN as part of a filesystem exported via NFS, you've just rendered the volume unusable by clients until they unmount and remount it, or until they reboot. We discuss this case in Chapter 14, "Data and Web Services."

11. Make the new LUN accessible to your users, and let your users back on the system.

If you have users who use disk space other than the affected LUN, then they will only be interrupted by the reboot. But the users whose data is on the LUN in question will be down for the entire period, which can run many hours or even a couple of days.

However, if you have installed a logical volume manager, you can save yourself a lot of effort and downtime:

1. Plug your new hot-pluggable disks into your disk array.

2. Create a new LUN on these new disks.

3. Use your LVM to combine the old and new LUNs into a resized LUN.

4. (If appropriate) grow your filesystem into the space on the resized LUN.

All of this work can be done during the day, without downtime or any adverse impact on your users. Life is good.

Managing Disk and Volume Availability

As evidenced in the previous section, there is no substitute for good planning. With that in mind, we offer some more suggestions for maximizing the availability of your disks, volumes, and data:

Redundant data paths and controllers.   Use at least two data paths and controllers. In order for this to work, your disk array, operating system, and LVM must support alternative paths to the same disk.

Redundant disk array hardware.   Due to all the potential single points of failure in any cabinet, it is always best to mirror between two or more disk arrays.

Cabinets and racks.   Never put all of the disks from one volume in the same rack. Mirror between separate racks and cabinets. Racks and cabinets are not failure-proof. They can collapse or topple; shelves can come loose and fall; liquids can spill down them; power cords can be pulled (most cabinets run on just one power cord); circuits controlling a cabinet can blow; they can be moved (most of them are on wheels, after all), pulling or breaking cables; ceilings can fall on them. And what happens if the doors on your cabinet get locked and you cannot find the key?

Cables.   Always run two sets of cables along separate and distinct paths. Never run them in the same conduit. Beware of electrical or magnetic interference. If pairs of cables are being run outside, never, ever put them in the same conduit: Backhoe problems are a real possibility. Always leave slack in your cables, and tie them down so that if they are pulled, the pressure point is the tie-down, not the connection to the system. And, of course, always use the screw-ins to fasten your cables securely into their connectors. Neatness in cable runs is good (but don't be a maniac about it). (We'll discuss cables and some of these other issues in more detail in Chapter 10, "Data Centers and the Local Environment.")

Power management. Don't plug mirrored devices into the same power source or the same circuit. Be sure that your disk arrays have redundant power supplies and that the array can switch from one power supply to another without interrupting its service, or that if a power supply fails, the remaining ones provide enough juice to keep the array running without interruption.

Filesystem Recovery

Windows and Unix filesystems do a lot of their work in memory. This work gets written to the disk periodically, but most of the time there are filesystem changes in memory that have not yet made it to the disk. If the system crashes, these changes never do make it to the disk. If a disk operation had begun and did not complete, filesystem corruption can result.

Normally if corruption does occur, it is minor and correctable, but it must be corrected. If a running filesystem stumbles onto a corrupt region, unpredictable results can occur, including a total system panic and crash. (The original design decision to perform so much of the filesystem's work in memory was made for performance reasons; it is much more efficient to save up small disk writes in memory and make a bunch of writes in a group. The downside to this design is the potential loss of data that was in memory and never written to disk.)

The likeliest time for corruption to occur is when the system is brought down abruptly. Therefore at boot time, the system must check its filesystems for corruption. Any corruption that is found must be repaired. To handle this task, Windows provides the ScanDisk utility, while Unix provides fsck (File System ChecK). Both utilities read every data block in the filesystem and check it for consistency. Even though more than 99 percent of the filesystem is just fine, all blocks must be examined. There are no shortcuts. These checks can take hours on a system with many large filesystems. Even a small filesystem can take an inconvenient amount of time to regain consistency. The rule of thumb is that fsck takes about a minute per gigabyte of disk space. During this period, the system is unusable.

Fortunately, one technology can overcome this loss of availability. A Journaled File System (JFS) can reduce disk check times by better than 99 percent. A JFS reserves a small chunk of disk space for a journal or intent log. When a write occurs that would cause corruption if only partially completed, an entry is written to the journal before the write is performed. The journal entry contains enough information for the filesystem to re-create the transaction. If the system crashes after the journal entry is written, but before the actual data write is performed, the fsck or ScanDisk will read the journal and re-create the data write. If the system crashes before the journal entry is written, then the transaction is lost. The parts of the disk where no transactions were occurring are simply not touched by the filesystem checker, resulting in a tremendous time savings. JFSs usually complete their `fscks` in a few seconds.

The size of the filesystem has no bearing at all on the duration of the filesystem check. With a journaled filesystem, the log consistency check can be completed in a few seconds. The end result is a great increase in overall system availability.

Key Points

- Disks contain data, one of the two most important assets of your entire business, and they must be treated as the critical resources that they are.

- Before you work to protect any other component of your system, protect the data.

- Mirroring (RAID-1) is the best way to protect your data from hardware failure online.

- It is better to mirror disks across controllers and between disk arrays than to confine mirrors to a single cabinet.

CHAPTER

8

SAN, NAS, and Virtualization

The fastest I/O is the one that doesn't move any data.
—Mark Erickson

In this chapter, we take a look at three storage-related technologies. Two of them (NAS and virtualization) have been around for quite some time, but their names haven't been as well known until more recent times. SAN, on the other hand, is a new technology that is most commonly associated with an older one, Fibre Channel. Fibre Channel was begun in the late 1980s, but SANs did not begin to take hold in the market until the late 1990s; the first recorded sighting of the term SAN was in a 1996 whitepaper from Gadzoox.

SAN and NAS are often seen as competitive technologies. In fact, the two are quite compatible with each other and are often seen moving the same data to different parts of the same enterprise.

Because the technologies are all storage-related, we are still on Level 3 of the Availability Index, as shown in Figure 8.1.

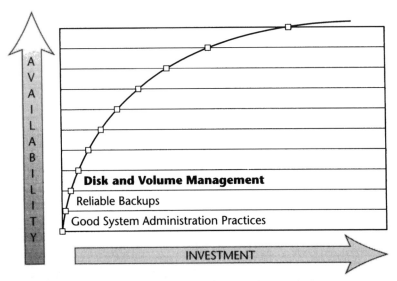

Figure 8.1   Level 3 of the Availability Index.

Storage Area Networks (SANs)

Back in the Dark Ages of client/server storage (the mid-1980s), disks were connected directly to hosts through several different interconnects, the two most popular being Integrated Drive Electronics (IDE) and SCSI. For the amount of data being stored and transferred at the time, this was a perfectly sound way to connect the high-speed computers of the day to their high-speed data storage devices. Both technologies allowed several (up to seven for SCSI and up to two for IDE) disks to be connected to the same computer interface, while data flowed at around 5 to 10MB/second.

As computer systems grew faster and storage requirements increased, SCSI disks no longer physically fit inside their server cabinets, and so they were put in external storage cabinets. But then SCSI's cable length limitations became a problem. Performance also became a problem because all those disks had to contend with the limited bandwidth and processing speed of their host computers. Fibre Channel was applied to this problem in the early 1990s, giving storage interconnects much higher rates of performance, and increasing the allowable distance between system and storage from just a few meters up to 10 kilometers or more.

Connections began to be made through a new protocol, called Fibre Channel Arbitrated Loop, which allowed more disks and more storage to be connected to an individual host. FC-AL was physically arranged in either the traditional loop structure, as shown in Figure 8.2, or with a hub in a star-shaped configuration that still functioned logically as a loop. Soon after, Fibre Channel switches started to come down in price (it was the high cost of these switches that forced early Fibre Channel configurations into hub-based loop configurations).

Once switches achieved more market acceptance through lower prices, the loop became a fabric, and SAN storage could be shared between more hosts in more complex arrangements than ever before. This new architecture, depicted in the previous chapter in Figure 7.5, greatly increased the throughput and ease of management of the network.

The difference between a hub and a switch is that a hub has a minimum of internal electronics; it merely takes a frame (essentially the same thing as a data packet in the SCSI world) and passes it on, with no processing being done to it along the way. A hub can only handle a single frame at a time, which can seriously limit the capacity of a SAN that depends on it. A switch creates virtual network routes between the devices that are communicating. A switch with 32 ports can have as many as 16 separate routes running through it simultaneously, as half of the ports are talking to the other half of the ports. Hubs are simple and relatively inexpensive; it is becoming fairly common to find Fibre Channel hubs being built into high-end RAID arrays. Switches remain independent boxes that are often mounted into a data center rack.

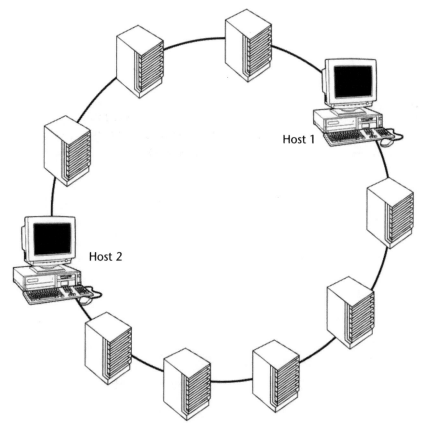

Figure 8.2   Fibre Channel arbitrated loop.

Whether the Fibre Channel is arranged in a loop, a fabric, or a combination of the two, it still functions as a network.

Since SAN technology is relatively new and standards have not been widely adopted, the components can be extremely expensive, although prices have begun to drop in recent times. We have seen cases where the cost of a host bus adapter (HBA, the card that plugs into a server allowing it to connect to a SAN) costs more than the whole server. The networking components that sit on the SAN, including hubs and switches, can also be prohibitively expensive. Costs will continue to fall over the next few years, but in the meantime, SANs will continue to be a significant expense for most organizations.

Why SANs?

Several significant benefits can be realized through the proper implementation of storage area networks. The following are some of these benefits:

- Storage centralization and consolidation
- Sharing storage
- Reduced network loads
- Faster backups
- Improved data access

Let's take a brief look at each of these.

Storage Centralization and Consolidation

Storage requirements have grown at dramatic rates over the last few years, as applications like email, file sharing, and web services have become more and more prevalent. As each of these applications become more widely used, in fact, each pushes the use of even more storage (for example, as more people use email, the amount of email that is sent to each email user increases). As a result, each host on a network must be connected to more and more individual disks. In order to effectively manage this growth, many system administrators have chosen to centralize and consolidate their storage, as it is easier to manage pooled storage and a smaller number of larger storage arrays than it is to manage lots of small islands of storage scattered around an enterprise.

As storage needs continued to change, and storage had to be reallocated from one host to another, administrators quickly learned how difficult it was to move this storage around. SANs allow storage to be placed into a centralized pool that can be easily allocated and reallocated between the hosts on that SAN. Administrators may have purchased enough storage, only to find that it has been connected to the wrong server. They no longer have to tell their managers that even though there is an unused terabyte of storage on *that* host, *bonnie*, we need to buy another terabyte so that we can have it for *this* host, *clyde*. With a SAN, the unused terabyte can be reallocated, entirely through software, from *bonnie* to *clyde*.

When storage is physically (or at least logically; SANs do not require all the storage to be physically colocated for it to be centrally managed) centralized, it can be administered from a central console, by a small team of administrators, often just one administrator. Centralized storage can also be backed up more easily to a centrally located set of SAN-capable tape drives or disks. The result of both of these centralizations is a reduction in complexity (complexity is, of course, the sworn enemy of high availability) and in management costs, freeing up resources for other projects.

SAN management is often performed with the combination of a whiteboard in the system administrator's office and a spreadsheet. Often, the information on the whiteboard and in the spreadsheet are not up-to-date, and sometimes they completely contradict each other. Modern SAN management software eliminates the need to use these old-fashioned tools, replacing them with modern methods that can build and maintain a full-blown database, and that can discover new storage and new hosts as they are added to the SAN, simplifying management even further.

One problem that has plagued SANs in recent years is that there are so many different vendors, each offering different products and components, with different revision levels. The result is a morass of combinations and permutations that ensure that virtually no two SANs have exactly the same combination of hardware, firmware, and software, and that nobody could possibly have tested all of the combinations. In many cases, the combinations are not only untested, but they genuinely don't work. The introduction of just one bad component can cause problems across the entire SAN in totally new and unexpected ways that can be extremely difficult to isolate. The promise of SANs cannot be fully realized until the vendors can develop a basic set of standards that allow all of the different vendors to play together. We sincerely hope that by the time you read these words most of these compatibility problems have been solved.

Sharing Data

Since there are many hosts connected to many storage devices in a SAN, the question invariably arises: Can we share data between the different hosts on the SAN? The answer is a very qualified yes.

The fundamental problem with two systems accessing the piece of data on the same disk at the same time is that standard operating systems and disk management software do not know how to arbitrate between these parallel requests, particularly if one of those requests is a write. The most benign outcome of such a conflict is probably a system crash from one or more of the hosts. Data corruption, potentially large-scale, is another potential, and far more serious, outcome.

There are SAN-based software packages available, often called *clustered filesystems* and *volume managers*, that permit multiple systems to have parallel access to shared data. The limitation of these packages is that they do not permit data sharing between systems running different operating systems. We expect this limitation to be overcome during the next few years.

A simpler application of shared storage is the migration of the right to access a set of disks from one system to another. In this case, *huntley* gracefully gives up its access to one set of disks, and they are passed to a second system, *brinkley*. This is precisely what happens in a clustered failover, which we will discuss in more detail in Chapter 15, "Local Clustering and Failover." This passing of data and disks from one system to another also occurs manually when an older *huntley* is being retired and replaced by a newer and faster *brinkley*, or when data and systems are being migrated from one data center to another on the same SAN.

Reduced Network Loads

In the mid-1950s, when the United States started to build the Interstate Highway System, a new network of high-speed, high-capacity highways was added to the existing infrastructure of smaller roads around the country. The result, of course, was a lessening of traffic on the smaller roads, as cars took to the newer and faster roads. But since the roads could support more cars, people bought more cars, keeping the roads quite busy. (So that's why the Interstate near your house is always under construction.)

As a new network of SANs is added to data centers and enterprises that previously had just LANs, the result is a significant increase in the amount of data that can be moved, as well as in the speed at which that data is moved. Of course, since SANs are bigger and faster, organizations implement new applications that take advantage of the new bandwidth, keeping the networks quite busy.

One of the biggest performance improvements that SANs have enabled is in backups. In many organizations, the single biggest load on LANs comes from backups. By moving backups from LANs to faster SANs, the results are less congested LANs and faster backups.

More Efficient Backups

With the introduction of SAN-aware tape drives and libraries, not only have the management costs of backups been reduced, but so have the hardware costs. With SANs, it is no longer necessary to purchase separate tape drives for each large data server. Instead, with proper backup software pushing the data, tape drives can be connected to the SAN and shared among the SAN-connected hosts, which are usually large data servers. The result is a significant reduction in the number of tape drives and libraries that are required for backups, saving the enterprise considerable amounts of capital.

A new technique has been developed specifically for SANs that can speed up backups even more. This technique, third-party copy, uses specialized hardware called *data movers* to copy data from disk storage to tape, without all of the network overhead that standard backup methods bring along. The result is backups that run even faster, and with less of an impact on hosting servers. Data movers are available from companies like Chaparral Network Storage and Crossroads Systems.

Generally, SANs are faster than LANs, and so backups that send their data across the LAN will be faster and more efficient that those that use a LAN.

A Brief SAN Hardware Primer

Like so many new technologies, SANs come with their own terminology and hardware menagerie. Although we cannot teach you all there is to know about SANs in this brief section, we will end our discussion of SANs with a quick look at the important hardware components that make up SANs and that you'll need to be familiar with if you are thinking about implementing one.

Three types of devices connect to a SAN: initiators, targets, and interconnects. Initiators put requests onto the SAN. Those requests travel through interconnecting devices until they arrive at a target. Targets service the request and send the response across the same interconnecting devices in the opposite direction, until they arrive back at the initiator.

Host bus adapter.   The host bus adapter (or HBA) is an adapter board that sits in a host computer and initiates all communication between the host and the SAN. If a device requests information from storage on a SAN, then that device requires an HBA. The device could even be a computer system, or an intelligent tape drive that does its backups directly from the SAN-based storage, or a data mover.

Switches.   The backbone of the SAN architecture, they provide a high-speed interconnect between different devices on the SAN, and they route blocks of data from one device to another.

Fabric.   The virtual infrastructure that is formed by all of the interconnected switches on a SAN.

Router.   A router connects two different protocols, such as Fibre Channel to Ethernet, in a many-to-one or many-to-many configuration.

Bridge.   A bridge is a router that only supports one-to-one connections. In the SAN world, the terms router and bridge are often used interchangeably.

Hub. A hub is simply a box with a number of ports that devices can be connected to. Hubs share their bandwidth between all connected devices, and do not introduce any intelligence or management onto the SAN.

To learn more about SANs, please visit the Storage Networking Industry Association's web site (`www.snia.org`). SNIA is the standards organization that actively promotes storage networking, and its membership includes nearly all of the vendors involved in the SAN space.

Network-Attached Storage (NAS)

In the earliest days of computing, IT architectures consisted of a central computer, called a mainframe, which was connected to large (for the time) monolithic storage devices. Users accessed mainframes via dumb terminals, which relied on the mainframe for all intelligence. When client/server architecture replaced mainframes, the intelligence that had been concentrated on the mainframe moved out to the edges of the network, as the dumb terminals were replaced by desktop workstations and, eventually, PCs.

Although users' workstations needed local storage for system maintenance and for a small set of operating system files that were local to each workstation, it was neither practical nor efficient for all of the storage to be replicated on each workstation. A method was needed to share files from the central server out to the workstation clients.

It was around this time that Sun developed its Network File System protocol (NFS, which we will discuss in more detail in Chapter 14, "Data and Web Services") and published the protocol specifications, so it quickly caught on and became the de facto standard for file sharing in the Unix environment. It has remained so ever since. NFS allowed users on distributed client workstations to access and share the files that were on the server as if they were local to their workstation, and started the client/server revolution in networked computers. Microsoft followed NFS a few years later with their Common Internet File System (CIFS), which has some architectural differences. Fundamentally, though, both protocols enable the easy sharing of files across a LAN.

NFS and CIFS are the two leading examples of Network-Attached Storage (NAS). Apple's AppleTalk is another example, but it generally runs only between Apple computers. NAS is a method of sharing filesystems from one server to one or more clients. The protocol handles the differences in architecture, so with NAS, it is possible, and in fact common, for a server running one operating system to share a filesystem with clients that run different operating systems. Since the filesystem is being shared, the client systems need not be concerned with the underlying physical disk hardware or layout.

Two primary kinds of computers can serve files in a NAS. One is a standard computer file server. Generally, in this environment, NFS is served by Sun or other Unix computers, and CIFS files are served by Windows systems. But there is at least one software product that allows a single server to serve the same files under both NFS and CIFS at the same time. It is called the TotalNET Advanced Server, or TAS, from LSI Logic (they acquired Syntax, the original developers of TAS, in 2002). In addition, a freeware, open source suite is available that provides file and print services to CIFS clients from Unix servers called Samba. For more information about Samba, please visit www .samba.org.

The other kind of NAS server is called a filer, or an appliance. Standard computers serve files while doing other general work. Filers, on the other hand, are dedicated systems that run small operating systems with limited capabilities beyond sharing files. Filers usually share files faster than general-purpose computers, and can do so to both Unix and Windows environments. Filers tend to be much more expensive than general-purpose computers, though, and offer limited additional capabilities. It can be difficult to cluster filers, to back them up, or to replicate their data without using additional computing resources beyond the filers themselves. While this limited functionality may seem like a knock against filers, in fact, their manufacturers offer it as a genuine benefit. By limiting the functionality of filers, manufacturers are able to squeeze every bit of I/O performance out of their systems, while keeping them extremely simple to use. Filers are managed with a minimum of effort, as there aren't very many buttons or knobs that require attention.

Filers offer other significant advantages, too, including consolidation of storage resources onto a single system and often-outstanding performance. Network Appliance (www.netapp.com) is one of the leading vendors of NAS filers. They have a large product line of both hardware and software to enable Network-Attached Storage.

SAN or NAS: Which Is Better?

So, which should you use, SAN or NAS? The answer to this question, like so many others we've discussed in this book, is "It depends."

Both technologies offer the ability to achieve higher levels of availability and high-speed data access, but each has advantages and disadvantages. In the end, though, it's not an either-or decision; you can easily implement both NAS and SAN if that is what your environment requires. Both can support varied levels of RAID on their storage. Both can share files without regard for their format or contents.

For applications where many servers will be sharing large amounts of data, SAN is better. SAN is better for large backups and for high-speed file sharing, where speed and bandwidth are the primary concerns.

In a SAN, hosts and storage communicate directly. In a NAS environment, the client does not communicate directly with the storage. Instead, requests go through another computer, a server. The server processes the request with data on its local disks and sends data back to the client via a multilayered protocol (NFS running on top of TCP/IP, running on an Ethernet, for example). As a result, given similar network hardware, SAN tends to run faster than NAS, although it is very difficult to make absolute statements about performance. If you are concerned about performance, be sure to run benchmarks that match your local environment as closely as possible.

In a NAS, servers deliver filesystems to their clients. Any mirroring or other volume management is performed at a lower level, and the clients do not see it. This greatly reduces the administrative overhead of NAS on clients. In a SAN, on the other hand, hosts on the SAN see disk blocks. Any work to combine or arrange the disk blocks must be done on each client. If SAN-based hosts attempt to write to the shared disks when or where they should not, the result can be data corruption, as the different hosts get confused about what is on the disks.

Building a SAN can be a very complex endeavor. Many different components from many different vendors are required, and not all combinations are compatible, or have even been tested together. It is very likely that SANs will become much easier to build and administer over the coming years, but they have a very long way to go before they are as easy to manage as a filer, which, as we said earlier, is little more than a black box with few, if any, buttons and knobs.

NAS tends to be a much less expensive solution to deploy than SANs, since it employs older and more standardized technology. While a single HBA for a SAN can cost around $1,000 (a number that is sure to drop significantly over time), a 100Mbit Ethernet card can cost less than $20. In a large network with lots of hosts, the cost savings for NAS will be quite significant. But the performance with NAS can be significantly slower.

NAS can be implemented on top of your existing Ethernet-based networking infrastructure (assuming the Ethernet has additional capacity, of course), while SANs require an entire new infrastructure based on Fibre Channel optical cabling, further increasing their cost.

SANs can stretch over greater distances than NAS. While it's difficult to say what the upper limit is for the size of a SAN (it seems to change every 45 minutes), 50–80 kilometers is a sure bet. If you need a SAN to stretch beyond that limit, it may be possible; speak with your SAN vendors. NASs can be stretched over several kilometers with the inclusion of repeaters and other expensive hardware, which will also slow down the performance of the network. If you wish to stretch a NAS over unusually long distances, be sure you work closely with your vendor and you benchmark everything very carefully.

OFF TO THE RACES: SOME THOUGHTS ON BENCHMARKS

Throughout this book, we often discuss application and data performance, and when we do, we usually mention benchmarks and performance analysis. Benchmarks are the best way to measure the performance of an application, but like so many other useful tools, they can be useful in the hands of a well-trained professional and dangerous in the hands of an amateur.

Nearly every vendor, hardware, operating system, networking, and application, offers benchmark results, and not remarkably, these results always indicate that their products are much faster than their competitors' products. This is, of course, because vendors naturally publish the benchmarks that make their products look best. And by publishing benchmarks, they hope that they will prevent their customers and prospects from taking the time to run their own, with results that may not be quite so positive.

The real questions are how can every vendor's benchmarks indicate that their products are the fastest, and how does this apply to your environment?

The answer is that most vendor benchmarks are useless to most of their customers. (It is very interesting to note, by the way, that some vendors have rather remarkable clauses in their sales contracts that specifically prohibit their customers from running performance benchmarks on their equipment for any reason.) Computer performance is the result of dozens of complex variables that can interact in unpredictable ways, and by finding the exact combination of variables that puts their product in the best light (and their competition in the worst), vendors can make some fairly outrageous claims that often have little validity in real-life scenarios.

To be fair, there are some standard benchmark suites that have been run reliably across different platforms and applications for a long time. Although these benchmarks certainly allow for a fairer comparison between different hardware and software combinations, unless the conditions under which they were run match your environment precisely, they are still not especially valuable.

When a comparative benchmark is taken, and only one variable has been changed, the result is an interesting study that shows the benefits of the new variable. But, again, whether that variable will work as well in your own environment cannot be determined without running similar benchmarks in that environment.

The only way to be sure that a product's performance will be adequate for your computing environment is to run your own benchmark in an environment that is as close to the production environment in which the deployed products will run as possible. That means that the test environment must include the same system hardware, the same storage hardware, the same networking and interconnects, the same type and size of data, the same applications, the same user loads, the same system loads, the same number of active users on the system, and so much more. What's more, all software and firmware must be at the same patch levels. Despite all of this, if you run the same benchmark 10 different times, you can easily get 10 different sets of results.

(continued)

OFF TO THE RACES: SOME THOUGHTS ON BENCHMARKS *(continued)*

Sound difficult? You bet it is. But it's the only way for your benchmarks to have any relevance to your environment. As soon as you change even one variable, the benchmark loses most, if not all, of its relevance. And if the benchmark isn't relevant, why take the time and effort to run it?

SANs are much more cutting-edge than NAS. They can feel much more like a science project than NAS. It is not yet impossible to call a single vendor and say, "Give me a SAN." On the other hand, there are plenty of vendors who can implement a complete NAS solution running on a LAN. As newer technology, SANs are much more vulnerable to sporadic and hard-to-diagnose problems, although that will become less and less of a problem as the technology matures.

NAS tends to come in a one-size-fits-all model, while SANs have many more variables and choices. SANs are usually custom-designed for the application that will use them, accounting for required performance, resilience to failures and outages, backup speed, budgetary requirements, and many other factors. While NAS takes these features into account, in return for their simplicity, you get fewer choices.

SAN-connected disks look and feel to their computers like local disks. Even disks that are spread over many kilometers for increased availability act and feel the same as direct-attached storage. NAS-based disks are not directly attached to the clients who access them, and so they are somewhat more difficult to manage. SAN-attached disks can, for example, be mirrored, even over long distances. NAS-attached disks must be mirrored on the system to which they are directly attached. In this way, SAN-attached disks have more flexibility than NAS disks do.

Hosts in a SAN are peers. They share their data, but all of the SAN-attached hosts are equal; no node is more important than another. In a NAS configuration, there is a hierarchical relationship between the hosts. One host is serving data to one or more clients. (As we will discuss in Chapter 14, NAS servers are often both servers and clients; it is important that the relationship between them be hierarchical to limit the effects of a failure of one of the servers. In a circular relationship, all servers can be adversely affected. In a hierarchy, only lower-level servers will be affected.)

A SAN is an excellent solution for applications with the following conditions:

- High bandwidth requirements
- Parallel applications (such as Oracle RAC)
- Distributed or shared applications
- Large amounts of data to back up on a regular basis

NAS is a superior solution when the following conditions exist:

- Centralized storage management is needed.
- There is a small amount of storage.
- Cost is a major deciding factor.
- Little or no growth is expected in the environment.
- Many different client platforms and operating systems are involved.
- Complex administration is not desired or appropriate.

Even that is not the end of the discussion, though. In the early days of SANs, the conventional wisdom was that it was either SAN or NAS. One or the other. Black or white. In fact, it is easy to combine SAN and NAS into a single infrastructure that many organizations find quite reasonable and sensible. An example of a joint SAN and NAS environment is shown in Figure 8.3, where the two networks are bridged by *GWbridge*, which serves as both a NAS server and a member of the SAN. *GWbridge* acts as the link between the two environments, retrieving data requested by its NFS and CIFS clients from the SAN.

Since the clients *manhattan, bronx,* and *queens* do not have or require significant amounts of local storage, there is no good reason to put them onto the SAN, especially considering the financial cost to do so. However, the hosts on the SAN, in the top part of the diagram, are larger servers, directly connected to large storage arrays.

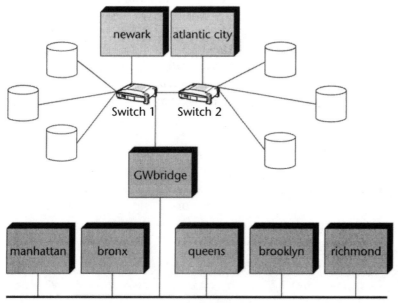

Figure 8.3 A joint SAN and NAS environment.

Storage Virtualization

Virtual is certainly one of the third millennium's favorite adjectives. We have virtual reality (www.vrs.org.uk, among others), virtual hospitals (http://vh.org), virtual libraries (http://icom.museum/vlmp), and virtual universities (http://vu.org). There are virtual florists (www.virtualflowers.com), virtual museums (http://archive.comlab.ox.ac.uk/other/museums/computing.html), and one global travel company who styles its web service as *Virtually There* (www.virtually there.com). And if you can't make it in person, you can even visit virtual Finland (http://virtual.finland.fi) and virtual Jerusalem (www.virtual jerusalem.com).

Webster's Dictionary defines virtual as "being such in essence or effect though not formally recognized or admitted."[1] A visit to the virtual florist may enable a web surfer to buy and send flowers, but she does so without the experience of actually visiting a flower shop. The smells are missing, as are many of the sights, certainly the three-dimensional ones (at least at this writing). She can enjoy much of the experience, perhaps enough of the experience to satisfy a particular need, but some parts of the experience will be missing.

When we turn the discussion to virtual storage, we start by looking at the fundamental physical components of online storage, namely disk drives.[2] Fundamentally, all disk drives store data and (usually) offer it up when requested to do so. Yet each device is quite different from the others in terms of performance, capacity, power consumption, physical makeup, and other characteristics.

A virtual storage device, then, is a storage device in essence, but it is not formally a storage device. That's not a very practical definition, though (perhaps it's a virtual definition). A more useful definition might be that a virtual storage device is a combination of one or more physical storage devices that are addressed by applications, users, and other devices, as a single device. A single computer system may contain one or more virtual devices. Virtual disks are more commonly referred to as logical disks, to differentiate them from physical disks.

One of the most interesting aspects to storage virtualization is that despite the attention that it has received in the press over the last few years, it is not new technology. The concept of storage virtualization dates back at least as far as the earliest specifications for RAID,[3] where disks are combined and addressed in combination as a single entity.

---

[1] www.webster.com/cgi-bin/dictionary

[2] Of course there are many other kinds of storage devices, including tapes and tape drives, CD-ROMs, DVD-ROMs, floppy disks, Zip drives, and a pile of different formats of memory cards. For the purposes of this discussion, we will only be concerning ourselves with disk drives.

[3] In 1988, a landmark paper called "A Case for Redundant Arrays of Inexpensive Disks" was published by the University of California at Berkeley. It can be found online at www-2.cs.cmu.edu/~garth/RAIDpaper/Patterson88.pdf.

As disk capacity and user requirements for disk space have grown, along with the speed of the media that connect the disks together, storage virtualization has become more important, and more applications have been developed.

Why Use Virtual Storage?

Data storage devices are simple devices with simple measures of quality:

Availability. If the data is not available, dependent applications will fail to function properly or in a useful manner.

I/O Performance. More and more, the speed with which data can be accessed determines the performance and even the viability of applications. For example, if data cannot be delivered at the rate required by a video player, a video-on-demand application is not viable. If credit card databases cannot be updated fast enough, queues of disgruntled customers develop at checkout lines. As we repeat throughout this book, performance is most assuredly an element of availability.

Cost of capacity. While the price of raw storage is falling at a dizzying rate, the consumption of storage is increasing at an equally dizzying speed. Therefore, the cost of delivered storage capacity remains a factor.

Manageability. Conventional IT wisdom says that the management of systems and components is the most rapidly increasing cost of owning and processing computer systems. The consensus among industry analysts like Gartner and Forrester indicates that over the life of a set of storage, management of that storage costs between 5 and 10 times as much as the initial purchase. Management costs therefore become an important measure of quality. In particular, storage devices that support effective management of more bytes of data by a single manager are seen as superior to devices that require more management. (Be wary, though, of claims that fewer administrators can manage one vendor's storage over another's. It may be a valid claim, or it may be nothing more than a false benefit that is derived from overworking system administrators rather than from any great economy that a product delivers.)

The case for virtualizing storage is equally simple. Storage virtualization improves one or more of these qualities, increasing the value that an enterprise can derive from its data storage assets. For example:

- *Striping* (RAID-0) data addresses across several disk drives to create a virtual volume increases I/O performance and extends the scope of management.

- *Mirroring* (RAID-1) data across two or more disk drives increases availability and performance.

■ *Aggregating* low-cost disk drives under software control decreases the cost of storage capacity.

These virtualization methods were discussed in more detail in Chapter 7, "Highly Available Data Management."

Types of Storage Virtualization

For our purposes, there are two primary kinds of storage virtualization: filesystem virtualization and block virtualization.

Filesystem Virtualization

Filesystems can also be virtualized in at least two ways. Remote file servers run filesystems that are perceived by client applications as running on the client computers, even though they are not. Two famous examples of this technology are NFS and CIFS, as discussed earlier in this chapter. More recently, technology that aggregates multiple filesystems into a single large file store has appeared. In both cases, applications access files without regard for their physical locations, while system administrators reap the management benefits of consolidated file storage for multiple applications running on multiple (possibly diverse) servers.

Block Virtualization

Block virtualization is the most common type of disk drive virtualization, and the one that we spend the remainder of this section examining. Under block virtualization, the disk blocks from a set of disks are logically brought together so that they appear as a single virtual block device, commonly called a *virtual disk* or *volume*. The disks may be combined to form mirrors and stripes, or they simply may be appended or concatenated together to increase available disk space.

Since the underlying physical structures beneath virtual disks are standard physical disks, applications that use physical disk drives can use virtual disks without modification. The applications can expect the exact same sorts of responses from their local operating system whether they are writing to real or virtual disks. When data is written to, or read from, a logical disk, the arrangement of physical disks within is irrelevant. Data is simply written to the volume. The control software (a volume manager, for example) takes care of distributing the writes to mirrored or striped disks.

Block virtualization can be managed by software that runs in three different places:

1. The RAID system or disk array.

2. The host computer system.

3. SAN infrastructure components.

We look at each of these in the following.

Block Virtualization in the Disk Array

When the virtualization takes place within a disk array, its reach is generally restricted to the array itself and any computer systems that are connected to the array. In general, a single instance of array-based virtualization software cannot support disks from multiple arrays.

The processors in RAID controllers often have the advantages of being highly optimized for their purpose and of having access to specialized auxiliary hardware for boosting performance. Most enterprise RAID systems can connect to and provide storage services to more than one application server, either through multiple parallel SCSI server ports or by connecting to a storage network.

Block Virtualization in the Application Server

When the virtualization takes place in host-based software, its reach is limited to the one system and any disks that are connected to that system, even if those disks are in multiple disk arrays from multiple vendors and connected to the host via different interconnection technologies.

Server-based volume managers are generally available for most computers at lower intrinsic cost than RAID systems. Volume managers typically enable disk drives of different types to be aggregated and virtualized. The virtual block devices presented by a RAID controller are often further virtualized by a volume manager running on an application server. This property can be exploited to improve I/O performance and data availability, for example, by mirroring or striping data between two RAID systems or by making virtual devices available on multiple access paths.

Block Virtualization in the Storage Network

The advantage to managing the virtualization in the SAN is that the reach of the virtualization is greater than with either server-based or array-based virtualization. The limit of either one server or one disk array is eliminated. There are, however, other disadvantages that SAN-based virtualization introduces.

There are two different styles of SAN-based virtualization, commonly referred to as in-band and out-of-band. Both styles have advantages and disadvantages, as compared with each other and compared with application server-based and RAID array-based virtualization.

> **In-band storage virtualization.**   Under an in-band storage virtualization model, a "virtualization box" sits on the SAN. All data traffic flows through the box, which manages all of the virtualization. (When this box manages the virtualization, it responds to a request to read from blocks 400 through 600 of virtual disk 1 by issuing the actual request to the

physical disk or disks containing those virtual blocks.) Today, the virtualization box is usually a standard small computer.

There are two problems with the virtualization box model. The first is that the box represents a bottleneck for the entire SAN. All SAN traffic must flow into the box, be processed, and then flow out again. If the virtualization is being handled by a single standard PC, it is unlikely that the PC can keep up with the I/O load. A larger system that could handle more traffic will, at least at today's prices, be prohibitively expensive. The second problem is more easily solved: The virtualization box is a single point of failure for the whole SAN. The solution is to cluster the box.

Out-of-band storage virtualization.   In an out-of-band virtualization model, traffic does not flow through the centralized virtualization box at all. Instead, the routing of traffic from the virtual disks to the physical disks is handled directly on the clients. Only the instructions and rules for the virtualization are handled on the central box.

There are still a couple of downsides to this model, though. Every member of the SAN that uses the virtualization must have software installed on it, which introduces administrative overhead, as well as consumes some CPU and memory on each client. If the clients are different platforms, or run different operating systems, then the code for each client must be managed separately and kept in sync. If a bug in one version of the software causes a client to write to the wrong piece of physical disk, data corruption is inevitable, and probably irreparable. While this data corruption could occur if all clients had the same OS, it becomes much more likely as the software variations increase.

Virtualization and Quality of Service

One of the trends that we see coming from this rediscovery of virtualization technology is the virtualization of service quality. In the past, the levels of service afforded to different critical applications would generally be defined haphazardly for each application. The use of backups, mirroring, clustering, replication, and other data and system protection methods would be applied to different applications as they were needed, but with little or no consistency from one application to the next.

Under virtualized Quality of Storage (QoS), an enterprise clearly defines a few (often three or four) levels of service that it wishes to make available to its applications. For our purposes, consider the service levels shown in Table 8.1. We have defined three levels of service, which we call Gold, Silver, and Bronze, and we have assigned each of our system applications to one of these levels of service.

Table 8.1 An Example of Virtualized Levels of Service

QUALITY OF SERVICE	DISK PROTECTION	SYSTEM PROTECTION	BACKUPS	APPLICATIONS	RELATIVE COST
Gold	Triple mirrored	Clustered locally and remotely	Daily fulls, with replicated indexes	ERP, CRM, customer-facing e-commerce	$$$$$
Silver	Double mirrored	Clustered locally	Weekly fulls, nightly incrementals	E-mail, software development, accounts receivable	$$$
Bronze	RAID-5	Not clustered	Monthly fulls and weekly incrementals	Accounts payable, payroll, marketing	$

We have, of course, chosen these levels of service and assigned these applications to them rather arbitrarily. Different organizations will have wildly differing requirements.

The point is that by virtualizing these levels of service, a technique that is made easier with SAN-virtualized storage, it becomes much easier to set and deliver service levels across the enterprise. It's also easier to determine how much each application must pay the system administrative staff to deliver their required levels of service. Obviously, gold service will cost a great deal more than silver or bronze, but for applications like ERP and CRM, which can be the lifeblood of the organizations who run them, it is worth the added expense to keep those applications running a greater percentage of the time.

Key Points

- NAS and virtualization are not new technologies, but rather are new names for things that have been around the computing industry for several years.

- NAS is a simpler and less expensive technology than SAN, and it is better equipped for sharing data in a client/server environment.

- SAN is a more complex and often very expensive technology that is best for moving data between servers with large data stores, and for clustering and parallel applications.

- Virtualization is a method for hiding the complex inner workings of a technology such as storage and replacing it with simpler and more flexible representations.

CHAPTER 9

Networking

I live in a crumbling and defective world.
—Scott Adams, in *The Dilbert Future*

Bob Metcalfe, inventor of Ethernet and technology writer, is fond of saying that the power of networked computer systems goes up exponentially; as you connect them together, their aggregate usefulness increases as the square of the number of systems. Metcalfe's Law has a dark side as well: The complexity of these systems and the number of potential failure modes also increase exponentially as they grow. Often, network failures cause the same symptoms as a server failure, and to the user sitting impatiently with an hourglass cursor on her screen: The server is simply "not there." Whether it's a failed router, a network flooded with unwanted traffic, a broken network interface card, or a server crash, the user is going to see the same client-side behavior until the problem is resolved.

Networking moves us up to Level 4 in the Availability Index, as shown in Figure 9.1. We've moved away from a collection of components treated as a single system to a network of things that have to operate together. In our discussion of SANs, the network fabric between hosts and disks represented something of a virtual cabling harness, with well-known endpoints and a well-managed topology. That specificity and neatness goes away at Level 4, so much of this chapter is devoted to looking at how things break when you are dealing with an open-ended system that includes "the Internet masses."

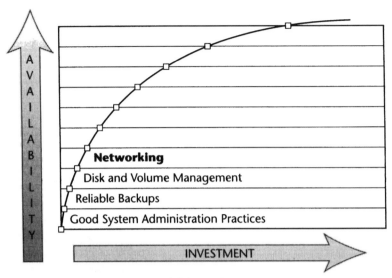

Figure 9.1 Level 4 of the Availability Index.

In this chapter, we look at several ways in which networks fail and methods that you can use to engineer reliability in the face of those failures. We also cover key network services, how you can determine whether your network is recoverable after any type of service failure, and how to detect certain network conditions that appear to be failures. As in previous chapters, we start with the fundamental building blocks and demonstrate how to assemble them without single points of failure, with an eye toward management and monitoring. Using the redundant host and redundant network design rules for building platforms, the following chapters will cover application-level engineering concerns to complete our bottom-up approach to high-availability design.

Network Failure Taxonomy

Network failures are difficult to detect with certainty, due to several factors, including the transient nature of many network overload or performance problems, the ability of IP networks to self-heal or route around single points of failure, and the tendency to equate periods of high network latency with network failures. This section covers the different types of failures that networks should tolerate in order to achieve a level of high availability, along with some mechanisms for detecting these failures.

Network Reliability Challenges

On the surface, adding redundancy and reliability to a network should be no more difficult than solving the split-brain problem that we discuss in detail in Chapter 15, "Local Clustering and Failover." However, all of a host's resources are contained within or controlled by the system. In the network, resources are highly distributed, have multiple points of control, and are subject to outside forces. Network reliability poses several challenges to the system management team:

Network failures come and go. A period of very high traffic, followed by a lull in activity, followed by another peak, may appear to be a prolonged failure. In this case, network latency and network failure produce the same client-side symptoms. Measurement and monitoring tools must be able to distinguish between the two cases, and network segregation techniques provide isolation and protection against some forms of traffic-driven meltdowns.

It's hard to define where the network is. A typical path from a PC to a server located in a machine room on the same campus will touch a switch or LAN concentrator in a local office wiring closet, a router or two in the same building, another router entering the data center building, and one or more machine room high-speed networking switches. Add in network interface cards on PC, server, routers, and switches, and you have a dozen or more points of failure. What if the backplane on a switch fails? Or one outbound interface card on a router? Each one of these pieces of equipment may be controlled by a different operations organization, adding a people angle to the complexity.

Latency contributes to perceived network failures. A router that is overloaded or dropping packets in the middle of a long network path will greatly impact end-to-end reliability. Network design and traffic management help to reduce network latency, or at least control it, but it remains an external factor in service reliability measurement.

Denial-of-service attacks are real. Most simply, a denial-of-service attack means that a user cannot get access to a host or network service because all of the input capacity is tied up dealing with bogus requests. Here's a simple example using the ever-popular bank teller model: Five people simultaneously cash their paychecks, take the amount in pennies and unwrap them, then ask to deposit the pennies by counting them. All other bank customers queued for a teller are stuck while the bogus requests are handled. All "real work" is held pending while the annoyance requests are serviced.

Load balancing is a scalability feature, not a reliability solution. Distributing input load over several servers allows horizontal scalability of a service; that is, the service capacity can be increased by adding more hosts that perform the same function (the "horizontal" notion probably comes from the profile you see entering the machine room, as the new servers increase the width of the server skyline). When a single server in a load-balancing configuration fails, or when one of the intermediate network components fails, recovery is still an issue. Reliability features can be added to load-balanced configurations to improve recovery time and overall uptime, but the simple load-balancing solution by itself does not improve end-to-end reliability. We'll look at horizontal scalability of web services in Chapter 14, "Data and Web Services."

Network access isn't as secure as it should be. Are all of the network interface jacks secured, or can anyone plug a random PC into the building LAN? Incorrectly configured hosts cause major network problems without any malicious intent. Network cables are also a common source of failures. Twisted pair cables are indistinguishable from telephone cables unless you look carefully at the RJ45 (or RJ11) connectors on the ends. Once you start running network cables in wiring raceways or near power circuits, you'll eventually find a mechanical failure that leads to a short, an open, or an intermittent failure in the network.

CLEANLINESS IS NEXT TO (NETWORK) CLEAVAGE

In a startup company, we used thinnet Ethernet to connect a few dozen workstations to our server room. We reconfigured partitions frequently to make room for new employees and ran the thinnet along the partition feet as a sort of informal cable raceway. After any minor network change, the cleaning service would, without fail (but entirely accidentally), vacuum up any cable that dangled dangerously far away from the sanctuary of the partitions. Next morning: network cleavage and some unhappy users. After the second or third time this happened, we got quite good at tracing the network segments from the repeater to successive workstations, breaking and testing the network as we went to locate the fault.

—Hal

Only end-to-end reliability counts in the networking arena. Redundant network interfaces and switches configured in pairs help to reduce the probability of a LAN failure, but without redundant routes, aggressive management and monitoring, and key service ruggedization, the overall client picture of reliability is greatly reduced. Adding this level of certainty to network services requires knowing how and why they break.

Network Failure Modes

Network failures create frustration because of the myriad failures possible when you combine host interfaces, cables, switches, routers, hubs, and network services like Dynamic Host Configuration Protocol (DHCP) or Domain Name Service (DNS). Understanding the different possible failures for a network of systems is critical for ensuring its availability; while you may not be subject to all of the corner cases, you need to know which ones are potential traps and how you'll avoid or manage your way out of them. Some of the most common network failures are:

Local network interface.   Typically on an I/O card with one or more network interfaces, the network interface represents the first point of potential failure between a host and the outside world. An I/O bus or partial backplane failure can make a network interface appear to have failed; however, these system-level failures usually cause other more easily noticed problems such as disk I/O failures or complete system crashes. In rare cases, devices on the I/O card fail, and the network interface is rendered inoperable.

Cabling.   Items subject to the highest degree of physical wear and tear tend to fail the most frequently. Cables connecting hosts to hubs or switches are near the top of this category, with failures that include a broken locking clip, causing the cable to fall out of the connector; a frayed conductor in the cable; or severe physical strain resulting in damage.

Network infrastructure equipment.   Hubs, switches, bridges, and other devices that sit below the IP layer are frequent contributors to network-level failures. It's not just physical failures that should give you pause; excessive load may cause packets to be dropped on the inbound side of a switch, resulting in an intermittent network outage.

Routers and route information.   At the IP layer, software, configuration, and even interoperability woes are also root causes of network outages. In 1998, AT&T lost part of a frame relay (FR) network due to a misconfigured router, resulting in a multiple-hour outage for some of its FR customers. Physical failures remain a possibility; however, IP networks are typically designed with some level of redundancy to handle router failures. That redundancy, reflected in the routing tables of hosts, is yet another source of network outages.

Key network services.   Even the simple act of deriving an IP address corresponding to a hostname requires talking to another host on the network, using a name service such as DHCP, NIS, or DNS. Networked filesystems like NFS and Windows SMB services, along with naming, directory, and security services, add to complexity of network operation. A failure in any of these services, caused by any of the failures previously noted or by a failure in the system software providing the service, usually results in a network outage.

Latency.   Excessive load, broadcast, Address Resolution Protocol (ARP) storms, or a denial-of-service attack render a network nearly useless as the useful throughput drops precipitously. While not a network failure per se, latency creates the illusion of an outage to the nodes connected to it, and it furthers our premise that performance is an aspect of availability.

The next sections explore the physical and logical failures in more detail, providing first-level detection mechanisms. Using this basis, we describe several approaches to building reliable networks tolerant of these failure modes.

Physical Device Failures

From a networked host's perspective, it is exceptionally hard to distinguish between a broken cable, a faulty switch, or a hub. Network interface card failures tend to occur quietly, while the others may result in "No carrier" or other messages indicating a network disconnect. In some cases, the network connection merely disappears, and the host is stranded on the wire. For simplicity, it helps to lump these faults into a single class, detected by the host's inability to send or receive packets. Recovery from these failures does require knowing the exact fault location and the appropriate repair steps needed, but for initial detection and system-level recovery, a simple algorithm should suffice.

Windows and Unix hosts track the number of packets sent, received, and dropped due to errors for each network interface. The netstat -i command in Unix and Windows (netstat -e in some versions of Windows) displays the packet counts. To detect a NIC or switch failure, look for an output packet count that isn't increasing even as you attempt to send network traffic; be wary of an input packet counter that doesn't increase; and also check for an increasing error count. Output errors are usually caused by repeated attempts to send a packet that result in a collision or can't complete because there is no network carrier.

For confirmation of a suspected network disconnect, try using ping to reach another, well-known host, or ping a router. Beware of pinging your own machine, since you may reach it via a loopback, or built-in network interface that doesn't actually send packets onto the network. Before relying on ping tests, test your operating systems to see how they transmit or don't transmit packets on the network. Also, choose your source well, using a well-run, rarely changed machine as a known, clean, starting point. One machine that tends to be very reliable in almost any network is the home machine of a system administrator. Unlike the oft-mentioned shoemaker (whose children always have the worst shoes), most system administrators make their machines among the most reliable ones on the network. Another good testing device is a network router, they seldom fail.

In the case of a switch or router failure, attempts to manage the device will fail, giving you an additional clue as to the location of the fault. Your first responsibility, however, is to get critical hosts connected to some well-conditioned network, so it's fair to lump all of these physical failures together under the same detection umbrella. Physical failures are usually addressed by switching to a redundant network connection, and can often be handled on a host-by-host basis. One host's NIC failure does not impact others. This is, of course, the easy case. The harder problem is when you have to get several machines to change their configurations at the same time.

IP Level Failures

Once you add system administration, configuration, and network services to the mix, the complexity of network failures increases in accordance with Metcalfe's Law. Things get more complicated exponentially, and it's essential to break detection and fault repair down into well-defined tests that are as independent and isolated as possible. We'll continue our list of sniffing techniques, providing more case-by-case details.

IP Address Configuration

The simplest failure at the network level is that a host ends up with the wrong IP address or with a duplicate IP address. Duplicate IP addresses often are the result of too few checks when updating DNS or NIS tables, or overlapping DHCP address space ranges. Once "Duplicate IP address" messages begin appearing, the host borrowing another's IP address can send packets without difficulty but may not receive any input packets (since they are going to the other host with the same IP address).

From the point of view of the misconfigured host, this problem typically appears as an intermittent network failure. The failure isn't permanent or easily traced, as the exact machine that receives packets destined for the duplicated IP address is determined by a race condition in answering ARP requests on the network. When any other node needs to locate the host corresponding to an IP address, it sends an ARP request. With more than one host believing that it owns that address, they all answer the request. The reply that arrives first may release an outbound packet; however, subsequent replies update the sender's ARP table with different information. In short, the host whose answer arrives last appears to own the duplicate IP address.

Incorrect IP information, such as a DNS entry that contains the wrong IP address for a hostname, typically results in one-sided traffic flows. Responses that take the misconfigured host's IP address from a request arrive without problems; however, services that look up the problem host's IP address in a name service will send their packets into the void (or to the wrong destination). Regular pings or heartbeats sent between well-known hosts should ensure that dynamic IP addressing like that provided by DHCP remains problem-free. However, the first line of protection is careful management of all network configuration services. We'll discuss change control and audit trail functions in Chapter 13, "Application Design," but for now note that many of these apparent network failures are due to system administration problems introduced by weak or unaudited processes.

Routing Information

Network connectivity is only as good as the routing information used by hosts to locate servers, clients, and service endpoints on the network. IP-routing algorithms attempt to handle redundancy and dynamic recovery from failures; however, they also introduce new complexities that result in sometimes-baffling failures. Asymmetric routes, incomplete or incorrect routing information, or networks with many hops between redundant connections also contribute to network failures.

Asymmetric routes occur when a client finds the server without problem but the server cannot send a reply back to the client because it lacks routing information. This is possible if the server is behind a firewall that blocks some routing information, if the server uses static routing information, or if a router along the path is sending incorrect route updates. Note that it's the server's return path that creates the network failure; if the client can't find the server, the client-side application will complain about an unreachable host or network.

A client sending a request on its happy way turns unhappy when the reply is discarded at the server, silently, due to an asymmetric routing configuration. NFS system administrators puzzled by `nfs_server: bad sendreply` error messages can thank asymmetric routes for their problems. This error is caused by an NFS server's inability to return a client request. Again, using the ping utility, or more prudent examination with a tool such as `traceroute`, the system administrator can locate the trouble spots and provide ongoing monitoring of the round-trip health of your network.

Technically, any host with two or more network interfaces can function as a router. This doesn't always mean that it should, however, as routing is CPU-intensive and will degrade performance for other applications. Usually, hosts that accidentally route packets do a poor job of it. Look for unwanted IP routing using `netstat -s` (in Windows or Solaris).

Finally, once a router fails, the network needs to construct a redundant path to the networks on the far side of the failure. If there are multiple routers connecting two networks, the secondary routers will appear in hosts' routing tables during subsequent routing table updates. For example, using the Routing Information Protocol (RIP), updates are sent by active routing hosts every

30 seconds. When a router fails, it stops sending RIP updates, and hosts relying on routes through that device discard those routing entries as soon as the updates stop. It takes about 30 seconds to establish a secondary route when there are no IP address topology changes and sufficient redundancy of routers. However, if a new network number is configured, or if a new host route is created to a new IP address, then clients may wait several minutes for this updated network information to propagate through all of the intermediate routers. This is, in fact, a strong argument for cementing a network numbering scheme early on, and then leaving it static as you build redundancy around it.

Congestion-Induced Failures

Sometimes your network problems stem from a simple case of too much traffic and not enough highway. Even with a well-designed, redundant, and highly reliable hardware base, spikes in network traffic or intentional attacks create the perception of a network or host failure. When the user is looking at an hourglass cursor, she doesn't really care what broke or is overloaded; she only knows that she's not getting data from the network. Congestion-induced failures fall into two broad categories: traffic congestion and denial-of-service attacks.

We do not cover causes and resolution techniques in detail here, as there are many good references for these topics, including the web sites of popular network hardware vendors such as Cisco and Nortel Networks. We look at each class of failure, give you some quick metrics to use for field identification of these beasts, and describe the general impact on reliability. Thoroughness in network reliability requires that you consider these cases, so our goal is to provide a baseline for including these failures in your operational and design processes.

Network Traffic Congestion

Network traffic overload causes data reliability problems in the same way that highway traffic overload causes personal reliability problems. How many meetings or shows have you missed due to accidents, congestion, or poor planning on the road? The same constraints apply to network traffic. Unusually high traffic levels can introduce temporary or sporadic network failures as packets are dropped by switches or routers that overflow internal buffers. Excessive latency can be introduced as these pieces of network equipment struggle to keep up with the resulting load.

Break down the traffic types and try to locate root causes, or use that information to enforce filtering, partitioning, or routing schemes. The following is a short list of symptoms and problems:

Excessive point-to-point or unicast traffic.   In short, too much talking at the same time, contributing to a network noise level that's not healthy. Historically, system administrators used the collision rate on a network to detect this background noise level, but switched, full-duplex networks have made collisions an anachronism. In some excessively high load situations, you'll see collisions on a full-duplex network, as a host attempts to transmit on one side of the cable and receives a late carrier on the receive side. Using a network sniffer or hardware monitor will give you a more accurate reading of load. Once you start loading an Ethernet over 50 percent of its capacity on average, you run the risk of severe slowdowns during peaks or bursts of activity. On a switched network, you'll need to examine the per-port statistics on packet drops, or switch packet loss to see if you are suffering load problems. Some loss may be attributable to short bursts; however, any kind of packet loss is a warning sign.

Broadcast packets.   The family of broadcast packets includes User Datagram Protocol (UDP) packets; Address Resolution Protocol (ARP) packets, used to locate the owner of an IP address on the network; and various PC file-sharing and -naming protocols like SMB and NetBIOS. Some examples of UDP broadcast are an NIS client looking for a server, a DHCP configuration, a network boot request, and RIP information sent by routers. Look at the level of broadcast activity using `netstat -s`, breaking it down into UDP and ARP broadcasts. Too much ARP activity could indicate a network that simply has too many nodes on it, or one that suffers configuration problems causing ARP requests to be forwarded or answered incorrectly. High levels of other broadcast traffic should be addressed with routers or other filtering devices. Broadcast storms, or endless streams of broadcast traffic, can be caused by hosts using broadcast addresses as their own IP addresses, mixing 0s and 1s styles of broadcast addresses (yes, there are systems that still interpret a string of 0s as part of a broadcast address), poorly formed ARP requests, ARPs for broadcast addresses, or incorrect forwarding of broadcasts over a router or filter that should suppress them. Part of your network operations process should include the ability to detect a broadcast and break the network into subsegments to assess and repair the damage at the source.

Multicast traffic.   Multicast packets are sent to a selected group of hosts. Those machines expressing an interest in the packets receive them; however, they do take up network bandwidth. Some data distribution products claim to do multicasting of data; however, they actually do serial unicasts of the same data to any subscribing clients. Watch for excessive load generated by data distributors, such as messaging products that are used in publish and subscribe mode (sending data from a few distribution points to multiple receivers) and multicast traffic that won't appear in broadcast packet counts. Again, a network analyzer or sniffer is your best approach to locating the head end of this problem.

Denial-of-service attacks.   Rather than filling up the network with packets, a denial-of-service attack fills up a network service's input queue with bogus or invalid requests. It's possible to have a denial-of-service attack that doesn't absorb all available network bandwidth but that still brings a network service to its knees.

Design and Operations Guidelines

You don't want to experience false positives and perform complete network failovers simply to recover from a period of peak load or a spike in traffic caused by a poorly configured client. Network traffic nightmares tend to repeat; that is, if you bring down one network with a problem, the same hosts and same configuration on a redundant network are likely to bring that formerly clean network to a halt as well. We offer some guidelines for design and operation of networks here, as a precursor to redundancy design guidelines. Typically, network operations is a separate entity in the data center, so it's a good idea to review these big rules around load management with all of the operations players, just to be sure infrastructure hiccups don't bring down a distributed service.

Know your baselines.   "It was faster on Tuesday" is the watchword of the underinformed system administrator. Without some knowledge of the typical packet counts, packet demographics (broadcast UDP, ARP, IP, TCP, unicast UDP, and PC protocols), or variations during various parts of the day or days in the work cycle, you'll have trouble identifying spikes or bursts as potential instigators of trouble.

Know your tools.   Measuring collisions on a switched network or looking for output errors instead of counting switch packet drops will ensure that you never find the needle in the haystack. Make sure that you know what your tools measure and that you can control the outputs under measurement. There's no point in taking a reading on something that can't be directly fixed by an operations person.

Routers, filters, and firewalls are good defense mechanisms.   They block broadcast packets and can be used to block other kinds of unicast traffic as well. Firewalls aren't just for external defensive positions. Gaining a measure of predictability on the network means having more control over what kinds of traffic actually enter and exit the network. This requires careful coordination with applications developers and users, but it's well worth the effort.

Use cache servers.   Web proxy cache servers do what their name implies—cache recently used static web content to reduce network load and improve throughput. They corral traffic and do not require application-level changes.

Networking is not a zero-sum game.   It's usually a positive-sum game. If you subdivide a network with a 60 percent utilization into three networks, don't expect to see a nice dip to the low 20 percent range on each one. Once you remove that bottleneck, nodes on each subnet will step up their activity, producing more load than before. When you stop choking someone, that person tends to fight back—and the same is true for networks.

Our focus on end-to-end system reliability necessitates some discussion of network loads, latencies, and failures, but our focus will primarily be on building redundancy into the network infrastructure to tolerate physical failures. In the case of a network that goes open loop, with excessive load, broadcast storms, or other unexplained incidents that send you into an *X-Files*–like state of weirdness, treat the problem like a physical failure and resort to a redundant network while you find the truth that's out there. We'll discuss ways to build in redundancy and handle failover now that you know what you're protecting yourself against.

Building Redundant Networks

Up to this point we've concentrated on what makes networks break, and how you might detect these failures. In this section, we describe architectures and designs for network redundancy, ranging from multiple networks to multiple paths through multiple networks. Some of these scenarios may seem far-fetched or impractical, or you may feel that you can condense multiple failure modes into a single problem area with a well-defined recourse. Remember our key principles: You need to spend money, but be sure that you spend it the right way. When you multiply the number of nodes on a network by the cost of adding redundancy to all of the infrastructure they touch, and add in the cost of managing those points on the network, the total cost of providing network redundancy can grow large. We walk through the basic connectivity options and some more advanced features to fully describe the building blocks, and then look at how to ruggedize network services on top of the resilient network infrastructure.

Virtual IP Addresses

One of the most critical design rules for networked, highly available systems is to distinguish a host's network identity from the name used for a host supplying a network service. If that sentence seems like it was written by political spinmeisters, but you still understood it, skip the following list of requirements. Otherwise, here's what makes Internet protocol addressing interesting when designing for availability:

- Every host on a network must have at least one IP address. That IP address matches some hostname. We've referred to these IP/hostname pairs as private or administrative addresses in previous discussions of failover mechanics. Private addresses are useful for things like `telnet`, `rlogin`, and `rdist`, where you need to ensure that you end up at a precise physical destination.

- Any network client looking for a service uses a hostname-to-IP-address mapping to find the required server. From the client's point of view, the IP address could correspond to a single physical location, a collection of machines, or a proxy service that forwards the request on to another server behind a firewall or redirector farm. The client doesn't really care; it only sees a logical location on the network. The converse is also true, though, in that clients want to find services at the same IP address over time. Reconfiguring clients to wander through the network looking for available servers isn't fast, easy, or reliable; clients should be able to rest assured that the IP addresses they use correspond to something that will be highly available.

- Services that are static or hosts that don't participate in any kind of redundancy scheme can use the same physical (private) name and logical (public) name. Your desktop machine is a good example; there's no need to give it multiple logical names.

- Services that move between hosts in an HA pair or services that correspond to one of several machines in a server farm use logical addresses that map to one or more physical addresses. Enter the concept of the virtual IP address.

Virtual IP addresses are redundant names given to a network interface that already has a private hostname. Most network interface cards support multiple IP addresses on each physical network connection, handling IP packets sent to any configured address for the interface. The second and successive addresses added are called virtual IP addresses and are used to create logical hostnames that may be moved between machines or scattered over several hosts using a redirector service.

Consider the two hosts in Figure 9.2, *norman* and *mother*. These are private names. There's also a logical, virtual IP address assigned to the single network interface on *norman* namely *psycho*. If the primary server crashes, the secondary can pick up that same logical (public) name, assign it to its single network interface as a virtual IP address, and the NFS clients using that service are none the wiser. Enabling a virtual IP address is as simple as configuring the appropriately named device with the logical IP address, here shown using the Solaris naming and configuration syntax:

```
# ifconfig hme0:1 psycho up
```

In this example, hme0 is the physical device instance, and the :1 notation indicates this is a virtual IP address assigned to that device. Usually, hme0:0 and hme0 are equivalent, and the :0 is suppressed for consistency with other Unix commands. Some systems impose a limit on the number of virtual IP addresses per physical interface; but if you're hitting the limit, you should reevaluate your network and naming architecture for overly complex designs.

Virtual IP addresses have a host of other applications in network redundancy, including virtual network numbering, which we cover shortly. They are also used to give a single host several names—a useful mechanism when hosting multiple services or using one machine to cohost several web sites, each with its own URL. For now, bear in mind that virtual IP addresses provide redundancy on the input side, allowing a machine to appear to have multiple personalities on any given network. Next, we make multiple connections to a single machine to provide reliable paths to those machines.

Redundant Network Connections

There are three fairly obvious approaches to redundant host connectivity:

1. Make multiple connections to one network.

2. Connect to more than one network.

3. Do both of the above.

You'll probably want to explore all of these options over time, so we proceed from the simplest redundant connection up to more complex multiple network numbering schemes.

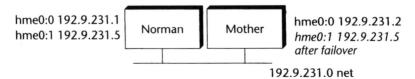

Figure 9.2 Virtual IP addresses.

Redundant Network Attach

Redundant network connections protect against failures in the network inter-face card, the I/O subsystem containing a NIC, or the cable connecting a NIC to some piece of networking hardware. To have redundant network connec-tions, you need at least two, with only one active at a time, similar to the way asymmetric failover works (For more on asymmetric failover, see chapter 17, "Failover and Clustering"). The hot-standby configuration is the simplest, involving a secondary NIC attached to the same IP network as the primary. To remove all SPOFs, the interface should be on a separate I/O bus, and even on a separate I/O card if supported by your server hardware, and definitely on a separate interface card. You want to make sure that failures in the card, the bus, or the bus-host interface don't bring down all of your redundant network connections.

Once you have the physical connectivity set, the logical configuration is a simple matter of monitoring the primary interface for failures, and then decommissioning it and bringing up the secondary:

ifconfig le0 down [bring down the old interface]

ifconfig le0 unplumb [remove system resources]

ifconfig le1 plumb [initialize the new NIC]

ifconfig le1 norman up [bring the interface up on the new NIC]

The secondary network connection retains the same hostname and IP address as the primary, so there is no impact on clients. Some operating sys-tems and some failover management systems support this network address failover (NAFO) capability and provide configuration tools for specifying interfaces to be treated as asymmetric redundant pairs, while in others you'll have to write the scripts to monitor netstat output and run the ifconfig scripts to effect the change. Because it's simple and does not introduce any client- or naming system configuration changes, redundant network attach is an elegant way to grant the first level of failure resiliency.

Multiple Network Attach

Multiple network attaches provide redundancy and a small measure of perfor-mance improvement. If redundant network attach points are an asymmetric HA analog, multiple network attach points are the equivalent of a symmetric HA pair. The key difference between the two network redundancy models is that in the multiple attach case, each interface has its own IP address and its own private hostname. Instead of moving the single IP address from a live to a standby interface, multiple network attach requires that you either instruct clients to use the new IP address or rebind a virtual IP address from the primary to the secondary interface. In this latter case, there's not a significant difference between treating the secondary interface as a hot standby or a live network connection, since it only represents the public name of the machine when it has the virtual, logical IP address bound to it.

Using multiple, distinct IP addresses allows you use both pipes at the same time. You can use load-balancing DNS (lbbindd) to round-robin between the different IP addresses. With lbbindd, successive requests for a hostname-to-IP-address mapping return the different IP addresses in turn. Some vendor implementations of DNS do this when multiple IP addresses are provided for a hostname, so check your documentation and verify operation before you build the public source of lbbindd. In the event of a failure of one network interface, clients attempting to connect through the dead interface will timeout or find that the host is not reachable. Those clients may query DNS again, hoping to get the alternative IP address(es), but this requires fine-tuning your applications to make them aware of the server configuration. Some applications also use a list of IP addresses, allowing connection code to try them in order until they find one that appears to be live. This approach allows the application to recover from a single failure and to seek out surviving network interfaces, but again, it's a client-side implementation. Without any clear, definite way to make the clients find the alternate IP addresses, failover using multiple network attach is a bit brittle. We discuss request distribution over multiple host IP addresses in more detail later in this chapter.

Realize that the small kick you get out of having two pipes between the network and host doesn't do much for performance. In order to gain input capacity, you'd have to be bandwidth-limited on that single network interface, in which case redundant connections to the same network get you two ways of looking at the same congestion. There are cases, however, where multiple client segments come into a switch and produce more than a single segment's worth of input for a server; using multiple switch connections in this case alleviates the bottleneck on the link between server and switch. Consider having 10 clients on a 100Base-T Ethernet switch; if all of the clients are reading from an NFS server simultaneously, it's likely the server is spewing out more than 100Mbit/second of output. Running two links between the NFS server and switch helps, provided the switch can handle the extra load on its internal bus. If the multiple attach points lead to two distinct switches and network congestion is a problem, you may see also some benefit from the multiple attachments.

Multiple network attach also raises the question of uniquely knowing a host's real name and IP address. Packets may be sent to any of the IP addresses, but replies will come with only one IP address in the source IP address field. Furthermore, all output to the single IP network will occur over only one interface, adding load to the output side of the pipe. The single output pipe is a result of having only one route to the outbound network—it's only one IP network, and therefore has only one current, lowest-cost route to it. In the previous NFS server example, in order for client requests to go over both switch-host legs, you'll need some of the clients to use each IP address, and some way to ensure a roughly even distribution of clients on each side. An example of multiple network interface attachments is shown in Figure 9.3.

Some operating systems fix the outbound IP address situation by remembering the interface and IP address over which a particular connection was built, and others allow this connection-to-IP-address persistence to be enabled as an option. Solaris calls this feature "IP interface groups," and it is enabled in /etc/system.

As you can probably see, though, with input/output load distribution, client-side knowledge of IP address distribution, less-than-predictable client failover, and the need to enable interface groups, multiple network attach is less attractive as a resiliency mechanism than it first appears to be. There are variations on this theme—redundant switches, multiple networks, and IP redirectors—that skirt these issues and are discussed in upcoming sections.

Interface Trunking

Trunking allows you to bundle several network connections together into a single virtual network interface that has roughly the aggregate capacity of the components added together. Think of trunking as the network analog of disk striping with RAID-0 to gain performance. Interface trunking combines some availability aspects with improved bandwidth between network and host, making it more attractive than multiple network attach in many respects. Trunking involves running multiple connections from a switch to a host, where both host and switch support trunking software that is interoperable. Today, that's far from a given, as there are no standards for how packets are distributed over the links in a trunk and how failures are tolerated. However, most server vendors have trunking software that will talk to the dominant switch vendor products—you have to do the research.

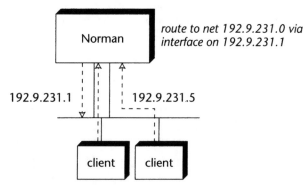

Figure 9.3 Redundant network interface attach.

A host that is trunked to a switch has a single IP address, much like the redundant NIC case. The switch and host handle the scatter and gather of packets distributed over the multiple network links, distributing data round-robin on each end. Because all of the links are active, trunking increases the bandwidth between switch and host. Furthermore, trunking software handles failures of the links transparently, so any NIC or cable breakdown is hidden.

A caution with trunking is that frequently it requires devices that have several network connections on the same card. This card then becomes a single point of failure. Of course, you can combine methods and trunk over two cards to two different switches, using the multiple network attach approach described in the previous section. Given that SPOF caveat, though, trunking is an excellent choice for alleviating server input bottlenecks while gaining protection from the most common network failures—cables and connectors that are subject to physical wear and tear.

Configuring Multiple Networks

Up to this point, we've looked at single failures between switches and hubs and servers. Aside from cable damage, network failures tend to fall into the excessive load, configuration error, or denial-of-service categories, where protection requires separate, redundant networks. When the primary network is deemed unusable for any reason, all traffic switches to the secondary network. If you're suffering from inconsistencies in configuration or severe load problems, turning on the clean network may be the best and most expedient way to restore order among the network citizens. A word of warning: Load-related problems simply move to the redundant network and cause headaches there; configuration problems can be resolved by going to a clean area where they don't exist and then taking the time to diagnose the sick network.

Redundant networks are commonly called *rails* (borrowing from the AC power distribution vernacular). When wiring a data center, independent power rails bring AC to the machine room from different circuits, and possibly from different sources as well. Similar design considerations are used in data center equipment with hot-swap and redundant power supplies. "Rail switching" within power supplies allows a server to switch to an alternate source of line current without interruption. The same notion of rail switching applies to taking all IP traffic off of one network and sending it over the redundant set of network rails.

The most difficult part of multiple network configuration is sorting out the IP addressing on each network. The simplest approach to multiple networks is to use multiple switches, with each switch connected to every server. In an asymmetric configuration, one set of switches acts as hot standby for the active set, and in the event of a failure, all interfaces on all servers failover to the second set of switches. This is essentially the redundant network attach on steroids, and it may prove more efficient to insist that all hosts failover together. If the problem is in the switch, or is a load issue, all of the hosts are going to attempt to fail to redundant connections anyway, so forcing the issue ensures a shorter MTTR. The downside to redundant switches is connecting a router to the network. The router will have to be made aware of redundancy and configured to route traffic over either interface as required. We're starting to bump into the "keep it simple" key design principle as we add complexity, and it requires that you step back at some point, look at the number of moving parts and things you need to manage, and balance that against the extra level of protection you get by investing in various network redundancy designs.

You can also run the network rails in parallel, with distinct IP network numbers on each. In this case, servers connected to both networks are merely multihomed, and have multiple IP addresses on multiple networks, a common situation that is easily handled by routers, switches, and clients. To effect a failover, however, you'll need to make sure that all client traffic gets sent over the correct network, usually requiring some of the client-side host searching tricks previously described. You can mix in virtual IP addresses and create an entire virtual IP network, using a third IP network number as the logical network and allocating an IP address for each host on this virtual network, as shown in Figure 9.4. For the hosts to see the logical network, they'll need a route to it, built using a metric of zero in the route command:

```
# route add net 192.9.235.0 norman-net1 0
```

This zero-cost route tells the host that it can reach all of the hosts on 192.9.235.0 via the interface for its primary hostname *norman-net1*. The cost of zero indicates that the network is directly attached to the host, and not on the far side of a router. Usually, the cost metric indicates the number of router hops taken to get to a destination; lower numbers indicate better or closer routes. Zero-cost routes tell you there are no routers along the way; the network is directly attached, and the route merely enables an alternate numbering scheme for the same physical connection.

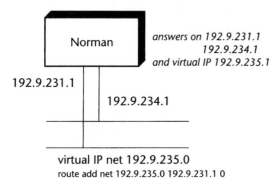

virtual IP net 192.9.235.0
route add net 192.9.235.0 192.9.231.1 0

Figure 9.4 Multiple networks.

When the primary network is taken down, all of the virtual IP addresses are assigned to the secondary network, and new routing information is added to each host to redirect outbound traffic to the correct rail. If your routers are capable of switching a network from one interface to another with a minimum of manual intervention, the virtual network approach works well. Delete the old zero-cost routes and add new ones, using the hostnames for the second network rail, to complete the failover for each host.

There's no hard requirement that all network interfaces failover in unison when using symmetric dual network rails. If you have a small number of servers, routers on each of the redundant rails, and a fairly small number of clients, it's easy to accomplish network failover merely by creating host routes and pointing them at the appropriate network side as shown in Figure 9.5. Using a virtual IP address of 192.9.231.1 for the first host, and network numbers 192.9.231.0 and 192.9.232.0 for the dual rails, clients can choose one rail or the other by adding a host route:

```
C> route add host 192.9.232.1 router-net2 1
```

This route command tells the client that it can reach the host at 192.9.232.1 via router-net2, which is connected to the 192.9.232.0 network. In the event of a failure, the client can redirect this host route to use the alternate router to network 192.9.231.0 with:

```
C> route add host 192.9.231.1 router-net1 1
```

Host routes are suitable for small client/server computing groups, because they grow linearly in size as more clients and servers are added to the mix. Host routes have the advantage of putting the client in control of its path to the server, and they don't require any router reconfiguration. They support multiple routers and can be easily automated on the client side by testing connectivity, making them resistant to a variety of configuration and naming errors. The downside, again, is complexity. For larger computing groups, use redundant routers and fully redundant networks and avoid making changes on a per-client basis.

In all cases, redundant network rails consume a large number of IP addresses, so ensure that you have enough network numbers or subnets and a sufficiently large number of free network addresses to accommodate your numbering and failover system. You can conserve IP addresses by using host routes to connect servers directly to routers, eliminating networks of two or three servers. Since clients match the longest portion of an IP address possible when looking for a route, they'll find host routes to servers first in their search. In Figure 9.6, the two routers connect four servers to the client network, using only one IP network with four host routes. Without the host routes, two IP network numbers would be needed, one for each group of servers, creating a configuration that scales poorly as additional servers are brought online.

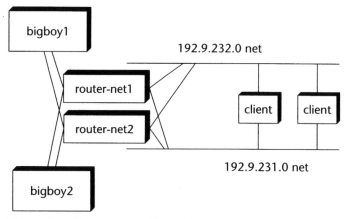

Figure 9.5   Host route configuration.

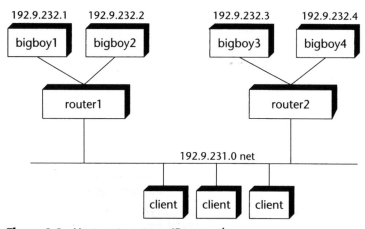

Figure 9.6   Host routes versus IP networks.

IP Routing Redundancy

Internet historians will tell you that IP was designed to help the ARPANET survive a nuclear attack that might take out major portions of it. Sounds impressive, but it's probably a magnified version of the truth: IP packets benefit from a flexible and resilient routing scheme. Internet Protocol remains a best-effort, hop-by-hop network protocol that implements redundancy through routing choices. Getting hosts onto multiple networks requires careful engineering of IP addresses and network numbers, but routing traffic between IP networks is relatively easy once you build in a level of router redundancy. You have two choices for IP routing redundancy: dynamic route discovery or static routes using the Virtual Router Recovery Protocol (VRRP).

Dynamic Route Recovery

Figure 9.7 shows a typical redundant router configuration. Network net3 is accessible directly via router r4 from network net1, and through either r1 or r2 and r3. The default behavior is to use the lowest-cost route as measured by the number of router hops between the networks, so packets going to net3 from net1 will use router r4. If r4 crashes or loses its routing information, packets can be sent via the higher-cost but equally good redundant route. IP once again proves its strength as a repairman of broken networks, but the time required to accomplish the repair isn't easy to determine.

Hosts using the route through r4 will notice that r4 stopped sending routing updates within a minute of its crash. Routing Information Protocol (RIP) updates normally are sent once every 30 seconds, so allowing for the time required to recognize an update was missed and for the time needed to update routing tables, 60 to 90 seconds go by before the routing information from r2 or r1 is used to set up an alternate route to net3. Transmission Control Protocol (TCP) sockets connected between hosts on net1 and net3 are oblivious to the change, since IP handles the packet shuffle and updates. However, it's possible for application failures to result during the time required to build the second route:

- TCP sockets set a timer that detects failure of either endpoint. The default value for this keep-alive timer can be as long as 2 hours, depending on your operating system; however, many network managers tune it down to several minutes to allow rapid cleanup of broken connections. As a result, a network that takes 2 minutes to reconfigure may result in broken socket connections.

- Applications don't always wait patiently for initial connections to a service. If an application was attempting to contact a network service on net3 when r4 failed, it's possible that the application will timeout and complain. A subsequent attempt should result in a success, but the user sees a temporary failure.

- Hosts on net3 may not know about a return path to net1 via router r3. If they were using router r4 as a default route and were not receiving RIP updates, then incoming traffic will reach net3, but responses will be undeliverable because no path exists back to the source on net1.

When you lose end-to-end connectivity, in either direction, applications on either side believe the other side has failed. Errors that occur during connection setup are easily traced back, but intermediate failures, once connections are established, generate calls to the help desk.

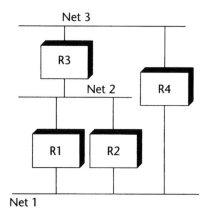

Figure 9.7 Redundant routing.

Static Route Recovery with VRRP

Dynamic route recovery is a good idea within your data center, or among servers that make up a large web site farm. When you're dealing with multiple networks with multiple routes between them, along with firewalls and packet filters, you want to have fine-grain control over your network topology. However, there are many cases in which you're going to have many smaller, single-outlet networks that tie into a backbone or larger network. Managing multiple routes, or multiple default routes, on many hosts becomes a large administrative chore; driving a consistent network address failover when a router or other outlet point fails is equally more difficult as the network grows in size.

Enter VRRP, which allows you to pair up routers to create "virtual routers" whose IP addresses migrate from a failed router to the redundant router. In Figure 9.8, each branch network is connected to redundant routers; each network knows the IP address of its preferred router as the virtual address managed by VRRP. In the event that router r2 fails, for example, VRRP will migrate the virtual IP address 192.9.231.200 to router r1, and all traffic from network 192.9.231.0 will flow to the backbone network through router r1. VRRP makes failover decisions on the basis of a master/slave relationship between router pairs, although it can also do load sharing between routers. Figure 9.8 shows two virtual IP addresses, with each router acting as a backup for the other. If desired, or required for load handling purposes, the routers can be configured to balance the load between them.

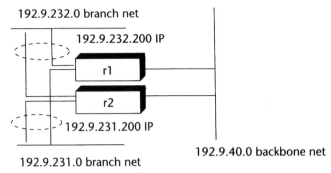

Figure 9.8   Virtual router interfaces.

Routing Recovery Guidelines

To make your network infrastructure more tolerant of routing problems, make sure that you combine routing techniques to aid recovery and early warning of problems:

Avoid single-outlet networks.   A network connected to the world through only one router has a single point of failure. Even using a host as a router only for emergency purposes leaves you a fallback position. Severe router problems may require several hours to trace and repair, leaving your network partitioned without the redundancy. Again, VRRP is a good answer here, but that means redundant routers at the single outlet. If you're connecting several hundred branch offices to a core network, that's several hundred redundant router pairs to operate as well.

Default routes are good—as long as there's more than one.   Using a default route means you don't need to accept routing updates and can turn off the somewhat noisy RIP protocol on your routers. If you do this, however, make sure that you have multiple default routes (one for each possible outlet from the network). Sending packets to a default router that isn't listening is as good as being without any redundancy. While it sounds counterintuitive to have more than one default, realize that default is only used to designate the route used when no better match can be found in the routing tables. Multiple default routes mean that you have several choices of last resort, and can select the route with the best availability or capacity.

Dynamic redirection is also good.   Ensure that your router sends ICMP redirect messages if it's asked to forward a packet better handled by another router. Without dynamic redirection, you'll clutter your network with reforwarded packets, possibly hurting performance.

Scripted intervention cuts down the time to repair. Aggressively monitor end-to-end connectivity, using ping or more advanced tools like `traceroute` that show you the path taken by a packet. You'll even find asymmetry in your routing tables using `traceroute`. Rather than waiting for a client to recognize a router failure and update its routing tables, use the `route` command to proactively flush the stale information and construct a new route. You can trim recovery times into the tens of seconds with aggressive monitoring, and also collect data to help locate the root causes of repeated router outages or problems.

Choosing Your Network Recovery Model

We've covered a few cases in which scripts or system administrator help is necessary to keep the network chugging along with its packets. Unlike system-level failover involving disks, network reconnection involves multiple points of control and many moving parts unless you use the static route driven failover pairs provided by VRRP. There are several configurations that make the case for manual failover as opposed to fully automated but very complex operations.

We assume automated failover as the default mode of operation through most of this book. However, network failover requires careful coordination of all hosts that need to be reconfigured, and partial failovers are often harder to sort out than complete shutdowns of a single network. We use this rule of thumb: If there's one point of control and one set of resources, automation is your friend. Multiple points of control, coordination of multiple resources, and multiple steps that have to coordinate with each other, and occur in order, argue for manual intervention. Some of the network redundancy techniques that rely on router information or route changes are ideal for automated care and feeding; others that require changing host routes, or ensuring that all hosts have switched to an alternate rail, are best handled by the network operations staff.

The key question to address is the MTTR. With active, aggressive monitoring and an on-call network staff, you can limit your manual failover time to the window in which the staff is alerted, problems found, and repairs made. With a 24 × 7 staff, this window gets smaller, and with well-documented failover processes you can be reasonably sure that the failovers will happen the right way the first time.

Partial failovers are to be expected in the automated network management world. Some hosts end up stuck on the primary network, because not all of them noticed the failure, or because scripts that triggered the failover failed on the dying network. If you account for the typical time required to dig through these failure modes, you can argue for manual intervention in the case of a complete network meltdown. To repeat a bit of our management dogma, aggressive, active network monitoring will aid early detection and repair, possibly eliminating the corner cases that require interruption of someone's beauty sleep.

Load Balancing and Network Redirection

In addition to explicitly making the intra-server room network highly available, you'll need to deal with a highly demanding user base that wants to be able to reach your servers, with low latency and high predictability. When using redundant servers to increase reliability, you need some way to steer traffic to all of them, in an equitable way, and then to redirect that traffic in the event of a failure. We look at two high-level approaches, one that uses DNS to have the clients do the work and a switch-based approach that gives you fine-grain control over load balancing and failure detection.

Round-Robin DNS

Round-robin DNS is useful in rack-and-stack clusters, or shared-nothing clusters where you achieve redundancy by building out multiple instances of web servers (we cover rack-and-stack, or horizontal, clustering in Chapter 14). Each web server has its own filesystem, its own IP address and hostname, and its own interface to the world. DNS does the heavy lifting by associating multiple IP addresses with the virtual hostname; for example, you may assign four IP addresses to www.blah.com so that incoming traffic will go (fairly evenly) to all four addresses over time. Some implementations of DNS do this automatically, circulating through all available IP addresses for a given hostname. In other configurations, you're going to need to get a copy of the publicly available load-balancing BIND daemon (lbbindd).

When a client gets an IP address via round-robin DNS, it will use it until the DNS lifetime has expired. Sites using round-robin DNS typically shrink the DNS lifetime to several minutes, forcing clients to rebind the hostname to an address more regularly and reducing the average window of an outage. Done well, round-robin DNS is a low-impact and low-budget solution with its own good and bad points, which are shown in Table 9.1

Table 9.1 Good and Bad Points of Round-Robin DNS

GOOD	BAD
■ There aren't any real failovers to manage; clients just find alternative servers when they get new IP addresses for the virtual hostname.	■ Downtime windows can still be minutes, or as long as it takes to spit out the defunct DNS mapping and get a new one.

Table 9.1 *(continued)*

GOOD	BAD
■ Scaling up is as simple as adding hardware and IP addresses, then mixing until blended. ■ With N servers, you're only taking down 1/Nth of the clients when a server fails, and even then the outage is limited by the DNS cache lifetime.	■ Reducing the DNS cache lifetime means more DNS traffic for you. You're trading availability for load. Best to beef up the DNS servers. ■ You're assuming that all clients have nice DNS configurations, and that they'll play by the lifetime and timeout rules, and not make mappings persistent or copy IP addresses into local state files. ■ Implicit load balancing doesn't take into consideration the duration of a connection. If every fourth connection is for a rather large file, and all other HTTP hits are for small graphics or HTML files, you'll find that a four-way server farm has a real hotspot where all of the large file transfers cluster. This is an extreme case, but it points to the unpredictability of load balancing via round-robin techniques.

What started off as a balanced point-counterpoint on DNS round-robin techniques ended up with an extra negative point. This isn't meant to dismiss round-robin DNS out of hand; in some cases it will be the best, quick solution you can implement. However, the Internet market seizes opportunity, and when web server farms became de rigueur, new and established players in IP switching filled the gap in IP traffic distribution.

Network Redirection

Network redirection is essentially a reliable DNS round-robin service in a box. An IP redirector assumes a well-known, public hostname and IP address, and then translates it into multiple back-end, private IP addresses. When combined with routing functions, the IP redirector can talk to back ends on multiple networks. Figure 9.9 shows a typical IP redirector configuration, using a redundant IP switch to avoid a single point of failure at the public/network interface. There are several variations on the basic redirector idea, ranging from simple IP address load balancers to stateful, packet-inspecting switches that perform load balancing and failover between back-end targets based on session information.

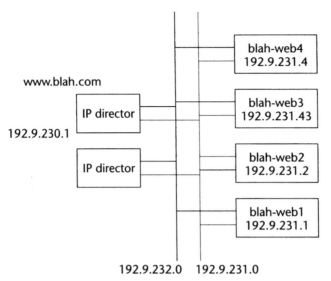

Figure 9.9 Load-balancing switch configuration.

Normally, you'll set up the redirector behind a firewall or external router, replacing what would be a single web server's network interface with the redirector complex. Because it uses only one public IP address, an IP director does not need DNS round-robin support. Clients resolve the public name through DNS, and are connected to the appropriate back-end server based on load, time, equal distribution, network radix or distance, or other metrics particular to the manufacturer of the IP traffic router. By eliminating DNS as a point of control, and by consolidating all load-balancing decisions into a redundant configuration, IP redirection provides the best solution for horizontal scaling (by adding more servers) and reliable scaling (by minimizing downtime). Clients will still notice that a web page isn't loading, but the next hit on that site will be directed to a different, and hopefully more functional, server in the farm.

What should you be sensitive to in choosing a network redirection configuration?

- Some load-balancing switches actually terminate incoming TCP connections and then act as a proxy to forward those connections on to the appropriate back-end server. In this case, when the back end goes down and the switch chooses a different server, the client's connection (to the switch) isn't impacted.

- Session state can be critical for preserving the user's experience. *State* in this case includes login credentials, shopping carts, last page visited or other navigation aids, or work in progress. We'll talk more about web and application servers and how they manage state for availability in

Chapter 13. At the network level, realize that you want your sessions to be sticky to the back-end server on which they were created, unless that server fails. Switches that can aid in redirecting requests to maintain stickiness are essential if you're creating applications with state.

- Don't rely on the source IP address of a request for a load-balancing algorithm because all traffic from a large service provider or enterprise may appear to come from a single IP address. Furthermore, some larger service providers such as America Online use a proxy that may change the source IP address of successive packets within the same session. Most switches work off of a load or availability indicator, or *health check*.

- Make sure your health check isn't intrusive to the back-end servers. If you verify the end-to-end health of your web site by invoking a URL that executes a web server plug-in to generate a large database query, each ping from the load-balancing switch is going to take a bite out of the performance of your database server. Testing the availability of back-end services should be as lightweight as possible while still yielding a reasonable up or down answer.

CAN YOU HEAR ME NOW? CAN YOU HEAR ME NOW?

Strolling through the backwoods has made the Verizon guy's tag line the current vernacular equivalent of "Where's the beef?" The commercial represents a brute-force health check of a network, but the idea isn't a bad one: Find the simplest way to detect that required services are available. Load-balancing switches that are web-server savvy will invoke any URL you specify to validate that the path from switch to properly functioning web server is available. One of our larger sites generates a huge volume of dynamic content, mostly using Java Server Pages (JSPs). To ensure that the web server, application server, and all intermediate compilers and filesystems were in order, the customer chose to perform health checks using a mostly empty page with a simple JSP template in it. Unfortunately, as the JSP was executed, it created other side effects, mostly creating load on the state replication engine that slowed the application server complex down. As the frequency of the health checks increased, the volume of side effects increased as well, actually impairing the operation of the site. Building a simple JSP template without side effects solved the problem.

—Hal

Dynamic IP Addresses

As mentioned in the previous section, source IP addresses are not a surefire way to identify a unique client. In addition to proxy rewriting by enterprises or service providers, you'll run into the most common source of dynamic IP addresses each time you plug a PC into your corporate network: the Dynamic Host Configuration Protocol (DHCP). DHCP servers hand out IP addresses to transient devices such as PCs and laptops that enter and leave the network without any administrator effort. Users with desktop PCs may use an entire range of IP addresses over the course of a workweek; users accessing network services from home through cable modem or DSL service providers also have their IP addresses allocated dynamically.

A related trend is Network Address Translation, or NAT. NAT has grown in popularity for two reasons: home networks that use NAT to allow multiple PCs to share a single connection upstream, and a dramatic reduction in the number of IPv4 addresses available. The dearth of 32-bit IP (IPv4) addresses has probably caused the increased use of NAT through home network or local network proxy devices. A NAT device manages all connections to its local devices, acting as a DHCP server for them and handing out "private" addresses that never are used beyond the NAT device's local network interfaces. The NAT device then talks to the outside world, mapping connections built by local PCs to the larger, outside network.

Bottom line: Don't build a network service that relies on the client or source IP address to determine where the request is coming from, or where the request should be routed. You'll either need to use cookies to create a session identifier or embed session information in a URL returned by your web and application servers. We'll cover this issue in much more detail in Chapter 13.

Network Service Reliability

With your network plumbing in good order, it's time to actually launch something down those pipes, so building reliability into the key network services is the next step.

Doing something interesting with a computer requires actually moving some data around on the network. The most interesting data tends to be that which is dynamic in nature (such as web pages with stock quotes) or valuable and persistent (such as payroll records in a database). Our discussion of failover management systems and data service reliability cover these data-moving services in detail. Underneath the interesting services are a chorus of supporting network services, such as naming, directory, security, and network management, all of which provide vital information to the higher-level data management service. Want to connect to a database to start perusing those most interesting payroll records? You're going to need to find the database first, and that means looking up a hostname in a name service and possibly finding the TCP port number corresponding to a network service name. And if you want access to your home directory so that your database extract has a place to land, you'll need another trip through the naming service and RPC binding service to find the NFS server on the other end.

We characterize network services as more informational than transactional in nature. If a name service answers a request twice, no harm is done. Replication tends to be a feature of configuration or built-in to the service, not an application level issue. While these services are hidden, they can't be taken for granted, and they need to be made as reliable as the data services above them.

TRAITORS TO TRADERS

Several years ago, one very prominent trading floor lost the use of its portfolio management application on a day when the fixed-income (bond) markets were particularly volatile. Interest rates moved, making traders froth at the mouth, and the network services felt the traders' pain. A router failure caused a naming service to become inaccessible, making the application fail without the ability to resolve key hostnames into IP addresses or the ability to allow users to log in. From the traders' point of view, the system administrators were traitors, having let them down in their moment of need, but the real root cause was buried several layers below the obvious failure point. The SAs have since put in redundant naming and fallback services, but it was an expensive lesson.

—Hal

Network Service Dependencies

To get a good feeling for the dependencies that exist in a typical environment, we're going to trace the average Unix login sequence and point out network service interactions. If you've ever wondered why it takes minutes to fire up your desktop, stop cursing the window system developers and look instead at what's happening on your own wires.

When you login to a Unix system and start your first shell, the following events occur:

- Your username and password are compared to the values provided by the naming system. If you're not using the local /etc/passwd file, that means going over the network to an LDAP, NIS, NIS+, or other network database to look up the right entry. Your group number is pulled from your password record, and is used to look up all group memberships in either /etc/group or another network database.

- Any authentication service, such as Kerberos, is contacted to generate session keys for your new log in session. Note that this is why klogin is required instead of rlogin or telnet when using Kerberos services; the login process needs to pass your authenticated credentials off to the ticket-granting server to set up your Kerberos session.

- The home directory listed in your password entry is checked for .cshrc and .login files, which are executed in that order. If your home directory is accessed via NFS using an automounter, this first access completes the NFS mount. Quotas on your home directory are checked, if enabled. NFS servers and name servers needed by NFS on the client side to determine IP addresses are now brought into play. If you're using an automounter, it may use NIS for its maps or for host-name resolution.

- The shell builds its hash table of executable commands by walking every directory listed in the PATH variable, checking for executable files. This speeds up response time at the command line; however, if you have a long path that contains several directories that are auto-mounted, starting a shell sets off an automounter storm.

- As your .cshrc and .login files complete execution, any other local commands you have added may touch other network services.

There are an awful lot of dependencies in something as simple as logging in. And we haven't even connected to a database or fired up a browser to check the market's opening yet. To make the higher-level services like NFS and databases reliable, you need to make sure that you have a clean, well-ordered, and reliable set of underlying network services. One of the better ways to map out your reliability issues is to build a dependency graph of all of the services required, starting with the service you're putting on an HA pair. Figure 9.10 shows a typical dependency graph.

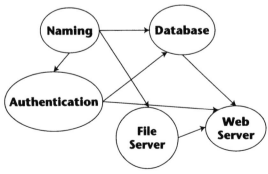

Figure 9.10 Service dependency graph.

In this example, a web server gets its HTML files from an NFS server, and its forms rely on a user database. The database, file server, and network management applications all rely on a name service. Furthermore, the database requires help from an authentication service, which is also called by the web server. This example is oversimplified; we lump all file server access into a single bubble, when in reality most web sites are driven by multiple servers. We also left out routers, configuration tables, and other software-driven services that could affect reliability.

These dependency diagrams should be directed, acyclic graphs. By *directed*, we mean that the relationship between the dependent and independent service is clear; an arrow points to the item that is dependent on something else. *Acyclic* refers to the property that there are no circle tours through the graph; if you start at any node, you can never get back to that same node simply by following the directed arrows. There are well-known algorithms for proving that graphs are without cycles; however, for the dozen or so dependencies you'll find, you can trace the possible paths out by hand. If you encounter a cycle, as shown in Figure 9.11, you have a deadly embrace between network services. If one goes down, it may crash another, leading to a deadlock condition that can't be broken through normal, automated methods. The example shows a pair of file servers that cross-mount each other; when one crashes, the other is taken out as well.

Look at the number of graph nodes that have no incident arrows; these are the root or independent services. Typically, it's naming, DNS and LDAP, and occasionally an authentication server. There are many design points to be drawn from these types of graphs:

- Make sure the root services are highly replicated and available, because failures will trickle through to appear in the applications that are at the end of the dependency graph.

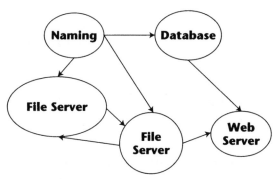

Figure 9.11 Cyclic dependency graph.

- Nodes with many arrows coming into them are highly dependent on other services, and are deserving of extra redundancy engineering and aggressive monitoring. Spend the engineering effort and money to make these services reliable, as they're likely to affect many users or many other services.

- Routers introduce dependencies when there's only one path between services. If you find a router in the middle of a graph, remove it by adding a redundant routing device.

- Your monitoring tools may have network dependencies as well. Something as simple as `netstat -r`, which checks routing tables, uses NIS to look up hostnames for gateways and network names. Stick with the `netstat -rn` form, using numeric representation of IP addresses, to make `netstat` a standalone management tool.

- A dependency graph with cycles represents a network that cannot boot itself. During the process of starting up, you'll hit a race condition in which some service may be waiting on another one, which is waiting on some other host that forms a dependency loop. Consider a host that issues a route command during booting to find a network service on the far side of a router. The route utility uses a hostname, which is resolved via DNS. If your only authoritative DNS server is also on the far side of the router, there's no way that host is coming up all the way. Remember, after a major reboot, your DNS cache servers may not be useful. Just because it worked fine right up until the failure doesn't mean you can boot your way out of trouble. Break the cycles and make your network more resilient to massive failures or recovery efforts such as blackouts or disaster recovery processes.

Naming and directory services are almost invariably at the top of the dependency charts, so we'll look at ways of hardening them and providing adequate capacity to prevent them from starting a Chernobyl-scale chain reaction on the network.

Hardening Core Services

NIS, NIS+, and DNS have built-in resiliency through replication. Each naming service allows multiple servers, at multiple points in the network, to answer requests with authority. Here are some basic design rules for making sure that these core services are well behaved:

- Never have just one server. Use at least two servers, in master/slave configuration or in primary/secondary modes for DNS. Keeping the servers close to their clients, ideally on the same side of a router or other filtering device, will prevent problems due to network connectivity or intermittent routing issues.

- Make sure you list more than one DNS server in DNS client's `resolv.conf` files. Have a fallback position of some high-level, well-known server that can be consulted when all else fails.

- Design a fallback plan, so that a catastrophic failure in the name service can be worked around using local files if required. This means making a master password file that is consistent with the NIS maps, and an `/etc/hosts` file derived from DNS zone information. This data probably exists already where the NIS and DNS maps are built, so putting it into a form in which it can be used to populate critical servers is not a major task. The fallback plan should be manual, as it requires changing several machine configurations, and it should detail the failure modes under which naming service priorities are changed or other key network services are bypassed in the interests of recovering from a network failure.

- Invest in change management and operational processes that leave audit trails and do consistency checks of generated configuration files. Being process-weak is a sure way to introduce a failure at the root of your graph.

- Watch for network topology issues that can lead to a partitioning or breakdown of the network services. Keeping NIS and DNS servers close to their clients helps, but also watch for web/proxy servers, authentication (when feasible), and directory servers. The number of services calling your NIS servers, for example, should give you an indication of how to scale these servers and what kind of load they experience at peak times.

Armed with network graphs, redundant rails, and solid processes, you're ready to make data management services available. Before leaving this chapter, though, we briefly visit some denial-of-service attacks and fit them into the broader picture of network-level reliability.

Denial-of-Service Attacks

A well-engineered network can be taken out by a malicious user that floods it with bogus requests, or a broken application that repeatedly sends a failed request to the server. Denial-of-service attacks that are the result of poor application design have the same impact on overall reliability as the highly publicized attacks discussed at security conferences.

Denial-of-service attacks fit into several categories:

- Traffic flooding, attacks based on the UDP echo protocol, in which a machine sends an endless stream of requests to a server. Some of the echo-based attacks you'll find described in detail on the CERT web site www.cert.org are called *smurf* and *fraggle*. These attacks attempt to overwhelm a system by presenting it with a never-ending input stream.

■ Attempts to crash the application or its network stack, such as the Ping of Death, which attempts to overflow the network stack of PCs with excessively long packets that require reassembly on the receiving end.

■ Connection attempts that fill up a service's queue and render the service inaccessible to other clients. The most well known are SYN attacks (named for the synchronize sequence numbers, or SYN step, in a TCP connection setup) that take down TCP-based services by flooding the input queue with bogus connection requests. The trin00 attacks in February 2000 that affected ebay.com and yahoo.com were distributed denial-of-service attacks that generated enormous connection loads for the Internet-facing web servers of those sites.

■ Attempts to start multiple copies of a service, consuming all available resources on the server. Usually an attacker will look for a well-known, frequently used CGI script or executable, and then connect to that URL in an attempt to have the server fork itself to death.

In addition to the obvious issue of careful packet filtering and closing known security holes in your web and application servers, your best defense against a DoS attack is to make sure your servers can handle very high connection backlogs, and that they discard half-completed connections quickly:

■ Increase the TCP connection queue depth to either its maximum value or to a reasonable upper limit given the rate of connections and typical network latency you'll be dealing with. Many operating systems allow you to increase the connection backlog into the tens of thousands. A reasonable rule of thumb is to take your maximum connection arrival rate (estimate using your HTTP logs over a period of 10 to 20 busy minutes) and multiply by three times the maximum latency for the network over which these connections occur. If you're running a web site that gets most of its traffic from AOL, figure your user-to-site latency could be in the 0.2-second (200-millisecond) range; if you get a maximum of 1,000 connection requests a second, then your queue depth should be 0.2 seconds × 3 × 1,000 requests/second, or 600. The scalar factor of three is due to the client-server-client-server round-trips required to establish a connection.

■ Many operating systems split the connection queue depth control into two variables: one for the incoming request queue (those in the first part of the handshake) and one for requests that are waiting on the second half. DoS attack requests won't make it off of the first queue, which lets the operating system prune that queue more quickly. Use the same rule of thumb above as a lower bound on the queue depth.

- If you find that you're subjected to a flurry of requests for the same network service application, you can limit the number of concurrent requests using the `xinetd` (`www.xinetd.org`) replacement for the standard `inetd` daemon that maps incoming TCP and UDP requests to associated server processes. `xinetd` will limit the number of connections, give you time-based access control so that you can open the gates only during certain periods of the day, and control the growth of log files to prevent a full filesystem from becoming a denial-of-service attack in its own right.

YOUR BARN DOOR IS OPEN

In addition to my day job, I run two small web sites for nonprofit organizations. Donated PCs with Linux are the system of choice because I can remotely administer, monitor, and whack them as needed. When attempting to log in to one system for some mail alias updates, I noticed that the system was unusually slow. A cursory look at the load average and running processes showed that sendmail had taken over the system: We were being used as an open relay to forward spam to several million people. Panic ensued; this was the primary email server for our organization, and people had grown to depend on it for basic communications and scheduling with a far-flung community. My reaction was fairly brute-force: Turn off `sendmail`, then check the `sendmail` logs for clues. I noticed that all of the spam contained what appeared to be URLs as part of the recipient's address, and that led me to the web server log files. Sure enough, someone had been using our `formmail` script to turn our web server into a mail relay—the log files had pages of entries showing execution of this CGI script. Mea culpa. I was using an old version of `formmail` with a known security hole in it, and some web crawlers managed to find it by looking for all variations of the URL `cgi-bin /formmail.pl`. Because we used mixed-case names for our scripts, our site wasn't hit as quickly as others that matched the all lowercase probes. Morals of the story: If you use publicly available software, stay on top of the web sites and mailing lists that support it to be aware of security holes. Keep up with your web server log files because they give you early clues about probes, crawlers, and other attempts to sniff out an opening in your site. Failing to do so is equivalent to walking around with your barn door open.[1]

—Hal

[1] For those readers who don't have elementary school-aged children at home, "leaving your barn door open" means you're walking around with the fly of your pants wide open. Not an attractive thing.

Denial-of-service attacks that fit into the malicious category are best handed off to the security team for evaluation. This is another topic we touch on for completeness, and to paint a picture of complete responsibility. Even well-designed services suffer when extreme conditions are presented to them; if you can quickly diagnose and recover from these corner cases, you'll present a more reliable face to the world.

THE BIG SECRET

Stories surrounding the online debut of Victoria's Secret catalog are now Internet apocrypha, used by vendors to sell more hardware and bandwidth by playing on the hope or fear that another customer will enjoy the same massive audience. Supposedly, the Victoria's Secret web site with streaming video, launched via ads during the Super Bowl, was swamped by user requests as soon as it came online. It wasn't just the Victoria's Secret site that suffered, though: ISPs passing streaming video to those who managed to get through had excessively high loads. All intermediate networks felt the brunt of the user crush.

—Hal

Assuming that incoming load doesn't contain any unwelcome surprises, and that the key network services are well behaved, you're ready to make your main network data services reliable.

Key Points

- Network redundancy can be achieved using multiple connections to the same network, multiple networks in an asymmetric configuration, or multiple live networks.

- Balance complexity and cost against benefits when choosing a network redundancy scheme, because you're affecting every client and server in the end-to-end system.

- Manual failover is a realistic and practical approach to shuffling multiple hosts between networks.

- Network services such as naming need to be among the most reliable you have, if you use them, because many other higher-level services and management utilities depend on them.

CHAPTER

10

Data Centers and the Local Environment

Occurrences in [the environment] are beyond the reach of exact prediction because of the variety of factors in operation, not because of any lack of order in nature.

—Albert Einstein

In this chapter, we move to Level 5 of the Availability Index, the Local Environment, as shown in Figure 10.1. Environmental issues tend to be less technical than some of the other Index levels. Nevertheless, the environment in which your critical systems operate can have a serious impact on system availability. If the processes and the environment around your systems are well run, they will probably slip into obscurity and never be noticed by your users unless they are the cause of a significant outage.

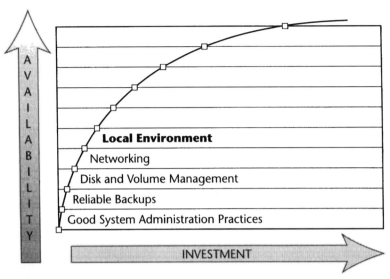

Figure 10.1   Level 5 of the Availability Index.

Data Centers

Administered properly, data centers can be wonderful places from which to operate critical systems. But just like anything else, if they are mismanaged, they can be bad news. Data centers are, in many ways, throwbacks to the days of large mainframe computing. Mainframes required carefully controlled temperature and humidity, and they needed to be placed where certain people could get regular access to them. Since they had specific power requirements, data centers represented a single place where 220-volt lines could be run, battery backup units could be installed, and large amounts of air-conditioning could be installed. Raised floors made it easy to hide the spider webs of cables that often emanated from these machines to terminals, printers, and tape units. Fire protection could be centralized there; old Halon[1] fire suppression systems could be deployed in a limited area.

Although most modern computers are not as picky about temperature and humidity as the older mainframes were, today's data centers have many of the same features. One reason for the similarity, of course, is that many modern data centers still have mainframes happily chugging along. In fact, some high-end servers from vendors like Sun and HP are looking more and more like

---

[1] Until 1994, fire suppression systems based on Halon, a liquefied, compressed gas that stops the spread of fire by chemically disrupting combustion, were commonly found in data centers and other facilities where water could not be used. In 1994, the Clean Air Act ended production of new Halon, but many facilities still use recycled Halon. Other chemicals have been introduced to replace Halon.

mainframes. As a result, power conditioning, fire protection, and environmental controls are still valuable and practical with today's systems. Modern fire protection systems are safer and cleaner than Halon, but in the data center they can still be centralized into a relatively small space. Power requirements run the gamut, and 220-volt lines are still common requirements for larger systems.

Data centers offer significant advantages and disadvantages as compared to leaving critical systems in regular work areas. The following are some advantages:

Centralized resources.   A data center is the perfect place to coordinate all the specialized requirements of large, critical machines: conditioned 220-volt power, fire protection, security, battery backups, raised floors, atmospheric control, and so on. If systems were deployed at random throughout the facility, those resources would need to be available everywhere. By limiting their deployment to the data center, a tremendous cost saving can be achieved.

Physical security.   Data centers work well to prevent inappropriate physical access to systems. But since they are centralized and they contain lots of large, impressive-looking equipment, there is a tendency to show them off through data center tours (see *Data Center Tours*, later in this chapter), which limit security.

But there are disadvantages too:

Limited possibilities for expansion.   If your systems need to expand beyond the capacity of your rack, it may not be possible to get another rack adjacent to the first one. This can lead to complicated and messy layouts of systems, as they spread themselves in a seemingly random fashion all over the data center, like fast-food toys in a family minivan. In that event, there may be issues with cable lengths, especially when SCSI is involved, that make such expansion impossible.

Putting all your eggs in one basket.   Centralizing your systems can be a double-edged sword. Countering all the advantages of centralization, that we discussed previously, is the prospect that a single calamity could strike the data center and wipe out most or all of the company's computing resources at the same time. Of course, this can be addressed by maintaining multiple data centers at separate facilities, a topic we cover at length in Chapter 20, "The Disaster Recovery Plan." Some people prefer to keep their clustered systems at opposite ends of their data center, to limit the impact of a localized external calamity such as a ceiling or floor collapse, or an overhead pipe leak.

Too much physical security.   Some security is critical, but too much security will do little more than impede the ability of system administrators to get their jobs done. In our experience, good security doesn't keep the bad guys out; if a bad guy really wants in, he will find a way. All that overprotective physical security does is slow down the good guys who have valid, often time-critical, reasons for getting into the data center.

Perpetual construction.   Like airports, it seems that data centers are always undergoing some sort of construction. Often that means large people who are unfamiliar with the nature of the equipment housed in the data center tromping around the floor in heavy work boots, climbing ladders, pushing equipment, moving ceiling or floor tiles, and plugging large pieces of heavy machinery with huge motors into the same circuits as delicate computer equipment. They are also likely to prop open otherwise secure doors, circumventing any attempts to maintain security. Invariably, dust is stirred up and gets sucked into fans and filters, impeding system ventilation. Power interruptions (planned and otherwise) are common hazards of data center construction, and sometimes broken pipes (water, heat, fire protection, and so on) will interfere with the data center's operations.

Be sure that when you consider placing systems in a centralized data center, you consider all of these issues.

Data Center Racks

If you choose to locate your systems in a data center, you will almost certainly mount them in data center racks. Just as with data centers, there are advantages and disadvantages to rack-mounting your systems.

Advantages and Disadvantages to Data Center Racks

The following are some advantages:

Neatness and organization.   Racks place systems and their components near to one another, and allow for system grouping based on ownership in a large organization or based on system function.

Security.   Most racks provide door locks to keep unauthorized personnel away from your systems. This makes it harder for cables, tools, and other components to simply vanish.

Centralized power.   Racks are rated for power capacity and provide ample, nearby power outlets for their components.

Cooling.   Good racks have high-powered fans in them and are designed to provide adequate ventilation.

Efficient use of space.   Racks enable systems to be arranged vertically, so that additional equipment does not require additional floor space. In most data centers, floor space is at a premium.

LIFT AND SEPARATE
_____

A system manager for a popular web site told me how he got "religion" about rack-mounted equipment. Two systems in an HA pair were sharing the same machine room footprint—one rested on top of the other. (Workgroup servers can be cajoled into this physical configuration by pulling their casters off.) When the machine on the bottom failed and needed to be replaced, a system administrator lifted the top machine, yanking all of its network cables free, and taking the live half of the HA pair offline.

—Hal

Of course, data center racks also have disadvantages, including the following:

Hard-to-relocate mounted components.   Since components are usually mounted directly to the rails of the rack, moving a system around can require more than one person, including one to remove the screws and another to hold the system so that it doesn't fall. The proximity of neighboring racks or badly opening rack doors may make it very difficult for more than one person to physically reach into the same rack at the same time without achieving new degrees of intimacy.

Cabling issues.   Commonly, cables in data center racks are tied together; moving a single cable from a bundle means disturbing all the cables in that bundle. Disturbing those cables adds risk and could affect the services that those cables provide. Also, in a data center rack, there is a single best path between two components, say, a system and a disk array. If the system and disk array are joined by two parallel cables for added availability, the physical arrangement of the equipment may make it difficult or impossible to run the cables along separate paths. (More on cabling later in the chapter.)

Tipping or collapsing hazards.   Racks are extremely heavy, often weighing 500 or 1,000 pounds or more after they are fully loaded. If the weight is poorly distributed (that is, the rack is top-heavy), someone leaning on it could cause it to topple over. While the effects of toppling racks can be pretty serious for the systems contained in the racks and those nearby, they pale in significance when compared to the impact of the racks striking or landing on an unfortunate person who happens to be wandering past the rack at just the wrong moment on his way to visit his own systems.

Rack wheels.   Most data center cabinets have casters on the bottom to make it easy to move them around the data center. They usually also have brakes on the casters, so that when the rack is in its final location, it stays there. It is not unusual for caster brakes to become unset (for example, they get kicked or a momentarily bored administrator plays with it with his feet). If the brakes are taken off, and someone leans on the rack, the rack may roll away, pulling on cables, connectors, and systems. It's not hard to imagine a rolling rack taking systems from other racks along for the ride.

Clearances.   This is generally a problem with or without racks: You need to make sure you have enough clearance from walls and other equipment to remove a board, drive, power supply, or other component from a system. If you place your racks in neat rows, the rows have to be set far enough from walls and each other so that the largest clearance requirement is observed. This is a good argument for keeping like-sized equipment racked together, and for carefully studying how you'll service equipment after it's bolted in.

A-DOOR-ATION

I was responsible for some systems that were stored in a data center rack. The systems had been inserted into the rack from the front and fastened to their shelves. We knew that it might be necessary to slide a board out of the very wide system chassis, and so we left enough clearance space behind the rack. Unfortunately, when we had a problem and had to actually remove one of the system boards, there was no way to get it past the back door of the rack. It missed the opening by less than half an inch, but that was enough to mess us up badly. We had to take the systems down, unfasten everything, and reposition the systems with enough clearance to get around the door. In the end, we had to repeat this action on four other nearby racks as well. Good testing would surely have caught this problem.

—Evan

Too much security.   If the doors on the cabinet are locked and the person with the keys is unavailable, you will have a problem if you need to access the system.

Effects of neighboring systems.   Apart from the possibility of neighboring racks falling over and striking yours, nearby systems are probably administered by administrators who have nothing to do with your systems. They may not show the same respect to your systems that you would show theirs. If your racks aren't locked, they might borrow components or loose tools from yours.

The China Syndrome Test

To call attention to another disadvantage of arranging critical systems vertically in the same rack, we offer an exercise that we call the China Syndrome Test. Take one of those huge 64-ounce (two liter) paper cups of soda pop available at many convenience stores in the United States. Fill it all the way up with real soda pop (no diet stuff, please; sugar works much better for this experiment). Carefully set it on top of the cabinet containing your critical rack-mounted servers. Now knock it over. Watch as the sticky soda pop flows into all the ventilation holes and onto the systems and disks! Marvel as it runs out the bottom of one case and into the top of the next! Panic as you consider what happens as the sugar-laden goo runs down into your raised floor! Lose your job as you realize that you have violated company policy that prohibits food and drink in the data center, and cost your company thousands of dollars!

Are your systems arranged to minimize the effects of such a spill? Or are both of your clustered servers arranged vertically in the same cabinet? Are both sets of your disk mirrors similarly vulnerable? What if the mess finds its way into your lone disk array? Would this spill take down critical servers? Chances are that they have already become soggy, sticky toast.

Rules prohibiting food and drink in the data center are important, but they are often violated—especially late at night and on weekends. Don't assume that such a policy will keep all such contraband out of your data center. It won't. Of course, many data centers have no such prohibition, and moreover, you don't have to restrict your worries to soda, beer, and little ketchup packets. Glycol-based coolant from the air conditioner or water from a leaking overhead pipe can have the same effect.

Disclaimer: Please don't try this at home, kids! We accept no responsibility if a reader actually performs this exercise on his systems. The China Syndrome Test is best performed as a Thought Experiment. Offer void where prohibited by law, common sense, or management dictum.

Balancing Security and Access

Physical security is an important part of any security model. If the bad guys can't get to their target, they can't hurt it. As a result, entry to data centers usually requires waving of some sort of electronic ID card through a scanner or entering a numeric code into a lock. Those are sensible security precautions, in that they will generally keep the bad guys out—unless the bad guy gets hold of someone else's ID card or learns the code.

Whatever security system you choose, and this does not just apply to data centers but to any environment that must be secured, it is very important to balance security with practicality. If a system in the data center is down and requires a physical visit by an administrator, the physical security system should not slow him down. If it can, then forgetting his ID card can add 10 or

15 minutes to system recovery time, as he goes back to his desk to retrieve the card. (If he left it home, add a lot more time.)

TRAPPING YOURSELF A MAN

At one particularly security-conscious organization, I was offered a data center tour. In order to enter the data center, we had to pass through something called a *man-trap*. One at a time, each of the five of us went through the outside door, into a tiny room, basically big enough for one person. In that room, the man-trap, I was electronically sniffed for explosives and had to show ID authorizing me for entry into the data center through a second door. After each of us passed into the data center, we began the tour. As we neared the back wall of the data center, I noticed an unguarded, open door that opened onto an unsecured corridor. On the far wall of that corridor was another open door, leading outside to the parking lot. I could actually see my car.

When I questioned the security of such an arrangement, I was told that there was construction going on, and that was the only door large enough to bring heavy equipment in and out. So much for the man-trap.

—Evan

If security is too complex or time-consuming, doors will wind up propped open, bypassing all security. Many data centers have proper security at the main door, but the administrators know that there is a back door that is permanently propped open or unlocked. That speeds recovery, but it obviously compromises security. After all, today's trusted employee might be tomorrow's saboteur.

Data Center Tours

Let's not beat around the bush on this point: Data center tours are bad. Unless there is some business-critical reason that strangers are permitted to wander around the data center, poking their noses into the racks and cabinets that contain some of the most fragile, expensive, and critical material assets your enterprise owns, visitors should be barred from the data center. In mainframe days, data centers were called *glass houses* because they always had a large window through which the curious could watch the goings-on inside, without being able to touch the equipment. That model has fallen out of favor and has been replaced by the tour.

With all the talk of data center security and corporate security in general, one might think that most corporate policies would prohibit strangers entering data centers. After all, a good data center contains a high percentage (100 percent?) of an enterprise's critical data and systems. A typical data center might have millions of dollars worth of delicate equipment that support the entire business for the enterprise.

Nevertheless, most companies encourage data center tours. Consider that a data center tour generally consists of one or two employees taking a group, often of six or seven or more, and herding them up and down rows of tall and noisy computer systems. Most data centers are basically the same, of course (there are always exceptions): There are rows upon rows of blue and beige boxes (maybe some purple nowadays), cabinets with smoked-gray Plexiglas doors, and a few large tape units. The raised floor consists of white tiles, with black stripes running between them. Some of the tiles have lots of little holes in them for ventilation. There are thousands of blinking LEDs, in the various racks and cabinets. Thick conduits and/or bundles of wires run overhead. And it's very loud, and probably pretty cold.

MY HARDWARE IS BIGGER THAN YOURS

I was taking a data center tour at a large financial company in New England. (It is rude to turn down tours, after all.) Among the rows of large boxes and the LEDs, I saw something that I had never seen on a tour. While many data centers put printed labels on their systems that identify the system's name, manufacturer, and model, these people had labeled their systems in a somewhat unusual way. In addition to the usual information, their system labels contained the system's function, and the original cost of the hardware. When I asked why, they told me that it was a matter of pride. All I could figure was that this gives a malicious tour-taker a road map to exactly which systems he wants to sabotage.

—Evan

With companies so eager to show off their data centers, it makes it very easy for a malicious person to gain entry, where they can lag behind their tour slightly and perform mischief. Imagine someone from your major competitor visiting your office on the pretense of a job interview. It's very common for technical job interviews to end with a data center tour. Once in the data center, the interviewee can fall a few steps behind his tour guide and accidentally trip over a power cord, lean on a power switch, or perform other mischief. Even the best-intentioned tour guest could cause trouble on a tour, by tripping on a cord, knocking something over, or hitting a power switch by mistake.

We'd like to see businesses return to the glass house model, where visitors can look but not touch.

You wouldn't take a stranger on a tour of the vault where the company stores its cash. ("And over here are our $100 bills.") Why take them into the data center? If they don't need to be there to do their job, don't let them in.

A DIFFERENT KIND OF BACKUP

On yet another data center tour, a system administrator was hurriedly bringing some equipment down the row that we were standing in. Everyone on the tour stepped aside as best they could to let him pass. In my haste to get out of the way, I backed into an old-fashioned line printer, and right into the power switch, turning it off. The printer was printing something, so the job was lost. I saw what I had done and quickly (and very smoothly) turned it back on. I don't think anyone noticed (except for the person who had printed the job).

Even well-intentioned and careful visitors to data centers can cause problems.

—Evan

Off-Site Hosting Facilities

The last few years have seen the emergence, and then the near total disappearance and reemergence, of companies dedicated to off-site hosting facilities for computer systems. There are still large companies who offer this service as a part of other offerings, most often consulting, but the small ones were casualties of the dot-com bust.

Early generation off-site hosting facilities (OHFs) consisted of a large room partitioned off with metal cages. Each cage had rigid walls that were made of thick welded and painted wire in a heavy frame, arranged in a grid pattern that went up to or just short of the ceiling. The open grid made ventilation between the cages possible and prevented too much heat buildup in any one cage. Cages were fairly small, and it was not unusual for one company to have several cages scattered around the facility. The floors were standard data center white raised floors. Cooling, humidity control, and power protection was centrally provided by standard data center air-conditioning devices.

After visiting a few of the early-generation off-site hosting facilities, we came away with some significant concerns about the level of security and protection that these sites offer. Even though facilities like these are hard to find anymore, if they even still exist at all, the lessons that they left behind are valuable and are worth exploring. These lessons included the following:

Physical security.   The holes between the wires were large enough for fingers, so any cords or systems that were near the edge of the cage were potential targets of mischief. If someone got into the facility with a broomstick handle, the person could inflict serious damage on many of the clients in very short order.

Public cable runs.   If your company had two cages located at opposite ends of the facility, and you needed to run cables from one cage to the other, those cables would pass beneath cages belonging to other organizations. Someone might be able to lift up a floor tile and intentionally or accidentally damage or break your critical data cable. There was no protection at all against that sort of calamity.

Anonymity.   In a most sensible move, cages were not labeled with the identity of their owners. However, many clients labeled their systems with asset tags that clearly identified the name of the company who owned them. Some administrators considered it to be a game to figure out who owned which cages.

Impact of others' problems.   If one cage had a fire or some other kind of serious physical problem, neighboring cages would be affected through no fault of their own.

Impact on recovery time.   If a system is located a 45-minute subway ride away from the main office, how will travel time impact recovery time, if a visit is required?

Physical space.   Is there room in the cage for all of the equipment? Can you arrange it without violating the China Syndrome model? Will there still be room to move around the equipment? Will you be able to repair one system without affecting any of the others?

Adequate cooling and power.   Early-generation OHFs were not prepared for the onslaught of customers that they saw. They did not have sufficient cooling or power, and customers were often forced to shut down their busy equipment to conserve power or to prevent overheating. Beware of large temporary cooling units in the aisles between cages; that's a sure sign of trouble.

Safe working conditions.   Small, cramped cages filled with lots of equipment and cables are a surefire recipe for trouble. There are tripping and banging hazards galore for system administrators under these conditions. The removal of raised floor tiles makes tripping and falling even more likely.

RUNNING HOT AND COLD

Once when I was working in an OHF on a very hot August day in New York, I walked past one cage, where a system administrator sat, furiously typing on his keyboard. Nothing unusual about that, except that he was wearing a down ski parka, zipped up to his neck, a wool hat, and fingerless gloves. Normal protocol at OHFs is that the administrators from different companies leave each other alone, but I had to ask.

He explained that he was sitting in the only remaining open space in the cage, and it happened to be right underneath an air-conditioning duct that was blasting ice cold air. The air was so cold that he simply had to have his ski parka to be able to work. I couldn't help but wonder what the people from OSHA[2] would have said if they had seen these working conditions.

—Evan

There was another serious concern that could not have been foreseen in the early, salad days of OHFs. The OHF is in every way a data center for its customers. If the OHF went out of business or closed a facility (which happened a lot near the end, sometimes without any notice), displaced customers were forced to quickly migrate their operations from the closing OHF to a new facility. In another context, a rapid, unforeseen data center migration is called a disaster and could easily result in extended downtime.

Electricity

There is no better way to bring home this book's mission statement—that achieving true high availability requires more than just installing failover management software—than to discuss electricity and electrical dependencies. A system that is functioning perfectly will, of course, stop instantly when its electrical supply is cut off. If two systems are connected together in a high-availability pair, and their electricity is cut off, they will both stop working. By providing electricity through separate paths, their power source, and therefore the systems, becomes more reliable. The farther upstream the power source paths can be separated, the more reliable the power supply gets.

Plugging both systems in an HA pair into the same power strip is obviously silly, especially if the power strip has a single on/off switch on it. Running both systems through the same circuit breaker is almost as silly, but much

---

[2] The Occupational Health and Safety Administration is the United States government agency that regulates workplace and worker safety.

more common, probably because it's a little harder to see which power outlets are on the same circuit.

The extreme at the other end is to obtain power from two different power grids or power companies. While this will provide system protection against some major outages, it can be prohibitively expensive and may introduce problems with grounding or other electrical issues.

POWERLESS

One customer I had was very concerned about power outages. He went to the extreme measure of running power to the building from two separate power companies. The problem was that they chose to run both lines into the building through the same power pole in the parking lot in front of the building. When a car knocked down that pole, power from both companies was interrupted until the pole could be re-erected and the lines rerun.

—Evan

UPS

Another way to defend your operations against power interruptions is through the use of a so-called uninterruptible power supply (UPS). The "uninterruptible" part is pure marketing. UPSs are nothing more than battery backups that will continue to provide power for a limited amount of time after electricity fails. But, like any other battery, they will cease to function after their power has been drained. The duration of the power protection is determined by the capacity of the battery unit and the amount of power being drawn. More capacity and less power drawn means longer life. More size also means more money; UPSs can be very expensive. When you increase the draw on the UPS by plugging new equipment into it, be sure that you get more and stronger UPSs; otherwise, your UPS won't last as long as you believe it will.

A few years ago, one of the American tire companies released a tire that they advertised as being able to be driven for 50 miles after it has gone flat. The marketing says that this will enable you to get to your destination or to a repair shop without stranding you in the middle of nowhere. Sounds great, right? It might get you to your destination, but the only way the extra 50 miles can get you to a repair shop is if you know that the 50-mile countdown has begun. If you don't know, then you are just stranded 50 miles farther down the road. (To be fair, the fine print on the commercial made reference to a required monitoring device.)

The same rule applies to UPSs. A UPS may get you to your destination (the restoration of regular power), but if it doesn't, then when the battery runs out your systems will go down just as hard as they would have before the UPS kicked in. Make sure that your UPS is smart enough to tell your systems or your administrators (preferably your systems) when it is running out of juice so that they can be brought down in an orderly fashion. Be sure you leave enough time and juice for the graceful shutdown of your databases, filesystems, and network services to complete.

UPSs can be used for minimal protection against downtime in two ways:

Very brief power interruptions.   In many parts of the world, especially during hot summers, it is not unusual for a one- or two-second power interruption to wreak havoc on unprotected systems. A fully-charged UPS will, in almost all cases, bridge the gap and keep your systems running through such a brief outage.

An orderly shutdown of the system.   When the power goes out suddenly, and systems are shut down "violently," filesystem damage can result. At the very least, a UPS should be used to give the systems time to shut themselves properly.

If the UPSs have more power, they can, of course, keep systems running longer. More power and more time from UPSs can cost a lot of money, and the value that they return must be carefully balanced against the cost.

An often overlooked fact about UPSs is that the more equipment you plug into them, the less time they will be able to keep that equipment running. More equipment will cause the UPS's power to drain that much faster. Test your UPSs from time to time and make sure that they still have the capacity you think they do.

Backup Generators

The other way to protect your systems against power failures is through the use of backup generators. We know of jet-engine-powered generators in at least two New York financial houses, and have seen elaborate diesel-powered generators in telecommunications hubs. Backup generators are no less likely to fail when they run out of fuel than UPSs are. The difference is that large diesel-powered backup generators can produce a lot more power.

MORE POWERLESS

One of my customers had a very expensive jet-engine-powered generator on the roof. One day the regular power went out, so it was up to the roof to start the engines. (He did have a UPS in place to bridge the gap between the time the power went out and when the generator could be started up.) Our guy ran up the stairs to the roof (remember, the power was out: no elevators), and, panting, tried to start the engines. Unfortunately, nobody had ever bought any jet fuel to power the generator, so it wouldn't start. When the UPS drained, they were out of power. The moral: Never assume; test everything!

—Evan

Cabling

The typical data center contains many miles of cables. From network cables to disk-attach cables (ESCON, FC, SCSI, or Ethernet) to serial and parallel cables to electrical cables, the floor under most data centers looks like a rat's nest. Some data centers will also have keyboard, mouse, and video cables that run to user workstations, and other cables that have been in place so long that nobody knows what they do. (But don't touch them; they might be really important!)

The time to address availability issues in cabling is when the cables are installed. Issues to consider include the following:

Cable labels.   Every cable should be clearly labeled. Labels should be on both ends of the cable, and if the cable is long, there should be additional labels every so often. Ideally the label should include what flows on the cable, where it starts and ends, when it went into service, the type of cable it is, and who to contact if there is a problem or issue with the cable. Since cables often undergo stress, it's important that the labels be durable; the ink must not smudge, even if it gets wet, and the labels must not be able to fall off of the cable.

Cable wraps and ties.   There is a natural tendency to make data center racks and cable runs as neat and organized as possible, mostly because it looks good. This leads to cables being tightly fastened with cable wraps to any appropriate surface. The really organized administrator will use cable wraps every few inches along the entire cable run to make sure that those cables are really tied down, and aren't going anywhere. Tying down cables is a bad policy; it sacrifices recovery time for neatness. By tightly tying cables down, you can create several problems:

- When a cable needs to be replaced, it requires opening (usually with a knife, although some more expensive cable wraps use Velcro to stay closed) all of those nice neat cable wraps to free the cable in question. Knives and critical data cables are not usually a good combination.

- Tightly tied cables make it almost impossible to move the systems that are attached to these cables. Since the cables have no slack to them, there's no way to move systems without freeing all of the system's cables. Knives again.

- Human nature is such that administrators are more likely to try to shift a system slightly rather than cut all those cable ties. Subtle movements can cause breaks in cables or connectors to become detached from their system.

- When it is necessary to swap one system for another on a rack, it is very difficult to do so quickly when cables are rigidly fastened to the rack. If the system in question is in the middle of a stack of systems on a shelf, then all of the systems above it must be moved up first, and then down (to fill the space just vacated). If there is not enough slack in the cables to handle that minor move, then, once again, cable wraps must be cut.

If you absolutely must use cable wraps, use the Velcro variety, rather than thin plastic locking strips (the more common and less expensive kind). Velcro can be easily opened and reclosed without the use of sharp objects.

Removing cables.   Clean up after yourself. Perhaps the toughest requirement in managing the cables in a data center is to remember to retire old cables when they are no longer needed. Cables and the systems they are attached to often outlive the people who installed them, and usually outlive the institutional memory of the cable installation. Nevertheless, it is very important to remove old cables to free up space for new cables. (Sometimes, though, it's easier to just move to a new data center.)

PULL ON THIS

When I was a system administrator for one Wall Street financial firm, we ran into a problem I'd never come across before. The space under the raised floor in the main data center was full. There was no more room to run any new cables. As a result, IT management announced a new initiative: They were going to go through all of the cables under the floor and remove the ones that were no longer active. Hardly any of the cables were labeled, so it became a huge testing effort to figure out which cables were active.

The task took several months and cost the firm a lot of money. If cables had been labeled, or if administrators had removed cables when they were no longer in use, or if someone had maintained a database of cables, the task could have been completed much faster for a lot less money.

In the end, they identified nearly two-thirds of the cables in the floor as unused and removed them.

—Evan

Multiple conduits.   Newer disks and networks often support the running of multiple, parallel cables between devices. While parallel cables can improve performance, the real gain is in availability. If a controller or HBA fails for one of the cables, data can continue to move between the devices using the second cable. If, however, the cables are run through the same conduits, and along the same paths between the two devices, the value in increased availability is limited. A single event could easily cut both cables, halting the flow of data.

We offer a rather extreme policy to help reduce the cable overpopulation problem: If a cable is not labeled, it should be removed from the floor. Large data centers will simply giggle at this suggestion, and perhaps they should. But small data centers, shipboard data centers come to mind, may find this is an absolute requirement. They do not always have the 9 to 12 inches of space under their raised data center floors.

Cooling and Environmental Issues

Although today's computer systems are less sensitive to overheating than systems from 10 and 20 years ago, it is still important to maintain reasonable temperature and humidity levels in your computing environments. Failure of an air-conditioning unit can result in the total failure of the data center. The effects of extended exposure to extreme heat or humidity can be subtle or, in some cases, can be quite noticeable.

The clearances between disk heads and their associated disk platters have become remarkably small. Heat can cause expansion in disk head arms, causing the disk head to make contact with the platter, destroying your disk and its data. The glue that holds the disk heads in place can soften or melt under extreme conditions, causing it to move out of line. In more extreme cases, solders could melt or the fire suppression system could go off, giving all the computers a nice, cool bath or sucking all the oxygen out of the room and causing a potential personnel problem.

If your data center or other computing environment is unmanned, even just some of the time, then it is imperative to install temperature sensors that can contact a human being who can come in and fix the problem. In the worst case, fixing the problem may mean shutting down the equipment, but since that will eliminate most of the heat generation, at least the equipment will be safe.

Systems should also have ability to shut themselves down if they begin to overheat. If a system detects an internal fan failure, it should be able to spin up other fans and notify the appropriate support personnel that maintenance is required. Look for thermal protection and thermal overload notification features. Ideally, the system notices it has a problem, since it may be local to a fan or airflow difficulty and not a machine room condition. However, you can achieve some measure of thermal protection with simple environmental monitoring and an "emergency power off" switch. That's a crude but effective method when the alternative is data corruption.

Possibly more serious than overheating is water penetration. If water (or soda pop) gets under your raised floor or starts accumulating on the true floor, all sorts of damage can occur, including short circuits and general component damage. Electronic devices don't generally cope well with water (or soda pop). Water could come from cooling system failures, building leaks, water pipe leaks, or even condensation. To protect yourself from water damage, install water and humidity detectors that contact people immediately when trouble is found. Often these can be part of the same system that detects fire or cooling system problems.

The most serious environmental problem is, of course, a fire. Fires can be extremely dangerous and possibly fatal to your personnel. Automated fire detection and suppression systems are a must and are required by law in most areas. Support personnel need to be taught to leave the premises immediately if the fire alarm sounds; a fire suppression system that removes the oxygen from the room will surely have unfortunate effects on anyone who stays in the room. Even an accidental discharge of the fire suppression system can have negative consequences, as you have to have equipment scrubbed before it can come back online.

If the fire is serious enough, the data center will have to be closed for some period. To keep critical applications running, even through as serious a calamity as a fire, consider implementing a disaster recovery (DR) site. We discuss DR in Chapter 20.

System Naming Conventions

One of the more emotional issues around system administration is system names. Some people want to be very serious with their system names, giving them names that are encoded with all sorts of information (for example, *ha4pv56d*...). Others want to use numbered system names (*Chi001, Chi002*, and so on). And still others prefer lighthearted or cute names, or names that come from a themed set (*sneezy, sleepy, bashful, dopey*, and so on) rather than names that are especially meaningful.

If you are naming desktop or laptop computers, then naming them after their owner is certainly appropriate. If a computer is not owned by an individual, then other schemes are required.

From an availability perspective, lighthearted names are the winning approach, but not by more than a nose. The value of coded names is clear; you can get a lot of information into a host's name, making it easy to organize the systems and to tell a lot about them from their names.

However, complex names violate our first principle of system design. They are not simple. When a new member joins the sys admin team, that person must learn, from scratch, the naming scheme so that she can go to the data center and reboot *ha4pv56d* and not *ha4pt56b*, when necessary.

A system name like *ha4pv56d* is more spelled than said. There is no opportunity when saying that name to sound anything out. As a result, you are reciting a list of six characters and a two-digit number. If instructions about *ha4pv56d* are being given over the phone, the opportunity for misunderstanding is great. Three of the eight characters are commonly misinterpreted over the phone without careful attention ("H... A... 4... P..." "T?" "No, P as in Peter... V as in Victor... fifty-six... D as in David..."). Imagine doing that with the operators at the pager service.

A name like *rocky* is said once, everyone knows how to spell it, and there is no room for confusion. Simplicity is good.

Then the question becomes what kind of naming scheme should you use. Schemes should always be open-ended sets, or, at least, sets that are so large that there's no reasonable way that you'll exhaust all of the possibilities. Snow White and her dwarves are a commonly used set of names that work just fine, until you get to the ninth system. (*snowwhite* would be the name for the eighth, of course). The planets (assuming that Pluto retains its status as a planet) work until you get to the tenth system.

Better schemes might be Star Trek characters from all the series (if you are into that sort of thing), Simpsons characters, Bible characters, musical groups and singers, mammals, fish, colors, street names in a large city, fruits, vegetables, and on and on. With a little imagination you can come up with a scheme that you'll never exhaust.

You might also choose to go with multiple schemes, a different naming scheme for different logical grouping within your organization, thereby encoding real information into the names.

I CAN NAME THAT HOST IN FOUR TALES

Back around 1990, I was consulting at one shop where they wanted to change the names of over 300 systems and bring them into one common naming scheme, but they could not think of a scheme that would be large enough to encompass them all. I offered cartoon and comic strip characters' names. After I assured them that I could, in fact, come up with 300 such names (I attribute it to wasted youth), they agreed. I spent the rest of the day coming up with a list of nearly 400 comic strip and cartoon character names, from nearly every discipline. They wound up with systems named *archie* and *jughead, scooby* and *daphne, lucy* and *linus, boris* and *natasha, jonny* and *bandit, clark* and *lois, zonker* and *thudpucker,* and on and on and on. That was as fun a day of work as I could ever remember.

Years later, I was consulting at a large telephone company in New Jersey, where I came across the strangest naming scheme I've ever seen. The guys in one group named the 15 systems in their workgroup after serial killers and murderers through history. They had *jripper, jdahmer, ggilmore, ahun,* and like that.

To end on a lighter note, I have one friend who makes sure that no matter where he works, there is a system called *elvis* on the network. This way, when he uses the Solaris ping command (`ping elvis`) to see if it is operational, he receives the uplifting message that "`elvis is alive`". The friend reports that he has often done the same thing with the name *paul,* but his attempts to name systems after religious figures have been squashed by management.

—Evan

When we got our first real dedicated VAXen in the Princeton Computer Science department, they were named after different ways they could misbehave: *quirky, flaky, down, panic,* and so on. The running joke was that we could call each other and ask "Is it *down?*" "No, it's *flaky.*" "You

mean is the machine named *flaky* not working?" "Yes, it's *down* right now."
Six machines and a few system managers made this both fun and
manageable, and there wasn't any large money riding on our ability to
quickly identify a troublemaking machine.

—Hal

Key Points

- Data centers and data center cabinets are valuable ways to maintain systems, but they are not perfect in all situations. Apply them with care.
- The time to take care of cabling issues is when the cables are installed, not when new problems arise. Label all of those cables!
- In system naming schemes, as in all areas, simplicity is the best approach.
- Remember that security and cooling are just as important to system availability as disk mirroring and clustering.

CHAPTER 11

People and Processes

Take away my people but leave my factories and soon grass will grow on the factory floors. Take away my factories and leave my people, and soon we will have a new and better factory.

—Andrew Carnegie

Why do builders skip the 13th floor of buildings, but book publishers aren't afraid to include a Chapter 11?

—George Carlin

It's been said that data is a business's most important asset. To say that is to overlook (and perhaps take for granted) a far more important business asset: the people.

In Chapter 11, we look at two important areas of availability, people and processes. Like Chapter 10, "Data Centers and the Local Environment," this comes under the heading of Local Environment, leaving us at the fifth level of the Availability Chart, as shown in Figure 11.1. You can implement all the processes that your business may need; processes that can make it a model of unmatched efficiency. But most of those processes require people to keep them going. It's people who will locate and fix bugs in software, it's people who will replace a failed board in a server, and it's people who will write the documentation that your systems need so that another generation of people can maintain them.

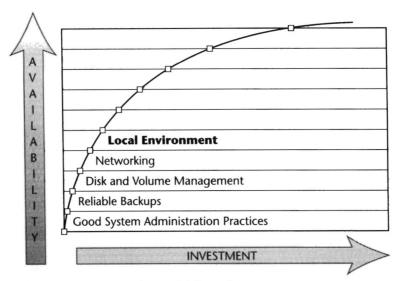

Figure 11.1   Level 5 of the Availability Index.

System Management and Modifications

Wouldn't it be nice if you could roll out a system and that would be the end of it? Imagine if you never had to revisit your systems for hardware, operating system, or application upgrades. As long as you're making wishes, how about a pony, too? Life just isn't that simple.

The first rule of system maintenance is that it will always be required. The trick is to perform the maintenance so that it has the least possible impact on overall system availability. The second part of that trick is to properly maintain your servers while still properly maintaining your personal life. Restricting all of your maintenance activities to Friday and Saturday nights after 8:00 P.M. doesn't leave a lot of time in life for much else. Of course, if your systems are used 24 hours a day, there may not be a noncritical time.

IN THE STILL OF THE NIGHT

At one job that I had, policy was that maintenance could only be performed on Friday nights. Work could only begin at 7:00 P.M., and then before any actual work could begin, a complete backup of the systems had to be taken. (These were development systems.)

One particular Friday night, backups completed at around midnight, and then we got to work doing a major system upgrade. Some time around 4:00 A.M. (I had come into work that morning at 8:00 A.M., having no idea how late the night would go), I made a mistake in judgment that turned out to be fairly serious. Due to a problem with the backups, this mistake caused the developers to be idled for nearly two weeks while files were manually repaired and recovered.

To this day, I blame my error (at least partially) on having been at work for 20 straight hours and having been alone for the last 8 of those hours.

—Evan

Maintenance Plans and Processes

The ideal way to perform ongoing system maintenance is to do so in a failover cluster (for more on failover clusters, see Chapter 15, "Local Clustering and Failover") and to work on one server at a time. Consider an active-passive cluster with two servers, *heart* and *soul*, that require maintenance. If *heart* is active, first perform the maintenance on *soul*, and then failover to it when your work is completed to make sure that the changes worked. If they did, then you can follow up with *heart* later. If not, you still have a perfectly good *heart* to go back to while you try again on *soul*.

Some other items will help to make your maintenance planning go a little better:

- If your systems are clustered or paired, additional complexities may be introduced by the very nature of the clustering. The best example of this is what happens when SCSI disks are shared between two servers. A SCSI chain cannot be broken while a system is accessing it. If the chain is broken (in other words, if the termination is removed), I/Os will fail, and users will be unable to work. (This is a SCSI-specific issue and does not apply where other disk technologies, such as Fibre Channel, are used.)

- Be sure to consider the ramifications of your work on other servers, clients, networks, and on your users in general.

- Always plan for the worst-possible case. (It's easy to plan for the best case!) What happens if adding new disks somehow wipes out the contents or formatting of the existing disks? What if that static shock you got when you opened the case destroys the motherboard?

- Never begin any significant system work without a plan to back out the changes. That could (and probably should) mean taking a full set of backups before you begin. It could mean designating a less-critical system that you would cannibalize if you have no spare parts and some unexpected hardware damage occurs.

- The best way to develop plans, contingencies, and a list of possible external impacts is to work with a team. Run your ideas past your peers and/or superiors. Peer review is a wonderful way for all parties involved to learn to improve their plans. In the worst case, your plans are perfect, so others can learn from your extraordinary wisdom.

System Modifications

The second law of thermodynamics tells us that disorder will always increase. That means constant change for your systems. However, when change is uncontrolled and undocumented, systems become unmanageable. The worst kind of change is the quick temporary change that "I'll get back to and make permanent tomorrow." Most of the time the temporary changes work fine, and there is no impetus to get back to them, nor to document the change. Hey, it's not permanent, right?

Things to Aim For

Some other things to aim for in the area of change control:

All changes must be documented.   This means leaving comments in the files that get changed; comments should describe the nature of the change and the reason for the change, and should include the name of the changer and the date(s) the change was applied. If documenting the change in a file is inappropriate, then document the changes offline in a notebook or other agreed-upon central location.

Try to limit the number of modifications applied at one time.   If you apply five changes at once and something immediately goes wrong on the system, it can be extremely difficult to figure which change caused the problem, especially if the changes are complex. Apply changes one at a time, until you can be sure that the change has fixed the problem it was intended to solve, and that it has not caused a new one.

Test everything.   Whenever changes are made to a production system, before the system is put back into production, the changes must be tested. As a bare minimum, tests should include the following steps:

- Bring up the server, and make sure it makes it through the entire startup routine.

- Make sure all filesystems are mounted and all databases are operational.

- Make sure all required server processes are running.

- Ensure that clients can reach their critical services and data on the server.

Different situations will require different and more thorough testing than this short list. The important thing is that anytime changes are made, proper testing is done and reported.

Automate the distribution of files.   Your operating system probably offers utilities to ease the distribution of files to several machines at once. There are also public domain utilities available on the Internet that have more features and flexibility than the standard ones. Use them! They were developed by people in a similar situation to yours and will probably handle your problems easily. Similarly, there are verification tools to make sure that files got to where they were headed. Use them to double-check your work. It is much faster to have a program check 20 machines for you than it is for you to manually log in to all 20 machines and poke around.

Use change management.   There are public domain and commercial utilities available for managing versions and changes in text files. These utilities allow you to roll back to previous versions of a file, if necessary, making it easy to back out the most recent changes. They can also generate a list of differences between one version and another. These utilities go by several names; SCCS, CVS, and RCS are some of the most commonly used and mature of these change-management packages.

Watch for system file changes.   Public domain utilities such as Tripwire can be used to keep an eye on certain key files so that if they get changed accidentally or maliciously, the system administrators are notified in a timely manner. The time to discover that files have changed is not during a failover or a reboot. Something as simple as modifying the order of entries in the /etc/vfstab filesystem mounting table on a Unix system can result in a never-ending stream of NFS errors when the server with the modified filesystem table reboots.

Software Patches

System vendors such as Sun Microsystems are constantly issuing operating system and application patches. Some patches are revised and upgraded 50 or more times each as problems are fixed that depend on previous fixes. Usually, it's not 50 fixes for the same bug, but 50 (or many more) fixes for different problems that grow in complexity over time, and all change the same kernel modules, library routines, or other system software components. It is almost impossible to keep up with all of them. On the other hand, patches are the best way to get up-to-date fixes to bugs and other problems that inevitably occur between product releases. Microsoft's strategy is to release only the most critical fixes as patches, and to roll other fixes into Service Packs, which are released only occasionally. This method makes it easier to keep up on the fixes that the vendor has released; however, it can significantly delay receipt of a fix or introduce new problems in legal agreements. Microsoft has been known to include new features and changes to their End User License Agreement in their Service Pack releases.

Managing patch revision levels and patch interactions is a challenge when vendors distribute them individually. Consider all the permutations of patches that may be installed on a particular system. Let's say there are just 10 patches available for a particular operating system, and each patch has three versions. Ideally, you want to be on the latest version of whatever patches you have chosen to install, unless other considerations prevent you from upgrading (an application may break with a later revision of a patch, or regression testing or end-of-month configuration freezes may prevent system changes for a few weeks). Each patch has four states: It can either not be installed at all, or installed in one of the three versions. Think of the 10 patches as digits in a base-4 (for the four states) numeral. Enumerating every possible value of every patch in every state yields a total of 4^{10} (or just over a million) possible permutations. It is unlikely that your vendor has tested every one of these combinations to ensure interoperability. Just for comparison, 50 patches with 5 revisions each yields 6^{50}, or roughly 808,281,277,464,764,060,643,139,600,456, 536,293,376 permutations (that's more than 808 trillion trillion trillion, or 808 undecillion). How many patches and revisions does your vendor have? What are the odds that he has tested all of the combinations and permutations? Undecillions-to-one, probably.

We recommend a two-pronged approach to selecting which ones to install. First, regularly contact the vendor, possibly as often as once per month, to obtain the most current list of recommended patches. Be sure that all of those have been applied on all of your systems, not just the critical ones, and that you are right up-to-date. Second, maintain a separate list of patches that are specifically required in your environment, and only apply those that are required, and keep those up-to-date as well. Don't apply patches or service packs to systems where they are not needed or recommended.

Unless a brand-new patch specifically fixes a serious problem you are having, don't just drop it onto your production systems without putting them through some acceptance testing. Either test new patches on less critical systems or wait a month or so before applying them at all so that others can test them and report problems. When a patch version number hasn't changed in a month or more, then it's probably acceptable to install it. If patch version numbers are changing all the time, keep away if you can.

When new service packs or jumbo patches are released, that is a good time to read online bulletin boards, Internet newsgroups, or trade magazines where such things are discussed. Get a feel from others who may have installed the updates for how they are working out. Try not to be the first one on your block to install patches or service packs.

Spare Parts Policies

If you choose to keep a spare parts inventory on hand, there are certain policies to follow that will help make your decision especially fruitful:

Inventory the parts that fail the most. This will have the greatest impact on MTTR, as you will not have to wait for shipping. You can replace these items as soon as they fail (or even before they fail, if you keep a close eye on system logs; see *Preventative Maintenance*). Disks and fans have moving parts, and as such fail a lot. A large system will have hundreds or even thousands of disks; if you are responsible for their maintenance, it is wise to keep spare disks around so that the failure of a single disk doesn't put a large chunk of critical data at risk. Part for part, though, power supplies fail the most often, so you should definitely stock them. It doesn't hurt to have some spare monitors on hand, either; there's no value in cannibalizing a good desktop system because you need a head for a critical system.

Inventory parts that are hard to get. If you find that a particular part is always back-ordered when you need it, it makes an excellent choice for inventorying. If you can wait for the part when there is no immediate need for it, everyone will be happier.

Test your stock. When parts come in, make sure that they work in non-critical systems. If they don't, there is no point to keeping them in inventory. Return defective parts before they are needed rather than when systems are down and waiting for them.

Rotate your stock. Always put the oldest parts into systems, rather than the newest parts. If a part is too old to use, then exchange it for a newer version. Determining the minimum acceptable hardware revision level means having regular audits of the spare parts stock done by your hardware service provider and asking your vendor for a list of the most current versions (or at least the supported versions) of the hardware in your stock.

Balance ease of access with proper security.   Make sure that authorized personnel can access the parts at any time of the day or night. However, if unauthorized people can get to the spares, the spares won't be there when you really need them.

Limit the number of system vendors and models.   Limiting the number of distinct parts you need to inventory will keep your costs down and will make it simpler to keep track of the parts you should have in inventory. Keep it simple!

Use multiple suppliers.   If third-party vendors can provide high-quality parts (rather than just the primary vendor), it is best to have more than one source for critical components. If one supplier is forced to cut off supply, discontinues older models of equipment, or has an inventory shortage, you can still get parts another way. The lone supplier represents a single point of failure; refer back to Key Principle #18 in Chapter 5, "20 Key High Availability Design Principles," for a discussion on single points of failure. However, if you choose third-party spare parts, be certain that the use of these parts will not void warranty or service agreements, that they are interoperable with all of your system configurations, and that they are of a sufficiently high quality where they will not jeopardize the health and well-being of these critical systems.

Preventative Maintenance

It is definitely better to find trouble before it actually strikes. Like living organisms, hardware components often get sick before they die. By monitoring system logs for recurring events like spurious memory errors, disk retries, and SCSI bus errors, you can predict the impending failure of system components.

If you can learn in advance that a component is nearing failure, you can replace it before it totally fails, and you can do so at a time that is more convenient than, say, the middle of the afternoon (on an equities trading floor). You can learn about potential hardware failures, especially disk failures, by keeping an eye on your system logs, and on your disk array logs, if you have a disk array. Watch and learn the symptoms of failures, so that you can fine-tune your detection mechanisms and even extend the break-and-fix cycle to do root-cause analysis.

Vendor Management

Some of the most important professional relationships you are likely to have are with your vendors, and specifically with their sales teams. In the computer industry, vendors are more than just salespeople. They can help with implementation, and they can provide knowledge and expertise that is unavailable through other channels (not to mention a nice meal, a free round of golf, or sporting event tickets every now and then). As part of developing reliable and resilient systems, we strongly recommend building and maintaining positive relationships with your key vendor representatives. Learn what resources your vendor has to offer. Take advantage of them. But don't abuse them; believe it or not, vendors are people too. Team with your vendors; if they like you personally and if they believe that you are straightforward with them, they are much more likely to go the extra mile for you.

Choosing Key Vendors

When you are deciding which product to buy, a significant part of the evaluation effort should go into looking at the company selling the product. With that in mind, we offer some tips that will help you succeed in product and vendor selection:

Promote vendor competition.   Don't make up your mind before you can speak with them all. Each vendor can give you key questions to ask their competitors; but play it fair. Tell each vendor you are going to do this. Give each vendor a chance to guess what the competitor might say, and to shoot it down in advance. Ask each vendor who he or she considers the competition to be. Give each vendor a chance to evaluate the competition; avoid vendors who are openly hostile or angry or just plain nasty toward their competitors. It's not a personal evaluation, but a company one. Most likely, the vendor who is nasty toward his competition is trying to hide something.

See what people are saying.   Look in magazines, both trade magazines and general financial magazines; visit trade shows and conferences; poke around the Web and through relevant newsgroups; ask friends and colleagues; and get out and really speak with vendor-provided references. Find out what people are saying about the company, its people, its products, and its support. If you can't find much this way, then the company may not be a big player. See what industry analysts like Gartner and Meta think of the company. Get references from your sales team and then call them; probably the best question you can ask a reference is "What's the worst thing about working with this vendor?" Sometimes, over a beer (one that the vendor buys, of course), you can find out the real poop about working for a company from its employees. Are the employees happy? Why or why not? Are these issues relevant to your doing business with them? Could they become more relevant if the problems are not fixed?

Test customer support. As part of any product evaluation process, place a test support call (just one should be plenty) to see how nice support people are, and how quickly they call you back. Determine the overall quality of the response. Be fair, though—don't burden or abuse the support people. Are patches and critical problem information made available on the Internet in a timely manner? Do customers have to go look for them, or will critical problem information find the customer? Examine vendor-generated statistics on average time to close support calls. What about their customer-support web site? Can you get real questions answered there without having to wait for callbacks from support engineers?

Look at the company's financials. During the Internet and stock market boom of the late 1990s, it was tempting to pick vendors on the basis of their stock performance. In fact, that's not the only or the best barometer to use. Instead, look at the company's entire operating picture. Do they have a lot of cash, or are they heavily in debt? Do the product lines you're interested in make money, or are they losing market share? Is there a risk you'll be buying into a product line that won't be around in a year? How are their quarter-to-quarter revenue numbers? Are they hitting their targets? Are you buying into a vendor that won't make it another year, given the current state of the market, and the company's cash flow and debt issues? Look at the company's price/earnings (P/E) ratio; a high (or not applicable) P/E ratio can indicate very low earnings, no earnings, or a money-losing company. Accounting tricks and charges for mergers and other unusual events can affect the way earnings are presented, so use it as a piece of corroborating evidence, not your primary decision factor on the financial front.

Some companies have policies that prohibit decision makers from owning stock in vendors to prevent even apparent conflict of interests. If you like a vendor enough to own its stock, make sure that your code of business conduct agrees with your investment decisions.

Look for a broad product line. If the company you are evaluating has a limited product line, that may not be a bad thing by itself, although remember that a one-trick pony (a company with only one product) may be acquired or squashed by a richer competitor. A one-trick pony may lack the resources to keep its product competitive over the long term. Of course, if a company has grown to be successful from just one product, as likely as not, it is an excellent product and should be evaluated on its merit too. If, on the other hand, a sales rep has lots of products to sell, it is in her best interest to keep you happy over the long term. The happier you are, the more of her other products you are likely to buy. If a vendor has only one or two products to sell, once you buy them, your long-term value to her may diminish, as she has nothing left to sell you.

Whom does the vendor partner with? Just about everyone partners with everyone else in the computing industry nowadays, even with the competition. Do you like the vendor's partners? Do you use the partners' products? Do you like those products? If a vendor you are considering does not partner with other vendors you use, how much trouble will that cause? What happens when a problem arises that looks like it's a joint problem between two vendors? Can the vendors work together to resolve it, or will they spend all their time pointing fingers at each other? Are the partnerships genuine, or just press releases? Sometimes partnerships are announced with a big splash and then terminated later under cover of night. A vendor who partners with lots of other vendors is more likely to be successful and to have products that are more universally interesting.

Look ahead. Get a nondisclosure presentation. See what the vendor is planning two, three, and four years down the road. Is it interesting? Is it believable? Does it fit with what they are doing today? Does it play to their strengths? Have they delivered on their promises reliably in the past? What is the company vision? Is it realistic?

Cross-platform support. Can the same product be delivered on all, or most, of your critical computing platforms? How similar are the products on different platforms? Can the different platform products be administered easily and centrally? If products are similar between different platforms, system administrative costs can be reduced significantly, as less training must be purchased to teach sys admins how to operate the products, and to keep them up-to-date later on. In many cases, if products are similar enough between operating systems, fewer administrators may be required, saving even more money. Even if you are running a single-platform shop, remember that that state of affairs can change overnight through a merger, acquisition, or change in CIO. It's best to be prepared.

Stick with your vendors. After you have chosen vendors you are happy with, try to stay with them. You should still evaluate products from other vendors, but once vendors are in and you are happy with their treatment, they should be treated as incumbents; don't kick them out unless the competition is clearly superior. If you show your vendors loyalty, they will show loyalty back to you, often with superior pricing, support, and perks.

Limit the number of vendors.   It is much easier to work with 3 or 4 vendors than it is to work with 20. You'll have to deal with less intervendor dissent and competition, and you'll spend less of your time in sales presentation meetings. However, if you limit your number of vendors down to just one, that vendor can represent a single point of failure. If you've put all your eggs in a single basket, and something does happen to that basket, you can be in a lot of trouble. Three or four vendors is probably the right number.

Working with Your Vendors

The single most important piece of advice on working with vendors is: "Work with them, and not against them." Be a partner with them, and don't always try and chisel every nickel and dime; they need their profits to support you. If they represent large and successful companies, it is unlikely (but possible, of course) that they are trying to rip you off; they want your goodwill too. Vendors want to build long-term relationships with their customers so that they will look at their other products and so that they can be a reference site in the future.

Keep in mind that if you mistreat your vendors, who, like you, are only human, *they can take their business elsewhere.* Just as you can choose between vendors, your vendors can, if their products and the market are any good, choose from many potential customers. If they like and respect you, you are more likely to get their time and resources. If you pay a reasonable price for their products and services, they will come back to you when they have new products they think you will like.

Expect honesty from your vendor. Not all of their products, especially if they have a large set, are superstars. There are going to be some junky ones in the mix. A good sales team will be up front with you and tell you that "you don't want *this* product, it's not that good yet."

The same rules that apply to working with salespeople apply to working with support personnel. If you return from a meeting and find two phone messages waiting for you, whom will you call back first? The person who is rude and screams and yells at you, or the one who is pleasant and only calls when he or she has a real need for your help? It's human nature; be the second kind of person.

Don't make every single support call into a crisis. If you do, your real crises won't be taken very seriously. When a support call is for a minor problem, treat it as one. You won't be sorry. When there is a genuine crisis, you will get better help, more resources, and probably a solution faster than you would if everything is a crisis.

Give your support personnel all the information they ask for. If they ask a question, they need the information to solve your problem.

On the other hand, there are plenty of incompetent support personnel answering the phones for good vendors. If you are unsatisfied with the response you get back from support, make sure your local sales team knows all about it. (If you like the support you get, tell them that too!) As a customer, you have the right to say, "I don't like that support person and I don't want to work with him anymore. Get me someone else."

Similarly, if your sales rep or another member of the sales team is a jerk, then you certainly have the right to go to his or her manager and ask for a different rep for the account.

The Vendor's Role in System Recovery

Whether it's hardware service to repair damaged components or bug fixes needed to prevent repeated system outages, vendor service plays a large role in system recovery and constraining the time to repair a failed system. Here are some issues and questions to consider when evaluating a vendor's ability to support you and your systems.

Service and Support

Telephone support.   Nearly all support calls begin with a phone call. When you call the vendor, how long does it take before you speak to anyone? How many push-button menu options must you parse before you get to a human being? How long before you speak to someone who can help solve the problem? How helpful are the people you speak with? Do they call you back in a timely manner?

On-site service.   When on-site service is required, how quickly can the vendor get someone to your location? Do they meet or exceed contractual obligations? What happens if the vendor fails to meet their obligations? Are the people they send able to solve the problem themselves, or do they spend all their time on the phone back to headquarters?

Spare parts.   How long does it take for the vendor to get spare parts to you? Are the parts stored locally, or must they come in from across the country?

Root-cause analysis.   This is often the trickiest part of problem solving. How good is the vendor at determining the ultimate cause of an outage? Do they have tools to help diagnose and solve problems? Do they keep going back to you with more questions and requests for ever-increasing amounts of assistance, or can they solve the problem on their own?

Bug fixes.   Once a software problem is isolated, can the vendor provide a patch (and the mechanism to apply the patch), or is an upgrade required to fix the problem? Patches are generally preferable, as they can be installed quickly and easily, and should be readily available via FTP or a web site.

Resolution times.   The faster the vendor can get your problem solved, the quicker your systems will be back in business. However, some vendor support organizations are more concerned with closing the support ticket than they are with genuine customer satisfaction (this is for statistical reasons: More closed calls is interpreted as higher customer satisfaction; that is not always the right interpretation). Who makes the ultimate determination as to whether or not a problem has been solved, the vendor or the customer?

Integration.   Will the vendor take ownership of multiple-vendor problems, or point fingers? Finger-pointing slows recovery; taking ownership and being willing to work with other vendors to solve problems gets systems back online faster.

Escalation

Know the escalation process.   How do you get a support call escalated? What does that mean? Does it help? How long before a problem gets attention from engineering? Whom do you call locally when things don't go right with support? Not everything can be an escalation . . . or nothing is. Don't cry wolf!

Know your customer service managers.   They can be your best ally when things go bad. Make friends with them. Call and email them to praise their people when things are going well at least as quickly as you call to complain when things go poorly. (People so rarely go out of their way to call with praise nowadays that your efforts will be remembered and you will likely be rewarded with even better service over time.)

Vendor Integration

Will your vendors support your configuration?   Are their disks interfering with my operating system? What are the supported combinations of releases?

Whom do you call first?   Which vendor is your best route to other vendors when the vendors pass calls to each other? How do you decide where to take your first call? What if that vendor is not the right one? Blind one-stop support calling is *not* highly available.

Vendor Consulting Services

Who knows a product better than the company and the people who produced it? If a complex or new product is to be installed on your site for the first time, take full advantage of the vendor's expertise. Use your vendors to implement new products, perform major upgrades of old products, and customize applications. They have most likely done this sort of work successfully before, and can do it again for you.

Yes, consulting services can be extremely expensive ($3,000 to $4,000 per day is not unheard of). But consultants have the ability and experience to get things done right the first time. And should the consultant run into problems, he or she should have a support network to fall back on. If your local personnel do the work instead and they run into problems, whom can they call? Many vendor consulting organizations offer fixed-price consulting. If the job is done easily and successfully, the hourly rate may be very high, but if things don't go as well, you are protected from hidden costs, and the vendor has incentives to get the job done quickly and efficiently.

As with all external services, there is always the chance that your consultant will be poorly qualified to do the job he or she has been hired for. That is an unfortunate risk that simply must be taken. If you get an unqualified consultant, you should speak to the company who provided that person, and make arrangements so that you do not have to pay for that person's time. A good consulting organization will make additional concessions to ensure your satisfaction and future business.

Security

System security, which by itself has been the subject of many computer books and seminars, is a critical part of system availability. The reason is simple: A breach in security can directly or indirectly cause downtime. Network breaches can keep your users out; deleted or damaged files can seriously impact your business.

Breaches can come from outside or inside. Watch out for corporate espionage. Protect your systems from disgruntled employees and ex-employees. (It is very important to keep your employees as gruntled as possible!) When people leave a job, if they were treated badly, they are much more likely to leave their ex-employer a going-away present. When employees (and especially system administrators) depart, change any passwords they may have had. Scan all of your systems for files owned by those users, especially scheduler files that may contain time bombs. If another employee needs to take ownership of some of the files of the ex-employee, it may be best if the work of going through the files to get the required data is performed on a standalone system, especially if you are concerned about trusting the ex-employee. These actions should be standard operating procedure so that it does not appear that you are acting against one particular ex-employee or another.

The following are some examples of other protective measures you may choose to employ:

Firewalls.   A *firewall* is a system that acts as a gateway between outside networks (including the Internet) and your internal computer systems. It monitors and restricts certain types of network traffic, and can keep hackers and other unwanted visitors from getting into your systems from the Internet. Be sure that your firewall systems are highly available; if they go down, your users may lose their ability to access external networks at all.

Data encryption.   Data on backup tapes or on your network that is left unencrypted can be read by anyone with the means and desire to do so. While it may not be easy to get to these tapes or networks, someone who truly wants to can probably do so. Data is the heart and soul of almost every enterprise nowadays; if you protect it like it is that important, you can ensure the long-term safety of the enterprise. Be careful, though, about shipping encrypted tapes and disks across international borders; there are laws restricting the use of long encryption keys in some countries.

Strong password selection.   Make sure that all passwords into your systems are secure. Passwords should include characters from at least two or three of the four character classes, and should be at least six characters long. The character classes are uppercase letters, lowercase letters, numbers, and punctuation. Passwords should never be a dictionary word in English or other popular language (Spanish, French, Japanese, and so on). Yet they should also be easy to remember, because passwords that are written down may as well not be set at all. (Remember the scene from *War Games* where Matthew Broderick opened the drawer on the administrator's desk and found a long written list of passwords?) An example of such a password might be: sa/ni/li. Why? The letters come from the first two letters of each word in "Saturday Night Live" (easy to remember) and are separated by a character from a different class. A more secure version of the same password would be: sa/n1/l1 because each letter i has been changed to a 1. If your operating system permits it, spaces make excellent characters for passwords, as many automated password crackers don't try spaces (until their authors read this passage, of course).

Protect passwords.   Don't give passwords to vendors or users who don't need them. If a vendor needs a privileged password to do his job, change it to something easy to remember while the vendor is around and return it to something harder when he leaves. Run a complete security audit after the vendor is done, looking for security holes left behind either as inadvertent side effects of the work or for more sinister purposes.

Limit administrative access.   Restrict administrative and privileged access very closely. Don't let more people get privileged access on your critical servers than absolutely need it. If remote administrative access is required, use secure shell (ssh) to build a tunnel rather than allow work as root to be done from a trade show or Kinko's public computing facility across a public network. Be sure that if you do remote work from an Internet café or other public location that you destroy any logs of your session that may remain behind on the public system.

Enable auditing.   While auditing certainly imposes a significant performance overhead (15 percent or more on some systems), and it requires significant disk space to hold all of the logged information, auditing can also help you track down intruders and keep track of system calls made by every running application. If you're suspicious about user activities, auditing gives you some data; if your intruders are good, however, they'll clean up behind themselves and leave few clues in the audit or system logs.

Establish policies for password and key escrow.   While password and encryption keys should normally be kept secret, allowing only one person to hold critical information of this nature is a single point of failure. If the one person who knows the encryption key to a critical corporate document gets run over by a bus or is hit on the head and suffers total amnesia, then nobody has the key. Critical keys and passwords should be kept in escrow, such as in a sealed envelope kept in a well-known, physically secure location like an executive office or safe deposit box. If the envelope is disturbed, then the associated keys and passwords must be changed and the envelope updated. Of course, if the passwords are changed for another reason, the envelopes must be updated too.

Data Center Security

Security has always been one of the most important features of data centers. With modern electronic-card–based access systems, access to secure locations can be carefully restricted and monitored. And yet almost every data center permits outsiders (vendors, visitors, and even the occasional school field trip) to wander through, oohing and aahing over the massive, expensive, and handsome equipment. Some data centers don't just permit tours, they promote them, inviting visiting job applicants, passersby, and homicidal maniacs into the rooms containing their most important computing resources.

In a perfect world, data centers would be completely off-limits to anyone who did not have a business-related reason to enter. Enough people have business reasons to enter, so data centers are often very crowded, even without allowing tours to wander through.

This topic is discussed in more detail in Chapter 10.

Viruses and Worms

The security issue that gets the most press nowadays is malevolent code: viruses and worms.[1] An entire industry has sprung up based around protecting systems from the malcontents and miscreants who write viral code. It's a constant game of cat and mouse between the antivirus companies like Symantec and McAfee and the hackers and crackers who write the viruses.

As we mentioned in Chapter 5, a few years ago, it was sufficient to update antivirus definitions every week or so. Nowadays, the conventional wisdom is that daily updates are usually enough, but more even frequent updates are required when a new and nasty virus hits the news.

There have been discussions about the next generation of malevolent code, which could, theoretically, infect all vulnerable hosts on the entire Internet in about 15 minutes. These so-called Warhol worms would not require human intervention, and might actively search for other hosts that they could infect, and spread themselves. Modern antivirus software would not be effective against this sort of attack. This may just be the kind of story that the media spreads to scare people, but it's not hard to imagine such a virus attacking the Internet in the next few years.

If you are looking for a good book on security, we wholeheartedly recommend Bruce Schneier's book, *Secrets and Lies* (Wiley, 2000, ISBN: 0471253111). It is an extremely informative, rather scary, and remarkably entertaining read on the usually-less-than-spellbinding topic of computer and network security.

Documentation

Nobody likes writing documentation. It is slow and tedious work that takes time away from more interesting pursuits, like putting out fires and solving critical problems. Many of the engineers who should write documentation are not native speakers of the local language, which can make writing extremely difficult. Of course, some native speakers of the local language are unable to write a coherent paragraph in any language. Nevertheless, documentation is

---

[1] A virus is a program that changes other programs so that they spread the virus; it modifies other programs on the same system so that it can spread itself further. A worm is a free-standing program that does not modify other programs; instead, it tricks the receiving computer into accepting and executing it.

vital to the long-term success of any system, computer or otherwise. It is impossible for one person to keep every tidbit of knowledge about a system in her head. Even if it were possible, that person (another single point of failure) might change jobs, go on vacation, or forget seemingly trivial details. Or worse, she might remember some detail incorrectly, causing even more trouble.

On the other hand, visit any established mainframe shop and ask to see the run books, and you'll find volumes of information, usually right up-to-date, describing how you start, stop, diagnose, and deal with every system and application that is in production.

Good documentation is as important to the long-term success of systems as any other component. Without it, new personnel will be hindered in their attempts to learn how existing systems are maintained. The more time it takes for them to come up to speed, the longer the systems are undersupported.

Another aspect to producing documentation is that if you are a really good SA, you may not have a lot of new problems to solve. Producing documentation may help justify your existence to upper management who don't understand the day-to-day work on system administration.

One reason that people are often reluctant to create documentation is the fear that documenting what they do will make them less valuable to the organization and may even make them expendable. This is just not true (at least most of the time). Documentation does not make anyone less valuable to the organization; just the opposite, it frees experienced personnel from the burden of maintaining older, less interesting systems and allows them to move on to newer projects. Without good documentation, they run the risk of constantly being pulled back into old projects.

So, what do you document? To start, we recommend the following:

- What to do when various critical events occur
  - How to start and stop an application
  - What to do when a failover occurs
  - What to do when systems fail completely
  - What to do when a site disaster occurs
  - What to do when the data center power will be shut down for a weekend
- Procedures for rolling out new systems and software
  - Servers
  - Clients
  - Applications
  - Monitoring tools
  - Physical data center changes

- Requirements for new applications
  - Log requirements
  - System standards
  - Interdependencies
- Network layout
- Hardware diagrams for every critical system
- A diary of all system and network outages, planned and unplanned, including the cause and the amount of downtime incurred

Start with that list, and see where it goes. Documentation should contain many cross-references to external documentation and to other parts of internal documentation so that you don't write the same information in more than one place. If someone else has written it down, use that person's copy. If different parts of the same documents disagree, which is inevitable over time without great care, a tremendous amount of time can be wasted trying to determine which passage is correct. Documentation should always be marked with a date and version number, with both updated whenever the slightest change is made.

There should even be a manual about the documentation itself. This manual should contain standards information for new and existing documentation— things like distribution models, update procedures, version numbering standards, formatting, storage standards, and so on. And all system documentation should include "update the documentation" as one of the steps to perform when a documented component is changed or added.

All the while, be sure that you keep things as simple as possible (always remember Key Principle #1!). People will have to read the documentation that you've written. If it is unreadable, or unusable, then there is no point to having it at all, and you'll have wasted a tremendous amount of your own time and created a great deal of frustration among your audience.

The Audience for Documentation

When you sit down to write anything (a book, a magazine article, a school essay, a diary entry, a love letter or anything else), the first question you must ask yourself is who the audience is for the document. In the case of system documentation, as mentioned in Chapter 5, some experts will say that it must be written at a very low and simple level so that anyone, from the janitor (or the CEO, as some wags will tell you) to the head of systems, could pick it up and recover a system from whatever ill may have befallen it. That is a surefire recipe for failure.

Documentation cannot possibly be written so that a total novice could recover a system from any outage. There are far too many variables and options that documentation cannot consider, and too much experience that a good system administrator brings to the table to make the right choices in a given situation. To write documentation for the total novice, you'd have to include the right commands in a text editor, such as `vi` or `emacs` on Unix, and specific line numbers of a file that might need to be edited. Every time the line numbers or the contents of adjacent lines in the file change, the documentation will be out-of-date.

Instead, target system documentation at the experienced system administrator who does not know your specific systems. On Windows systems, the target would be an MCSE. On Unix systems, the target should simply be experienced SAs. Emphasize in the documentation the things that make your systems unusual or unique rather than things that might be seen as commonplace. Use your digital camera and include pictures, use that drawing program you never get to use and include diagrams, and include screen shots where they will clarify a complex point. But don't overuse graphics, or, like any tool, they will lose their effectiveness.

Documentation cannot possibly be all things to all people; keep the documentation as simple as possible, and aim it at the people who will actually use it.

Documentation and Security

The same experts who will tell you to aim your documentation at unskilled personnel will also tell you that the documentation should be spread around loosely, with copies stored all around the enterprise, as well as in employees' cars and homes.

That, too, is a recipe for disaster. System documentation must, by its nature, contain privileged information, such as passwords, account names and numbers, and home phone numbers. This is not information that you want everybody to have. Each time a single one of these numbers changes, all copies must be retrieved and updated; the more copies there are, the harder the task of updating becomes.

More importantly, when a holder of the documentation leaves the company, her copies must be retrieved. Of course, if the holder has been planning to leave for some time, there is no guarantee that she hasn't copied it and given a copy to her new employer or some other inappropriate third party. Most companies can't be bothered collecting badges from departing employees, so how likely is it that these manuals will be collected?

Documentation should be maintained online, but stored offline. Maintain it online so that it can be easily changed; store it offline so that it can be accessed whether systems are up or down. Store an additional copy off-site, in a reasonably secure place that can be accessed by key personnel in an emergency.

Reviewing Documentation

Documentation should be regularly reviewed and tested. If documentation sits for months without review, testing, or updating, it will fall out-of-date and be worse than not having documentation at all. The best way to test documentation is to hand it to newly hired members of the team. When a new system administrator comes on board, it often takes several weeks or months before he becomes truly productive.

One way that he can add value from day one is to sit down with the documentation and follow it. Do, or at least simulate (if it would be destructive on a running system), what it says, and see how it goes. Once he is done, he should report on his findings and make the appropriate updates to the documentation.

This method of review will not always be effective, as there may not be new members joining the team often enough, but it makes an excellent start. If too much time passes between reviews, a more senior team member should perform the same exercise.

System Administrators

The most important people to the long-term successful operations of your computer systems are your SAs. System administration, especially in the Unix world, is learned almost entirely through on-the-job experience and by making mistakes (often one and the same). There is very little formal training in how to be a system administrator. There are lots of courses and books that teach the various skills required to administer systems, but there are so many varied skills involved that it is very difficult to become a totally well-rounded SA without doing it for a while first.

The skills, obvious and otherwise, required by a good SA include the following:

Backup engineer. Must be able to take and administer backups, and locate and retrieve tapes easily and quickly. Must also arrange for off-site storage of copies of the tapes, and quick and easy retrieval in an emergency.

Evaluator of equipment and software. Must be able to examine new products, both hardware and software, cut through the marketing double-talk, and determine what products will adequately meet requirements.

Hardware engineer. The first line of defense for swapping bad disks may be your system administrator; CPU and memory module replacement may be handled by your hardware service provider or by your own staff if you've chosen break-and-fix self-service.

Software developer.   SAs are always writing bits of code to automate key tasks.

Help desk. An SA is the first line of defense when users run into any sort of problems, and depending on the enterprise they work in, they are often on call 24×7.

Chameleon.   To properly support users, an SA must understand the business that their users are in, whether they're involved in equities trading, manufacturing, e-commerce, software development, or physical warehousing.

Deputy fire inspector.   The SA is ultimately responsible to make sure that the cables running under or on the floor, above or near the ceiling, and up and down the elevator shafts and stairwells are up to local fire codes.

Security expert.   The SA must maintain firewall machines at a proper level of security (strict enough to keep intruders out, but loose enough to let valid data and users pass through unimpeded), ensure that high-quality passwords are chosen, and ensure that departing employees' files are purged from systems promptly. Windows administrators must make sure that antivirus software is up-to-date.

Technical writer.   The SA is ultimately responsible for documentation that must be written for future SAs and for the current staff (if any), who cover for him during vacations and training.

Quality assurance engineer.   Before new applications can be rolled out, they must be tested. Unless there are dedicated QA engineers on staff, this task falls to the SA staff too.

Technical trainer.   When the user community needs to understand a new work-related technology, it falls to the system administrators to make sure the users are adequately trained.

New technology expert.   When some new whizzy high-tech toy comes along, even one that is unrelated to the systems he maintains or the business, the SA is expected to understand it and to explain it to her users, whether it be programming language, operating system, palmtop computer, video game, DVD player, or new computer hardware paradigm.

World Wide Web whiz.   The SA is expected to know about all the new and cool web sites, and web languages, and be able to answer her users' questions about them.

Town crier.   Bad news (such as system outages) must be reported to his user community.

Diplomat. Bad news (such as system outages) must be reported to his user community in such a way as to not make the users attack him with pitchforks and torches.

Detective. When system problems occur, it is up to the SA to track them down and solve them.

Network technician. In general, the SA is responsible for maintaining and troubleshooting networks and associated hardware.

Salesperson. Once the SA has decided on a particular product or technology, he must then go and make the case to management in order to get the project funded.

Relationship builder. To be successful, a good SA needs to develop relationships with the support and local sales teams from all key vendors, his users, management, customers, the local help desk, and his peers in other departments.

Night owl. A large percentage of the work an SA is responsible for must be done at night or on weekends, and usually after working a full day and week.

(Is it any wonder that most SAs have a very hard time explaining to non-technical friends and relatives, never mind their user community and their management, exactly what it is they do for a living?)

Every site, and often every system, has different methods for maintaining their systems. Every time an SA changes jobs, he needs to learn the new model and combine that with preexisting skills and experience in order to become truly useful in the new environment.

Since system administrators are the people who have to implement all of the stuff we discuss in this book, along with countless other technologies, you don't want to be replacing your people all the time. Keep your system administrators:

Happy. Give them interesting work. Don't micromanage. Ask them what makes them happy, and try to deliver it. Let them decorate their cubes. Keep some simple food and drink around for late-night work. Don't make them dress up.

Relaxed. As long as the systems are running well, there's nothing wrong with letting them occasionally surf the Web or maintain a personal web page during the day if they want to. (Remember all those late nights and weekends!) In Chapter 5 we talked about the six computing environments you might need, with the last one being the playground. Don't be afraid to let your system staff run free in the playground, because they may just come up with the next big process improvement.

Responsible.   If your SA is responsible for the proper functioning of a particular system, then she needs the authority to change things as she sees fit. It's not fair or reasonable to assign responsibility without granting the authority that goes with it.

Interested.   Make the work challenging and fun. Make the workplace a pleasant place to spend time. Keep things as high-tech as possible.

Motivated.   Reward good work. Let your SAs have cutting-edge equipment and software if they are good at what they do. Feed them; there's no better way to get late-night work out of them.

Well compensated.   If you won't, somebody else will! Top-grade system administrators are very hard to find and well worth the extra money that they cost.

Educated.   Send them to training and conferences like USENIX and LISA, and user conferences, regularly. Let them stay on the cutting edge of technology. There are entire user groups, like the 24×7 Users Group, dedicated to system and physical plant availability.

Well read.   Get them the magazines and books that they need to keep up on current trends in technology. One good tip from a magazine will pay for the magazine for many years to come.

Around!   If you have frequent personnel turnover, it will be very difficult to maintain your system availability.

Don't undervalue your important people. Make sure they want to keep working for you.

Internal Escalation

System administration is a 24×7 job. Unless someone is on-site 24 hours a day, as is realistic in larger sites with full-time operations staffing, the daytime staff will be responsible for off-hours crises too. There is virtually no time that is guaranteed to be totally free of responsibility. Someone needs to be reachable at all times of the day or night in case of emergency, even on holidays and weekends.

The best common way to reach the on-call person off-hours is via pager. Pagers are better than cell phones when one member of a team is on call, because the team can make sure that the pager is in the right person's hands, and users need not be concerned with the schedule. ("Let's see, it's Tuesday night. Does Jonathan or Madeline have the pager, or is it Hannah's turn tonight? I'd check online, but, of course, the system is down.") Some organizations report success with Nextel's long-range walkie-talkie system, but for that model to work, a user who might call for support must have a Nextel, or the user must call a central dispatcher who has one. Pagers are simpler (simple is good!), and everyone knows how to get a message to a pager. Other organizations pass around a shared cell phone in the same way they might share a pager; that is a good system, but it can be much more expensive than using a pager, and then the on-call SA will probably be stuck carrying two cell phones.

An internal escalation policy must be set into place, with a primary person, a secondary person, and an emergency backup person. If the first person does not respond to a page after a given period of time (often 30 minutes), the backup person is paged and given 30 minutes. After 60 minutes have passed, the third person, usually a manager, is paged. Since the first two people know they will be in trouble if the manager gets paged, it is generally in their best interests to respond quickly.

LEFT A MESSAGE WITH YOUR SPOUSE

Very early one August Sunday morning in 1988, the Stern phone rang. My wife, Toby, answered to hear a computer-generated voice, which she promptly hung up on. A few minutes later, the same call, same voice, same hang-up. "Who is it?" I asked. "Some computer telling me something about the temperature of a pie," she answered. Voice-generation software being somewhat infantile at the time, I recognized the caller—the environmental monitoring system in my startup company's machine room. At 5:30 A.M., the temperature wasn't "pie," it was "high"—like over 100 degrees. Our rooftop chiller had failed sometime over the weekend, and the machine room was quickly roasting the disks with the product we planned to introduce at the following week's trade show. One call to the 24-hour HVAC service, 150 feet of garden hose, and a few hundred dollars worth of fans dropped the temperature to the point at which we could safely restore power to the machine room, and by Monday things were back to normal.

Moral of the story: When you're on call, your family is on call with you. Make sure that everyone knows how the escalation path reaches you.

—Hal

In addition to pagers, home phone numbers should be centrally available, and email can also be employed as a backup method. Email is the weakest approach in an emergency, especially if the email system is affected by the emergency. Even if email is available during the emergency, unlike pagers and cell phones, it requires an action by the recipient to pick it up.

Late-night phone calls and pages can be reduced through the use of automated processes that take care of the most common and invasive problems. But if late-night support work is unavoidable, a tremendous amount of time can be saved by giving your administrators remote access to servers so they can log in from home and correct problems without having to get dressed and drive to the office at all hours of the night. Remote access can speed up the initiation of repairs by two hours or more. Many companies pay for their SAs to have high-speed Internet access in their homes via DSL, cable modems, or some alternate method.

But arrangements must still be made to grant SAs access to the facilities at all hours of the day or night. In order to ensure success, SAs must have keys and access cards to the facility and to any important rooms inside, codes to deactivate burglar alarms, emergency phone numbers, appropriate security clearance and passwords, and any access codes to use phone lines at off-hours. The bottom line is that your SAs must have complete 24×7 access to any and all parts of the facility that they may need to get to when a crisis is in progress. The worst thing that could happen is for your SA to get up at 3:00 in the morning, get dressed, drive to the office, and then be barred access to the systems he needs to get to. Never let that happen. An occasional dry run, as unpopular as that idea may be, is probably appropriate.

Trouble Ticketing

Ease the burden on your people through the use of automated problem detection and reporting tools. The marketplace is loaded with these sorts of tools; they come from hardware and operating system vendors with their equipment, as well as from vendors who specialize in such products, such as Computer Associates, BMC, and Tivoli. These packages allow users to submit their own problem reports too.

Whatever product you use, make sure that trouble tickets and reports include as much detail as possible. These reports need to be reliable, detailed, accurate, verifiable, and documented. The less work an SA has to do to research the problem, the more time she can spend solving it or moving on to the next problem.

Key Points

- Bad documentation, inadequate testing, and poorly educated users and administrators can be just as damaging to system availability as technical failures.

- Treat your vendors like people, and in turn they will take better care of you.

- Realize that your system administration staff is like engine oil. It's only a commodity when it's on the shelf. When they are working for you, it's your responsibility to take care of them.

- Security, a topic worthy of many books all by itself, is a critical part of system availability.

CHAPTER 12

Clients and Consumers

Blessed is he who expects nothing, for he shall never be disappointed.
—Benjamin Franklin

We have built a base of redundancy constructs centered around your data, its management, and the environment in which everything is housed. An end-to-end availability design needs to consider the consumers of the services, as well as the network that delivers the well-behaved services from the data center to the client machines. In this chapter, we examine the issues surrounding client availability, ranging from having clients for users to various impacts of service failure on client applications. We're at Level 6 in the Availability Index, as shown in Figure 12.1. Clients sit squarely between the data center environment and the application layer, because they represent the user interface to any availability hardening. No clients, no availability.

What should available services expect of their clients? To paraphrase our founding father, "Not much." There may be cases where a complex Web-based application needs to persist and restore in-flight state information, but we'll cover that as a server-side problem, not a client issue. This is purely about the client side of the problem—that is, we're assuming the applications that are running on the clients aren't highly available themselves, but need to preserve the best possible user experience in the face of failures. In Chapter 13, we'll go up another level in the Index to explore application design consideration for making them more fault-resilient.

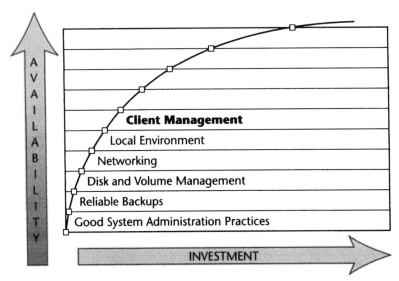

Figure 12.1   Level 6 of the Availability Index.

Hardening Enterprise Clients

There are two types of clients: enterprise clients that live on one of your networks and are managed by your own resources, and Internet or public clients, over which you have zero control and often zero knowledge. In an age of mobile laptops and hotel-style offices, you lose some measure of control over your enterprise clients, but you still have responsibility for their correct operation on your network. The two biggest problems you'll face are eliminating client disks as SPOFs for business-critical data and re-creating client systems quickly in the event of a failure or request for replacement.

Client Backup

Proliferation of data on the desktop puts you at risk for data loss. Files and databases contained inside the safe glassy confines of the data center are protected by the data management design rules we've laid down already, but you can't protect what you can't see. PCs with large internal disks have turned into one of the largest potential single points of failure for data loss in the enterprise. Loss doesn't have to mean that the disk fails in a small whirlwind of smoke; failure in the desktop sense includes data inaccessibility because your user dropped her laptop, or spilled coffee into it, or suffered laptop theft where the data goes with the rest of the hardware.

There are not many elegant solutions to the problem. The following are some ideas to reduce the number of potential failures due to the loss of PC data:

Synchronize to a network folder.   In its simplest form, you create a folder on a networked drive, one per user, that acts as the backing store for a "briefcase" of documents that users take with them. Your goal is to treat the PC as a cache for the networked fileserver, so data loss from the cache is handled by reloading it from the network folder. There is a fair bit of user behavior to dictate in this scenario, but it's the easiest approach. Rely on your normal backup and restore procedures to manage the network folder, and you've taken a giant step to ensuring the long-term survival of PC data. You may be able to use network synchronization features of Windows, or the briefcase local copy model, to automate this process as much as possible. Similarly, there's no requirement that the network folder be hosted on a PC server; you can host it on any server that speaks the native file-sharing protocols used by your clients.

Make a network folder the default for file locations.   A variation on the preceding scheme is to ensure that all of your user defaults for file locations, in all personal productivity applications, default to a network drive. This makes disconnected operation more difficult, so users who are frequently mobile are going to create local copies of documents. However, the extra work required in locating the local folder should make the users more sensitive to copying that data off of their personal machines as soon as they're near an office again.

Create a drop box for key documents.   This solution is not as transparent to users as using a networked folder, but it is appealing to the email junkies. Users email documents for archival to a common alias, which either saves the emails in a disk archive (good) or merges them into a common mailbox (bad). You can create some elaborate mail sorting and saving scripts using the `procmail` tool (`www.procmail.org`). Restore requests are handled by forwarding the user's original email back to him or her. The common mailbox can get very large, and you may sort through thousands of documents looking for the right one to restore. File-based archives can be scanned with scripts and have return emails automatically generated.

Build public area docking stations with tape backup devices.   "Docking station" is used loosely here; you don't need to invest in all new PCs with docking station capability. A local backup station could be a tape drive and a USB cable, or a large-format Zip drive and a stack of blank disks. What you need to ensure is that PCs have the right software to do local backups or copies to the external media type (this is part of client provisioning, covered in the next section). You can get somewhat dictatorial with this approach, requiring that completed tapes or disks be dropped off with a local administrator (executive or systems flavor), providing you with a low-cost way to take attendance at the docking stations.

Rely on your users to give at home.   And you'll find your users' home backup tapes orbiting somewhere alongside the checks that are in the mail.[1]

Avoid using the inbox as a filesystem.   POP3-based mail servers copy messages from the server into the client. Lose the client, lose the mail. Furthermore, inboxes grow large with saved documents in them; if users want to mail key files to themselves, reinforce the idea that those documents should be saved into mail folders, preferably mail folders on the server or network fileserver folders that get backed up regularly.

Back up your PC.   There are several products that automatically back up the contents of your PC to a centralized server. The best of these do it whenever the PC is connected to a network and optimizes the data that it backs up. (For example, it wouldn't back up each user's copy of Microsoft Word—if they are all the same, why back up each copy?) Done properly, the data from a lost or corrupted PC could be rebuilt in a matter of hours. But don't waste resources backing up your MP3s.

If you go down the local PC backup route, make sure everything that is critical to the user is on the backup file list. You want user configuration files like web bookmarks as well as hidden but critical local data stores like the inbox from a POP3-based mail client. Once you've removed SPOFs from client-owned data, you can worry about the total loss of a client and how quickly you can create a new, functional client system.

Client Provisioning

This may seem obvious, but the key issue in client availability is making sure there are clients to be used. Many trading floors keep fully built spare machines sitting in the electronic on-deck circle, ready to be plugged into the network in the event of a hardware failure. When all of your configuration, application, and user data is network-based, you can get a quick client recovery. There are many cases, typically involving PCs with large local software application counts, that require a process for mastering or provisioning desktops. You'll need to optimize the provisioning process to reduce the MTTR for

---

[1] We're not implying that users are lazy or stupid, rather that doing backups is a time-consuming and uninteresting task. Neither of us are very religious about regular backups, creating the situation where the cobbler's children have terrible shoes.

a client desktop failure. If the user can't get work done because there's no machine on which to do it, you have an availability problem.

Physical damage such as coffee, flood, fire, drops onto hard surfaces, and theft are the more likely, but not the sole causes of new desktop provisioning. Users who attempt to add new hardware, install device driver patches or other fixes for reported software bugs, install incompatible releases of key drivers, or get hit with a virus that infects places other than the address book require that their PCs be reloaded from the ground up. This process is referred to as provisioning or mastering, a tip of the propeller hat to the recording industry in which a master tape was used to cut record albums. There are several commercial tools for loading specified configurations onto raw hardware, including local software distributions and configuration files. You may also choose to create a golden CD mastering disk with software and FAQs to be given out to users on a regular basis.

THE KILLER APPLICATION

One of our early PC applications was a chemical structure-drawing tool. The graphics were pretty, and the user interface predated Windows 3.1 and most of the more elegant Macintosh designs. It was a DOS application, and the application took full advantage of DOS failure modes while under development. At one point, we were looking for a memory corruption problem where data was being written into a piece of memory that was far outside the application's bounds. So far outside, in fact, that the application was writing into the DOS File Allocation Table (FAT) that represented the in-memory filesystem data. The next disk write usually wrote out bad data to the disk, and after a few minutes the test PC was reduced to a vegetative state. We got very good at reloading PCs from floppies, downloading our application, and starting over. Quick provisioning ideas kept the QA team busy finding bugs rather than shuffling floppies.

—Hal

What goes into a provisioning effort? The following are some key provisions:

- Key applications, such as productivity tools, browsers, and networking software.

- Antivirus scanning, as well as the default configurations to enable it. There's no point in reloading a machine that was taken down by a virus with user files that may have been previously infected.

- Configuration files such as bookmarks and browser preferences.

Remember that one of the constraints on availability is MTTR. Automate your client provisioning, and keep a good supply of spare desktops on hand to reduce your MTTR and eliminate user-introduced variations that lead to future problems.

Thin Clients

Thin clients are one extreme endpoint in client reliability. "Thin" refers to the lack of local disk, local operating system, or user-visible processing; most thin clients are either X terminals or extended terminal devices like Sun's SunRay client. Thin clients improve client-side reliability by taking away opportunities for bad configuration, viruses, undocumented changes, and local disks to bring down clients. Client-side availability becomes a function of physical device availability and network connectivity. Reducing the number of moving parts a user can interact with helps reliability because it removes potential failure entry points.

The overall user perception, however, is dependent on the client device as well as the servers that run user applications and drive the interfaces to these thin clients. Part of the problem shifts from client-side software to server-side applications. Moving your entire office to a thin client model but hanging all of those clients off of a nonclustered single large server ensures that when you have your first system reboot, all of your users are going to be angry. Thin clients work well in conjunction with the application conditioning and server clustering patterns we cover in the next several chapters.

Once you've gotten a grip on the hardware side of the client equation, it's time to look at how client applications behave or misbehave when the data services they're consuming fail.

Tolerating Data Service Failures

Client applications have a hard time detecting the difference between a successful server failover and a fast reboot. Most database applications will recognize that a server connection has been broken, and it will try to reconnect to the server and restart in-flight transactions. Other types of clients may not be so optimistic, or they may require system administration changes to make them tolerant of short breaks in service that are handled by failover systems. Fileserver clients are probably the biggest culprit in this class. Everything in this section applies to both enterprise and Internet clients; however, since it's unlikely that you'll be providing NFS service to the general public, the database and web services sections are most pertinent to public network clients.

Fileserver Client Recovery

Setting up a high-availability pair for an NFS fileserver is only half of the battle. You'll need to be sure that your NFS clients are tolerant of breaks in service and continue to retry requests and recover gracefully from server outages. Again, the clients don't really see the difference between a single server reboot and a failover; your goal is to use failover to make the time to client recovery as short as possible. You also want to be sure there are clients at the ready.

NFS Soft Mounts

The default mode for mounting NFS filesystems is with the hard option, indicating that the client should continue to retry operations until it receives an acknowledgment from the server. The alternative to hard mounts is soft ones, in which a request is retransmitted a few times and then the client gives up. Five retries is the default, although this parameter can be set as a mount option.

NFS soft mounts and reliability do not mix. Data integrity has to have the highest precedence. NFS soft mounts do not ensure data integrity on the server or application correctness on the NFS client.

If your goal is to make sure that servers recover quickly and clients continue from where they were waiting, you cannot use soft-mount operations to give the clients a chance to abort operations in progress. Some system administrators prefer soft mounts to hard ones because they allow clients to break operations that are stuck on NFS servers that have crashed. Note that this is precisely the behavior you're seeking to fix by investing in availability techniques in the first place. You want clients to be as insensitive to the server's state, and even the server's identity, whenever possible. Mixing hard mounts and the "intr" mount option to allow NFS operations to be interrupted may give you control of the NFS clients more quickly than a server failover, but it kills the application process that was hung on the nonresponding server. Again, your goal should be to improve server reliability to the point where client-side behavior isn't your concern. You can focus your attention on a room of NFS servers, but it's nearly impossible to scale up your system administration staff to handle floors of NFS clients in various states of hanging and abnormally terminated applications.

What happens if you use soft mounts, and a client request times out? The process making the system call to the filesystem that was converted into an NFS call will eventually run into trouble. On a call to get the inode information from a file, possibly as the result of an ls command or part of the file opening sequence, a null structure will be returned to the calling process. A well-written process will detect an empty structure and complain (see *Boundary Condition Checks* in Chapter 13, "Application Design"). Most applications, however, will dump core when they attempt to use the zero-filled values in that file information structure. Similarly, an attempt to read a page from a file that fails returns a zero-filled page; a failed write operation leaves a hole in the file on the server. Both of these failed operations cause data corruption. Writes that fail on soft mounts are particularly tricky to identify because the error may be returned to the calling process long after the error occurs (again, see the following text for more details on why this happens).

Big rule with NFS servers: If you make them highly available, make the clients highly patient and persistent in sending requests until they are serviced. Soft mounts are a poor man's way of regaining client control; they were introduced in the early days of NFS when server uptime was measured in days, not months. With improvements in operating system reliability, network engineering and hardware improvements such as switches, and the introduction of server-side redundancy, soft mounts no longer really have a place in NFS environments. You'll get better predictability from server-side controls, and you'll only get control over data integrity with hard mounts.

Automounter Tricks

Another common approach to improving NFS client resistance to failures is to use the automounter (or the publicly available amd) to load-balance across multiple, replicated servers. We discuss the merits of replicating fileservers in Chapter 14, "Data and Web Services" (it's done primarily to improve performance and improve reliability when many geographically dispersed clients are involved). The automounter on the client side is not an availability technique for the long haul. Replicated filesystems give you load balancing and some measure of protection against servers that have gone down for long periods of time, but they don't give you the rapid recovery of an HA pair.

When the automounter is given a list of fileservers for the same mount point, it tries to find the one "closest" to the client by matching network numbers. Once network distance is determined, the automounter then pings each server by calling its null procedure (as described in *Detecting RPC Failures* in Chapter 14) and measuring the response time; the fastest local network server is chosen. Mounts are only completed on the first reference to a filesystem; once the server's volume has been mounted on the client, the automounter is no longer involved in references to that filesystem. If a server is down while the automounter is searching for a potential server, you'll safely skirt it. But if that fileserver later crashes after a client has mounted it, the client is blocked waiting on the server. Replicated filesystems don't help at this point because the client has file handles, mount information, and other state tying it to the particular server that serviced the mount on the first reference through the automounter.

Many system administrators find the amd alternative attractive because it has a set-aside feature. When a fileserver in a replicated list stops responding, amd moves the mount point aside, and the next reference to that volume causes a fresh mount from a different server to be completed. This has the nice feature of preventing the next process from stumbling into a crashed server, but it doesn't help the processes that already have operations in progress on open files on the now-defunct server. Those processes are blocked, waiting for the server to recover. The set-aside feature and soft mounts may be used to essentially fast-crash applications that get caught waiting on a crashed, replicated server; soft mounts mean that the process will eventually recover from its wait and can be killed and restarted. When it is restarted, it will use the new and improved mount point for the same filesystem. This is a bit heavy-handed, since it requires restarting a client application and is far from transparent; it's going to require at least a user adept at sending interrupt signals to a process or system administration help.

Sun's Solaris operating system includes a client-side NFS failover feature that works for replicated, read-only volumes. When multiple servers are listed for the same filesystem and one of the servers crashes, a client will recognize the failure when NFS requests begin timing out repeatedly. At that point, the client unmounts the volume, chooses another server from the list, remounts the filesystem, and renegotiates all of the open file handles in use, using mount path information and permissions stored on the client side. Client-side failover is useful for replicated volumes that are subject to random outages, such as those in a development environment that is not well controlled, but it is less deterministic than recovering the server quickly. In general, replicated volumes should be used for performance and ease of administration; each replicated server may be part of an HA pair to ensure shorter maximum time to recover from failures.

In the Windows NT arena, file sharing resembles NFS soft mounts. When a server fails, the mount eventually times out. If the server recovers quickly enough, then the client resumes the mount. Clients run a process known as a *redirector* that intercepts file references and sends them to related processes on the server. The redirector binds to a specific remote server instead of one in a list of replicated servers. NT does offer network-based file locking, although it is not implemented by default. In general, if you're providing an NT fileserver to NT clients from a Unix host, you'll want to go down the high-availability path.

Database Application Recovery

Database clients are much easier to recover than NFS clients. When the database server fails, client applications determine that they have lost their server connections and can abort in-progress transactions. Some transactions may have rolled forward when the server recovered, so clients need to reconnect and check on the status of in-flight transactions before restarting them. In general, database client libraries handle reconnection, transaction restart, and recovery gracefully. When using an HA pair, the IP address and hostname used for the data service migrate to the secondary server, so clients reconnect to the right machine. The generic case is the easy case.

It's possible for stored procedures or triggers to fail on an otherwise normally functioning database. These failures may be due to internal database problems; errors in the logic, external problems such as a full log device or lack of data table space, or a lack of available memory on the server. Client applications must check the return values of stored procedures, looking for all possible failure modes and exception conditions. Also watch out for long-running transactions. Clients that set timeouts (or deadman timers) for some transactions may inadvertently abort transactions that are blocked by a large SELECT or other transaction that consumes most of the database engine's cycles. Application developers may be tempted to break up the single large transaction into several smaller ones, performing part of the work in each transaction. This attempt to break the logjam works well if you are certain that the other transactions are lookup- or read-oriented, and won't change data that impacts parts of the broken-up transaction that occur later in the overall timeline. Part of the advantage of a single, large transaction is that you're guaranteed to have the database state remain consistent during the course of the entire work unit. You need to manage your recovery time exposure against the smallest logical unit of work done by the application. You want the right answer with the least application work, provided it gives you the right recovery window.

Replicated database systems also pose problems for client applications. If a client is going to failover to a replicated system that uses a different IP address and hostname, it must know how to connect to that server. Some application frameworks and client libraries support lists of IP address and hostname pairs that represent a search path for applications, giving them some of the benefits of the NFS client using replicated NFS servers with the automounter. Many publish and subscribe state management systems use this technique to ensure that clients can find a valid, functioning server on the network even after a primary server has failed, without requiring IP address and hostname information to migrate (which might confuse the configuration of the state multicasting engine).

Finally, most database applications require a client login to authenticate the user to the database server. Even if the client application reconnects after a server failure and restarts in-flight transactions, the additional step of logging in with a password makes the failover visible to the user. If you can automate the authentication step, by using a tool like expect or by caching the user password in memory (encrypted, of course), then you can make database-client reconnection completely transparent to the user. Even without a failover management system, this is a good developer practice, as it reduces the impact of server failures on the user community.

Web Client Recovery

Web clients have the easiest recovery path of all application types discussed. When a web surfer notices that a page isn't loading, the conditioned reflex is to hit the Stop button, followed by one or more tries on the Reload button. With replicated web servers, the first reload should start a new connection, routed to a different server, which completes the HTTP operation successfully. If the failure occurred at the level of a cache or proxy server, there will be a small performance hit as the cache reloads, but aside from the user-driven click-and-start operation, the failover to alternate servers happens automatically. Web sites that use load-balancing switches that terminate TCP connections on the switch (with independent connections to the back-end web servers) won't even have this minor effect on clients, because the switch-client TCP connection isn't broken by the failure of the web server. On the other hand, if the switch fails, causing a failover to a redundant switch, then the clients will see a pause and potential reload situation.

Pages that are forms-driven or are used to create shopping baskets on the server side introduce a bit more complexity. Most browsers ask if the user wishes to repost form data; this is re-sent to (hopefully) the new server when the page is reloaded. Any transactional back end called through a CGI script should be hardened the same way other transactional data management services are handled—a topic that we cover in more detail in Chapter 13. If the shopping cart or other back-end state is maintained only in the web or application server, then client recovery involves having the user on that client log in again and reestablish the last known state, either replacing items in a cart or renavigating to the same location in the web site. Stateful web sites are much more likely to use state replication or other techniques to persist in-flight, per-user information to minimize the client impact. We'll cover stateful web sites and other recovery techniques for back-end web and application servers in Chapter 14.

Clients that are viewing secure pages using Secure Socket Layer (SSL) connections will have to reconnect to the server. Pages that use the `https:` URL type to specify an SSL connection reestablish the SSL connection after a failure. The client picks up the same server-side information as when the original SSL connection was built, so this is largely transparent to the client. There are a few sites, however, that blindly take a client into a secure page area without requiring some kind of login or user authentication. The user verification process creates back-end state; once you have user credentials stored on the server, you're in the same client recovery situation as the preceding shopping cart example. Since SSL is typically used to secure financially or personally sensitive transactional information such as credit cards, username, and passwords, user may need to reauthenticate.

Servers can minimize the different types of client disruption by treating a loss of user authentication or other server state as the same problem as a session timeout (when the user leaves the client system idle for too long; time-outs are used to prevent unattended systems from being used maliciously). There's no problem in presenting the same page used when the user's session times out or when you want to reverify user credential information. A simple user-intelligible message about restarting a transaction or verifying work done to the point serves to make the user verify that everything has recovered properly, and that you're proceeding from a known point.

Critical design point: Make sure the back-end state is recoverable, so you can present the user with a well-formed, consistent page explaining what to do next after a back-end failure. The client only knows what the next page of web content tells it to display, in addition to storing any session or login recovery cookies that might have been saved by the server. Again, from the client perspective, this is largely transparent; however, you'll find users who turn off cookie-setting in the browser for privacy or anonymous browsing reasons, and then the session restart mechanisms that aim for transparency break. The onus of responsibility for session recovery is going to fall primarily on the web and application servers and on the application architects who must determine how best to mask failures from the user. Warnings about proper operation requiring cookies, or more explicit reauthentication schemes for the cookieless users both help. We cover cookies and sessions in Chapter 14.

Consumers of high-availability services are fairly easy to condition to handle server-side failures and recovery. Make sure that client configurations are consistent with server failover mechanisms, and clients should see little, if any, disruption when your HA system kicks into gear. However, applications on both client and server can still fail because of other errors caused by system failures or internal problems. We'll now go on from looking at a client system as a nonactive participant in a server-side availability plan to an examination of applications that need to be made highly available.

Key Points

- Even though client systems may not be highly available, users will need some way to access the well-conditioned services you've built. Make sure there are client systems that are physically and logically available to users.

- The widespread use of PCs with large internal disks poses a risk to valued data loss. Get critical data onto servers where you can employ the backup schemes that form the base of the Availability Index.

- Client systems should not normally be affected by reconfiguration or recovery of highly available server systems; however, there may be client application effects that need to be handled as transparently as possible.

Application Design

Architects and interior designers revile and battle each other.
—Stewart Brand, in *How Buildings Learn*

Stewart Brand's book is a wonderful resource for all architects, whether you're working with silicon, steel, or sofas. The preceding quote captures the tension between those who design structures, like availability platforms, and those who make things happen within them, namely those who design the applications that run on those platforms. We've been describing availability building blocks in series of more complex layers, starting with a foundation of data management and working up through network redundancy. Applications fit in at Level 7 of the Availability Index because they need to be well conditioned before you think about clustering them or adding other external recovery mechanisms around them. Systems and applications compose an application platform; that is, they are the pieces you use to support an application that actually does something interesting.

Unless you run benchmarks for a living, you probably don't just run a database; you run an application that talks to the database.

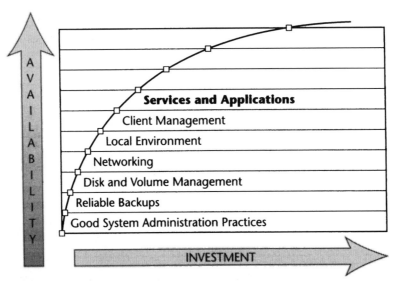

Figure 13.1   Level 7 of the Availability Index.

There are two aspects to application recovery: First, how does the application react when a data service fails, and second, what else might go wrong within the application code that would cause a failure? Sometimes it's the application to blame, dumping core or behaving erratically when the network and all of its services are just fine. In this chapter, we add to our analysis of design rules and building blocks with an investigation of application-level recovery, starting with a list of failure modes and application reactions, then we take a brief look at internal application failures, some process-level replication techniques. We conclude with an overview of good developer habits that improve overall system reliability.

Application Recovery Overview

Service availability only ensures that a data management service like a database is at the ready on the network. In the previous chapter, we looked at what might happen to client systems that don't tolerate failures well. On the server side, your user-level applications may not be able to access these data management services if they are not configured to deal with redundancy and get confused after a server failover. Applications may not deal with failures in a gentle manner, resulting in application crashes or endless streams of errors while they try to recover or reconnect to the wrong server. Application-level reliability is a trap for finger-pointing: The front-end team blames the back-end team for making their part of the application crash; the web designers insist they didn't do anything on the edge that would make a browser seize up; the database team blames the middleware selection for failing to route transactions after a failover, while the middleware team insists it's a database recovery problem. Developing good detection and prevention techniques will help you sort through these situations.

Application Failure Modes

From a network application's perspective, a server failover is indistinguishable from a fast reboot. (For more on failovers, see Chapter 17, "Local Clustering and Failover.") The client needs to reconnect, restart any in-flight operations, and continue from where it left off. If the application happens to be running on the machine that crashes, obviously it will be restarted when the machine comes back up. These are the two extreme cases, where there's a clear failure and recovery at the system level. But what about nonfatal system or software logic faults? These can impair or crash an application, even while the system is still running. Commercial failover management systems often let you try to restart a crashed application at least once before taking down the entire server, so you'll need to make sure your applications tolerate these soft crashes well.

The following are the application failure modes we dissect in detail in this chapter:

Improper handling of a server restart.   Networked applications must be able to detect the corner cases when data management services restart or failover, such as a long break in service or an aborted transaction. Many of these conditions are the same for server reboot and failover, so ensuring proper restart behavior is a good idea even without high availability or other server management software in place.

Nonfatal system or external failures.   How does your user application react if it can't find a remote server? What if a disk quota is exceeded and a write operation fails? None of these conditions is strong enough to cause a failover immediately, but they may have adverse affects on applications. When a disk fills up, failover isn't going to help, as the overflowing disk is going to be imported on the other side of the HA pair. Persistent failures, such as a network segment that fails and requires redundant routing, or a disk that presents media failures, may be handled automatically, but you want to be sure your application will tolerate the intermediate failures well. There's little point in having automated recovery if the user-level application has already failed.

Internal memory and state management.   In the vernacular, this category is filed under bugs. We restrict our discussion to memory-corruption problems and their detection. Memory-related problems are probably one of the most common sources of application-level failures. Developer difficulty with memory management was one of the key drivers behind the memory access constraints in Sun's Java environment.

Logical faults.   Examples of these include looping or hung code, deadlock conditions, improper handling of unexpected input, or merely wrong answers. We'll include some boundary condition handling in this category (these are also known as bugs).

Many of the topics in this chapter may seem like commonsense items, but even obvious application safety mechanisms fall by the wayside when customer deadlines, urgency of bug fixes, or upcoming trade shows in Las Vegas demand swift development. "Damn the torpedoes, full speed ahead" works in the movies, but not in the real world when you've got a beeper attached to your waist. It pays to invest time with the developers up front to be sure the applications under development fit your models for cost, complexity, and time to recover, and that the development and operational camps are aligned in terms of priorities. This often means crossing political boundaries and offering some value in return for a series of meetings. Set your sights on the level of continuous application uptime that you need to achieve, and you can generally coax all of the teams into the same goals. Our goal in this chapter is to show you where the torpedoes are and what you can do to avoid them.

Application Recovery Techniques

Investing in application recovery is akin to the message sent out by health management organizations: If you do a good job of early detection and prevention, you won't get too sick. Given that software failures account for a large portion of system failures, your applications need to be sensitive to the different types of faults they'll hit. That's another reason why investments in applications come before investments in clustering software. Why make a bad application failover between hosts, instead of fixing the application? Job one is to decide how you'll react to each type of failure. These are cost-time-benefit evaluations, balancing the time required to implement a recovery technique against the cost of having or not having that recovery, with the possible benefit of the automated recovery considered. There's no sense in adding checkpoint features to a database application if it can be easily restarted and the database handles transactional integrity. On the other hand, if an application crash runs the risk of corrupting data or propagating wrong answers, you'll want to invest in taking the necessary steps to keep your data flows clean.

We've broken down recovery techniques into five major categories. We'll provide an overview of these categories here, and then dive into detail on how the most appropriate ones apply to each type of data management service crash, nonfatal system error, and internal logic problem.

Detect and retry.   Images of "Abort, Retry, Fail?" haunt DOS-literate users. This is the simplest approach, and while it seems obvious, you need to be sure your application "tries enough" to achieve reconnection to a data service or recovery. In the event of memory exhaustion or network disconnects, for example, it's possible for an application to punt and simply crash, or for it to sleep for a few seconds, try to wait out a short-term memory deficit or network glitch, and then retry the failed call again. Patience is sometimes rewarded.

Gentle shutdown.   Faced with a case of memory exhaustion that doesn't resolve itself quickly (perhaps another application has a memory leak and has consumed the entire machine), or a floating-point exception that can't be fixed, it's necessary to save state and make sure files are left as consistent as possible. User-level applications should try to fail gently, leaving clear messages for users about what happened and what to do next.

Crash, burn, and restart.   A variation on the gentle shutdown, when either the application exits abnormally due to a signal, exception, or other internal failure or when the failover management system decides to kill it because it's not responding. In most cases, the failover management software will try to restart the application at least once before declaring the entire system unusable and instigating a failover to a secondary server. On the application side, recovery isn't always possible, but in the case of violent client-side death, users usually know what to do when they see their application window vanish or end up looking at a Blue Screen of Death for a few minutes. Again, in this chapter we're focusing on the user-level server applications only, which generally have lengthy restart times.

Restart from a checkpoint.   Checkpoints are the application equivalent of putting your PC in hibernate mode—they save all relevant in-memory state to disk so that it can be reloaded later on. Restarting from checkpoint assumes, of course, that your application generates checkpoints and that you have a valid checkpoint file somewhere. If your failure was caused by an internal application error, like a memory exception, restarting from a checkpoint may result in you taking the same exception later on. Applications that handle streams of requests may be able to recover from a checkpoint, since the new request stream may go through different code paths in a different order. Memory exceptions and other internal errors are often exposed randomly, so mixing up the input may allow you to continue past the fault. Further, if the problem was caused by poorly conditioned input that slipped past the default boundary checking, then executing past that request may eliminate the problem as well. As we discuss at the end of this chapter, checkpoints are useful if you have a long startup or recovery period for an application, typically one with significant internal state or computation required to regenerate that state.

Escalate to a higher management authority.   Otherwise known as *pager pandemonium,* this technique is used for nonfatal system faults that can and should be resolved with human interaction. Disks that fill up, networks that appear partitioned or unreliable, or memory exhaustion may not be fixable through a failover. The time to repair these failures is dependent upon the time to locate someone who is available, awake, and accessible to fix the problem. Escalation paths, as we discussed in Chapter 11, "People and Processes," are critical for continuous operations.

It's always a good idea to have an application clean up as much as possible if it fails, or if it knows that it's going to fail. For some fatal exceptions, this isn't possible, but even problems like floating-point exceptions often give the application a chance to be notified and deliver some last-gasp information useful for tracking or preventing the problem in the future.

Kinder, Gentler Failures

When an application is terminated by the operating system, there isn't much it can do. Its open files are closed, locks released, and other resources returned to the system pools. In some cases, the operating system may deliver a signal to the process, allowing it to perform some last-minute cleanup or diagnostic message printing. In other cases, where applications recognize failures for which they have no recovery path, it's up to the application to exit gracefully under pressure. One example is a database client application that tries to reconnect after a failover, finds it can't reach the server, retries a few more times, and finally gives up. The application should at least give some warning to the user about the state of the last known transaction and the reason for the failure. When users are expected to call the help desk to report application outages, the application can help its own cause by reporting problems automatically to the help desk facility and interactively to the confused or angry user.

What else goes in the kinder, gentler application failure bucket? Ensuring that all files, counters, and indexes are kept consistent helps. The operating system will close files automatically, flushing out whatever data was queued for the disks. If there is additional information the application needs to ease recovery, or if an indication of the last action of the application is helpful, then this data can be written as well, provided the internal application failure doesn't prevent it from doing so. When developers add last-gasp features to applications, these should be self-contained, simple, and use a minimum of system calls. A memory access failure, leading to an exception, may be caught with a signal handler that prints out some diagnostic information. However, if the diagnostic routine tries to allocate memory to format a print string, the diagnostic routine is likely to fail as well.

Providing as much information as possible about memory-related problems such as access protection faults may be helpful to developers looking to fix the problem. It won't help bring the application back quickly; you'll need to restart the application or do a failover to recover. Note that Unix operating system failures, or panics, are sometimes due to memory access problems within the kernel. Other application-specific failures, such as floating-point exceptions, should also deliver a signal to the offending process. If possible, the process can take corrective action—sometimes these failures are due to code that attempts to be more precise than input or data items allow, resulting in an underflow or divide-by-zero problem. In other cases, a floating-point exception is entirely unexpected, and dumping out whatever state information is relevant will help in diagnosing the problem further.

None of these graceful exit techniques improves recovery or reliability; they merely make life easier the next time by helping your development teams locate and eliminate problems or by gently steering users to corrective action. However, the best failure is one that doesn't happen, so we're going to turn our focus to preventing application-level failures, starting with adding resiliency and recovery in the face of system resource exhaustion.

Application Recovery from System Failures

External events such as a disk filling up can cause application failures. In this section, we look at system-level failures that create headaches for applications, and some common workarounds or early detection steps. We also cover network programming interactions and dependencies, since some network-based applications don't restart well after they have failed and been restarted. We cover the easy ones (memory exhaustion and I/O errors) first, then look at how network failures impact application flow.

Virtual Memory Exhaustion

Even with large physical memories, systems can exhaust their virtual memory. In some operating systems, this happens when swap space or paging files are full; in others, it's when the sum of physical memory and swap space is allocated completely. In either case, virtual memory exhaustion is an external, system-level failure that can crash, confuse, or otherwise impair the reliability of an application. The two most common causes of virtual memory depletion are memory leaks, in which one or more processes grow in memory consumption until they occupy all of memory, and endless forking (spawning) of new processes due to a bug in a script. Even forking a large application can cause a temporary shortfall as the system cleans up the copy of the large application to make a process container for a new job.

When you run out of memory, normal processes start to act like denizens of the twilight zone. Checking all return values from `malloc()` is the first step in reducing memory-related failures, but that only tells an application if there's enough virtual memory left to satisfy a request of the stated size. An application may try to dynamically allocate a full megabyte of space, and fail, but the system has 512KB free. On the other hand, the system may be down to only a few tens of kilobytes of available memory, and out-of-memory errors start to pop up in many places:

- Attempts to create new processes fail because there is not enough memory left to copy the parent process's state.

- Attempts to dynamically allocate memory, even in small cell sizes, also fail because there is not enough virtual memory left.

- Network applications attempting to create sockets to the machine cannot complete their socket connections, because there is not enough memory left for TCP data buffers and socket control block structures. Similarly, attempts to create new sockets on the memory-starved machine also fail because the necessary kernel data structures cannot be allocated.

- System calls fail, often producing the EAGAIN error on Unix systems, indicating that the error is temporary and may be recoverable, but at the time of the call there were not sufficient resources to complete it. Generally this indicates a lack of space for I/O buffers.

How do you resolve a memory shortfall? If the problem is due to a memory leak, killing the offending process should restore order to the system. When memory exhaustion becomes a chronic problem, it's time to look at resource management tools as described in Chapter 19, "Virtual Machines and Resource Management." If it's an overall load issue, or a process that has gone out of control forking copies of itself, then system administrator help is often required to reboot the machine or kill the root process in an attempt to clean up all of the rampant children processes. Remote help isn't always a possibility, as a machine in a memory contention fight may not have the resources to open up a new telnet or rlogin session. This is a corner case that may best be handled with automated failover management systems, adding memory exhaustion to the list of monitored conditions that make a machine go out of service.

I/O Errors

For the most part, I/O errors are caught and suppressed by the data integrity techniques discussed in Chapter 7, "Highly Available Data Management," such as disk mirroring and RAID-5 redundancy. If you start building in redundancy at the data storage level, disk errors due to media failures, I/O failures, or systemic failures in the disk storage unit should never be seen by the application. In the rare event that a disk failure manages to bubble up to the application level, you'll want to be sure that the application handles it cleanly.

Read errors are usually obvious. Instead of a buffer full of data, you get back zero bytes and some indication of an error. Make sure that the error isn't that the input pipe is empty; there's no point in going through corrective action only to find out that the problem was a zero-length input item. The gray area between what volume management systems provide and what applications demand is filled with failures in write operations on filesystems. On raw disk partitions, write operates synchronously, and there is no intervening data structure to add to the complexity of the problem. Working through the filesystem, the `write()` system call is asynchronous in Unix operating systems, meaning that the actual data block is written to a disk after the system call has returned. In the event of an uncorrectable disk system failure, errors are returned to the calling process in a later `write()` call or when `close()` is called on the file (see *Return Value Checks* later in this chapter).

Two filesystem-related problems compose this gray area between predictable disk systems and well-defined system call behavior. First, what happens when the filesystem fills up? The lack of space is detected immediately, causing the `write()` operation to return an error with some indication that the disk is full. No data is queued; no asynchronous reporting is needed. The application just realizes that it's staring at a full closet while holding an armful of dry cleaning. In some cases, this problem resolves itself when a large temporary file is removed, but usually it requires help from the SA staff to enforce good disk usage habits. What should an application do? Generally, retry a few times if the shortfall in disk space is expected to be resolved quickly; otherwise, do as gentle a shutdown as possible, given that there's little or no room in which to write out a checkpoint image.

The second problem: user quotas. Quotas are like payphones installed in your home to control garrulous teenagers. Seems like a good idea until you need to make the critical call to your client and you're without change or a calling card. To be fair, quotas allow large time-sharing systems to ensure that individual users don't inadvertently seize control of a filesystem with downloaded files from the Internet and PostScript output from graphics-laden presentations. If a write operation fails because a quota would be exceeded, it's up to the application to notify the user (and possibly the SA authorities) via other channels, and then again either wait it out or gently fail. With an NFS-mounted filesystem, the quota may be exceeded on the server side, and there is no immediate notification, since the quota check is done once the call reaches the server, not at the local client side. A good rule of thumb is to manage disk space carefully and aggressively on servers, and avoid the use of quotas except in interactive, many-user environments.

Database Application Reconnection

Ideally, a well-written database application recognizes a broken server connection and rebuilds it, without notifying the user of any problems. Transactions that were aborted or backed out can be resubmitted, possibly with user authorization. If there's a possibility that another transaction occurred while the system was recovering, the client-side application may want to ask permission before blindly sending a backed-out transaction again. Consider the case of a stock trading system, where a trade bookkeeping system is locked out for two minutes during a failover. When the client is connected to a live system again, the market may have moved away from its previous price point, making previously submitted trades less profitable. In this case, the database application should notify the user of the failure and let the user make the choice to resubmit or discard. In most cases, early notification results in the user solving the problem through another channel when time is critical.

Less-than-perfect database applications abound. They cause user headaches in a variety of creative ways:

- Instead of reconnecting, they crash or sit disconnected from the real world.

- They force the user to log in again, or to provide other startup information. The surest way to annoy a time-stressed user during a failover is to require more user intervention.

- They remain strangely silent as soon as a disconnect or transaction abort is detected. When you're driven by transactions, it's best to let users know exactly where those transactions stand. If there's a sign of trouble, tell the user so that corrective action can be taken in other ways.

We looked at issues for desktop applications that use databases in the previous chapter. On the server side, a database application needs to be able to recover itself, often independently of the database server. Server-based applications may need to notify the users of failures that require manual intervention, so recovery requires coordination of the server-resident and desktop-resident application components. If you're using a browser-based (HTML client) front end to your application, then generation of the appropriate error and user information pages is the responsibility of the server-side application alone.

Network Connectivity

A well-functioning application that needs to use network services is at risk of network connectivity impacting its predictable behavior. To continue functioning normally, the networked application relies on routing, remote host availability, and name service configuration. The most common error is that a host or network is unreachable, meaning that either the network is partitioned because of a routing failure or some intermediate routing information is no longer valid, so that clients on one end of the network can't find the servers on the other end. Assuming that you've done a bare minimum of redundant network design with multiple routers and rapid detection of outages, connectivity failures reflecting network outages should be short-lived. On the other hand, without network redundancy, you need an alternative plan—either another server for the same service or some way to stall the requesting application. If you are merely waiting for the routers to reestablish end-to-end connectivity, a short wait-and-retry loop should make your application tolerant of these network hiccups.

A second network connectivity problem is when your application and a host undergoing failover or reboot engage in a network footrace to see if the server can start listening on a port before the client's request arrives there. If the server wins, there's no visible impact; but if the client wins, it may see a "port unreachable" message indicating that the remote host was there but nobody was home on the desired port number. Again, if you assume that the remote service is on its way back to full health, then a short timeout and retry should establish a connection on the next attempt.

Another set of network problems has to do with connections reset by peers. This is the networking equivalent of "I don't like you anymore." Usually, a network connection reset occurs when one end of the connection reboots, telling the other end to drop as soon as it's able to do so. Resets can also be sent on connections that do not respond to any traffic for a long time, typically at the expiration of a keep-alive timer that sends periodic probes to the other end to be sure someone is still listening even if there's no traffic on the socket. When a database server reboots, all of its clients see their TCP connections reset by peers, and they have to reconnect. This should be handled transparently by applications; there aren't many worse ways to annoy a user than indicating that an application has to be restarted because the socket connection code is buried somewhere in the startup sequence.

Finally, network applications have to be sensitive to connection request timeouts. If the TCP connection can't be built up when there's a valid route, one or more of the following problems is at work: The remote host has crashed; the remote side's connection queue is too small; there's a network latency problem or some piece of network hardware is dropping packets; or a bona fide denial-of-service attack is under way and absorbing all of the server's capacity. Your best approach, from an application perspective, is to try several times before declaring the remote server inaccessible. Consider the typical user reaction to 404-type errors from browsers. Users want applications that produce meaningful diagnostics when they have trouble reaching remote servers. Your tolerance for pain in this case is at the threshold where a user goes to click on the equivalent of the browser Stop button.

Restarting Network Services

Recovering services by restarting applications on an otherwise functional host requires that you tune network traffic parameters to allow the same TCP/IP ports to be reused. Anyone who has restarted a database on a machine without rebooting has probably seen "Address already in use" error messages, caused when the database listener processes attempted to bind to a well-known port for incoming requests. If the server can't bind to the port, clients won't be able to find it at the agreed-upon location, and to the clients, the server is still down even though the host is running and the application has restarted. Guaranteeing that well-known addresses can be reused is critical for restarting applications without a complete cold start via server reboot.

Only two knobs need to be turned to ensure that server processes can reuse their previous network registrations. First, make sure that you are specific that a socket address can be reused, by handing the SO_REUSEADDR option to a setsockopt() call (using Berkeley socket semantics). This system call indicates that even after the socket owner crashes, the socket's port number can be reused later on by another process. The second knob is a TCP/IP configuration control that sets the TCP keepalive interval and the close_wait interval, both of which are used to determine when a socket that has one end closed is really, totally, most sincerely dead. The defaults for these values are generally in the range of several hours—not exactly the timeout you want before you restart an application in an attempt to recover a service without a reboot.

Here's where your challenge as a high-availability system architect arises: Set the timeout too small, and heavy network congestion coupled with lossy networks (such as clients connecting over the Internet) may result in discarding sockets that are functional, but moving little data. Set the timeout too high, and you might as well reboot or failover to another server because you'll have to wait for the entire timeout period before restarting the application that wants to reuse its previous port registration. Using a lower bound of 3 minutes is fair—meaning that you can restart applications after 3 minutes of a crash. Any network connection that remains data-free for three minutes is suffering from other problems, and abnormally terminating a socket connection is the least of them.

Network Congestion, Retransmission, and Timeouts

Losing a network endpoint because of a router or server crash is an extreme case. More frequently, you'll find network connections between application and data service provider slowed by congestion or server load, causing the lower levels of the network stack to run through their timeout and retransmission algorithms. The TCP part of TCP/IP guarantees that transmitted bytes get to the destination in the order in which they were sent, without data loss; often this requires resending data in smaller chunks, or retransmitting pieces that were dropped in transit because of overloaded network equipment.

Application reliability bumps into network reliability when you have an application that manages its own timeouts and retransmissions. NFS over UDP is an example; if the NFS client code believes that a request has been lost because no reply was received within a timeout window, it retransmits the request. The NFS server understands how to deal with duplicate requests, a definite possibility when you are dealing with a client that retransmits without knowing whether or not the original (or previous) request was received. Applications that set their own dead man timers may run into reliability problems when they use TCP connections to back-end data services, because TCP guarantees delivery of bytes written to a socket. The TCP stack manages the buffering of data and retransmission of segments to achieve this promise. You run into application problems when the timeout values selected by developers are too short relative to the latency experienced on the application's network. Running in a data center environment, with well-managed networks and closely watched routers, this shouldn't be an issue; but with clients on the Internet at large, possibly separated from the server by 100 to 200 milliseconds of network latency, you may run into dueling timeouts.

Figure 13.2 illustrates this problem on a time line. At time *t0*, the application sends a full buffer of data. With a slow network, TCP experiences timeouts waiting for an acknowledgment from the receiving end at time *t1*, and the TCP stack begins to fragment it into smaller packets for delivery, adjusting the transmit window to accommodate network latency and congestion. By time *t2*, TCP is still busy pushing data through the network, but the application has grown impatient. Having decided that the other end must have disconnected or otherwise dropped data, the application establishes a new socket connection (TCP socket #2) and retransmits the data. In reality, the original buffer of data was still in flight to the receiving end when the application timed out because the effective network latency was long compared to the application's choice of a reasonable timeout. The process may be repeated at time *t3*, and with sufficient network latency, the transmitting end may never successfully complete a round-trip data exchange with the far side because it times out (and stops waiting for a corresponding reply) before the request even crosses the network. Result: Your application appears to hang.

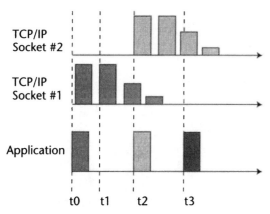

Figure 13.2 Network timeouts.

Here's a brief discussion of network parameters and some general guidelines for how they affect network retransmissions:

- By default, TCP won't send a second small, initial packet over a socket connection until the first one is acknowledged. This behavior, known as the Nagle algorithm, prevents a sender from overwhelming an already busy receiver; however, on slow networks it tends to make performance worse. Turn the Nagle algorithm off by setting the "no slowstart" option on the socket in your application code, particularly if your application sends a series of small packets.

- You may want to set the TCP option to send more than one initial segment over a TCP connection, ensuring that PC clients get enough data to start the bidirectional flow over the socket. Some TCP/IP stacks won't start returning data until they see a full TCP segment arrive. The TCP option for this is set in the operating system; in Solaris it is called `tcp_send_initial`.

- The default timeouts used by TCP to determine when to retransmit a segment are also tunable. In the example in Figure 13.2, this timeout controls the window between times *t0* and *t1*. There are usually two parameters, also set in the OS, that control the initial timeout and the smallest value for the timeout. They may be set as low as 100 milliseconds, which is simply too short for applications that have clients connecting via America Online or other large ISPs. Consider cranking the initial and minimum timeouts up to 500 milliseconds. The parameters in Solaris are:

  ```
  tcp_rexmit_interval_min
  tcp_rexmit _interval_initial
  ```

That completes the list of external failures that may impact application reliability. To be thorough in our discussion of application operations, though, we need to take a brief look at ways in which applications fail through nobody's fault but their own.

Internal Application Failures

Probably the most common cause of application-level failures is improper memory accesses. The usual suspects include array indices that go past the end of the structure, use of a null pointer,[1] using an uninitialized piece of

---

[1] Null pointers are one of the most common application problems. When an application walks through a list of objects and attempts to go past the end, or allocates a new pointer to a chunk of memory but doesn't assign it an actual memory address to which to point, you have a null pointer. They show up in Unix systems most commonly as segmentation violations.

memory as a pointer, yielding a random data address, and overflowing a buffer with unterminated or unexpectedly long input.

Memory Access Faults

Accessing the wrong piece of memory or attempting to access an invalid piece of memory produces either a segmentation violation or a bus error if you're on a Unix system, or a general protection fault on a Windows system. In any language, the cause is the same—a piece of code used a memory address that wasn't valid and ran into memory that didn't belong to it, or memory that shouldn't be accessed because it was in a red zone between valid segments of a process. Dereferencing a null pointer, or using it as a base for an offset into a data structure, produces this red zone fault, where the resulting data address points into the invalid first page or so of an application's address space. There is little help for these kinds of faults after they occur. Mostly your work is preventive medicine in terms of testing and using memory-checking tools that look for invalid pointer arithmetic.

Memory leaks are another class of fault that can cripple an application. When a data item is dynamically allocated, it can only be found if there's at least one pointer to it in the process's address space. Reassign a new value to the last pointer, and the data item is *orphaned*—left in the address space without any way of being reclaimed or returned to the pool of available memory cells. If this orphaning process happens regularly, the process has a memory leak and will grow to consume all available resources on the machine.

Memory access faults don't always cause application termination. If the problem results in a pointer being moved to another valid location in a valid page, then you'll corrupt data and possibly get the wrong answer, but you won't suffer an application crash. More common are wild pointer references that cause the text segment—the executable instructions—of a process to be damaged, or that damage the dynamic linking information so that a future library call goes into hyperspace. When an application scribbles into memory that contains instructions, the next attempt to execute those instructions causes either random results or a fault in which the operating system realizes it's trying to execute an illegal instruction—a random value written into memory as opposed to instructions generated by a legitimate compiler. Applications that crash with illegal instruction errors or data alignment errors generally suffer from wild (uninitialized) pointer problems. In nearly every case, there's some element of data corruption, making it a chore to determine what's valid and where to pick up from a well-known state.

PARTY LIKE IT'S 1999

Part of our Year 2000 application remediation kit was a set of libraries that had all of the date functions updated to handle four-digit years and make assumptions using a sliding window about two-digit years. These libraries were dynamically linked into applications, so that old code didn't need to be recompiled to operate correctly with the date fixes. One customer reported that as soon as they linked with the new libraries, their application began to dump core, so obviously there was a problem with the libraries. Upon further inspection, it turns out the problem was that their code was stomping on memory. With the old dynamically linked libraries, this memory corruption didn't hit anything vital, but with the new libraries the memory overrun caused a memory access exception. 1999's code may have introduced undetected data quality problems, but the party was over just before 2000. When a change in libraries or the link order of object files causes a new memory problem to appear, but the error seems to be coming from an innocuous piece of code, it's likely that some of your program structures such as link tables or the stack are damaged by a memory corruption problem.

—Hal

Memory Corruption and Recovery

How do you know that you're suffering from memory corruption? First of all, attempts to solve problems involving wrong answers or invalid calculations usually involve adding output statements to the code. If these make the symptoms disappear, you have a memory-stomping problem that was rendered less fatal by the introduction of new code and data structures. Similarly, moving or adding data items may hide the problem, or changing from dynamic to static linking rearranges the code segments so that the damage is hidden for a longer period. None of these answers is sufficient, because they only defer the point at which the application will use an invalid piece of data and crash.

Some application developers attempt to recover from an invalid memory reference by catching the signal delivered by the operating system. In Unix, when you get hit with a SIGSEGV on an invalid memory access, you're probably in irreversible trouble. Flush out some state, if possible, and pick a point at which to restart the process from a known good state, using a checkpoint if one exists. In highly sensitive and time-critical operations, it may be beneficial to add intermediate checkpoint and consistency checks on vital data items. Like the checkpointing process described later in this chapter, there is a cost to performing these checks, and they can't be done on every item after every reference, or you'll slow your whole application down to the speed of a simulation. On the other hand, running a checksum on some key, in-memory data items and comparing it to a known good value from time to time may help detect when any of those items is damaged by a bad, but not invalid, memory reference.

Hanging Processes

Our final flavor of internal failure is the good, old-fashioned infinite loop. Generally, loops are caused by unexpected input that sends the input parsing routing into a cycle or a deadlock on threads or other scheduling facilities that results in a deadly embrace followed by a break followed by another deadly thread embrace. Even network events, such as having a client disappear when a server is sending a UDP packet to it, can cause a loop, because there's no way of knowing that the system responsible for the next event in the processing chain has disappeared. There are a few ways to deal with habitually locked-up processes:

- Use an application-level heartbeat to learn whether the application has returned to its main loop or listening state. It if gets caught processing a request, the heartbeat stops and the equivalent of a failover management system can step in and kill it with the intent of restarting it, or can try to send it secret input to grab control of the application.

- Make sure you understand the deadlock detection and back-out procedures for whatever scheduling facilities you use. If you need to back out or reschedule a task, don't just blindly go down the same path; execute with a delay or out-of-order to prevent future deadlocks.

- Don't mix and match locking mechanisms. If two applications are locking the same pieces of data in different orders, or using different granularities of locks, eventually they're going to deadlock and get stuck in a deadly embrace, where each one waits for the other.

Most of these issues won't affect system administrator– or architect-level work. We include them to be sure that you know the warning signs of a variety of failures and common courses of corrective action.

Developer Hygiene

In a USENIX keynote address years ago, John Perry Barlow remarked that the early American West was inhabited by adventuresome, aggressive men with poor hygiene—a situation that resembled the frontier of the Internet at the time. We're not going to make disparaging remarks about anyone's personal grooming. We want to concentrate instead on the adventuresome and aggressive parts, and how to balance the need for speed in Internet time with the good grooming required to ensure that your network applications run reliably.

No matter how much diligence the system administration staff and operations design architects apply to a problem, you still run the risk of a poorly written application reducing availability. This section is not meant as an exhaustive list of how-to techniques for application development, code quality standards, and secure applications. Instead, use this as a checklist of minimum functionality required to eliminate the most common mistakes at the application level.

Return Value Checks

Programmers tend to pick system calls out of manuals and programming examples to accomplish a specific function without concern for how that function might fail or otherwise impact the application. The best example is the behavior of the Unix write() system call. Delivering acceptable write performance to a filesystem requires that the write operations be done asynchronously; that is, the write() system call returns as soon as the operating system has copied the data into a memory buffer and scheduled the disk write, possibly for some future time. Asynchronous writes are one of the things that makes filesystem checking so laborious, because information about the file (like its last update time and size) are modified at the time of the write() system call, but the data blocks aren't updated until the write operation percolates to the top of the I/O queue.

What happens if there's a problem finishing a write operation? Let's say a disk has a media error. There's no way to tell the application about the exact write operation, because the system call that schedules it has come and gone. Instead, the operating system returns an error with the next write() call, even if that succeeds. As a result, the application cannot tell precisely which write operation failed, and if the application developer doesn't arduously check the return value from write(), the failure may be missed entirely. When a file is closed with outstanding write operations, the close() system call waits for the writes to complete and reports any errors back to the application. Errors from any outstanding write are compressed into the single return value, even if multiple, different errors occurred. Here's an example involving a network client and a remote write() operation: If an NFS client writes to a filesystem and exceeds a hard or soft quota, the write on the remote end may be aborted. The client won't know about the quota problem until the write hits the server; the server can only report the issue in a subsequent write() call. Applications that continue to stream data to the server even after a reported failure essentially dump that data down the bit bucket, since enforcing quotas on the server suppresses new writes to a user's home directory. Net result: a hole in a file, or at least some incomplete filesystem data.

What are the issues? First, always check the error return value on a system call, even a trivial one like `close()` that can never fail. (Yes, closing a file can return an error if there was an I/O problem not reported back to the application previously.) Next, I/O errors reported back through the `write()` system call do not necessarily correspond to the operation scheduled by that call. Whenever there's an error on an asynchronous call, whether it's `write()` to the filesystem or an explicit asynchronous I/O thread, you need to back up in the output file and determine exactly where the error occurred. Finally, failure to heed error return values can lead to data corruption or application failure. When a `write()` operation fails, it can leave a hole in a file, since successive completed writes will move the file pointer ahead and fill in data beyond where the failed operation should have done its work. When the file is read at a later time, the hole is returned as a block of zeros, which is likely to cause problems for the reading application expecting something else, or for an application that was attempting to use the block as part of its text segment.

BUILT-IN TESTING

During my first summer job that involved writing code for a Unix system, I ran into a stumbling block in the form of a memory management problem that insisted on dumping core on me. Being (at the time) a strict adherent to the `printf()` school of debugging, I began to isolate critical sections of the code in an attempt to find the pointer overrun. Frustrated, I compiled a greatly function-reduced version of the code and called it "test." Typing "test" at the command line prompt returned no error; adding some more `printf()` debug lines also yielded no error, but no output either. I was stymied and began to distrust my compiler options and filesystem search path. The problem, of course, is that the shell has a built-in function called "test," and if you execute it on the command line, you get back either 0 or 1, not `printf()` output. Using `./test` to explicitly call my code snippet worked, and eventually led me down the path of finding my root cause sloppiness. Lesson learned: Know what it is you're testing, including everything in the application linkage and execution path from code to libraries to configuration files.

—Hal

System calls have a well-defined interface to an application, and therefore have a nice way of handing errors back to the calling process. Life is a bit more complicated for problems that arise in the normal flow of control of an application. In addition to aggressive checking of error values from system calls, developers need to perform regular checking of bounds and input values.

Boundary Condition Checks

Remember the Internet worm incident of 1988? The Morris worm used a buffer overflow problem to inject its code into a running process; many of the Unix security holes discovered since have also utilized a buffer overflow or improper input checking as a vector. Boundary condition checks, where you test the assumptions of a developer against the randomness of the real world, are an important reliability feature because they prevent spurious crashes, wrong answers, or security holes. Checking input values against constraints is another cost/benefit trade-off; if you run every value through a sieve of checks, you'll burn a nontrivial amount of CPU and user time. If you worry about the index into an array exceeding the dimensions of the data structure, you can have the developers trace back the code to where the index is calculated and determine what inputs affect the index value, or you can insist on periodic bounds checking.

In general, you want to question odd results or outcomes that are dependent on seemingly unrelated events such as link order or inserting of debugging statements. Here are some guidelines for making your life easier in terms of instituting and testing boundary condition checks:

- Utilize testing and development tools that look for boundary condition exceptions, memory leaks, and other internal structure problems. Most vendors' in-house compiler suites include this functionality today, and it's available from third parties like Rational/Pure Atria.

- When there's an input, make sure you span the entire dynamic range expected, and then cover all of the unexpected values. A FORTRAN application expecting a positive integer value may try to digest a negative number that shows up in the input file; the developers will be quick to point out that no rational person would use a negative number for something as obvious as, say, the number of iterations of a simulation. But connect applications together in a script, mix in some 32- and 64-bit type casts that may sign-extend values, and fairly soon you're passing the wrong input value to a long-running application. Test the unexpected.

- Watch out for testing results that vary each time you relink or rebuild the application. In particular, if an application works well when statically linked but fails when dynamic linking is used, you're looking at a buffer overflow or boundary problem. The different linking techniques rearrange data structures such that in one case, the error damages something critical, and in the other, it merely steps on memory in a nonfatal way. Both applications will fail, at some point.

- Use a programming language, such as Java, that hides memory allocation and size matching problems from the developers. Java applications don't suffer from random results caused by buffer overflow or index values out of bounds because these structures are handled opaquely and dynamically.

EXPECT THE UNEXPECTED

Opening slide from a USENIX talk: /* not reached */ **is the surest way to be sure that piece of code will be executed. If there's a code path that can only be reached through the right combination of bizarre inputs, corner cases, and ill-advised user actions, it will happen. Test this combination, and see how the application behaves; at the least make sure it complains nicely and produces diagnostics.**

—Hal

Boundary checking from a technical perspective requires that you understand how an application will handle or mishandle the entire range of inputs and index values. There is also a business aspect to boundary checking—is the application doing something that makes sense? The second aspect of boundary condition checking is to add these business-rule-driven checks, sometimes called *value-based security checks*.

Value-Based Security

Assume you have an inventory application that lets you move from 1 to 1,000 widgets at a time between warehouses. The lower bound is simple logic; the upper bound is set by the size of a truck or the number of widgets in a packing crate. What if a user requests a transfer of 547 widgets, but only 13 remain in the source warehouse? The request is perfectly well formed, but it doesn't make sense in the business context. As an application developer, you have no insight into these business rules. As someone charged with improving reliability and predictability, you need to capture these rules and cast them as simple boundary condition checks that can be added to the application.

THE $300,000 LETTER

Several years ago, a Wall Street trading firm received some negative press for processing a perfectly valid trade for the wrong security. A trader had written a ticket for several thousand shares of Verizon-predecessor NYNEX, ticker symbol NYN, but, probably due to sloppy handwriting, it was read as symbol NVN during trade entry. NVN was another valid symbol, only instead of a high-volume, well-known utility stock, it was a small bond fund that traded only a few hundred shares a day. The resulting sell order for NVN sent the stock into a downward spiral, until someone noticed that the order size and average volume simply didn't make sense. The firm found the error, corrected it by buying back the NVN and properly selling the NYN, but not until a number of holders of NVN had the color drain from their faces. Net effect: several hundred thousands of dollars in slippage as prices had moved while the trades were unwound. How do you fix something like this? Checking the size on a ticket versus the average volume is a start—and is now standard practice for trading floors. Wall Street adopts the exceptions and corner cases as standard practice quickly to prevent the same mistake from being made twice.

—Hal

Typical business rules that need to be included in application logic include checks for quantity desired versus quantity on hand, or average size versus requested size; time and sequence problems; and dollar amount or value of a transaction versus the permitted or valid amount for that user. Some of the more complex uses of value-based security entail adding authentication checks for certain transaction types, such that first-level employees cannot move millions of dollars, or employees below VP level cannot adjust salaries more than 15 percent without additional authorization. Typically, value-based security can be enforced by a database, using stored procedures or triggers to run additional checks on the records about to be inserted or modified, but it can also be done at the application logic level.

Logging Support

If you assume that you're going to have problems with applications at some point, you'll be well served by insisting that applications log messages when practical. As with nearly all other topics in this chapter, it's a balance between logging everything and computing nothing; logging is overhead and consumes disk space. If you chose to write out a 500-byte log message for every transaction, you'll be logging 50KB/second at 100 transactions a second. Let that application run for a few days and you've filled up a filesystem. In general, log all fatal or near-fatal but recoverable problems; log anything that might help with performance modeling or prediction; generate period logs of response time and load metrics; and log anything unusual, such as input that comes close to a boundary condition.

How do you add logging support? Writing to a log file is the most obvious approach, although some applications use a centralized logging facility like syslog in the Unix operating system. Here are some practical concerns for logging activities and log entry formats:

- Logs are almost always read by people, so make them easy to parse by carbon-, not silicon-, based readers. Not everyone reading the log will know that "mkttfxcp" is the "make trade ticket FIX-compatible" step, so take the time to spell out exactly what happened, where, and why.

- Sequences of events help determine why a failure occurred; timestamps that are coordinated across all log entries help tremendously. Make sure that you're using a common time base such as the Network Time Protocol (NTP, visit www.ntp.org) and include a timestamp in every log entry. It's going to be hard to diagnose problems at the millisecond level via logs, so you can stick to minutes and seconds in the timestamps.

- Nobody can digest megabytes of logs, even with significant doses of caffeine. Keep the logs short, using circular log buffers or trimming the logs frequently. The exception is logs that may be used for tracking security incidents; if you're going to go back through the logs looking for patterns, you'll want to keep them accessible and complete.

- Logs should be located where the operations staff can find them, but not in a public place so that nonprivileged users can glean information from them. The /var/log directory is an ideal place on a Unix system, because it is persistent across reboots and expected to contain files that grow over time. Don't use temporary directories, because your logs may vanish after the mysterious reboot you're trying to explore. Don't use filesystems limited in space, or those that are already under high load, because logging will fill up the disk and add to its write load.

- Think of logging as primitive engineering journalism; use the five Ws: who, what, why, when, and where (and don't forget the H: how) did something fail, or why was the log entry made? If there's a reference point back in the code such as a routine name, or a trail (routine XYZ called by routine ABC), leave those clues for the folks who will read the log entries later on.

Process Replication

Process-level replication ensures that you have another copy of a server at the ready, with all of the intermediate, in-memory state and supporting data it needs to take over for a primary or peer process. Web sites frequently use process replication by running multiple web servers on multiple small machines. Replication at same-system, process level buys you the shortest time to repair, because you can redirect client connections or route transactions to a replicated process in near-real-time. To be complete in our discussion of replication, we also look at checkpoint and restart techniques typically used to restore a system to a well-known state after it has been running for a long period of time. Checkpoint and restart and process replication are similar in their efforts to reduce time to repair a server fault; however, process replication can take you from minutes to seconds, while checkpointing is most commonly used to go from hours down to minutes. We look at each technique and provide thoughts on its ideal applications.

Redundant Service Processes

Redundant service processes are used to provide more CPU cycles for an application. The simplest example is the implementation of NFS in the Unix operating system, where the nfsd server-side process spins up multiple copies using multiple threads of execution. Each nfsd thread can handle a different incoming request, and adding threads adds parallelism and headroom to the NFS server. The best-case scenarios for redundant service processes are applications that have little state retained between requests, and where the requests can be multiplexed over a single incoming connection.

The usual startup sequence is something like this: A master, or controller process, creates sockets for incoming connections and requests, and then creates (forks) subprocesses that do the actual work. The more subprocesses, the more capacity (subject, of course, to the physical limits of the server). Since all of the subprocesses inherit the open file descriptors from the master process, they all are connected to the stream of requests and have control, configuration, or other utility files open when they are started. How does this provide redundancy? All processes can read from the same socket, allowing for a demultiplexing of requests on the back end. If a process dies, others can continue reading from the same input stream. The master or controlling process may choose to spin up another subprocess or run with fewer worker processes.

Think of the overused bank teller example as a model for multiple service processes. Once the bank opens the front door (the common input socket) and sets up the ropes to define the teller queue, all of the tellers are essentially identical. If one teller leaves for a bathroom break, the line's progress slows. Astute branch managers notice lines heading for the door, and add tellers or step in themselves to help absorb the volume. Any state information, such as your balance, credit, and identification, is stored in a back-end database where it can be equally accessed by all tellers. The advantage of the multiple teller model, like that of the multiple process model, is that a failure or grand pause with one server does not impact the others; you get a very rapid failover at the application level or continuity of service through the multiple back ends.

Redundancy at the process level has limitations. Each process must ensure that it remains independent of others, not moving file pointers or modifying shared file information. Output must be coordinated and serialized so that there is no contention from the writing processes. If there is intermediate state managed by the worker processes, that state needs to be broadcast to all the processes, since a future request looking for that state information might end up on another process. Ideally, you want as little state as possible managed on the server side within the application process; state belongs in a database or filesystem where it can be made recoverable, persistent, and easily accessed from any process. Note that with multiple processes trying to coordinate read and write access to files, and passing information through the filesystem, you may get better results and fewer development headaches by using a small database table to accomplish the same thing.

Multiple server processes can run on multiple servers. Classic example: httpd daemons running on a web server farm. They contain no state that lives beyond the scope of an HTTP connection; they are identical from the point of view of a client, and they are easily replicated. If you choose the multiple-server approach for scale or host redundancy reasons, make sure you use a load-balancing network distribution model as described in Chapter 9, "Networking." Running multiple server-side processes buys you protection against application-level or logic faults; running them across multiple servers gains the additional protection against hardware, operating system, and peripheral failures as well. Designing an application to fit the multiple-server model is complex, because not all applications can be stripped of their state. When you want the benefits of application-level process replication but have to deal with state information, you need process state multicast support.

Process State Multicast

State multicast, or reliable multicast techniques, are used to distribute updates from one process to all of its peer processes on the same server or on the same network. Implementations range from serial unicast, in which the updating process sends updates to each receiver in turn, to actual usage of Internet multicast class addresses with verification and logging to ensure that all recipients see all intended data. Most of the products in this space come from the middleware vendors such as Vitria/WebMethods, TIBCO, and BEA Systems.

State updates are useful when an application has to maintain some in-memory information about transactions to process incoming requests. This might be an open order table or an in-flight transaction history or a list of available slots in a scheduling system. This data is also recorded in a persistent disk store somewhere, but the time required to query the disk system through a database or filesystem often makes it impractical for real-time request processing. The in-memory state offers a compromise, representing a cache of the persistent copy of the data. As such, the problem of state replication resembles that of processor cache snooping, ensuring that all CPUs in a multiprocessor system see all updates to shared, cached data addresses.

When you're designing hardware, though, you can set the hard-and-fast rules. In software, and over a network, you need to deal with a variety of failures and with a longer time scale. Be sure you understand the constraints and guarantees you're getting from any kind of replicating middleware:

- *What are the delivery semantics?* Do you get delivery of messages *at least once, at most once,* or *exactly once? At least once* means you may get duplicate messages if the middleware believes a message was lost on the network. *At most once* means you have no duplicates, but lose messages that are eaten by the network or by overloaded servers. *Exactly once* is the transactional, ACID-property-friendly behavior that's ideal, but often the slowest and hardest to guarantee. (ACID properties are covered in detail in the *Database Servers* section in Chapter 14, "Data and Web Services.")

- *Deal with duplicate messages.* If you may get duplicates, make sure you know how to suppress them or filter them out. In some cases, duplicates are immaterial and can be ignored. If you get the same quote on a stock once or five times, only the last reported quote really matters. Similarly, if you run the risk of falling behind in processing state updates, determine if you can compress the updates and take the last one or the net-net change of all of them. Being flexible with the update stream allows processes to pick up and remove slack from the distribution system.

- *What's the latency under load?* As with queuing systems, you want to be sure the distribution middleware holds up with increasing request volumes.

As you compare various state replication techniques and application issues to handle duplicates, lost messages, and updates, the process replication problem bears an uncanny resemblance to a transaction replication problem. The same concepts are involved, and the same constraints and concerns should guide your selection of technologies and designs. With some good groundwork and developer guidance, you can build a system that tolerates failures at any level, from the hardware to the application coding.

Checkpointing

Not all processes handle short-lived requests. Reliability engineering also has a place in the scientific and modeling worlds, where codes may run for several hours, days, or weeks. Taking a hit because of insufficient memory or a network error in the middle of a weeklong simulation run incurs about 50 hours of recovery time to get the simulation back to the point of failure. Given that most simulations are run to reduce time to market, wasted simulation cycles and dead time are not easily forgiven. You need to add reliability at the process level to ensure rapid recovery of long-running jobs.

Checkpointing can be done at the application level, with extra code to handle writing out critical state information; it can be done using a job scheduler or tool such as the Load Share Facility (LSF, from Platform Computing), or it can rely on operating system support for preserving an entire process and its in-memory state at any point in time. Checkpoint-restart facilities are not common, so we'll stop at this brief mention of them. All of the techniques and issues described in the following text apply to OS-level support as well, but we're going to focus on more application-controlled techniques to allow restart and recovery.

What kind of failures scare the scientific coder the most? Obviously, resource shortages such as memory, swap space, and filesystem space represent threats to the completion of a long-running code. There are also issues of poorly conditioned inputs, application bugs, and floating-point exceptions that can cause a finely tuned, sensitive piece of code to crash if given slightly erroneous inputs midway through the simulation. With checkpoints made along the way, the application can back up to a well-known point in time and restart, perhaps with finer input checking or resolution of system resource constraints.

The most obvious approach: At well-defined intervals, copy out state information such as in-memory matrices, file I/O position indicators, locking information, counters, and intermediate results. After ensuring that the disk I/O has completed, and that the state variables dumped are consistent with each other, the application can continue. When the application is restarted, it should check for the existence of a clean checkpoint file or have a flag passed on the command line indicating it should resume a checkpointed operation. You'll need to manage the time required to create the checkpoint and write out the state information as an overhead factor; if it takes you 6 minutes to write out state for a 200GB memory segment, you don't want to do this every 10 minutes. Once an hour reduces your duty cycle to 90 percent, with 10 percent of the time spent writing out checkpoints.

Balance the checkpoint interval against the difficulty in backing out changes made since the last known good point. If you're walking through a file, updating records, make sure the checkpoint contains a copy of the file as it was at the time of the checkpoint, because you may update another 3,000 records before crashing—how do you back out those changes when the checkpoint file reflects the total system state 3,000 records ago? Coordinate file I/O, lock files, counters, and other indications of progress with the data recorded in the recovery area, and you'll be able to move backward in time to recover from a variety of faults.

Operating system or job control level features such as LSF and OS checkpoint merely make the checkpointing process easier for in-core state. You'll still have to worry about file I/O and interactions with other data services such as databases. Make sure you understand all of the dependencies of an application, and you can engineer a recovery technique that provides rapid recovery as required. Your job, as you've probably deduced from other sections of this book, is to make the choices in trading off complexity, time, cost, and resiliency.

Assume Nothing, Manage Everything

Sounds like being a parent of a toddler.

As availability becomes part of the management vernacular, application developers are going to work more with operations staff to define the critical instrumentation points and test vehicles for applications. In addition to the process-oriented, straightforward system administrators, you'll find experts in toolsmithing and data collection—true tweakers and tinkerers. Take advantage of system administrators with these skills by codeveloping the right points of instrumentation with meaningful data collection intervals and values. Your application developers may be very proud of the performance data that their code produces, but if it's not correlated to system resource usage via timestamps or doesn't measure the scarce resources from an operational perspective, it's not useful data. At the heart of the matter is defining the "critical to quality" metrics that can be extracted from an application, and then jointly developing the instrumentation, collection, and analysis tools with operations. And if "critical to quality" rings a bell, it's the defining metric for six-sigma efforts, as discussed in Chapter 2, "What to Measure," making your analytics data-driven and sensitive to variations in the data.

No matter how well designed something is, and despite all of the effort put into testing, verification, and logging, something is going to break. You may get hit with something subtle, like a filesystem filling up such that your database can no longer log transactions, or you start dropping incoming mail. Perhaps most vexing is the universe of user inputs, which range from the bizarre and unexpected to the truly random, usually when a user's mouse wanders and changes window input focus on your application. If you weren't expecting a 22-character string of the letter *d* as input, and your application crashes or, worse yet, takes down a server-side application, you'll learn to expand your input testing to cover the completely irrational but possible cases. When you take no assumptions for granted, when everything is suspect, and when you itemize, prioritize, and then test your risk tolerances, you're ready for production. Or so you assume.

Beware of quick hacks meant as stopgap measures. They tend to live on and have other applications piled on top of them. Unless the quick hack really is an overnight or hour-long fix to buy time to get the real solution in place, you'll find enough application weight heaped on your quick fix to compress it into something resembling architectural rock. Once in place, the fixes don't come out. Remember that COBOL programmers thought of two-digit years as a necessary hack to get around short-term memory constraints; few thought such techniques or assumptions would still be in place two or three decades later. Your quick and dirty fix is the next person's millennium bug.

Baking in the reliability aspects at design time isn't sufficient for smooth, predictable operations. You'll also need management, operations, and backup support to ensure that you handle all failures as predicted, to repair outages within your expected time windows, and to bring the world back to a state of serenity. The next chapters deal with the most complex operational aspects: eating your own clustered systems cooking.

Key Points

- Applications need to be tolerant of data service failures. NFS and database servers crash and recover, and your applications should be ready and waiting for the service to resume.

- External system conditions and intermittent network outages affect application reliability. Understand them and deal with them.

- Replicating processes, or checkpointing them for restart, will help for very long-running computational applications.

- Developers share the responsibility for application correctness. They need to test return values, institute boundary condition checking and business-rule conditions, and accept the entire range of possible but unexpected input streams.

CHAPTER 14

Data and Web Services

The repairs [that Big Ben's resident engineer oversaw] were intended to give the clock two centuries of reliable service before the next major overhaul.

—Stewart Brand, in *The Clock of the Long Now*

Reading Stewart Brand's description of his tour of Big Ben, you can't help but be struck by how our computing time scales pale in comparison to those used to measure availability of physical structures. At this point you should feel like an architecture student who has studied material strength and wind shear until all hours, but still hasn't built a building. As we've moved up the stack of the Availability Index, we're getting closer to the mechanisms that let you build strong buildings out of replicated components. However, not every application fits the clustered system model of reliability; in some cases simple redundancy and effective networking strategies provide sufficiently large MTBF and small MTTR metrics as well as excellent scalability. At Level 7 in the Availability Index, shown in Figure 14.1, we've moved squarely into the data center and will build upon the networking, client and consumer configuration, and disk management strategies covered to this point.

We open this chapter with analysis of how NFS and database servers recover at the application level, and we look at how you distinguish a multiple-instance approach (replication) from a bigger instance solution (clustering). We build on the notion of shared state applications by looking at the core services that run web sites: web, application, and directory servers. Finally, we wrap up with some thoughts on the emerging web services architectures and how they can be made more reliable.

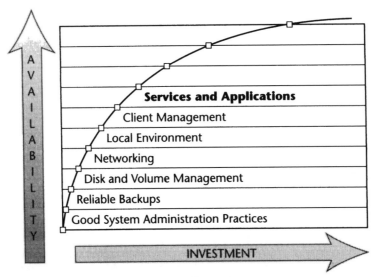

Figure 14.1   Level 7 of the Availability Index.

Network File System Services

Sun's Network File System (NFS) was introduced in 1985 as a way to share disks over a network. With several million networked computers now using NFS to share data, it's become a de facto standard, and in many cases, NFS uptime determines web server uptime. Unix researcher Rob Pike once said, while describing parts of his Plan 9 operating system, that "everything is a file, and if it isn't, it should be." If files dominate your world, whether they be user home directories for developers or HTML files served up by dozens of web servers, you need to make your NFS service as reliable as possible. We start by figuring out how to detect an NFS server failure.

Detecting RPC Failures

The network filesystem was designed so that network failures and server failures appear the same to an NFS client. The client continues merrily (or somewhat merrily) resending requests until a reply arrives, oblivious to whether the request or reply was lost on the network, was damaged in transit and discarded, or simply has reached a server that has gone faceplate-up. As a result, it's difficult to tell whether an NFS server has actually crashed without trying to talk to the server itself.

NFS relies on the remote procedure call (RPC) framework to send requests from client to server. As its name implies, RPC makes a remote system appear to be part of the local one, completing the request and returning results (in this case, data) to the calling process or system. The NFS system uses multiple RPC-based programs:

- The NFS mount protocol, or rpc.mountd, used to locate filesystems available for clients and to check permissions. If the mountd daemon disappears, clients will not be able to complete any new mounts, although existing mounts will continue to function normally. If you're using the automounter or amd, and the mountd daemon freezes or dies, the server is essentially dead to you.

- The NFS data server, called nfsd, usually runs as a set of threads in the server's kernel. It's possible for all of these threads to block or get hung, making the NFS server unresponsive. Since the NFS code lives inside the kernel, a crash of the NFS server-side code brings down the operating system in a hard crash or panic.

- Network locking services used for carrying file lock information between clients and servers. The rpc.lockd daemon and its supporting cast of processes (described shortly) need to be functional for network locking activities.

- The server's RPC port-binding daemon, or rpcbind (once called the portmapper). rpcbind's job is to assign TCP or UDP port numbers to RPC programs, and to return those registrations to inquiring applications looking for a particular service by its RPC program number.

If any of these daemons suffers a failure or locks up and stops responding to requests, NFS is dead in the water. There are two simple ways to check up on the health of your NFS server: Call the RPC server and verify that it answers trivial requests, or actually try to move data through the NFS server.

Every RPC server, regardless of its platform, implements a null procedure, or nullproc, that does absolutely nothing useful but returns upon successful receipt of a request (it's extremely tempting to call this the management procedure). RPC registrations and null procedures can be verified using the rpcinfo utility. Start with rpcinfo -p host, and look for the registrations of all required RPC services. Using the RPC procedure name and number, use rpcinfo -T tcp host prognum to ping the null procedure of the service. Use rpcinfo -p host to determine the program numbers of registered services, and use rpcinfo -T tcp and rpcinfo -T udp to ping the actual service daemons. If you get a response, the server is at least listening to requests. This simple round-trip ping is used by the NFS automounter when multiple servers are listed for a mount point to measure fastest response time.

What if your NFS failure is due to a disk problem or a bad interaction between NFS and the local filesystem? The NFS service null procedure doesn't test anything deeper than the RPC and TCP/IP stacks and the most top-level RPC service code. You have two choices. First, you can hope that disk-related problems are detected by your RAID or disk array configuration and are handled automatically. Second, you can attempt to test all of the interactions between filesystem, NFS, and the disk system, which requires that you try reading or writing some well-known file. To make the test conclusive, be sure that you're really moving data to or from a disk, and not just the local client's disk cache.

One way to be certain that you're sending data through to the server's disk is to create a new file and write a timestamp or some other easily verified contents into it. Read the file back on another machine or on the server, since it is cached on the client that created it. If you're a purist and want to test the whole chain, write a simple program to create a file, obtain an advisory file lock on it, write some data into it, close the file, open it for reading with a new lock, and read the data back. File locking turns off all NFS data caching and ensures that you write the data through to the server and read back the file from the server's disks. Involving the ever-popular network locking service makes sure all of the RPC daemons are in full operation. Yes, this is complex, which is why there are commercial failover management systems to test NFS data services for you. For more on file locking, see *File Locking* coming up in the chapter.

If you're going to write your own failure-monitoring agents, make sure they don't block (that is, prevent the monitoring application from continuing to execute until the completion of a system call). A crashed NFS server won't respond to your monitor requests, leaving the monitor hung in a noninterruptible disk-wait state. If you're running the monitor from the secondary server, avoid testing file reads and writes as you can hang the monitoring script on the machine that is about to become the primary, creating a deadlock or at least a complicated failover scenario.

When your NFS server goes down, and you're sure of that, your thoughts immediately turn to its resuscitation. Making sure the failover server takes over, quickly, requires some additional design work on your part.

NFS Server Constraints

NFS presents the best case for a failover management system because the client-side work is baked right in by design. Clients silently and cleanly rebind to the secondary server after a failure, provided it retains the same filesystems and IP address/hostname pairs as the failed primary. Not only can NFS clients not distinguish a failed server from a broken network, they generally can't differentiate one server from another that presents the same filesystem and host naming conventions.

Inside an NFS Failover

To better understand how to improve NFS failover times, it helps to have a rough idea of what happens when a secondary machine seizes the day (or disks) and assumes the role of primary NFS server. On the server side, there are only a few important steps. First, the secondary machine grabs the IP address and hostname of the primary, using some of the tricks described in the previous chapter. Next, it checks each imported filesystem for consistency, mounts each one, and NFS exports the mount points. If there were outstanding file locks, the secondary server would attempt to recover them, and from that point on, it's off to serving files.

Clients see a slightly harsher reality from the time the server stops responding until the newly exported filesystems are accessible on the secondary:

They hang. Processes accessing files or directories on the failed server are stuck in disk-waits and cannot be killed. Even something as innocuous as starting a new shell can hang the client, since the shell walks its directory and command paths.

They repeat themselves. Clients will retransmit requests to the server, after waiting for a timeout period. The timeout period doubles after each unanswered request, and after the fifth attempt, you see the "NFS server not responding" message on the client.

They eventually get turned upright. When the secondary server comes back to life, the client's requests are answered, and it continues where it was previously stuck. This assumes you're using hard NFS mounts on your clients. Chapter 12, "Clients and Consumers," discusses the scourge of soft mounts and why you don't want to use them in section *Tolerating Data Service Failures*.

Failovers that happen quickly may fly under the radar of the dreaded "NFS server not responding" messages that signal problems to even the most naive users. A server has to stop responding for the better part of 2 minutes for client-side messages to appear. If you can complete the failover faster than that, few, if any, users will notice through explicit error messages.

Optimizing NFS Recovery

How do you achieve a nirvana in a world dominated by a relatively old network protocol? The following are some rules you should follow:

NFS should be the only application on the server. NFS is an application, even though it runs in the kernel. Don't mix IP routing or name services or the occasional small database with NFS. First, multiple services make failover much more complex, and second, you want your servers concentrated on spitting files out onto the network. Performance is a reliability factor, and you should focus on optimizing each server for its intended purpose.

NIS, NIS+, DHCP, NT domain, and DNS servers belong on other machines. Yes, this is a rehash of the previous point, but it's one that is skirted so often that it bears repeating. If you're relying on an NIS server running side-by-side with the NFS server, and you need to fail the NFS service to a secondary machine, you're going to have some temporarily unhappy NIS clients waiting to rebind to a server. You may accomplish NFS failover quickly but then wait minutes for NIS clients to timeout and rebind to the secondary (or a different) server. Separate the servers and spare yourself the headache. Naming services can be run on small, easily replicated servers, while NFS belongs on a disk-heavy, NIC-loaded box.

Cross-mounting is evil. Cross-mounting, or having NFS servers mount each other's disks, is a recipe for a deadly embrace where NFS servers crash and hang each other. *Network Service Dependencies* in Chapter 9 outlined a graphing strategy to prove that your network is free from dependencies in core services. Add NFS to that service graph and ensure that you are still service cycle-free.

Journaled filesystems speed recovery. Once the secondary machine starts its takeover procedure, one of its first steps is to verify the consistency of the filesystems it is inheriting. The Unix filesystem check (fsck) utility can take an extremely long time to check large volumes—up to a minute per gigabyte of filesystem under duress. Since you failed over in midstream, without quiescing clients or attempting any cleanup on the primary server, you're under duress, and long fsck times are not out of the question. Journaled, or logging filesystems, solve the problem by eliminating the fsck step. With a journaled filesystem, recent modifications to the filesystem are written into a log, as with a database. When the filesystem needs to be checked for consistency, the update log is replayed to flush out all of the filesystem redundancy and self-check data. Instead of crunching block-by-block through every file, logging filesystems cruise through an update history and complete in a matter of seconds per gigabyte. Some journaled filesystems do not perform as well on writes and modifications as their naked cousins; however, it's worth sacrificing the write performance, if any, to gain the better recovery time.

Treat WebNFS like vanilla NFS. WebNFS, the http competitor that allows you to use an nfs://host URL notation to walk filesystems via your browser, is really just NFS on the server side. You'll probably want to be more careful about security and auditing the content you make available via WebNFS, but the redundancy and availability rules are the same.

File Locking

File locking and NFS were never meant to mix gracefully. The problem stems from differing design constraints of stateful and stateless systems. Stateful systems remember information about previous requests, such as the holder of a lock or the byte range requested. Stateless systems retain no information between requests. It's easier to recover stateless systems, since they don't need to go back and rebuild their internal remembered state based on what clients tell them about previous requests. On the other hand, stateless systems can't handle every situation. File locking is stateful and requires coordination between the applications that use it. NFS was meant to be stateless so that it would recover from server crashes quickly. NFS servers therefore require an adjunct protocol to handle the locking functions. As a result, file locking makes NFS server recovery more complex. Fortunately, few applications use NFS-compatible file locking, making this less of an issue in practice.

NFS-compatible is stressed for a reason. You can only do advisory, or gentleman's, locking over a network. Mandatory, or blocking, locks are not supported across machine boundaries because the crash of a client holding a mandatory lock would render a file inaccessible by other clients. Advisory locking provides a primitive access-allocation scheme that is essentially interoperable with PC filesystem locking. It's good enough for most of its uses.

What happens when the primary crashes and the secondary takes over? It's not a whole lot different from the case when the primary recovers by itself. Before going into the gory details of recovery, you need to understand how NFS monitors file lock holders. When a client-side process requests a file lock, the request is passed outside of the NFS RPC service to the network lock manager (NLM) RPC service on the server. The lock is acquired, the client is notified, and the server and client then begin monitoring each other. Clients with NFS locks verify that they still want what they previously requested, and servers verify that the requesting clients are still around and functioning as they were when the lock request was made.

The status monitor (`rpc.statd`) makes sure that locks are freed or restored in the event of a system crash on either side. If the client crashes, the server removes its locks when the client stops responding to monitor probes. A server crash causes each lock-holding client to be polled. Clients are given a short grace period in which to reestablish their locks.

When performing an NFS failover, you need to make sure the directory used by the status monitor to note lock holders is included on a shared disk set that migrates to the secondary server. This may require passing a command-line option to the status monitor so that it can find the state directory in its nondefault location. In addition, locks can only be acquired from the public, or virtual, hostname of the NFS server, since that's the name that moves and will be contacted for lock restoration by the clients.

Some operating systems support an option for mounting a filesystem without network locking, using `-llock` or a similar flag in the mount syntax. If your applications want to coordinate locking intramachine, without any regard for other applications on the network, this is sufficient. Unless there's a specific requirement that processes on different clients coordinate locking with each other, local locking or no network locking is ideal. You want to ensure that all of your applications agree on locking mechanisms, possibly including a long timeout waiting for a lock that is in transit between servers. If some of your clients don't renegotiate locks after a server failure, avoid using locking at all—think about databases instead.

USE BIG GUNS

In the first Indiana Jones movie, Harrison Ford is confronted by a saber-wielding maniac who threatens him with moves normally reserved for circus performers. Ford resolves the situation with a single shot from his gun. (The oft-told and probably apocryphal story is that the script originally called for a much more elaborate fight scene, but Ford was ill that day and decided to avoid the fight.) Such is life when you depend on gentlemen's agreements about access—if you rely on applications to coordinate their own access to files and obey advisory rules, at some point you'll have to support an application that's packing the equivalent of a large gun. When you have applications that don't play nicely in the locking sandbox, ensuring serialization of access and consistency requires an even larger gun in the form of a database.

—Hal

We cover database recovery and consistency later in this chapter. For now, realize that we're not fans of file locking for a reason: It has a bad return on complexity and it's not foolproof. Gaining availability means getting rid of those fool-susceptible things like applications that don't cooperate or users that remove files others have in use, creating stale file handle problems. Now that we've blasted file locking, it's time to deal with stale file handles.

Stale File Handles

Probably the most common complaint we hear about NFS failovers is that they aren't transparent to clients suffering from stale file handle problems. The short, snappy answer is that stale file handles are a bug, not a feature of failovers, and well-conditioned NFS failover systems don't produce lots of errors. Before we rail on stale file handles, you'll need a bit of background.

NFS clients identify every file and directory with a file handle. Locally, you'd use an inode number and filesystem number to locate something on a disk; however, over the network you need to know the server's identity and also the modification history of the file. An NFS file handle is an opaque, or server-specific, structure that contains the server's IP address, the filesystem ID number on the server, the inode number on the server, and the inode generation number. The last item is used to make sure inodes that are reused don't get picked up by file handles that referred to their previous lives in older, deleted files. Let's say two clients are working on the same file, and one of them deletes the file and creates a new, unrelated file on the same server. Because of the way inodes are allocated, it's highly likely that the new file reused the inode most recently freed, so the second client's view of the file is now invalid.

A popular cause of stale file handles is multiple clients accessing the same files or directories. One client removes a file while another is working on it, and the second client gets a stale file handle error. These situations are typical of software development or web authoring environments, where files are shared by multiple users and may be modified by several people during the course of a day. Stale file handles that arise from user access collisions can't be fixed with failovers or HA pairs; you'll need to use a source code control system to serialize access to the files that are being manipulated from multiple clients.

Much more common in the failover scenario is the situation where the filesystem ID numbers are not kept consistent between primary and secondary. In most operating systems, the filesystem ID number is assigned in the order in which the server mounts filesystems. Change the order, and the filesystem ID numbers change. This means that seemingly innocent changes to your /etc/vfstab or your FMS's mounting configuration file can paralyze all of your NFS clients when the server reboots or fails over; make sure that your system administrators add new filesystems to the end of the filesystem table to make the upgrades and reboots as transparent as possible. If the secondary fails to preserve the filesystem ID numbering of the primary, all NFS clients will see stale file handles after the failover, because one component of the file handle no longer matches their pre-failover view. The only way around the stale file handle morass is to reboot the client (or fail back to a happy primary).

EVERYTHING YOU KNOW IS WRONG

One night in the early days of a startup, we decided to add some disk space to our primary development server. While we had the guts of the machine arrayed on the floor, it seemed like a good time to juggle some directories and make better use of the space. We did full dumps of the filesystems and restored them in their new, larger homes. As soon as we rebooted the upgraded server and exported the enlarged filesystems, the network essentially came crashing to a halt. The server's CPU was pegged, and the blinking lights on our network hubs were twinkling at high speed. Looking at the client closest to the machine room door, we saw a stream of stale file handle error messages. The network was full of NFS requests and immediate replies of "stale file handle," resulting in retries by the clients that firmly believed they had valid file descriptors. In our predawn haze we realized that we had invalidated every file handle held by every client system when we shuffled the disks. The restore was successful, but it also made everything the clients knew about filesystem IDs and inode numbers ancient history. We went on a rebooting spree, and things settled back to normal—or as close to normal as you get in a startup.

—Hal

We've spent the early part of this chapter lamenting the lack of strict transactional control for client access to shared data in files. When you want transactions, you want a database, and with it comes a new set of challenges for optimizing recovery times, which are explored in the section that follows.

Database Servers

Databases provide transactional, recoverable access to persistent storage. You can argue about the merits of object-relational or relational or next-generation databases, but the basic mechanisms are the same. Database systems obey the ACID properties:

Atomic.   Transactions are demarcated and either complete or do not complete. There are no partial insertions or updates.

Consistent.   All parts of the transaction complete, and all modifications that make up a transaction complete within its scope.

Independent.   Transactions do not affect each other, so that one failure is isolated from other successful completions.

Durable.   Even after a failure, committed data is accessible and correct, while uncommitted or in-flight transactions can be backed out, restarted, or discarded.

Atomic and independent transactions are the domain of database management systems. Making sure that the database is available, that it can be recovered quickly, and that it provides a consistent view to clients falls under the availability umbrella, so we focus mainly on the "C" and "D" parts of the property sheet—consistency and durability.

Managing Recovery Time

As with NFS servers, it's helpful to know what happens when a database server fails and goes through a takeover cycle, and how clients are likely to react to that chain of events. We look at the usual failover and recovery cases, and then go into the more sinister setting where the failure also causes the database to be corrupted.

Database Probes

The first order of business is to be sure you truly have a database failure and not merely a break in the action. Some database transactions can be intense and long-running, making the server appear to be unresponsive when it's crunching through millions of records. Unlike NFS clients, who resend requests that appear to have vaporized, database clients have to respect state, transaction boundaries, and sequencing that are enforced by the ACID properties. It would occasionally be nice to have the ever-popular interest rate calculation example (where an application applies interest to some accounts, crashes, and then starts over again recrediting interest to the first few accounts updated before the crash) performed a few dozen times on your bank account, but database application designers are smarter than that. In the cases where the IT people fail, the bean counters pick up the error; there's always another level of management. You want your failover management system to check several test points in the database.

Listener processes or back-end reader/writer processes may fail, leaving the data incommunicado with the server; or the database engine may seize up or the SQL interpreter fail, allowing the database to receive requests but not do anything useful with them. It's a good idea to check the operation of the database, using a short piece of SQL that looks up values in a small table reserved for the purpose of a health check. Think of this as the `nullproc` equivalent for databases; you may want to use the internal statistics tables of the database, since you know you'll be testing something that resides deep inside the database engine.

If you're using raw disks for the database, there's not much benefit on your insistence that the test actually tickle the disk. Without a layer of filesystem and other kernel code between the database and the disk, you can rely on the disk management subsystem to recognize and repair disk failures. Checking the database health using an in-memory table is sufficient in most cases. Of course, if you're using a database on top of a filesystem, you may want to go through the whole database-to-disk path to be sure the filesystem internals aren't causing problems.

Database Restarts

Preserving the ACID properties of a transactional system requires more work on recovery. It's also not completely invisible to clients connected to the system, as we'll see shortly. When the primary database server fails, the secondary does a cold start of the database, either as a second instance in a symmetric configuration or as a new database instance in a master/slave setup. The first order of business is to get the disk sets from the primary to the secondary, just as in an NFS server takeover. If you're using raw disks for the database, the disk consistency check will happen at the database level, so the failover system just has to move ownership of the disk sets. When the database gets layered on a filesystem, however, you have the same recovery time headache inherent in an NFS server—namely, checking the filesystems for consistency. The database will still have to confirm that its data structures and transactions are clean, so this data storage consistency check only gets you partway there.

RAW OR COOKED?

Should you run your database on raw disks or cooked filesystems? This is the "tastes great" versus "less filling" debate of the digerati. (Although some database products have a definite preference for one or the other, most database applications run adequately in either environment.) This was the issue that caused the most debate and discussion between your two authors.

Hal, taking the "less filling" argument, prefers raw disks for their ease and surety of recovery, and their enhanced performance. Evan takes the "tastes great" position and prefers filesystem-based databases for their ease in backups, the ease in restoring a single filesystem from tape, and for all of the features that modern filesystems can deliver.

In some ways, the debate boils down to a safe-or-fast issue. Raw disks have one less layer of operating system overhead between the spindle and the SQL, and therefore reduce complexity (generally a good feature for critical systems). Filesystems can add the issue of recovery: If you're recovering a 300GB database on a filesystem and you have to `fsck` the whole disk farm, you'll learn that the "mean" in mean time between failures has other, more personal interpretations besides the mathematical one. Attempt to turn on journaling for the filesystem and you end up logging every disk update twice—once in the database and once in the filesystem. This is going to impact your update and insert rates. What if an application core dump fills up the data space filesystem you were counting on for the next hour's worth of inserts? You lose automatic recovery when a system administrator has to figure out why there's no more disk space left for the database tables and logs.

On the other hand, more advanced filesystems add the ability to checkpoint and roll back filesystems, which can eliminate concerns over database corruption; and they also add the ability to perform block-level incremental database backups, which can reduce backup times by 98 percent or better over fulls.

Filesystems that cache pages provide an additional performance boost for read-only or read-mostly systems: Much of the server's memory is used to cache database blocks, eliminating disk I/O and improving response time. Known as *supercaching*, this additional layer of in-memory caching can boost performance tremendously, especially for very large databases on large memory machines where the elimination of disk I/O improves whole-table scan times by orders of magnitude.

Again, Hal's preference for reliability lies with the raw disk design, in the most general case. It's simpler to manage, and it eliminates nasty interactions between filesystem effects and your database. Your mileage will vary depending upon the filesystem, operating system, and database system you've chosen, and the benefits of supercaching may thoroughly outweigh the recovery aspects. (If you're doing a read-only database, you're probably not going to worry about checking filesystems because they're not modified at all.) As Hal points out, "Sometimes cooking can be hazardous to your health."

Evan can't help but wonder if Hal has ever eaten bad sushi. This is not intended to sound like a commercial—but VERITAS Software has a product called Quick I/O that sits on top of their journaling filesystem. It has the advantage of making the database space part of a filesystem. However, Quick I/O removes the usual filesystem overhead of logging, journaling, caching, and buffering to deliver raw disk performance. For more details, pick up the whitepaper describing Quick I/O use and implementation with Oracle from either company's web site.

When the database engine starts up, it goes through its redo or undo log files to locate transactions that were in-flight when the failure occurred. These logs were brought over to the secondary from the primary, along with the data spaces, and are the critical component for rolling back any incomplete transactions. Typically, the database system completes any transaction that was in progress that can be completed, and that was acknowledged as complete to the client system. Transactions that weren't acknowledged, weren't completed, and can't be rolled forward are backed out. So much for your duplicate interest payments; you either snuck in under the wire or the client system recognizes the failure and knows it's safe to resubmit the whole transaction. Replaying the log files is the largest component of database recovery times, and shortly we look at how you balance performance and transaction shapes against recovery.

Once the database has completed its cold start, you are left with a system that is internally consistent, obeys the ACID properties, and is ready for action again. In NFS server recovery, there's nothing else to do because the clients were tapping their network fingers, retransmitting, and waiting for the server to recover. Database systems, however, are not stateless with respect to the clients. They see their database server connections get dropped, and they may see transactions abort or return error codes, requiring some client-side cleanup.

Surviving Corruption

Some database shops insist on checking the consistency of a failed database before bringing up the redundant server, thereby eliminating the possibility of running with bad data. While database corruption is a rare event, once it happens you'll be spooked by the thought for a long, long time. Databases are supposed to enforce the ACID properties; however, durability is remarkably difficult when the database is corrupted.

What causes database corruption? In addition to the usual issues of bugs in the system, you need to look out for external impacts on the database's storage. Random processes that write to the disk, or database processes that write bad data, can blow out log files or data spaces. If you're using a filesystem for database storage, you run the risk of user-level processes with root permission writing or corrupting named files and wiping out your database. If this sounds fatal, it is. We were tempted to title this section *Death of a Database (Salesman)*, but respect for Arthur Miller and our high school English teachers won out.

There is no silver bullet that enables you to fix database corruption. You need to recover from a redundant copy of the database, or restore from tapes, or roll back to some well-known, precorruption state. Corruption introduced as a result of database bugs may make this process difficult, which is why the database vendors tend to fix these issues rather quickly. We'll look at replication techniques and cost trade-offs in Chapter 18, "Data Replication."

Unsafe at Any (High) Speed

"Do it quickly or do it safely" sounds like something the metal shop teacher drills into your head before you turn on your first power tool. The quick-or-safe trade-off also exists for database systems. The more you focus on high performance, the more you risk increasing the recovery time. Database insert and update performance comes from increasing the depth of the replay logs, and from caching more structures in memory. The deeper the logs, the longer they take to replay. The intent is to allow the system to catch up and flush out the logs once a peak in inserts or updates has passed, but if you happen to crash at the apex of the performance peak, you'll have an extra-long recovery window.

Transaction Size and Checkpointing

You can attempt to strike a balance between transaction size and recovery time. Consider the difference between a transaction that updates every customer record in a single SQL statement and one that walks through the index sequentially, updating each record as a separate transaction. Clearly, the second approach takes longer, as it eliminates any benefits of caching and bulk data retrieval that the database might perform for you. Large transactions are the norm, but they aren't always the easiest to recover.

Database crashes between separate transactions mean the client program can pick up where it left off, possibly repeating the one transaction that was in-flight at failure time. This requires that client-side applications know how to walk through the table, and also how to determine what the pickup point is; a client-side crash will require the application to query the database to find its last update. Involving the client in the reliability design makes recovery easier but makes the client more complex. It also requires you have the political clout to get the application designers to sit down and consider recovery issues when doing their design. If you're successful, you'll have an easier time in the data center and might consider using your newly found spare time to run for public office.

Another independent approach is to trim the logs more frequently. This process, called *checkpointing*, forces the database to verify that any transaction represented in the logs is written out to disk, and then to discard the related log file entries. There's another balance between performance and recovery in setting the checkpoint interval: A longer checkpoint interval means that you can survive higher peaks of logging activity; a shorter interval means that you clamp the recovery window based on the depth of the log file. If you build in sufficient disk I/O capacity, and the database storage can handle the activity using whatever CPU and memory resources are required, more frequent checkpointing will be a win in the longer run.

You'll probably want to try smaller transactions and more frequent check-pointing. Both introduce minimal complexity and don't require major server-side changes. The next step is to use a parallel database to improve recovery time, but this, too, comes with a performance consideration.

Parallel Databases

Parallel databases like Oracle Real Application Clusters (RACs) use multiple database engines on a single, shared disk set or on multiple, independent (shared nothing) disk units. The goal is to provide a single view of a large database with more than one host, operating system, and database engine underneath it for performance and reliability. Note that a parallel database in this context is not just a database that parallelizes activity using the operating system's threads model; that form of parallelization is expected and provides a solid performance improvement. We're going to look at the case where you have multiple servers and multiple database engines, and have to coordinate availability and performance between them.

Scaling up with multiple engines sounds nice in theory, but the drawback to parallel databases is coordinating inserts, updates, and cache information between the instances. The problem is about as complex as trying to get a group of your friends to decide where to go for lunch. Who's driving? What restaurant? Who should reserve the table if you arrive there out of order? The coordinator among your cohorts is probably the largest or loudest person; in the parallel database world this function is performed by a distributed lock manager, or DLM.

The benefit of a parallel database is that the recovery window is reduced to the time required to back out in-flight transactions on the failed node. Consider a two-node HA pair running a database. When the primary fails, the secondary has to restart the whole database engine and roll the transaction log. In the parallel database, the second database node rolls the relevant portion of the log for the failed node and continues with its existing work. There's no cold start, only a warm recovery, making the typical time for database restart much shorter.

And there's the rub. Reread the previous section where we pointed out that replaying the transaction log is the greatest contributor to database recovery time. In insert-intensive or update-heavy environments, the transaction log is going to take a relatively long time to recover, whether it be on a parallel database or an HA pair. For read-mostly or read-only applications, parallel databases offer both performance and recovery advantages because there's little work involved in failing one node over to a sister node in the parallel cluster. In general, parallel databases can be slower for heavy insert and update work than their single-instance relatives, given the overhead of the distributed lock manager and multiple cache instances to be maintained.

This holds true for shared nothing and shared disk parallel databases. In the shared nothing case, a transaction has to be routed to the instance that owns the most data for the work required; if portions of the database owned by other nodes are needed, you start routing traffic on the server interconnect, resulting in higher overhead than a shared disk DLM. Shared nothing databases are good for decision support or warehousing work in which you apply transactions to all rows of the database, and parallelization at the node level is trivial. Of course, these types of marketing applications tend not to be highly available, so you can make the performance-versus-recovery trade-off without negative consequences.

There are cases where shared nothing, parallel solutions are ideal, typically where ACID properties and state persistence don't involve shared disk systems but rather in-memory transient data. Web and application servers fit this bill nicely, because there's little connection state or in-flight user state such as user login data. When state information can be shared between systems over a network, stored in memory, it opens up several replicated, parallel server reliability strategies. We continue our look at data service reliability with an analysis of the types of applications that fit the stateless replicated server model.

Redundancy and Availability

Avoiding single points of failure means creating redundancy at the component or system level. Many people immediately equate server reliability with clustering, thinking of two-way or four-way clusters that share a single disk system or SAN. However, there are many data services that don't rely on shared, on-disk state, or have very little state that needs to be shared between nodes. Redundancy can be accomplished by stacking like-sized boxes next to each other, with load balancing and some simple error detection. There are three basic approaches to server redundancy:

Multiple independent instances of the server, with no state sharing between them. Web servers and blades (see *Blade Computing* in Chapter 22, "A Brief Look Ahead," for more on blades) fit this model well, as what's happening on one web server has no impact on connections to another one. This is the classic rack-and-stack model, which we cover in the subsection on *Web Server Farms* later in this chapter.

Multiple instances with some sharing. If there's user session information involved, it needs to be copied to all of the servers in the farm. Typically, this is much lighter-weight data transportation than copying files or database logs, and it's memory-to-memory copying without disks involved, so using four, eight, or more servers isn't unusual.

Disk-based state sharing. The cluster classic, and the subject of the next few chapters.

Why the distinction? Why not just use clustered servers for everything? For many user- (or consumer-) facing services, scalability is just as critical as availability, so the horizontal, shared nothing model balances the need to scale simply with a recovery model that replicates just enough state to keep users happy. This is why we're still at Level 7 in the Availability Index—this is about applications and getting the most from application-level redundancy via a simpler, more easily configured mechanism than clustering. Not every web-oriented service benefits from rack-and-stack, though: For example, LDAP availability or web servers that contain their own filesystems don't.

Multiple Instances versus Bigger Instances

What's the best way to get high performance and high availability for a network service? Is the best configuration a stack of low-end boxes, or a pair of high-end, symmetric multiprocessing servers using a commercial failover product? There is no single right answer for all configurations, because the "bigger boxes versus more boxes" depends on the code paths taken by applications through the operating systems, the amount of state generated and accessed, and the eventual scale required of the service. The pendulum of system design seems to swing between the extremes of very large, scalable symmetric multiprocessing (SMP) servers and very thin, racked-and-stacked blade computers. How do you decide whether to go deep—big boxes—or wide, with many smaller ones?

Dismissing this question with "it depends" is the easy way out. You deserve a set of guidelines, and you'll get them, based on the code path ratio—the percentage of time server application code spends in user space, rather than in the kernel.

Routing packets and running NFS are system-level work. Doing I/O for a database and locking pages are system-level work; running the database optimizer and interpreting SQL statements are user-level work. Web servers shuttle files from the disk to the network, typically mapping the data from one controller to another and rarely coming up to the light of user level. Pure web servers have code path ratios of close to zero (mostly system work); databases can range from 80 percent user work to 10 percent or less user work, and NFS is nearly 100 percent system work, with a resulting code path ratio of close to zero as well.

If you can estimate your code path ratio within about 25 percent, you're ready to go through the decision tree for the rule. You'll need some data about the applications to be run on your highly available servers, and the client population they serve. Answer the following questions to determine how the code path ratio rule applies to a given application:

Is on-disk state involved?   If the user applications create on-disk state, then the state needs to have persistent, single-source storage. State can be records in a database or changes to a password file or even history files that are referenced in the future. Applications with state need to be run on deep (vertically scaled) SMP servers, since the state is very difficult to replicate across many small machines and frequently the operating system acts as a single, large cache for the on-disk state.

Are clients server-agnostic?   If the clients don't care about the identity of the server providing them with data, they are suitable for a wide (horizontally scaled) strategy. If clients need to know the identity of a server (NFS file handles, for example), then you need to go deep with HA pairs. Databases can go either way—a read-only database of stock quotes or a data mart has no persistent state, so clients can send their SQL to any available machine. Inserting records into a general ledger, on the other hand, creates state that is better handled by a single, large multiprocessor server in an HA pair.

Is the code path ratio close to zero?   The closer you are to zero, the more the model fits the stack of boxes approach. With a small code path ratio, the operating system can become a rate-limiting factor in performance. Adding copies of the operating system through multiple servers is your best path to high performance and rapid failure recovery. This rule comes third because the server and state limiting requirements can make the code path ratio meaningless. NFS has a nearly "ideal" code path ratio (almost zero), but NFS relies on server-client relationships and the state represented by files to which those clients are writing.

Of course, there are times when you can't build a bigger box, and you simply need more servers to meet performance demands. There are also recovery time windows smaller than the relatively uncontrolled database failover, typically where you're serving users on the Internet for whom the Stop button is hit at the first sense of web site slowness. Scaling web services—web, application, and directory servers—and making them reliable requires a mix of server and state replication.

Web-Based Services Reliability

Web-based services are the core functions that run web sites, whether for internal (intranet) or public-facing (Internet) use: web servers, application servers, directory servers, and the glue between them. Web services in the trade press refers to a specific set of protocols and application development standards that we address at the end of this section. We use the more generic term to cover the key functional areas that are used to build network-delivered applications, focusing on how to make them reliable and scalable.

Web Server Farms

Web servers are now the classic rack-and-stack appliance—you scale the site by adding web servers and using network load balancing to distribute requests across all of them. Making a farm of web servers reliable requires that you ensure that each server has network connectivity and will receive incoming requests, that each server has access to the right set of HTML and other content files, and that user connections can be reestablished to another web server if one fails in the middle of a session.

The following are some key Web server reliability design points:

- Treat all web servers as NFS clients, and put your content on one or more large NFS servers. Obviously, the NFS servers need to be made highly available, which can be achieved through standard clustering, as described in Chapter 15, "Local Clustering and Failover." Further improvements in availability can be achieved by sharing critical filesystems between members of a SAN.

- If each web server has its own files, ensure that they are consistently updated so that all of the web servers appear the same to the outside world.

- Secure Socket Layer (SSL) requests can consume large portions of the web server's CPU. Consider using an SSL accelerator board, or a switch that offloads SSL processing from the web server and sends cleartext HTTP traffic to the web server.

- Make sure your connected TCP/IP sockets get connected to a surviving server when their original destination endpoint server crashes. If you're using a load-balancing switch, it should remove the failed server from its list of available servers and reroute requests destined for that server elsewhere. Some switches actually hide the web server failure by proxying TCP/IP connections between the public network side and the web server side. If the server failure is visible to the client in terms of a TCP/IP socket termination, then it's up to the application to reconnect to the server. Most applications are intelligent enough to recognize failures on a TCP/IP connection and to reestablish it.

Many sites collect session information such as user login credentials, navigation histories, shopping carts, and other in-flight data. We refer to this collection of data as *session state*. Session state on the web server also includes HTTP connection information. State data used by objects on the web server typically gets embedded in a URL that is handed back to the client via a redirect operation, so the next client access (to the returned URL) returns enough information for the server to remember the client's state. The following is an example of a URL that contains state information:

Original URL:

```
http://www.buyjunk.com
```

User logs in on the home page and is redirected to:

```
https://www.buyjunk.com/main.html?uid=abcdef&cart=xyz123
```

In this example, the `uid` and `cart` parameters in the URL are consumed by objects on the `main.html` page, providing sufficient session-level data to process successive requests. It's critical that the session state used not depend on anything that might be in memory or on disk on the web server, because a web server failure will cause loss of state and create an inconsistency for the client. In cases where user state needs to be preserved across multiple sessions or needs to be preserved in the event of a web server failure, an application server is often used to manage the session information.

Application Servers

Application servers also fit into the horizontal school of scaling, using replication for availability. However, since application servers need to run the bulk of the business logic on the web site and handle connections to existing systems, they generally consume more CPU horsepower than web servers. While a web server may be optimized for a 2- to 4-processor system, application servers generally run on 8-way up to 24-way multiprocessing servers. Replication of these larger servers is occasionally referred to as *diagonal scaling*, a cross of vertical scaling with bigger systems and horizontal scaling by stacking boxes.

Business logic—the core of a network application—usually needs to have some persistent information about the user or series of requests being processed. If you shop on amazon.com, for example, your session information includes your login data if you're a registered user, whatever is in your shopping cart, and your recently viewed items, all of which control your experience on the site. Obviously, some of the data is dynamic and is generated on the fly by the application server; other data is persistent across logins and even across access points. When you leave work and revisit a site from home, if your shopping cart still has items in it, or your preferences have been reloaded, your state was permanently maintained, or persisted, somewhere by the site.

Before looking at the availability options for preserving state across sessions and across failures in the web server complex, we should look at how requests get routed to the appropriate server containing session state.

Figure 14.2 shows how a request hits a set of load-balancing switches and then gets handed off to a web server. The web server will look inside the request to see if there's an indication of which application server instance holds the session state. This identifier could be part of the URL or, in most cases, is part of a cookie that the site sets in the user's browser as soon as the session information is created. Using this cookie, the web server steers the request to the appropriate application server, where the user has some session-level information such as login credentials. What happens when a web server fails? Because the ultimate back-end destination is coded into a cookie or the URL, any web server can do the routing; the load-balancing switch pair reroutes incoming requests to a new web server after a failure. Getting application server requests to the right place is known as making them sticky, a critical part of making replication invisible to the end user.

The stateless parts of the request routing chain—switch, network, and web servers—recover easily from failures. What about a failure in the application server? In this case, the web servers will have to reroute requests to a new application server instance. If the recovering application server has enough session state to handle the new requests, the user doesn't see any impact; if the application server has no previous knowledge of the session, the user may have to log in again or may get nonintuitive error messages. It's up to the application servers and the applications running on them to be certain that session state can be persisted or re-created on any application server instance.

There are four ways to preserve session state:

- Do nothing.
- Store it in a cookie.
- Use memory-level replication in the application server.
- Write it to a database.

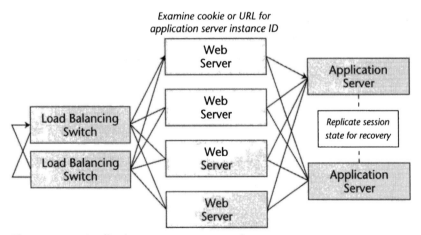

Examine cookie or URL for application server instance ID

Figure 14.2   Application server request routing.

If the application does nothing about its state, after a failure the user will have to log in again, or otherwise provide enough information to get back to a previous point. Repeated user logins that are an expected part of the site experience (perhaps you timeout logins after 5 minutes, so failures can masquerade as shorter-than-average timeouts) require no other redundancy strategy. Saving state in a user cookie has several limitations: the amount of data you can put into the cookie, privacy concerns that may restrict setting cookies on the user's browser, and the need to constantly fetch information from the cookie. Cookies are useful for remembering where a user last was on a site, or for providing cross-session user identification. If you've noticed that sometimes a site like amazon.com welcomes you back, it's because your user information was provided in a cookie requested by the site when you hit their home page.

Doing nothing or using cookies are overly simplified where availability and the user impacts of failures are minor design concerns. Sites that need to be continuously available and never interfere with user operations need to keep session state in memory, or in a form that can be reconstituted on the fly if needed. The easiest approach is to use the in-memory state mechanisms offered by most application servers, and to turn on state replication or state sharing across instances of the application servers on your diagonally scaled servers. As you add to the state maintained in a session, it gets replicated to other servers; if one application server fails, the web servers routing requests will choose a different instance, and that new instance already has in-memory state for incoming requests. The state replication engines keep each application server running as a warm spare environment for the working set of user sessions.

An alternative to using a pure application server solution is to write state information into a database, and then have a new session retrieve any necessary state from the database after a failure. There's no need to replicate the session state between application server instances, because each new session fetches the last known state from the database, with the application server acting as a cache for the truth maintained by the database. This session preloading is done under application control, not by the application server, so it lacks the transparency offered by the application-server-only approach. Conversely, using a database gives you transactional guarantees about the state information after a failure.

What approach is best? Many sites use a combination of all approaches, having databases for long-lived state that needs to survive across user sessions (items in a shopping cart or user preferences) and the application server level, in-memory replication for dynamic content generation, navigation information, or user privilege state. What are the trade-offs? The following are a few:

Frequent state updates.   Replication may fall behind the current user session, since each transfer of state between application servers is a transactional update—to memory, which is faster than disk, but still involves significant handshaking overhead. Advantage: database.

Recovery time.   If your database fails, your application servers pause while it recovers; your MTTR for the web site is at least as long as the MTTR for the database server. Without a database, the MTTR is much shorter because you only have to wait for the web server layer to start redirecting requests to alternative application servers. Advantage: application server.

Large numbers of sessions.   Each one is doing inserts and updates in your database. Tuning of the database is critical, unless you prune down the state to make replication sufficient. Advantage: slight edge to application server.

Performance.   Avoiding the database query is going to be a win; using memory as a cache for the interesting data will keep you running at memory speeds. Advantage: application server.

Long-term persistence.   Want your users to find that saved item from three months ago? You don't want the equivalent of plaque building up in your application servers. Write it to a database and retrieve it based on a user cookie. Advantage: database.

Scale.   In a pure database-centric state management solution, you scale by adding another application server that's a client of the database. On the other hand, you need to scale your database to handle the additional number of users, sessions, and queries. Advantage: the solution with the most manageable complexity, as complexity is going to introduce points of administrative failure.

There are no cut-and-dried rules for making the web-based services routing sequence reliable; you need to balance your requirements for scale, recovery time, and real-time performance.

Directory Servers

A directory server is a database-like, networked repository that is optimized for hierarchical, read-mostly access to its data. Directory servers are frequently referred to as Lightweight Directory Access Protocol (LDAP) servers, although technically LDAP is the protocol that is used to talk to the server that contains the directory. Directory servers are used most commonly in the web-based services realm as places to store configuration data for the web site, user registration information, and other data that needs to be shared by many access points.

Why not just use a database for everything? Directories are optimized for reading, so they will typically provide better performance in the real-time world of the Web. Directory servers also use replication between a master server and several slaves, making reliability a function of choosing any available server. Directories also have a hierarchical (tree) structure, allowing entries to be organized to match organization charts, product data, or other data that fits the tabular or table-of-tables model. Databases excel at transactional integrity, high-volume updates, and inserts, so typically you'll find both directories and repositories behind the web and application server façade of a web site.

The following are some considerations for making directory servers reliable:

- Determine what the rate is of updates and the volume of updates. Directory servers replay updates from the master to the slaves, and high volumes of updates may slow down normal directory service.

- Ensure that you have enough slave servers to continue to provide high performance lookups even if one or more slave servers have crashed.

- Validate that the *window of inconsistency*—the longest time period from when you make a directory update until that update is reflected in all slave servers—is within the bounds of what your web-based applications can tolerate. If applications want strong read-back semantics— that is, they want to see changes reflected in the data repository as soon as they're made—you're probably going to need to use a database for the rapidly changing, instant-replay data.

Web Services Standards

Web services are enjoying the peak of their popularity in the trade press. Hailed as a new way of assembling applications from smaller components, web services represent (perhaps) delivery on the promise posed by object-oriented computing—being able to connect application components together with minimal developer effort. The so-called WUS standards, coupled with Extensible Markup Language (XML) data representation, form the core of the web services universe:

- Web Services Description Language (WSDL, pronounced whiz-dull— the *W* in WUS) allows developers to describe what their web services do in terms of semantics and programmatic interfaces.

- Universal Description and Discovery Interface (UDDI—the *U* in WUS) is a lookup service for web services interfaces. Need to find a server that has an instantiation of a particular service? UDDI provides the equivalent of telephone directory service for you.

■ The Simple Object Access Protocol (SOAP—the *S* in WUS) is used to send XML messages between applications. SOAP most commonly uses http as its transport layer, making it another flavor of web traffic that builds on the reliability mechanisms outlined earlier in this section.

■ XML is used to encode data in machine-independent fashion. One of the historical problems in application interoperability has been agreement on data formats; XML makes the data self-describing so that data interchange is a function of programming rather than *a priori* format discussions.

So what's the big deal about the big four standards? Web services allow developers to assemble applications out of components, with a simple, small footprint of standards defining how those components are identified, located, described, and able to communicate with each other. Efforts such as Web Services Interoperability (WS-I) are creating profiles of the standards that form templates for interoperability of applications across multiple operating systems and developer environments. Think of web services as a sort of TCP/IP for applications—the right building blocks to make networking easy, but the simplicity comes with additional responsibility for the developer (as we saw in Chapter 9, "Networking").

How do you make web services reliable? This is largely an open question, even with several years of work on the basic standards. The following are some guidelines for developers and deployers of web services:

■ UDDI and WSDL typically are built on top of registries like directory or database servers, with web server or application server interfaces. Web services implementations that depend on looking up interface information on the fly are going to be dependent on the availability of the UDDI and WSDL services; they need to be made highly available.

■ Dynamic assembly isn't the same as reliable assembly. When you are choosing a service implementation, it's critical to know what *best implementation* means—most reliable? most scalable? Initial deployments of web services between enterprises should center around services where the deployment characteristics, including security, can be well defined to ensure that the quality of the assembled service meets the service level requirements of both parties.

■ In addition to the reliability of the network services on which the WUS standards are built, web services that cross boundaries between systems need to be aware of security, performance, and transactional consistency issues. Assembling services with dependencies on long-running back-end services may not meet the real-time goals of the users of that service.

Applications that use web services asynchronously, that is, they call several components and assemble the results without waiting for all calls to complete in order—run the risk of having some calls succeed while others fail. In this case, the application needs to undo successfully completed transactions that are part of the larger sequence of steps that is being backed out. Known as *compensating transactions*, the application is responsible for backing out changes that can't be made permanent without the entire series of transactions having run to successful completion. Compensating transactions are the subject of serious database literature.[1]

We raise the issue here because this is another case where a much-heralded new technology—in this case web services and their associated standards—reinforces the need for some basic computer science and reliability engineering. Users measure systems by what they see. If users see inconsistency as the result of some train of execution, then standards for developers have not served the right audience.

Coming down the pike in the web services world are new proposals for reliable transports at the SOAP level, such as Web Services Reliability (WS-R) and Reliable HTTP (HTTP/R). Even with reliability at the SOAP level, applications still need to be engineered such that they produce the correct results, with predictability in performance and security implementations that meet the needs of users and system administrators.

Key Points

- Pay attention to the recovery characteristics of the applications you're making highly available. Some, like databases, may affect clients as they restart; other services like NFS are sensitive to consistency in configuration information.

- Reliability doesn't always equal clustering. When the state information that needs to be shared between data service nodes can be memory-based, look at state replication and network load balancing to achieve horizontal scale rather than building a bigger vertically scaled box.

- Standards for application developers, such as the web services WUS footprint, only provide a framework for making applications easier to develop. You still need to ensure that your applications deal with the aftereffects of a failure, recovery, or restart.

---

[1] Jim Gray and Andreas Reuter's *Transaction Processing* is the gold standard in the area.

CHAPTER
15

Local Clustering and Failover

"I think she's dead."
"No, I'm not."
—Monty Python's Flying Circus ("The Death of Mary, Queen of Scots")

With this chapter, we reach the eighth level of the Availability Index, Clustering (see Figure 15.1). It is very interesting to note that when most people think of high availability, they tend to think of this particular technology. The first commercial failover and clustering packages for Unix were called high availability software, and that terminology has stuck over the years. That is unfortunate, because, as we've been saying since the start of the book, high availability is not defined by the technology, but by the demands placed on the system by its users, and is met through appropriate protection methods by its administrators to deliver application availability.

The most complex component of any computer system is the host. The host consists of dozens of components: CPUs, disks, memory, power supplies, fans, backplane, motherboard, and expansion slots; most of these in turn consist of many subcomponents. Any of these subcomponents can fail, leading to the failure of the larger component, which will in turn contribute to the failure of the host. If parts are required to fix a failed component, it could take days for the parts to arrive. If the outage can be fixed by a simple reboot, or other manual action, the duration of the outage (the MTTR) will be as long as it takes for someone to do the work, plus the time it takes for the system to recover.

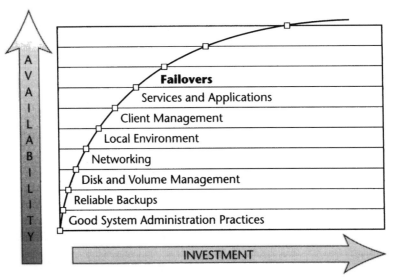

Figure 15.1 Level 8 of the Availability Index.

Clustering, by the modern definition, means that there is a second system[1] configured as a standby for a primary server. If the primary server fails, the standby node automatically steps in and, after a brief interruption in service, takes over the functions of the original primary. Since the standby server can step in and quickly take over for the primary, downtime due to a failure in the primary is limited to that takeover time.

In this chapter, after a brief diversion to take a look at the history of clustering, we examine server failover, the physical components that make up a cluster, and how best to configure them to maximize the cluster's availability.

A Brief and Incomplete History of Clustering

It would be arrogant to assume that modern forms of clustering software are the only ones that have ever been available, or even that they are necessarily the best.

The most famous early commercialization of clustering took place at Digital Equipment Corporation (DEC; they were acquired by Compaq in 1998; Compaq was in turn acquired by Hewlett-Packard in 2001). DEC's VMS operating system was introduced in 1978, and it quickly achieved great success. In an attempt to maintain and grow that success and to compete with fault-tolerant

---

[1] There can, of course, be more than one standby system in a cluster, and far more complex configurations. We discuss clustering configuration options in detail in Chapter 17, "Failover Configurations."

systems sold by Tandem (ironically, in 1997 Tandem was also acquired by Compaq), DEC began to introduce their VMScluster in 1980 and continued enhancing it well into the 1990s.

VMScluster was a distributed computer system, made up of multiple, then-standard VAX CPUs and storage controllers, connected by a high-speed serial bus, which supported simultaneous connections to as many as 16 nodes. VMS was extended to permit each major system facility to run on each CPU in the cluster; the CPUs communicated with each other on the serial bus. Two key pieces of software were developed: a distributed lock manager to manage multiple CPUs trying to write to the same disks and a connection manager that determined which CPUs were active at any particular time and coordinated their efforts.

The result was a single distributed operating system that ran across multiple CPUs. Services were delivered continuously as long as a majority of the CPUs and their OSs were operating. Functionally, VMScluster delivered nearly continuous operations, with little or no interruption when a CPU or OS failed.

In 1991, a Wall Street financial firm was concerned because their trading systems, which ran Sybase's RDBMS on SunOS, were having failures. The failures interrupted the firm's ability to trade and cost them a lot of money. They contracted with Fusion Systems, a small New York City consulting company, for Fusion to produce software that allow a system that had failed to automatically migrate its services to a dedicated standby system that would take over and continue running the services.

Although the firm did not deploy the product, Fusion turned this project's output into the first commercially available failover software for SunOS, called High Availability for Sun. It was a very limited product; early releases only supported failing over to a dedicated standby system (this configuration is called asymmetric or active-passive failover) in two node clusters.

Around the same time, Hewlett-Packard released SwitchOverUX, their first entry into the clustering space. In 1992, IBM acquired their first clustering software, HA/CMP, from a small company called CLaM Associates (now called Availant), making it available for AIX. After a few years, HA/CMP became the first clustering software that supported as many as 16 nodes in a cluster. It was designed specifically for NFS and could not be used with other applications.

Later, in 1992, a group of former Sun SEs in Silicon Valley decided that they could write a better failover product. They formed their own company, called Tidalwave Technologies, and wrote a product called FirstWatch. It was better able to support symmetric or active-active failover in two node configurations (for more on clustering configurations, see Chapter 17). FirstWatch was also easier to install and configure than the Fusion product. Tidalwave had entered into an agreement for Qualix, a California reseller, to exclusively sell First-Watch, which is why many people at the time believed that FirstWatch was a Qualix product.

In 1993, another small Unix company, Pyramid Technology (which was later acquired by and merged into today's Fujitsu Siemens Computer Corporation), came out with its own clustering product called Reliant. In 1994, VERITAS Software licensed Reliant and made it available via OEM to several Asian vendors.

In the spring of 1993, Fusion was acquired by OpenVision. High Availability for Sun soon evolved into OpenV*HA, and later became Axxion HA. VERITAS Software acquired both Tidalwave and FirstWatch in 1995, although they could not sell the software for several months, because of the exclusivity agreement with Qualix.

Sun Microsystems entered the clustering space in 1994 with a product called SPARCcluster PDB (Parallel Database), which was sold exclusively for Oracle's Parallel Database product. At the end of 1995, Sun released the first version of their general-application Sun Cluster product.

When VERITAS merged with OpenVision in 1997, they acquired Axxion HA, too, which gave them two formerly competitive failover products (one of which they could sell). Around this time, IBM introduced their second and more general failover product, HACMP, for AIX systems, and scrapped the NFS-only product around this time as well.

In 1997, Qualix (later acquired by Legato) released their first HA product, called Qualix HA, for Sun, and allowed VERITAS to sell FirstWatch. Other system vendors began to introduce and modernize their own failover products at this point, including Hewlett-Packard's MC ServiceGuard for HP-UX and Microsoft Cluster Server. VERITAS released their cross-platform VERITAS Cluster Server in 1999 (which meant that VERITAS has sold at least four different clustering software products in their history).

In many people's minds, VMScluster remains a superior product to all that came later because it did not take several minutes to failover when a system crashed; instead, it continued operating almost seamlessly. We often hear the question, "If DEC could do instantaneous failover in 1980, why can't Unix or Windows do it today?" VMSclusters were closed systems; all hardware had to be purchased from DEC, and there were few choices available. This made it much easier to write hardware-specific operating system and application code that enabled much of VMScluster's functionality. Today's systems are open and support many different varieties of hardware; it has become much more difficult to support a truly distributed operating system.

VMSclusters are much more closely related to today's fault-tolerant systems, from vendors like Tandem, NEC, and Stratus, than they are to modern clustered open systems, despite the latter's unfortunate appropriation of the word *cluster*.

Server Failures and Failover

When a computer system fails, it can take hours, or in some cases days, to diagnose the failure. If the failure is an intermittent one, it can take even longer; some intermittent problems are never reliably diagnosed. If it turns out that the source of the problem is hardware, a replacement for the failed part must be obtained, and then someone who is capable must be called upon to replace it. If the problem is in software, a patch to the application or to the operating system must be obtained, if it even exists (it may have to be written first). Assuming the fix works, the host must be rebooted, and recovery must be initiated from any damage that the failure may have caused.

Sometimes you'll find yourself in the finger-pointing circle game, where the hardware vendor blames the OS vendor, who blames the storage vendor, who blames the application vendor, who blames the hardware vendor again. All the while, of course, your system is down. If the failed server is a critical one, this sort of hours- or days-long outage due to vendor bickering is simply unacceptable.

What can you do? You could take your applications off the Unix or Windows server you've installed them on and put them on a multimillion-dollar fault-tolerant server instead. Unfortunately, a fault-tolerant (FT) server, which is designed with redundant hardware (often triple-redundant hardware; there is at least one quad-redundant system on the market) so that if one component fails others can instantly step in and take over for them, may still not offer adequate protection. Although the FT vendors may make enhancements to their drivers and operating system, FT systems are no less vulnerable to software issues than more conventional systems. What's more, by their nature, FT systems are closed systems that do not offer the flexibility or connectivity of conventional systems, because those benefits can introduce risk to the system. It is difficult to migrate existing applications to FT systems, because they are not always compatible with conventional systems. FT systems are popular in certain high-end applications, such as gaming (casinos and lotteries), and air traffic control, where the benefits that they provide offset their cost.

A more practical and less expensive solution is to take two or more conventional servers and connect them together with some controlling software, so that if one server fails, the other server can take over automatically. The takeover occurs with some interruption in service, but that interruption is usually limited to just a few minutes.

To ensure data consistency and rapid recovery, the servers should be connected to the same shared disks. The discussions in this chapter assume that the servers are located within the same site, and generally in the same room. Migrating critical applications to a remote site is a disaster recovery issue, and while it seems similar to the local case, it actually introduces many new variables and complexities. We will discuss replication and disaster recovery issues starting in Chapter 18, "Data Replication."

The migration of services from one server to another is called *failover*. At minimum, the migration of services during a failover should meet the following criteria:

Transparent. The failover should be no more intrusive to the clients who access the server's services than a simple reboot. This intrusiveness may not be reflected in the duration of the outage, but rather in what the clients must do to get back to work once services have been restored. In some cases, primarily databases, it may be necessary for the user to log back in to his application. Nonauthenticated web and file services should not require logging back in. Login sessions into the server that failed over do, with today's technology, still require a re-login on the takeover server.

Quick. Failover should take no more than five minutes, and ideally less than two minutes. The best way to achieve this goal is for the takeover server to already be booted up and running as many of the underlying system processes as possible. If a full reboot is required in order to failover, failover times will go way up and can, in some cases, take an hour or more.

The two- to five-minute goal for failovers is a noble one and can be easily met by most applications. The most glaring exception to this is databases such as Oracle or DB2. Databases can only be restarted after all of the transactions that have been cached are rerun, and the database updated. (Transactions are cached to speed up routine database performance; the trade-off is a slowing of recovery time.) There is no limit to how long it might take a database to run through all of the outstanding transactions, and while those transactions are being rerun, the database is down from a user's perspective.

Minimal manual intervention. Ideally, no human intervention at all should be required for a failover to complete; the entire process should be automated. Some sites or applications may require manual initiation for a failover, but that is not generally desirable. As already discussed, the host receiving a failover should never require a reboot.

Guaranteed data access. After a failover, the receiving host should see exactly the same data as the original host. Replicating data to another host when disks are not shared adds unnecessary risk and complexity, and is not advised for hosts that are located near to each other.

The systems in a failover configuration should also communicate with each other continuously, so that each system knows the state of its partner. This communication is called a *heartbeat*. Later in this chapter we discuss the implications when the servers lose their heartbeats.

When a failover occurs, three critical elements must be moved from the failed server to the takeover server in order for users to resume their activities and for the application services to be considered available once again:

1. *Network identity.* Generally, this means the IP address that the server's clients use. Some network media and applications may require additional information to be transferred, such as a MAC address. If the server is on multiple networks or has multiple public network identities, it may be necessary to move multiple addresses.

2. *Access to shared disks.* Operating system, and in particular filesystem, technology generally prohibits multiple servers from writing to the same disks at the same time for any reason. In a shared disk configuration, logical access must be restricted to one server at a time. During a failover, the process that prevents the second machine from accessing the disks must reverse itself and lock out the original server, while granting access only to the takeover server. Note that not all operating systems provide this technology.

3. *Set of processes.* Once the disks have migrated to the takeover server, all the processes associated with the data must be restarted. Data consistency must be ensured from the application's perspective.

The collection of these elements is commonly called a *service group*. A service group is the unit that moves from cluster member to cluster member. Sometimes called a *virtual machine*, the service group provides the critical services that are being made highly available.

A cluster may have multiple service groups, and depending on the software that manages the cluster, there may not be any limit to the number of service groups. Service groups must be totally independent of each other, so that they can live on any eligible server in the cluster, regardless of what the other service groups might be doing. If two or more service groups cannot be independent of each other (that is, they must be together on the same server at all times), then they must be merged into a single service group.

Logical, Application-centric Thinking

One of the more interesting aspects of working with systems that failover is the new way you must think about the server pair and its services and resources. Normally, you think of a computer system as a single box, with a single network identity (though it may have more than one network address), that runs one or more applications on its local or perhaps network-attached storage.

A collection of clustered servers must be thought of in a nontraditional way. The bottom-line component is no longer the server, but rather the service group. The computer is merely an application or network service delivery device. Just as a disk is subsumed under a host when you enable data redundancy, the server is subsumed under the service when you add in host redundancy. The server becomes just another term in the overall service-delivery equation.

The computer itself is the least interesting component of an application-service delivery mechanism. Any computer that runs the right operating system and is made up of the same basic hardware components can deliver this service (albeit not always optimally). The computing hardware itself is an interchangeable commodity. If a computer dies, you should be able to remove it, replace it with another computer, and continue operating as before. Failover Management Software (FMS; we'll discuss this term at the beginning of Chapter 16, "Failover Management and Issues"), the software that automates the failover process, performs this swap automatically, moving the service group to a second computer that has been predesignated and configured for this function. In some environments, the second computer is actually waiting for a service group to arrive. In other environments, the second computer is performing other functions and will accept the service groups in addition to what is already running there.

In a clustered environment, an IP address does not connect you with a particular computer, but rather a particular service group that is using that name at that time. The name, and the IP address, might reside on either machine in a redundant pair, or on any machine in a larger cluster. It should not matter to your users which computer is running the application, only that the application is running, and that they can obtain the services that the application provides.

THE NUMBER YOU HAVE CALLED . . .

In the spring of 1999, my family and I moved to a new house. The new house is less than a mile from our old house in the same town. We were fortunate in that we were able to bring our phone number with us to the new house. People who called us did not need to concern themselves with which house we were in. When we moved to the new house, the phone number rang the phones in the new house (and curiously, in both houses for about an hour).

This is exactly what happens in a failover. A phone number is just a network address, after all. Someone who called to talk to me (OK, my wife; nobody ever calls to talk to me.) didn't care which house (computer) was serving us (the application), only that he reached the person (service) that he was looking for. Despite your change in physical location, the very same logical network service is still being provided.

—Evan

Disks and storage devices, similarly, may not be associated with a particular server. The data, and possibly the application code itself, can move between servers.

The unit that performs a particular service is no longer a single computer, but rather the pair or cluster on whose computers the application may be running at a particular moment. It should not matter which computer runs the service, as long as the service runs.

Consider that the cluster acts as a black box providing a particular service. Your users connect to a network address and exchange data with that address. Assuming that the speed at which the responses return is adequate, it doesn't matter to the user what is providing the service. Theoretically, the server could be a Unix computer, a Windows computer, a mainframe computer, or even a fast-typing monkey with a keyboard. As long as the service is being provided and the responses are accurate, the users should, at least in theory, be happy. There are technical reasons why a particular server is used, and why you'd never mix server types, but purely from a user's perspective, it truly should not matter which type of system is doing the work.

Failover Requirements

A failover pair or cluster requires more than simply having two servers placed near each other. Let's examine the various components that are required to turn the two servers into a failover pair. (We elaborate on each of these required components in the next section, and we discuss larger and more complex combinations of servers later on.) A simple cluster is depicted in Figure 15.2.

The components that are required to build a cluster are the following:

Servers.   You need two servers—a primary server and a takeover server. (We refer to the takeover server as the "secondary server" in some cases, but it's the same idea.) A critical application that once ran but has now failed on the primary server migrates to the takeover server in a process called failover. The servers should be running the same operating system version, have the same patches installed, support the same binary executables, and as much as possible, be configured identically. Of course, clusters can grow larger than two nodes, but the basic premise is the same; an application moves from one node to another. Whether a cluster has two nodes or 2,000 nodes, the application still migrates in the same basic manner.

Network connections.   There are two different types of network connections that are required to implement failover, and a third that is strongly recommended. A pair (for redundancy) of dedicated *heartbeat networks*, which run between all the servers in a cluster, is a basic requirement.

The heartbeat networks allow the servers to communicate with and monitor each other with a minimum of other traffic, so that each server knows immediately if something has happened to another cluster member that requires its action. The heartbeat network must be dedicated to this purpose so that news of a problem on one system arrives at its partner with no delay.

The second type of network connection is the *public*, or *service, network*. This is the network that carries your user and client data. The third type of network connection is the *administrative network*, which allows the system administrators a guaranteed network path into each server, even after a failover has occurred.

Disks.   There are two different types of disks required for failover. The *unshared disks* contain the operating system and other files that are required for the operation of each system in the pair when it is not the active server, including any software required to initiate and maintain the failover process.

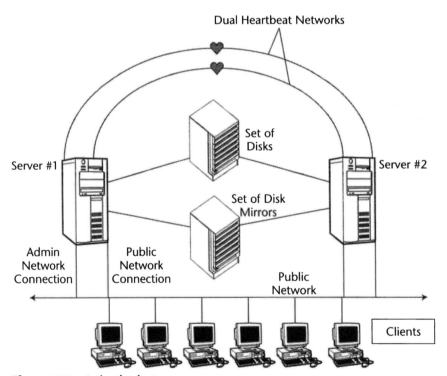

Figure 15.2   A simple cluster.

The second type of disks is the *shared disks*, where the critical application data resides. These are the disks that migrate back and forth between servers when a failover occurs; they must be accessible by both servers in the pair, even though they will only be accessed one server at a time. All disks, both shared and private, that serve a cluster should have some sort of redundancy; mirroring is generally preferred over parity RAID.

Some FMSs use a configuration called *shared nothing* rather than shared disks. In a shared nothing configuration, the data on one server are replicated via a network (LAN or WAN) to the other server. This is a less desirable configuration for local failover because of the added complexities and dependencies, especially on another network, that are introduced. Shared nothing configurations are fine for wide area failover, but for local failover, where the systems in question are located close enough together that SCSI and/or Fibre Channel specs are not exceeded, shared disks are a far superior and more reliable solution.

Application portability. A vitally important but often overlooked element of failover pair design is the requirement that the critical application(s) can be run on both servers in the pair, one server at a time. Most often, the bugaboo is licensing. If your application won't run on both servers, one at a time, you do not have high availability. Speak to your application vendor; many vendors will provide a discounted license to run on a backup server. (Your mileage may vary.) But it may be necessary to purchase two complete, full-price licenses to permit your application to run on either server as necessary. If it is necessary, then it is. Nobody said that achieving HA was going to be cheap or easy. In some cases, applications bind themselves very closely to the hardware on which they run; those sorts of applications will have particular difficulty when it comes to failing over. It is vitally important that as part of any implementation of clustering software sufficient time is spent testing all aspects of the failover.

No single point of failure. An ideal design principle, rather than a physical component, this is still a very important guide to building clusters. If there is a component of your failover pair whose failure will cause both servers to become down or otherwise unavailable, then you will not achieve high availability. It is important to look at all components, internal and external, on your systems. For more on single points of failure, please refer to Key Design Principle #18 in Chapter 5, "20 Key High Availability Design Principles."

Servers

The fundamental requirement when designing a cluster is that there be at least two servers. The servers must be the same platform (that is, the same processor type, and ideally the same model to reduce complexity), and should be running the same operating system release with the same patch releases. The servers should offer similar performance, via identical memory and processor speed. Ideally, the servers in the failover pair are completely identical.

Using identical servers will help reduce the cluster's complexity, conferring all the benefits of simple systems—ease of management, brief learning curve, fewer parts to break, and so forth.

While it is not an absolute requirement, it is generally preferable if clustered servers have similar performance parameters. If one server in a cluster, *ozzie*, is noticeably faster than its partner, *harriet*, then after *ozzie* fails over to *harriet*, users may complain about the decrease in performance. This may lead the administrator to manually switch operations back to *ozzie* before the problem that caused *ozzie* to fail in the first place is completely fixed, or at a time when the brief outage might inconvenience the user community. By configuring the systems with identical performance parameters, you can increase availability simply by reducing the number of times that a failover must take place.

Differences among Servers

Some vendors release variations of their CPUs that have subtle differences. Each generation may have unique instructions that allow for different optimizations in applications, or may require operating system support in terms of a kernel architecture. Sun's earlier SPARC chip families, for example, had several kernel architectures, requiring minor variations in the SunOS or Solaris operating system. When a processor supports special memory access modes or fast block copying, and an application such as a database takes advantage of them, you must be certain you have identical processors in each server—or you'll need differently optimized versions of the database on each node. While these differences are hard to detect, there are no guarantees that these differences won't, at some point in the future, make two machines incompatible in the same failover pair. This unlikely incompatibility becomes a moot point if the hardware is all the same.

In the Microsoft world, there may be similarly subtle differences between the various Intel architecture CPUs that run Windows operating systems. Processors made by Intel and AMD are supposed to be perfectly compatible, but it is not hard to imagine that there could be minor differences that won't appear for years after their initial implementation. Not all Windows NT systems are binary-compatible: HP/Compaq/DEC's old Alpha chip could not run the same code that runs on an Intel Pentium processor, for example. The same vendor may have several chip lines running different operating systems, or the same operating system on multiple chips. The matched set of operating system and processor must be consistent if you want to be sure you're getting a consistent applications platform on all nodes in your cluster.

Vendors may have dozens of different system models. As with patch releases, it is unlikely that any vendor has tested every single combination of systems that can possibly be built into a failover pair. Never be the first to do anything when production machines are involved. Stick with simple configurations; use combinations that are well known and well tested.

Failing Over between Incompatible Servers

It is amazing how often system administrators suggest creating clusters composed of incompatible systems, such as a Windows server and an HP-UX server. Why? The argument goes, "Since we already have both systems, why can't we connect them together and fail back and forth?" There is an apparent cost savings if you can combine two systems that are already on hand. This is, unfortunately, a surefire recipe for failure. In order to successfully failover between incompatible hardware, a number of issues would need to be addressed:

Failover software. Both systems would need to be able to run compatible versions of the failover management system that could communicate with each other, and we are not aware of any examples of commercial failover software that work across multiple OSs, even under the best of conditions. The FMS would have to handle a multitude of combinations of hardware. Each server type has many variations (kernel architectures, as described previously, are just one example), and when you add another whole class of server, the permutations increase dramatically.

Applications and data formats. The application would need to function identically on both servers, despite differences in hardware architecture. It would also need to read data written by the other server, on a potentially incompatible filesystem, or in an incompatible format or style (word size, big-endian versus little-endian, and so forth). An application vendor who is willing to give a discount for an extra failover server license may be less willing to do so when the failover server is from a different vendor, assuming that their application even runs on both platforms.

Network interfaces. The heartbeat networks become more complicated when the NICs on each server are of drastically different types. If the network technologies are incompatible, then a network bridge or other hardware may be required that adds complexity and potential failure points.

Disks. In addition to all the other disk requirements, the shared disks must also be physically compatible with both servers. While interface cards don't need to be the same for both servers, they must be able to operate in a dual-hosted environment, with the other, probably incompatible, card on the same bus. This can be an issue with SCSI-based disks but will probably not be an issue in a SAN.

Administration.   This would be a very difficult situation for a system administrator, who would need to be proficient in the administration of both operating systems, scripting languages, and hardware environments. Work performed on one server would need to be translated to the operating environment of the other before it could be applied there. It is safe to say that this environment would more than double the amount of day-to-day tinkering required to keep the systems operating properly when compared to a more traditional cluster.

Support.   When there are problems, which vendor do you call? It is not hard to imagine that one server might cause some sort of subtle problem on the other. Then what? If, as we previously noted, it is unlikely that a vendor has tested every possible combination of its own servers in a failover environment, what are the chances that two competing vendors have tested every combination of their servers working together?

Despite all the negatives, it is likely that the introduction and widespread acceptance of storage area networks will turn out to be the first steps down the long path to make incompatible system failover a reality. From a hardware perspective, SANs solve the shared disk problem, the first step to more complete vendor partnerships that can solve the other problems, enabling incompatible system failover in limited combinations. But not any time soon.

Networks

Three different types of networks are normally found in a failover configuration: the heartbeats, the production or service network, and the administration network. For more detail on networks, please see Chapter 9, "Networking."

One caveat that applies to all of these network types: Some operating systems support virtual network interfaces, where more than one IP address can be placed on the same NIC. While these virtual IPs can be used in some failover scenarios, beware of introducing a single point of failure. For example, will the failure of a single NIC bring down both heartbeat networks?

Heartbeat Networks

The heartbeat networks are the medium over which the systems in a failover pair communicate with each other. Fundamentally, the systems exchange "Hi, how are you?" and "I'm fine, and you?" messages over the heartbeat links. In reality, of course, the heartbeat packets are much more complex, containing state information about each server and commands from one server directing the other to change states or execute some other function.

Heartbeat networks can be implemented over any reliable network link. Most often, simple 100Base-T Ethernet is the medium of choice for heartbeats, since it is inexpensive and pervasive and it does not require any specialized hardware or cabling. Using a faster or more complicated network medium for your heartbeats will add absolutely no value to your cluster, so why spend the money? Besides, these other media can be less reliable than good ol' 100Base-T. Fast networks are ideal when sending large streams of data, but heartbeat messages are short and relatively infrequent (on a network traffic time scale).

The primary purpose of heartbeats in a cluster is so that one server learns of the demise of one of its partners when the heartbeats stop. However, heartbeats can stop for several reasons besides a downed partner server. By running dual, parallel heartbeat networks, with no hardware at all in common, you can sidestep the impact of the most common causes of improperly stopped heartbeats, which include a failed NIC, a broken network cable, a network cable that has been pulled out, or the failure of a network hub.

There are a few other events that might cause heartbeats to stop. These require somewhat more careful resolution but can also be handled:

Heartbeat process has failed.   If the process that sends the heartbeats fails on a node, heartbeats will stop on all networks, regardless of how many networks are involved. The process that sends the heartbeats must, therefore, be monitored and/or made locally redundant. If it stops, it should be automatically restarted by another process. This is a function that your FMS should provide. Sometimes FMS will offer an additional level of testing by sending ICMP packets (pings) to its partner host. Pings are not always useful (occasionally they will report success, even if the rest of the system is down) but can add value as a final test.

Remote server is running too slowly.   This is a trickier case. If server *odds* is running too slowly to report heartbeats to *ends* in a timely manner, *ends* may mistakenly assume that *odds* has failed. To reliably fix this, *ends* must leave enough time for *odds* to send heartbeats, thus slowing down detection. In return, *odds* must make sending heartbeats its highest priority, so that even if it is extremely bogged down, *odds* can still squeeze off one extra CPU cycle that goes to sending heartbeats. Again, minimizing the latency on the heartbeat network helps, as it gives *ends* more time to receive and process the heartbeat before it starts wondering what happened to its partner. A good FMS might be able to monitor not just the existence of heartbeat packets, but of the frequency of the packets. If *odds* senses that *ends* is slowing down, perhaps it can become a little more tolerant of longer durations between packets for a short period of time. Assuming that the operating system provides the functionality, a good FMS product will place itself on the real-time scheduling queue and offer an option to not be on it too.

Low-level system problem takes all networks offline. If a server, *wine*, cannot see any of its networks, it is not serving any useful function at all. A good FMS package should shut *wine* down immediately, since, after all, should *wine* decide to access its shared disks after *roses* has accepted a failover from it (because *wine* has no network, it cannot learn of the failover), data corruption is almost certain to result. Another option when a still-operational clustered system suddenly loses all network connectivity is for heartbeats to be routed across shared disks. We have not found a commercial failover product that adequately handles shared disk heartbeats, especially in larger clusters, so we don't consider that a viable solution.

Copper no longer conducts electricity. If this occurs, you have bigger problems. Like electricity. Like the laws of physics.

ELEVATOR TO NOWHERE

Some people find our closing worry about copper and electricity a bit facetious, but it has a real dark side as well. Large magnets and moving wires can cause copper to *induct* electricity—when you move a magnetic field around, you can create an unexpected electrical charge in an electrical conductor like copper wiring. Not everyone keeps large magnets around, unless they happen to be near a large motor, such as one used to power an elevator.

One customer complained of intermittent failures that seemed to occur late in the afternoon nearly every weekday, especially on Friday. After traces of power, network, system, and disk cabling, eventually the root cause was found to be electromagnetic noise inducted into various poorly shielded cables by an elevator that ran in a shaft outside one wall of the machine room. (And you thought we forgot everything from freshman physics.)

—Hal

Of course, the ultimate protection against one of these false positive conditions is human intervention. When heartbeats fail and an alert goes off, a knowledgeable human being can attempt to log in to the servers, evaluate their conditions, and decide what action to take. This is not always a pleasant option, as failures can occur at all hours of the day or night, any day of the week. The human intervention may also introduce delays that are unacceptable in a critical production environment. It may not be practical (or desirable) to wake up your system administrator at 4:00 A.M. Sunday morning, nor to chain him to the table with the system console on it 24 hours a day, so that he can log in to a server and check its condition. It is also impractical to pay SAs to sit at the console 24 hours a day. So we settle for an automated solution.

What should happen when the heartbeat stops? If everything else is configured properly, and you have accounted for the most common false positive events, there are basically two options. You can assume that if the heartbeat has stopped, the other system is really down, or you can still require manual intervention to make sure that it really is.

Nearly every site that uses an FMS has configured it for automatic failover. A handful of sites still choose to require human intervention when a failover is necessary. These people are particularly concerned about the systems getting into a state called *split brain*, where both servers believe that they should be the primary one and try to write to the shared disks at the same time. Good FMS takes extreme measures to make sure that split brain does not occur. In reality, it almost never does. When planning your systems, make sure that you have planned for some manual intervention to handle the very rare case when split-brain syndrome occurs. (For more information on split brain, see Chapter 17.)

We will discuss the steps that are required for manual failover in detail in Chapter 16.

Public Networks

In order to provide the service for which it was deployed, the server pair needs to be connected to at least one public service network. This network should also be the home of the client workstations who get their critical applications from these servers, or at least be connected to a router that gets to those client workstations. The public network is the visible face of the server pair. Of course, the servers may serve more than one public network to their clients and, therefore, have more than one visible face.

Redundant Network Connectivity

Like all hardware, Network Interface Cards (NICs) will fail from time to time. Ideally, the most critical NICs will have backup cards on the same host, and connected to the same network, to which their services can be migrated in the event that they fail. It may not be necessary to have one spare card per NIC, but certainly one spare card per subnet served is a worthwhile goal. Good failover management software will take the networks served by one NIC and migrate them to another NIC on the same server without requiring a full failover. You can also configure redundant public networks and move all traffic from one network to another. We discussed network interface redundancy and public network redundancy in Chapter 9.

In a failover configuration, since both servers must be configured identically, both servers must be physically connected to the same public networks, whether standalone or redundant. Otherwise, it will be impossible for one server's services to be migrated to the other, and the fundamental requirement for transparency will be lost.

Moving Network Identities

When a failover occurs, the IP address and logical hostname used by the primary server need to migrate to the takeover server. Normally, this is done by reconfiguring the public network interfaces on the takeover server to use the public IP address. Simple on the surface, the process is made more complicated by the mapping of hardware or MAC addresses to network or IP addresses.

Every system has a unique MAC address, a 48-bit value that can be used by all interfaces on that machine, or set individually for each interface. Every network interface has a unique 32-bit IP address. The Address Resolution Protocol (ARP) is used to determine the mappings between IP addresses and MAC addresses; when a host wants to send data to a particular IP address, it uses ARP to find the MAC address that goes into the packet header indicating the right network hardware destination. It's possible for all interfaces on the same host to share the same MAC address but answer to different IP addresses (one per interface); this is the way many Sun systems are configured and is a source of confusion for someone looking at the network interface configuration tables. When a client sends an ARP request and gets a MAC address matching the known IP address as a reply, that MAC address is cached on the client for anywhere from 30 seconds to several hours, eliminating the need to "ask before speaking" repeatedly on the network.

What happens when a failover occurs, and the IP address associated with a data service moves to another machine with a different MAC address? At that point, the clients that had cached the IP-MAC address mapping have stale information.

There are several ways around this problem:

- When the secondary machine configures the public network interfaces with the public IP address, it may send out a gratuitous ARP. A gratuitous ARP is an ARP request for a system's own IP address, meant to inform other listening network members that a new IP-MAC address mapping has been created. Hosts that hear the gratuitous ARP and cache it will update their tables and be able to find the secondary server using the same IP address as before. Their IP-MAC address mappings are different, but the client and client applications see no impact. However, not all machines or operating systems send gratuitous ARP requests, and not all network clients pick them up and do the right updates with their information.

- You can move the MAC address from the primary to the secondary node. In this case, it's best to create your own MAC address on the public network interface; when the primary configures its public network interface, it uses this MAC address, and after the failover, the secondary machine configures its public network with the same MAC address. There are two ways to choose a private, new MAC address. The first is to change one of the first six 4-bit values in the address. MAC address prefixes are assigned in blocks to vendors, so all equipment with the 8:0:20 prefix is from Sun Microsystems.[2] If you choose 8:0:21 (which is not assigned to any company) as a prefix for a private MAC address (keeping the same 24-bit suffix), and verify that you have no other equipment using that address, you should be safe. The second way is to follow some of the guidelines for locally assigned numbers in Internet RFC 1597, which is already rather dated. You'll need to be sure that the primary recognizes that a takeover has occurred and goes back to its default or built-in MAC address; you also want to be sure that if the primary reboots and comes back as the secondary node, it also uses its built-in default MAC address rather than the locally created, public one. The advantage of moving the MAC address is that clients don't have to do a thing. The IP-to-MAC-address mapping stays the same, since you move both the logical IP address and MAC address to the secondary host. However, some network media do not support migrating MAC addresses, and more and more clustering software does not support it either.

■ Wait for the clients to realize that the host formerly listening on that MAC address has gone away, and have clients send new ARP requests for the public IP address. If ARP entries are only cached for 30 seconds, this means that there's a 30-second MTTR before a new ARP request is sent, and the clients see a short pause (probably no longer than is required to get the secondary machine up and running anyway). You'll need to be sure that the client application can tolerate this delay, and that your ARP cache entries timeout quickly. Many system administrators tune the ARP cache expiration period up to over two hours, reducing the volume of ARP traffic on the network, but making it impossible for clients to recover from an IP address migration quickly. In short, you want to keep ARP cache timeouts at their minimum levels on all clients of HA systems, because you want to be sure they'll find the new server after a takeover, even if the client misses (or ignores) a gratuitous ARP sent by the secondary server.

There are other side effects of moving MAC addresses between hosts. Switches and hubs that track MAC addresses for selective forwarding need to handle the migration. Not all equipment does this well. You want to be sure that moving a MAC address doesn't trigger a spanning tree algorithm that splits the network at a switch that believes a loop has been created through improper connections or cabling. We took a closer look at redundant networks, moving IP addresses, and the use of virtual addresses for ease of management in great detail in Chapter 9.

---

[2] IEEE maintains an online database of MAC prefixes and the companies who own them. If you are interested, visit http://standards.ieee.org/regauth/oui/index.shtml.

IP Addresses and Names

There are three different kinds of hostnames that a system might have in a failover configuration; each type maps to a type of network, as discussed previously. One is its *private name*. This is the name found in system configuration files, and the one that shows up if you ask the host for its name. Depending on how the network is configured, that name may or may not be resolved on the network. If your machine's private name is *shirley*, that does not necessarily mean that other hosts on the same network know the machine as *shirley*.

The second kind of name is the *public name*. This is the name that maps to IP addresses that other systems on the network know about. In a failover configuration, this name and IP address should not map to a particular machine, but rather to the application that is requested through that name.

The third kind of name is the *administrative interface name*. That name may or may not match the system's private name. It's probably best if it does, but it does not have to. For example, in a configuration with an administrative network, one public network, two heartbeat networks, and an NFS server, a pair of servers might use the following hostnames:

- *laverne* and *shirley* are the real hostnames. They are the names assigned to the administrative network interfaces, which means that only the system administrators will access the systems using these names. They refer to physical machines and not logical services.

- *milwaukee-nfs* is the logical hostname. It doesn't correspond precisely to one interface, but will instead be bound to the primary server's (*shirley*'s) public network interface by default and migrate to the takeover server's (*laverne*'s) public network link during a failover.

- *shirley-net1* is the administrative hostname assigned to the public network on the primary server. Similarly, *laverne-net1* is the administrative hostname on the secondary server. Further discussion of administrative networks can be found in the next section.

- *shirley-hb1*, *shirley-hb2*, *laverne-hb1*, and *laverne-hb2* are the hostnames for the interfaces connected to the redundant heartbeat networks. (Note that some FMSs do not require IP addresses or hostnames on their heartbeat ports.)

Moral of the story: You're going to use an awful lot of hostnames and IP addresses. Make sure that you have a sufficient number of subnets available and IP address space to allocate for each server pair. Also, keep the names obvious, and use suffixes indicating what net, what kind of network, and what number the interface is on a net if required. Refer back to Key Design Principle #1 about simplicity: It counts when you're sorting through 14 network interfaces, trying to figure out why a secondary server can't send NFS replies back to clients connected through a router.

Administrative Networks

In some failover configurations, the takeover server will boot up with no network connectivity, apart from the heartbeat connections to its partner server. The side effects of this lack of public network connectivity at boot time can be seriously detrimental to the server. Naming services will fail, as will email, network printing, and any other network services. If a public network interface is not present, the initial implementation of the FMS will be greatly complicated because those services will need to be disabled at boot time, only coming to life when the server receives a failover.

It is best to configure failover servers with an additional interface connected to the public network. We call this network connection the administrative interface because it is used solely for administrative purposes. Besides providing basic network connectivity and services, this connection allows system administrators a guaranteed connection to a particular server rather than to an anonymous server providing a particular service. The administrative interface allows an administrator to log in to a failed server and investigate the cause of a failover before the server is put back into public use.

This interface should not be publicized to users, as it is not highly available and does not provide them a guaranteed route to their applications.

Just because you think that your administrative and heartbeat networks are private does not mean that they are. Clever and misconfigured dynamic routers have been known to find and use networks that they should not. Make sure that the $-$PRIVATE flag is set on any network routes that should not have public traffic flowing over it.

Disks

There are two kinds of disks in any failover configuration. There are the *private* disks that contain each host's private system information. These disks are dedicated to one, and only one, server, so they should be electrically independent from the *shared* disks, which can be accessed by both servers in the pair. The shared disks contain the critical data that is needed by the applications for which the servers were made highly available in the first place.

To maximize system availability, all disks must have a level of redundancy, as discussed in Chapter 7, "Highly Available Data Management." Ideally, all disks should be mirrored from one disk controller to another, and from one disk cabinet to another. If the system is important enough to cluster, then the system is important enough to have its disks mirrored.

Private Disks

Private disks contain the operating system, the system identity, swap space, and the FMS executables. In order to start the clustering software at boot time, it must be located on the private disks. These disks are generally located inside each server, although that is not a requirement. In fact, it is better that the private (or system) disks be physically located external to a server. This way, if a server fails, no surgery to extract the disks from one server and to install them in the other will be required, thereby delivering a quicker MTTR.

Private disks, by definition, cannot be connected to multiple hosts. Only one server can and should ever see the data on these disks.

The entire contents of the private disks should be mirrored. Some may argue that swap space need not be mirrored. This is simply not true. If the disk containing critical application data in swap fails, then at the very least, the application will stop working. Most likely, though, the server will stop working and possibly crash, resulting in a failover and causing some downtime. Highly available systems are designed to avoid preventable causes of downtime such as these.

The requirement of private disks calls attention to a serious bit of administrative overhead associated with systems that failover. Many administrative files on the two systems must be kept in perfect synchronization. Most FMSs do not offer tools to help with this synchronization; it must be maintained manually. Unix files like /etc/system must be the same on both sides; when you change one, it is vital that you change the other. Failure to do so will result in failovers that fail to failover.

In the Windows world, most applications write critical data into the system registry, an area of disk that cannot be directly shared with other nodes. In order for an application to properly failover within a cluster, the same registry information must be available, and kept up-to-date, on all nodes where the application might run.

Shared Disks

Shared disks are the disks that contain the critical data. Both systems need physical access to these disks, although it is critical that only one system at a time access them. If both servers try to write to shared disks at the same time without specialized software in place, data corruption is virtually inevitable. If one system simply tries to read the disks while the other writes, the reader will likely run into problems when the data it is reading changes unexpectedly. Access to shared disks must be limited to only one node at a time unless specialized software that specifically changes these rules is in place.

When you share disks, you are actually sharing data. There is more than one way to share data among the nodes in a cluster. The most common and preferable way is called *dual hosting*. In this model, both servers are physically connected to the same disks at the same time. Access is arbitrated by external software that runs on both servers. When a failover occurs and access to the shared disks migrates from one server to the other, all the data successfully written by one server is guaranteed to be accessible by the other.

The other method of sharing data is through a technology called *shared nothing*. In this model, data is replicated across a network (usually either the heartbeat network, or another parallel private network) between the servers. Shared nothing is a much more complicated model, since it requires a functional network and a functional host on the other side to ensure that the writes actually succeed.

Another significant issue with shared nothing clusters is as follows. When server *agony* is healthy and functional in a shared nothing configuration, it replicates data to *ecstasy*. When *agony* fails, it fails over to *ecstasy*. While *ecstasy* operates, *agony* may not be functioning, and so *agony* will not be able to keep current on updates to *ecstasy*. When *agony* is repaired and is ready to go back into service, additional work will be required to refresh its data to match *ecstasy*. Depending on how much data is involved, it could take a long time, and a tremendous amount of effort and network bandwidth.[3] If *ecstasy* were to fail during that refresh period, *agony* could not take over. What's far worse, though, is that if an event occurred that brought **both** *agony* and *ecstasy* down—a power outage, for example—after *ecstasy* had taken over. When the power was restored to both nodes, neither would know which node was running as the primary before, and therefore, neither would know that *agony*'s data was out of date. If *agony* came up as the primary, it would begin replicating data to *ecstasy* immediately, and the result would be two hosts with two different sets of data, neither set complete or correct.

Dual hosting is a superior method for sharing disk data, although it requires specific hardware that permits this dual hosting. Not all disk or controller hardware can handle the dual hosting of SCSI-based disks and arrays, especially in the Windows world. Check with your vendors before you make blind assumptions. SANs are another way to achieve dual-hosted storage. For more on SANs, please refer to Chapter 8, "SAN, NAS, and Virtualization."

When configuring disks for use on critical systems in a cluster, it is important to remember the availability enhancing techniques that we discussed in Chapter 7, including mirroring, RAID, and multipathing.

Disk Caches

A disk cache is a chunk of memory that is used to hold disk data before it is written to disk, or to hold data that is read from the disk before it is actually needed. Since memory access can be 1,000 times (or more) faster than disk, there are tremendous performance implications by using disk cache. From an availability perspective, prereading (or prefetching) disk data has no implications. However, writing data to the cache that never makes it to disk can have significant availability implications.

---

[3] This is only the case for software- or host-based replication and does not apply if hardware replication is used, as hardware-based replication can update its remote side even if the host has gone down. For more on the different types of replication, see Chapter 18, "Data Replication."

Normally, when an application writes to a disk, the disk tells the operating system that the write has completed, so that the application can move on to its next task. When a disk-write cache is employed, the disk reports successful completion of the data write when it is written to the cache, not when it makes it to the disk. Since a cache is nothing more than memory, it is volatile; if power is lost to the cache, its contents are lost with it, regardless of whether or not they made it to the disk.

Write caches can live in the disk array, or on the host's disk controller. Caches in the disk array are fine, as long as they have battery backups. Caches without battery backups will lose their cached data if power to the disk array is lost. A write cache on the system controller board is not acceptable in a failover environment. When a failover takes place, the cached data is locked inside the cache, and the other system has no way to access it, or even to be aware of its existence. Prestoserve and Sun's Storedge Fast Write Cache are two examples of system-based disk-write cache boards. Although they can do an excellent job of improving I/O performance on a standalone system, those boards are not acceptable or supportable in shared disk configurations.

Placing Critical Applications on Disks

One of the more interesting questions that comes up as engineers configure HA systems is where to place the executables for critical applications. There are, of course, two choices: You can place them on the private disks, along with the boot and system information, or you can place them on the shared disks along with their associated data.

If you install the applications on the shared disks, the good news is that you only need to maintain one copy of the executables and of the associated configuration files. If you need to make a change in the application configuration, you only need to make it in one place.

If you install the applications on the private disks, then you must maintain two copies of the executables and of their configuration files. Changes must be made twice; otherwise, a failover will not guarantee an identical environment on the other side.

However, with just one copy of the applications, it is almost impossible to install an upgrade to the application safely, and with the ability to roll back. With two copies of the application, and system *mason* active, you can install the upgrade on system *dixon* and failover to *dixon*. If the upgrade was successful, then *dixon* should take over, running the upgraded application correctly; you can then upgrade *mason* and move on. If the upgrade fails, however, then you need only fail back to system *mason*, and try the upgrade again on *dixon*.

This is one of those cases where there really is no single right answer. What we can tell you, though, is that more often than not, we have seen a single copy of applications installed in clusters, rather than two copies. In most cases, upgrades are just not performed enough to justify the extra work associated with managing two separate sets of configuration files.

Applications

The last, and most important, component of a service group is the critical application itself. The good news is that most applications will just run in a clustered environment. There are, of course, exceptions to this rule, but they are few and far between. As long as applications write their data to disk on a regular basis and do not only preserve it in memory, they can usually function in a cluster without modification.

We speak specifically of applications that run on a single node at a time in a cluster. There are more complex applications such as Oracle RAC that can run simultaneously in multiple hosts. These types of applications are very complex and may introduce issues that can reduce performance or availability. On the other hand, when properly implemented, they can offer significant increases in availability above the norm. But parallel applications are the exception rather than the rule.

For most applications, the most pressing issue is whether or not a copy of the application is licensed to run on a particular server. That is, in fact, a vital test that must be run during configuration of a cluster. Every application must be run on every eligible system in the cluster, just to make sure that it really works there. In some cases, enabling applications to run on every server will require getting a multitude of license keys from the application vendor, even if the application will only run on one node at a time. Some vendors will discount failover copies of their software; others will not. It is reasonable to assume that a vendor will discount their product if it is totally inactive on other cluster nodes; if it is running on multiple nodes, expect to pay for it multiple times.

As we discussed previously, sometimes an application will bind itself very closely to the server on which it runs. In this event, it may be difficult or impossible to move an application to a different node in a cluster. One example occurs on Windows systems, where an application may write some critical information into the system registry. If the same registry information is not available on other nodes in the cluster, then the application cannot run on those nodes.

Larger Clusters

Thus far, we have limited our cluster discussions to small clusters of two nodes. When SCSI was the predominant medium for connecting disks and systems, that was pretty much a hard limit. All of the early clustering software packages (apart from VMScluster) that we discussed at the start of this chapter pretty much had a hard limit of two nodes in a cluster. Even if the software was marketing with claims of larger limits, it was nearly impossible to implement larger clusters.

With the advent of SANs, cluster sizes have grown immensely. Today's products support clusters of 32 and 64 nodes, with larger clusters likely, especially as blade computers become more prominent (for more on blade computing, see Chapter 22, "A Brief Look Ahead"). Although cluster configurations can grow quite large, some shops have been reluctant to grow clusters beyond a certain size. The largest cluster in production that is running on commercial FMS that we are aware of is a 20-node cluster running VERITAS Cluster Server on Solaris. Most clusters tend to stay smaller than that; with 7 to 10 nodes being the most common size after 2-node clusters (which are easily the most popular size). When clusters get larger than that, configuration files get large, and the clusters can become harder to manage. Plus, in the unlikely event that the FMS itself causes an outage, the effects become much more significant when that likelihood is multiplied across many servers.

In terms of the technology covered in this chapter, very little actually changes when you discuss larger clusters. Shared disks are still required, albeit SAN-based disks. Each host still needs its three kinds of networks. And, of course, critical applications are required; without them, there's little point to clustering at all.

Probably the biggest change due to the increase in cluster size is in the heartbeat networks. When cluster sizes exceed two nodes, it becomes necessary to use hubs to build the heartbeat networks. When you use hubs to manage your heartbeat networks, make sure that the hubs do not add latency to the traffic, and merely forward packets on to their appropriate destination. Each heartbeat hub should be on a separate power source.

Larger clusters also enable many more complex and economical failover configurations besides the traditional active-passive and active-active. We will examine cluster configurations in detail in Chapter 17.

Key Points

- To maximize application availability, you need a second system that can take over the application if the first system fails.

- Be sure your application can actually run on the takeover server.

- Think of your computer as a service-delivery mechanism. Your applications need not run on any one particular system, but rather on any of the systems in a cluster.

- Plan out your IP address space and host-naming conventions carefully. You're going to use quite a few of them, and you want to be sure you can easily identify hosts and host-network connections.

CHAPTER 16

Failover Management
and Issues

Success is never final, but failure can be.
—Bill Parcells

In Chapter 15, "Local Clustering and Failover," we introduced clustering and failover, and the components that are required to implement a simple cluster. In this chapter, we look at the methods and technologies for enabling the failover, and compare manual methods of detection and failover to a more automated approach. We also examine some of the issues that you're likely to run into while implementing a clustered solution. We'll build on this foundation in Chapter 17, "Failover Configurations," where we will discuss some of the more commonly used cluster and failover configurations.

In terms of building up our Availability Index, we remain at the eighth level, Clustering, as shown in Figure 16.1.

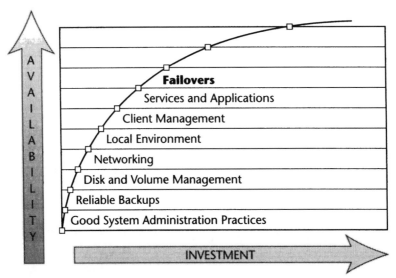

Figure 16.1   Level 8 of the Availability Index.

Failover Management Software (FMS)

In the previous chapter, we introduced the term failover management software, or FMS. Since this term describes something that has been around for several years, you may well ask why we would create a new TLA,[1] when the software has been called "high-availability software" for so long.

Besides attempting a small social experiment to see if we can introduce a new term into the vernacular, we use FMS because of the ambiguity that is implicit in the term high availability software. As we said in Chapter 15, the expression high availability has been corrupted by corporate marketing departments throughout the computer industry and has lost its meaning. Similarly, high availability software has very little meaning; any of the software that we discuss in this book could be considered high-availability software, as it adds availability to the systems on which it runs.

We figure that if it actually adds value to the language, the term failover management software will catch on. If system administrators and end users find a preferable phrase, then they will use that. We offer FMS because we haven't found one that we like better.

---

[1] Three-letter acronym.

Component Monitoring

All failover management methods start from the same point; they require that the key components of the system be monitored—the components whose failure would cause critical applications to stop delivering their services. The quality of each failover management method can be determined, at least in part, by the quantity and variety of components that are monitored and the mechanisms chosen to monitor those components.

Hardware is generally the easiest part of a system to monitor. Are the disks accessible? Is there network connectivity? Is the system up and running? There are relatively easy tests for monitoring the current state of each of the hardware components. Plus, there are relatively few different varieties of hardware components, so fewer different kinds of tests need to be created and managed. The test that monitors one disk, for example, can be used to monitor all of the disks. While there certainly can be gray areas when monitoring hardware (for example, it can be difficult to tell the difference between a down system and one that is running so slowly that it does not reply to queries), it is still easier to monitor hardware than applications.

There are several ways to monitor the health of an application. The easiest, most general, and weakest monitoring method is to examine the system's *process table*. The process table is a list of the programs that are running on a system at a particular point in time. The process table offers information such as the amount of memory and CPU each process is consuming, when the process began running, and so forth. (The precise set of information will vary from operating system to operating system, and often on the command-line arguments or other options that determine exactly how the command will run.) The process table does not provide any indication, however, that the process is running properly. There is no way to tell from the process table if the application will respond to a query, or if it is hung or in some other way operating improperly. All the process table will tell you is whether the process is running.

Since the process table is not reliable, there must be a better way to find out if an application is running properly. There is, but it is much harder to implement. You must query the application itself and see that you get an appropriate and timely response. For some applications a query is easy. For others it can be almost impossible. Querying a database server is easy, for example; accepting queries is a fundamental part of what database servers do. If you have an application that sends a basic SQL query to a database and watches for a response, you have a simple monitor for that database. If the database doesn't respond to the test query, it won't respond to genuine user requests.

Unfortunately, the reality is a little more complicated than that. You must be sure that you are testing the right things. If the test query asks for the exact same data on each query, then the database may have cached the answer in memory (databases do that to improve performance). The database will provide the right answer, but the test is not properly or completely exercising the database or the hardware behind it. A good test query will exercise the disk. If the disk has failed, the database will not receive a response. Does the query originate on the same system that the database runs on? If so, you may not be adequately testing network connectivity. As we have said from the start of this book, availability is an end-to-end proposition, so tests must be end-to-end as well. Otherwise they do not simulate the user experience and will not detect the kinds of errors and failures that users see.

WHAT YOU SEE IS NOT ALWAYS WHAT THEY GET

A large media corporation was demonstrating their very popular news headlines web site at an executive meeting inside their headquarters. The web site came up, but none of the graphic images appeared. Naturally, the executives were mortified, and they contacted the external company who hosted their images to find out what was wrong.

The external company was able to see all of the web site without any problem at all. The executives began pointing fingers and calling the people at the external company all kinds of names.

In the end, it turned out that the problem was with the Internet connection out of the headquarters building. End users who wanted to see the news were always able to reach it. Don't assume that all problems are global, or even external, ones. So often, it's the simplest things that cause the biggest problems.

—Evan

So, your test query must exercise the disk, the network, and the database application itself. An example of a thorough test is one that writes something different and verifiable to a database across a network, and then reads it back. Since the data is ever-changing, the database cannot cache it. Probably the best and easiest way to test a database is with a script that gets the date and time, writes it to a special table in the database, and then reads it back, comparing the original date to what it reads from the database. If they match, the database is performing properly. If not, there is cause for concern.

Specific application testing is especially complicated because every application type will require its own specialized test method. Every vendor's database must be queried in a different manner. Web servers must download a small web page. File servers must provide file data. Homegrown applications must provide their own testing methods as well. And all of these tests must exercise all of the components that any user's use of the application will exercise.

Who Performs a Test, and Other Component Monitoring Issues

Who performs the test? Is it performed by the host on which the application is running? That model requires less hardware overhead, but if the host itself is misbehaving, the test results can be skewed. And surely the host cannot test for its own overall well-being. If the testing is performed from a separate host, then those tests must have some intrinsic redundancy as well, so that they function even if multiple hosts in the cluster have failed.

There are other issues as well:

- When a test fails, does it hang, or does it timeout quickly and report the failure to its application? If it hangs, or causes new problems, then the test is unacceptable. Tests must be totally unobtrusive, atomic, and hang-proof.

- What if the timeout value is set too low, and the test times out before the application has a chance to respond to the query? On the other hand, if the timeout value is set too high, unnecessary delays will be added to the identification of and recovery from a serious problem.

- How often do you run the test? Running it too often can put an extraneous and unwelcome load on the systems and networks being tested. But running the test too infrequently could result in a failure going undetected for an extended period.

- Some applications simply do not invite easy and nonintrusive testing. For those applications, process table examination may be required as a last resort. Otherwise, it may be necessary to monitor a process that is dependent upon the one that cannot be monitored.

- What happens if the test itself is broken? How do you determine that? What monitors the monitor? And what if the monitor's monitor fails? What monitors the monitor's monitor? And what if that fails? The best solution is to have two monitors on each node in the cluster; among the duties of each monitor is to watch the other monitor. If the first monitor sees that the second monitor has stopped, it must start a new second monitor. At the same time, one of the two monitors is responsible for communicating with other cluster members. Implemented properly, this is a reliable model. (Note that we are specifically not advocating triple redundancy. That is a waste of time and energy.)

When Component Tests Fail

Once your test has found what it believes to be a problem, then what happens? First, the test must be rerun. If the first failure is a fluke, it is certainly better to know that and not to overreact than it is to act hastily upon failure detection and affect services that were, in fact, functioning normally.

Let's assume that the failure detection is genuine; that a key component has actually failed. The next hurdle to clear is to decide upon the appropriate action to take. The correct action will vary based on your environment, on which component has failed, and on the way your system is configured. (Of course, with an automated FMS, these decisions have been made long before the failure occurs. They are usually made at installation and configuration time.)

For example, if the failure is in an application, the choices are to do the following:

- Ignore the failure, and allow the system to continue running without the failed application.

- Send notifications out to key people via appropriate methods (email, pager, etc.), so that the right people can take the right manual action.

- Attempt to automatically restart the application a predetermined number of times, and if the application cannot be restarted, then:
  - Ignore the failure.
  - Send notifications.
  - Initiate a failover.
  - Reboot the server.
  - Halt the server (secondary server will take over).
  - Initiate a failover to the secondary server without attempting any restarts.

For most applications, the most reasonable choice is to attempt to restart the application on the same system, and after a given number of failed attempts, initiate a failover. While failovers are a fine way to recover from one of many different kinds of failures, failovers are, in and of themselves, not desirable. If the application can be safely restarted in place, without requiring the work (and intrinsic complexity and risk) of a full failover, higher levels of availability can be achieved. The application may be able to be started on the same node faster than if it were failed over to another node.

Of course, not all applications fit the mold. Some database applications fare better if a database administrator is given the chance to examine the cause of the failure, and to repair it and any ancillary damage before the database is restarted.

When the application being monitored is a homegrown one, the developers should be made aware of the monitoring requirement early in the development process, so that the testing can be done in as nonintrusive a way as possible.

If the failure is in a hardware component, then the choices are basically the same as for software, but there are some additional options. If the failed component is a network interface card (NIC), it is possible to move the IP addresses that were housed on the failed NIC to a dedicated standby NIC that is in the same host and attached to the same network. In that case, the system can completely recover from the failure in the time it takes to detect the problem, and migrate the IP addresses to the new card, which should take no more than a few seconds. (However, some client applications such as databases, may need manual assistance to reconnect.)

When a disk fails, and it has been made properly redundant (that is, mirrored or RAID-5), the only action that is required is notification. The failed disk must be replaced, an activity that is most assuredly a manual one. But since the data on the failed disk is protected, it need not be replaced immediately; the system administrator may choose to wait until a more convenient time to perform the work (keeping in mind that some level of redundancy has been lost). All the while, the system will continue to operate. If the failed disk is further protected with hot spares, then no redundancy will be lost as the system automatically (and logically) replaces the failed disk with the hot spare. If the failed disk sits within an array that supports hot swapping, then the disk can be replaced without any service interruption.

Time to Manual Failover

So now our automated testing software has determined that a failure has occurred. For our purposes, we have concluded that a failover is the best way to recover from this particular failure. There are two ways that this failover might be initiated: manually and automatically. In a manual failover, all the work to respond to the already identified failure lands squarely on the shoulders of the system administrator.

> **Before anything else can happen, the system administrator must find out about the problem.**   She could be notified via pagers or email, or her users could start screaming or storm her desk carrying pitchforks and torches. Of course, for this to work, she has to be near her desk or phone (and not using it) or be carrying her pager. What if she is out of the building at lunch or in the bathroom? What if the failure occurs late at night or on a weekend?

Once she has learned of the problem, she must get to the servers, as a failover often requires physically touching the failed system. She must get to and enter the data center, or whatever room the servers are located in. That could require the use of pass cards, or waiting for and then riding on an elevator, which can cause unfortunate delays. (In some Wall Street banks and trading firms, it may be necessary to switch between two or even three elevator banks to get from the floor that houses the users to the floor containing the data center.) She has to locate the server in the data center. Servers and rows of cabinets may all look the same; she has to find the right one. Finding the right server also assumes that she knows the correct name of the server that has failed (as we discussed back in Chapter 5, "20 Key High Availability Design Principles"); servers with meaningless names or names that are similar to other servers can cause confusion. If she messes up and begins working on the wrong server, she'll cause all sorts of new problems, while not fixing the ones that sent her to the data center in the first place.

Once our system administrator has identified and located the right server, she must perform the correct steps to recover from the failure. If she manages several clusters, one hopes that the recovery steps are the same for each cluster. If they are not, then they need to be clearly posted on or near the servers, and, of course, kept up-to-date. Does the procedure require a complete reboot? Does it just mean running a predesignated script and throwing some A-B switches (to move control of the disks from one host to the other)? How long will it take? Of course, if she has to read the documentation, it will take her that much longer. And any manual process, especially one that is not regularly tested and rehearsed, is more prone to error than a well-tested automated process.

Manually initiated failover seems less expensive than automated failover, but in practice, it rarely is. In a shop that already has a knowledgeable operations staff located near the servers 24 hours a day, 7 days a week, manual failover may be workable. But most shops cannot afford these luxuries, and so automated failover is the prevalent solution. Manual failover requires rapid response times, a reliable and quick notification system, and full-time presence. It is very difficult for even the best shops to provide all of these things, and to maintain them at acceptable levels every single day of the year (even holidays).

When you are considering manual versus automatic failover, ask yourself the following questions. If you are satisfied with the answers, then perhaps manual failover is right for you:

- What happens when one knowledgeable operator is at lunch and the other is in the bathroom at the moment something fails?

- What if a failure occurs late at night in the middle of a long holiday weekend?

- What happens when knowledgeable administrators abruptly leave the company? How quickly can they be replaced and their replacements trained? What happens during the interim?

- What happens when the satellite that relays pages to pagers gets knocked out of orbit, as happened in 1996. (The resulting outage lasted several days.)

- What happens when procedures are not followed properly, and as a result, systems get damaged worse than before the alert?

- What happens when your knowledgeable people cannot gain access to the servers, or cannot find the servers when a failure has occurred?

Automatic failover software addresses these issues. It will respond automatically to a failure and respond in preprogrammed ways. It knows which host has failed and which hosts are eligible to take over for it. It can be used to identify loads across nodes in a large cluster and to determine which node is best able to handle the additional load that the downed resources will require.

Homemade Failover Software or Commercial Software?

Another option for implementing an FMS is to write it in-house. In our experience, homemade FMS consists of code that one or two system administrators wrote in their copious spare time to manage failover for one or two particular pairs of servers. Since their salaries are preapproved expenses, it may seem that having them write this code is a wonderful idea, as the project looks like it is free. But who is left doing the job the administrators were hired to do while they are writing and testing this code? But putting that aside, let's compare the likely results of this coding effort to our key HA design principles:

Homegrown FMS is not mature code. Nobody else has tested it. You are placing your critical systems under the care of code that has never been rolled out anywhere else and has never recovered a production application or system before.

Homegrown FMS is version 1.0 code. As it is new and untested, it will inevitably have bugs. The only way to discover the bugs is to use the code. Testing the code in production violates another principle.

Homegrown FMS has no reference sites. It also has no USENET newsgroups to discuss problems and issues with other users, or any user conferences, magazines, books, or any of the other ancillary features that mature, widely installed code offers.

Homegrown FMS has little or no support.   Whom are you going to call for help when it doesn't work on a weekend or in the middle of the night? What happens when the authors leave the company? They take the support with them, and you are left with none.

Your homegrown FMS may handle the easy failure cases well, but there are many corner cases that do not occur very often. Nevertheless, these oddball cases must be handled by any worthwhile FMS. The developers must first think of them, and then write code to address them. Since they seldom occur, these cases will probably not be adequately tested; when they do occur, can we be confident that the code will handle them properly? Decisions must be made in advance regarding the best way to handle these situations. Commercial FMS solutions have examined these and have either worked out ways to handle them (hopefully the best ways to handle them) or have given the user configuration options that he can choose from at install time.

The following are some examples of corner cases:

- What if a clustered host loses connectivity to the public network?

- What if a clustered host loses all of its heartbeat links? How can we be sure it has really failed?

- What if an application is running and can read cached data from memory, but cannot access certain disks or data?

- What happens if both servers in a failover pair boot at the same time? Which takes charge? Does it matter?

- What if the takeover server has problems and cannot accept a failover when it is expected to?

- What happens if a failover script has an error in it and cannot run to completion?

- What if a server is too busy to send heartbeats for awhile?

- What happens if a few heartbeats get corrupted on their way to the other server?

- What if the FMS daemon crashes or is manually killed?

- How do you handle extreme levels of network or system latency?

- What happens if the Name Service goes away and your software can't resolve IP addresses?

- What happens if the routing tables get messed up and heartbeats start routing over the public network? Or worse, what happens if public traffic goes over the heartbeat network?

- Are you sure that after running for months, your homegrown software won't have a memory leak or a socket descriptor leak? Maybe your algorithms for requesting and releasing memory are flawless, but what about the underlying libraries or scripting language?

- Can you maintain the proper cluster state if only your HA software is restarted while all services remain running?

- What happens if the file permissions to config files or scripts change, or if the files are corrupted while the HA software is running?

Good, mature commercial FMS has run into all of these issues and many others and should be able to handle them.

Commercial Failover Management Software

Commercial FMS offers many advantages over homegrown versions. The software is likely to be mature, well tested, and robust. It should be available with support 24 hours a day, 7 days a week. It should install easily and communicate with third-party monitoring frameworks (including Tivoli, Solstice Domain Manager, HP OpenView, BMC Patrol, and CA Unicenter), and it should be able to monitor many popular third-party applications, including databases, web servers, email servers, and file servers. If you have unusual or homegrown production applications, the commercial FMS should be able to easily extend itself to monitor them. If your environment requires manual intervention for failover, good FMS will permit that too. It should be customizable for just about any configuration you may have. The vendor should offer regular enhancements and upgrades, and it should be possible to install those upgrades without incurring any downtime at all.

We offer a brief discussion of some well-known commercial FMS (contact the specific vendors for up-to-date and complete information about each product):

VERITAS Cluster Server (VCS).   The market leader across all platforms for clustering, VCS is available on Solaris, HP/UX, Windows, AIX, and Linux. First released in 1999, VCS handles all of the basic functions of FMS, along with support for cluster reconfigurations without stopping the critical applications, and automatic propagation of cluster changes. VCS also supports SAN environments, rule-based failover, and dependency rules in its supported configurations of up to 32 nodes on most platforms.

Microsoft's Cluster Server.   Available only as part of MS Windows Enterprise Edition or above, MSCS supports four-node clusters, growing to eight nodes in Windows .NET Server 2003. 2003 is also the first version of Microsoft Cluster Server that supports automatic propagation of cluster changes, the ability to remove a node from a cluster without stopping the cluster, and much easier setup than earlier versions.

Sun Cluster.   Available on Solaris only, Sun Cluster supports clusters of up to eight nodes, made up exclusively of Sun servers and generally Sun disk hardware, although limited support is available for third-party disk arrays. Sun Cluster can be quite complex to install, and Sun requires that its consulting services be sold with it. Sun says that coding customized agents is quite simple and that SC supports diskless servers in a cluster.

HP's MC/Serviceguard.   Available on HP/UX and Linux, MC/Service-Guard is HP's highly regarded clustering software, primarily targeted at its high-end servers. It supports all networks and most critical applications, and has a reputation for being fairly complex to implement. A node may be temporarily removed from a cluster (which may be as large as 16 nodes) for maintenance without affecting other cluster members.

IBM's High Availability Cluster Multi-Processing (HA/CMP).   Available for IBM's AIX systems only, it is not quite as robust or flexible as products on other platforms. It can be quite complex to install as well.

There are many other products in this space as well, including Legato's products, Co-StandbyServer for Windows and Automated Availability Manager (AAM), and a slew of Linux-only products from vendors like Red Hat, Debian, SuSE, and Kimberlite, to name a few. HP also offers TruCluster for (formerly DEC/Compaq) Tru64 systems, and Novell offers Novell Cluster Services for its systems.

When Good Failovers Go Bad

Introducing new technology, such as failover management, into your environment can bring on new problems. These issues are all unique to failover environments; they have no parallel in the single-host world. To be fair, they are quite rare, and you could run clusters for years without ever seeing them.

Split-Brain Syndrome

The first of these phenomena that are unique to clustered systems is called *split-brain syndrome*. The bane of FMS, split brain can occur when the servers in a clustered pair completely lose contact with each other while remaining otherwise operational. Both nodes believe that their partner has gone away and that they are the remaining healthy node. As a result, both servers attempt to take over.

The fundamental cause of split brain is that there are two completely separate data paths between the two servers; they communicate with each other across LANs, but the actual data that flows between the systems lives on disks and does not travel on the same networks. If the LANs fail, disk connectivity is not affected. Ideally, data and communications would flow over the same media, but that solution has not been built with adequate reliability into any mainstream commercial products. Normally, the two media, and therefore the two systems, are in sync and have an accurate idea of what is happening on their partner system. If they fall out of sync, though, that's when the trouble can begin.

If the shared disks fail and the network continues, that's all right, because the systems can continue to communicate with each other and initiate appropriate action to bring disks back online.

If all of the networks fail but the shared disks continue to function, that is when the trouble begins. The backup server thinks the primary has failed, since it has stopped replying to heartbeats, and so it takes over. The primary thinks the backup server has gone away, but that is not a condition that requires any specific action on its part (apart from perhaps issuing a warning), so it continues writing its data. With conventional disk technology in a clustered configuration, the very worst thing that can happen is for two or more servers to write to the same disks at the same time. Standard versions of today's operating systems, filesystems, and applications do not support multiple systems writing to them at the same time.[2] The inevitable result is data corruption and application confusion (which results in system or application crashes).

When a cluster is working properly, all of the member systems are in sync and know the state of all the others. When split brain occurs, the hosts (brains) get out of sync and begin acting separately.

Our advice is that while you should be concerned about selecting FMS that will detect and do its best to prevent split brain, you may not be able to absolutely guarantee that it will never occur. Detecting split brain and forcing a proper recovery is a very difficult problem that not all FMS packages can solve at all, much less solve well. We are not suggesting that you reject all FMS packages that don't handle split brain, just that you are sensitive to the causes of this problem and try to manage around them. As the old joke goes, if you tell your doctor, "It hurts when I do this," the doctor is likely to say, "So don't do that," and charge you (or your HMO) for an office visit. We give you some pain-avoidance ideas at a lower price.

---

[2] There are nonstandard filesystems, such as the VERITAS Cluster File System, that support multiple, parallel writes. Even if the filesystem can handle the multiple writes, it is doubtful that your application could.

Causes and Remedies of Split-Brain Syndrome

There are several scenarios that could result in split brain. However, all of them are extremely rare, or could only be initiated manually. So even though we are devoting all this space to this discussion, understand that split brain hardly ever actually occurs in nature.

Multiple Heartbeat Failure

Split brain can be caused by several different sets of circumstances that involve multiple failures of heartbeats. Split brain can occur under the following conditions:

- If all of the heartbeat networks between the servers fail simultaneously.

- If all the heartbeats run through the same network hub, and that hub fails, because of, for example, loss of power, internal failure, or someone hitting the power switch.

- If the heartbeats run through separate hubs, but all the hubs share a common power source, such as a single circuit, power outlet, power strip, or even electric utility company, and that power source fails.

- If a single multiport NIC is used for all heartbeats on a cluster member, and that card fails.

In rare circumstances, it's possible for the TCP/IP stack of a system to lock up completely or to become corrupted, possibly because of a denial-of-service attack (see Chapter 9, "Networking") or a system memory exhaustion problem (see Chapter 13, "Application Design"). It's extremely rare for the TCP/IP stack to fail on its own without the root causes of that failure also bringing down the server or causing another failure, but it can happen. Another extremely unlikely event is the simultaneous failure of all of the NICs that operate the heartbeats. Solid-state components such as NICs do fail, but only very seldom. If failed NICs are routinely replaced quickly, the odds against a second failing so as to cause a larger problem are so astronomically high that you probably need not be concerned.

As we said, split brain is rare. But it is still worthy of discussion, if only for academic reasons.

Fortunately, there are several remedies that can be designed into the FMS and into the system hardware configuration that can keep split brain from taking hold.

Some of the issues that can lead to a loss of network heartbeats are symptoms of poor overall system design: the presence of single points of failure. The heartbeats should never all be plugged into the same NIC or network hub; doing so creates a single point of failure. If separate hubs are used, they should not share the same power source any more than clustered systems or mirrored disks should use the same power source.

Of course, the loss of multiple heartbeats could be a genuine indicator of a problem. To recognize and properly handle split-brain conditions, some FMSs use the public network as a backup heartbeat medium. Often, public networks are designed to be a little more bulletproof than heartbeat networks, or at very least they are designed to use different network hardware than the heartbeat networks. If all of the heartbeat networks do fail, the public network represents another independent network over which heartbeat traffic can flow. Because of its very nature, of course, the public network is not a particularly reliable medium. (If it were, heartbeat networks would not be necessary.) After all, there are probably dozens or hundreds of devices connected to a public network, and dozens of unmonitored and unused network drops scattered around the enterprise, which are vulnerable to attack. See Chapter 9 for more details. Not all FMSs can use the public network as a backup. Check with your vendor.

Some FMSs may also permit the use of a shared disk for heartbeats. In this scenario, all of the hosts in the cluster take turns reading and writing status information to predesignated locations on a shared disk. Disk heartbeat permits heartbeats to be exchanged even if all networks totally fail. Depending on the FMS and disk management software that you employ, that disk may have to be dedicated to heartbeating, or there may be a limit as to how many clustered nodes can share it. Some FMS packages may exchange less information when using disk heartbeat than they do when using network heartbeats, thus reducing some other aspect of the product's performance. In theory, shared disk heartbeat makes an excellent third heartbeat medium. Again, ask your vendor. We are not aware of an FMS vendor who has delivered an ideal implementation of shared disk heartbeats.

Another protection method against split brain is enabled at the disk hardware level. Some disks, disk arrays, or software volume management products have an internal write-access flag that indicates which server is writing to the physical disks at any particular time. When a server attempts to write to the disks and finds that the flag indicates that the disks are owned by another server, it knows that the other server is already writing to the disks. What happens next is a function of the FMS. Ideally, when a system that sees its disks cannot be written to, it will immediately shut itself down. This is desirable: a soft power-down as soon as the former primary system detects that its disks are no longer solely its own for writing purposes, thus protecting the disks against potential data corruption.

The FMS can introduce yet another level of protection against split brain. The most general description of an FMS is that it constantly monitors all of the system's resources, and when these resources reach a particular state, the FMS performs a predetermined function. In the case where a server loses all of its network interfaces, heartbeat and public, then the server is simply not serving anyone. It is not doing anybody any good by continuing to operate; the only thing that a server in this state can be doing is bad: writing to its shared disks and corrupting data. So, when the FMS detects that all network interfaces have failed on a particular server, it might choose to immediately shut down the server in the most direct and speedy way possible. If the shutdown takes too long, though, writes, and therefore data corruption, can still occur.

Suspending and Resuming the Operating System

Another scenario that can cause split brain can occur when a system administrator or operator performs an unfortunate action, and the system responds in an even more unfortunate way. In the Sun world, if the user hits the Stop key[3] and the A key at the same time on a Sun console keyboard, or the Break key on a terminal configured to be the console, the system is suspended and it drops into firmware mode. (The firmware is sort of the operating system that runs the operating system.) On older Sun boxes, unplugging and reconnecting the console keyboard has the same effect. In the Windows world, NT can be suspended from the Start menu and reactivated by turning the server back on after the suspension has completed. A system administrator can suspend an HP-UX system by typing Control-B on the console. IBM AIX, on the other hand, has no such functionality.

In a clustered configuration, there is no way for the partner system to tell the difference between a suspension and a true system crash or other failure, since in either case all communications from the suspended server are stopped. So, naturally, a good FMS will begin the process of taking over all the processes from the suspended system.

If the suspended system is then unsuspended (in the Sun world, type "go" to the "ok" monitor prompt[4]), you have a problem. Both systems think that they are the masters; both systems think they own the disks; both systems think that they own the network address (two systems with the same network address can cause widespread network problems). It gets ugly very fast. The problem is not with the suspension of the OS, but rather with its resumption.

The recommended fix for this particular problem is not a very technical one, but it can be as effective as any of the more technical ones for the other problems previously discussed. The fix is: *Don't do that!* Make sure that anyone who has access to the keyboards of your critical systems understands the implications of resuming a suspended OS on a clustered system and that they simply never do that.

Of course, simply saying "Don't do that" seems kind of glib, and we don't mean to be glib. (Well, maybe a little.) But you wouldn't walk over to a production Windows server and type "format C:" on the keyboard, would you? Why not? Because you know better. (If you don't know better, please keep away from our production Windows systems.) That's the same reason you

---

[3] Or the L1 key for old-timers like your authors.

[4] Or c on old systems that use the > prompt.

shouldn't resume a suspended OS in a failover configuration. Resuming a suspended OS may not be quite as obvious as typing "format C:", but with appropriate education, it can be. There is a more technical solution to this problem, but in the interest of completeness, and in keeping with our design principles, we present the simplest first.

It is possible to disable or remap the Stop-A key combination on Sun consoles. But that doesn't help the people who use terminals as consoles and can still hit the Break key. It also does not prevent someone from unplugging the console keyboard and plugging it back in, which can have the same effect. The Stop-A capability is, in fact, provided for a reason; there are times when it is necessary to hit Stop-A to halt and then reboot a system that gets messed up. Since Stop-A is not the problem, disabling Stop-A is not the answer. The problem is with resuming the OS, so that is what should be disabled.

Again on a Sun box, the NVRAM can be modified to print out a message when the OS is suspended that says something like, "This system is running in a clustered configuration. Once the OS is suspended, resuming it via 'go' could have serious consequences. Please reboot." But of course, once the message scrolls off the screen, its value is lost. It is also possible to remove the go command from the monitor completely. That would make it impossible to resume the OS after a suspension, thus protecting the system from the uninformed.

On Windows systems, the Suspend menu option can be removed from the Start menu, thus eliminating the possibility of suspending the system; the power-on switch cannot be removed.

The ultimate fix for split brain in two-node configurations, at least under today's technology, is to use serially controlled power switches. The first system, *hall,* has a serial port connected to a power switch that the second system, *oates,* is plugged into. *Oates* has one of its serial ports connected to an identical switch that *hall* is plugged into. When *oates* takes over after a failover, it takes the additional step of sending the signal to its serial port to cut off the power to *hall.* Ideally, this step is performed before *oates* actually takes control of the disks. Serially controlled power switches are not a suitable solution for configurations with more than two nodes, though. Determining which server gets to turn off which other server and under what conditions will give you a serious headache. Although such devices may exist, we have not yet come across a cluster-controlled power switch that could be managed by FMS. Your goal in dealing with split-brain syndrome is to minimize the window in which data corruption can occur. A quick power-down, even a hard one (by pressing the power switch), and its associated risks are probably less risky than running with two systems writing to the same disk set.

Most of the fixes for split brain involve the use of good design techniques and eliminating single points of failure and needless complexity. We believe that once those techniques are employed, the likelihood of split brain occurring is infinitesimal.

Most FMS users and most clusters will never see a single instance of split brain, even in the largest data centers, but if you know how to detect and disarm it, you should be able to survive this rare occurrence.

Undesirable Failovers

There are two basic kinds of undesirable failovers: *ping-pong* failovers and *runaway* failovers. Both can be prevented by a good FMS.

A ping-pong failover can occur if there is, for instance, a massive shared disk failure. System *crate* cannot access the disks, and so it shuts down, initiates a failover, and reboots. *Barrel* takes over and also cannot reach them. So once *crate* reboots, *barrel* fails back to it. This process continues until a human intervenes. A good FMS will support some sort of state locking, where if *crate* fails to *barrel*, *barrel* will hold the critical resources until a human intervenes, fixes the problem, and unlocks the state. In some cases, ping-pong failovers can cause data corruption.

Ping-pong failures can also be prevented by disabling automatic reboot. If *crate* crashes, it is best if it does not automatically reboot, but rather awaits some human intervention.

State locking will also help prevent runaway failovers. In a runaway failover, *samson* crashes and *delilah* takes over. In an effort to diagnose the problem with *samson*, the system administrator reboots *samson*. Immediately upon completion of the reboot, *delilah* sees that *samson* is back, gives up the critical processes, and fails back to *samson* before the system administrator has even begun trying to identify the cause of the original failure.

If, however, *delilah* can lock control of the cluster's critical resources after it takes over, then nothing that happens on *samson* should cause *delilah* to fail back to *samson*. Once the system administrator is satisfied that the problem is fixed, then, if he chooses, he can manually induce *delilah* to switch back to *samson*. (Availability is increased, though, if *delilah* is allowed to keep running the critical resources even after *samson* comes back up.)

Verification and Testing

Designing a highly available system will lead to several sessions where you're sitting in a room, huddled with developers, managers, businesspeople, and the system administration staff, trying to decide what to do when all of your networks fail or when an application refuses to restart on a server. Performing some thought experiments during this part of the design phase will prevent you from ending up in an unknown or unmanageable state later on; it's time well spent on verifying your decisions and implementation ideas.

State Transition Diagrams

A state transition diagram shows you how the system flows from one well-defined operational state to another, during the course of certain events. In the diagram, the states are shown as bubbles, while the transitions between the states are labeled with the events or failures that take you from one bubble to another. A very simple state transition diagram is shown in Figure 16.2, where a system has four operational states: (1) OK, (2) Application Recovery, (3) Primary Network Down, and (4) Manual Recovery. Every arrow is labeled with the event that takes you to another state, such as the application failing, a successful recovery of the application (via the FMS), or the failure of the primary or secondary network.

As shown in Figure 16.2, the system is normally in the OK state. If the primary application fails, the system starts recovery (by restarting the application on the same server, for example), and when completed, it goes back to the OK state. If the primary network fails, the system moves to the lower-right-hand state; again, an application fault and recovery loops into the Recovery state and then back to the starting point. But what if something happens during application recovery? At that point, or if the second network fails after the system is already in the Primary Network Down state, manual recovery begins. It's clear when the system is automated, moving between states, and also clear when there have been enough failures or complex, multiple-mode failures that require a human being to make decisions.

Why would you spend the time drawing one of these? There are many motivations to develop and maintain state transitions:

- You can get beyond the single-failure mode of most FMS packages. What do you do if you suffer a second failure while recovering from the first? What are the kinds of failures you want to worry about handling in succession?

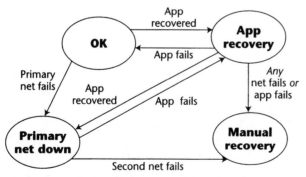

Figure 16.2   A simple state transition diagram.

- The fewer states your system can occupy, the easier it is to understand. As you develop a transition diagram, you may find a few states that are essentially the same, or that with minor process modifications they can be made to be the same. For example, in Figure 16.2, there's no real reason to have "OK" and "Primary Network Down" be separate states; since both have essentially the same event transitions, they can be merged together. When you reduce the number of possible outcomes, you make it easier to diagnose a system failure.

- Well-defined states, whether they describe the system as operating or failed, are just fine. It's the unknown or ambiguous states that can be trouble. Are you sure that your system won't end up in the twilight zone if several things fail at the same time? Do you know that you'll end up in a state where the FMS kicks in and tries to right the boat, or that you'll be able to begin a manual intervention process that gets administrators in front of consoles quickly? If you end up doing neither, you're looking at a system that may be down for an indeterminate period of time.

- You need to draw the line between automation and manual processes. If you can determine those states in which your FMS will throw up its hands and cry, "Uncle! Call the system administrators!" you'll know where you need strong escalation and people management processes. (Of course, if you actually hear voices coming from your FMS, it may be time for a nice, long vacation.)

- Not all issues are necessarily apparent when the first design wave is through. If you haven't proven that the designed system can be operated, or that it meets the operational requirements of your staff, you'll need to walk through a state diagram to show that you have all of the necessary expertise at the right locations.

Going through this process early on can save you time and money later. A design error that leaves you without a path to recovery may be more complex and more difficult to fix once developers have started. If you need the application team to accommodate certain failure cases, they're going to need to know up front.

The other benefit to state transition diagrams is that they let you visually compare the trade-offs of different solutions. Let's say you have a 10-minute automatic failover whenever a network becomes unusable, driven by monitoring scripts that watch network traffic and communicate among themselves to time the failover (we talked about this case more in Chapter 9). If the downtime you are trying to shorten down to 10 minutes would replace a 15-minute manual process, you may decide that the extra few minutes of recovery time are acceptable in the one transition that occurs during an infrequent failure, or that the work required to improve failover time by 5 minutes is just not worth it.

Testing the Works

Testing is the castor oil in the design phase and the maintenance process of a highly available system. It's always the first activity that goes away (except perhaps for documentation) at crunch time. In many shops, of course, it's always crunch time, and little or no testing ever takes place.

Unfortunately, without adequate testing there is no way to tell if your procedures and safeguards are going to work. Good testing always finds holes and inefficiencies in procedures. Testing catches those quick "Oh, I'll put together a more permanent solution next week" fixes that always seem to work their way into systems, even in the best-run shops.

Since systems are always evolving, with applications and procedures being added and modified all the time, testing must be done on a regular basis. Failovers should be tested at least once a quarter. In order for testing to be thorough, it must include the following:

- All documented procedures must be tested. In an emergency, it is likely that written procedures will be followed blindly. If they don't work exactly right, the result may well be chaos. The only thing worse than no documentation is bad documentation.

- Since it is virtually impossible to target documentation at inexperienced personnel, the target audience should be experienced system administrators who are not familiar with the particular idiosyncrasies of your local systems and environment.

- When testing your standards implementation, make sure that systems and applications meet the documented local standards. Know what all test results should be before the test is run.

- Test your backups by restoring a couple of them on a regular basis. If you cannot restore your backups in a test environment, you won't be able to restore them when a disaster occurs.

- Test any critical process whose failure may cause downtime. Consider less obvious potential SPOFs, like building access scanners or locked doors.

Besides periodic procedural testing, it is also important to test applications and how they perform in high-stress situations. Always remember that long service times and failures are indistinguishable to the average user. How does your system perform as load averages increase, especially when they do so over long periods of time? What breaks first? Fix those things, and move on to second- and third-level failures. Bad assumptions made in buffer or counter sizes will often be the first things exposed.

Test the sort of problem that may not bite you for a while. The Y2K problem is an excellent example of this. Programs that were written in the 1970s that were believed to be temporary were the worst culprits for Y2K. Test unusual calendar alignments, like leap years (remember, the year 2100 is *not* a leap year!). Check for assumptions that may be broken in months with 6 weeks in them; if August 1st falls on a Friday or Saturday, then August stretches into the beginning of a 6th week on the 29th or 30th. Of course, it is difficult to test dates after 3:14 A.M. GMT on January 19, 2038, on Unix systems, as that is when their clock counters run out. (Yes, another Y2K-like crisis is approaching.)

Managing Failovers

Like security, entire books have been developed on system management. Rather than provide a primer on system administration habits, we zoom in on a few of the aspects of system management that are particularly relevant to running a failover management system.

System Monitoring

Automated failovers are great to ensure that your systems recover quickly from most outages. But they are not enough. You must monitor your systems for any variety of error conditions, including system resource exhaustion (filesystems or memory fill-up), super-high CPU loads (which can resemble outages), network failures, and so forth.

Most systems have automated monitoring tools that help trouble find your SAs, rather than the other way around. If the SAs don't have to spend time looking for problems, they are free to solve problems that find them, or to properly implement new systems. Framework products like BMC Patrol, Hewlett-Packard Open View, Tivoli Global Enterprise Manager, and Computer Associates' Unicenter will monitor your systems for a variety of potential problems and then notify a preselected group of administrators via pagers, email, telephone calls, console displays, or other alarms. Generally these applications use a protocol called SNMP (Simple Network Management Protocol) to detect and pass on information about these errors.

Make sure that your FMS and any homegrown or third-party applications are capable of sending SNMP notifications, so that any tool that subscribes to the pervasive SNMP standard is capable of monitoring it. This way, new applications can seamlessly merge themselves into the existing environment without requiring a new infrastructure.

When selecting a system monitoring protocol or tool, as we said in our key design principles back in Chapter 5, be sure to select technologies that are mature and that have reference sites and web sites as sources of good information about successful deployments.

Consoles

Every computer system needs to have some sort of console. A console acts as a master terminal, often allowing access even when all other system resources are down. Boot messages and other critical startup information appear on the console screen. The problem, though, with fixed, attached consoles is that they make it very difficult to perform system maintenance, such as reboots, without being in the same room as the system. If a system requires emergency work in the middle of the night (or any other time), fixed consoles require that your system administrators get in the car and visit the data center.

If your operating system supports text-based consoles, connect a terminal server as your console, rather than a fixed and local console. GUI consoles, such as Windows operating systems generally require, are not practical for remote system management. Text-based consoles enable your system administrators to access systems from anywhere in the world, at any time of the day or night. Few things are more frustrating to a system administrator than having to get up at 3:00 A.M. on a Sunday morning and drive to the office to repair a down server, only to discover that a single command she could have given to someone over the phone, or typed in herself, would have fixed the problem. If she could have logged in from home, the system would have been back online faster, and she could have gone right back to sleep. It's also wise if your system administrators have high-speed network access from their homes; such a program will probably pay for itself the first time that a system administrator is able to bring a system up from home without having to drive to the office.

Of course, if you arrange for network access to system consoles, you open up a potential security hole. Be sure to enforce good passwords on the terminal server ports to keep out intruders. Otherwise, some of these reliability measures will come with undesired side effects. It is best to enforce the use of tools like ssh to encrypt traffic that flows across otherwise unprotected networks.

If your server has a CD-ROM drive on it (and don't they all nowadays?), and it isn't being used for anything else, keep a copy of the operating system CD in the drive. Then, if it becomes necessary to reboot the system from the CD, nobody need visit the system to get it ready. This also helps keep track of where your operating system CDs are; lost OS CDs are a common factor in increased MTTRs. Some people have debated the wisdom of this advice from a security perspective. The truth is that if your system consoles are adequately protected, then there should be no security issue at all.

As a final measure to protect your consoles, you should log all data that appears on the console to a system log file, and then automate the examination of these log files for notification of problems. If you decide to build your own log notification system, consider a method where console messages that do not generate alerts are written to a file, and any message that does not appear on the exclude list generates an alert via pager or email. Creating a list of console messages that generates higher levels of alerts is also wise. Avoid a system where unknown or new messages are routinely overlooked.

Utilities

Most likely, whatever system problem you are trying to solve or information you are trying to collect has been previously solved or collected by someone else. Before you spend a lot of time writing a homegrown single-use application, do a web search for something like it. Usually it is much easier to customize an existing application for your purposes than it is to write something from scratch. The customization process is also much less prone to error.

The following are some examples of useful public domain software:

Perl. A very useful programming language that was designed by and for system administrators. It runs on just about every major operating system.

Tripwire. A Unix utility that watches a list of key system files and notifies the administrators if the files are altered.

Top and wintop. These utilities return as output a list of the processes running on the local system, arranged and sorted any number of ways. Top is the Unix version; wintop is the Windows version.

Ntp. A cross-platform clock-synchronizing utility. All the systems on your network synchronize their clocks with a preconfigured time server, or with an external server such as an atomic clock located out on the Web.

If you do find it necessary to create your own utilities, use the command-line interface, rather than a Windows-based one. It is not hard to imagine a scenario where the person who dials into the server to fix it only has access to a slow line on a dumb terminal from very far away. A command line interface makes the repair process much simpler; no specialized hardware is required.

Time Matters

Regardless of the type of system or the method you choose, it is imperative that all systems in a cluster be time-synchronized. Applications and operating systems can get confused when a fundamental assumption is violated: that time always flows in the same direction, forward, at the same rate of one second per second. If systems are out of time-sync, it is possible for one system to create a file with a timestamp that a second system regards as being somewhere in the future. Results can be most inconsistent and confusing. The Unix make utility, for example, will not behave properly when a file's timestamp occurs in the future.

The public domain application `ntp` is the best utility we have seen to synchronize clocks between multiple systems. Unlike Unix's `rdate` command or a manual clock set, `ntp` resets clocks slowly and gradually over a period of time, allowing the time to be changed without applications on the server even being aware of the change. The `rdate` command changes the date of one server to match another, but it does it all at once, often resulting in time seeming to move backward on the server whose date changes. On Windows, there are similar products, such as WinSNTP and Timeserv.

Other Clustering Topics

In this section, we look at some other topics related to clustering and availability that may not fit in other places but are certainly worthy of our attention.

Replicated Data Clusters

We discussed replicating data between clustered nodes briefly in Chapter 15, but we feel that it is worth discussing a little further at this point.

In a replicated data cluster (RDC), data is shared between the clustered nodes by replicating it from one node to the other, rather than by sharing disks between the nodes. We'll discuss more about the mechanisms and choices related to data replication in Chapter 18, "Data Replication." For the purposes of this discussion, you need only understand the differences between shared data (where all systems in a cluster can see and access the very same disks) and replicated data (where each system in the cluster, usually a two-node cluster, has its own independent copy of the data, and updates are sent between the systems across a network).

We believe that when there is a choice between replicated data clusters and shared data clusters (SDCs), SDCs are always preferable. The differences and advantages of shared data clusters are quite clear.

RDCs require the extra step of keeping the data in sync between the two clusters at all times, and in real time. Keeping real-time synchronization between two systems' data sets requires synchronous replication (where the data must be sent to the remote system as part of each write to the local system). Synchronous replication cannot help but introduce I/O overhead, slowing down all the production work. As we've discussed, performance is an important element of availability. Slow performance decreases availability. The performance impact is generally a bigger problem with hardware-based replication than it is with software-based replication. (We'll defend this statement in Chapter 18.) What's more, since RDCs require additional processing steps, additional components, and a functioning LAN or WAN over which the replicated data is sent, RDCs add complexity when compared to an SDC, as well as more elements that can fail, thus violating Key HA Design Principle #1.

When disks are shared, SAN-style, between the nodes in an SDC, the data need only be written once, twice when mirroring is in place, with all writes performed locally. (Disk mirroring does add a small amount of performance overhead, but in most cases, that overhead is not noticeable and is certainly not significant.)

But the real problem with RDCs is what happens after a failover. Consider two hosts, *eatdrink* and *bemerry*, configured asymmetrically (only because it's simpler; the principles would apply equally in a symmetric or a larger SAN-based cluster configuration) in an RDC that uses software replication. *Eatdrink*, the primary, is working and servicing its users, and replicating data over to *bemerry*, the takeover host. When *eatdrink* fails, *bemerry* takes over; its data is an up-to-date and current copy of what was on *eatdrink* before it failed. During the time that *eatdrink* is down, writes that reach *bemerry* do not get replicated back to *eatdrink* because there is no way for *eatdrink* to process incoming data packets.

When *eatdrink* is fixed, it cannot take over for *bemerry* until its disks have been refreshed with the changes that occurred on *bemerry* while it was down. This refresh can require manual intervention and will certainly require time and network bandwidth before it is completed.

Let's also consider what would happen if during the time when *eatdrink* is being refreshed with the changes from *bemerry* (or before that refresh has begun), there is, for example, a power failure that shuts down both systems. *Bemerry* is the only system with current data; the data on *eatdrink* is still out-of-date. It is difficult and may well be impossible for clustering software to determine which host's data is more current. If *eatdrink* comes up as the primary, it will immediately begin to replicate updates to *bemerry*. Once those replications begin, it becomes virtually impossible to reconcile the two data sets between the two separate sets of disks. The inevitable result will be lost or corrupted data.

If during that same period of time *bemerry* had a failure that required a failover back to *eatdrink*, *eatdrink* would take over but would not have current data, causing the loss, probably permanently, of any transactions that never made it back to *eatdrink*.

In a hardware replication model, the issues are different, since the receiving system does not need to be operating for the data to make it to its disks. But the actual details will vary based on the model and vendor of the hardware involved. Some hardware disk arrays can only replicate in one direction, or replicate better in one direction than the other. It is quite possible that some hardware-based replication sidesteps all of the issues and would be satisfactory for an RDC. We have not found one yet.

We are not arguing, however, that RDCs are always bad. They are not. There will be situations where an SDC is out of the question, particularly when the nodes are too far apart from one another to allow disk sharing. But if you have the choice between an RDC and an SDC, we recommend choosing the SDC.

Distance between Clusters

How far apart can nodes in a cluster be so that they can still share disks with each other in a cluster? When SCSI was the predominant media to connect disks and their systems, that was a pretty easy question. SCSI cables could only go so far before their signal quality suffered and data loss occurred. The actual distance depended on the variety of SCSI being employed (see Chapter 7, "Highly Available Data Management," for more details on SCSI varieties), although it never exceeded about 30 meters.

The answer to that question becomes a lot more complicated in Fibre Channel world, but at the same time, the supported distances increase dramatically. Early versions of Fibre Channel imposed a limit of 10 kilometers. That limit appears to have been completely lifted, as vendors are offering Fibre Channel and SAN devices that can send data 50 to 100 kilometers, and in some cases even farther than that, without signal degradation and data loss. (We'll discuss the disaster recovery implications of building a shared disk cluster that extend tens or hundreds of kilometers in Chapter 20, "The Disaster Recovery Plan.")

The bottom line, though, is that the maximum distance by which SDC nodes can be separated is a function of the hardware and networking technology, not of the FMS. If networking advances permit nodes to be separated by thousands of kilometers while still sharing and mirroring disks, there is no reason that an FMS package couldn't support clustering over the same distance. If your FMS vendor imposes artificial restrictions that interfere with your ability to deploy your clusters where you want, and over distances that your networking vendor supports, you probably should consider a different FMS vendor.

Load-Balancing Clusters and Failover

A significant marketing advance in the FMS space over the last few years in something called *load-balancing clusters* (LBCs). This is where we'd like to give you an easy definition of LBCs, if one existed. The problem is that there are actually two significantly different definitions for LBCs.

The first definition describes the feature that most enterprises believe they want their clusters to support. It says that an LBC is one where the cluster is automatically able to determine when a member host becomes too heavily loaded to provide expected levels of service. When the FMS detects that a host is running too slowly, it automatically and proactively takes one or more of the otherwise healthy service groups from the slow node and switches them over to another node in the cluster.

The problem with this feature is that critical applications that are being actively used will temporarily vanish from the network as they are switched over to another node in the cluster. The user may not have been aware of the performance problem, but he will likely be all too aware of the application disappearing. If the application that gets switched over is a database, restart time for a database can be considerable, as the in-flight transactions from the database are processed by the database. That switchover time becomes artificially imposed downtime.

Definition two only comes into play when an unscheduled failover is taking place in a cluster larger than two nodes. When a failover has been deemed necessary, the FMS looks around the cluster at the usage levels of the different nodes and restarts the failed application on the lightest loaded node. Depending on implementation, the FMS may make one scan of the cluster for all of the applications that need new homes, or it may rescan for each application placement. The definition of *lightest loaded* can be quite interesting and can vary depending on which resources are monitored in order to make that determination. Does the FMS look at CPU load, I/O response time, number of processes, or something else? There isn't always one right answer, especially if the hosts in the cluster are of varying sizes and capacities.

Unfortunately, both of these can rightfully be called load-balancing failover, since definition one initiates failover to balance the cluster's load, while the second balances the load whenever a failover occurs.

Be sure that when you ask for load-balancing failover from your FMS vendor that you are getting the definition you want, and that what you want delivers the functionality you expect. Also be sure the functionality can be disabled on a service-by-service basis.

Key Points

- Be sure that your component tests actually test the right things, and that they emulate client processes that depend on them.

- If you decide to go with manual rather than automatic failover, be very sure that the inherent delays are tolerable in your environment.

- The most reliable takeover server is one that isn't doing anything except waiting to step in.

- You'll have to expend more energy on management tools and management processes when you're using failover management software. If you're going to the effort to make the systems reliable, you have to improve the operational management as well.

- Go through thought exercises first to determine what you need to manage and what will happen under any operating condition.

- Be aware of issues like split-brain syndrome or undesired failovers, and have the management processes in place to identify and resolve them within the constraints of your FMS and operational tools.

CHAPTER

17

Failover Configurations

*One only needs two tools in life: WD-40 to make things go,
and duct tape to make them stop.*

—G. M. Weilacher

In this chapter we look at some of the specific configurations that we have seen used for cluster design, and then at some of the issues commonly (and not so commonly) seen when implementing them. For the sake of organization, we have broken up the most commonly seen failover configurations into two groups: two-node configurations and common larger configurations.

On the Availability Index (see Figure 17.1), since we are still discussing clustering, we remain for one more chapter on Level 8.

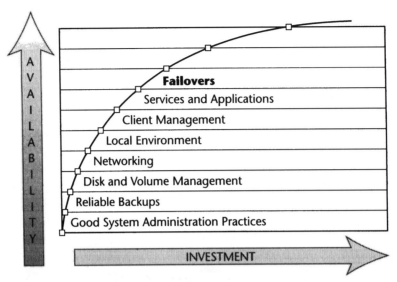

Figure 17.1   Level 8 of the Availability Index.

Two-Node Failover Configurations

The simplest and most common failover configurations are the two-node variety. There are two basic types of two-node configurations: *active-passive* or *asymmetric*, and *active-active* or *symmetric*. In an active-passive configuration, one node is active and does all of the cluster's critical work, while its partner node is a dedicated standby, ready to take over should the first node fail. In an active-active configuration, both nodes are doing independent critical work, and should either node fail, the survivor will step in and do double duty, serving both sets of services until the first node can be returned to service.

Active-Passive Failover

Active-passive failover, as shown in Figure 17.2, is the baseline cluster configuration. Every cluster configuration is a variation of this model. In an active-passive configuration, there is one master server, called *rhythm* in this example, which provides all of the critical services within the pair under normal circumstances. It is connected via two dedicated heartbeat networks (as explained in Chapter 15, "Local Clustering and Failover") to its partner server and dedicated backup node, *blues*.

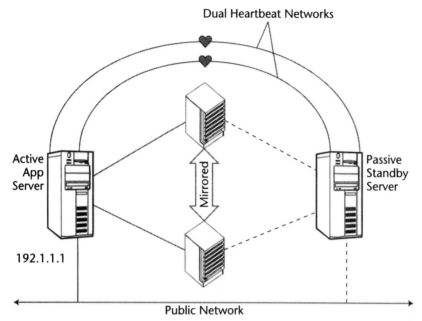

Dual Heartbeat Networks

Active
App
Server

Mirrored

Passive
Standby
Server

192.1.1.1

Public Network

Figure 17.2   Active-passive configuration, before a failover.

Both servers are connected to a set of dual-hosted disks. These disks are usually divided between two separate controllers and two separate disk arrays, and the data is mirrored from one controller to the other. (Of course, the configuration works just fine if the mirrors are on a single controller or in a single cabinet, although the resultant configuration is just not as resilient or as highly available as it would be with separate controllers and separate cabinets.) A particular disk or filesystem can only be accessed by one server at a time. Ownership and conflicts are arbitrated by the clustering software.

Both servers are also connected to the same public network, where the users sit. The servers share a single network (IP) address, which is migrated by the FMS from one server to the other as part of the failover; this virtual IP address is not permanently assigned to a particular server. Only one server in the pair actually owns the address at a time, and any ownership conflicts are arbitrated by the failover management software. As we discussed in Chapter 16, "Failover Management and Issues," the other host's public network identity is limited to its administrative network address, an address that is only for the use of system administrators, and not for regular users.

Active-Passive Issues and Considerations

The biggest issue when examining the issues of active-passive versus active-active failover is, of course, the cost. Fundamentally, with active-passive you are buying two hosts to perform the work of one. One host sits largely idle most of the time, consuming electricity, administrative effort, data center space, cooling, and other limited and expensive resources. However, active-passive configurations are going to be the most highly available ones over time. Since there are no unnecessary processes running on the second host, there are fewer opportunities for an error to cause the system to fail. In general, largely due to the extra expense and administrative overhead, only the most critical applications run in an active-passive configuration.

After an active-passive failover has completed (see Figure 17.3), the takeover server has control of the associated service group. Since both hosts in a shared-disk two-node cluster directly access the same disks (at different times), as long as the disks and all connectivity are in place, there is no question that the takeover host will see the same application data as the failed host.

How Can I Use the Standby Server?

Probably the most common question asked about active-passive failover configurations is "How can I use the standby server?" It is most difficult to justify to the people who approve technology spending that they need to buy two identical servers, thus doubling the expenditure, while only actively using one of them at a time. So the obvious suggestion is to find some activity that can realistically and safely be performed on a standby node. This most commonly asked question is usually followed by this suggestion: "What about my developers? Can I put them on the standby server?" Of course, this is probably the worst thing to do with that standby server.

The key question to ask when evaluating a potential activity for its fitness to be placed on the standby server is "How likely is it that this activity will cause the server to be unable to accept a failover?" To correctly answer this question, you must consider the likelihood that whatever activity is taking place on your standby server will cause that server to crash, hang, freeze, or have its critical files altered. If the activity on the backup server causes a critical failover not to complete, extended downtime will almost certainly result. Another inevitable result will be you on the hot seat, trying to explain to your management why all the money that they spent to implement a highly available system did not do what it was designed to do.

We have categorized many of the activities that a business might consider for placement on the standby server into four levels of advisability: Bad, Acceptable, Good, and Best.

Level 1: Bad

Probably the worst activity to put on standby server is full-blown code development. (We say full-blown to differentiate it from database development, which is generally constrained by the database itself and is discussed under *Acceptable*.) By their nature, developers write untested code with bugs in it. (This is not intended to disparage any particular developers; the first pass on just about any code is going to contain bugs. If your developers do not write code in this way, we recommend giving them a handsome raise. They are well worth it! Or they are lying to you.)

Application bugs can produce all sorts of effects, including but not limited to system crashes, system lockups, depletion of one or more system resources (such as memory or CPU), or leaving the system in a state that makes it unable to accept a failover. (Obviously, bugs can also have much less serious effects on your system, resulting in simple compilation errors or program failures. We are not concerning ourselves with them, only with the kind of bug that can prevent a clustered node from accepting a failover.) If your management has just spent lots of money to make their critical servers highly available, and just when you need to use the standby for a failover it is unavailable, everybody looks really bad, and the money that was spent to shore up these systems will be deemed wasted.

Allowing developers on the standby server also violates at least two of our key design principles from Chapter 5, "20 Key High Availability Design Principles":

- Development and production environments should be totally separate from one another.

- The code running on these critical systems is not mature. The code is brand-new and full of bugs; that makes it totally unsuitable for inclusion in a cluster. Note that any code that runs on a cluster member is running in that cluster.

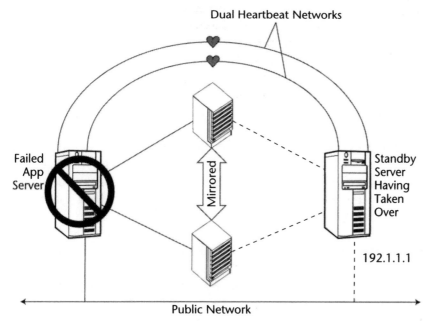

Figure 17.3   Active-passive configuration, after a failover.

Even worse than just letting developers work on the standby box is allowing them to have privileged (administrator or root) access on the standby box. If developers have that level of access, you may as well grant them privileged access directly on the main server. When developers are hard-pressed to find the cause of a system-level bug in their code, they start to look at the OS and network configuration and, hence, start playing with configuration files and restarting services and, worse yet, systems. With privileged access, they can override the FMS's protections against disks being accessed on multiple hosts. Plain and simple, this condition should never be permitted to occur. It is nothing less than a surefire recipe for calamity.

Arguably, an even worse application for the standby server is to use it for QA testing. In a QA environment, the testers are out to find bugs and other problems in the code that is being tested. If they do their job and find bugs, their successes could have serious impact on the server's ability to accept a failover, making it unavailable at the critical time and once again making the decision makers and influencers who recommended clustering look foolish and wasteful.

Level 2: Acceptable

Unlike raw code development, database development often has some constraints on it. Database development generally takes place within a mature database application, such as Oracle, DB2, or SQL Server, and the actions performed by the code are more likely to be restricted to database-related activities. If your database developers are writing code that might hang or crash the standby system, then their work should be classified as Bad. If their work is only going to impact the database environment on the takeover server, rather than on the whole system, then it can be classified as Acceptable.

One of the leading arguments for putting developers on the standby server is that it's easy to kick them off when their system is needed for production. Since the developers might be kicked off their server at any moment, it means that they must change the way they work, saving their work far more often than they might otherwise. If they forget to save frequently, then they could lose their work when a failover occurs. It also gives the perception that their work is of limited value to the overall operation, since they may be asked to stop working at any time without warning. In organizations where we have seen this model implemented, it has a detrimental effect on the morale of the developers and causes them to place less value on their own work and contributions to the organization. In most cases, it just makes them angry.

What's more, while critical services are running on their development server, the developers are unable to do any work, resulting in a slowdown in their performance, and delayed deliverables. An additional cost to the business is the direct result of their idle time; they are collectively sitting around doing nothing, while collecting their wages and other benefits. You're choosing one kind of downtime for another. When evaluating the overall cost of building a cluster in this manner, be sure to include the cost of idling developers and delayed deliverables.

Level 3: Good

So, we've decided that we shouldn't put our developers on the standby node in a two-node active-passive cluster. What does that leave? What *can* we run on the standby node?

It is certainly okay to put another production-quality application on the standby node. Because of the nature of clustered systems, the applications must be totally independent of each other, using separate disks and separate networks. They should have no dependencies of any kind on each other. Within that constraint, it's just fine to put, for example, one instance of a database on one node and a second, separate, instance on the other node. Or a database instance on one node and a file-sharing service, such as NFS or CIFS, on the other.

It's important to understand, though, that running any applications on the standby node increases the risk of that node not being available when it is required for a failover. A system that is busy running an application is measurably more likely to go down unexpectedly than is a node that is not running any applications.

In our experience, though, for most applications and enterprises, the additional risk introduced by running truly well-tested and mature applications on the standby node is more than outweighed by the cost savings of actually using the standby node. When the alternative is to idle the standby system and buy two more hosts to cluster the other application, the cost savings are clear.

Level 4: Best

If maximum availability is the primary factor, and cost is a distant second, then the very best way to configure a pair of failover servers is to dedicate the standby server as a pure standby server, running absolutely no other applications on it. For many of the most critical applications, this configuration is fairly popular. But in other shops, where the costs of dedicating a server outweigh the availability benefits of putting one application in a cluster, this configuration turns out to be prohibitively expensive.

However, by dedicating the standby server, you virtually guarantee its availability when it is needed. The rule is quite simple: The less the server does, the less risk there is that it will fail at an inopportune moment.

Active-Active Failover

The active-active failover model (see Figure 17.4) is very similar in appearance to the asymmetric model. The main physical difference is that in active-active each server will usually have more than one connection to the public network (although virtual networking eliminates multiple connections as an absolute requirement).

The real difference between active-active and active-passive is that in active-active, both hosts are running critical applications at the same time. Each host acts as the standby for its partner in the cluster, while still delivering its own critical services. When one server, *greeneggs*, fails, its partner, *ham*, takes over for it and begins to deliver both sets of critical services until *greeneggs* can be repaired and returned to service.

From a pure cost perspective, active-active failover is the better way to go. It makes much better use of your hardware dollar. Instead of incurring a more-than-100 percent hardware penalty, the only additional cost in building the cluster is the cost of running dual-connect disks and heartbeat networks, and obtaining the clustering software. Those costs are much more manageable and are generally acceptable for all but the least-well-off organizations.

There are two fundamental downsides to active-active configurations, but they are relatively minor and usually acceptable. The first, which we discussed in the *Level 3: Good* section, is the risk that one of the servers will be unable to take over from its partner when it is required to, because of a problem with its own critical application. If all of the applications in the cluster are well tested and mature, the risk here is acceptably low. The second downside is in the inevitable performance impact on the takeover host when it begins performing double duty. If you are concerned about this performance impact, there are basically two ways to handle it: (1) Buy extra CPUs and/or memory for both servers so that they can more easily handle the additional load (but remember what we said about applications expanding to take up all available resources) or (2) decide not to worry about it. After all, if you buy extra hardware to account for the periods of double duty, it is difficult to ensure that this hardware will be used exclusively at takeover time only. More likely, the additional hardware capacity will be sucked up by the resident application and will still be unavailable to ease the load when it is required. When you consider that either server will likely be running in dual mode far less than 1 percent of the time, you will see that the concern about performance after a failover is much ado about nothing. If you can afford the extra hardware, great. Get it. If you cannot, don't worry. It's not going to be a very big deal, and in most cases it's better to have two services running a little slow than it is to have one service stop running completely. Figure 17.5 shows what a symmetric pair looks like after the failover has completed.

It is important that the servers be truly independent of each other. You cannot have one server in the pair act as a client of the other. Taking the example of NFS, if servers *livelong* and *prosper* make up an active-active failover pair, and *prosper* is the NFS client of *livelong*, then if *livelong* fails, *prosper* will be impacted by the failure; it will hang, and most likely not recover. The failover will fail, and downtime will result. Interdependencies like this should be avoided in any kind of clustered configuration. We cover dependencies on network services and ways to identify these interlocking server issues in Chapter 11, "People and Processes."

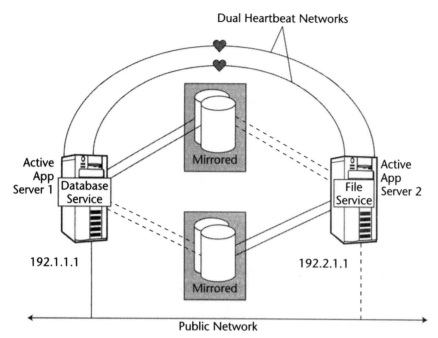

Figure 17.4   Active-active configuration, before a failover.

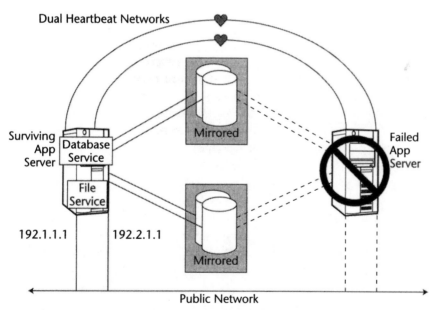

Figure 17.5   Active-active configuration, after a failover.

Active-Active or Active-Passive?

So, the question remains: Which configuration style is better? As with so many of the questions that we examine throughout the book, the complete answer is not entirely clear-cut. Active-passive is unquestionably better for pure availability. But because of the added implementation costs, it is just as unquestionably more difficult to sell it to management.

From a cost perspective, active-passive is superior. It requires fewer systems, and as a result, less space, less electricity, less cooling, and less administration.

In the end, like nearly everything else we have discussed, it depends on your needs. If your applications are so critical that you need to squeeze every possible iota of availability out of them, then active-passive is the way to go. If rare outages are tolerable, then active-active clustering should be fine.

If you believe that active-passive is truly the way to go, but your management is not convinced, we recommend selling it to them the same way you might sell life insurance. Clustering software and configurations are just like life insurance, after all. Although nobody likes to admit it, system outages are inevitable. When they occur, they cost money, and depending on when they occur and the importance of the system that has failed, they can cost a lot of money. The parallels to life insurance are obvious.

FAILOVER AS LIFE INSURANCE

Every few months I send my life insurance company a check. In return for that timely payment, I receive . . . nothing! (Not even a lousy calendar.) And personally, I hope that relationship continues for a very long time. If I were to stop paying those bills, the insurance would go away, and when my family finally needs it, they won't get any of the benefits. (Personal note to my wife: Relax, I have no intention of stopping my life insurance payments.)

If your company chooses not to invest in a standby server, then when it needs it, it won't get the benefits that a reliable standby server can provide.

Just as I (at least in theory) eat right and exercise so that I will live a long, healthy life, and therefore get to keep making those insurance payments and keep getting nothing in return, we build our computers with spare NICs, mirrored disks, mature applications, and all the other stuff we have discussed. Someday, despite my best efforts (and although I really don't like to think about it), that life insurance policy will finally pay out. And despite your best efforts, someday that critical server is going to fail. When it does, you'll want the most reliable server backing it up. Otherwise, downtime will be the inevitable result. The most reliable takeover server is one that isn't doing anything, except waiting to step in.

—Evan

However, more than four out of every five two-node clustered configurations that we have been involved with over the years have been active-active configurations. Realistically, they are more economical, and the risks that they bring along are acceptable for most environments. Once again, your mileage may vary. Choose the configuration that makes the most sense for you.

Service Group Failover

Back in Chapter 15, we defined a service group as a set containing one or more IP addresses, one or more disks or volumes, and one or more critical processes. A service group is the unit that fails from one server to another within a cluster. In the early days of clustering software, especially in active-passive configurations, each cluster ran a single service group, and when that group was on a system in the cluster, that system was active; otherwise, it was not. There was no concept of multiple service groups.

Later, when FMS grew more sophisticated and active-active clusters began to appear, two systems shared two service groups. When the cluster and its components were operating normally, there was still just one service group allocated to each server.

As servers grew larger and able to handle more capacity, it became clear that each server could easily manage more than one service group without suffering any significant performance impact. If a cluster member could manage more than one service group, it was reasonable to require that each service group must be able to failover separately from any others. Otherwise, the multiple service groups would, in reality, be a single service group, and no advantage would be gained.

The introduction of multiple service groups to clustering added value because they gave FMS the ability to failover intelligently. Service groups could be split up between multiple nodes in the cluster after some members of the cluster had disappeared. Service groups could failover to less heavily loaded systems, or be reapportioned between nodes based on just about any rule set.

For service groups to maintain their relevance and value, they must be totally independent of each other. If because of external requirements, two service groups must failover together, then they are, in reality, a single group.

Service group failover, as shown in Figure 17.6, is, therefore, the capability for multiple service groups that ran together on one server to failover to separate machines when that first server fails. In this figure, we see two nodes: *fish* and *chips*. *Fish* has two active service groups, A and B, and *chips* has two other service groups, C and D. Each group can also run on its respective partner server; A can run on *chips* as A', and so on. Even though the service groups can move separately from *fish* to *chips* and back again, the advantage of this scheme, from an availability perspective, is negligible.

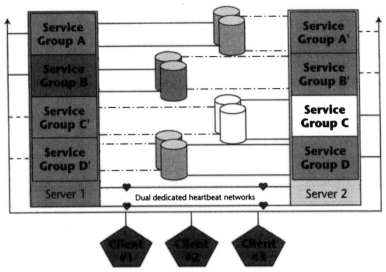

Figure 17.6 Service group failover.

Early implementations of service group failover were designed for two-node clusters, since that was all that was available at the time, and it was marketed as a huge advance in clustering software. It was not; the capability was there, but service group failover in a two-node cluster offers practically no additional value. As FMS has grown more sophisticated, service group failover has gone from being an overmarketed, underachieving feature to one that is taken for granted.

Service group failover and SANs have been the two critical technological advances that have enabled larger clusters.

Larger Cluster Configurations

As storage area networks and commodity-priced servers have permeated the computing world, clustering software has grown in popularity and become more sophisticated.

N-to-1 Clusters

In a SCSI-connected world, building more than two hosts into a cluster is immensely complex. Consider the SCSI-based four-node cluster shown in Figure 17.7, where four nodes are actively running, and the fifth node is designated as a standby for the other four. The standby server requires at least 10 SCSI bus connections (two each for the four primary servers, plus two more for the standby's local private disks, and two NICs for heartbeats, one for an administrative network connection, and at least four for public connections for the four primaries. Assuming no virtual IP, that's seven NICs. That adds up to a minimum of 17 external interface cards to support 4-to-1 failover. No wonder, then, that it was extremely rare to find clusters larger than two nodes before SANs began to appear.

Clusters larger than two nodes make it less expensive to deploy dedicated backup nodes. Instead of requiring one node to act as a dedicated standby for one active node (a 100 percent overhead), as in a two-node active-passive cluster, consider a three-node cluster where two of the nodes run critical applications and the third is a dedicated standby for either of the first two (a 50 percent overhead). Instead of requiring four nodes, arranged in 2 two-node pairs, you can save 25 percent of the hardware costs by only purchasing three nodes. If you carry that principle further, you can use the single backup node to protect more hosts, say, 10 (10 percent overhead) or 12 (about 8 percent overhead), in a larger cluster.

This model, where some number of clustered systems failover to a single dedicated standby node for the whole cluster is called *N-to-1 failover*.

The other serious limitation of SCSI-based *N*-to-1 clusters is that since only the "one" node (the backup for all the active systems in the cluster) can see all of the disks, when the failed node returns to service, it is necessary to fail its services back to it, freeing up the one node to takeover for another set of service groups. As you will see, failing services back isn't necessary for *N*-plus-1 clusters.

SANs have greatly simplified the construction and design of *N*-to-1 clusters, as shown in Figure 17.8, where we have taken the same 4-to-1 cluster depicted in Figure 17.7 and migrated it to a properly redundant SAN infrastructure. (For more about SANs, please refer to Chapter 8, "SAN, NAS, and Virtualization.")

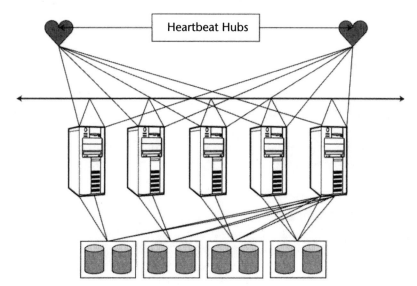

Figure 17.7   A 4-to-1 SCSI-based cluster configuration.

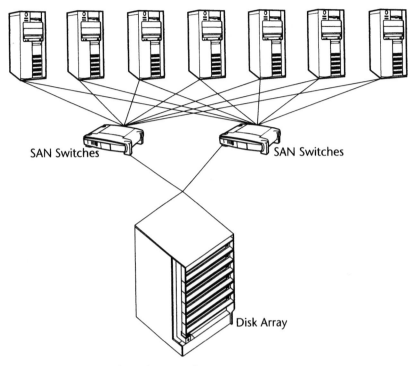

Figure 17.8   A SAN-based 6-to-1 cluster.

An interesting difference between the SAN-based cluster in Figure 17.8 and the SCSI-based one in Figure 17.7 is that in the SAN-based cluster, the hosts are all identically attached to the storage. In the SCSI-based cluster, one node, the 1 node in *N*-to-1, has many more connections to the network, and, so, must be bigger. It has to have the backplane slots to permit making all of these connections.

N-Plus-1 Clusters

As we described previously, SCSI-based *N*-to-1 clusters have a serious limitation. They must incur extra downtime after the cause of a failover has been repaired, so that the migrated services can be moved back to their original host. The added overhead required to configure all nodes to be able to see all the disks and to run all of the critical applications is huge, adding SCSI cables and a lot of complexity.

In a SAN-based cluster, all the nodes can see all of the disks, so there should not be a need to migrate applications back to their original homes. If we take this observation to its logical extreme, we develop a new type of cluster configuration that we call *N-plus-1*, shown in Figure 17.9 as 6-plus-1.

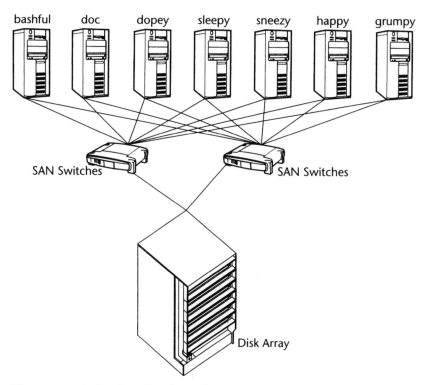

bashful   doc   dopey   sleepy   sneezy   happy   grumpy

SAN Switches   SAN Switches

Disk Array

Figure 17.9 A SAN-based 6-plus-1 cluster.

In Figure 17.9's 6-plus-1 cluster, we have a total of seven nodes, including *grumpy*, which is running as a dedicated standby. Should *bashful*'s services fail, they will be automatically migrated over to *grumpy*, who becomes the new home for these services. When *bashful* returns to service, it joins the cluster as the new standby, so that when *dopey* crashes, its services will migrate over to *bashful*. Over time, the layout of hosts and services will not match the original layout within the cluster. As long as all of the cluster members have similar performance capabilities, and they can see all of the required disks, it does not actually matter which host actually runs the service.

N-plus-1 will provide availability superior to *N*-to-1, since no manual return to normal is required when *bashful* returns to service.

If *dopey* fails before *bashful* has been put back into service, then, of course, there is no dedicated standby host for *dopey*'s service to move to. What happens next depends on how your FMS handles the situation. Lesser quality FMS will take *dopey*'s service groups and move all of them to some other host in the cluster, say, *doc*. With an eye toward load balancing, high-quality FMS will take those same service groups and divide them up between the surviving hosts in the cluster. Very high-quality FMS will decide where to place the applications around the cluster based on the current loads of all of the hosts in the cluster; extremely high-quality FMS will make the determination based on historic system resource consumption, considering CPU and memory consumption, and I/O rates, along with the types of applications that are currently running on the system. The last option will generally result in the most accurate level of load balancing, though perhaps at the cost of a brief delay in failover time.

As clusters begin to grow to 15 or 20 nodes or more, it's possible that a single standby node will not be adequate, especially if it is down for repair for an extended period. We have begun to see larger clusters built in an *N*-plus-2 style, where, for example, 20 nodes are clustered together, but only 18 of them run critical applications at any time. The remaining two are configured as dedicated standbys.

We expect to see cluster sizes grow dramatically over the next few years as blade technology begins to enter the mainstream marketplace. With that in mind, we suggest that a roughly 10 percent system overhead is a sensible level.

High-quality FMS should be able to handle just about any mixed-and-matched cluster configuration that makes sense.

The astute reader may have noticed that there is no material difference between the configuration layouts in Figures 17.8 and 17.9. That is correct. Since there is no hardware difference between the two configurations, we recommend using *N*-plus-1, rather than *N*-to-1, in clusters that are larger than two nodes to take the best advantage of hardware resources and to maximize availability. If there is a serious downside to this configuration, we have not been able to identify it.

How Large Should Clusters Be?

Unfortunately, it's difficult to make a clear recommendation on the maximum size of a cluster. It would be very nice to be able to tell you that clusters shouldn't be larger than, say, 27 nodes. We cannot do that.

We also cannot say that clusters can grow in size without limit, subject to the capabilities of your FMS. The FMS itself can represent a single point of failure, and we have seen organizations who are leery of running all of their critical operations in a single cluster for just that reason. This is especially true if your FMS requires the cluster to be shut down in order to make configuration changes within the cluster.

The natural tendency is to grow clusters as large as possible and necessary to limit the number of management points. (From a simplicity perspective, it's pretty much a wash: Ten 2-node clusters are roughly just as complex as two 10-node clusters. In the end, you are just moving the complexity from one place to another.) However, as you put more responsibility on the FMS, it can become a single point of failure itself. Since the S in FMS stands for software, FMSs are no less prone to failure and errors than other applications. A bug or configuration error in an FMS could, in some instances, cause the entire cluster to fail. By limiting the number of nodes and critical applications in the cluster, you limit the impact of a failure in the FMS.

KILL THE BUGS

A friend of mine was the lead developer on an early clustering product called FirstWatch. He imposed a rule on his team: No new code can be added to the product unless all medium- and high-level bugs have been fixed, tested, and closed. He says that if he were developing some retail middleware, he would not have been as careful, but because FirstWatch was a product that customers came to count on to deliver increased levels of availability, he felt the extra precautions were absolutely necessary. He believes that the engineering teams for most clustering software are at least as careful as he was with his code, and that they tend to have more rigorous test suites.

—Evan

That being said, we expect to see cluster sizes increase dramatically over the next few years as the acceptance of blade technology widens and (see Chapter 22, "A Brief Look Ahead") these small, inexpensive, single-tasking commodity-style computers are introduced to the mainstream. There have been discussions of how to manage clusters of hundreds or even thousands of physically very small nodes that might all be located in a single data center rack. (We would, of course, recommend putting them in more than one rack, as one rack represents a single point of failure.)

Given today's technology, there's probably no need to grow clusters beyond 15 to 20 nodes. However, when blades make themselves felt in the market, that recommendation will surely change.

Key Points

- The most reliable takeover server is one that isn't doing anything except waiting to take over for a failed one.
- You'll have to expend more energy on management tools and management processes when you're using failover management software; if

you're going to the effort to make the systems reliable, you have to improve the operational management as well.

■ Go through thought exercises first to determine what you need to manage, and what will happen under any operating condition.

CHAPTER

18

Data Replication

What we have here is . . . failure to communicate.
—The Captain (Strother Martin) in *Cool Hand Luke*

As we move on to discuss replication, we move up to Level 9 on the Availability Index, as shown in Figure 18.1. Replication most commonly means file and data replication, but as we will discuss in Chapter 19, "Virtual Machines and Resource Management," processes can also be replicated to make them more highly available, and as we discussed in Chapter 16, "Failover Management and Issues," process states can also be replicated to increase their availability. In this chapter, we limit our discussion to the replication of files and data.

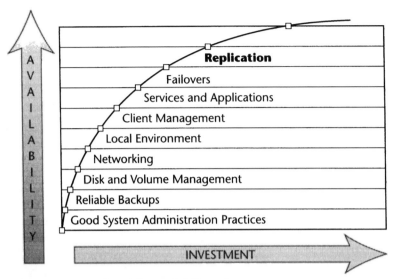

Figure 18.1 Level 9 of the Availability Index.

What Is Replication?

Replication is the copying of data from one system and its disks to another system and its completely independent and redundant set of disks. Replication is not the same as disk mirroring, because mirroring treats both sets of disks as a single, logical volume with enhanced availability, while replication treats the disk sets as two completely independent items. Mirroring is confined to a single computer system, while replication moves data from one system to another. When replication is done properly, the same ACID properties present in database systems will be in the replicated databases. (See the *Database Servers* section in Chapter 14, "Data and Web Services" for a discussion of ACID properties.) The end result is two consistent and equally viable data sets ideally in distinct physical locations. Since it further increases the data's availability, replication further increases your disk space requirements above RAID-1 or RAID-5, because each replicated disk set is usually a separate volume unto itself, with its own RAID implementation. Depending on the implementation, you could choose to replicate from a RAID 0+1 set to a RAID-5 set, or to a non-RAIDed set at your DR site. What you gain in return for the investment in disk spindles is the ability to recover from a large variety of performance and operational outages quickly, and with predetermined downtime.

Why Replicate?

An enterprise might choose to replicate its data for several reasons:

- Probably the most popular use of replication is for disaster recovery. Sending data over a wide area network to a remote site means that the data will be protected in the event that something happens to the facility that contains the master server. It is this use of replication that leads us to place replication so high on the Availability Index. Other uses are valuable, but are not as critical to achieving high availability. Wide area replication, in fact, enables (but does not define) the 10th and final level of the Index, disaster recovery.

- Data can be replicated from one system to another within the same facility. In this model, the destination system can work on and with the replicated data independently of the master. The destination system might be used to generate reports, mine data, or perform tape backups, all without affecting the original copy of the data, or impacting the CPU, and therefore the users, of the master.

- Some FMS packages use replication to share their data. As we said in Chapter 15, "Local Clustering and Failover," even though some vendors recommend it, we maintain that data sharing via replication is inferior to data sharing via shared disks.

Two Categories of Replication Types

Replication types or styles can be categorized in two ways:

- By the amount of latency they introduce (none, a little, or a lot)
- By the entity that manages and initiates the replication (hardware, software, filesystem, or an application)

Within both categories, each type has its distinct advantages and disadvantages, and we spend this section discussing them in some detail. In some cases we mention specific vendors who offer products in each area. The two replication categories are independent of each other. In other words, each initiator-based type of replication can create any amount of latency.

Four Latency-Based Types of Replication

The four types of replication, relative to the latency that they introduce, are: (1) synchronous, (2) asynchronous, (3), semi-synchronous, and (4) periodic, or batch-style, replication. The impact on both network and system performance decreases as you move from synchronous to batch style, but in return, the data on the destination system is more and more out-of-date.

Latency-Based Type 1: Synchronous Replication

Synchronous replication is the copying of data from the master system, *ebony*, to its destination, *ivory*, in real time. As a block of data is written to *ebony's* disks, the block is sent across the network. The data must arrive at *ivory*, which must acknowledge receipt of the data by sending a packet back across the network to *ebony*. Only once it has received the acknowledgement does *ebony* report to the application that generated the write that it has completed.

Since every single write causes a round-trip on the network (once when the data packet itself travels to the remote site and once when the acknowledgment makes the trip back), writes can be significantly delayed under synchronous replication. That delay is called *latency*. The latency is not only caused by the length of network cable and the time it takes for data to traverse it at roughly the speed of light, but also any additional delays caused by equipment, such as routers, switches, and repeaters, located along the network. This equipment may simply receive and then resend the data, or it may receive the data and perform some processing on it before sending it on. In either case, these devices introduce additional latency to the replication process.

For systems that are located in the same data center, the same building, or even in the same neighborhood, the performance impact of synchronous replication will be acceptable on all but the busiest systems. Once the distance between the systems exceeds about 20 miles, the overhead that the latency introduces may start to have some mild impact on some busy applications, and once it exceeds about 50 miles, the delays will likely become unacceptable for many applications. These distances are, of course, just a suggestion, and your (ahem) mileage will surely vary. The reasons for this variance include the amount of data and the number of packets being replicated, the method of implementation of synchronous replication that you choose, and the amount of equipment between the two sites.

In return for this delay, synchronous replication provides the ultimate in data integrity. It ensures that the data on *ivory* is as up-to-date as it can be. *Ebony* cannot generate its next write until the current write's acknowledgment has completed the round-trip and been received on *ivory*. As a result, every write that makes it to *ebony's* disks also makes it to *ivory's* disks. This means that if something happens to *ebony*, all of its data is guaranteed to be present and up-to-date on *ivory*. For some extremely critical applications, this guarantee is worth the impact on performance. For others, the impact will be too great, and different options must be considered.

MAINTAINING WRITE ORDERING

When data is replicated from one system to another, the data can be replicated so that write ordering is maintained, or so that it is not. In general, of the types that we discuss, only the last one, periodic replication, fails to maintain write ordering.

When write ordering is maintained, data that is written to the master host, *country*, will be written to the destination host, *western*, in the same order it is written to *country*. If a single database transaction generates a series of 50 disk writes, those disk writes will hit both hosts' disks in the same order. As a result, if *country* crashes or suffers another interruption in the middle of its replication, the data on *western* is incomplete (as some of the writes did not get replicated), but it is consistent. A good database can work through a situation where data is incomplete but consistent.

If *country's* writes are sent to *western* in any old order, then it is likely that write number 50 will reach *western* before, say, write 14 does. If, for example, write 50 is a confirmation of the data in the rest of the transaction, but some of the transaction's data is missing, that's a problem.

The bottom line is that if your data is not replicated in the same order in which it was originally written to *country*, when *country* goes down, the data is likely to be corrupted and unusable on *western*. That likelihood defeats the entire purpose of implementing replication software.

Another important advantage to synchronous replication is that since the data is replicated as it is written, it isn't just guaranteed to be on *ivory*, but it is also written in the same order that it is written to *ebony*. While that may seem obvious, it is not always the case with asynchronous and periodic replication. Since the data on *ivory* must always be written in the same order as it is written on *ebony* (remember, it is sent one write at a time; there is no other way for it to be written), the data on *ivory* is always consistent and usable. If something happens to *ebony* that forces a switchover to *ivory*, the data on *ivory* should be ready to use at any moment. We discuss the implications of data arriving in a different order in the sidebar.

Different implementations of synchronous replication will introduce different levels of latency. We strongly recommend that anyone considering a synchronous replication solution arrange for competitive performance benchmarks among all of the vendors they are considering. As with all benchmarks, be sure that the test emulates as closely as possible the type, size, and amount of data that you will likely experience in production; otherwise, the benchmark is useless.

Latency-Based Type 2: Asynchronous Replication

Under asynchronous replication, data is stored locally in a log on the master system, *pratt*, and sent across the network to the destination system, *whitney*, when network bandwidth or system performance permits. Often, depending on the rate of incoming data, data will be replicated just as quickly as it comes in. If the rate of incoming data is more than the network or system can handle at that moment, write transactions will stay in the master system's replication log until their turn comes around, when they will be replicated in the order they arrived.

Writes are confirmed back to *pratt*'s application when they are written to the log on *pratt*, rather than when they are written to *whitney*. As a result, the impact on *pratt*'s application performance is minimal, and often will approach zero. Since writes under asynchronous replication are read from the log and sent across the network in the same order that they arrived in the log, the data on *whitney* is always as consistent and usable as it is on *pratt* at all times, even if it is not perfectly up-to-date. Some vendors offer variations on asynchronous replication that do not guarantee write ordering. In reality, those variations are periodic replication (see *Latency-Based Type 4: Periodic, or Batch-Style, Replication*), which does not generally guarantee write ordering on the remote system.

Unless you are confident that your users and applications can withstand the delays that most synchronous replication solutions introduce, make sure that any replication solution you consider can perform asynchronous replication while maintaining write ordering and data integrity.

The downside to asynchronous replication is that, depending on the rate of incoming data on *pratt*, the data on *whitney* may be some number of writes behind *pratt*. For most applications, this is an acceptable trade-off in return for the improved performance of asynchronous replication. The logic here is that a failure that results in switching over to the remote host is an extremely rare event, one that may only occur once every few years. If a handful of the most recently applied transactions (the only ones that should ever be affected) do not get replicated to the remote side and are lost in one of these extremely rare events, that is a worthwhile trade-off to protect all of the rest of the data, and while maintaining acceptable levels of application performance.

If properly implemented, asynchronous replication is acceptable even over extremely long distances. We are aware of at least one implementation of asynchronous replication where data is created in Atlanta, Georgia (in the southern United States), and replicated to Munich, Germany. By all reports, performance is quite acceptable.

Another downside to asynchronous replication is that it puts a nearly constant load on the network connecting the sites (network load is also an issue with synchronous replication). While that is all right for many enterprises, some may find that unacceptable and may wish, instead, to confine the traffic to a particular time of day, say, late at night, or simply to have more control over when the network will have this traffic flowing across.

Latency-Based Type 3: Semi-Synchronous Replication

Semi-synchronous (or "semi-sync") replication is a method that was created by EMC for use in their SRDF (Symmetrix Replicated Data Facility) product, to bridge the gap between synchronous replication, with its performance problems, and asynchronous replication. SRDF does not support a form of asynchronous replication that maintains write ordering, so semi-synchronous gives their users another option besides synchronous replication.

Semi-sync is designed to improve the performance of SRDF in configurations where regular synchronous mode's latency is too great to maintain reasonable application performance. Semi-sync reduces synchronous replication's performance impact by having the local disk array acknowledge the completion of a write to the application *before* propagating the data to the remote disk array, eliminating the latency caused by data transmission.

The benefit of semi-sync is dependent on the application, the workload, and the speed at which replicated data makes the round-trip between the primary and secondary nodes. EMC says that there is a benefit only if it takes longer for writes to reach the local Symmetrix than it does for them to cross the SRDF link.

On the downside, though, EMC acknowledges in their documentation that the use of semi-sync may result in inconsistent data at the remote site if there is a crash at the primary site, which, of course, is the primary purpose of using the software. EMC also says that under some circumstances the use of semi-sync mode with applications that do not defer their writes is not recommended.

Latency-Based Type 4: Periodic, or Batch-Style, Replication

The final type of replication goes by two different names. Under periodic, or batch-style, replication, data is saved up, and from time to time is replicated in a batch, all at once. Write ordering is not maintained, so during a replication cycle, the data that has reached the destination is not consistent. This means that if, during the replication cycle, the master system fails, the data on the destination system is not usable. The advantage to this style of replication is that it gives system and network administrators some control over when the network will be impacted by the additional load that replication introduces.

Another important disadvantage to periodic replication is that the data on the destination system is very much out-of-date. If the data is updated via replication every 4 hours, for example, then on average, the data on the destination is 2 hours out-of-date. If an emergency causes a switchover from master to destination, as much as 4 hours of committed work can be lost. For most critical applications, this significant loss of data is considered unacceptable, and as a result, periodic replication is not considered acceptable for disaster recovery situations. Periodic replication is generally much more useful as a way of getting data to other systems for backups, data mining, and other non-critical uses.

If periodic replication is to be used for disaster recovery, then it is critical that additional copies of the data be maintained. The remote side will require a multisided data mirror, and while the replication is active, one side of the mirror must be broken off to receive the updates, while the other sides of the mirror hold their static (and consistent) copy of the data. Once the replication cycle has completed, the sides that were not updated will be reattached to the updated copy and will be brought up-to-date. Some implementations will require a similar process on the sending side, as a copy of that mirror is split off from the active copy, so that it does not change during the replication. Disk vendors love this method, as it allows them to sell multiple sets of disk spindles to keep up with all of the copies of the data set. Note that if it becomes necessary to recover from an older copy of the data (because of a failure during the copy), the data you'll get dates back to the previous round of replication.

YOUR DATA IS ALL WET

Consider replication as a bathtub with the drain plug open.

For asynchronous replication, if you turn on the water just a little, it drops straight down the drain without delay. If you turn the water on harder, you will overwhelm the drain's ability to let the water out, and water will back up in the tub, but it will eventually all drain, especially if you periodically turn down the incoming flow. (If the drain cannot keep up with the incoming water, you'll need a fatter drain pipe. In replication, you'd need additional bandwidth.) This metaphor fails only in that the water cannot possibly be taught to drain in the same order in which it came in. The only way to guarantee that in a bathtub is to tag all the water molecules and line them up accordingly. (In our experience, tagging and queuing water molecules is not usually worth the effort.)

Under synchronous replication, water comes into the tub one glop[1] at a time. The next glop is not permitted to enter the tub until the last one has totally drained. As a result, in a busy system, glops can get backed up. In theory, though, they will eventually all drain.

With periodic replication, the drain plug is closed, and from time to time it is opened to allow all of the gathered water out. The water does not drain in any particular order and is all sent down the pipes in the seemingly random order that it makes it to the drain. Just so long as all the water gets out.

—Evan

[1] Glop is a technical term that is commonly used in the bathtub replication business.

Five Initiator-Based Types of Replication

There are five types of replication, based on which software initiates the replication: (1) hardware, (2) software, (3) filesystem, (4) application (usually database), and (5) transaction monitor. We discuss each in detail.

Initiator-Based Type 1: Hardware-Based Replication

Hardware-based replication is the clear market leader for replication. EMC and their SRDF is largely responsible for the early market success of replication, as they were the first vendor to widely introduce it for open systems, after first developing it for the mainframe market. Other disk array vendors have joined them in the market, including Hitachi and their TrueCopy replication solution.

Hardware replication does its work external of the system where the applications run, on a CPU located within an external disk array. As long as you can connect the array to a system, that system's data can be replicated.

On the receiving side of hardware replication, there must be an identical disk array; the software that performs the replication only runs on specialized arrays. There is generally no way to open the replication process and extend it to another vendor's hardware. Similarly, hardware replication often requires a particular type of network (ESCON, for example), which is not commonly found in Windows and Unix shops. More recently, hardware-replication vendors have introduced the capability to convert their ESCON data packets to the more prevalent TCP/IP network, although doing so can have a significant performance impact, as the packet must be stopped, encapsulated, sent on its way, and unencapsulated on the remote side.

Some hardware-replication vendors, including EMC, do not support asynchronous replication because they cannot guarantee write ordering of the data on the remote side.

Using the Data on the Remote Side

One of the implicit limitations of most replication solutions is that the data on the remote side is not usable while replication is active unless special measures are taken to make it available. The remote data, by its nature, must be read-only because it is being changed in a manner that most applications do not understand. Even in a read-only state, the data should not be used. If you are reading a file on the remote side through the local filesystem, and suddenly that file is deleted by the replication tool (because it was deleted on the primary side), how will your application and filesystem respond? It's hard to predict, but you can be sure that the result will not be a good one.

By taking a snapshot-style copy (as discussed in Chapter 7, "Highly Available Data Management") of the remote filesystem and splitting it off from the one that is receiving the replicated data, you can create a copy of the filesystem. Changes that are made to this snapshot are not permanent (they will be lost when the snapshot copy is destroyed, or updated with new changes from the primary), so even though the read-only nature of this copy may not be continuously enforced, it is certainly true.

In between the Two Sites

Wide area replication between two remote sites requires additional networking hardware from companies like CNT, Inrange, or Nishan Systems. These companies make the hardware that converts the replicated data into the appropriate format for replication across wide area networks. The disk array vendors rely on these companies to provide the wide area links between their arrays, as they do not provide this functionality themselves.

One of the methods that these companies use is called *dense wavelength division multiplexing* (DWDM). We mention it mostly because it's very cool. DWDM takes data from multiple protocols, including Fibre Channel, FICON, ESCON, and Ethernet, and converts them into optical signals, which are sent across a fiber optic network as light. As shown in Figure 18.2 (that we wish could be in color), a DWDM converter takes each incoming channel, converts it into a different frequency of visible light (i.e. color), called a *lambda*, and merges the colors together into a single stream with a prism. The stream is then sent across the network at very nearly the speed of light (bends in the cable can cause reflections, which can slow the signal down slightly). The colors are then separated on the remote side by another prism and converted back into data, and the data is sent to the appropriate destination.

The result is that a single strand of fiber optic cable can run many parallel data streams at very high throughput rates, each with its own color.

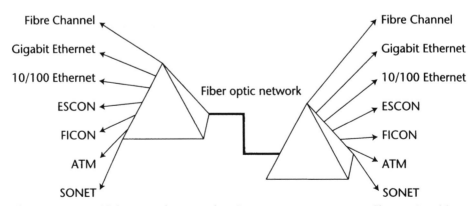

Figure 18.2 Multiple network protocols using DWDM on a common fiber optic cable.

Initiator-Based Type 2: Software-Based Replication

Software-based replication is generally performed by volume management software, such as the extension to VERITAS Volume Manager, called VERITAS Volume Replicator (VVR). Software-based replication offers more flexibility than hardware-based replication, usually at a lower cost.

The following are some of the advantages of software-based replication:

- There is no requirement for the disks to be a certain type or brand; the software replicates from its own logical volumes (as described in Chapter 7) to another system and its set of logical volumes.

- There is no requirement for a specialized network; a standard TCP/IP network is usually just fine. If you add software-based replication to an existing WAN, it is likely, however, that your network will see a rather substantial decline in performance and throughput due to the additional data traffic.

- Because of its open nature, software-based replication tends to be a less expensive solution than hardware-based solutions, especially when considered from end to end and including disk and network hardware.

- Surprisingly, benchmarks reveal that software-based replication tends to have far less impact on systems and applications than hardware solutions do. (More on this in *Is Software Replication Really Faster?*.)

- There are no specialized hardware requirements for repeaters, protocol converters, or wide area networking hardware.

- Because of the way that hardware-based replication copies its data, generally you'll usually need to keep more copies of the data on separate sets of disks than you will with software-based replication, saving you money on hardware.

One disadvantage to software-based RAID is that you can only replicate data between systems that support the software that does the replication. With hardware-based RAID, you could replicate data from your Amiga to a Palm OS PDA, as long as you can figure out how to connect those to the disk arrays.

Is Software Replication Really Faster?

In our experience, and counterintuitively, software-based replication is actually faster than hardware-based replication. The following are some of the reasons why:

- Software replication solutions generally replicate smaller blocks of data than hardware-based solutions. Less data means that the transactions finish faster, and with less network traffic being generated. Smaller chunks also mean that less unchanged data is replicated. A small local write can generate a much larger replicated write via hardware-based replication, which usually replicates data in the same-sized chunks each time. The same local write on most software-based replication products will send less data while replicating.

- Hardware-based replication adds its overhead when it performs the write; that's when it begins the process of spawning off the replicated copy of the data. The moment of the actual disk write is the slowest part of the transaction. By spawning the write at that point during the process, the slowest part of the transaction is made even slower. Software-based replication is done much earlier in the process so that more of the writes wind up being done in parallel, making better use of resources.

- While it's certainly true that hardware-based replication's work is done on an independent CPU located inside the disk array, it can still have a significant effect on the computer system's CPU. So that it does not get swamped by incoming replication requests, some hardware solutions will put the CPU into an uninterruptible disk-wait state while the transaction is sent across the network and the confirmation is making the return trip. During a disk-wait, no other activity can be performed on the host CPU. On a busy system with a lot of data being replicated, this will seriously slow down the host as its CPU essentially stops working for the duration of the replication.

- Some hardware-replication solutions do not use TCP/IP as their native network. Unless your enterprise uses one of these other networks (such as ESCON), it may be necessary to slow down the delivery of each data packet across the network by encapsulating it inside a TCP/IP packet and then unencapsulating it on the other end. The encapsulation also serves to make the packet larger, further slowing down the replication process.

We certainly understand that product improvements are being made all the time and that what is true about performance as we write this material may or may not be true when you read it. Therefore, we once again urge our readers to carefully evaluate the performance of any replication solution that you may be considering, and that you run relevant benchmarks to determine which solution will balance the best data protection with the least impact on application and system performance.

Initiator-Based Type 3: Filesystem-Based Replication

When you boil it down to its base components, filesystem-based replication is much like tape backup: a point-in-time copy of the files in a filesystem.

Hardware- and software-based replication, tape backups, and database products include fancy vendor-based tools, while filesystem-based replication tools are generally utilities that are included as part of the operating system.

It is rare, though not unheard of, for filesystem-based replication to be used as a solution for DR. By its nature, filesystem-based replication is very similar to the periodic style of replication we discussed in the previous section: From time to time, the contents of a filesystem (or just the changes since last time) are collected and sent to the destination site. Filesystem replication is best used, then, to make a copy of a filesystem whose contents don't change very often, or perhaps to make a one-time copy. If contents change regularly, it is best to consider another method, such as hardware- or software-based replication.

One excellent use of filesystem replication occurs when you have enough developers to outstrip the capacity of a single server, and the users are demanding multiple servers' worth of development tools, library files, and manual pages. Multiple servers provide a basic level of redundancy against the failure of any one server and can remove performance bottlenecks by distributing the client load over several servers. Replicated read-only file servers can also be dropped in behind web servers, providing load balancing across multiple sources for the same content with the same measure of availability and performance. To be fair, though, this technique of replicating among colocated servers is falling into disuse as SANs are able to fill that niche without requiring separate copies of the data on each server. SANs can be configured to protect the data against most types of outages; for more on SANs, see Chapter 8, "SAN, NAS, and Virtualization."

Like mirroring, filesystem-based replication is not a substitute for backups, because replication only preserves the current state of the filesystem. If you need to restore your boss's email file from last Thursday, not even Siegfried and Roy[2] could make it appear from a current remote copy. You need a multiple-level backup strategy. (As we discussed in Chapter 6, "Backups and Restores," remember, backups are always your last line of defense against total and irrevocable data loss.) Replication is also not a snapshot mechanism, as we introduced in Chapter 7. Snapshots may give you a copy-on-write filesystem, which allows you to go backward in time and look at the filesystem before any particular change was made to it. Snapshots are useful for recovering damaged or missing files, because they track changes to files. However, those changes are usually only tracked on one filesystem, making it just as susceptible to single-site failures as a normal, non–snapshot-based system.

Archive Distribution

Most filesystem replication techniques rely on checkpointing (taking a point-in-time copy) of the master filesystem. All of the files that have changed since

---

[2] The actual Las Vegas magicians, not an eponymous pair of replicated or clustered systems.

the last copy are rolled into a package, which is sent across the network, and the changes are applied on the remote side. The simplest approach is to direct a built-in backup utility, such as Unix's dump, to create a file that contains an image of the entire filesystem, and copy that image to an empty filesystem of at least the same size on the destination server. If you're going to be taking these backups several times a day, you'll want to have multiple landing spots on the destination servers in case your copy process happens to crash in mid-stream, much as we discussed previously under periodic replication, leaving you with at least one good, albeit slightly out-of-date copy.

A completely safe way to work around the risk of a crash during the replication is to use tapes for the replicas, restoring the tapes at the remote site. For exceptionally large replication tasks, on the order of hundreds of gigabytes or terabytes that change every day, consider using tapes to alleviate network congestion and improve your remote restore bandwidth. To paraphrase the Andrew Tannenbaum quote we used at the start of Chapter 6, never underestimate the aggregate bandwidth of a station wagon carrying a load of tape cartridges to your disaster recovery site; with enough tape drives (and some fancy driving) you should be able to re-create the primary location at better than DS3 WAN speeds.

Another approach is to use cpio and tar in Unix or one of the many variations on zip utilities in Windows to create what's commonly called a zip- or tar-ball. This method isn't much different from a full backup, although some backup utilities are smart enough to do multiple passes on filesystems that might be changing while the dump is being taken. If you are modifying the filesystem while also making your tar archive, you run the risk of sending a corrupted or inconsistent replica to the slave servers. Unix's cpio utility, long overshadowed by its cousin tar, is especially useful for checkpointing because it allows you to provide a list of files via standard input that it should work on.

If you want to have consistent home-brew utilities for your Windows and Unix systems, consider a Unix-like shell package for Windows that will let you use find and other Unix staples. Remember, though, to hearken back to the key design principle about homegrown software; you can surely find commercial tools that are multiplatform and more stable over time than anything you'll write and support yourself.

A less efficient and less safe but inexpensive method is the use of remote access and copy scripts. In their simplest form, they amount to remote mounts of a filesystem via NFS or CIFS, followed by a script that copies selected files onto the local disk. Remote access has the single advantage of working across different operating systems so that you can access an MVS system and copy files from a Unix server to it, or use an NT filesystem share to copy files from an NT fileserver onto a VMS server for safekeeping.

The following are some risks of an archive-based replication approach:

- Failure during the copy or remote restore steps
- Distribution of a corrupted, inconsistent, or incomplete archive
- Orphaned files on the remote sites
- Running out of space to receive the updates on slave servers

Note, too, that NFS and CIFS are not particularly fast protocols, so you will probably not get the greatest possible performance out of this method.

Be aware that you need to think about hardware failure in the midst of a copy operation; how long does it take to recover the primary or replica systems and then restart or back out the copy and begin a new, clean take? You're creating manual intervention after a system failure. For a first pass at replication, and for many high-update environments, archive-level distribution works well because it's low-impact and easily tended to by the system administration staff.

Distribution Utilities

Somewhat more complex are distribution utilities like rdist and its secure cousin sdist that uses the ssh secure shell to create a secure wrapper around the data being transported. rdist is almost always built into Unix systems, and versions are publicly available (one is available from the Free Software Foundation's GNU web site at www.gnu.org) for consistency in options and configuration across multiple-vendor Unixes. By comparing the local and remote timestamps, rdist will only send files that require updating on the remote site, conserving network bandwidth and time. It also has limited error checking and a powerful, though amazingly complex configuration language, allowing you to specify replication at the filesystem, file tree, or subtree levels, or even down to the individual files that you need to keep synchronized.

In exchange for this flexibility, rdist is more complicated and can break in more colorful ways than a simple dump-and-restore process. You need to be wary of network outages (even temporary ones) that could cause rdist failure. File and directory permissions can also create problems for rdist, so it's best to carefully test configurations and replication by hand a few times before putting an rdist-based system into production.

Designed to work on local area networks, rdist doesn't incorporate encryption or any other security features to prevent unauthorized or unintentional exposure of data. Furthermore, it may not be the best tool to push files outside of your internal firewall to an external or DMZ-located web server. You can use sdist to wrap up the whole transfer in an ssh session so that outsiders can't see the file content, or you can use an FTP script to push files from inside the firewall to the outside. If you need to move complex packages of files, consider bundling up the FTP script using expect to script drive the command-line interactions with firewalls and remote authentication systems.

Tips and Tricks

What we've described are bulk-loading techniques that allow you to manually move all or part of a filesystem from one server to another one with a high degree of confidence that what you'll get on the other side is functional and essentially complete. The following are additional tips and tricks that should round out your arsenal of big filesystem slingshots:

- Read-only doesn't imply "never changes." Filesystems that are mounted read-only may change on the server side, and the client eventually has to realize that the data changed and has to reload its copies (which may have been cached for a long period of time). This means that NFS clients mounting read-only filesystems should not set arbitrarily long attribute cache timeouts, or they'll fail to notice the server-side changes.

- Versioning helps make sure you know what is where. When you're replicating web server content to 40 servers in 8 countries once an hour, there will be failures. At some point, you're going to have to intervene manually and decide what updates need to be propagated around the world to catch up with failed distributions. Having timestamp or timestamp and version number files included with distributions makes your life much easier.

- Checksum-generating tools like Tripwire help even further by verifying the integrity of what you've copied over. Get in the habit of putting a checksum in your distributions so that you can use it for timestamps, content integrity checking, and debugging purposes.

- Sparse files wreak havoc with utilities that read files block by block. A sparse file is an efficiently laid out file with intentional holes in it. Around the holes, blocks are allocated at random points in the file; the holes appear where no blocks have been allocated. These holes read back as zeros, and can cause a file-oriented copy to grow tremendously in size. Database applications, even NIS or NIS+ systems that use DBM files, tend to create sparse files. If you're using Perl scripts that create and maintain DBM database files, or other tools that create index files based on block numbers, you probably have sparse files around and should be especially careful when copying them. Improperly copying sparse files is a common cause of suddenly and unexpectedly running out of disk space.

- Large files are becoming commonplace, and all utilities should know how to handle a 6GB log file or a transaction log that's greater than the default 32-bit file size limit of 2GB. Make sure all file transport products can handle files larger than 2GB, or you'll find that you corrupt files and/or truncate them during the replication process, often with no error messages.

■ Be sensitive to the time frame for propagating file changes. Web content that's created hourly as a summarization of news items should be pushed at least hourly; if your web server is a Windows share client and caches files for 2 hours, it's going to miss one of those updates. Change management becomes more of an issue when you're dealing with complex software packages and supporting tools.

Software Distribution

We're going through this exhaustive discussion of filesystem replication and software distribution techniques because improperly replicating files will produce a client-side reliability issue: Clients that have the wrong versions of something, or that try to mix-and-match old and new versions, are invariably going to cause intermittent and vexing failures. Since these techniques tend to be manual ones, there is a greater tendency for error than in the lower-level and totally automated techniques we discussed previously.

Software distribution is a special case of filesystem replication because of the number of ways it can go wrong. At the basic level, there's nothing special you'd do for a software package or a set of developer libraries as opposed to taking an intraday checkpoint of a mail spool or a home directory. The following are a few more rules to live by:

■ Versioning of the entire package, including libraries, tools, header files, and intermediate object files, is critical. Once you've spent half a day convinced you have a bug in your code or in your compiler, only to find that you were mixing an old header with a newer library, you'll make sure you use versioning on every file that gets replicated. This requires that you maintain parts lists of the files that need to be kept together, at the appropriate revision numbers. Some shops just use consistent version numbering so that all files must have the same version number, regardless of their age or quantity of updates. List mastering is worth the effort if you're going to be copying all or part of that tree around your network.

■ Applications with local configuration requirements, such as printer lists or user authentication tables, need to be separated into the fully replicated parts and the locally managed pieces. If the package you're working with doesn't allow for easy separation of the custom and common components, consider using a shortcut or symbolic link to a nonreplicated area for custom files. Every distribution will have the same link, pointing to a per-machine area with local information in it. Devout

Unix *automounter* and *amd* users will find ways to build hierarchical mounts or multiple mount points that layer local information on top of the common base package.

■ Don't change binary images in-place. Make sure you do the distribution to a new directory, and then move the entire directory into place. Clients that were using the old binary will continue to do so until another reference opens the updated file. If you replace files on the fly, clients that are paging text (instructions) on demand from them may become confused and crash when the text pages change underneath them.

An example of software replication helps to illustrate these rules. Consider how you build up a directory in which local tools, libraries, manual pages, and other locally important files reside. The standard approach is to have one tools directory on a large file server that all clients share; changes are made to the file server, and all of the clients see them within a short window. Note that the quick-and-dirty method introduces a SPOF at the file server and isn't scalable for performance. If your client load is going to increase over time, you'll need to be able to crank up the horsepower of the tools directory server at the same time, and that means multiple copies of it, close to where its users are on the network.

The single tools directory also leaves you open to process weakness in change management. What if your latest software installation has a broken install script and trashes the tools directory? With replication and change management you have built processes to recover from internal corruption. Test a new or modified tool by building a new area within the shared directory, verifying operation using the master, and then pushing the replication to the slave servers.

Initiator-Based Type 4: Application-Based Replication

Database replication buys you protection against several disasters: corruption of your primary database, failure of an operational system when the MTTR is measured in seconds not minutes, and in some cases protection from a full-fledged physical disaster. Database replication can rely on variations of file distribution tricks, using log replay, built-in database features such as distributed transaction management, or third-party transaction processing and queuing systems that guarantee delivery of transactions to multiple database instances on multiple servers.

Log Replay

Database log replay is the simplest approach to database replication. Taking a page from the filesystem replication playbook, a database logs all changes to permanent structures, typically in an undo or redo log that is used for rolling the transaction forward in the event of a system failure. Log replay involves manually (or via a scheduled script) copying these log files to another machine, and then reapplying the transactions from the logs to the replica databases using the recovery manager, creating a similar copy of the primary database with some minor changes, including, but not limited to, timestamps and transaction IDs.

One concern with log-replay-style replication is that it is possible for some transactions to fall into the gutter between the primary and secondary database machines, if the primary crashes and takes its log files with it before the final transactions are copied from the log. If you replay the log file, then accept five new transactions in the primary database, then suffer a crash, those five transactions won't make it to the secondary server.

Another concern with log replay is that the database on the remote side is not, in fact, identical to the one on the primary side. As a result, it would be more difficult, and, in fact, probably impossible, to take an extract from it and apply that extract back to the primary side, in the event of data corruption. As we mentioned previously, timestamps and record identifiers are going to be different on the remote side. If it were necessary to copy the replicated database back to the primary database server, serious confusion and corruption will result.

However, database log replay is a relatively big win because it requires no application changes to implement replication. The database administrators can configure the log copy and recovery steps, setting the time interval between copies and the verification of updates on the replicated machines. Some applications are better suited to this technique than others. The following is a brief checklist of features that allow an application to fit the log replay model:

- *Applications that can easily detect missing transactions when connecting to a database for the first time and that know how to find the right starting point.* This is a critical consideration for stating that no changes are necessary to the application. If the application can look for transactions that fell into the gutter, then it will tolerate log replication well.

- *Low volumes of inserts and updates so that the log files do not grow rapidly.* Applications with high rates of change generate large log files and can induce a backlog on the replica database servers as they struggle to keep up.

- *Applications that can tolerate a small time skew between the live and redundant sites.* If the primary site goes down and the application has to reconnect to the redundant site, it may have to wait for several transactions to be played through the recovery manager before it can reconnect to the database. This delay is likely to be similar to the delay imposed by a failover.

In some cases, asking the user for verification of a missing transaction (resulting in a user query of the secondary database) is warranted or desired; this puts recovery with precision back into the hands of the end user and helps ensure the integrity of the data. In some cases, if a few minutes have gone by between the time of the original transaction and the time the redundant database is available, the user may no longer wish to resume the old transaction. One example is that of a trading floor, in which a user may choose to hold a trade that was not accepted by the primary database if the market has moved adversely during the recovery window. It's better to let the user make this call than to blindly apply the transaction under a different set of environmental conditions.

LOG-ROLLING COMPROMISE

At one trading institution, tensions arose between operations people running a trading system and businesspeople looking to real-time reporting of activity to help identify trades that went outside of acceptable risk levels. The operations crew felt that adding a risk management step would slow down trade reporting, possibly introducing some regulatory issues. How to get through the impasse? Log replication to the rescue! Logs from the trading system were copied to the risk management system, where they were used to insert transactions into the risk management database as if it was directly connected to the trading system. The trades were entered into risk management in real time, plus the log transfer interval of a few minutes, making everyone happy and eliminating a possible bottleneck on the trading system.

—Hal

Database Replication Managers

One step above database administrator–directed log transfers on the replication food chain are commercial database replication management products. Some, such as Oracle Replication Server, are offered as part of the database management system, and others, such as Quest SharePlex, are third-party products. To replicate databases, a database replication manager application walks through the log files and copies the transactions to one or more replica databases. Instead of relying on the recovery manager to roll the logs, the replication manager mimics an application performing the workload represented by the log files. The process that picks apart the log files and reconstructs the transaction is commonly called a *transfer manager,* and it can write to one or more target machines that have a local replay manager acting as a database application.

Replication is typically done asynchronously; that is, the log files are scanned by the manager after the transaction has already been applied to the primary system, and without any locking or checkpointing to ensure that the transfer manager and the primary application coordinate updates to all databases. As a result, it's possible for the transfer manager to be several transactions behind the primary application database, slowed by the time required to walk the logs and apply transactions to the secondary machines.

As with log replay, there are design considerations for database replication managers:

- The relationship between insert rate, update rate, and the log transfer manager's ability to extract transactions must be clearly understood. Under high insert and update conditions, does the transfer manager run into contention for access to the log files?

- The longest delay you'll see under extreme conditions must be known. One way to accomplish this is to watch the number of transactions that go into the log transfer manager queue. If you can only replicate 10 transactions a second but have insert peaks of 50 transactions a second, you'll push 40 transactions a second off into the transfer manager. You may end up with a delay of a few minutes while waiting for the replicated databases to absorb these load peaks.

- Some database replication managers can fail completely once the load exceeds a certain level. These solutions are not appropriate for large-scale operations with heavy-duty levels of transactions. Speak to your vendor and determine their rated limits for transaction throughput.

- What happens when the primary database fails? Does the transfer manager fail as well, requiring applications to do the "ask then restart" recovery outlined previously? If the transfer manager continues to apply updates, how can a client application determine when it's acceptable to connect to another copy of the database?

- When the primary returns to service, what happens to the log transfer manager? The secondary database (now acting as the primary) has probably reinserted all of the transactions that were entered into the queue in the transfer manager at the time of the primary failure. Should the transfer manager flush its queue? Should it remain quiescent until restarted by the database administrator?

As with all commercial tools, you should get better results using the commercial tool rather than building your own log transfer mechanism. Be sure to look for third-party tools that handle log transfers before you delve into log copying.

Initiator-Based Type 5: Transaction Processing Monitors

Transaction processing monitors (TPMs), now sometimes referred to as transactional middleware, are your best bet for hard, reliable database replication. They're also the slowest and hardest to implement, a trade-off you'd expect for a solid guarantee. You can use some distributed transaction features of some databases to accomplish the same results described in this section, with the same upsides and drawbacks.

Two-phase commit (see Figure 18.3) ensures that two databases are updated in a consistent manner transaction by transaction. The TPM, or resource manager, makes sure that both systems can proceed with the transaction, then it applies the transaction to each, verifies completion, and completes the higher-level transaction it is managing for the application. If either side fails to complete the transaction, the TPM can roll back the side that succeeded, aborting the transaction. TPMs do not require that the transactions be the same; they are commonly used to ensure that updates to multiple, different databases occur as a single transactional unit.

The problem with two-phase commit is that it's slow. The TPM has to coordinate with each database, and every intermediate transaction has to complete before the application is notified of a successful transaction. So what is the advantage? Recovery is no different than reconnecting to a single database. After all, the TPM was managing all updates in lockstep, so if the application sees the last transaction rolled back, it's been rolled back in all copies of the databases. You'll need to make sure your application uses the appropriate transaction interfaces supported by the TPM and databases, and this may require some application coding changes. You'll also need to make sure you can find the redundant copies of the database and reconnect the client application quickly.

1. You ready?
3. I'm ready
   5. Commit
7. Done

Resource Manager

2. You ready?
   4. I'm ready
6. Commit
   8. Done

Figure 18.3   Two-phase commit.

So how does having a redundant, live copy of the database allow for predictable failover times? The trick is moving the point of control from the system administration domain, where systems monitor each other for failure or signs of failure, to the application domain, where the application itself or the transaction processing monitor drives recovery via a timeout or dead man timer.[3] Let's say you want less than 10 seconds of downtime for any transaction. After submitting the transaction, set a timer for 8 seconds; if the timer expires, then you can forcibly abort the transaction, apply it to the secondary system only, and proactively declare the primary system dead. Of course, you may want your application to begin queuing updates for the primary, or to note that the primary fell behind at a certain time so that it can be recovered later. Many TPM systems allow dead man timers to be set by the resource manager coordinating the transactions, proactively alerting applications if the entire set of updates cannot be performed within the desired time window.

What do you do if you can't trade off insert and update performance for fast failover times? Look for an intermediate solution that guarantees transactional integrity but allows for asynchronous updates to the replica systems. So-called asynchronous, or reliable, queuing mixes the best of the TPM and log replication models.

Queuing Systems

Most transaction processing monitors operate in a bulletin board, or memory-based mode. Transactions that are in-flight are posted to the bulletin board until they are committed to all systems. Recovering a bulletin board system is similar to recovering a database; the log of applied transactions results in roll-forwards or rollbacks to bring the transaction monitor into a state of consistency with the databases it is front-ending. A reliable queue, or transactional queue, uses disk-based transaction waiting areas to ensure that no transaction accepted by the queue is ever lost. Reliable queues that allow transactions to be inserted and processed later are known as *store-and-forward queues* or *asynchronous queues*.

Examples of reliable queuing systems include the IBM/Transarc Encina RQS, IBM's MQ Series, Microsoft's MSMQ, and BEA's Tuxedo/Q and MessageQ products. There are other commercial products that perform some of the store-and-forward distribution of messages but lack strong recovery or replication features. Use the design rules and requirements in this chapter to help guide you through product selection; you may not need all of the transactional recovery if you handle corner cases in your application.

---

[3] A dead man timer is a mechanism where any sign of activity from a system resets the timer. When no activity occurs, the timer counts, and when it reaches its expiration point, it acts as though the nonresponding system has failed.

Applications can send their transactions into the queue and then continue with other tasks, safe in the knowledge that the queue manager will forward the transactions on to their next destination. Generally, it's a bit faster to insert a transaction into a queue than into the whole database, because there's no data manipulation work involved in the queue. The transaction is copied to disk and logged, and the writing application is free to continue. The queue manager then forwards the transaction on, possibly replicating it to other queues on multiple machines, or doing the replication in-place by replaying the transaction across several machines before removing it. Queues allow transactions to be routed, merged, and distributed without impacting the application, provided the application can handle asynchronous notification of transaction completion or failure, and that the application is "pipelined" enough to benefit from asynchronous operation.

WEDDED ASYNCHRONY

When talking about asynchronous queuing systems, I often point out that they work best in optimistic designs—that is, in cases where you try to cover the average case instead of the oddball but serious failure mode. After I used the term in a conversation, a customer asked me, "What do you mean by asynchronous but optimistic transactional systems?" It's a model that was popularized inside of Sun by Alfred Chuang (who went on to become the A in BEA Systems), but the examples seemed particular to Sun and computer sales operations. Here's the example I used to explain asynchronous operation:

Consider how you and your spouse manage your checkbook. In a synchronous world, you would write checks together, go to the ATM together, and even balance the checkbook register together in a true fit of marital bliss. This model is impractical because it assumes you're physically together and in total agreement for every single financial transaction. In real life, you operate asynchronously; you each visit the ATM separately and write your own checks, confident that your spouse won't suddenly withdraw 99 percent of your available funds and head for Las Vegas.

Your ability to handle your own slice of the financials is the asynchronous part; the assurance that most transactions don't produce exceptions is the optimistic part; the monthly discussion over who gets to sort through receipts and checks to balance the checkbook and produce the truth is the transactional part. Eventually, all assumptions are cleared and exceptions processed, and you're back running asynchronously again.

—Hal

   Applications that can operate optimistically while recovering an asynchronous queue are ideal. It's possible to execute ahead, with the optimistic assumption that transactions in the queue won't interfere with or invalidate transactions being currently processed. As the queue of transactions is applied, those assumptions are tested and any exception conditions are handled, allowing the system to continue functioning even while it performs recovery. This is vaguely similar to a disk mirroring system that does disk rebuild after hot-spare replacement on the fly. The system makes the optimistic assumption that you won't suffer another failure while it is copying data onto the new disk, and it allows the mirror repair to proceed asynchronously with respect to the other disk activity that is generating independent I/O operations.

   Be careful not to leave single points of failure when designing with queues. If you leave the receiving queue on the same machine as your primary database, but have the queue write to two intermediate queues on other machines, you're exposed if one of the intermediate machines crashes and leaves the queue inactive during the downtime. See Figure 18.4 for an example of two databases that populate an intermediate queue used to replicate the transaction stream into two disparate databases. If the intermediate node fails without any redundancy, transactions in the queue are left in limbo until the node is repaired. When using asynchronous queues, keep the queues close to the databases that they're responsible for updating so that they fail and recover consistently with the database servers.

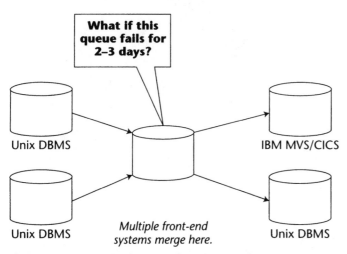

Figure 18.4   Two databases with an intermediate queue.

Other Thoughts on Replication

In the remaining portion of this chapter, we discuss some other thoughts and issues relative to replication.

SANs: Another Way to Replicate

In Chapter 8, we discussed SANs. One of the characteristics of SANs is that they allow data and disks to be shared over moderate to long distances. If your data centers are located on the same SAN, then you achieve the results of replication without having to introduce the accompanying complexity.

In Figure 18.5, we show a model where two hosts that are located on opposite sides of a SAN, each connected to a local set of disks that is mirrored to the other host, achieve the same basic goal of replication; their data is copied to a remote location where it is protected in the event that something happens to the primary site.

As SANs mature and become less complex and more reliable, this alternative to replication will become more prevalent and will likely replace replication for short-haul work of this nature.

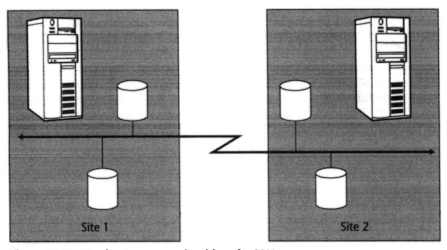

Figure 18.5 Two hosts on opposite sides of a SAN.

There are two big advantages to this sort of remote disk sharing. The first is that the data on both sides of the SAN is always kept in sync; data is not delayed the way it can be in asynchronous replication. Another advantage is in clustering. By clustering nodes on opposite ends of a SAN, you can get the best of both worlds: You can treat the nodes as a local cluster, while still having the additional protection that only a separation between nodes can provide.

More than One Destination

Standard replication solutions are perfectly reasonable methods to enable the extra cautious to send their data to more than one site. Some replication solutions will permit a single site to branch out and replicate to multiple sites in parallel, while others require daisy chaining equipment and sites.

In the parallel model, as shown in Figure 18.6, data comes in to Sheboygan (Wisconsin), it is simultaneously sent out to destination sites in Walla Walla (Washington), Wollongong (Australia), Ypsilanti (Michigan), Weehawken (New Jersey), and Addis Ababa (Ethiopia). As the data reaches the master server in Sheboygan, the data is replicated synchronously to some of the closer sites and asynchronously to sites that are farther away. This model can be very quick and will help ensure that your data is adequately protected. However, the complexity that we left out of Figure 18.6 (and have shown in Figure 18.7) is that you need to interconnect all of the sites, so that if it becomes necessary to migrate operations from Sheboygan to, say, Ypsilanti, Ypsilanti still needs to continue replicating data to all of the surviving sites. In fact, all sites need to be able to communicate with each other. As more sites come online, it becomes necessary to add network links from all existing sites to the new site. Even though, as we said, this will ensure a high level of data protection and availability, it will also ensure a high level of cost, as networks can be very expensive, especially when run over long distances.

Figure 18.6 Parallel replication to multiple sites (simple version).

Figure 18.7 Parallel replication to multiple sites (complex version).

In the daisy-chained model, as shown in Figure 18.8, data is replicated from the main site in Kalamazoo (Michigan) to Bird-in-Hand (Pennsylvania), which then sends it to Hoboken (New Jersey). Hoboken receives the data and sends it to Leighton Buzzard (Great Britain). The advantage in the daisy-chained model is that each site need only be able to communicate with the sites before and after it in the chain. (Of course, then each site and network link become single points of failure for the entire operation; it might be better to link each site to three or four others.) The disadvantage is in the performance. As you move away from the master, each site will each be a greater number of transactions behind the master, and so of less value to take over should something happen to the master.

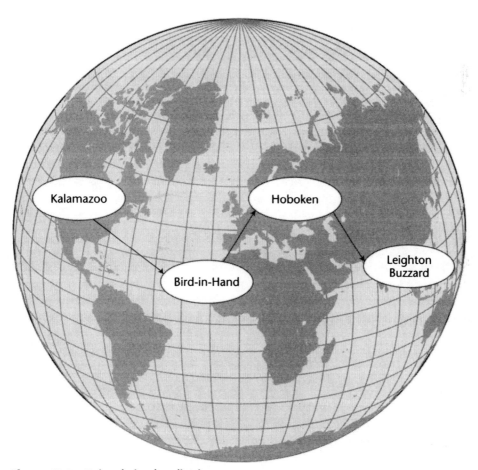

Figure 18.8   Daisy-chained replication.

Remote Application Failover

When data is replicated to a remote site, that simply means that the data is there, but for most situations, the data alone is not sufficient. If replication is done properly, then the application executables and configuration files are there as well. But even that does not ensure that the applications will start themselves automatically during a disaster recovery. In order for applications to automatically start themselves at the DR site, some additional software is required that can do the following:

1. Figure out that the main site has gone away.

2. Tell the replication software to promote the DR site, making it the new replication master.

3. Automatically bring the key resources online.

4. Start the critical applications at the DR site.

It is important that any software that might make these decisions for you require some sort of minor human intervention. It would be inappropriate for software to make the decision to migrate operations to your DR site all by itself. In the unlikely event that the software mistakenly decides that a site-to-site failover is required, the result will be a very expensive error, as well as unplanned and planned (as you move operations back) episodes of downtime.

Remote application failover can reduce recovery time after a disaster, especially if your DR site is normally unmanned. Applications will begin to come back online in minutes, regardless of how long it might take for system administrative staff to physically reach the DR site.

Another important aspect of remote application failover is in the networking. Most of the time, the DR site is on a different subnet than is the primary site. Even if applications are brought up on the remote side, client systems on the Internet or at other company facilities will not be able to find them if they are on different subnets. Any application that you use to failover applications to a new subnet must be able to tell clients of the change. Later releases of the Domain Name Service (DNS) allow you to create an alternate list of IP addresses that it knows about but does not make active until it receives a signal from another application. This feature is a very important one to make sure that automated failover to a remote site can be successful.

VERITAS and Legato both have applications that can automate remote application failover, as do some of the system vendors.

Key Points

- When you are evaluating replication tools, you have many choices. Before you start, understand all the choices so that you can make the right decision the first time.

- If the two replication sites can be on the same SAN, that is the best approach.

- To maximize data integrity, but with the greatest impact on performance, use synchronous replication. To minimize the impact on performance, but with a reduction in data integrity, use asynchronous replication.

- Software-based replication is often more flexible, faster, and less expensive than the more prevalent hardware-based replication.

CHAPTER

19

Virtual Machines and Resource Management

What is real? How do you define real? If you're talking about what you can feel, what you can smell, what you can taste and see, then real is simply electrical signals interpreted by your brain.

—Morpheus, in *The Matrix*

As systems have become larger in terms of memory, CPU, and I/O channel counts, there has been a corresponding trend to subdivide these big boxes into smaller, more flexible units for management. Each of these subdivisions looks and feels like a standalone system, but because they're carved from a larger box, they are virtual machines. Virtual machines (VMs) are not a new technology. They go back to the earliest days of mainframe computing. In fact, the VM in the name of IBM's old mainframe operating system stood for Virtual Machines. After falling into disrepute for many years, painted with the mainframe brush, virtual machines have begun to make a comeback.

From an availability perspective, we're near the top of the Availability Index, at Level 9 as shown in Figure 19.1. Your availability return on investment is lower than for more fundamental redundancy planning such as backups and clustering, but virtualization and resource management will yield availability improvements in terms of predictability.

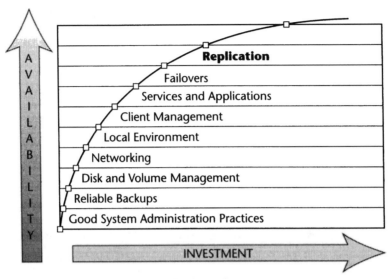

Figure 19.1   Level 9 of the Availability Index.

In this brief chapter, we look at three abstraction levels for machines:

- Systems divided into independent partitions
- Multiple virtual copies of the operating system within a single virtual (or real) system
- Scheduling of resources within a single system to control predictability and ensure service level agreements

This chapter isn't meant to be a full tutorial in the configuration aspects of each topic. Rather, we want to relate the issues of resource management to making systems predictable. Going back to our definition of availability as making sure users can get their jobs done, virtualization of machine resources and allocation of those resources to tasks aids in availability planning by offering the ability to cap user-visible latency.

Partitions and Domains: System-Level VMs

Whether you call them domains, partitions, or logical partitions (LPARs in mainframe parlance), the first level of VM abstraction is to subdivide a large server into several smaller virtual servers. There's no hardware effect in this subdivision; it's all done via software that reroutes the logical connections of the backplane. This soft cabling allocates hardware system resources to create multiple, independent machine instances. Each domain or partition runs its own copy of the operating system, can be booted or crash independently, and has its own complete view of the network, IP addresses, memory, CPU, scheduling, and all other functions controlled by the OS.

One of the advantages of domains is that you can shuffle resources between them, in many cases while the system is running. Have a large workload that needs another four processors? Borrow them from the QA domain, run the job to completion, then put the processors back into the degraded QA domain for normal operation. Dynamic reconfiguration of hardware involves draining CPU and memory boards of data, then detaching and reattaching them to appropriate domains. This hardware-level VM capability is frequently controlled by a console or command-line function available to a privileged user only.

VMs can be created, destroyed, and reallocated very quickly and easily under software control. One of the most common uses for software VMs (such as VMware, www.vmware.com) is to allow a user to run more than one operating system on a PC or workstation. Once the host software has been installed on the physical system, it can be used to create new virtual machines, each one of which could run a different operating system. A sophisticated user or administrator could choose to run Windows XP, Windows 2000, Windows NT, Solaris for Intel, Red Hat Linux, and SuSe Linux at the same time on six virtual machines on the same Intel-based computer.

As with any technology that touches system resources, there are good and bad aspects of partitions and domains in the reliability engineering world:

Good.   Running multiple environments on the same box. Separate environments for each stage of the deployment lifecycle were highlighted in Chapter 5, "20 Key High Availability Design Principles" (Rule #9). To many managers, that means separate boxes with increased footprint, increased physical management woes, and more cost. Combining environments in the same physical server, using partitions to slice it into production, QA, and development environments, gives you a lifecycle in a box. They're isolated, as if they were on separate servers, but with the advantage of running inside a single box.

Bad.   When the big box fails, so do all of the partitions. As we observed way back in Chapter 2, "What to Measure," hardware is a relatively rare cause of system downtime; system problems are usually software related. But when the partitioned box fails, all of its partitions fail with it unless the failure can be constrained to a single domain of resources that is logically isolated from other domains.

Neutral.   You can failover from one domain to another one. By failing over from one virtual machine to another inside the same physical computer, you can recover from non-hardware system failures without having to incur the expense of additional hardware.

Good.   Those different environments might be at different revisions of the operating system or at different patch levels, or contain different product releases of your application. Think of partitions as offering a sort of double buffering for change management and release management.

Bad, at times.   Let's say you're running a large database application in one partition. You want to drain memory and CPU resources out of this domain for another slice of the server that has become too slow. However, the full-blown database is using 500MB of shared memory, which can't be drained, and it requires another 500MB of memory for process images. You may not be able to resize domains as small as you want if they're running resource intense applications.

Below the abstraction level of an entire server, we can virtualize at the operating system level.

Containers and Jails: OS Level VMs

There are times you want to create multiple, independent execution environments within a single operating system instance: to create multiple virtual domains for web hosting, to isolate applications with varying security requirements, to corral an application that needs significant OS-level configuration, and to provide a restricted environment for applications that are running in a nontrusted or semitrusted mode. Some of the more common implementations of OS level VMs, known as containers or jails, are Solaris containers, HP's vPar virtual partitions, and the use of `chroot()` jails in the Linux space (do a `google.com` search on Linux jails for a gaggle of articles on their creation and management). On a finer-grain level, there's also the Java Virtual Machine (JVM), which abstracts the hardware, operating system, and network resources of a system into a controlled execution environment, providing security controls and exception handling.

You can run multiple containers inside of one operating system. In the `chroot()` (change root) case, the jail is a top-level process that runs with a specified directory as the root directory for the filesystem tree seen by that process. Within this filesystem view, you create (or copy) device files, libraries, executable images, and necessary support files, but nothing else. The process running inside of the jail sees a slimmed-down view of the world, without the ability to see anything outside or above the jail. `chroot()` jails are used most commonly for FTP servers, both to restrict the filesystem areas seen by FTP users and to minimize the number of executables that can be run from within an FTP session. This partitioning of filesystem and executable resources is also useful for web servers, where each web server image supports a different domain; by putting each web server into its own jail, you can prevent them from interfering with each other from an HTML and CGI file perspective.

What's the availability benefit profile of containers?

Good.   Limited view of the system means limited risk. What you take away can't be used as a vector for a security incident, so containers improve availability through simplicity.

Bad.   All of the containers run inside of a single OS image. If the parent OS panics, then the containers go with it. Compared to system-level partitions, where each partition runs its own OS instance, containers provide less protection from operating system failures.

Good.   Processes are isolated. Code that tends to behave badly in terms of needing its own view of the filesystem, or writing to log files that would normally be shared by other processes, can be run in separate containers without the developer having to create multiple operating system configurations.

Neutral.   Containers do not govern execution of the processes inside. If you're running 10 containers inside of your operating system but want to ensure that none of them consumes more than 10 percent of the system's memory or uses more than 20 percent of the CPU, you need to implement resource management in conjunction with containers.

Resource Management

Resource management isn't thought of as a canonical part of availability; however, it's essential for providing predictability in quality of service. There are several knobs to turn in the resource management domain:

Process scheduling.   Normally the Unix scheduler tries to allocate CPU cycles evenly, giving priority to processes that were waiting for I/O to complete. The default behavior isn't ideal if you want to skew scheduling in favor of critical, user-visible processes or push various housekeeping tasks into the background. In addition to the default round-robin scheduler, many vendors offer a fair share scheduler that allows you to create classes of processes and CPU (and memory) allocations for each class. There are also batch schedulers that take specified processes and only run them when the system is otherwise idle.

Bandwidth management and allocation.   We looked at the end-to-end networking problem in Chapter 9, "Networking"; if your packets aren't making it from application to database server or from client to web server, you have a perceived availability problem. When you are dealing with congested networks, or looking to enforce a minimum quality of service, bandwidth management is a tool that carves out slots for traffic.

Job scheduler.   Process scheduling handles tasks that are already running; a job scheduler sequences tasks to ensure they run in the correct order. From an availability perspective, job scheduling is a critical tool to prevent memory thrashing. If you're going to run several large processes that will each use, for example, 75 percent of your system's memory, don't run them in parallel. The CPU scheduler will keep them all running with equitable slices of processor time, but you'll spend most of your life waiting for memory to be paged in or swapped in because the large processes are thrashing the system. Sequencing large jobs eliminates resource contention.

Resource management.   This is fine-grain, explicit control over CPU and memory allocation to a process or group of processes. Resource management subsumes fair share scheduling by adding a memory high-water mark and memory/CPU usage policies to the basic process prioritization scheme.

What do you use to improve system availability and response time? Depending upon the types of processes you're running, and your requirements for response time and predictability, probably some combination of all of these virtualization techniques. Figure 19.2 shows how the different control points work together.

A database server and database application share one OS image, which is run inside of a system domain with its own dedicated CPU, I/O, and memory resources. To ensure that the database application takes precedence over other jobs, resource management is used to set policy, as well as to prevent the DB application from suffocating the DB server if it experiences a memory leak. Large jobs are mapped into a second domain, running its own copy of the OS, with explicit job scheduling to prevent thrashing of the resources mapped to this second OS instance. On the left-hand side, multiple web servers are placed into their own containers to isolate them for security purposes. Then those three containers are placed into a single OS image that runs in a third domain.

Where are the availability benefits?

Good.   Controlled execution of processes prevents thrashing and allows you to gain better control over quality of service delivery. Moving resources between system-level domains also lets you apply horsepower where and when it's needed without shuffling processes and configurations between separate servers.

Bad.   There's no explicit redundancy created with any of the virtual machine technologies, although improved response time and predictability mean fewer false negatives reported by users.

Good.   Resource contention can lead to application or system hangs, or excessive network loading. Explicit execution control reduces the probability of availability problems caused by a badly behaved application.

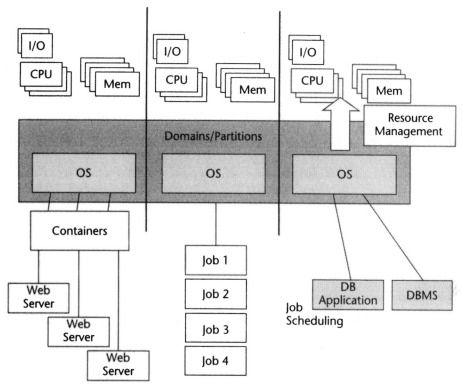

Figure 19.2   Composition of control points.

Key Points

- Partitioning and control of resources provides another axis for controlling predictability.
- Applications that may cause availability problems through excessive resource consumption or configuration complexity benefit from resource management and operating system containers.

The Disaster Recovery Plan

It's the end of the world as we know it, and I feel fine.
—Michael Stipe (R.E.M.)

There is so much to say about disaster recovery (DR) that we could surely write an entire book on the subject. Needless to say, we have not chosen to do so. Instead, we have elected to offer an overview about many of the topics that must be considered for a complex enterprise to survive a disaster. For our purposes, a disaster is an event that knocks an entire facility offline.

Back in Chapter 3, "The Value of Availability," we introduced the concept of the outage lifecycle timeline, and we used it to demonstrate how the right level of protection can allow an enterprise to reduce the effects of an outage to a tolerable level. It is important to note here that the timeline and all of its characteristics hold just as well for a disaster as they do for a local outage, such as a disk failure. We made the point then, and we make it once again: A disaster is no different from other kinds of outages, except that the disaster takes the outage's effects and spreads them over a wider area, and applies them to more components.

Our entry into the realm of DR brings us to the top level, Level 10, of the Availability Index, as shown in Figure 20.1. This discussion continues into Chapter 21, "A Resilient Enterprise," where we take a look at a most remarkable story: the real-life story of the New York Board of Trade, and their experiences on September 11, 2001, when their building, adjacent to the World Trade Center towers in New York, was destroyed, and they were able to resume trading less than 12 hours later.

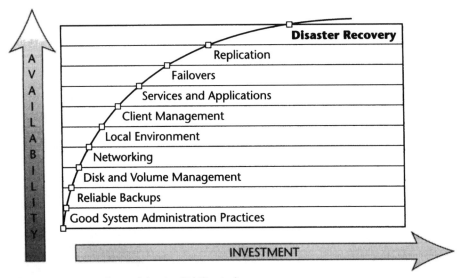

Figure 20.1 Level 10 of the Availability Index.

In this chapter, we look at developing a disaster recovery plan. The goal is to give our readers a starting point from which to launch a full-fledged disaster recovery program. We do not pretend to include every single element that you might need in your plan. Instead, we hope to give an overview that includes many of the most important points to hit and the elements to include in your plan. Much of the chapter is written in lists, giving you a starting point to create your own DR checklists. Once we finish developing the plan, we discuss testing and exercising the plan, and then we wrap up with a look at how disasters can affect people. As with the rest of this book, our emphasis in this chapter is on technology rather than management or business operations.

Should You Worry about DR?

As we have been saying since the start of the book, as an enterprise moves through the different levels of the Availability Index, they incur ever-increasing costs, as they attempt to keep their systems operational despite all sorts of outages.

Now that we have reached the top level of the chart, it is worth pointing out we've lost most enterprises by now. Not a lot of organizations, especially smaller ones, can afford the level of protection that a full-blown DR plan provides.

Nevertheless, any organization could be struck by a disaster. Those who decide that they cannot afford a full DR plan have made another decision, either directly or implicitly. That second decision says that in the event of a disaster, if there is no alternative, the organization will close up shop and send its people home. They have decided that the cost of implementing a DR plan is not worth it, and it is more sensible and makes more economic sense for the business to simply shut down if a disaster occurs.

This can, in fact, be a most sensible and rational business decision. There are plenty of businesses whose business model simply cannot justify the expense of a DR plan. It can be extremely expensive to find and obtain real estate for a DR site, and then to stock it with equipment and invest in the manpower that is required to operate the site.

Unfortunately, there is a third class of organization who have not decided anything and simply have not gotten around to developing a DR plan. Those organizations must make the decision: What do we do if a disaster strikes? Can we afford to develop, test, and implement a plan, or do we just give up and go home? Every organization must make this decision. We cannot tell you which way to go, only that the decision must be made. Otherwise, it could be made for you, and you may not like the outcome.

Three Primary Goals of a DR Plan

Before you can put together a disaster recovery plan, it's important to understand why you are taking the time and effort to put the plan together in the first place. What are the main goals of a DR plan?

Before September 11, 2001, a large number of organizations would say that they put their plan together to make sure that their business survives a disaster. Since September 11, some new and improved priorities have begun to sneak into many organizations' plans that have given us the following goals, which are generally considered in the order shown here.

Health and Protection of the Employees

Employers have recognized that without their employees, they don't have a business. The companies at the World Trade Center in New York who lost large percentages of their employees on September 11, 2001, found that even though they were able to recover most or all of their computer data, they were utterly devastated and demoralized by the human loss. The emotional loss and stress experienced by the survivors, who had lost dozens and even hundreds of friends and colleagues, were something that nobody expected or could possibly have been prepared for. Corporate knowledge and experience that was never written down was lost and had to be rediscovered. Beyond that is the moral obligation that some businesses feel to protect the people who have chosen to work for them. As a result, enterprises are changing their priorities to increase the value of the individuals who make up their employee base.

The Survival of the Enterprise

Like a living, evolving organism, the ultimate goal of an enterprise is to survive, grow, and continue into the future. All of the principles that we have discussed throughout this book for protecting data and computer systems go a long way to ensuring that survival. Ultimately, public companies have an obligation to their shareholders, private companies have an obligation to their owners, government entities have an obligation to their citizenry, and educational institutions have an obligation to their students and faculty to carry on, and to continue providing the services that their customers are accustomed to receiving and paying for.

The Continuity of the Enterprise

Beyond just survival, an organization needs continuity through a disaster. It needs to be able to pick up where it left off before the disaster as quickly and seamlessly as possible and to carry on. An enterprise's survival is, of course, a prerequisite for continuity, but in order for the survived business to be worth maintaining, it must be able to get back to its normal work, under conditions that are acceptably close to normal as soon as possible. Failure to do so will put the future of the enterprise itself at risk.

What Goes into a Good DR Plan

Many things combine to make a DR plan into a good DR plan. Each of them requires attention to detail and thorough verification. Ultimately, the DR plan is a complete collection of the information and procedures that are required to recover the systems and procedures that make an enterprise successful. The following are some of the critical elements in a good plan:

Documentation and prioritization.   Identify the essential hardware, software, networking, and other elements that are required for everything to come up at the DR site.

Selection of the DR site.   There are many criteria that go into the selection of a DR site. Choosing the wrong one could leave you unable to get to the site in an emergency or with a site that is rendered unusable by the same disaster that took out the primary site.

Identification of the key people and their backups.   Which people are critical for the success of your DR efforts? What if those people are not available at the time of the disaster? Who can take their place?

Creation and training of recovery teams.   It is not appropriate for DR responsibilities to lie with individual people, as those people may not be available when they are needed. Responsibilities should instead rest with small teams of people, any of whom can do all of the jobs for which the team is responsible. This may require training, but that training is critical for the success for any DR efforts.

Development and implementation of tests and exercises of the plan. An untested plan is just a piece of paper. Any plan, especially one on whose back the survival of the enterprise relies, must be thoroughly and regularly tested. All parties must be confident that the test, in its current form, will work, and that the enterprise will survive and continue after a disaster strikes.

Constant revisiting of the plan.   Are newly added systems included in the plan? Do they get backed up? Is their data replicated? Who is responsible for the recovery of these systems at the DR site? What happens when primary people leave the company? Does the plan get updated to reflect personnel changes?

Preparing to Build the DR Plan

The steps that we outline in this section are arranged in a logical order that may vary slightly in different enterprises. We cannot be much more specific than that because every enterprise will have different priorities that must be taken into account in preparing to build a DR plan. What's more, many of these steps can, and should, be performed in parallel.

1. *Identify the Recovery Coordinator and a backup.* Ultimate responsibility for the success of the recovery will fall to a single person. That person should not be doing all the work during the recovery, but rather should do the bulk of his work before the disaster. His responsibility is the development and maintenance of the plan, and overseeing the ongoing implementation of that plan. He should control the DR budget and make sure that anyone who needs training or other resources gets those resources in a timely manner. When it comes time to exercise the test, that responsibility ultimately falls to the coordinator too. His responsibilities will reach across most, if not all, of the critical departments in the organization, and so he must be a bit of a diplomat on top of everything else. He should work closely with a designated backup person so

that, once again, if something happens to the coordinator, all of his efforts are not lost.

2. *Identify and prioritize business functions.* It is impossible for all functions within an organization to receive the same degree of attention and priority during and after a disaster. The time to decide which functions are the most important is during the development of the plan. It is vital that all affected managers sign off on this prioritization, and that when personnel changes occur, new managers sign off anew. Among the items that need to be identified and prioritized are the following:

- *Business units and their functions.* Every organization has business units that are more and less critical to daily operations. Priorities may be determined by simple contribution to the corporate bottom line, by the amount of time the business unit can stand to be down, by the amount of time it takes to restore the business unit to service, or by some other internal measurement. All units should be prioritized so that the limited number of hands that will likely be available after a disaster to restore them know exactly what to do, and in what order.

- *Workgroups and their functions.* Within each business unit are workgroups, and they must also be prioritized if they have their own systems, data, and applications that must be restored. The same logic that went into prioritizing business units may apply, or some other business-unit–specific logic may make more sense.

- *Order of server restoration.* Within the workgroups, some applications are going to be more important than others. Many organizations, for example, run on email. If the Microsoft Exchange, Lotus Notes, or sendmail servers are down, nothing can get done at all. While other systems, such as an old VMS server, may hold older and less important data, or archived data that the workgroup could live without for months. Any prioritization should go down as far as the individual systems and applications.

- *Critical documentation.* Within each workgroup function, there are books, papers, manuals, and other printed matter that are a fundamental part of day-to-day operations. If that material (online or offline) is not duplicated and maintained up-to-date, at the DR site, work could be disrupted.

MY UNIT HEAD CAN BEAT UP YOUR UNIT HEAD

Although I have never heard of an actual case, it is very easy for me to imagine a situation where all of the affected unit heads have not signed off on a list of recovery priorities. After a disaster occurs, managers and employees will be coping with levels of stress that they may have never encountered in their entire lives, and under these conditions, individual behavior cannot be predicted. Usually calm and rational people may suddenly be given to huge temper fits, punctuated with physical violence. (Of course, there are many stories of people who become amazingly helpful in the wake of a true disaster, too. It is very difficult to predict an individual's behavior when she is in a situation with never-before-experienced levels of stress.)

With this in mind, I have often imagined the scenario where a pair of particularly stressed out unit heads decide that each of their organizations is the more important one and should be restored first. It is easy to imagine that such a situation could come to blows.

By recording unit priorities in the DR plan with the appropriate (and up-to-date) signoffs, you can help reduce the likelihood that resident hotheads won't beat the stuffing out of each other in the middle of the DR site's data center during a recovery, but there are no guarantees. Just stay low, and give them plenty of room.

—Evan

3. *Identify a DR site.* One of the fundamental decisions that must be made in putting together a DR plan is where the DR effort will take place. Exactly what location and what kind of facility will you use for your disaster recovery? We discuss this topic in more detail later in this chapter.

4. *Estimate time to recover.* The only way to estimate when the first systems will return to service is to have an idea of how long critical restoration steps will take. It is very important to know, for example, how long it will take to:

   ■ Get critical people to the DR site to begin the recovery process.

   ■ Locate the most current version of the DR plan document.

- Locate and deliver off-site backup tapes to the DR site.
- Rebuild the backup indices from hundreds or thousands of tapes.
- Restore data from backup tapes (if that's how the data is to be recovered).
- Start up critical applications at the DR site.
- Propagate network changes to the user community so that they can find the DR site on the network.

5. *Develop a methodology for off-site storage.* How will data be protected from a disaster at the primary site? How will it get to the DR site? Will it be carried on tape? Will tapes be duplicated across a network? Where will tapes be stored? How will they physically make it to the DR site in the event of a disaster? Will data be replicated? Asynchronously or synchronously? Will different applications be treated differently? (Almost certainly . . .) How?

6. *Build phone lists.* Who needs to know what's going on? Who needs to know that they must change what they do in direct response to the crisis that is in progress? What managers and executives must be notified? How does word that a disaster has been declared find its way into the organization? The best way is through a telephone chain, where all critical people have a copy of the list and are responsible for calling the next people down the list until they find a real person who can carry the message forward. Phone lists should include all phone numbers where these people may be: home numbers, work numbers, and mobile numbers should all be part of the list. In some organizations, alternate contacts, such as spouses or children, may also be listed; if there is difficulty reaching a critical employee, perhaps someone else knows where he is.

7. *Develop a distribution model for plan documents.* Conventional wisdom on plan distribution once said that copies of the plan should be everywhere. That wisdom is being challenged more and more. Plans contain a great deal of confidential information. In the preceding item, we endorsed including home phone numbers of company executives. In upcoming items, we recommend including passwords and critical bits of information like account numbers. While this data is critically important in a disaster, if it falls into the wrong hands, it can create a disaster all by itself. We explore this topic in some more detail later in this chapter.

8. *Identify and train company spokespersons.* Who will represent the company to the press, and to employees? If your organization is large enough to have a public relations department, those people are usually the best for being a liaison with the press, but if you don't have such a

group, then someone in the organization needs to take on that role. In a disaster that is localized to your organization, and even in some that are not, you will likely have to field calls from the press; all calls should be directed to the right person, who has been properly trained. Otherwise, incorrect or counterproductive messages can get out. Someone else must be identified who will be the voice of the company to your employees. The best person for that role is often the CEO, or perhaps the chairman of the board; someone who employees trust and respect, and whose word carries some weight. Her goodwill must be employed to make the employees feel comfortable about their company and their jobs after the disaster.

9. *Create and staff recovery teams.* Recovery teams should include the people who know their areas the best, without regard for ego, but rather with regard for appropriately speedy recovery from the disaster. Your organization may need more recovery teams than we have suggested, or you may find that some of the teams that we have identified are not appropriate. At a minimum, team leaders for each appropriate group must be identified, and their management as well as the individuals themselves must agree to the selections. Once the team leaders are in place, then the rest of the teams must be staffed; the responsibility for team staffing usually falls to the team leaders. It is inappropriate for any one individual to be an active member of more than one recovery team.

The following are the 12 recovery teams that we have identified:

Disaster Management Team. This group oversees and coordinates the entire DR effort. The recovery coordinator will likely head this team, which should be staffed by representatives from all key business and operations areas around the company. During a recovery, all of the other recovery teams will report in to this team on a regular basis.

Communications Team. This group includes representatives from the public relations group, if one exists, and is responsible for all communications with executive and upper management, the press, FEMA, the police, the employees and their families, and any other organizations that wish to speak with yours. Any communication requests that come in to other parts of the company must be redirected to this recovery team.

Computer Recovery Teams. These teams work together and separately to restore all of the computer-related functions in an organization, after a disaster. An organization may have more or fewer teams, combining some and eliminating others. These teams will work very closely together throughout the recovery to make sure that, in the end, all systems, networks, storage, applications, and data are restored.

System Recovery Team.   This team will be broken into several sub-teams, one for each system platform found across the organization. A typical modern organization might have a Windows team, a Solaris team, an HP-UX team, and a mainframe team. There should be a single leader to whom all system recovery teams report. This team's goal is to get all critical systems back online after a disaster.

Network Recovery Team.   This group is responsible for getting the LANs and WANs, and all of the associated equipment (routers, switches, hubs, etc.) back online at the DR site.

Storage Recovery Team.   These people are responsible for restoring the SAN to service (if one exists), and to make sure that all disk and tape drives are accessible by their systems after the system recovery team has completed its job.

Applications Recovery Team.   Once the system and storage teams have completed their tasks, the applications team takes over and works to get databases and other applications back online.

Data Management Team.   This group is responsible for getting data restored to the systems where it is needed, and for physically managing backup tapes. They are responsible for making sure that the tapes make it to the DR site after the disaster.

Vendor Contact Team.   This team is responsible for contacting all of the enterprise's vendors and maintaining that contact as necessary throughout the recovery period. All requests for vendor contacts from any of the computer recovery teams, or any other recovery team, should be funneled through the vendor contact team.

Damage Assessment and Salvage Team.   Depending on the nature of the disaster, this team might spend its time back at the site of the disaster, trying to determine the state of the original site, or trying to salvage any equipment or data that might be salvageable. This group would also be responsible for signage, and for roping off areas of the facility that may be dangerous or inaccessible.

Business Interface Team.   Lest we forget about the business (or primary function of the enterprise), a team must be designated that is responsible to the business itself to make sure that their needs are being met and their priorities are being addressed by the recovery efforts. If the business is working to bring back a particular group first, then it is important that the business interface team be made aware of it so that the efforts in IT match the business's efforts. At the same time, this team makes sure that the business folks don't interfere with IT's efforts. The latter point is especially true when the business-people are former engineers who think they still know everything.

Logistics Team.   All of the details that are part of the recovery effort are handled by the logistics team. They make sure there is food, water, space to work, and telephone service, and they handle all of the other unimportant tasks that would cause the entire recovery to fail if they were overlooked.

10. *Collect system-specific information.* Information about how to start up, shut down, and reboot all critical systems and applications must be identified and collected into the DR plan. Network administration groups must inventory their equipment and completely diagram all of their networks (LAN, MAN, WAN). Each system and storage administration group needs to collect hardware and software inventories. Inventories should, at minimum, include vendor name, software or firmware release, passwords, serial numbers, vendor contact and support information, and relevant platforms and operating systems. Any other procedures, such as tape restore instructions, must also be included here.

11. *Collect confidential information.* A great deal of the information that will be in the DR plan is, by nature, sensitive and confidential. In the financial services industry, for example, certain key account numbers and passwords may have to be included. The home phone numbers of upper management and executives will need to be included in the plan, as well as a complete list of alternate operating locations, even secret ones.

12. *Collect local information.* Employees may not know how to get to the DR site, and they may not be familiar with the area where it is located. If you include maps and directions (including public transportation, if any), along with airport and hotel information, a list of local restaurants and takeout places (especially ones that deliver), a list of useful radio stations, and other relevant local information, you can help your relocated staff feel more comfortable at their new, albeit temporary, homes.

13. *Identify critical forms and supplies.* If your business requires specific forms for printers (what about blank paychecks?), for example, or other hard-to-get supplies, it would be wise to identify these materials, and make sure that there is an ample supply of them at your DR site.

14. *Don't forget the people.* Your people are going to need different levels of assistance, depending on the nature of the disaster. Some will need psychological assistance, others will need financial assistance, and others will need to have their loved ones taken care of. Regardless, everyone will need to know where to report to work, or if they should just stay at home.

15. *Ongoing training for all involved parties.* All recovery team members and probably all technical employees should undergo training for disaster awareness and emergency procedures. This will help ensure that everyone performs to their abilities in an emergency situation.

Choosing a DR Site

One of the fundamental decisions that must be made when a business decides to implement a DR plan is where the recovery site will be located. There are some basic requirements that come into the decision-making process, some more obvious than others.

Physical Location

The physical location of the DR site relative to the primary site is one of the most important considerations. It can't be too close or it could be affected by the very same disaster, but it can't be so far away that it is difficult or impossible to reach in all circumstances.

In the days that followed September 11, 2001, the United States' Federal Aviation Administration (FAA) took the unprecedented step of shutting down all air traffic in the United States. New York–based businesses that wished to relocate their operations to a DR site could not fly there, and so if the site was more than a few hundred miles away, they could not get their people to the site.

On the other hand, there are unverified stories of organizations who operated their primary site from one World Trade Center tower with their DR site in the other tower. Clearly that was too close.

If a visit to the DR site requires any form of public transportation, it may be inaccessible in a disaster. If employees can drive there, they could easily get stuck in evacuation or panic-driven traffic jams.

IN THE UNTAMED WILDERNESS THAT IS NEW JERSEY

I know of at least one major New York financial institution whose DR site is in the bucolic New Jersey suburbs, roughly an hour's drive outside Manhattan under the best conditions. Although this site is manned 24 hours a day, seven days a week, if it were not, it would be necessary for their system administrators to make their way to this remote site after a disaster. If the system administrators live in Manhattan, it is extremely unlikely that they have cars, leaving them no way to get to the New Jersey suburbs in such circumstances.

—Evan

On the other hand, two sites located 300 miles apart along California's San Andreas Fault are not well insulated against a single disaster. Two sites along the North Carolina coast, even hundreds of miles apart, could both be taken out by the same hurricane.

Considerations in Selecting DR Sites

A common choice among Wall Street firms is to set up their DR site across the Hudson River in New Jersey, just a couple of miles away. In many cases, you can actually see one building from the other. Although this is a fairly common practice, it gives us cause for concern. It is not hard to imagine certain types of disasters that might take out both locations.

Other things to keep in mind when considering DR site locations:

Can you reach both sites from a single SAN? If so, you can save a great deal of complexity and money by mirroring your data within the single SAN between disks located at each site. Or, as we discussed in Chapter 6, "Backups and Restores," you could take tape backups from disks at one end of the SAN with tape drives at the other, automatically giving you off-site tapes that really aren't off-site at all.

Do the sites share utility services? Are utilities such as electricity and telephone service provided by different companies at the two sites? Or can a single mishap cause both your main site and your DR site to lose, say, electricity for an extended period of time?

Is the DR site near medical facilities? This is a good idea all the time, not just when considering DR sites. It's always better to be close to a hospital or other medical facility, but in times of crisis, it can be even more valuable. Besides the obvious easy access to medical care, roads near hospitals tend to be the first ones cleared after a major snow or ice storm, making access to nearby buildings that much easier.

Is it a low-key site? Some buildings are famous sites, like New York's World Trade Center, and while that makes them prestigious addresses, it also makes them more prone to a malicious attack. If your DR site is in a building with another company's sign on the outside, you could find yourself in trouble because of their relationships or political standing. It's generally best not to let the world know the location of your DR site.

Is it big enough? Is the site big enough for your current operations, or is there a danger that growth at the primary site will outstrip the capacity of the DR site? Do you just need space for computers, or do you need workspace, conference rooms, offices, or desks? Like the New York Board of Trade, which we discuss in Chapter 21, does your business have unique space requirements that would make it difficult to relocate just anywhere?

TORNADO ALLEY

One end user that I dealt with in the Midwest United States proudly told me that their DR site is a safe 10 miles away from their main site. Since the disaster they are most concerned about is tornadoes, that sounded pretty reasonable to this lifelong resident of the East Coast. Then they sheepishly admitted that both sites are right in the heart of the same tornado alley, and despite the distance, they felt one tornado could conceivably wipe out both sites.

—Evan

Other Options

Now that we've made selecting a DR site so difficult by pretty much eliminating the whole world, we offer a few suggestions that might make it easier.

Does your enterprise have multiple offices in different locations? Would it be possible for your facility to trade space with the other so that you can each provide DR facilities and possibly even manpower for the other location? The DR plan might be a little more complex, since work prioritizations would have to take into account the regular work going on at the site in addition to the incoming DR work, at least until personnel from the other site can make it to the DR site and take it over.

You can also achieve this end by putting some regular production work at your DR site so that the site is staffed for other reasons. That way, the production staff at the DR site could drop their regular work and concentrate on disaster recovery if it ever became necessary.

Another approach for smaller enterprises that don't have multiple offices is to find a partner or other organization with whom you could swap space in a similar arrangement. We recommend staying away from direct competitors, but an organization who shares some of your company's board members (if you are a publicly held corporation) might make an excellent choice for a DR swap.

There is another option, which in fact is one of the most popular. You can choose to farm out your DR site to a shared DR facility offered by a company such as Sungard to IBM Global Services. We discuss shared DR facilities later in this chapter.

THE WATER DOWN BELOW

For protection from flooded basements, one site had not one, but two backup servers in two separate basements in separate buildings. The data center also had two backup generators. Unfortunately, one of the basements didn't have enough space for both the server and a generator, so they put both generators in the same basement. Of course, the two-generator basement was the one that flooded, and sure enough, power was lost.

—Evan

DR Site Security

How secure is your DR site? The issue of DR site security has two different thrusts, both of which must be addressed and managed.

- Can anyone access the equipment when no emergency condition exists? Should anyone be able to access it? If the site is a shared site, and regular operations take place there, then a degree of regular access must be granted. If some of the systems at the shared DR site are dedicated for pure DR, those systems must be protected from regular access and reserved only for DR preparation and testing. If unauthorized or undocumented access to the DR systems can be gained, those critical systems are uncontrolled, and there is no guarantee that when they are needed for a recovery that they will be in any shape to do their jobs.

- When an emergency is declared, can the people who need access to the site get it? Or will a team of system administrators be standing in front of the security guard's desk carrying bags and boxes of tapes arguing that they need to get into the DR data center. (Make sure that the DR plan designates a team whose responsibilities include notifying the security guard at the DR site that he's about to receive visitors, if that's an appropriate action in your environment.)

Any DR site security plan must take both sets of conditions into account. Is the site appropriately secure under normal operating conditions, and when a disaster is declared, can the right people gain easy and rapid access to begin their recovery efforts?

How Long Will You Be There?

When most organizations design their DR site plans, they assume that they will be at the site for a week or two, possibly as long as a month.

As we spoke with organizations that survived the World Trade Center attacks, one of the common themes that we heard was that nobody ever expected to totally lose the towers. They assumed that the buildings were permanent, and that they'd be there forever. DR plans assumed that companies might require a temporary relocation to their DR site after a relatively small event like the 1993 terrorist bombing (small only when compared to the September 11, 2001 attacks) or a weather-related calamity.

The idea that the towers could be destroyed simply didn't enter into the planning for most of the organizations involved. When you make your DR plans, it is important to consider all possibilities. Unfortunately, buildings really can be destroyed through acts of terrorism and through accidents. Is your enterprise ready for such an eventuality?

Distributing the DR Plan

Plan distribution is one area where we disagree with what can be called the conventional wisdom on the subject. As we said earlier, conventional wisdom says that the DR plan should be widely distributed, with copies of the entire plan made available to anyone who has any reason (or possibility of a reason) to need it. Some organizations we have seen leave printed and bound copies of the plan on every bookshelf or near every fire extinguisher. Others give most or all employees a copy and ask them to leave it in their cars, their homes, or anywhere else they regularly find themselves. Such wide distribution is seen as a requirement because when the disaster strikes, everyone must be able to get their hands on a copy of the plan to begin the recovery process.

What Goes into a DR Plan

Consider the information that goes into a DR plan. If the goal of the plan is the recovery of the business, even when people and systems are temporarily or permanently unavailable, the plan document must contain a great deal of sensitive information. Among the confidential information that should be in a well-written DR plan:

- Home phone numbers
- Passwords, both privileged and regular

- Account numbers
- Emergency procedures
- Calling trees
- An organization chart
- Locations of other sites within the organization, some of which may be secret
- Proprietary information that you do not want your competitors or the press to get their hands on

If your organization has decided to widely distribute a plan that contains all of this sensitive information, there are several concerns that come to mind. What happens when a planholder leaves the company? Can you really get the plan document back? If the planholder has made photocopies of the plan, it really doesn't matter whether you get them back or not. If the planholder is leaving you for a competitor, that competitor is surely going to be interested in the contents of your DR plan, just as you would be interested in theirs.

Can you implement a policy to retrieve DR plans from departing employees? Does your enterprise do a decent job collecting security badges? If not, how likely is it that they can retrieve other sensitive documents?

One approach to improving security of the plan documents might be to uniquely number every page of every copy of the plan, and to use colored paper that does not photocopy well. Even these measures have limitations, though, and the truly unscrupulous will find ways around them, too.

If you have a plan with a truly wide distribution, how do you issue updates? A DR plan is a living document that changes in the aftermath of DR testing, whenever new systems and procedures are introduced to the organization, and whenever passwords or personnel change. It could become a full-time job for a team of people to keep track of who has which versions of the plan, who has turned in old ones, and who has received appropriately updated copies. As we said earlier, the only thing worse than no documentation is bad documentation, because it will be followed regardless of how out-of-date or incorrect it is.

Of course, when you put passwords in the plan document, you violate one of the prime directives of security and password management: Never write down your passwords. Widely distributing a document that contains passwords just compounds the problem.

So What Should You Do?

So, if every copy of the DR plan is a double-edged sword that can both save the company and destroy it, how do you handle document distribution? Our recommendation is as follows:

- The recovery coordinator should have a complete and current copy of the plan stored off-site, possibly at home.

- The backup coordinator should also have a copy stored off-site.

- One printed copy of the plan, along with a CD or diskette copy of the entire plan (possibly both) should be stored at an off-site location, most likely at the DR site itself.

- If there is a secure on-site location that the coordinator and the backup have access to, two copies should be stored there.

- Each recovery team leader and a single designated backup should have a copy of that team's part of the plan. There is no reason, for example, for the application recovery team to have a copy of the logistics team's plan. It does them no good to do so.

- All plan distribution and recovery is the responsibility of the recovery coordinator.

That's it. No more copies than that. Plans should *not* be ubiquitous. The key people should know about the plan, know where to find copies, and know the procedure to get their hands on them. The military calls this "need to know" access, and it seems to be the best approach for DR plan distribution.

The Plan's Audience

Another area where we disagree with conventional wisdom is in who the target audience for the plan is. Many experts on the subject have said that a DR plan should be written so that anyone from the most experienced system administrator all the way down to the CEO could pick up a copy of the plan and run with it.

While a plan probably could be written this way, it would almost certainly result in a separate disaster. As much as he might want to take an active role in the recovery, it is not appropriate for the CEO to sit down at a keyboard during a disaster and work the recovery. Even in the unlikely event that he has the experience necessary to lead the recovery, he probably has other things that he should be doing. He should leave the recovery efforts to experienced people who have done this before.

AN ENTERPRISING CEO

Our suggestion that the CEO should not take over the recovery efforts flies in the face of those episodes of *Star Trek: The Next Generation* where Captain Picard takes over the helm and pilots the Enterprise out of a tough spot. Even if Captain Picard is a very experienced helmsman, he is, at best, rusty at it and should leave the job to the regular helmsmen who usually pilot the ship.

All he is doing is putting the ship at unnecessary risk and satisfying his own ego, while hurting the morale of the regular crew. I have this mental image of the regular helmsman standing just off camera, muttering under his breath about what a better job he could do than that old man.

—Evan

A plan that was written for the CEO or even a custodian to follow would require a level of detail that is totally unmaintainable. On a Unix system, for example, you might need to edit a file as part of the recovery. The plan, therefore, would need to include instructions in using a text editor such as *vi*. The inexperienced person at the keyboard would need to be told every single keystroke. To edit line 300 of a file, he'd need to type "300G" into vi, and that would have to be clearly spelled out in the instructions. When the structure of that file changes, and the line to change becomes number 301 instead of number 300, the plan document would need to be revised. It is simply impossible to maintain the plan to that degree and then distribute it every time a minor change was made.

What's more, even the best-written plans have flaws. If an inexperienced person is executing the plan, and he runs into difficulty, he won't have the experience necessary to figure out how to solve the problem. It's just not possible to account for all conceivable problems in the plan. If it were, then anyone could read the right book and become truly well versed at any skill. Life just isn't that simple.

If the plan is written with too much detail, it will slow down and probably confuse the target audience.

The way to solve this problem is to rethink the audience for the plan. The reason conventional wisdom says the plan must be written for a broad audience is that the skilled system administrative staff may not be available at the time of a crisis. So, by writing the plan for this broad audience, in theory, anyone could step in and bring the systems back. We have established that that model won't work.

Instead, the plan should be targeted at people who have general experience in the relevant technical area for that part of the plan, but who lack specific organizational experience. In other words, the Solaris part of the plan should be written for experienced Solaris administrators who are not familiar with your enterprise and your specific system design. The Windows portion should be written for an outsider Microsoft Certified Systems Engineer (MCSE), and the network portion should be targeted at people who are experienced with relevant network technology, without knowing the specifics of your environment.

If the members of your experienced system administrative staff become unavailable for an extended period, you can hire consultants from the system and network equipment vendors themselves, or from third-party consulting organizations, and they can apply their experience to your environment's specifics and move as rapidly as possible through the recovery.

If you target your plans and procedures at the totally inexperienced, you will wind up with a disastrous recovery attempt.

Timelines

One of the outputs that management may expect from a DR plan is a specific timeline. "OK," they'll say, "the disaster has hit. When will my application be back up?" Unfortunately, it doesn't work quite that way. The reality is that everything always takes longer than you think it will, especially in a crisis situation when you don't know how many people, which people, or what skills you'll have at your disposal during the recovery period.

Timelines that obligate the recovery team to complete certain tasks in a particular time window are much too specific to circumstances. Unless a lot of extra time is built into the timelines, they are surefire recipes for failure, but worse than that, they are recipes for incredibly visible failure. After all, in a disaster recovery, everybody's watching. Their jobs (and yours, for that matter) may depend on your ability to get the systems working again.

A much better approach, and one that is more likely to succeed, is to develop critical paths to success. Rather than saying that task A will take an hour, task B will take 35 minutes, and task C will take 8 hours and 19 minutes, develop a set of critical paths for tasks, as shown in Figure 20.2. Microsoft Project is an excellent example of a tool that can generate critical paths and help determine which tasks need to be performed in what order, while also keeping track of costs and deadlines.

By arranging critical paths for tasks, you can determine where personnel shortages may occur before they actually do, enabling you to bring more people into the teams that may create bottlenecks.

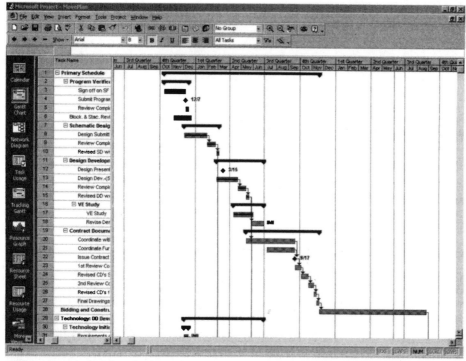

Figure 20.2 Critical paths for tasks.

Team Assignments

As we have been saying throughout this chapter, it is important to assign teams to tasks, rather than assigning individuals. An individual may not be available during a disaster or may behave in unpredictable ways in the face of all the unexpected stress that is coming his way. Therefore, it is best to assign small teams to tasks. Each team should have a leader and a basic hierarchy. That hierarchy may just include the designation of a backup for the leader, although some organizations may choose to assign complete hierarchies from top to bottom.

Assigning People

Assign people to do the things they are best at. Sometimes you'll have senior people in your organization who have moved on from a task that they were very good at so that they can learn new skills. This is an excellent thing to do to advance one's career, but in a disaster it is quite reasonable to ask these people to return to their previous roles, at least for the duration of the crisis, if they are the best people for the job.

In addition to a team leader, who coordinates all specific tasks, there must be a team spokesperson. The spokesperson is the only team member who is authorized to speak to the overall recovery coordinator or anyone else outside the team. If all team members answer questions and communicate outside of the group, they are not performing the tasks that will bring the organization back online. What's more, doing so will add a great deal of confusion, as mixed messages reach the outside world. Some organizations will choose to have regularly scheduled meetings among all of the teams' spokespeople, so that all the teams know what overall progress is being made, and so that they receive any other situational updates that conditions require.

There is another role that must be assigned. You can call this the team's den mother (or father). This team member watches the efforts of the rest of the team during the recovery and makes sure that everyone is eating, and drinking fluids, and getting rest, and even taking brief breaks from time to time. (No, this probably should not be their only task, but it is one that must be taken seriously.) In a crisis, some people will work and work and work until they drop. At some point, they become exhausted and start making mistakes in judgment. The den mother's role is to make sure that nobody gets to that point.

On some teams, especially smaller ones, the team leader may also be the spokesperson and the den mother (but then the leader needs someone else to be her den mother, perhaps the backup leader).

Management's Role

What should upper management be doing in a DR scenario? Management's role is a very simple one: Get out of the way! In any organization, management is there to make the big decisions. Hopefully, for example, the CIO decided to invest in a solid DR plan. Once a disaster has been declared (and it may well be the CIO who declares the disaster), it's time to sit back and see how the plan does. The CIO has spent thousands or millions of dollars to make the plan effective; here is where he realizes his return on that investment. If the big decisions haven't been made by the time the disaster strikes, it's too late.

If the CIO is constantly on the phone asking the recovery teams for updates and information and completion estimates, he is distracting them from their primary goals. If the CIO is wandering around and is constantly in the face of the recovery teams, he risks slowing them down and/or intimidating them while they are trying to work.

On the other hand, if the CEO or other corporate executive takes an occasional walk just to quietly look over the teams as they work, that is a good thing. It shows calm and decisive leadership, faith in the troops, and an understanding that he can't really help right now. That sort of visit can be quite helpful to team morale. If he comes in with food or drink, all the better.

Communications back to upper management should be through a coordinated effort among the spokespeople for each team, back to the master spokesperson, who can then relay information to upper management. Information must, of course, also flow in the opposite direction so that teams learn what is going on at the corporate level and on other teams.

How Many Different Plans?

We once again go against conventional DR wisdom when we tell you that it is not realistic or practical to create a different DR plan for every single eventuality.

Some people will say that organizations should have one DR plan for a tornado, one for a fire, another for an electrical outage, and more plans for every other conceivable emergency situation. This approach quickly becomes unmanageable, as plans become similar, with only slight differences. Changes must be made in all the right places in all the plans, and each plan has to be collected and redistributed when it changes. This is in total violation of our #1 Key Design Principle, which calls for maximizing simplicity wherever possible, and is a recipe for contradictory plans.

No plan can possibly account for everything. Table 20.1 shows just four examples of extreme long shots. Just because something can happen doesn't mean it will.

Table 20.1   Long Shots

EVENT	LIKELIHOOD
Annual chance of a person being struck by lightning*	4,289,651 to 1
Lifetime chance of a person being killed by poison*	1,174,000 to 1
Chance of the Earth being pulled out of the solar system by a passing star†	2,200,000 to 1
Chance of hitting the U.S. Powerball Lottery‡	120,526,770 to 1

* Source: National Security Council (USA)
† Source: University of Michigan Study
‡ Source: Multi-state Lottery Association

Of course, just because something is a long shot doesn't mean that it won't happen, so it is still necessary to make some preparations, even for long shots.

So, how many different plans do you need? The easy answer is, of course, just one. But two is probably a better answer. There are two totally different classes of disaster. One is an internal disaster, where only your organization is adversely affected. A major building fire is one example of such a disaster. The other class of disaster is the external one, where civil authorities and possibly the military are involved. An example of an external disaster might be a terrorist attack, a major weather event like a tornado or hurricane, or an earthquake.

In an internal event, it will be easy to get support from unaffected external organizations, both civil (police and fire departments) and commercial (vendors). If the event is external, it could have a significant impact on the ability of these organizations to respond to your needs.

Therefore, we conclude that the best approach is to write and maintain one plan with different contingencies, based on the nature of the disaster. Two parallel plans will probably overlap so much that it would be difficult to keep them synchronized. By maintaining a single document that contains all reasonable steps and contingencies, you can minimize the amount of redundant effort that goes into maintaining multiple copies.

Shared DR Sites

So far in this chapter, we have made the assumption that you would choose to manage your own DR site, rather than farm it out to one of the companies that can manage a facility and equipment for you. Working with a company like Sungard, who, for a fee, will provide computer equipment and space for a company's DR efforts, can definitely provide real advantages. The advantages that they can provide include the following:

Experience. Since these companies have been offering these services for some time, they are good at them, and as a result, they can deliver them with fewer time-consuming and expensive mistakes. They can help determine exactly what levels of protection their clients' critical systems and applications require.

Financial savings. They deliver these services to many clients at the same time and so are able to make more efficient use of their resources, producing savings that they can pass on to their customers. They can often deliver similar services to what a company might be able to put together itself, and they can do it for less money. Your organization need not hire specialized DR experts, as you can use the ones that the DR facility offers as consultants, as necessary.

Additional resources.   These organizations have a great deal of experience helping companies design, implement, and test DR plans. They can help carry out the actual plan when the disaster strikes, and they can help with advance preparation. These services are usually available for an additional fee on top of the standard charges for providing space and equipment. In addition, different service providers offer a variety of services, such as mobile recovery units, where a bus or large recreational vehicle full of computer equipment rolls into your parking lot to help provide additional resources after a disaster. They can also provide assistance in locating a private DR site that meets your organization's particular requirements.

Remote site security.   Since they administer the DR site for all of their clients, they manage the security and can make sure that only the right people have access to the site and the equipment, when they have been authorized to do so.

Ongoing maintenance of the plan and the recovery site.   Their experience and expertise can help their clients with the maintenance of their DR plans, especially as resources and personnel change.

But there are also some disadvantages to the services that these organizations offer. As with the advantages, some of them will affect each potential customer differently. If you are considering using one of the companies that offers this service, please don't be dissuaded by what we write. Speak to a representative of the company, and make sure that what she says applies to them as well as to their competition. The following are some of these disadvantages:

Shared equipment.   The basic level of service offered by most shared DR sites calls for hardware to be shared among all customers. It is allocated to disaster-stricken organizations on a first come, first served basis. If the disaster is widespread, there is a risk that if you don't get to the DR site quickly, you may not get the recovery hardware you expect. To be fair, the shared DR providers that we have spoken with all say that they have never had to turn away a single customer because of a lack of resources.

Loss of control.   Since the computer equipment is shared, there is no guarantee which system will be allocated to your enterprise in a disaster. Therefore, any work that is required to bring that system up must be performed after the disaster has struck. There is no way to prestage the data, or to set up site-to-site failover. Systems that you own and control can have replicated data and preloaded operating systems and applications preloaded before any disaster, obviously speeding recovery times.

More complex testing.   When you control your own DR systems, you can schedule DR tests at whatever time is convenient for your organization.

When shared DR facilities are involved, testing must be coordinated with the facility, and with any other company who might wish to conduct their own tests at the same time. Some facilities also charge additional fees to run tests, especially extended tests. These fees may discourage some organizations from doing testing, making their recoveries less likely to succeed.

Our recommendation is to look carefully at both options. Smaller organizations will likely find that it makes more sense to use a shared facility, while larger organizations will probably find that they have sufficient internal resources to do it all themselves.

Equipping the DR Site

What sort of equipment do you need at your DR site? What we offer in the following is not a complete list, but it makes a good starting point. Once again, different organizations will have different requirements for exactly what equipment they need at their DR site. The following are some of the items you will need:

Computer equipment.   For our purposes, it all starts with computer equipment. Do you have enough systems, both servers and desktops, to recover and then resume operating your business? Will there be a decrease in performance and service? Is everyone whom the decrease might affect aware of the limitations that will be imposed by a switchover to the DR site? Have they accepted them?

Network equipment.   Do you have sufficient bandwidth at the DR site to interconnect servers, clients, the Internet, and remote users? Do you have private connections to your suppliers and customers? Do those connections also go to "their" DR sites? Network equipment includes LANs, WANs, and all of the additional networking equipment.

Storage.   Do you have all the disk drives, tape drives, and other storage devices that you'll need at your DR site?

- *Disk drives.* Do you have sufficient disk space at the DR site to hold everything that you need right away? Is the storage accessible by the systems that will need it? Is the storage appropriately mirrored? If your primary site survived, or if you have an additional DR site, you may want to make sure you can replicate your data to still another site.

- *Tape drives and tapes.* One of the lessons learned in the aftermath of September 11, 2001, in New York was that a lot of organizations did not have enough tape drives at their DR sites to restore their data and systems quickly. Since it takes longer to restore than to backup, you may need more tape drives in your DR site than in your primary site. You'll also want to start taking backups, after you've settled in at the DR site. Do you have enough tapes on site for that effort?

- *SANs.* Do you have a SAN infrastructure at your primary site? Is it replicated at the DR site? Can all systems access the data and files that they need at the DR site?

Printers.   Does your business use specialized printers? Or do you just use standard ink-jet and laser printers? Do you have sufficient printer capacity at the DR site once business gets back to normal? Do you have spare ink and toner cartridges? Do you have enough paper? Are there specialized business forms (like paychecks, for example) that are required at the DR site to keep the business functioning?

Scanners.   If your business requires scanners, bar code readers, or other specialized input equipment, an adequate supply must be maintained at the DR site.

Other specialized equipment.   What equipment does your business use that may be hard to obtain in a crisis, or that gives you a competitive advantage? Is there equipment that regulations require you to use in order to operate your business, like time clocks or specialized lighting?

Regular office equipment.   Does your DR site have copiers, postal meters, cabinets, office supplies, desks, chairs, phones, a PBX, whiteboards, fax machines, paper, writing instruments, pads, trash cans, spare mobile phones, walkie-talkies, televisions, VCRs, PC projectors, and all the ordinary stuff that an office needs to function in the twenty-first century?

Items for comfort and well-being.   It's safe to assume that employees will be spending many hours at the DR site after a disaster. It's important to make sure that their basic needs are being met, and that they are as comfortable as they reasonably can be in a difficult situation. This means that ready-to-eat food, bottled water, eating utensils, soap, can openers, soft drinks, coffee, sugar, radios, flashlights (with spare batteries), first-aid kits, and other basic (and slightly more than basic) comforts should be provided, and freshened every once and a while, so that workers are not eating three-year-old bags of pretzels while recovering the business. It might not be a bad idea to leave a small petty cash supply on hand as well, just in case.

Other things.   Since you cannot possibly know the nature of the disaster before it strikes, it is best to stock the DR site with some basic construction and repair equipment like hard hats, work gloves, hand tools (hammers, nails, screw drivers, crowbar, saw, etc.), and even boots. Plywood and tarpaulins can make it easier to affect temporary repairs, water pumps can help clean up nasty situations, and of course, large heavy-duty trash bags can help with cleanup. Brightly colored police tape, oak tag, thick markers, whiteboards, and dry erase markers can help with inside communications, while orange traffic cones and road flares can help with outside communications.

Is Your Plan Any Good?

Once the plan has been developed, it has to be tested. As we said earlier in the book, an untested plan is just a piece of paper.

There is some semantic question as to whether or not you call a run-through of your DR plan a test. A test, after all, is graded, and the taker of the test either passes or fails. In a DR test the goal is not as simple as pass/fail, but rather to make the plan better for the next time.

It's very important to remember, as a test proceeds, what is being tested. You are not testing the participants in the test, but rather the plan itself. If a participant makes a mistake during the test, the fault is most likely with the test, and not with the participant. Some instruction wasn't clear, a diagram was wrong, or there was some other error that caused the participant to interpret the plan improperly. The fix is with the plan, not with the person.

As we discuss going through the plan, we use the term exercise rather than test, because we see the process much more as an ongoing attempt to make the plan better, rather than as a chance to fail.

Qualities of a Good Exercise

A good exercise does more than just work through the plan. The exercise offers side benefits as well, including the following:

Builds teamwork.   Employees with similar skill sets who may not see each other or get to work with each other very often are suddenly afforded the chance to team up and work together on the DR exercise. Unspoken hostilities have the chance to be rectified privately, or to come out (which can help them to be resolved before a real disaster puts everyone to the test), and new friendships and alliances can be made across the organization.

Challenges all participants.   DR exercises allow employees to do things that they don't usually get to do. They are given the chance to think on their feet and exercise brain cells that don't always get worked out in day-to-day work. It's a change that many employees find refreshing and rewarding.

Presents realistic situations.   Without actually scaring people into believing that a cloud of toxic gas is really floating toward the facility, or that there has been a terrorist attack, a good exercise still allows its participants to get into the activity and treat it as though it were real. In return, the exercise must feel real enough that participants really can get into it without being asked to suspend their critical thinking too much. Some suggestions for making exercises feel more realistic are offered in the section that follows.

Allows participants to take an active role.   One reason that participants often report enjoying a DR exercise is that they get to do stuff. They can get out from behind their desks and move equipment or put up police tape. They get to solve problems and then act on the solutions. Tests can be fun and, once again, represent a change from the daily routine.

Provides excellent training.   When participants have the opportunity to extend themselves and do new things, they learn new and useful skills. Sometimes the skills are only useful to a DR situation, and other times participants learn general skills that can help them in their jobs or in their personal lives.

Exposes leaders to management.   A significant career opportunity can be afforded to the people who lead a DR test. Because their roles are very visible, if handled properly, a DR test can offer them the opportunity to demonstrate their leadership and management skills to corporate management. All participants, not just the leaders, have the opportunity to rise above the pack in a DR exercise and make themselves better known up the management chain. Whether the impression they make is good or bad depends on the apparent success of the exercise and how well the individuals conduct themselves as the exercise goes on.

Planning for an Exercise

Before an exercise can take place, the organizers, usually led by the recovery coordinator, must spend a lot of time preparing. Basic exercises are not going to be executed as surprises. As an organization becomes more advanced, and early exercises have been deemed successful, then a surprise exercise can be attempted, but not before. The following are some of the preparations that must be in place for an exercise to have a chance to be successful:

Seek management buy-in.   Obviously, without the total buy-in of management for a serious disruption in workflow for a day or so, no exercise can possibly be successful. Management should be pushing for a DR exercise to take place, rather than acting as any kind of hindrance.

Identify the staff for the exercise team.   Everybody who is taking part in the test needs to know about it in advance. They will need to clear the event with their management ahead of time, who, of course, should be delighted to let their team members participate in the exercise.

Select exercise observers and evaluators.   Some participants should be held out of the exercise and instead be given the important role of observing and evaluating the exercise. These people are specifically prohibited from helping in the actual exercise in any way; the active participants should treat them as if they are not even present. Observers should take notes, write down their observations and comments, and then deliver a presentation at the postmortem meeting.

Determine the scope of the exercise.   Exercises that take place early in the life of the DR plan are not going to be end-to-end in nature. Rather, they will look at particular aspects of the plan, such as restoring backups or bringing up applications on new systems. Early exercises should be briefer in nature than later, more comprehensive exercises. Before an exercise begins, all participants should know what elements of the plan are being worked on, and what elements are not.

Set objectives for the exercise.   As with just about any project with objectives, exercise objectives should meet five basic criteria:

- *The objective should be achievable.* There's no point in setting up an exercise where the objectives simply cannot be reached. You will discourage your participants and ensure that nobody wants to take part next time around.

- *The objectives must be, well, objective.* They should be set up so that opinion and judgment is minimized or eliminated, and the criteria can be determined impartially by any observer.

- *The objective should be quantifiable.* An objective cannot have the exercise aim to "do well." The aim must be to achieve something that can be put into numeric form, like "improve recovery time by 30 percent over last time."

- *The objective should be relevant.* All objectives should be relevant to the DR process. Objectives that involve unrelated events or criteria should be eliminated from the exercise. They should also measure qualities that participants can actually affect by doing their jobs.

- *The objective should be trackable.* Participants should be able to determine as they go along how well they are doing against an objective.

Develop and publish the exercise schedule.   There should be no secrets in early exercises. Everyone should know where to be, what to do, and when to do it, though with many of the specific details held back until the exercise begins. As we said, later tests can include surprises, but basic information about the early ones should be public. As the process is refined, surprise exercises can be introduced.

Build a large scenario for the disaster.   The place for surprises and secrets is in the nature of the exercise. If participants know that the exercise is to take place on Tuesday, and that they should allow the whole day for it, that's good. They should not know what the scenario for the exercise will be. The actual details should be kept a total secret from as many people as possible until the event unfolds.

Brief the participants.   All regular participants and observers need to know what is expected of them as the test goes on. They need to know that they themselves are not being evaluated, but rather the DR plan is being evaluated. All participants, not just the observers, should all feel free to make comments on how things can be improved, what felt and went well, and what felt and went wrong.

Possible Exercise Limitations

Any exercise will have limits as to how real it can be. You may, for example, choose not to involve customer service or production every time you perform an exercise because of the potential impact on their operations. They must be included in some tests, though, just to make sure that they, too, are DR-ready. Anytime an exercise could affect production, customer service, or other critical departments, written executive buy-in will certainly be required.

You may also run into limits imposed by other parts of the organization, who are not willing to take part in anything that might disrupt their day-to-day activities, or by groups who are unwilling to allow their personnel to take part in the exercise. Since exercises cost money, you may also run into some budgetary resistance or political problems, such as determining whose budget the cost of the exercise should be charged to.

If the exercise does have limits, those limits must be clearly spelled out to all participants so that they do not do anything that affects a group that is not taking part. As part of the exercise, participants should simply explain what they would do that crosses beyond the predefined limits, without actually doing it.

Make It More Realistic

You can have some fun and make your exercise more realistic. Be creative. Play with your favorite photo manipulator software and make photos of damaged parts of the building or neighborhood. Get some yellow police tape and traffic cones and cordon off inaccessible areas of the building. Strategically place some actual broken equipment (we are not suggesting that you break stuff, just find some old equipment). Make audio- or videotape of fake news reports describing the unfolding scenario; if you work for a major company in a small town, you might even be able to get someone from a local television or radio station to lend a hand.

If the exercise feels real, you will get more and better participation from your teams. And their level of enthusiasm, and even fun, will increase.

To make the scenario even more real, take people out of play. Suddenly announce that two key people are unavailable for the duration of the exercise. Make other people scramble to cover for them. Take entire rooms or building wings out of play. Declare that a backup tape (or a set of them) is no good, or that some systems or data are damaged and cannot be used. Use your imagination. Make things bad, but not so bad that the remaining team members cannot solve the problems and get back online with a reasonable effort.

Ideas for an Exercise Scenario

Looking for some ideas for the exercise scenario? Have no fear; we have a nice long list of them for you. We've broken them up into five types of scenarios with examples of each. We hope that you can take the list and expand on it, and develop your own ideas, especially if there is a chance that exercise participants have read this book and have seen this list.

Technological Accidents

Technological accidents are generally accidents that have wide-ranging effects, not just to your business, but to the general vicinity.

Chemical spill or toxic gas leak.   It's dangerous to have any contact with the cloud that results from the gas leak, or with the chemicals that have spilled. And, of course, the evil chemicals are heading right at our facility.

Power failure.   An especially tricky one, as it is often very difficult to know how long a power failure will last. When do you decide to declare it a disaster rather than just wait for the power to return?

Natural Disasters

One form or another of natural disaster can strike just about anywhere at just about any time. They can be rather geography-specific; it's probably best not to worry about disasters that cannot happen where you are, and concentrate on more likely ones. For example, we are not aware of any sinkholes striking Southern California, or active volcanoes in New England.

Earthquake.   An earthquake tends to be a widespread situation that occurs with no warning. Although earthquakes tend to be restricted to certain geographies, there is a school of thought that says that earthquakes can strike almost anywhere.

Flood. A flood can come on suddenly, especially if the facility is located near a stream or river, or can result from predicted heavy rains.

Sinkhole. More of a problem in Florida and the southeastern United States than other places, a sinkhole is when a hollow section of ground collapses, often because of an underground spring drying up, for example. Entire buildings can be swallowed up in a sinkhole. They can begin without warning, and then spread either slowly or quickly in just about any direction for tens or even hundreds of meters.

Fire. The exercise should pretend that the fire suppression system in the data center was activated. There is no need to actually activate it. One realistic, though morbid, twist would be to throw a curve into the scenario that someone was trapped in the data center when the Halon dumped.

Business Crises

These are scenarios that may have a greater impact on the business as a whole, rather than the IT environment. Nevertheless, they can affect IT and so must be included as possible scenarios.

xSP failure. A particular favorite over the last few years. When companies like Exodus and Global Crossing closed down their shared data center facilities, the result was that companies were forced to relocate their data centers with little or no warning. That is exactly what happens in a disaster and so must be addressed in a DR plan.

Loss of key supplier. What do you do if the only supplier to a key component of your company's primary deliverable goes out of business or is purchased by one of your competitors? Depending on the nature of your company's business, this may or may not be relevant.

Labor problems. This could be a strike, for example, that affects your business directly, or one that affects a supplier, a shipper, or the docks where key supplies are received and readied for delivery. It could be a local transit strike that makes it impossible for key employees to make it to work. Different types of businesses have different vulnerabilities to labor issues.

External Threats

These threats are ones in which your business is probably an accidental participant, or at least one where the effects can be wide, and your business is just one of many victims.

Terrorism. In the wake of September 11, 2001, terrorism has become the primary, and sometimes the sole, focus of many organizations' DR plans. This is not appropriate. The likelihood of any of these other scenarios has not decreased one bit; you could still have an earthquake whether there are terrorists or not. While it is certainly important to think about what a terrorist act could do to your business, don't do so to the exclusion of all other threats. A terrorist attack could, of course, take on many forms including a bomb threat, an actual bombing or other attack, or a biological threat. Any of these would make an interesting exercise scenario.

Virus/worm. Today's Internet viruses and worms tend to hit when people open the wrong email attachment or visit the wrong web site. Some experts believe that the method by which they attack will become much more dangerous over the next few years. There are even some doomsayers who speak of a future virus that could shut down the entire Internet, spreading to all corners of it in just 15 or 20 minutes. If you decide to use a virus or worm scenario, it's best to keep up on the technology and to understand what could realistically happen. You should also be sure that your exercise doesn't inadvertently release a real virus onto your network.

Civil unrest. Riots or other forms of civil unrest can have a serious impact on local businesses. If you are located in a region where there is even a slight possibility of such an event, it is best to be prepared for it.

Foreseeable Events

Sometimes disasters are predicted, often by the weather service.

Hurricane. The result of a hurricane could be flooding, moderate wind damage, a loss of power, and closed roads over a moderate to large geographic area.

Tornado. A tornado tends to be predicted, but generally only strikes a small area. That area could be hit by serious wind damage to buildings and property, power loss, and fire.

Other Scenarios

Obviously, there are many other kinds of scenarios to consider, some general, and some very specific to a line of work or a specific organization. Be sure that whatever scenario you choose is realistic in terms of how likely it is to strike, in terms of how it looks and feels to the drill participants, and in terms of the little extras that you add to better engage your participants. If the exercise scenario feels cheesy or thrown together at the last minute, you are not likely to receive the same level of participation.

After the Exercise

As part of the exercise, the coordinator must schedule a postmortem meeting, which should take place as soon after the completion of the exercise as reasonably possible. The evening after the exercise is probably too soon, and the teams should go out for additional team building exercises, over good food and appropriate beverages, rather than go back over the day's efforts.

When the postmortem does take place, every participant should attend. The observers should deliver presentations about the exercise, and what they felt went well and what went badly. Participants should be encouraged to offer their own commentary, and everyone should feel free to comment on and discuss all aspects of the exercise.

It is important to remember that the postmortem is not for sniping at other participants who made mistakes, misinterpreted instructions, didn't give their all, or did anything else that might be seen as objectionable. Instead, comments should be positive in nature, aimed at improving the process for the next round of exercises.

No comment is too trivial or too big for the postmortem. This meeting should represent the end of the exercise for all participants, except for the recovery coordinator, who will take the comments from the postmortem and incorporate them into the exercise for next time.

It will probably be appropriate for the coordinator to collect the results and the comments, and produce a report for the senior management team.

Three Types of Exercises

There are three types of exercises for DR plans: a complete drill where the entire plan is executed as if the disaster were real; a tabletop simulation where people in charge of recovery discuss how they would react in different disaster situations; and a telephone drill, where the communication plan is tested. A more detailed discussion of each of these follows.

Complete Drill

Most of what we've been discussing as a DR exercise comes under the Complete Drill heading. A complete drill basically requires that people get up out of their chairs and do the same sorts of things that they would do in an actual disaster. Complete drills are large undertakings that normally affect many areas of the enterprise and cause a great interruption in regular day-to-day activities.

No matter what limits are in place, some impact on production is almost inevitable as part of a complete test, and so efforts must be coordinated with them.

The bottom line is that complete drills can be extremely disruptive to a business, but not as disruptive as an actual disaster. Complete drills are the only way to make sure that your DR plan actually works. If the plan doesn't work, then exercises are the only way to find out why not and what you can do to fix them for next time.

In some ways, a complete drill can be more difficult than a real disaster, because in a real disaster, no effort is required to protect production. A real disaster will have 100 percent participation and enthusiasm, whereas a drill will surely have something less than 100 percent. On the other hand, there is virtually no danger to life or property during a drill, which unquestionably makes a drill less stressful than a real disaster. Plus, if it is run well, a complete drill can be a lot of fun for the participants.

A complete drill should be run once or twice a year after the DR plan has reached an appropriate level of maturity. That maturity can be gained by running a series of tabletop drills first.

Tabletop Drill

In some ways, tabletop drills can be as much fun as complete drills. In a tabletop drill, the recovery coordinator gathers together representatives from each of his recovery teams, sits them around a conference room table, and describes a disaster scenario. The rules of the drill are that this disaster is now unfolding in real time. Without getting up from the table, or calling in other people, the team members describe and discuss exactly what they would do, according to the plan, in a particular situation.

A tabletop drill is an excellent way to work out the kinks in a new DR plan without upsetting the entire organization. Although there is no need for fake newscasts or to actually cordon off parts of the building, the coordinator can still make the drill more realistic by throwing some curves at the participants. He can still take people or rooms out of play, and he can change the nature of the disaster on the fly, to make sure the whole scenario is realistic.

There should be at least one or two observers at tabletop drills, who can watch the proceedings and take notes for the postmortem. The coordinator will generally be too busy to take notes or make general observations.

Phone Chain Drill

The third kind of drill is the most basic. At any hour of the day or night (although day is better if he wishes to keep the goodwill of his participants), the coordinator picks up his phone and calls the first person on the telephone chain. He informs that first person that this is a phone chain drill, and he should call the next person on his list. (He should, of course, have a copy of the phone chain list accessible at all times.)

Each person in the chain should call the next person in turn, and if he cannot reach someone, he should call the next person, until he actually reaches someone. The last person on the list should call the coordinator to close the loop.

The goal of the test is to determine if someone cannot be reached, or if someone does not have his phone chain list to continue making calls. The guilty will learn and, everyone hopes, will do better next time.

The Effects of a Disaster on People

No discussion of disasters and disaster recovery can be complete without including a section on how people are affected by and react to disasters. As we have said, people are an enterprise's most important assets. Without people, there is no enterprise to carry on.

Typical Responses to Disasters

Experience has shown that in the days immediately following a regional disaster, just 40 to 60 percent of employees will show up for work. This rule held for the Oklahoma City bombing in April 1995, the tropical storms that hit Houston in the summer of 2001, as well as in New York in the days following the September 11, 2001 attacks. And it's not going to be the best 40 to 60 percent of the your employees who return.

Why will attendance be so low? After a major regional disaster, people's priorities change. Instead of work being near the top of their priority list, suddenly a myriad of other priorities get in the way. Where do people want to be when there is a major stress event going on? Some people want to be with their families. For some, that means going to work and spending time with their adopted family at the office; for others, it means going home and telling the people who are important to them that they love them. Some people who are not family-oriented may want to be alone. Others will want to throw themselves into their jobs and yet may be so distracted or upset that they are unproductive.

BASIC NEEDS

In the 1960s, renowned psychologist Abraham Maslow published his theory of self-actualization, which included what he called his hierarchy of needs, a list of basic requirements that all human beings need. The most basic needs (and we are skipping tons of his work here) are food, clothing, and shelter.

One modern interpretation of those basic needs is that people need money, information, protection, and facilities for themselves and their families, and once those needs are met, they can move on with their lives. When basic needs are not being met, people tend to concentrate their energies on satisfying those needs, to the exclusion of all else.

People can be hurt in a disaster, either physically or psychologically, and they need to tend to those injuries before they can work. Some will need to take care of family-care or home repair or other issues at home before they can work.

WHATEVER THEY NEED

At one firm that was devastated by the September 11, 2001 attacks, I know of at least one system administrator who, after the disaster, simply disappeared. For two weeks, his employer and his colleagues (who were incredibly busy attempting to recover the business) did not hear a word from him. Then, as mysteriously as he left, he returned. His employer did not ask any questions and welcomed him back to work as if he had never left.

The lesson here is that the firm was enlightened enough to understand that different people respond to high-stress situations in different ways. Behavior that might normally be grounds for dismissal is tolerated (just once) when the circumstances are sufficiently unusual.

Sometimes people really do just need their space.

—Evan

Before an employee can give his full attention to his job, he must know that his family is safe and cared for. That may mean day care, elder care, or pet care. It may mean making sure that there is sufficient food in the house or that the family is protected from additional dangers, real or imagined.

If the enterprise's operations have shifted to a DR site that is some distance away, many employees will be unwilling to relocate. Others will take advantage of the situation and choose not to work for some period of time, and still others will be unable to work because the disaster has shut down their department or function.

However, once the initial shock of the disaster passes, studies find that people really do want to return to work, as long as their basic needs are met. Work restores a level of normalcy to their lives, and many people will bury themselves in work to help them forget the effects of the disaster.

What Can the Enterprise Do to Help?

The enlightened enterprise can do many things to make sure that the needs of its workers are being met after a disaster. It can encourage idled workers who wish to be busy to donate their time to disaster relief operations, to visit the homes of other employees to help them out with repairs or child care or whatever they need. Workers could volunteer to help the local police or government, or, if local laws permit, they could even open a small day care center to allow other employees get back to work.

Employees will return to work faster, and with greater faith in their employer, if the employer goes the extra mile to help the employees when things are tough. Different employees, of course, have different needs. The best way to understand what an employee needs in a time of crisis is to ask. For example, some will have a need to provide or obtain care for family members. Until her family members are properly taken care of, the employee's thoughts will not be on her job.

Many employees say that the most important thing that their employer can do in a disaster is to make sure that paychecks keep on coming. Some people will need advances on their pay, and those should also be made available. Whether workers are idled against their will or are unable to work for a period of time, it is important that they continue to be paid without interruption, even if they must be asked to take vacation or sick time along the way. Workers who travel to the DR site might be worthy of bonus pay or of having their families sent to be with them on weekends.

Allow the people who are working to do their jobs with a minimum of interference. Allow lower-level people to make more decisions in a crisis, especially when it comes to spending. Timeliness is never more important than during a crisis, and if efforts are interrupted so that some executive can rubber-stamp minor purchases, recovery times will be delayed. Let people work where it makes sense for them to work. If they can do their jobs from home, let them. Don't overwhelm workers with meetings and requests for communications; let them work.

Different people need different things in different degrees. Some need information; others need protection or companionship or to be left alone. Others need psychological assistance or to attend to their families. The bottom line is that most people have never experienced the level of stress that comes with a full-blown disaster. They need to handle it in their own way.

Keep the information flowing. Everyone should know his roles and responsibilities in the recovery. Depending on the nature of the disaster, the press will need to be informed; there should be a single source giving a consistent message to the press. Employees should have a toll-free number to call for regular updates on the status of the recovery. Employees need to know that their jobs will survive the disaster; and if the jobs will not survive, they need to know that too.

Lest you think that we have strayed too far from the topic of high availability, remember that any recovery effort requires people. If people are not working, no recovery can take place. Get the people back to work, willingly, and your organization will recover faster.

Key Points

- A disaster is the largest "R" in MTTR that you'll ever have to deal with. By developing and then testing your plans thoroughly, you can confidently reduce that recovery time and get your users back to work faster.

- Disaster recovery is incredibly complex and prone to failure. By paying attention to the details, you can increase the likelihood of a successful recovery.

- There is no recovery, nor enterprise, without people. If you treat your people well, they will treat you well in return.

CHAPTER 21

A Resilient Enterprise*

The harder I work, the luckier I get.
—George Allen

Unlike the other chapters in this book, this chapter is a snapshot of an ongoing story. By the time you read this chapter, it will not reflect the current state of affairs at the New York Board of Trade. The point of this story is to describe the efforts and accomplishments of a dedicated group of people faced with a set of horrific circumstances that they could not have imagined, not in its being up to the second. Even when the story is 50 years old, it will still be interesting and relevant to anyone who is attempting to design and implement a disaster recovery solution.

At 8:46 A.M. on Tuesday, September 11, 2001, an airplane struck 1 World Trade Center in Lower Manhattan. The New York Board of Trade, located at 4 World Trade Center, a nine-story building adjacent to Tower Two, ceased trading and evacuated their building. By eight o'clock that evening, despite the total destruction of that building and its computer systems, the New York Board of Trade was ready to resume trading.

* This chapter is reprinted, with some minor modifications, from *The Resilient Enterprise*, a book produced by VERITAS Software in the spring of 2002. It appears here with the permission of Richard Barker and Paul Massiglia of VERITAS Software, as well as many others who worked on the book, and with the gracious permission of Pat Gambaro and Steve Bass of the New York Board of Trade.

The story behind this recovery is a fascinating one that demonstrates the personal and corporate qualities that are required to be able to recover quickly from a disaster of previously unimaginable magnitude.

The New York Board of Trade

The New York Board of Trade (NYBOT) is a commodity trading exchange with a history of well over 100 years. They trade options and futures on coffee, cocoa, sugar, cotton, and orange juice, as well as several financial indices and currencies, including the New York Stock Exchange Composite Index, the Standard & Poor's Commodity Index, and the U.S. Dollar.

Unlike equity financial instruments, whose traders sit in front of computer screens and execute trades in a relatively calm and orderly manner, through electronic trading systems, NYBOT's trading environment is quite frenetic. Some call it organized chaos. They trade in trading pits or rings, in a style called *Open Outcry*. Buyers and sellers stand, literally facing each other, on three or four steps arranged in a ring, as shown in Figure 21.1, and buy and sell these commodities based on orders from their customers. For example, the farmers who grow cocoa sell cocoa futures, and companies such as Hershey and Nestlé buy them. Prices are set through a verbal bid and ask process, where a seller might offer some cocoa (called a "lot") at a particular price (called an "ask"; a buyer's offer price is called a "bid"). If several buyers are interested in that lot, they might bid the price higher in an attempt to buy it, until only one buyer is willing to pay the new bid price. If there are no buyers at a particular asking price, the price might fall in an attempt to generate some buy orders. When an order is executed, its price is entered into NYBOT's computer system, and the prices of the most recent transactions are publicized instantaneously within the pit, and to the outside world. This process sets market prices for these commodities on a worldwide basis.

The result is a trading environment that operates at a very high noise level. Since the key to getting the right price on an order is to be heard by the person with whom you wish to deal, it is usually necessary to yell louder than the next trader. There is also much jumping up and down, waving of hands and papers, and jockeying for position in an attempt to get attention.

There is never just one trading pit or ring actively trading a commodity at a time; pits work in pairs. There is a pit for futures on a commodity ("I want to buy a lot of cocoa that will be delivered in March..."), as well as options on those futures ("I will pay you now for the right to buy a lot of cocoa to be delivered next October at a price we agree on today..."). The two pits are physically adjacent and active simultaneously, which just adds to the noise level.

Figure 21.1   Two of NYBOT's trading rings.

Another important difference between trading pure financial instruments like equities and trading physical commodities like cocoa and sugar is that if someone purchases a lot of sugar and doesn't resell it to someone else before its expiration date, it will be physically delivered to him. Although some of the traders want and expect to take delivery of the commodities that they buy, there are also speculators who try to take advantage of inefficiencies in the market, and may buy a lot planning to sell it before its delivery date.

What's more, since NYBOT trades in physical commodities, they have additional responsibilities; they must grade and certify their products, and store them in certified warehouses. Plus, all information about these activities must be available to any of their members at any time.

There are roughly 1,000 members of NYBOT; members are the only people who can make trades. Roughly 600 traders trade at NYBOT on an average day. Altogether, there are about 1,500 people working at NYBOT, including members, support staff, and so on. NYBOT services a community of roughly 10,000 people, although the precise figure would be very difficult to discern. The community includes growers, millers, farmers, buyers, sellers, and so on; all the people who are directly and indirectly touched by NYBOT's activities.

NYBOT makes their money on commissions. They get a fee for every contract of every trade that is completed in their trading pits. Besides Hershey and

Nestlé, other NYBOT customers include the companies that produce Tropicana, Minute Maid, Maxwell House, Folgers, various clothing brands, as well as the growers and mills that produce the raw commodities that go into these products. NYBOT makes a significant amount of additional revenue by distributing their commodity pricing information to their customers and to ticker service bureaus.

When NYBOT was housed at 4 World Trade Center, they had 13 trading pits, which allowed them to trade multiple commodities at the same time. Trading in the agricultural commodities would last for anywhere from four to five hours a day, depending on the commodity. Trading in the financials lasted from 7 to 18 hours per day. Typical daily NYBOT trading volume across all commodities was about 72,000 lots. As with other exchanges, when the trading day is done, much work remains. This back office work is the process of settling trades, and making sure that what was bought matches what was sold, and generating all the associated paperwork and audit trails.

The First Time

Shortly after noon on Friday, February 26, 1993, a bomb went off in the basement parking garage beneath the World Trade Center complex. The exchanges that were then called the Coffee, Sugar, and Cocoa Exchange (CSCE) and the New York Cotton Exchange were located in 4 World Trade Center (4 WTC), a nine-story building on the southeast corner of the complex about 100 feet away from the South Tower (Tower #2). Staff at both exchanges felt an explosion, and their lights blinked. Soon, they learned that a bomb had gone off. The explosion caused their facility to lose power, heat, and data center cooling, and the building was evacuated.

CSCE maintained a disaster recovery plan in 1993, which consisted of a migration to a cold backup site at Sungard Recovery Services in Philadelphia. The Cotton Exchange outsourced their computer management. CSCE's plan called for their system administrators to travel to Philadelphia, install an operating system on these cold systems, and install their applications and data. The recovery process was expected to take between 24 and 48 hours to complete.

Almost immediately upon the evacuation of 4 WTC, several system administrators headed down to the Philadelphia cold site carrying backup tapes.

The hole in their recovery plan was that there was no backup site from which to trade. Thus, even if they could get their computer systems back online, without access to their building, it would take at least 30 to 60 days before they could acquire a new site and install everything that would be required to allow them to resume trading.

On Sunday morning, February 28, New York City said that it could be a week or two until the exchanges could get back into the building. Later that day, the situation changed, and limited power (but no heat or air-conditioning) was restored to the WTC complex. This allowed the exchanges to reenter their building, where they could prepare for a limited trading day on Monday. Meanwhile, CSCE's system administrators who had gone to Philadelphia had reconstructed February 26's trading day and closed out processing so that their computer systems were now ready for the next day's trading. In 1993, all transactions were paper-based, and so it was relatively easy for the back office people to resubmit the transactions manually.

On Monday, March 1, trading resumed, but in a limited manner for just two hours a day. All back office computer functions were performed at the alternate site in Philadelphia, because while basic electric power had been restored, the air-conditioning systems remained off line. The computer systems could operate, but since they could not be cooled they would overheat if allowed to run for too long.

The exchanges continued to trade in this fashion for about two weeks, until the city was able to construct a temporary five-story structure adjacent to the World Trade Center complex to provide air-conditioning and heat to the entire WTC complex. At that point, the system administrators who had gone to Philadelphia were recalled, and CSCE computer operations were restored to 4 WTC.

One of the most remarkable and noteworthy things about this event was how the other exchanges in New York (the New York Stock Exchange and the American Stock Exchange) all pulled together and offered CSCE temporary equipment to help see them through their difficulties.

No Way for a Major Exchange to Operate

When all the dust had settled, Pat Gambaro, who was the Senior Vice President of Trading Floor Operations and Systems at the time, realized that this was no way for a major exchange to operate. CSCE needed a solid plan in the event that another disaster forced a relocation; they could not live with 48-hour delays in migrating their computer services. Besides, when working with cold site providers like Sungard, there is no guarantee that an incoming customer will actually get the equipment he needs; equipment is doled out on a first come, first served basis.

In advance of this disaster, there was not nearly enough time spent planning, and as a result, far too much time was spent scrambling after it had hit. So, Pat proposed to CSCE's Board of Managers that he develop a thorough disaster recovery plan that included a dedicated, hot recovery site for their computer systems, rather than a cold site, and, if possible, space for trading if the primary trading floor was rendered unusable. A hot computer site meant that all computer data created at the main site would be replicated to the hot site almost immediately after it reached the disks at the local site; this would allow them to recover from a disaster much more quickly than if they had to restore everything from tape. The Board encouraged Pat to look into acquiring such a site. Even as he looked for a site, he was developing cost estimates.

The costs associated with creating a second trading floor were more than the Board was willing to absorb, and so that part of the proposal was set aside, so Pat revised his proposal to include only a hot site for recovering their computer systems. The Board was reluctant to spend that money, too, but they agreed to a compromise. Pat would bring in an outside consultant to review his proposal and see if it made good business sense.

In the end, the consultant agreed with Pat, but felt that his recommendations did not go far enough. The most important fact that the consultant identified was that when that the CSCE was unable to trade, it cost them $350,000 per day, and it cost their business partners $3,500,000 per day. When they heard those cost numbers, the Board quickly decided that a hot site for their computers made a lot of sense. Soon, work began to identify an appropriate location for such a site.

CSCE began working with Chubb Recovery Services (later acquired by Comdisco, which was acquired in 2001 by Sungard Recovery Services), who, after an extensive search, found them a site in Brooklyn. However, before CSCE was ready to act, Chubb offered an alternate location in a building they had just acquired in Long Island City, Queens. This new site was on a separate power and phone grid from the World Trade Center, and had plenty of telephone service and redundant power. Furthermore, there was adjacent vacant space that could potentially be converted to a backup trading floor.

Chubb and CSCE worked out a deal that would allow CSCE to be the first tenants in the new building with a low rent. Although the Board had decided not to proceed with the alternate trading space, Chubb was very interested in helping CSCE build one. While they had built computer recovery sites before, Chubb had never built an open outcry trading environment; they felt that this could help them move into new business areas.

When the cost estimate came back at about $1.2 million, the Board had to say no. When Chubb offered to split the cost 50/50, the Board was still unwilling. However, when Chubb offered to pick up $1 million, leaving only $200,000 in costs to CSCE, the Board agreed, and work began.

Annual rent for the hot computer site would be about $50,000. When the Board learned that the rent for the whole site, including the trading floor would cost $200,000 a year, they initially did not want to spend the money. Pat kept working to change their minds until they finally agreed in early 1995. Each year at budget time, Pat had to go through the same efforts to justify this expense.

The Queens trading space was completed in 1995 with just two trading rings. In the event CSCE needed this trading floor, the plan called for the commodities to share the floor and trade in limited sessions of roughly 2 hours apiece, just as they did after the 1993 terrorist bombing.

But, before they could actually build this new hot site, they needed to end their contract with Sungard for the cold site in Philadelphia. In return for getting out of the contract prematurely, CSCE contracted with Sungard for the development and ongoing maintenance of a Business Continuity Plan (BCP) document. The BCP, roughly the thickness of a medium-sized city's phone book, described the recovery of every process and activity, manual or automated, in every department within CSCE after a disaster. There was also an individual concise document for each department. An incident management team was put together to oversee the plans. The BCP also included specific instructions for each employee as to where they should go after the disaster occurred. Sungard was also responsible for maintaining the document through personnel and procedural changes. The plan also included specific plans for information technology, a quarterly testing schedule, and just about everything else that a good disaster recovery plan should include.

Steve Bass, then the VP of Information Technologies, developed a scheme that allowed CSCE to place hardware at the Queens site at no cost. Although physical space there was still at a premium, another cost that the Board watched very closely was the cost of computer hardware. When NYBOT upgraded their system hardware at 4 WTC, the old plan was to retire the old hardware, and either donate it or recycle it. The new scheme called for them to take the old hardware, move it to Queens, and use it there for recovery purposes. Once a system was retired a second time, then it would then be donated or disposed of. This plan pleased the Board, as it allowed them to get their recovery site without having to purchase all new hardware.

In 1998, CSCE merged with the New York Cotton Exchange ("Cotton") to create the NYBOT. One of the biggest challenges that faced the merging organizations was how to reconcile the fact that CSCE had always managed their computer technology in-house, while Cotton had always outsourced it. Steve prepared a lengthy paper justifying CSCE's position that their computers should be managed in-house for the merged entity, NYBOT.

After a long series of debates, Steve and Pat prevailed, and systems administration was brought in-house. By doing so, they were able to be more nimble with their technological responses and development, allowing them to remain ahead of the technology curve in the years to come.

One reason for the debate on outsourcing was that it would be necessary to upgrade and enhance the BCP. All of the processes and procedures that the inclusion of the Cotton Exchange added had to be added to the BCP. However, as they were before the merger, computer management costs continued to be a major concern. Since the three-year agreement that was signed in 1995 with Sungard was expiring, the BCP upgrade was accomplished with Steve's in-house staff, and only minor help from Sungard.

Since information technology costs were still a concern, when Steve and Pat approached the Board to ask for additional funding to expand the Queens site to accommodate the new commodities and personnel acquired in the merger, they were unable to get the money. This meant that the recovery site did not grow to support the additional capacity that was necessary to keep all of NYBOT's products running after a disaster.

The last major shortcoming in the plan was in the recoverability of their back office applications. They knew that they could switch over all of their trading operations to the Queens site in about 15 minutes. However, without the ability to recover back office operations, they could not close their trading day, or perform other important, but less critical functions. Because of the ongoing budget tightness, Steve and Pat had to develop a low-cost or cost-free scheme to back up these functions.

One of the compromises that they made at the recovery site to save money was that there would be limited space for NYBOT's staff to work. The plan was that some of them would report to work at the recovery site, while others would work from home. The administrators were given suitable access from home (paid for in full by NYBOT), and would be expected to report there in the event of a disaster. This would be inconvenient, but since the system administrative staff's presence was not considered critical to the business, this made sense. The Long Island City facility held limited space for offices, trading pits, facilities, and all of the other things that NYBOT would need to operate long-term.

There was another implicit assumption being made throughout NYBOT's disaster plans, which was most evident in this lack of space for system administrators. Long Island City was seen as a temporary home. The plan did not consider the possibility that the entire World Trade Center building might be lost. They figured that if there were a fire or other calamity, they might be out of their WTC building for a week or two, or a month at most. They did not consider the possibility that the World Trade Center could be totally lost. Needless to say, this assumption would not prove to be a valid one.

Y2K Preparation

NYBOT saw Y2K coming before it became a public issue. The system administration staff began to prepare for Y2K as far back as 1997, and they had all of their internal applications totally compliant before 1999 began. In 1999, when their regulatory agency, the Commodities Futures Trading Commission (CFTC), sent all the forms and paperwork to NYBOT for Y2K certification, Pat told them that they were already done. It took a while to convince them, but once the CFTC believed that NYBOT was truly prepared, they asked for and received permission to use NYBOT as an example for their regulated organizations, to show them what to do, and how to do it.

Just because NYBOT was ready, that didn't mean that all of their partners were. So, there was still plenty of work to do to make sure that systems were compatible, and there were still many tests, milestones, and deadlines to meet, but NYBOT was way ahead of the curve. Pat and Steve describe most of this effort as busy work for the staff, since they were so well prepared.

Pat and Steve had nothing but good things to say about their staff. The systems management organization grew from 6 people in 1994 to over 60 at the end of 2001. They have kept very current on technology, and so have been able to implement new technology that has made their trading environment increasingly competitive. Besides Y2K preparation and Disaster Recovery, they were also early adopters of client-server technology, and are now (early 2002) implementing hand-held wireless devices to get customer information and orders closer to the traders in the pits. They raved about how well their staff has performed over the years in trying circumstances, and without the amounts of funding that they really wanted, and how despite that, the staff has allowed NYBOT to remain on the cutting edge of technology, and far ahead of competitive exchanges.

One of the biggest internal problems with which Pat and Steve had to contend was the unwillingness of their customers, the traders, and other NYBOT members to come visit the Queens site so that they could see where their money was going, and what the recovery facilities looked like. They were unable to persuade traders to come in and do a weekend day of mock trading, nor to close down WTC for a day and do a disaster drill. Nobody would seriously consider it. They even went so far as to charter buses and cater a lunch for the traders. Logistical problems messed that day up, and so even that endeavor failed.

The system administrative staff had spent many days in Queens, testing every aspect of the facility that they could. They had done mock trading, even in volume, and they knew that every system at the recovery site worked as advertised. Testing was done every quarter. But since the traders and users were unwilling to visit, there would still be logistical complications if they ever needed the site. Complete testing was just not possible without a greater degree of cooperation.

Since Pat and Steve could not get the traders' cooperation in solving the potential logistical problems, they needed the next best thing. In 1999, as part of Y2K preparation, they developed a comprehensive "Member Disaster Recovery Packet." The packet, which was given to every member, user, and trader, contained directions to Long Island City, operations information, and a plan for allocating scarce trading floor space and telephones, and other scarce resources.

The packet included key radio stations, web sites (the disaster recovery plan was on the staff intra-web site, and would failover to the Queens site transparently if necessary), home phone numbers, addresses, local restaurant and hotel information, street and subway maps, vendor contact information, driving instructions, contact information for pretty much everybody at NYBOT, and all sorts of other relevant information. The BCP was the official source of information about which system administrators were expected to report to Queens and which ones would be required to go home. It also included trader booth assignments at the Queens site, along with booth phone numbers. It even included a wallet-sized card that members could carry at all times with the most important information on it. Since the information was made available on paper and electronically via NYBOT's web site, there was no excuse for anyone to be without it.

Two of the most important issues introduced in the Y2K BCP were the concepts of shared space and staggered trading schedules. The Queens site had just 2 trading pits, rather than the 13 at 4 WTC. In order to continue trading under these cramped and limited conditions, they needed to develop a plan to share the trading floor by staggering trading schedules. Instead of trading simultaneously for four or five hours a day, as each commodity did at 4 WTC, at the recovery site they would be forced to limit their trading to just 90 minutes a day. All around the trading pits are trading booths: small cubicle-like spaces with telephones, where orders are sent to the brokers and all the paperwork associated with the trading is done. At 4 WTC, there were 600 booths. In Queens, there were just 100. This meant that users who were accustomed to having four or five booths might be relegated to just one or two. And instead of having access to the booths all day, traders would only have them for a 90-minute interval each day. After one broker's time expired, another broker would take over the booth and its phones.

Of course, just because all this was written into the plan doesn't mean that anyone had ever tried it.

In the end, though, after all of this preparation, and as it did for so many other organizations, January 1, 2000, came and went without incident for NYBOT.

Once they got through Y2K, a new push began. The system administrators worked to change the corporate culture to get all users to put all of their files and other data online and on the servers whose data regularly got replicated to the recovery site. If they failed to do so, individual user data would be lost in a disaster.

In early 2001, the information technology group began to push their testing efforts harder than ever before. Everyone who could work from home was able to work from home, and this capability was regularly tested, and all expenses to do so were picked up by NYBOT. The goal was to make sure that even if a user had no work space in Long Island City, he would still be able to get his job done, albeit remotely. Quarterly testing remained the target, and everybody whom they supported seemed much more willing to take part in testing than they ever had before.

Every system at 4 WTC had a backup system operational in Queens, and they all worked. When problems occurred at 4 WTC, and processing switched over to Queens, users could not tell; the switchover was totally transparent to NYBOT's users. Testing for the second quarter was done on July 12, and the third quarter's round of tests was scheduled for September 18. It never occurred.

NYBOT was about as well prepared for a disaster as they could be. Sadly, one occurred anyway.

September 11, 2001

As the first plane struck the World Trade Center complex on September 11, Pat was stuck in routine morning traffic, waiting to drive into the Holland Tunnel from New Jersey. He heard a news bulletin of a still-unidentified explosion at the World Trade Center. Immediately, he picked up his cell phone and called his office. He spoke with Walter Hines, NYBOT's CFO, who had felt the explosion shake their building violently, but he didn't yet know what it was. The Executive Floor Committee (the members who help coordinate daily floor operations) had calmly decided that it would be wise to evacuate the building. The phone call ended calmly, with a simple "talk to you later."

Since it was early in the day, there weren't too many people at work at NYBOT yet. There were about 200 to 250 people there altogether, 100 active cocoa traders (cocoa trading had begun at 8:00 A.M.), 50 financial traders, and 25 to 50 support staffers. There were also a handful of coffee traders who had arrived, as coffee trading was scheduled to begin at 9:15.

Next, Pat's wife, Adele, called him, and said that a plane had crashed into Tower 1. Like most people, Adele and Pat assumed that it was just an accident. She saw the pictures on TV, including the fireball and the big hole, and she was very concerned, but no more than that. Before they got off the phone, she saw the second plane hit. That changed everything. Pat was still half a block from the Holland Tunnel toll plaza, and he was stopped right there. Port Authority Police immediately closed the tunnel, and turned everyone around. Having no place else to go, Pat returned home, arriving there just after Tower 1 collapsed, at around 10:30.

Steve was at Penn Station in midtown Manhattan having just arrived on a commuter train from his home in Pennsylvania. He was unable to get any kind of information. The police closed Penn Station, and said that there was some sort of police action in progress at WTC, but nothing else. His first clue that there was something serious going on was when the police appeared and forced all the taxi cabs out from their taxi stand underneath the station.

The 250 or so NYBOT evacuees reached the street very quickly, as most of them were on the eighth floor of 4 WTC. Most of them got downstairs in time to see the second plane hit Tower 2. When they saw that, many of them panicked and ran south and east, which would take them away from the complex, but not toward any particular river crossing or landmark. They just wanted to get away from the scene as quickly as possible. At least one of the evacuees is a long-distance runner, and without really thinking about it, he ran five or six miles uptown away from the scene before he stopped to think about what he was doing or where he was.

Forty-five minutes later, when Tower 2 collapsed (the second building attacked was the first building to collapse), it fell onto the adjacent building number four, and in addition to the horrific loss of life that it caused, it totally destroyed the entire $25 million dollar NYBOT operation in that building, including almost $3 million in computer and networking hardware and infrastructure.

Pat was uniquely qualified to be the nerve center of the whole recovery operation. His house became a communication center and clearinghouse for the welfare of employees, utilizing all four phone lines running into his home. Cell phones were basically useless due to a combination of system overload and loss of access points. Many of NYBOT's personnel had Nextel cell phones/walkie-talkies, the walkie-talkie portion of which continued to function, but otherwise communications were very limited.

When Steve and Pat first spoke, they decided to declare an official NYBOT disaster with Comdisco, and that was the message sent around to all employees via phone, Nextel, and whatever other communications method could be found. The disaster declaration meant that the recovery effort in Long Island City would commence immediately.

Even though Pat was stuck in New Jersey, Steve was not. He began to make his way to Long Island City. There were no cabs, no buses, no subways, no cars, no nothing. So he started walking the roughly 3 ½ miles from Penn Station to the Long Island City site. Steve arrived at 12:30 P.M., and was the first NYBOT person to arrive there. Others began filtering in over the next four to six hours, most of whom had walked the nearly seven miles from the World Trade Center, after several detours. A couple of information technology executives were stuck in California at a conference. (They flew home once the restrictions on air travel were lifted.)

Steve spent his time on the phone, mostly, coordinating efforts with his users, system administrators, members, vendors, suppliers, and so on. Plus, his staff was calling him to make sure that recovery efforts were on track. Steve and Pat spoke several times throughout the day.

Because of the published and well-publicized plan, Steve's IT staff knew what to do. Some were supposed to go home and work from there. Those who were able to get there did so. Others reported to Long Island City, as they were supposed to.

Largely because the BCP included everyone's phone number, by midnight on the 11th, everybody at NYBOT had been accounted for. Three exchange members had been killed, all of whom were elsewhere in the World Trade Center complex that morning, including one who was at a meeting at the Windows on the World Restaurant. In addition, Pat's cousin, with whom Pat was very close, and who worked for Cantor Fitzgerald, was killed in the attacks.

Although this discussion is concentrated on the computer impact of the disaster, it is very important to point out that there was a significant emotional and psychological impact on the NYBOT members and employees. As a result, NYBOT arranged to have therapists and medical personnel on-site in Queens for two weeks after the 11th to help their members and staffers cope with the previously unimaginable levels of stress that the attack created.

As the system administrators arrived in Queens, they began bringing the recovery computers online. Once the systems were up, there was some important work that needed to be done: cocoa and some of the currencies had begun trading that morning. Before anything else could take place on the systems, the trading days for those commodities had to be closed. This was completed by 7:00 P.M.

And just a few minutes after 8:00 P.M. on September 11, NYBOT had completed their disaster recovery process. Their systems were ready to begin trading again.

Getting Back to Work

Even as the systems came back online, Pat remained at home on the phone, speaking with Steve, the NYBOT Board, regulatory agencies, users, traders, members, and employees. He received calls from other exchanges, including The New York Mercantile Exchange (NYMEX), The New York Stock Exchange (NYSE), The Chicago Mercantile Exchange, and The Securities Industry Automation Corporation (SIAC), offering anything that they had to help the NYBOT recover. Pat said that it was very gratifying to see the level of camaraderie and cooperation that these events brought out in everybody. However, it would have been very difficult for NYBOT to take advantage of the offers of computer hardware, as there are no standards between the different exchanges. NYBOT's primary hardware platform is Tandem. The NYSE's, for example, is not, and so it would have been very difficult, if not impossible, to get NYBOT's applications in a usable state on NYSE's platforms in any reasonable time period.

But getting started at Long Island City was not easy, as many of the organizations with which NYBOT communicates were also taken out by the attack. As a result, although everything was working as designed in Long Island City, they had networks that were no longer of any value because they were running to demolished or empty buildings (like the World Financial Center, located across the street from the site of the World Trade Center). They had never established network links between LI City and these partner organizations' recovery sites.

On the night of September 11, Pat and Steve got off the phone at 1:30 in the morning. Steve slept in a chair in the Long Island City facility.

The next morning, Pat made it to the DR site, having managed to drive to Queens from New Jersey. That task became much more complicated in the following days, as local authorities imposed restrictions on automobile access into Lower Manhattan and closed many river crossings in the New York area. When he arrived, he confirmed that everything had gone according to the plan, the systems were ready to go, and trading could begin.

When members and traders began contacting Pat and Steve later in the day on Wednesday the 12th, they wanted to know when they might be able to begin trading again. They assumed it would be Friday or Monday before they'd be ready, but, no, trading could resume immediately, at least from a computer perspective. In the end, though, that became a moot point, as all trading on all New York-area exchanges was suspended until Monday, September 17.

Before traders even arrived, there was an operational problem to contend with. Even though the staggered trading schedule (90 minutes for each commodity) was going to be in effect, there was no place to gather the group of traders who were waiting to take the trading floor. They needed the ability to gather and prepare themselves without impeding the active trading that was already in progress, as well as a way to more easily move the active traders out of the trading area when their time expired. The answer: more space. In a great stroke of luck, the only other tenants in the Long Island City building had moved out months before, so there was a tremendous amount of available space in the building. NYBOT quickly made a bid and acquired the space.

Once the space was acquired, Comdisco (the owners of the building) set to work preparing it to NYBOT's specifications, and in just a couple of days the space was ready to be used as setup space for incoming traders. (Comdisco assures us that under normal circumstances, this build-out would have taken a couple of weeks, if not longer.) Comdisco had obtained and set up tables, chairs, phones, and workspaces. This first upgrade greatly reduced tension throughout the organization, as it allowed members a space to work that was not on the trading floor, or in the way of active traders.

Since trading was not scheduled to resume until Monday, few members had any plans to visit the Queens site before then. However, Pat, Steve, and the Board realized that Monday morning would be total chaos, what with most of the 1,000 members arriving at once, all looking for their familiar booths, trading pits, phones, and other facilities. Many of them would not be familiar with the staggered schedule and would expect to trade all day as normal. As this would not be conducive to trading, it was decided to announce a mock trading day on Saturday, September 15.

On Saturday morning, everyone was asked to come in and acquaint themselves with the plans and policies that had been set up for Monday, and to do so on the staggered schedule. In reality, there were no plans to mock-trade anything. The point of the exercise was to bring everyone in to reduce Monday's chaos. (After all, since the system administrators had done a great deal of test trading, they already knew that they could trade successfully in Queens.) Saturday also gave NYBOT a chance to reissue badges and other paperwork that had been lost on the 11th.

What they learned was that, despite its availability, many members had neither seen nor read the disaster recovery packet. Others complained that while they had two or three (or six) booths at WTC, they were being limited to just one at the recovery site. Nevertheless, the overwhelming reaction from the members was a combination of pleasant surprise, amazement, and genuine relief. They were amazed to see that what they had been paying for all those years was real, and they were relieved because it would likely save their jobs. Suddenly, all of the funds that Pat and Steve had been fighting for all those years over objections from many quarters turned out to be money well spent.

The Saturday session revealed one very serious problem: The main telephone switch in the Queens building did not work. This meant that on Monday there would be no telephones in any of the booths for any of the traders. Pat contacted Mayor Giuliani's office on Saturday to get Verizon (their local telephone company) to come in and repair the failed switch. The Mayor's Office was exceptionally cooperative, and, in fact, had identified them as one of their three top priorities (along with the NY Stock Exchange and the NY Mercantile Exchange). Just in case Verizon could not get the switch working, later on Saturday Steve and Pat went out and bought 250 cell phones (cost for phones and service: $70,000) as a backup in case the new switch didn't work out. But, on Sunday afternoon, Verizon was able to get the switch working, and each booth had its two working phones. Even so, when members arrived Monday, cell phones were handed out on a limited basis, and they were used as extra lines for booths that needed more than two lines. The phone switch, however, held up just fine.

Trading began on time at 7:30 A.M. on Monday, the 17th, with cocoa, as per the staggered schedule. Normally, cocoa is a lightly traded commodity, and the pit at 4 WTC where cocoa was traded had room for about 60 traders. On this day, though, over 150 traders were crammed into a much too small space. Witnesses said that it reminded them of a Tokyo subway at rush hour. In the end, though, the abbreviated trading session went without any major hitches; the traders handled any disputes themselves, and trading itself was successful and completed on time. By the end of the day, NYBOT had traded 140,000 lots of all commodities, which was almost double the volume of a normal day. The additional volume was attributed to pent-up demand, and the volatility to market uncertainty.

In addition to the overcrowded trading conditions, NYBOT was also the center of a great deal of press attention, so on top of all the traders, there were a slew of newspaper and television reporters, along with representatives from the Mayor's Office.

NYBOT accomplished all of this trading activity amidst another serious problem. It became apparent early in the day on the 17th that two wired phones per booth would be completely inadequate, especially with the compressed trading day. To be successful, each booth needed at least six phone lines. The only way to achieve this increased capacity would be to bring in a new and larger phone switch. So late in the day on the 17th, the Mayor's Office was once again contacted, this time to request a new 1,200-line telephone switch, with the highest possible priority. With air travel and crossings in and out of New York severely restricted at this time, getting a switch delivered to Queens was no easy task.

Nevertheless, the Mayor's Office was able to cut through immense amounts of red tape, and on Wednesday, a U.S. Army helicopter flew to Long Island City with a 1,200-port telephone switch (a piece of equipment roughly the size of a standard computer rack). Four days later, in time for the Monday, September 24 trading day, every booth had four new phone lines running to its four new telephones, giving each booth a total of six lines and six phones. NYBOT estimates that under normal circumstances, it would have taken 30 to 60 days just to obtain the phone switch, and longer to get it installed and all the lines run and phones installed.

Chaotic Trading Environment

So, while trading went on successfully at this early stage of recovery, and as indicated in Figure 21.2, the quarters were kind of cramped. Making things more complicated, though, was that trading was very rushed. When NYBOT traded at the World Trade Center, each commodity traded for four to five hours per day. At the recovery site, trading was limited to just 90 minutes, with a 30-minute changeover period in between commodities. During this 30-minute period, the traders had to complete their trading and wrap up their trading days (a very complex manual process), the system administrators had to change all the display screens to reflect the correct data for the next commodity to be traded, and all the traders had to physically leave the floor with enough time for the next set of traders to come in and take their places.

Adding to the chaos was the telephone and booth sharing. An example of the small booths NYBOT used in Long Island City is shown in Figure 21.3.

Figure 21.2   Actively trading at the DR site.

During the course of the trading day, several sets of traders would occupy each booth. The telephones and telephone numbers in each booth were assigned to the booth, not to the traders; they were shared among all the occupants of a particular booth. A call to one of the six phones in row one, booth one at 9:00 A.M. might reach a cocoa trader; the same phone at 11:00 A.M. might reach a coffee trader. At 2:00 P.M., a sugar trader may answer.

After some time passed, and everybody got accustomed to the new arrangements, things got a little more efficient, and so the changeover time was reduced from 30 minutes down to 20, adding 10 minutes to the trading day for each commodity. Without the full cooperation of the brokers and the entire NYBOT staff, this switchover would simply not work. Pat reports that the brokers have shown remarkable levels of cooperation.

Before September 11, sugar traders traded an average of about 30,000 lots in a four-and-a-half-hour trading day. Since September 11, average trading volume has risen somewhat, but all the trades were being completed in just 90 minutes. That means that the rate of lots traded roughly tripled, from about 6,600 per hour to more than 20,000 per hour. What's more, since NYBOT trades manually rather than electronically, there is a tremendous amount of post-trading day activity that must be done to close the day. Because of the compressed schedule, all of that work must be done in less than the half-hour (now 20 minutes) that the traders have to clear the floor.

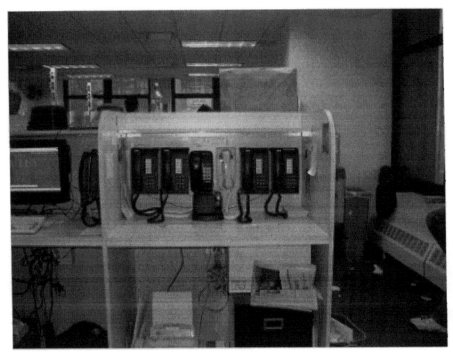

Figure 21.3 A shared trader's booth at the DR site.

NYBOT has been able to add an additional 100 phones to the trading recon-
ciliation area, as well as provide additional trading input terminals. Both of
these improvements have resulted in increased efficiency in trade reconcilia-
tion, and a little less work that needs to be done on the trading floor.

Another unforeseen complication was with the financial instruments
traders (U.S. dollar, and foreign currencies) who also traded at 4 WTC. The disaster recovery plan for them was to fly to Dublin, Ireland, where they would
resume their trading activity on NYBOT's Dublin trading floor. Their
exchanges quickly learned that flying anybody anywhere in the days after
September 11 was going to be difficult, so the decision was made to find some
space for them within the Queens facility. Adding to the complexity, because
the financial traders work with exchanges at other facilities, they do not get to
set the hours in which they trade. In order for them to trade, they must do so
at all hours that trading is done. This means that they cannot share the facilities at NYBOT with other commodities; instead, they must have their own area
in which to trade. They don't need trading pits, but they do need full-time
phones and booths to trade from, reducing the pool of booths available to be
shared among the commodities traders.

Improvements to the DR Site

By rearranging seating and other facilities, NYBOT was able to add a pair of smaller trading rings for orange juice and cocoa, the two commodities with the fewest traders and lowest average volume. By clearing those traders away from the main rings, they have been able to extend trading on the other commodities. By early February 2002, 12,000 square feet of trading space was available, more than double the space they had on September 17. They added two more rings by mid-February 2002, allowing even more trading for longer periods each day.

Additional facilities are being added to Long Island City beyond trading space. Upstairs, away from the trading area, a small lounge and lunchroom are being put in, as well as a coatroom to get coats off the trading floor. The additional space will also include conference rooms, offices and cubicles for staffers, and additional trading preparation space, including more telephones and data entry space for traders. This additional space will further reduce the amount of work that must be done on the trading floor at the end of each commodity's session.

AUTHOR'S NOTE

The last 8 months have been an extremely busy and productive period for our friends at the New York Board of Trade. Although they remain in their DR site in Long Island City, New York, they have made arrangements, and construction is expected to begin very soon on their new primary site in Manhattan. While planning has been going on for the move, they have continued to upgrade the Long Island City site, making it more productive for the different groups of traders, and more comfortable for the long term.

NYBOT is taking a very bad situation and making the best of it. They are taking particular advantage of new technologies, and their new trading floor will have some of the most modern information sharing technologies on any trading floor of its kind.

In early 2002, the trader transition area was relocated from the first floor to the second floor, and a whole new trading floor was built out in its place. Normally, the building of a new trading floor can be expected to take 6 months or more, but they were able to accelerate the process, and completed the floor in just 2 months.

* * * * *

In its new location, the transition area spread out to cover a lot more space, and included many of the amenities that the traders had done without since the relocation. The additional space gave the traders and support staff telephones, PCs, and space and equipment where they could enter their trades, as well as a lounge, a coat room, a vending machine area, offices for the executives, and space for other critical functions like compliance and trade clearing.

The addition of the new trading rings brought the total number of rings to eight. These new rings made trading much easier and more comfortable and meant that commodities could trade more hours a day than at any time since 9/11. For example, cocoa trades for nearly four hours a day, or only 1 hour less than at the WTC.

Eight rings, of course, is not 13, and so the commodities were not all able to trade in the hours of the day that they would like. The cotton and orange juice traders would prefer to trade with morning hours, but are unable to, due to the lack of trading space. Doubling up on trading space with other commodities is still a procedural requirement.

New Data Center

While the construction of the new trading rings was going on, Steve got approval from the Board to open a new backup data center in Lower Manhattan.

Steve's biggest concern since NYBOT had moved to Long Island City was that the building created a single point of failure for the entire operation. He saw that it would likely take a year or more before a new trading site could be operational, so he campaigned for a secondary separate site for a data center. This new site would give NYBOT a couple of substantial benefits. It would allow them to get the data center away from the trading floor, thus eliminating Long Island City as a single point of failure, and it would give Steve a place to house his IT staff.

With the Board's approval, Steve signed a lease for the new data center space in February. At WTC, the data center was over 6,000 square feet. Because of the remarkable reduction in the physical size of their servers, Steve was able to lease just 2,000 square feet of space, and that included offices that were not included in the 6,000 square feet they had before. What's more, the lease for the new data center was much less costly than any real estate they had leased in the last several years.

Once the lease was signed, the build-out began. Staffers, many of whom had been working from home most of the time since September, began to move in during early April. The data center was completed at the end of June. Almost immediately, the Lower Manhattan site became the DR site for Long Island City's data center. Two weeks after its completion, NYBOT ran their first DR tests. The tests were successful, and at this writing, they have been replicating data from Long Island City to the new site without incident for over two months.

Everyone felt a lot more comfortable once the Lower Manhattan data center came online and Long Island City was no longer a single point of failure. The Manhattan data center also ensured that they can relocate the development staff from Queens, removing a lot of the people from that site, freeing up space and other resources. Not only didn't they have a backup site before Manhattan came online, but they were using their production systems for development, a state of affairs that had made Steve very uncomfortable.

The New Trading Facility

Within days of the migration to Queens, Pat and his staff began the search for a new trading facility. They looked at nearly 20 different sites over a period of several months before they found the right one. They settled on the New York Mercantile Exchange building at 1 North End, overlooking the Hudson River. 1 North End is an ironic choice because of its location, just a block and a half west of the World Trade Center site.

The prospect of returning to the same neighborhood has made some of their members and employees uncomfortable, but from a business perspective, 1 North End is the right choice for NYBOT. Since they are relocating back into their original neighborhood, now called The Liberty District, they are entitled to federal money to rebuild their facilities. NYBOT received a piece of the $20 billion that Congress allocated to rebuild Lower Manhattan. They also received direct, personal appeals to return to the neighborhood from New York City's Mayor Michael Bloomberg and New York State's Governor George Pataki, as well as from some of the economic agencies who are chartered with rebuilding Lower Manhattan in the wake of the attacks.

Before The New York Mercantile Exchange ("The Merc") built and moved into its building at 1 North End, the New York Cotton Exchange and the Coffee, Sugar and Cocoa Exchange (before they merged into NYBOT) had been in discussions with them and their other sister exchange, The New York Commodities Exchange (Comex), to build a shared building. When negotiations went too slowly, the Merc went ahead and built their own building for themselves and the Comex, whom they had acquired.

In mid-2003, NYBOT moved into the seventh floor of 1 North End, a floor that had been roughly half vacant for several years, sharing the floor with the Comex. As part of the move, the trading floor was completely renovated. Comex moved to the formerly empty portion, and NYBOT took over Comex's vacated area. This design is the result of months of designs and redesigns, and nearly 40 sets of plans. The plan was in many ways like a jigsaw puzzle; space had to be found for Comex's 8 trading rings, plus the 13 that NYBOT would have. Since the floor has only one proper entrance, there needed to be sufficient space so that the various groups of traders could move to and from their trading rings without getting in each other's way.

The trading floor is a triple height space, with a 30-foot ceiling. It extends up through the 8th and 9th floors, but it does not use up all of those floors. Remaining space on those floors will be used by both exchanges for office space, trade clearing, and other administrative functions. Additional space on 7 was allocated for cafeterias and other trader amenities. In addition to the trading floor space on the 7th floor, NYBOT will have space for trading support staff on the 8th floor and executive offices on the 13th floor.

In the end, NYBOT will have just over 13,000 square feet of trading floor space at 1 North End, and the Comex will have slightly less. The 13,000 square feet is approximately the same amount of trading space that they had at the World Trade Center.

Before they completed the move to 1 North End, NYBOT operated without a disaster recovery site for their main trading floor. The data center functions in Long Island City will continue to be replicated to Lower Manhattan until the move to 1 North End, at which time the direction of replication will be reversed.

Future Disaster Recovery Plans

The first step in NYBOT's future DR plans was taken very quickly: They have separated their data center from the building in which the trading floor is located. The attacks simultaneously cost them both their trading floor and their data center. By putting the two in separate buildings, NYBOT hopes that a single event can no longer disable both functions.

The current plan is for NYBOT to hold on to the Long Island City site for the time being, and perhaps permanently, depending on how their other plans go. But they have other options.

One DR option is to merge their DR plan with the Merc's. The Merc has their DR building on Long Island,[1] and NYBOT could take some space and move their DR environment there.

Another idea is to speak with other exchanges in other parts of the United States, and discuss the possibility of trading DR space with them. In this model, NYBOT might wind up with a DR trading floor in Chicago, while a Chicago exchange uses some of NYBOT's space in either Long Island City or 1 North End. Steve acknowledges that traveling to Chicago could be very difficult in some circumstances, so a remote DR site would serve as an additional DR site rather than the primary one.

At this writing, these decisions have not yet been made.

---

[1] Long Island City is not located on Long Island, but rather is part of Queens, one of the five boroughs of New York City. Long Island is located several miles east of Queens.

The Technology

Perhaps the most exciting thing about the move for Pat and Steve was that since they got to redesign the trading space from scratch, they got to investigate and implement new technologies to accelerate and enhance the trading process.

The Outcry for Open Outcry

One technological option that was quickly dismissed was eliminating the Open Outcry method of trading and replacing it with a more modern and technological, but less personal, electronic trading system. NYBOT remains committed to the Open Outcry method of trading, as it best supports their customer base and their agricultural products.

The primary advantage that Open Outcry offers NYBOT and their customers is price discovery. In an electronic trading environment, traders simply match anonymous deals within the system; the highest bid price is matched to the lowest sell price, and so on. On an equities trading floor a specialist will trade a particular stock, say, General Motors (GM). On NYBOT's floor, there may be 30 traders, each having his own customer base and all of whom may want to buy and sell the same future or option.

Open Outcry traders generally know more about their customers, and so are able make trades while keeping their long- and short-term needs and/or strategies in mind. Since electronic trading is anonymous, it is impossible to acquire this knowledge. In an electronic system, it is possible for a trader to withhold information when it is to his advantage. In Open Outcry, that is not possible, since the work is concentrated in the hands of fewer people. An Open Outcry trader is kept continuously up-to-date on the activities of the market in which he trades and the activities of his fellow traders. He uses this knowledge to advise his clients in an ongoing manner. Therefore, in an Open Outcry environment, there is no need for specialized researchers, as there is in electronic trading. Research opinions come directly from the traders on the floor.

Another factor driving electronic trading on equities exchanges is the demand for 24×7 trading. Pat says that he sees no such demand for his commodities, so there is no need to start moving in that direction. At this time, the daily three or four hours of trading in each commodity is plenty for their markets' participants.

Pat's beliefs were demonstrated very strongly in the days that followed September 11, 2001, as trading on worldwide commodities markets was greatly reduced during the four days that NYBOT was forced to suspend trading. It turned out that the other markets were waiting for NYBOT to come back online and resume their price discovering.

Despite the obvious advantages of Open Outcry in a small commodities marketplace, it is a very expensive way of doing business. Open Outcry requires more equipment and more real estate than electronic trading. But Pat firmly believes that Open Outcry is the way to trade for their customers and their commodities. One of their competitive exchanges did do away with Open Outcry and went electronic; Pat says that that exchange has not gained any volume, and may have lost some volume to the NYBOT.

Modernizing the Open Outcry Process

Just because NYBOT has decided to stay with older methodology for their trading environment does not mean that they have decided to force their traders to use primitive tools to get their jobs done. On the contrary, since the decision has been made to stick with Open Outcry, Steve and Pat have been able to update their traders' tools, permitting them to exchange information and trade faster and more efficiently than ever before.

Above the new trading rings at 1 North End, the walls are lined with brand-new lightweight flat screen monitors. These modern 8-pound monitors replaced the ancient and very heavy monitors that lined NYBOT's older rings. Each trading pit is surrounded by roughly 80 flat-screen displays, mounted on a series of custom-designed lightweight trusses.

Figure 21.4 The new and improved trading booth.

The photograph in Figure 21.3 shows the rather bare-bones trading booths at Long Island City, where the work of research and customer contact took place. Information was shared on large message boards and monitors spread along the walls throughout the trading area. Traders and brokers were forced to scan a 70-foot-wide area to find all of the available information.

Figure 21.4 shows a prototype of the trader's booth that NYBOT installed for their traders at 1 North End. The goal is for each trader in his booth to be totally self-sufficient, with his own telephones and computer screens for internal and external connectivity along with a printer and fax machine. Traders can enter their trades in the booth instead of traveling to a common trade-entry facility. To reduce the number of crossing cables, each booth's phones are wireless. Each booth has its own lightweight overhead flat-screen monitors with displays that are totally customizable on a booth-by-booth basis. By putting monitors in each booth, Steve believes there is less eyestrain for traders, and the data that is displayed will be more useful to each trader. Pat says that they will be able to deliver more information to each trader for less money with localized displays than they can with large centralized displays.

The new site at 1 North End also has an entirely new electronic system for entering trades, a new order management system, and improved connectivity to their back office functions. Information is provided to the traders that they never had access to before, including market analysis and recommendations, news, weather, information from the other financial markets, and worldwide market conditions specific to their commodities. Traders get real-time audit trails, online risk management, and faster delivery of information. The result has been a significant cost savings, since fewer people have to handle paper in the back office, allowing the exchange to handle more volume (quicker trade closure yields more trades), which translates to additional income for NYBOT and its membership.

In addition to the upgraded displays and information sharing, NYBOT has put another significant improvement to the trading process in place. They have implemented new communication technologies, putting wireless, touch-screen PDA-like devices in the traders' hands that enable traders to receive orders automatically, without the use of a telephone, and in return, submit execution data. Orders are seen and their information is sent to the order flow provider almost immediately. Order receipt and execution turnaround completes much more quickly with these new electronic tools, which also allow NYBOT to send trading information directly to the back office for final dispensation.

Even though NYBOT has made it clear that they plan to retain Open Outcry as their trading vehicle, all of this new technology must still be sold to their traders. Concerns such as lost jobs or lost business still linger in their minds. However, where possible, NYBOT will deploy new technology strategies on a nonmandatory basis to improve its Open Outcry platform.

The Effects on the People

The time since the recovery has been a very interesting one for Pat and Steve on many levels. As a direct result of their efforts, they have been rewarded by NYBOT, with Pat having been made Senior Executive Vice President of NYBOT, and later named Interim Chief Operating Officer of the entire organization. Steve was made NYBOT's Chief Information Officer.

Even before things settled down at NYBOT, Pat and Steve started to become major industry celebrities. In the month of September 2001 alone, just the first three weeks after the terrorist attacks, NYBOT was written up over 230 times in publications and on newswires around the world, ranging from the *Wall Street Journal* and *Fortune Magazine* to *The People's Daily* in China, the *Times* of London, the *National Post* in Canada, and even *Progressive Farmer* magazine. In the months that followed, NYBOT's recovery was written up in thousands of periodicals, and was shown on television programs all around the world.

Then the conference invitations started to come in. Pat and Steve have spoken at conferences put on by The Federal Reserve Bank, The Futures Industry Association (four times), The Commodities Futures Trading Commission (three times), The Vanguard Technology Transfer Institute, and at two different VERITAS Software conferences.

In their year-end awards for 2001, *Information Week* magazine named Steve one of their co-CIOs of the Year, citing all the work that he and Pat put into their business recovery plans. They also made a point of contrasting the frantic pace of work at NYBOT with Steve's easygoing manner.

In the months that followed, requests for interviews and appearances have continued. During the week of September 11, 2002, Pat appeared on CNNfn, CNBC, the BBC, and New York City's NY1 cable news channel, and NYBOT was written up once again in dozens of newspapers and periodicals around the world.

NYBOT, led by Pat, has begun to lobby the CFTC to get all exchanges and member organizations up to certain levels of disaster preparedness. They believe that these organizations have an obligation to their customers and to the general public (who are, after all, the ultimate consumers of these commodities) to ensure that they survive disasters. Pat has taken slight advantage of some of his speaking engagements and has publicly lobbied to make these changes. Though the CFTC did not take maximum advantage of the attention that they and their efforts received during Y2K preparation to promote disaster preparedness, the CFTC has used Pat well at CFTC-sponsored forums to promote disaster preparedness, and it is hoped they will be able to get appropriate regulations in place sooner rather than later.

Shortly after the recovery was in full swing and it was clear that NYBOT would, in fact, survive, Pat Gambaro received what he believes to be the nicest compliment of all, one that put all of their efforts into perspective. "Don't just think about how your efforts managed to keep the exchange trading," Pat was told, "think, instead, of all the people who still have jobs because there is a market to sell their commodities. Think of the growers, the buyers, the millers, the clerks, the customers, and everyone else who gets their income directly or indirectly through the efforts of NYBOT. Your work ensured that all of those people continue to have a steady income, and are able to continue to feed their families."

But the loss of NYBOT would have had an even larger impact. Consumers of chocolate, coffee, cotton, orange juice, and the other commodities that NYBOT trades would all be impacted as well, either through a shortage of these commodities, or through higher prices, since the loss of NYBOT would lead to at least temporary market inefficiencies.

Despite all of the attention and accolades that they have received, Pat and Steve are remarkably humble about their accomplishments. They say that they were just doing their job. The people whose livelihoods Pat and Steve saved through their most remarkable efforts would probably have a bit more to say on the subject.

NYBOT derived another, perhaps less obvious benefit from their efforts. As they put together their plan, they were forced to take an extremely close look at how their business operates. They had to examine processes and procedures and interactions that most organizations never take the time to see. As a result, they were able to better refine existing procedures, and make their overall business more efficient.

The most important lesson that Pat and Steve learned from their endeavors is to never lose sight of their goals, and always strive to reach them. If they had given up in their attempts to build and maintain a disaster recovery site every time the Board turned down their requests for funds, NYBOT would most likely not have survived the World Trade Center attack. Pat endured a great deal of ridicule and verbal abuse in his stubborn efforts to maintain a recovery site, but he was not deterred. In the end, and without exaggeration, his and Steve's efforts allowed NYBOT to remain in business after a calamity that destroyed many less well-prepared organizations.

Summary

By just about every measure, the disaster recovery efforts at NYBOT were a smashing success. There were some problems, of course, particularly with the telephones (both the failed switch, and the undercapacity of the lines in each booth), and the lack of space around the trading floor for staging. Nobody had expected the total loss of the WTC site (like so many others, their plans assumed a temporary loss of access), and so NYBOT's disaster recovery plans did not take that into account.

Probably the most remarkable thing about NYBOT's story is simply that it is so remarkable. Not to take anything away from the job that Pat and Steve did, which was stupendous, but they got all of these accolades and attention for essentially doing their jobs. They worked very hard, and fought against the odds, and were the recipients of a healthy dose of luck, but in the end, they were simply totally successful at their jobs. As a result of their efforts, NYBOT recovered from the biggest man-made disaster that had ever struck the United States quickly, and pretty much according to plan.

If all enterprises gave disaster recovery an appropriate level of attention, instead of making it the first place from which to cut spending when budgets tighten, and if the people responsible for disaster recovery were as diligent and stubborn as Pat and Steve, these accomplishments would simply not be remarkable. They would be the norm. After all, Pat and Steve are not superhuman, and there is no reason that anybody who reads this chapter could not do exactly what Pat and Steve did.

In telling the NYBOT story, we could have spent pages discussing their networking infrastructure, hardware, and storage platforms. We chose not to. We also chose not to describe the precise method through which they got their data from The World Trade Center to Long Island City. Instead of concentrating on technology, we wanted to emphasize the preparation, the thought, the care, the attention to details, the arguments, and all of the hard work that went into NYBOT's effort.

How many enterprises could not only survive the total destruction of their headquarters and data center, but be back online in less than 12 hours, with their business and customers essentially intact? Could yours?

CHAPTER 22

A Brief Look Ahead

All probabilities are 50%; either a thing will happen, or it won't.
—Colvard's Premise

Computers in the future may weigh no more than 1.5 tons.
—Popular Mechanics magazine, 1949

The future becomes completely clear just after it arrives.
—Evan Marcus

What sort of self-styled industry pundits would we be if we didn't take a look at the future? In this chapter, and in no particular order, we take a quick look at a number of technology trends that we think are going to be important, or at least interesting and relevant, to the field of high availability over the next few years.

Please note that all predictions are based entirely on the information that was available to us when the book went to press. When you are zipping around in your flying car several years from now, and you read this book and see how ridiculous these predictions look in retrospect, please be kind.

iSCSI

Internet SCSI, or iSCSI, is a network-based protocol for sending SCSI commands and data over TCP/IP networks. Traditional SCSI, as we discussed back in Chapter 7, "Highly Available Data Management," is limited to very short distances, but through the use of iSCSI, the same functionality can be extended over the much wider distances that IP networks support. The practical result of iSCSI is that storage and data on storage devices can be directly accessed across any IP network, without the data having to be routed through a remote computer system first, as is required by NAS solutions like NFS and CIFS, resulting in technology that is functionally equivalent to a SAN.

iSCSI SANs can do pretty much the same things that Fibre Channel SANs can. What makes iSCSI particularly appealing is that it does not require an entirely new networking infrastructure as newer technologies like Fibre Channel do. iSCSI will require Gigabit Ethernet as a minimum, and more realistically, probably 10Gbit, so new NIC and other network components will probably be required, but it should not be necessary to run new networking cables.

Networking monitoring and trouble-ticketing tools that function on today's LANs will continue to work, without changes, on iSCSI. When a SAN is implemented, new monitoring tools are an absolute requirement.

Fibre Channel is very good at moving data with only a little overhead on simple networks, but it has trouble handling unreliable links and more complex network topologies. TCP/IP (and therefore iSCSI) is much better at handling complex networks and unreliable links, but does so with a great deal of I/O overhead, which is not acceptable for storage I/O.

iSCSI is a mostly software-based solution that solves traditionally difficult problems. There is at least one relatively new hardware device, called a TCP/IP Offload Engine (or TOE), which speeds up TCP/IP traffic by performing in custom hardware some of the network protocols that have traditionally been performed only in software.

Working against iSCSI is the ever-widening acceptance of SANs, which reached the market first, although not as cleanly as its proponents would like to acknowledge. It does seem as though SANs have much better marketing than iSCSI, and marketing has always been more important to the broad acceptance of technology than any actual technical advantage.

The killer advantage that iSCSI has over Fibre Channel for building SANs is cost. iSCSI can be implemented for a fraction of the cost of SANs, and organizations that have not even begun to examine SANs may decide that iSCSI is a better way to go.

One potential outcome of the market conflict between iSCSI and Fibre Channel-based SANs has already begun to hit the market. Cisco has a device that routes traffic from a Fibre Channel SAN onto an iSCSI network; this method of joining the two networks together may well turn out to be the panacea that drives both types of SANs into wider acceptance.

InfiniBand

The InfiniBand architecture is a very high speed interconnect between servers that are physically close together. InfiniBand speeds can reach 30Gbit per second, with extremely low latency. Unlike the better-known PCI bus, Infini-Band is point-to-point; it requires a switch to connect multiple devices, and software for node management. It was originally designed to offer faster I/O to computers with ever-increasing CPU and memory speeds, because there were concerns whether other I/O transports, such as PCI, would be able to keep up with the demands that the other components were placing.

When InfiniBand was first announced, expectations were extraordinarily high. It was going to replace every networking infrastructure in existence, and probably put an end to world hunger. Once expectations were ratcheted back, and InfiniBand was targeted as a data-center-only solution to interconnect servers at a very high speed, it became a much more realistic proposal. InfiniBand makes great sense as a clustering interconnect, and as a way to share and move extremely large amounts of data relatively short distances. (A good cluster interconnect is one that can send relatively small amounts of data over short distances at high speed with very low latency. Cluster members need up-to-the-second information about state changes in other members. A good storage interconnect, on the other hand, needs to be able to share large amounts of data, with high speed, as well as with moderate, but predictable, latency.)

Although it will require new hardware, InfiniBand does not require an expensive new wiring infrastructure because the systems it will connect will be physically close together. It will, however, require dedicated switches and other networking hardware. Until it is more widely accepted, systems will require an adapter board that will allow a connection to be made into the InfiniBand network fabric. Although InfiniBand supports copper cabling at distances of up to 17 meters, and fiber optic cabling at distances of up to 10 kilometers, with as many as tens of thousands of nodes in a single subnet, the early applications involve systems and storage that are physically close together.

Products that actually support InfiniBand have not reached the market in large quantities yet, but the InfiniBand Trade Association (`www.infinibandta .org`) lists more than 75 different hardware and software vendors, both large and small, as having joined. Of course, joining an industry association is very different from delivering products that support it. Recent developments have indicated that vendor support for InfiniBand is wavering, and there are many in the industry who believe that it will soon wind up either with a radical repurposing or on the great scrap heap of promising technology that never found market acceptance.

Global Filesystem Undo

Human error is one of the leading causes of system downtime. When system administrators make mistakes, those mistakes can have huge impacts on the systems, data, applications, and users that the administrators are responsible for. When a regular user makes a mistake, generally he is the only user affected. When an administrator makes a mistake, she can affect all of her users. Recovery from administrative mistakes can take days or even weeks.

One way to reduce the impact of human error[1] is to design systems that allow administrators to have a second chance when they know they've made certain types of mistakes. This is especially valuable, since the really difficult work of system administrators is usually done off-hours, especially in the middle of the night, when they may not be as alert or attentive as they are during the day.

The way to give administrators a second chance is through a technique called *global undo*. As the name implies, global undo would allow an administrator who has made a mistake to do the equivalent of typing a Control-Z in Microsoft Word and put things back the way they were before the mistake.

Obviously, there are other ways that system administrators can make mistakes besides messing up filesystem-based files, some of which *may* be repairable through global undo, such as database modifications and the applying of OS-level patches. Others, such as network configurations, take place external to filesystems, and would require other methods to facilitate recovery. But if global filesystem undo can repair many, or even most, situations, it would be very helpful and useful.

There are two ways to achieve global filesystem undo. One is by logging every single change, data or configuration, that is made to the every file in every filesystem on the entire computer system, and preserving that log for a known period of time. In this way, the administrator could roll the system back to a point in time before the error. The problem with this is that it's a complex and time-consuming system that requires a great deal of extra disk and computing resources.

A simpler and more practical approach is for an administrator to decide that he is about to begin a risky process, and take a snapshot of the filesystems. If he does something wrong, he can roll back to the snapshot. If the error occurs when he has not taken a snapshot, then he is no better off than he was without this capability in place. On the other hand, the system will not suffer the drag on resources that it would if all system activity was being logged at all times.

From an availability perspective, global filesystem undo is the most exciting of these future trends, at least in the short term. It appears to be a moderately complex implementation of existing technology that can have a very large impact on system availability. And when you combine this idea with virtual machines (discussed in Chapter 19, "Virtual Machines and Resource Management"), the problem becomes much easier to solve.

---

[1] You can totally eliminate human error by firing all of the humans and hiring monkeys or dogs in their place. Then it's not human error anymore, but simian or canine error instead. You'll also save money on salaries. But the raw number of mistakes and the cost of cleaning services will likely increase significantly.

The technology to deliver this capability largely exists today. It is just up to a vendor to package it up properly, customize it for the relevant operating environments, and make it available. A form of it will likely be available through manual snapshots by the end of 2003. System administrators have been using Tripwire (`www.tripwire.org`) and similar packages to generate checksums and digital fingerprints of system configurations in security circles, looking for changes that may have resulted from intrusions. Expect to see more widespread use of configuration management tools like *Cfengine* (`www.cfengine.org`) to automate the process and rulesets to create, edit, and distribute configuration information.

Grid Computing

The SETI (Search for Extraterrestrial Intelligence) at Home project (`http://setiathome.ssl.berkeley.edu`) has been doing gridlike work for many years. SETI@home takes data from radio telescopes that are scanning the skies, breaks it up into small pieces, and parcels those pieces out to users across the Internet who have signed up to take part, and who dedicate their PCs to the effort, when they aren't doing anything else. Anyone who finds evidence of extraterrestrial intelligence in the data that her computer analyzes expects a significant reward, and most likely some serious notoriety. Nobody has collected so far. With nearly one-and-a-half million CPU-years logged so far, this effort has been called the largest concentrated effort of computing power in history.

SETI@home is the best example of grid computing that we have been able to find. By breaking up huge amounts of data into bite-sized pieces, and sharing them among millions of computers, they have achieved the same goals as the developers of grid computing initiatives.

The grid is seen by some as the next step in the evolution of computing: a model where all computers in a particular logical or physical region (a data center, a company, a country, or perhaps the whole world) are joined together to share computing resources. Systems with idle resources would make those resources available to the rest of the grid. Proponents of grid computing often speak of a utility model for computing, where you could plug an appropriate device into the wall, just as you would plug in a table lamp to get electricity, and you would receive computing cycles. That "appropriate device" would probably be a computer, without a great deal of processing power, but just enough to know how to successfully connect to the grid and communicate with it.

Before grid computing can achieve wider acceptance, there are many hurdles that will need to be cleared, the biggest of which is probably security. If someone else can run a process on my system, who's to say that the process won't work some mischief on my system and steal passwords or install some form of malware? At the same time, if my process runs on some anonymous system, who's to say that the other system won't in some way affect (either innocently or maliciously) the running of that process and cause it to return bad data, or to snoop on what the process is doing?

One argument against the grid is that today's computers already have far more processing power than their owners actually need, and that PDAs and portable phones will likely follow suit before too long. With that in mind, grid architectures may only be useful for a handful of the most overwhelmingly processing-intensive applications, such as weather forecasting, factoring prime numbers, and SETI@home-like projects.

Another important concern that must be addressed before grid computing can achieve wide acceptance is accurate process billing. If you are running a process on my computer, I would certainly expect you to pay me for the resources you are consuming. If grid resources become truly worldwide, political questions come into play as well: What if a process sent from one country is run on a computer in a country where the process is illegal in some way, and how can these concerns be policed? Is it appropriate for one company to run processes on computers owned by a competitor? Policy and resource allocation, as discussed in Chapter 19, will prove to be a fundamental enabler for large-scale grid computing.

Early-adopting commercial entities must begin to implement small grids internally to make better use of their existing computing resources. To be fair, at this writing there are very few commercial applications that can take advantage of the grid. New techniques must be developed to encourage the production of parallel applications, as well as distributed applications for highly partitioned computing.

Grid computing today is centered on computational tasks, but there's no reason the concept of local clusters of resources, dynamically allocated and provisioned, can't be applied to storage as well. Consider the problem of creating temporary, large storage for media files like high-quality digital images or video clips. If you want to share your child's soccer pictures with the other members of the team, there's probably no reason to point everyone at an archive site when a grid storage node would provide lower latency, being closer to any point of presence for any ISP used by team parents.

From an availability perspective, grid computing could be the ultimate extension of clustering and replication techniques such as those covered in Chapter 15, "Local Clustering and Failover." If computers and computing power become true commodities like electricity, then the availability of a single computer becomes irrelevant. All computers become instantly replaceable by other computers. If a critical process is being run on the grid, perhaps it would be run on multiple computers at the same time. If one of those computers failed to respond, others would complete the task anyway. The user might never even know.

For more information on grid computing, visit www.gridforum.org.

Blade Computing

Blade computing is sort of the complement to the grid. Computers and storage are getting physically smaller and smaller, to the point where a properly loaded data center rack could hold hundreds of small, totally self-contained computers. These small computers, called blades, are already available from many system vendors. The thinking is that running hundreds of small computers results in more computing power for less money than running a single large system.

Of course, running hundreds or thousands of computer systems of any size introduces all sorts of new problems. For blades to be truly practical, a technology that can centrally manage large quantities of servers must be brought to market. That solution will need to manage servers from different vendors, that sit in separate racks, even in different data centers or buildings. The application that comes closest to delivering this functionality today is clustering software. With clustering software, an administrator can manage several nodes at the same time, although not as many as a large blade implementation will require; today's clustering software can generally only manage small to medium-sized clusters, containing up to 32 nodes. That is inadequate in an environment that may have thousands of blades. After all, a single data center rack can hold more than 200 blades.

What you can expect to see is a model where each blade runs a single application. The distribution of these applications is controlled by a piece of software that runs on a couple of blades, but not all of them. If a blade fails, its application is failed over to another blade that was sitting idle, waiting to take over. What's even more interesting is the prospect of instant blade provisioning, where the blade is kept totally blank. When circumstances dictate that a blank blade must be allocated, a copy of the appropriate OS is installed on it (Windows NT, Windows 2000, Windows XP, Linux, Solaris on Intel, and so on). With the operating system image provisioned to the blade, you'll layer middleware or applications images, and finally point the blade at a networked data repository. Once the data is in place, the blade can join the network and begin serving the application and data. In this view, the computer has become a complete commodity.

The pricing model for blades will likely be such that if one fails and cannot be easily repaired, the administrator will remove the system from the rack, throw it away, and replace it with another blade held in reserve. The cost of these blades is expected to fall to under $500 over time, and probably much less than that. The cost to repair one of these systems will be greater than cost to replace it. So, the commodity system becomes a disposable commodity.

The cost of a blade can be kept low by building it on commodity processor hardware (Intel processors are the most common), running a free or nearly free operating system such as Linux, and connecting the system to low-cost commodity storage.

There are still some technological issues that work to keep blades from achieving wider acceptance. It is impractical to connect blades together in a SAN when an HBA (the adapter board that connects a computer to a SAN) costs more than the blade itself. And until solid management tools can be developed, it will remain very difficult for system administrators to trade a few large systems in for hundreds or thousands of smaller ones. Designing applications that can be run in multiple, separate operating system instances remains an issue; there are obvious choices like web and application servers, and emerging models such as finely grained clusters of database servers. Blade and grid computing are likely to drive acceptance jointly, as application development and application assembly models such as web services are mapped into fine-grain compute elements.

Global Storage Repository

The OceanStore project at the University of California at Berkeley (http://oceanstore.cs.berkeley.edu) is probably the leading public example of a global storage repository, a model where computer systems from all around the world are linked together to create a massive library of storage, which is available to any system that joins the project. There are rumors of commercial software and hardware vendors working on similar projects, although no official announcements have been made.

The goal of these global storage repository projects is to create a persistent data store that could potentially scale without limit, and permit every computer user in the world to use its resources. When a computer uses repository data, it makes a local copy and modifies it on its own disks, rather than going back and forth to the central repository, thus improving performance.

In a project of this magnitude there are a seemingly infinite number of issues that must be addressed, including security, data integrity, heterogeneity, capacity management, file versioning, file locking and contention, network bandwidth and capabilities, and, of course, overall availability of the whole system. It must also be absolutely certain that the data that a user believes she has committed to the repository has truly made it there and can be retrieved by other users.

Data is stored in read-only form, with versioning, across hundreds or thousands of different systems, with only fragments stored on each system. But each file stored with great redundancy, so that even the loss of many of the systems would not cause files to be lost. In order to ensure adequate performance, there will be internal monitoring tools that collect and analyze all sorts of system data, and make sure sufficient resources are being directed where they are needed within the repository.

The LOCKSS project (Lots Of Copies Keep Stuff Safe, see `http://locks.stanford.edu`) creates a highly available document archive by copying files to geographically and logically dispersed locations. Avi Rubin's work on Publius (`www.avirubin.com`) extends the notion of highly replicated storage to detect and correct censorship, online defacing, and other content corruption problems. Cheap networking and cheap disks are combining to create more powerful archives than simple local filesystems.

RETURN OF THE SON OF USENET

In 1986, there was an effort to create a Usenet recipe book. At the time, I submitted my mother's recipe for kugel, a sweet noodle pudding with vaguely Russian roots. It was one of the three things I knew how to cook. Seventeen years later, I received an email from a friend telling me to do a google.com search on "Mom Stern's kugel." The matches returned span multiple continents, imperial and metric measuring systems, at least half a dozen languages, and archives that go back about 20 years. It's the same recipe, now copied so deeply into the fabric of the Internet that I couldn't rescind it if I wanted to. I believe this is the electronic equivalent of the definition of a good kugel: It's so dense it sinks in mercury.

—Hal

There are several functioning examples of rudimentary global storage repositories on the Internet today. The late, lamented music-sharing service Napster was the first well-known case, and its spiritual descendants (KaZaA, Gnutella, Morpheus, WinMX, Audiogalaxy, and so on) have ensured that this technology will exist far into the future. A recent check of KaZaA found over 3,500,000 active users sharing nearly 800 million files totaling almost six million gigabytes (six petabytes) of data. So, anonymous, global, distributed file sharing is alive and well.

Autonomic and Policy-Based Computing

Autonomic computing is a term that IBM is popularizing. It is an approach to self-managed computing systems with a minimum of human interference. The term comes from the body's autonomic nervous system, which controls key functions, such as heartbeats and digestion, without conscious awareness or involvement.

As computing power, storage capacity, network bandwidth, and society's dependency on computers has increased over the last few years, so has the complexity of computing systems. As the number of computers has increased, the need for talented system administrators has increased, too, but the supply of these skilled individuals has not increased significantly. Although there are certification programs, there is no real training ground to learn the ropes of system administration. Every system administrator we know had to learn on the job. (When will a forward-thinking university offer a degree program in computer system administration?)

At some point, probably fairly soon, it will become necessary for systems to become much easier to manage so that they do not require significant amounts of routine administration. Ideally, they should require no routine administrative tasks like allocation of filesystems, shuffling of computer resources, or job scheduling. System administration as a discipline will continue to be of critical importance, though, as the function that determines the policies to be implemented by self-managing systems. The goal of autonomic, or policy-based, systems is to eliminate the emphasis on the mundane and create time and flexibility for policies to be defined, implemented, and measured.

Another term that falls under the heading of autonomic computing is *zero administration*, which is best described as zero routine administration. A certain amount of administration will always be required, if only to take the system out of the box, carry or wheel it to where it will be located, and plug it into power, networking, and storage. It will be a long time before those are the only actions required to deploy a new system. Another approach to zero routine administration is *zero scale administration*, where only the first machine needs to be configured. Its configuration is then replicated automatically to other machines that are designated to receive it. This approach ties back to blade computing and is about the only way to manage the thousands of small systems that administrators may be forced to manage.

Cars are incredibly technical machines with thousands of parts inside that the average person can learn to operate with a minimum of training. Routine maintenance on cars takes place every few months. Autonomic computing says that computers should be able to operate reliably with a similar amount of maintenance and administration.

Most users want to use their cars without having to understand how they work. The automotive industry has come to understand that, and it's possible for someone to own a car for many years without ever having to do anything more technical than pump their own gas. The vast majority of computer users want the same level of convenience. They don't want to see Blue Screens of Death or have to concern themselves with backups, security issues, software patches, or upgrades. They want to be able to sit down at their respective computer and simply have it work at any time, all the time. Users expect the same level of service as from, say, the phone system: When you pick up the phone you get a dial tone.

True autonomic computing will seamlessly handle varied file formats, deliver extremely high levels of availability by diagnosing and repairing problems before they affect users, and operate through a natural language interface rather than through keyboards and complex sets of commands. Their data will be automatically protected so that users will not need to be concerned with system backups or viruses. Performance agents will examine the activity on the system at any given moment, and optimize resource allocation to deliver the best possible performance to the user. Newly connected devices such as printers will automatically configure themselves and announce their presence to the network, without requiring any user activity or system reboots.

Achieving this vision of pure policy-based computing requires that the basic discovery, connectivity, and monitoring tools become much more network-focused than system-, or single-box–, focused. Identifying a disk or memory failure on a single system is relatively straightforward because the system is well connected and predictable in its configuration; when you add the dynamic element of networking to the inherent unreliability and lack of predictable performance on a network, you have a much more difficult problem to solve. Whether it's autonomic, policy-based, or zero routine administration, these systems will change the shape of availability planning with new tools and new degrees of control for administrators.

Intermediation

Amazon.com shows us that the Internet isn't a disintermediating technology; it's one that creates new forms of intermediation. Amazon.com is the new channel between publishers and the public, just as ebay.com creates a new intermediation channel for small-scale collectors. Intermediation provides opportunities for creating more reliable and trusted computing models than are possible in the real, two-party world. For example, using an online payment service to transfer funds for an item you bought on eBay eliminates the need to send credit card information to an unknown entity—if you trust the payment provider and believe you're going to get the goods (due to eBay feedback ratings), then the three-party system creates more trust than is possible in a two-party system.

FROM RUSSIA WITH LOVE?

One October afternoon I received a brown-paper package tied up with string, return address somewhere in the Ukraine. At the height of the anthrax mail scares here in New Jersey, I was tempted to microwave the package for several minutes. Despite all of the jokes about "My Favorite Things," the contents, in fact, were something I wanted—a Russian hockey jersey to add to my growing collection. I found the perfect item on eBay, won the auction, and paid for it using Billpoint, eBay's credit card payment service. The seller received funds in whatever currency she wanted; I was fairly certain I was going to get the jersey because her feedback rating was quite high and she had a perfect record of delivering as promised on jersey auctions. eBay's intermediation allowed me to complete a transaction on the Internet that I never would have done in the real world out of fear of having my credit card number stolen.

—Hal

While intermediation reigns in the business-to-consumer Internet space, it hasn't found applications yet in the operations world. However, the same model may prove valuable for creating networks of web services or other fine-grain service points, where an intermediation facility brings producers and consumers of services together in a trusted environment where SLAs are consistently described and enforced. Increased intermediation means you need to have models and metrics for trusting other providers of software or network services. It also means that your reliability is a function of your own systems and those that you're relying on from third parties.

Software Quality and Byzantine Reliability

Fault-tolerant hardware systems use multiple implementations of components, running in parallel, to provide redundancy if any individual slice of the system fails. We have discussed how to provide redundancy for easily partitioned, scalable applications like web servers, where multiple instances of the application can be run, with state sharing, across multiple operating system instances. But what if you're dealing with a stateful application that occasionally gets the wrong answer? How can you improve the quality of software with respect to logical faults as well as external failures? One concept that's not new is *Byzantine reliability*,[2] in which multiple implementations of a chunk of code are run in parallel and vote on correct outputs.

Historically, Byzantine reliability models haven't held up because each implementation of the object was subject to most of the same failures—that is, there was too much correlation between the typical coding faults you'd find in multiple attempts to create independent software. Being able to craft applications in smaller pieces—whether it's through web services or other Java objects—will probably make Byzantine reliability more attractive.

PATCHES IN SPACE

One of my first jobs was developing software at a company that had done some of the test environment for the Space Shuttle back in late 1970s and early 1980s. The shuttle, like other spacecraft, requires extremely complex software reliability models. As one of the directors of engineering told me, "Once it's launched, you can't get patch tapes to it." Multiple gyroscopes are used to provide navigational integrity, and in some cases, multiple implementations of software are used to reduce the likelihood that a logical fault causes a system failure.

—Hal

Outside of Byzantine reliability models, we expect to see more of an emphasis on getting the right result propagated from CPU to memory to disk system. Hashing, digital signatures, and encryption of data paths are becoming more the norm because of SSL and crypto accelerators. Even if the software isn't working correctly, preventing data corruption is the first order of business.

Business Continuity

The events of September 11, 2001, put business continuity into the trade and public press. We have discussed availability of systems to tolerate single faults, and disaster recovery to deal with multiple, catastrophic physical failures, but

---

[2] Byzantine in this context refers to a theoretical computing problem known as the Byzantine generals. In this exercise, an army commander sends out his generals to scout the enemy. Some don't return, and some return compromised by the enemy as spies. The commander's task is to devise an algorithm that allows him to determine which generals are lying and which generals are telling the truth. Practical applications of this idea aren't plentiful, but voting algorithms for reliability are based on the same ideas.

business continuity is a strategic planning element. Business continuity is related to disaster recovery: DR describes the IT mechanisms for bringing a functioning system back online, while business continuity describes the policies and processes for keeping things running while you're executing the DR plan. Business continuity covers a wide range of topics, such as the following:

- Delegation of responsibility and decision-making authority in case key executives are affected by a disaster.

- Regulatory requirements for reporting, data preservation, and auditing capabilities while operating from a DR site.

- Putting bounds on the recovery times and systems capabilities for a DR site; business continuity becomes the requirements analysis for a DR plan.

- Relationships with suppliers, distributors, and other partners, such that the business is able to function (even at a reduced level of output).

Business continuity makes sure the enterprise is capable of running after any number of large-scale failures. Disaster recovery ensures there are IT systems to run that business. And availability planning keeps the IT systems running through smaller-scale failures. As we become adept at solving problems at one level of complexity, the issues get larger and more abstract.

Key Points

- Technologies evolve over time. Each new trend carries some impact on your availability planning.

- Adopt a portfolio management approach to emerging technologies, prioritizing the benefits, risks, and impacts of a new trend. Venture capitalists make many bets on companies, hoping that one or two generate large returns. You have the same responsibility to do prudent investigation of applicable technologies, exploring the one or two with most promise in more detail.

CHAPTER

23

Parting Shots

"Say good night, Gracie."
"Good night, Gracie."
—George Burns and Gracie Allen

There is a very interesting and not unexpected side-effect to spending your time designing high availability into systems. You gain a much better overall understanding of many of the aspects of the systems that you are responsible for. Whether you are a hands-on system administrator, a manager of system administrators, or a corporate technical officer, as you move through the discipline that is high availability, you quickly learn about system capabilities, disks, networks, backups, personnel issues, best practices, and all of the other topics that we have covered in this book. You learn the value of spending a little more money for high quality when it is needed. This information will make you more successful at your job.

How We Got Here

In the Introduction and again in Chapter 3, "The Value of Availability," we discussed the concept of an availability index, which is no more than a fancy way of saying that the higher the level of availability you need, the more money it will cost you. That money is an investment in the continuing operations of the systems that make your business work, and in turn your business. Failure to put the right money in the right places could, in the end, cost you and your business dearly.

The money that you spend on protecting your systems is really spent on protecting your applications. Your applications in turn run your business. Spending money (and time) to design HA into your systems is an investment in your business.

You almost certainly have a life insurance policy that will protect your family in the event that something happens to you. You have property insurance on the physical plant that makes up your business's facilities. But most businesses do not carry insurance on their systems and applications, and they fail a lot more often and for a lot more reasons than buildings or people do.

High availability in all of its forms is life insurance for your business. You wouldn't raise a family without insuring yourself, and you shouldn't run a business without insuring it and its systems. Life insurance salespeople sell life insurance as an investment, not as a simple expense. HA is the same thing. If your income is $35,000 per year, would you get $1 million in personal life insurance? Probably not, although you might. If your income is $250,000 per year, would you buy $25,000 in life insurance? Again, probably not. You buy insurance according to your personal needs. As your needs change, you reevaluate your insurance needs.

If your downtime costs $100,000 per hour, is it worth an extra $25,000 to shorten every outage by 30 minutes? Of course it is. But the same $25,000 solution may be a complete extravagance for a small business whose outages cost $500 per hour. Every business is different. Every business has different requirements. The trick is to spend appropriately for your business's needs—and to reevaluate that spending as your needs change.

Ultimately, it all comes down to figuring out how much your downtime actually costs you (factoring in any government or industry requirements and the potential for civil action or legal penalties) and then balancing the amount you spend against that. There is no single set of rules that applies to every business, just as there is no single insurance policy, or even type of insurance, that applies to everyone.

Once you know the cost of downtime, and the cost of eliminating that downtime, you can measure just what you're getting for your money. What are the users experiencing, and how is that related to the areas in which you've made investments? Correlate the user-visible aspects of the system to those that you've made most available, and you have a closed-loop process. Whether it's Total Quality Management (TQM), six-sigma methodology, or the latest process promoted in the *Harvard Business Review*, you're going to have to work with data.

Many sources for inspiration and skills transfer are available from noncomputing fields. Stewart Brand chronicles Danny Hillis's endeavor to build a clock that will last for thousands of years in *The Clock of the Long Now*; he also writes about the design implications of physical buildings and structures that endure for decades in *How Buildings Learn*. Smart engineers have been making reliable and available products for hundreds of years, and that prior art is available for us to leverage into the world of short time scales and big web sites.

Demand for availability design and verification skills will continue to grow. That's why we transcribed our knowledge in this book. It also means that the state of the art isn't standing still. We hope that with this introduction to the skill sets and design choices involved you've become a member of this growing class of highly valued individuals.

Thank you very much for your attention and interest. We sincerely hope that the advice contained herein will help make your systems more highly available, and your enterprise more successful.

Index

2209384

Made in the USA